BLACK LIVES IN THE ENGLISH AR[illegible]
1500–1[illegible]

To Forgotten Histories

Black Lives in the English Archives, 1500–1677

Imprints of the Invisible

IMTIAZ HABIB

LONDON AND NEW YORK

First published 2008 by Ashgate Publishing

2 Park Square, Milton Park, Abingdon, Oxfordshire OX14 4RN
52 Vanderbilt Avenue, New York, NY 10017

Routledge is an imprint of the Taylor & Francis Group, an informa business

First issued in paperback 2020

British Library Cataloguing in Publication Data
Habib, Imtiaz H., 1949–
Black lives in the English archives, 1500–1677 : imprints of the invisible
1. Blacks – England – History – 16th century
2. Blacks – England – History – 17th century
3. Blacks – England – History – 16th century – Sources
4. Blacks – England – History – 17th century – Sources
I. Title
305.8'96042'009031

Library of Congress Cataloging-in-Publication Data
Habib, Imtiaz H., 1949–
Black lives in the English archives, 1500–1677 : imprints of the invisible / Imtiaz Habib.
p. cm.
Includes bibliographical references (p.) and index.
ISBN 978-0-7546-5695-1
1. Blacks–England–History–16th century. 2. Blacks–England–History–17th century. 3. Great Britain–Race relations. 4. Blacks–Race identity–Great Britain. 5. Ethnology–Great Britain–History–16th century. 6. Ethnology–Great Britain–History–17th century. 7. Minorities–Great Britain–History–16th century. 8. Minorities–Great Britain–History–17th century.
I. Title.

DA125.N4H33 2007
305.896'04209031–dc22

2007000383

ISBN 13: 978-0-7546-5695-1 (hbk)
ISBN 13: 978-0-367-64991-3 (pbk)

Contents

List of Figures and Tables

Figures

Tables

Preface

A project such as this is likely to be a hazardous undertaking. To be able to collect scattered, fragmented, and historically disregarded records of black people from four centuries back, and to talk about them with authority and coherence consistently, is a daunting task. Furthermore, to conduct that conversation in a manner that is compellingly meaningful to archivists, historians, and literary scholars alike requires skills nothing less than polymathic, something hard to achieve in today's climate of specialized training. As anyone who has worked with early modern English records of any kind knows, confusion—of order, content, and therefore meaning—is not the exception but the rule in such sources. Then there is the demand of mobility, of travel to innumerable English national document repositories and local archival centers, even if that is beginning to be alleviated somewhat by the advent of electronic access to catalogs and to transcribed as well as digitized texts. Still further, there are the problems of reading physically deteriorated records and deciphering their handwritten contents. These facts, together with the severe constraints of time and expense imposed by the other obligations of one's professional and personal life, make such an endeavor a test of one's mental and physical endurance. Success can only be a relative term here. What sustains the effort is a conviction in the general intellectual gain of such a project and the hope of the specific benefits it might offer to others who might follow where it leads.

The precise moment of conception of this work was my discovery of Roslyn Knutson's seminal but still little-noticed essay, "A Caliban in St. Mildred Poultry," in the spring of 2000. In what was for me its lucid and gracious introduction to the empirical side of early modern English race study, it instantly confirmed the growing suspicion from my own work on race in the period up to that point of the necessity of establishing a documentary database of black records in order for this fledgling and contested field to grow significantly. The earlier work of Eldred Jones, Follarin Shyllon James Walvin, Peter Fryer, St. Clair Drake, Peter Erickson, and Paul Edwards had offered tantalizing evidence of that necessity, but Knutson's essay made it lucidly do-able. That essay showed me the form and the location of such materials and what was needed for their study. To her therefore must go the primary acknowledgment of this book.

Of course, the growth of a book, however desultory (and the desultory moments in the history of this book's writing were frequent), is also the growth of one's intellectual debts to many, through what Kim Hall has aptly called "the alchemy of conversation." Such conversations, whether brief and single, or extended and multiple, have a lasting effect. They help to convert the nebulosity and tentativeness of a possible writing idea into the palpability of a job that can be done. Conversations first with Margo Hendricks, and then Martin Orkin, and subsequently with Alan Nelson and Susan Amussen, stick gratefully in my mind, because of the reassurance they provided for instincts that I was nursing fearfully alone. Briefer but also nourishing exchanges with Ian Smith, Daniel Vitkus, and Steve Mullaney drove the project to the certainty of completion despite its exhausting demands. Over the years, the friendship and intellectual support of Charles Whitney has been valuable, and in the case of this book, quietly comforting. Dr. Maggie Scott at the Dictionary of the Scottish Language Project in Edinburgh, Marika Sherwood at the Institute of Commonwealth Studies in London, Roland Mellor at the University of California, Los Angeles, and Richard Bailey at the Henry Machyn Diary Project at the University of Michigan all provided both specific clarifications of some of the problems in records that I was pursuing and general cooperation in the interests of my research.

The first and most immediate source of intellectual support is, however, my own institutional colleagues. They are the ones who suffer daily the tribulations of each other's work, and they are the ones whose implicit or explicit expressions of empathy provide the validation of one's work that sustains its quotidian progress. Among my colleagues at Old Dominion University, the intellectual camaraderie that I have received from Jeff Richards has been invaluable, generally in all my professional work, but most crucially in this one. Invested unequivocally in the overall aims of my research agenda from the very beginnings of my career here, Jeff shared the excitement and the difficulties of this particular project in its entirety almost on a daily basis. An ever-present, always willing second mind with whom to probe the unseen pitfalls and untangle the endless obscurities of my journey, and an unflagging endorser of the merits of this project, Jeff gave me the intellectual and emotional prop I desperately needed to complete what was otherwise an impossible journey. All scholarly work is intrinsically collaborative, but Jeff's contribution to this book goes well beyond the casual inclusiveness of such a word. Without his encouragement, this book would surely have suffered an early death.

Given the range of cross-disciplinary knowledge and methodology needed for a work such as this, my colleagues in the History Department have also been sources of assistance. Annette Finley-Crosswhite and Chandra Desilva provided not just the general benefit of an informed interest in my work but also helped me meld literary and historical analyses in a manner that did not cut corners with either. Chandra Desilva was also a formal mentor and investor in this work in his capacity as Dean of the College of Arts and Letters, and his ever ready and always generous financial support of the costs of the preparation of this book for publication were only the institutional reflections of his overall intellectual involvement in the scholarly conversations on race in which this book participates.

In the year following my discovery of Roslyn Knutson's essay, a trip to the Guildhall Library and to the London Metropolitan Archives began what was to be a relationship with them lasting until the present moment. In fact, if Knutson's essay was the initiator of this work, the two London libraries and their staff were its continuous enablers, in person and at long distance. Unfailingly courteous and helpful in their guidance through the alien and often bewildering worlds of their materials, with Stephen Freeth at the Guildhall Library and Steve Gardam at the LMA even generous enough on occasion to supply me gratis with more than what I had asked for, the Guildhall and LMA library staff helped to transform for me the topic of black records from the initial excitement of a writing idea to the developed maturity of a book project. That what I found in the Guildhall library's documents, and what I partly demonstrated in Michael Wood's documentary film on Shakespeare's life called "In Pursuit of Shakespeare," would, in turn to my surprise, become the occasion of the library's *thanking me*, is also, in retrospect, a part of the library's extraordinary connection with the substance of my work in this book.

In the transformation of my project from a tempting idea to a practical reality, the Folger Shakespeare library in Washington, D.C. was another powerful friend. Its collection of printed and microform documents were treasures that I fed on hungrily and with increasing aggressiveness as the life of this book grew. The overall helpfulness of the general staff made the quick location of arcane items I needed a expected reality whenever I was there, while in the book's closing stages, the expert assistance of Erin Blake and Tina Smith in the library's portraits and photos department in both selecting and preparing images I needed for use in this book made the complexities of that part of the project far less terrifying than what they would have been.

Other libraries, local and abroad, helped to sustain my journey once it had started, and to keep it going through its recurring moments of despair. In Virginia, the Swem Library located at the nearby College of William and Mary offered what the Folger located farther away could not—quick checks on some records in its microform collections. A little farther away, the extensive collections of the University of Virginia's Alderman Library and the Eisenhower Library at Johns Hopkins University frequently made equally available documentary sources that were otherwise hard to find. Local libraries, such as the Mariner's Museum library, and the libraries of Christopher Newport, Hampton and Norfolk State Universities, also occasionally enabled the location of simpler items of research quickly and inexpensively.

In England, a host of local document repositories helped me to locate and identify a variety of records available nowhere else. The librarians and local historians who came forward instantly to respond to my inquiries, often at long distance, not only resolved questions convincingly but also revealed to me information about the contexts and locations of some records that I otherwise would not have known. Nikki Taylor at the Northamptonshire Archives, Margaret McGregor at the Bristol Record Office, Madge Dresser at the University in the West of England, Rory Lalwan at the City of Westminster Archives, Slan Mogridge of the Hackney Archives Department, Edward Small at the Surrey Historical Centre, Michael Carter at the Centre for Kentish Studies, Sue Hill at the Southampton City Council, Steven Hobbes at the Wiltshire and Swindon Record Office, and Jenny Cutis at the National Archives of Scotland all provided confirmations and corrections of the status and provenance of record originals that rescued me from the helplessness that my distance from these locations inevitably cast me in. Their assistance considerably bolstered my confidence in the validity of this project. In London, Robert Yorke of the College of Arms, and Lindesey Jones of English Heritage both supported my project by rushing the images from their collections that I wanted, on good faith alone rather than on completed paperwork, so at not to delay publication.

Inevitably, the prohibitive expense of frequent overseas and substantial local travel necessitates conducting large amounts of the endless research required for a book like this by long distance, by inter-library loan. In this, Beverley Barco, Stuart Frazer, and their colleagues at ODU's inter-library loan unit performed the miracle of supplying my endless research items whenever and however I needed them with the speed and efficiency that made the frequent wrong turns and dead-ends of my inquiries instructive points in the book's progress rather than signs of its hopelessness and futility. That they did this over the several years of this book's gestation, without complaint or comment, is certainly part of the reason for the book's successful completion. Also among ODU's library staff, Karen Vaughan's willingness to assist in the preparation of the images used in this book contributed to the health of its progress, especially in its closing moments.

The human costs of protracted scholarly projects appear most acutely in one's personal life, in one's immediate family. In the long and grueling years of this book's voyage, my constant companion has been my wife Rosy, whose dedication to my project included, astonishingly, her cheerful accompaniment to distant libraries and her investment of many hours in struggling with me over many unreadable records. Her unflagging belief in this work, and her unhesitating identification of weaknesses in its development were strengths that fed its growth. The book also profited from the labors of my daughter Reema Habib and my son Ameet Habib, who performed many of the chores of the book's preparation, and caught many errors to which my eyes were blind. That my family was denied the full benefit of my company in the years spent in the writing of this book is a loss that cannot be made up, only forgiven.

In the end, the most fundamental act of faith given to this project was that of Erika Gaffney of Ashgate Publications. The sure confidence that she showed this work from the very outset, and the unflagging patience with which she guided and nourished it through its recurrent setbacks and difficulties, perhaps did more than anything else to ensure that this research came to fruition. The book's debt to her is a profound and abiding one.

Imtiaz Habib
Old Dominion University
Norfolk, VA

Acknowledgments

Grateful acknowledgment is hereby made to the following organizations for their permission to reproduce in this book material owned by them:

The Editors, *Journal of Narrative Theory*, for permission to reprint in revised form sections previously published by them in 36/1 (2006): 1–13 of their journal as an essay titled "Indians in Shakespeare's England as 'the first-Fruits of India': Colonial Effacement and Postcolonial Reinscription."

The College of Arms, London, for the image of John Blank in the Great Tournament Roll of Henry VIII.

Commander Jose Barardo and Isabel Alves, of the *Barardo Collection*, Lisbon, for the painting *Chafariz d'el Rei in the Alfama District, Lisbon.*

English Heritage, London, for the painting by Gillis Van Tillborough titled *Sir Henry Tichbourn Distributing the Dole.*

The Folger Shakespeare Library, Washington, DC for the etching by Wenceslaus Hollar titled *Black Woman* and the colored map of London by Frans Hogenberg titled "Londonium Feracissimi Angliae Regni Metropolis."

List of Abbreviations

AHTS	*Accounts of the High Treasurer of Scotland*
APC	*Acts of the Privy Council*
BCB	Bridewell Court Books
BL	British Library
BMI	Boyd's Marriage Index
CollSP/E	*Collection of State Papers relating to ... Queen Elizabeth*, ed. Haynes
CompSP/D	*Complete State Papers Domestic*
CSP/D	*Calendar of State Papers Domestic*
CSP/Sp	*Calendar of State Papers Spanish*
DSL	*Dictionary of the Scottish Language*
GL	Guildhall Library, London
HCA	High Court of the Admiralty
IGI	International Genealogical Index
L&P HVIII	*Letters and Papers ... of the Reign of Henry VIII*
LMA	London Metropolitan Archives
NAS	National Archives of Scotland
NatArch	National Archives
PN	Hakluyt, *Principal Navigations*, ed. Goldsmid
RA	*Returns of Aliens*, ed. Kirk and Kirk
REED	Records of Early English Drama

RSM	*Returns of Strangers in the Metropolis*, ed. Scouladi
West.Arch	City of Westminster Archives
WRNCRO	Winiwick Register (Burial), Northamptonshire County Record Office.

Introduction

The Missing (Black) Subject

I

Studies of racial formations in early modern England have always had to deal with an uncertain knowledge of the actual numbers of black people. The stumbling block in the resurgent "moment" of race in Renaissance studies has been, in the absence of information to the contrary, the reluctant acknowledgment that "actual" black people were probably a "tiny" population.[1] Scholars have been unable to regard historical blacks in the reigns of Elizabeth and her immediate successors as anything more than stray figures in an "anecdotal" landscape, too accidental and solitary to be even a historical statistic.[2] Such current assumptions are merely reinforcements of the pronouncements of earlier scholars, who insisted that the Elizabethans did not know black people.[3] Yet, obscure, truncated and largely inaccessible documentary records, which are only now becoming fully available, paint a very different picture about the size, continuity and historical seriousness of the black presence in England in the sixteenth and seventeenth centuries, well before English black populations become known through the transatlantic slave trade.

---

1 Peter Erickson, "The Moment of Race in Renaissance Studies," p. 35. Even in the odd instance when scholars are impelled to assert that there were "fair numbers of black West Africans in England in the sixteenth and seventeenth centuries," they do so by blind faith rather than on the strength of documented evidence, as for instance Eldred Jones did a long time ago in his *The Elizabethan Image of Africa* (p. 17). By "black people" here and throughout this book, I mean people particularly from the African continent, including Egypt, but expediently from the Americas and India as well, in conformity with the endemically loose way an early modern English cultural consciousness sees them, as for instance Samuel Purchas does in his *Purchas His Pilgrimage*, p. 559. The only precision of the term "black" as a typological identifier of people—for the early modern English, and consequently for this study—is as a loose category of the non-white, non-English (as distinct from white but non-English people). "Black" in this study is thus "Negro," "Ethiopian," "Egyptian," "moor"/"blackamoor," "barbaree"/"barbaryen," and "Indian" (including orthographic variations thereof for all of them). The study's use of the word also includes geographic names by themselves, such as Guyana or Guinea, where for the early modern English they function openly or implicitly as regional identifiers of people of color. Anthony Gerard Barthelemy in *Black Face, Maligned Race* (pp. 1–17), Michael Neill in "'Mulattoes,' 'Blacks,' and 'Indian Moors'" (pp. 273–77), and Margo Hendricks in "Surveying Race" (pp. 15–20) all offer useful demonstrations of the propriety of adhering to a taxonomic looseness in tracing sixteenth- and seventeenth-century English constructions of colored people.

2 Kim Hall, *Things of Darkness*, p. 13.

3 G. K. Hunter, *Dramatic Identities and Cultural Traditions*, p. 32.

For instance, buried in the documentary minutiae of Elizabeth I's household records for the years 1574 and 1577 are several items of expenditure for two black individuals in her domestic staff, the one described as "a littel blak a More," and the other simply as both, "Thomasen, a woman dwarf," and as "Tomasen, the woman dwarf," respectively, the former apparently a page and the latter a female member of her personal entertainment staff.[4] Earlier in the century, obscured in the myriad desiderata of the ritual royal disbursements of Elizabeth's father and grandfather, are regular compensations to a black trumpeter named "John Blanke." Throughout the sixteenth century and the next, in the private household inventories of Tudor aristocrats, as well as in the casual entries of the parochial churches with which their estates or residences are associated, are notations about "Negroes" and "blackamores" or "blackamoors." For example, included in the elaborate instructions of Edward Stanley, the third Earl of Derby, to his domestic staff in 1568 is the incidental prohibition of his "slaves" from sitting at tables. Mentioned without explanation in the lavish household accounts of Robert Dudley, the Earl of Leicester, are his orders of payment to his "blackamore" in 1584, and to "Mr. Rawles" in 1585. Noted briefly in the baptism records of St. Luke's church in Kensington for 1597 is the baptism of Walter Raleigh's 11-year-old Guyanian boy "Charles," while tersely listed in St. Clements Danes' burial lists for 1601/02 is Robert Cecil's "blackamoor servant Fortunatus." Located unobtrusively in the extensive rolls of the Earl of Dorset's servants at Knole, his estate in Kent, for the period 1613–1624 is a "John Morrocco, a Blackamoor," and a "Grace Robinson, a Blackamoor," the latter also inexplicably remembered by Lady Anne Clifford in her *Diary*.

At the same time, hidden in the vast archives of parish churches within London and without, all through the Tudor and Stuart reigns, are voluminous cryptic citations of "nigro," "neger," "neygar," "blackamore," "blackamoor," "moor," "barbaree," "barbaryen," "Ethiopian," and "Indian." In London's northeast, in St. Mary the Virgin, Aldermanbury, a "Jhon the Blackamore" is said to have been baptized in 1565 and buried in 1566, and in St. Martin in the Fields "Margareta a Moor" is reported buried in 1571, in Christchurch Newgate Street on the city's west side the burial of Mr. Jucent's servant "Thomas Blackmore" is attested in 1579.[5] Towards the

---

4 Thomasen has been identified by some scholars as being black. See Item 139 in the Index. Henceforth, all records mentioned in this document will be cited in parenthesis in the document itself by the item number with which it occurs in the Index. The records cited below in this Introduction are only a sample of the total body of records presented in this book and listed and fully described in the Chronological Records Index at the end of the book. The full text and details of all records, including the ones referred to here, can be found in the Chronological Record Index, and in the discussions of each of them in the book's particular chapters in which they occur, in each of which they are identified parenthetically by the Item number that they have in the Chronological Records Index itself. Such Item number identification for each record mentioned here is for that reason not included in this Introduction.

5 All approximate parish locations and neighborhoods of early modern London and its environs provided in this book are derived from a combined consultation of the Agas and the Braun and Hogenberg maps of London in the 1570s reproduced in Prokter and Taylor, eds., *A to Z of Elizabethan London*, on pp. 2–29 and 32, respectively. In referring to London locations, I am assuming more or less the greater London area of today rather than the London

city's southwest, on the river, "Domyngo a Blackmore['s]" death is recorded in St. Ann's, Blackfriars in 1587/88. On the east side, transcribed in St. Botolph's church in Aldgate are the deaths of "Suzanna Pearis a blackamoore," "Symon Valencia a blackamore," and "Robarte a negar servant," all in 1593, while in nearby St. Olave's Church in Hart Street are described the demises of "Isabell a blackamore," "Francisco a nigro," and "Peter Marley, a blacamore" in 1588, 1590, and 1594, respectively. Across the river, south of the city, in the diocese of Southwark, a black family by the name of "Reasonable" is documented as living in St. Olave Tooley Street, where "Jane, d[aughter] of Reasonable, blackmor" and "Edmond, s[on] of Reasonable, blackmor" are listed as dying in 1591 and 1592.

Scattered across the four compass quadrants of London and its liberties, symptomatic documentations of black people continue in the seventeenth century. As a "Christian Ethiopia" was baptized in St. Dunstan and All Saints in Stepney in 1602, so was a "Richard a Blakmore" in St. George the Martyr, Southwark in 1609. In 1616, "Peter a blacamore … from Mrs Locksmiths" was buried in St. Dunstan in the West, while "An East Indian was Christened by the name of Peter" and publicly baptized in St Dionis Backchurch in central London. "Nicholas a Negro of unknown parents … at the age of 3 yeares or thereabouts" was baptized in St. Margaret's Westminster in 1619/20, while "Barbaree, servant to Mr. Smith" was buried in St. Peter, Paul's Wharf in 1623. The death of "Anthony, a poore ould Negro aged 105 yeares," occurred in Hackney in 1630, and "Sara Reide … a blackamore['s]" baptism took place in St. Dunstan, Stepney in 1659.

In the same period, inscribed fragmentarily in legal, taxation, medical and civic archives is the varied impress of black working lives. Immured within the ponderous substance and verbiage of sixteenth- and seventeenth-court documents are instances of black people answering to the laws of the land. A black Guinean diver's testimony on his employer's behalf in an Admiralty case in 1547/48 was protested by the prosecution because he was a slave. In a Court of Requests hearing in 1587 the newly purchased Ethiopian servant of a Portuguese merchant was the object of his master's desperate complaint because he refused to obey him. Sometime between 1588 and 1599, in a lawsuit filed in the Court of the Queen's Bench and heard in the Court of Chancery, the blackamoor servants of a prominent London Marrano Jewish physician's kinsmen were made to offer *by proxy* incriminating evidence against the physician after his death. Noted dryly in laconic tax returns are identifications such as "Lambert Waterson, denizen, barbaryen, tenaunte … [who] goeth to his parish church" in St. Giles in the Fields north of London in 1568, "Ferdinando a Blackamore" in All Saints, Staynings in 1582, and "Clar a Negra at Widdow Stokes, Maria a negra at Olyver Skynners, Lawse a negra at Mr. Mittons, Marea a Negra at Mr. Woodes," in Tower Ward in 1598. On occasion, written into stray medical records in London and in the country, are accounts such as Simon Forman's diagnosis in 1597 of "Polonia the blackmor maid at Mr Peirs" as suffering from "a fever …

defined by early modern English city limits. In the subsequent chapters of this book all London locations cited will be referenced parenthetically in my text itself by the map coordinate and page number of the location in the Agas map in Prokter and Taylor.

[and] faint heart full of melancholy," and a Court of Wards' postmortem in Chester, Cheshire of "George Blackmore" in 1617.

Even with their enigmatic brevity, such references register black lives in many visible professions. In addition to the vocational activities evident above, namely trumpeter, diver, royal page, entertainer, laundress, servant, and maid, black professional service caught in these documents includes that of a professional soldier of the kind that the decorated Peter Negro is in 1548, needlemaker of the type William Harrison remembers working in Cheapside in the early 1550s during Mary Tudor's reign, and metal worker of the sort that Symon Valencia is in St. Botolph, Aldgate in 1593. Also noticeable are goldsmiths, such as Andrew and Henry Blackmore in St. Mary Woolnoth in 1626. Indeed, in one instance an entire group of black people in a neighborhood setting is caught in a casual London newspaper comment in 1645.

Yet, despite the plentifulness of black people in early modern England that such documentary materials reflect, they do not, for the most part, appear in contemporary accounts of the land and its peoples as a distinct, considerable population. In his influential encyclopedic *Description of England* in 1577 William Harrison remembers only the black needlemaker in Cheapside in the reign of Mary Tudor cited above but declares emphatically "As for slaves and bondmen, we have none."[6] Following him, Thomas Smith and William Camden, in their magisterial accounts of the country in 1583 and 1586, are oblivious of any English black populations. Foreign accounts of England in the later decades of Elizabeth's reign are not any different. The Duke of "Wirtemburg" describes violent, dangerous street scenes in London in 1592 but no black people anywhere.[7] Paul Hentzner, the German traveler, sees Negro figures in a tapestry in Whitehall in 1597, but no living black people.[8] Thomas Platter, a Swiss visitor to England, recounts crowded London playhouse scenes in 1599 but mentions no blacks. The English reports of Juan Fernández de Velasco in 1604, Otto Prince of Hesse in 1611, Peter Eisenberg in 1614, and Valentin Arithmœs in 1617 fare no better either, notwithstanding their detailed and often critical recollections of English social practices.[9] Meticulous English urban and national chronicles at the end of the century and in the next are equally devoid of any citations of black inhabitants of the land. John Stow, while providing the most minutely informed and historically authoritative tabulation of Elizabethan London's neighborhoods and residents in 1598, has only a casual, ambiguous comment about black monks in Blackfriars but no other references to black people.[10] Between 1631 and 1684 John Evelyn, while faithfully chronicling numerous social and public events in London, has no memory of any black persons in England, even though he remembers seeing one in Milan,[11]

6 *The Description of England*, ed. George Edelen, p. 118. Although it is clear from the context that Harrison's phrase "bondmen and slaves" does not refer to blacks, they do not figure as a class of people at all in his taxonomy of English social structure.

7 In Willam Brenchley Rye, ed., *England as Seen by Foreigners: In the Reigns of Elizabeth and James 1*, pp. 1–52; see esp. p. 7.

8 Paul Hentzner and Sir Robert Naunton, *Travels in England and Fragmenta Regalia*; see p. 37.

9 Rye, *England as Seen by Foreigners*, pp. 115–24; pp. 141–45; pp. 175–78.

10 *A Survey of London* (1598), ed. Charles L. Kingsford, 1:340.

11 John Evelyn, *The Diary of John Evelyn*, p. 250.

which is all the more surprising since his close friend, Samuel Pepys, has several intimate accounts of black individuals in his *Diary*. Thomas Fuller in 1662 faithfully lists detailed histories of notable English personalities, regions, commodities, and resources, but cannot recall any blacks anywhere in such histories.[12]

So, are black people in early modern England an invisible, secret population? Not slaves officially since a reformist English Protestantism disavows slavery publicly even as it advocates its expedient usage,[13] nor properly a part of the medieval serfdom of *villeinage*, since that is a practice badly decayed by the sixteenth century,[14] and not quite belonging to the new practice of indentured servantship either because its precise articles of contract are for a color-coded English cultural practice almost certainly not usable for illicitly acquired blacks, early modern English black people miss the minimum humanizing visibility of legal definition. Tudor and Stuart poor laws—such as those of 1531, 1536, 1547, 1550, 1552, 1555, 1563, 1572, 1576, 1598 (2), 1601, 1610, 1647, 1649, and 1662 (which gives parishes the right to remove any newcomer deemed to be a burden)—do not see black people even when they see

---

12 Thomas Fuller, *The Worthies of England.*

13 Occasional papal edicts against slaving practices, such as the *Sicut Dudum* of Pope Eugene IV in 1435 condemning the enslavement of peoples in the newly colonized Canary Islands; Pope Pius II's letter in 1462 gravely warning against the enslaving of baptized Africans; and the *Sublimis Deus* of Pope Paul III in 1537 describing the enslavers of the West and South Indies as allies of the devil and declaring attempts to justify such slavery "null and void" (Parker Pillsbury, *Acts of the Anti-Slavery Apostles*, pp. 830–31), corroborated in English common law deriving from the Magna Carta (William Quigley, "Five Hundred Years of English Poor Laws, 1349–1834," p. 76), are reflected in conventional English disavowals of slavery such as the court rulings of 1569 ("Matter of Cartwright," 11 Elizabeth 1, in John Rushworth, *Historical Collections*, p. 468) and 1587 (Court of Requests 2/164/117; Index Item 163); in the denials of Sir Thomas Roe abroad in India in 1616, when he declines the Mughal emperor's offer of an Asian slave because "in England we had no slaues, neyther was it lawfull to make the Image of God fellow to a Beast ...," and in 1617, when he turns down the Mughal emperor's offer to sell him three "Abassines" (Abyssinian, i.e. Ethiopian slaves) because "I could not buy men as Slaues, as others did, and so had profit for their money ..." (*The Embassy of Sir Thomas Roe to the Court of the Great Moghul*, journal entries of March 23, 1616 and November 6, 1617 respectively, pp. 150 and 445–46), and of Richard Jobson in West Africa in 1620, who when offered slaves by a local chief said "Wee are a people that do not deal in such commodities, neither did we buy nor sell one another" (cited by Robin Blackburn, "The Old World Background to European Colonial Slavery," p. 96). At the same time, an expedient slavery is defended by the foremost Elizabethan jurist Sir Edward Coke in Calvin's Case in 1608, in which he rules that "all infidels are in law perpetual enemies" (Thomas Bayley Howell, ed., *Complete Collection of State Trials* 2:559), and complicatedly defined by the political philosopher John Locke in 1679 when as the justifiable product of a just war: "a state of war continued between a lawful conqueror and a captive" (*Second Treatise of Civil Government* 2:4, 24), both deriving from Pope Nicholas V's *Romanus Pontifex* Bull of 1455 sanctioning the war against and enslavement of non-Christian people whose primitive living practices are in violation of natural law (extracted in Frances Gardiner Davenport, ed., *European Treaties*, p. 23).

14 Sir John Baker, "Human Rights and the Rule of Law in Renaissance England."

the poorest in English society.[15] At the same time, throughout the fluctuating history of Tudor and Stuart legal definitions of aliens, including the repeated Elizabethan censuses of aliens in London and elsewhere,[16] the focus is on European religious

[15] The orders are, respectively, "Concerning Punishment of Rogues and Vagabonds" (22 Henry VIII c. 12); "For the Punishment of Sturdy Vagabonds and Beggars" (27 Henry VIII c. 25); "For the Punishment of Vagabonds and Relief of the Poor and Impotent Persons" (I Edw. VI c. 3); "Touching the Punishment of Vagabonds and other Idle Persons" (3 & 4 Edw. VI. c. 16); "For the Provision and Relief of the Poor" (5 & 6 Edw. VI c. 2); "For the Relief of the Poor" (2 & 3 Philip & Mary c. 5); "For the Relief of the Poor" (5 Eliz. I c. 3); "For the Punishment of Vagabonds and for Relief of the Poor and the Impotent" (14 Eliz. I c. 5); "For the Setting of the Poor on Work, and for the Avoiding of Idleness" (18 Eliz. I c. 3); "For the Relief of the Poor (39 Eliz. I c. 30); "For the Punishment of Rogues, Vagabonds and Sturdy Beggars" (39 Eliz. I c. 40); "For the Relief of the Poor" (43 Eliz. I c. 2); "For the Charitable Relief and Ordering of Persons infected with the Plague" (1 James I c. 31); "For the Due Execution of ... Laws ... Against Rogues ... and Other Lewd and Idle Persons" (7 James I c. 4); (1647 & 1649) "Ordinances of Parliament for the Relief and Employment of the Poor and Punishment of Vagrants and other disorderly Persons in the City of London"; "For the better Relief of the Poor of this Kingdom [Act of Settlement]" (13 & 14 Car. II c. 12); for a description of these laws, see Paul Slack, *The English Poor Law*, pp. 59–62.

[16] Irrespective of whether alien status is not an issue in post-conquest England because the government of William the Conqueror itself is foreign, as F. Pollock and F. W. Maitland held (*The History of English Law* 1:458–62), or whether it is legally constructed from Anglo-Saxon times to the fifteenth century exclusively in terms of a person's place of birth or origin in a location other than that of the time of such construction, or whether such constructions are also based on the person's status as "free" or "unfree," as in the writings of Glanville and Bracton, as Keechang Kim has recently argued (*Aliens in Medieval Law*, p. 9), and irrespective of how any or all of these ideas are replaced by or combined with allegiance to the monarch (i.e. state) as a criterion for the consideration of English subjecthood or citizenship from the fifteenth century onwards in the expositions of John Fortescue (*De Laudibus Legum Angliae*, p. 30) and Thomas Littleton (*Tenures*, fol. xiv r), and irrespective of how both traditions collide contradictorily in the early modern period in the pronouncements of Edward Coke in "Calvin's Case" in 1608 (Howell, *State Trials*, 2:638–96), such constructions do not extend to black people in Tudor and Stuart England, who remain, like animals, an un-legalized entity. This is true even if they fit the convenient summary of legal restrictions on aliens in England that Daniel Statt offers in his study of seventeenth- and eighteenth-century English alien legislation based on his culling of the standard legal historians of England such as W. Holdsworth, W. Blackstone, and A. K. Cockburn, that includes stipulations such as that the alien "could own no real property, he could have no legal heir, … he could bring no legal action that related to property, … he had no political rights, could not vote or hold political office," and could not employ "fellow aliens" ("The City of London and the Controversy over Immigration," p. 46). These stipulations, which permanently include the government's *de facto* right to search and seizure, are the overall product of both a variable Tudor monarchic fear of French and Spanish Catholic penetration of the security of the state, and of a selective monarchic pandering for popular support in times of crises to perennial English mercantile instincts of opportunistic protectionism against Italian, French, Dutch, and Spanish trade and craft activities within the country. Beginning with Edward I's Ordinances of London in 1285, Richard II's 6 Richard II c. 10 in 1382, Henry IV's 5 Henry c. 9 in 1399 and his 18 Henry IV c. 4 in 1439, Edward IV's 3 Edward IV c.3 and c. 4 in 1464, and Richard III's 1 Richard III c. 9 and c. 12 in 1483, some of the more signal instances of this legislative history include the

refugees. The fact that (a) most blacks may technically have been foreigners or aliens in terms of the histories of their arrivals and (b) English poor laws and local government were not set up to cater to outsiders, does not mitigate the fact of their exclusion from civic sight, particularly since they became a settled population in England. More than being even foreign or poor, black people are unnamable entities. The one time the law does openly identify them, it does so in a gesture of exclusion, as in Elizabeth's unsuccessful orders of 1596 and 1601 deporting "negars and blackamoors" from the realm, and which in their abruptness and singularity are acts that merely reinforce their effacement rather than the palpability of their English existence. Unseen in civic record, and hidden as references to them most frequently are in secretive parish archives,[17] where they are further obfuscated by (a) the eccentricities of improvisatory parish documentation that is incomplete, inconsistent, and discontinuous, (b) non-standard orthography, and the opacity of early modern English cultural naming practices, and (c) the pressures of the conversion process, whereby ethnic identities disappear under Christian names, Tudor–Stuart black lives are imperceptible in the cultural acknowledgments of the age. Even when they are visible, as in the popular representations of the English public theaters—such as in the plays of Thomas Kyd, Christopher Marlowe, Ben Jonson, and William Shakespeare—their historical reality fades under the deformative force of cultural metaphor and becomes exotic fiction.

Unsurprisingly, in seeming consequence of all of the above, early modern English black people are untraceable in the work of both social historians of the age such as Lawrence Stone, Peter Laslett, Steven Rappaport, A. L. Beier, Ann Kussmul, Ian Archer, F. F. Foster, Joan Thirsk, Paul Slack, Jeremy Boulton, Paul Griffiths, and Lena Orlin, and traditional literary scholars of the period such as Louis Wright, Samuel Schoenbaum, and G. K. Hunter, despite the fact that all of them use sophisticated cross-disciplinary methodologies and deal extensively with primary documents of the time. Even for traditional and post-structuralist scholars alike who have focused on historically ignored population groups in Elizabethan and Jacobean England, such as Linda Yungblut in her study of the xenophobia about strangers, aliens, and foreigners, and Patricia Fumerton in her tracking of the cultural life of vagrants respectively, black communities have not comprised an analytical category.[18]

---

statute of 14–15 Henry VIII c. 2 in 1523, which is revived and instituted permanently in 1529 in 21 Henry VIII c. 16, forbidding aliens to keep more than two fellow alien associates and making them submit to search and regulation, and to swear allegiance to the king. 32 Henry VIII c. 16 extends these restrictions to aliens and denizens. That black people are outside the consideration of even such restrictions demonstrates starkly how in the early modern period generally they are a people beyond the penumbra of political and civic legislation. For an account of the intensive Elizabethan surveys of aliens in London see Linda Yungblut, *Strangers Settled Here amongst Us*, pp. 17–25 and 86–92, and Ronald Pollit, "'Refuge of the Distressed Nations,'" pp. D1003–D1008.

[17] See the essay by Paul Griffiths, "Secrecy and Authority in Sixteenth and Seventeenth Century London", and Ian Archer, who observes, "Parish clerks were careful to conceal the existence of controversies" (*The Pursuit of Stability*, p. 84).

[18] It is appropriate to point out—in a footnote—that when Linda Yungblut does see black people—"two 'blackmores' were reported living in London at the time of this survey"—she

II

Emerging scholarly attention to this problem over the last four decades, while useful in tabling the issue, has been spotty, diffuse, and generally ineffective in its findings. W. E. Miller's solitary enumeration in 1961 of four Elizabethan London tax assessments identifying four black people in All Hallows parish was followed by Eldred Jones's two publications in 1965 and 1971 that broadly and tentatively searched for an empirical Elizabethan knowledge of black people. In between Jones's two works, Thomas Forbes, in his study in 1969 of the parish registers of St. Botolph, Aldgate, cited in the preface of his book, without any further attention, a list of entries of black people that he had found. Two similarly brief but helpful works were Robert Fleissner's pieces in 1976 and 1978 on the mannerist parallels between George Herbert's poem "Aethiopissia" and the "Dark Lady" of Shakespeare's *Sonnets,* and on the "Moor's Nomenclature," respectively. The trend toward documentary evidence in Miller and Jones, and the encouraging cue in Forbes's prefatory list, grew over the next two decades into the work of the black social historians Follarin Shyllon, Paul Edwards, James Walvin, Peter Fryer, and St. Clair Drake. But they focused more on the more relatively visible periods *after* the emergence of the slave trade in the latter half of the seventeenth century; historical blacks in the England of Elizabeth and her immediate successors were a minor and occasional presence in their data. That is even truer for the most recent example of this kind of study, Gretchen Gerzina's *Black London.*

On the other hand, the instinct for analyses of modes of representation in Fleissner, in gravitating in the same period as the work of Shyllon and the others into the full blown critical excursus of literary scholars such as David Dabydeen, Ruth Cowhig, Eliott Tokson, Anthony Gerard Barthelemy, and Jack D'Amico, while importantly foregrounding race and blackness as neglected topoi in Elizabethan and Jacobean literary studies, further occluded the materiality and consequent historical import of the black presence in the earlier centuries of the English early modern age. With the advent in the late 1980s of post-structuralist exegesis of early modern English race formations, the proliferation of such modes-of-representation studies in a constellation of analytical axes—cultural materialist, black studies, feminist, postcolonial—has eclipsed the subject of the historical presence of black people in Tudor and Stuart regimes even further and relegated it to the status of an unfashionable scholarly hobby-horse and naïve intellectual interest.[19] The only exceptions have been Roslyn Knutson's brief but important study in 1991 of notations of black people in several London parishes, Duncan Salkeld's committed electronic essay in 2000 about black prostitutes in late Elizabethan London court records ("Black Lucy"), Virginia Mason Vaughan's electronic notice in 2001 of blacks in the Harleian Society's published

---

relegates them to a footnote: p. 21, n. 39. See Margo Hendricks's comment on this scholarly sleight of hand in her essay, "Feminist Historiography," p. 371.

[19] I am referring to the work of Michael Neill, Peter Erickson, Martin Orkin, Emily Bartels, Joyce Green MacDonald, Margo Hendricks, Kim Hall, Ania Loomba, Jyotsna Singh, Dympna Callaghan, Arthur Little, St. Clair Drake, and Catherine Alexander and Stanley Wells, and my own work.

transcriptions of Tudor and Stuart London parish registers in the Folger Shakespeare library's holdings, and Margo Hendricks's essay in an anthology on early modern women's writing, insisting on the need for scholars to now turn to archival work on a historical black presence in early modern England.[20] Also exceptional has been Marika Sherwood's dogged if informal pursuit of black records in the Tudor and Stuart years. Equally notable is the work Susan Amussen has started recently on historical black people in England in the later seventeenth century. But these exploratory excursus have been little noticed and remain together with the works of Miller and Jones and the citations of Forbes, as well as peripherally that of Shyllon, Walvin, Fryer, and Drake, part of a minority trend in current scholarship. As the editors of the first recent scholarly attempts to explore the history of black people in Europe announce at the very beginning of their volume, this is a "neglected" subject, and as another contemporary scholar has put it, one that is still in its "infancy."[21]

Indeed, the triumph of theory in a poststructuralist age might seem to be the prohibition of the real. The threatening specter of essentialism translates factuality into the unknowable, renders ambivalent if not disallows the value of the archive. Yet, theory needs "a local habitation and a name" on which to mark itself, an ontology for the semiology of its performative life, without which its epistemological dividend misses its material effect. This lacuna develops into a compound loss in the otherwise rich aggressiveness of current deconstructions of racial formations in the early modern age in England cited earlier, in which the topoi of the racial other cannot transcend its constructionist abstraction and remains an ideology only, rather than an ideology that includes also, and is mandated by, the impress of the literal. The resultant scenario can be described thus: what is little looked for, and what is therefore non-existent, is also what is/should be unknown because it cannot be known. This in turn reinforces the conventional contemporary mistruth: there were no actual people of color in early modern England; references to them in popular media of the time are metaphoric; and the period is race-innocent. Thus, theory might seem to conspire with the natural fragmentariness and obscurity of the documentary life of the early modern English episteme to block the real of the racial in the corrective reconstructions of the age.

III

It is the contention of this book that the substantial archival evidence of black people in England between 1501 and 1676 exemplified above contributes significant,

---

20 "Feminist Historiography," pp. 374–75. Hendricks's call is paralleled by Kim Hall, both together representing a response to Ania Loomba's suggestion that scholarship should now move away from historical "black presence studies"; see Loomba's "The Color of Patriarchy," p. 26, and Kim Hall's measured rejoinder in her essay "Object into Object: Some Thoughts on the Presence of Black Women in Early Modern Culture," p. 349.

21 T. F. Earle and K. J. P. Lowe, eds., *Black Africans in Renaissance Europe*, statement in book's summary on the opening page; Vera Lind, "Africans in Early Modern German Society: Identity – Difference – Aesthetics – Anthropology." Electronic essay available at http://www.ghi-dc.org/bulletin28S01/b28lind.html. 12.9.05.

irreversible, and hitherto unavailable materialities to current understanding of racial discourse in sixteenth- and seventeenth-century England. These records mark the empirical intimacy of the English construction of the racial other, and of the national-imperial drive that is its most immediate occasion, both parallel to and independent of such formations in the travel literature of the period.[22] If, as Jacques Derrida has said, "what is no longer archived the same way is no longer lived the same way,"[23] it follows that archives write lived lives. As in the "repressed archive [lies] the power of the state over the historian," so "there is no political power without access to the archives."[24] If "[t]he "archive always works, and *a priori*, against itself," and if it reveals as much as it suppresses,[25] it is these archives that will publish the very secrets that they were meant to guard. As such, in documenting the presence of black people in Shakespeare's England, these datasets will de-mystify decisively the subject of the black presence in early modern English cultural history. If, in Michel Foucault's terms, the archive is "the system of discursivity" that establishes the possibility of what can be said,[26] these archives register the imprints of the invisible black within the most visible cultural episteme of the West.

In presenting these archives this book will, thus, marry productively, in the manner called for by Duncan Salkeld,[27] the hard pragmatism of traditional history with the constructionist convictions of poststructuralist theory in general, and postcolonial

---

[22] I mean here typically the well-known writings of John Mandeville, Leo Africanus, William Towerson, Richard Eden, Richard Hakluyt, and Samuel Purchas, among others, which have been traditionally regarded as the obvious sites of early modern English racial construction; see, for instance, Emily Bartel's essay "Imperialist Beginnings: Richard Hakluyt and the Construction of Africa."

[23] "Archive Fever," p. 18.

[24] Sonia Combe, *Forbidden Archives*, p. 321, cited by Derrida in "Archive Fever," p. 10 n. 1 and p. 10, respectively.

[25] "Archive Fever," p. 14.

[26] *Archaeology of Knowledge* p. 129.

[27] "Those who see a neutral history as the only one worth striving for (and if it can't be had, the very possibility of history is denied), throw the whole thing in because they demand the impossible. Theirs is a kind of all-or-nothing position which asserts that since genuine difficulties attach to historical/textual interpretation, it must follow that *all* interpretation is in the end 'fatally flawed' or futile. But only a hopelessly naive belief in the absolute conceptual purity of an intellectual discipline could be so flawed. Any view of historical interpretation which disavowed total conceptual purity would have not a single glove laid on it by this form of critique. Most people can accept that all sorts of difficulties and unknowns intervene with primary source material, empirical evidence, contextual bias and establishing agreement, since these are precisely what makes the study of history interesting and worthwhile. But no one needs to assume, as some postmodernists do, that since the history writer cannot step outside her language, community and time, her narrative of the past is 'fatally' disabled. There is, of course, no stepping 'outside' the language of our communities and so too, of course, there is no pure vocabulary of 'fact' that an imagined 'neutral' history could articulate. Once that illusion is dispensed with, and it is allowed that there simply are no non-evaluative discourses, the need to generalize about the fallibility of interpretation drops away, and more complex considerations of what makes an interpretation more or less persuasive come into view." Salkeld, "Making Sense of Difference," p. 5.

theory in particular, in which the strengths of the one are appropriated by the other, so that the facticity of the archives becomes the mandate of theory and the construction of theory writes the reconstructed facts of the English early modern age. Enabling the visibility and historical impress of black people in Tudor and Stuart England necessitates several heuristic transactions. Generally, since "archivization produces as much as it records the event,"[28] to navigate the archives is also to construct them. To secure access to the historical subjects of such records from the casual crypticity of parish record, arcane legal testimony, and casual household inventory listing, will involve doing what Paul Voss and Marta Werner have described as "read[ing]" their "minimum signs with maximum energy."[29] To extract a sense of a living community from such records despite the refraction inevitably imposed on them by the mediation of their recorders, such a community will have to be conceived, in the sense of what Patricia Fumerton has called the "virtual subject" of "nowhere people," as archival subjects that occupy a virtual space in the map of visible history.[30] The same virtuality of black archival content reckons with the inevitable transience of the abodes of disadvantaged early modern groups, particularly in London, and translates the scattered incidence of black people in the archives into the signs of a community that is identifiably cogent in its epistemic context and broad regional location. In the quantification of virtual black subjecthoods, the inscrutability of numbers cannot make what figures of black people the recovered records yield seem to be absolute, symptomatically indicative as they instead are of a larger unquantifiable population, and the semiotic quotient not of a demographic curiosity but of a historically significant reality.

The term "community" applied to early modern English black people here, and elsewhere in this study, is used in neither of the two senses in which Ian Archer has said the term is used in modern sociological scholarship, namely "locality" and "social organization."[31] Rather, cued by James Walvin's construction of the idea of such a black community as comprising "individuals distinguished from white society by their blackness, no matter how widely separated they might be,"[32] it is meant to denote a group of people bound by a common history of direct or indirect English enslavement, benign or brutal, and having common ethnic or cultural characteristics, not as a group of people who necessarily share a common interest and communicate with each other or who even know each other but as a term that is a starting point for identifying a set of people in the historical significance of their plurality. What Archer says about the "marginalized groups" of "subsistence migrants" in early modern London applies in a much starker sense to the early modern English black community as a whole that is this study's subject: "access to a key instrument of socialization was denied them. Rather they found themselves eking out an existence on the margins of economic life …" According to Archer what precludes such subsistence migrants from "a key instrument of socialization" is their exclusion from "the membership of the household of established citizens that apprenticeship

28 "Archive Fever," 17.

29 "Towards a Poetics of the Archive," p. ii.

30 Fumerton, "London's Vagrant Economy," pp. 220–21.

31 *Pursuit of Stability*, p. 58.

32 *Black and White*, p. xiii.

entailed."[33] For many early modern English black people, however, their location even in aristocratic households did not provide such socializing identifications, since they existed there as nameless chattels. Their commonly dispersed, unnamed existence is what makes them, in this study's purview, a historical community. But that early modern English black people can constitute a community even in the traditional sense of the term cited above (a group of people who share a common interest and communicate with each other or who even know each other) is evident in the one rare reference cited earlier, about their neighborhood activities near the Portuguese ambassador's house in London in 1645.

If the un-seeability of early modern English black people is also due to the sedimented racial etymology of their naming, the re-seeing of this population has to bypass traditional onomastics. As Ann Stoler has argued, racial thinking is not subsequent to social order but constitutive of it. Racism is not only a colonial reflex fashioned to deal with the distant other but a part of the very making of Europeans themselves, a setting up of the privileged hierarchies through which the European order itself will function.[34] Racial naming proceeds not from the fixity of essence but from its very ambiguity, which is to say that it fixes difference on that which resists difference, on that which is human/white but not quite. Thus, racial naming may *appear* to be a neutral descriptor of difference, unless it is realized that racial taxonomies produce difference in the very act of cataloging it.[35] In this sense, the English adoption of the Spanish-Portuguese word "negar/neger" for black, and "mourao" for Moor, may *seem* neutral, but the descriptive act in this derivative naming is a distancing separative gesture that only sometimes strains toward explicitness through other supplementary descriptors such as the prefixed variant "blackamoor" or the geographic locator positioned as surname, "guinea," 'ethiope," "barbary."[36] At other times, the racialism of the naming of the black is buried within the opacity of the chosen nominal term standing by itself. Thus, if "niger," meaning black in Latin, becomes "negro" meaning a black person in Spanish-Portuguese, and "negre" in middle French and "neger" in early modern English evolve with the same meaning[37]—that is a racialization process because it essentializes a physical attribute; a color becomes an essential determinant of a person which then is made to signify the entirety of the individual (without the same happening to white people in that moment). The word cannot be neutral, irrespective of whether the negative, racializing connotations show up obviously in it. As Alden T. Vaughan put it,

> in each language the word for "black" carried a host of disparaging connotations. In Spanish, for example, "negro" also meant gloomy, dismal, unfit, and wretched; in French, "noir" also connoted foul, dirty, base, and wicked; in Dutch, certain compounds of "zwart"

33 *Pursuit of Stability*, pp. 61–62.

34 Stoler, *Carnal Knowledge and Imperial Power*, p. 144.

35 Ibid., p. 207.

36 For discussions of the etymology of moor meaning a black person, see J. A. Rogers, *Nature Knows No Color Line*, pp. 72–74.

37 *Webster's New Universal Unabridged Dictionary*, p. 1203; *The Oxford English Dictionary*, 1:79; in that same main entry, however, the *OED* also cites "negerous" as "barbarous."

> conveyed notions of anger, irascibility, and necromancy; and 'black' had comparable pejorative implications in Elizabethan and Stuart England.[38]

To this can be added J. G. Jackson's comment that "no African was ever called 'negro' before or without enslavement, present or past."[39]

Two examples of visibly negative uses of descriptions of black people include the description of a "morisco," i.e. a Moor, as a worthless slave in the 1547/8 Admiralty case cited earlier (which is also the year that the word "blak e more" is first used in Andrew Boorde's *Introduction to the Book of Knowledge*), and John Minsheu's definition of "negro" as "a great lipp'd fellow" in his dictionary of 1599.[40] In the semantic mutation of "niger" to "negar," and of "morisco" to "moor" to "blak e more" and "blak a more," the racial etymology is additionally obfuscated by, and hidden under, other traditional associations of those words with which that etymology uncertainly coexists, such as field for "moor," and "blackmore" as a customary English surname.[41] The hidden negativity of the early modern English naming of black people applies to the variable Tudor and Stuart semantics of "black" as well, which indistinguishably includes both a black-haired, black-eyed, or tawny Caucasian, as well as an African (as in the instance of "reasonable, Blackman" cited above, whose racialization is visible only in the additional descriptor "blackamore" attached to his children).[42] The finding of early modern English black people will therefore have to proceed with a certain amount of reasoned intuition, in which the identification of individuals will have inevitably an approximate rather than an absolute accuracy.

IV

Given the virtual materiality of black people in the archives that is this study's project to render, the 448 records that will be presented comprise a catalogue that is neither definitive in ambition nor documentarily puristic in substance. To aspire to definitiveness in the detritus of personal, mercantile, legal, and governmental minutiae cannot be a feasible prospect because the accidental, discontinuous, and impossibly dispersed nature of the survival of such details ensure for them a state

---

38 Alden T. Vaughan, *Roots of American Racism*, p. 6.

39 *The Story of the Moors in Spain*; cited by Cedric Robinson, "The Inventions of the Negro," p. 332.

40 The first use of "blak e more" by Boorde is cited by the *Oxford English Dictionary*, 1:223, which also cites in the same headnote William Thomas's definition of the word in his *Italian Gram* the following year as "a man of Ethiopo." For Minsheu's definition of "negro" see Ian Lancashire's *Early Modern English Dictionaries Database* (EMEDD).

41 For "moor" as field see Patricia Hank and Flavia Hodges, *A Dictionary of Surnames*, p. 54; and for "moor" as both field and dark, see Reaney and Wilson, *A Dictionary of English Surnames*, p. 243.

42 For "black" as meaning dark see L. G. Pine, *The Story of Surnames*, p. 90; Charles Wareing Bardsley, *English and Welsh Surnames*, pp. 445–46; William Arthur, *An Etymological Dictionary of Family and Christian Names*, p. 77. For "black" as meaning both dark and fair, see Hank and Hodges, *A Dictionary of Surnames*, p. 55. For "blackman," "blakeman," as meaning dark man, see Reaney and Wilson, *A Dictionary of English Surnames*, p. 31.

of perpetually incomplete recovery.[43] Furthermore, as one early modern European demographic historian has put it, "detailed compilations [of demographic data] run the risk of rapid obsolescence."[44] The book's aim is not to recover a black population of any particular size, but to establish its very presence in early modern England, in considerable plurality, range of locations, and periodic continuity, that together demonstrate black people to be a known even if denied ethnic group rather than stray individuals encountered by few or none. Likewise, the collection of black records presented here is framed by dates that are not incontestably perspicuous but reasonably cogent. The general expository logic of the opening date of 1500 is that it marks the beginning of British and European cross-oceanic explorations and hence of contact with non-Europe, and that of the closing date of 1677 is that it highlights the first year in which British slavery is, albeit briefly, made official.[45]

The second limitation is mandated by the fact that against the inherent heterogeneity of these materials what creates them as an archive is simply the commonalty of their references to black people. They cannot be subjected to the kind of deep-structure unpacking used in traditional historical analyses, namely their examination in "the full field of language in history," prescribed by Carolyn Porter and demonstrated by Cynthia Susan Clegg, who cites her,[46] not only because "the archive is always only partially decodable,"[47] but also because materials such as these do not exist within

---

43 The comments of Paul Voss and Marta Warner about the fundamental fragmentariness of *all* archives are worth noting: "The history of the archive, on the one hand, a history of conservation, is, on the other hand, a history of loss. The archives of antiquity have long since vanished; we receive their contents as fragments or only as citations in later works. The contents of the English monastic libraries, scattered at the time of the Dissolution … have been only haphazardly and incompletely recollected … Moreover, the complex relationship between the archive and memory is not confined to the forces/agents of the outside but inheres in the interior dynamics of the archive. Even if the historical winds never destabilized the archives, their ultimate stability would not be guaranteed; the archive's dream of perfect order is disturbed by the nightmare of its random, heterogeneous, and often unruly contents. The dream of those secret or disconcerting elements ('errors,' 'garbage') located at its outermost edges or in its deepest recesses, defile codification and unsettle memory and context …" (pp. i–ii). "Founded in order to preserve the official records of successive cultures but comprised of material 'citations' often wrenched out of context, the archive is necessarily established in proximity to a loss—of *other* citations, citations of *otherness*" (p. ii).

44 L. R. Poos, "Historical Demography of Renaissance Europe," p. 796.

45 In 1663 England chartered the Company of Royal Adventurers—renamed the Royal African Company in 1672—which officially designated blacks commodities, or chattel, to be exchanged across the Middle Passage in the slave trade. This company held a monopoly on slaving, transporting nearly 90,000 slaves from 1673 to 1689, when all Englishmen were granted the right to trade in slaves (James Rawley, *The Transatlantic Slave Trade*, pp. 151–77). In 1677, in the court case *Butts v Penny*, involving a suit to recover possession of 100 slaves, it was held for the first time that slavery was legal in England because black people were infidels and the subjects of an infidel prince, and therefore without the rights enjoyed by Christians (A. Lester and G. Bindman, *Law and Race*, p. 28).

46 Carolyn Porter, "Are We Being Historical Yet?," p. 782; Cynthia Susan Clegg, "Archival Poetics and the Politics of Literature," p. 118.

47 Voss and Werner, "Towards a Poetics of the Archive," p. ii.

the plane of visibility that source documents of traditional historical scholarship have. Such records as this study deals with do not have for their recorders the already-established contextual value that the supplementary connected illumination of a cultural habit of documenting such subjects can provide and that is recognizable *as such* by the requisites of modern historical research. As a stand-alone instinct of preservation that is for the most part neither exclusively public nor private in what it preserves—the compost of human miscellany, the marginalia of mundane litigation, and the gloss of incidental private observation—these black records represent an unprecedented subject of early modern English memory that lacks the pre-established form that can historically identify it. Even if the black contents of the parochial church registers are part of data produced by Tudor monarchic promulgations ordering minute civil surveillance from the middle of the sixteenth century onwards, such dictates specified only purpose, not format: recording black people *per se* was not the charge given to the Church Wardens and parish clerks.[48] Thus, as the black records exceed the inter-documentary connectivities that one might bring to bear on them, so they resist the notions of documentary formalism that conservative scholarly expectations might demand of their assemblage as archives.

As the energy of this compilation is directed primarily to establishing a hitherto unavailable *critical mass* of information about the historical existence of black people in Tudor and Stuart England irrespective of any methodological self-consciousness that might accrue therefrom, its source attestation will variably include unpublished manuscript, transcribed print material, and even electronic media. Use of the last-named source is in acknowledgment of both, the impracticable time- and cost-intensive difficulty of direct examination of *all* early modern English manuscript records of the sort discussed above, and of the recent initiative of British national document repositories to release on the world wide web in the form of individual articles as well as online searchable catalogs partly scanned and transcribed sample manuscript contents of materials in their possession, including advertisements of those pertaining to black people.[49] As public announcements, such releases provide

48 The exact phrasing of the order, which was issued on September 5, 1538 to every parish in England and Wales, was as follows: "By the authoritie and commission of the most excellent Prince Henry by the Grace of God Kynge of Englande and France … I Thomas Cromwell, lorde privie seal … do … give and exhibite unto you theise injunctions following, to be kept observed and fulfilled upon the paynes hereafter declared … That you and every parson, vicare and curate within this diocese shall for every churche kepe one boke or registere wherein ye shall write the day and yere of every wedding christenying and burying made within yor parishe for your tyme and so every man succeeding you likewise. And you shall insert every persons that shall be so wedded christened or buried." Except for one change—in the amount of the penalty for failure to keep this injunction—the order was reissued *in toto* in the reigns of Edward VI and Elizabeth. See J. Charles Cox, *The Parish Registers of England*, pp. 2–5; W. E. Tate, *The Parish Chest*, pp. 43–44.

49 One description of such an initiative is the following: "Since 2001, 'Black and Asian Londoners: Presence and Background 1536–1840' (BAL) a major research project at London Metropolitan Archives (LMA), funded by the British Library and Re:Source – The Council for Museums, Archives and Libraries, has been uncovering fascinating evidence of the Black and Asian presence in London, stretching back over four centuries. Over 1,000 Anglican Parish

usable replicas of documentary substance and legal verifications of their locations. Whereas these releases by individual institutions can provide only a piecemeal database, this work collects and consolidates them into one body of information. Within this aggressive inclusiveness, all the records presented here are identified by print or current institutional location, frequently both in conjunction with each other, as for instance citations from the published volumes of transcriptions of London parish registers that are checked and cross-sourced with the manuscript originals, which helps to minimize the errors often contained in the former.[50] The records themselves, of which the book will be a discussion, make up the entries of the Chronological Index of Records, each of which is numbered and appears with date, geographic location, transcribed content, and source, with additional explanatory notes for some. The numbered format facilitates quick reference to a record for discussion, while the running chronology helps to make visible patterns in the flow of this data across the two centuries of its range.

There are three basic types of evidence of black people that this compilation will present. These are (a) government records, (b) personal references, and (c) parochial church notations. The first type includes monarchic promulgations, government accounts, law cases, and national chronicles mentioning black people. The second comprises descriptions of, and allusions to, black people in letters, household accounts, and diaries and personal papers. The third constitutes entries in local parochial church registers and ecclesiastical courts, documenting the christening, marriage, and deaths of black people in that neighborhood, including wills made by them or mentioning them. Whereas all three categories share a variable opacity of ethnic identification in their contents, the data of the first category is the most indisputable but the least numerous, and the second relatively more revealing of black personal history but distant and disconnected from, and uncorroborated by, the data of the other two categories. This is the type of black record that Kim Hall

---

Baptismal Registers have been searched for entries of Black and Asian people and the results have thrown up interesting insights into Black and Asian history in the capital … Over 2,000 references to Black and Asian Londoners were found in registers from all over London. Tower Hamlets, Westminster, Southwark, Camden and Greenwich each had more than 100 Black and Asian people." <http://www.bl.uk/collections/britasian/britasialondon.html> date seen 9.29.04. The total number of references mentioned here covers a range extending into the beginning of the twentieth century, whereas the present study is concerned only with the sixteenth and seventeenth centuries. Since the present study was begun before projects such as the above were started, and without awareness of them, the statement quoted provides a nice confirmation of the validity of the research agenda of this book, literally as in the following statement: "BAL has clearly demonstrated the amazing research potential in archives not only for academics but for those interested in their own rich local, personal and community histories."

[50] For a discussion of the frequent inaccuracies of early modern English parochial church records, see Eamon Duffy's *The Voices of Morebath*, pp. 17–24, and E. A. Wrigley's more historically wide-ranging but analytically detailed essay, "How Reliable is our Knowledge of Demographic Characteristics of the English Population in the Early Modern Period?," pp. 274–75; both contain sizable bibliographies of literature on this topic. These inaccuracies, however, concern dates and financial notations more than they concern the individuals mentioned. Needless to say, neither work is concerned with references to black people.

has described as anecdotal. The last category's distinction is not only that it is the predominant source for records examined in this book but also the most inclusive. The data extracted from parish registers and ecclesiastical courts is based on conservative and permissive criteria of selection, containing entries that cite black people not only in the rhetorically underlined forms recognized and accepted by traditional history such as "a/the blackamore/blackamoore" or "a/the moor" or "a/the negro," but also those that use other forms of black names and without any emphases, such as "Rose Blackmoore," or "Henry Blackemer," or "negus" or "morian," or even "blackman." Representing what in this book's view are the extinct variations of the more recognizable morphologies of black names, and the non-standard orthography and improvisational documentary habits of the local clerical record keeper, these kinds of entries, while being the most uncertain in the authenticity of their black content, are nevertheless included here in order to compensate for the over-conservative, mutually reinforcing, multilayered assumptions of traditional early modern history that have made black people in Tudor and Stuart England absent by default.

Such data as is presented in this work is inherently correctible, as all such data must be, but such corrections can occur only after the fact, that is after the project of making visible what has been rendered invisible has seriously occurred. It must also be clearly understood that this project is not interested in early modern English social history *per se* as it is traditionally constructed, except in those points and aspects where that history includes or connects to, or should include or connect to, black people. The book's discussions of the records of black people may often appear to be of speculative and symbolic value. But in the project of reconstructing the irrecoverable history of early modern English black people speaking from silence is not a willful disregard of an axiom of scholarly wisdom. It is a sober assertion of the obligation of a necessary risk and one that redeems a difficult task from being one that is not attempted at all.

V

This presentation is cued principally by the empiricism of the works of Miller, Jones, Forbes, Edwards, and Knutson, and peripherally of those of Shyllon, Fryer, Walvin, and Drake, and less centrally and eclectically by the theoretical conversations of Neill, Orkin, Hall, Little, MacDonald, Loomba, Singh, Hendricks, and my own earlier work, as well as the larger race, postcolonial, and theoretical excursus from which those conversations derive. This syncretic critical ideology informs the discussions of the records and fuels their argument, even as the fundamental purpose of the discussions remains to provide a coherent way to read the records themselves. The discussions of the records are organized in five chapters dealing with records of black people in early sixteenth-century Britain, in Elizabethan London, in seventeenth-century London, and elsewhere in England, with the last two chapters examining records of black people in the English provinces, and East Indians and other people of color in London and in the countryside. The book's "Afterword" analyzes the frequency ratios, demographic patterns, and locational impact of the records as a whole.

The particular argument that this study exemplifies is that the black archives demonstrate the vanishing circle of the bare life of the black between the beginning and end points of its early modern English narrative across both sides of the visibility sight line, from the bare life of the black encountered as unprocessed/never-seen phenomena by an insular English consciousness to the bare life of the black as the politicized racial subject processed and seen by a burgeoning English colonialism as the exception of a primitivism meant for reprogramming in its own image in menial usage. The excluded inclusion of the former and the included exclusion of the latter completes the arc of invisibility of the black subject from unrecognized life to undeveloped life, the present-absentness of both ends of this transformation describing the self-disappearance of black life in early modern Europe's cultural optics, its virtual subjecthood. This argument, while implied in the discussions of the records, is formally articulated in the "Afterword," providing a perspective on the records' significance after the records themselves have been experienced by the reader.

Chapter One

Early Tudor Black Records

The Mixed Beginnings of a Black Population

'Born where they are not christenyd'

I

The beginnings of human subjecthood, both political and racial, lie in the evolution of difference. Sameness is not visible, and the very act of differentiation is an instinct of epistemological seeing. From the family, through the community and the kingdom or the state, human bodies are tracked, identified, classified, and, through that, politically constructed. Such construction is not visibility, however, as it is only one kind of created sight that substitutes for the thing-itself. In the fictional sight of the collective seeing unit—the family, the community, or the state—subjecthood appropriates personhood and stands in for it. Personhood, the thing itself, is the excess out of which subjecthood is restrictively carved, the latter being a defining insculpture that is an effacement of the original. The visibility of the political subject is the invisibility of the human being. To deal with the beginnings of black people in early modern England is therefore to deal with absences, with the non-visibility of a presence whose communitarian processing has to write the grammar of its sight in order to reveal the objects of its view.

In the white, isolated Northern consciousness of the early modern English, unweaned as yet from the sameness of its phenotypical being, black personhood is phenomenologically cast in a fluctuating scale between the novelty of the exotic and the repugnance of a difference that is as yet unknown. As the entropic exchange between the xenophilic and xenophobic impulses defaces the contours of the black subject's knowability, the latter haunts the limits of civic sight, a phenomenon present but not recognized. Its sighting, which is its recordation, is a cryptic, uncertain, mark bereft of the paratactical desiderata that can render it intelligible to critical analyses. Whereas all the records of black people presented in this book have a varyingly uncertain luminosity, some early Tudor black records occupy an irrecoverable heuristic aporia—orthographic and archival, as well as historical. Such records are mere palimpsests of human presence, the outlines or substances of whose narratives no ancillary light can sharpen, and who must therefore be read as the models of their own meaning. To track the early modern English black subject's archival beginnings is thus to negotiate the disjunctive history and indeterminate logic of early modern English archival culture itself.

There are seven possible complementary avenues of a minimal visibility into the fundamental opacity of the early Tudor records of black people. These constitute, therefore, five heuristic caveats in the procedures of their reading. First, catalogic typology will have to be considered as a key of identity, whereby the nature and history of each kind of record is a clue to the social knowledge and hence communal imprint of the black individual cited by it. Second, the black person's namelessness when encountered will have to be regarded as a pre-Christian identity marker, as the visible residue of an individual history before the effacement of baptism has occurred, and therefore as the trace of an earlier historical self in the process of its obliteration. Third, a given or improvised surname of the black subject when present will have to be parsed as a sign of ethnographic and geographic origin, following the basic logic of traditional onomastics. Fourth, the aggregate of record citations will be regarded symptomatically rather than literally, that is, as the prognosis of a population size rather than as its proven range. Fifth, the extreme sparsity of incidence and crypticity of content of the early Tudor records of black people necessitate more of an extended case-by-case analysis of these records than will be desirable or possible with those of the other periods examined later in this study. Sixth, the meaning of the records will be constructed as theoretical hypotheses that will contribute transparency and coherence where there are none, that is to say, as the projective historiography of material that otherwise has no history. This could be described as the assembling of the elements of a methodology to write history from absence, from the simulacra of data rather from data itself.

II

It is a truism to say that the wealth of scholarly knowledge about the second half of the sixteenth century in England has obscured the lack of a correspondingly adequate understanding of the nature of political and cultural life in the reigns of the earlier Tudor monarchs. If a fuller awareness of the complex nature, origins, and impact of the Reformation has only recently begun to be available, that increase in historical knowledge has still not extended to the England of the first Tudor king. Scholarly disagreements about whether Henry VII was avaricious or fiscally efficient (Elton), a cautious traditionalist (MacFarlane, Guy), or an innovative modernist, and whether that England was an oppressive or a progressive one,[1] merely underline the fact that the later fifteenth and early sixteenth centuries represent what one historian has termed "a gap" in early modern English history.[2] Among the relative imponderables of Henry Tudor's political life, his variable internationalist projects are significant for a reason that has been of little value for traditional historians: the unpredictable and still little-known consequence they had in starting an influx of black people into England.

Having achieved the monarchy against improbable odds, and having lived on the fringes of the royal advantages that both the mainline Yorkist and Lancastrian families had accrued, and therefore being bereft of the formidable familial

[1] G. R. Elton, *The Tudor Revolution in Government*, pp. 410–17, and *Studies in Tudor and Stuart Politics*, pp. 40–41; K. B. McFarlane, *The Nobility of Later Medieval England*, pp. 276–82; John Guy, "Henry VII," Microsoft Encarta Online. For a useful summary of this debate see S. J. Gunn, *Early Tudor Government 1485–1558*, pp. 2–8.

[2] Gunn, *Early Tudor Government*, pp. 7–8.

connections that such advantages traditionally bred,[3] Henry's reign had to be focused on consolidating his power in both national and dynastic terms, that is, in inventing his monarchy in original ways.[4] If within the kingdom that resulted in aggressively taxing the nobles to simultaneously break their power and fatten his treasury (following the axiom that a poor king is a weak king), in the foreign context it meant both exploring new familial alliances for himself and initiating new projects of overseas exploration to seize territory, increase trading goods, and establish markets, as such projects were being pursued by Spain and Portugal. These strategies may have been a canny mixture of both cultivated ideology and vicious self-interest, but the twin latter projects in particular started a new demographic phenomenon that while being hardly noticeable at its inception was to continue steadily and grow in effect over the next two centuries. Whether Henry had wanted to forge a "different" England from that of his predecessors, his foreign initiatives introduced into the country the colored/black "other" against which an early modern English "difference" was to define itself.

If the treaty of Medina del Campo, in the proposed match between Henry VII's son Arthur and Ferdinand and Isabella's daughter Catherine that is its central feature in both its 1489 and 1496 versions, has for England the allure of a commanding position in pan-European politics, one of its unforeseen consequences is that it connected England with a country that has a large black population in it. Hardly acknowledged in most European scholarship, this population was partly derived from Iberian and Andalusian black Moors defeated and enslaved in the *reconquista* in the twelfth century and seized from West African coastal states in Portugal's brutal Christianizing assaults on those regions in the later Middle Ages, and was partly the result of an increasingly voracious Portuguese expeditionary slaving trade with Africa over the fourteenth century, the consequences of which spilled over inevitably into neighboring Spain.[5] The latter phenomenon, of which the Venetian

---

3 Fortescue, *De Laudibus Legum Angliae*, trans. S. B. Chrimes, pp. 52–53.

4 A. F. Pollard, *The Reign of Henry VII*, p. xvii.

5 A refreshing recent study of this neglected topic, and one whose approach and assumptions are very similar to those of this book, is T. F. Earle and K. J. P. Lowe, eds., *Black Africans in Renaissance Europe*. The earlier study, still very detailed and authoritative, is that of A. C. De C. M. Saunders, *A Social History of Black Slaves and Freedmen in Portugal 1441–1555*; for an account of the spreading of Portuguese slave markets to Spain in the fifteenth century see pp. 28–29. James Pope-Hennessey pinpoints the beginning of Portuguese importation of Africans as slaves in either 1441 or 1444, with ten brought back in 1441 and 250 in 1444 (*Sins of the Fathers*, pp. 8–13, 42–44). The latter date is confirmed by Didier Lahon, who cites Gomes Eanes de Zurara's eyewitness account in 1450, the *Cronica de Guine* (in Earle and Lowe, pp. 261–62). Either of these dates, 1441 and 1444, therefore marks the exact beginnings of the European slave trade. For a readable general history of the origins of the Portuguese importation of Africans from the Congo as slaves from the middle of the fifteenth century, see David Lopes's essay "The Destruction of the Kingdom of Kongo," which shows how, starting from the four Africans that Diego Cao brought back to Portugal from his first visit to the Congo in 1482—and which seems to parallel the earlier experimental importation of Africans from the northern Guinea coast in 1441 by Antam Gonçalvez for Prince Henry cited by Pope-Henessey—the numbers swelled quickly to the thousands by the

state is also a part,[6] rather than Columbus's American project at the very end of the fifteenth century, is what properly constitutes for early modern Europe the idea of a new world discovered, as Benjamin Braude has importantly pointed out,[7] from which flowed unimaginable material wealth and human discovery. Estimated by some to be around 150,000 at the start of the sixteenth century, and "one-tenth of the population of Lisbon and Seville," and in the "thousands," black people of unassimilated ("bossal") and assimilated ("ladino") varieties are a common syncretic feature of the early modern cultural life of the Iberian peninsula as a whole.[8] They exist on a wide social stratum that extends on occasion from menials to skilled craftsmen to military and religious professionals even to distinguished men of letters (such as Juan de Valladolid, the black magistrate in Seville in 1462; the African poet scholar Juan Latino, who taught Latin and Greek at the University of Granada in the first half of the sixteenth century and who eventually wrote an immaculate Latin epic on the Battle of Lepanto called *Austriadis Carmen*; and the African Moor of Granada Al-Hassan Ibn-Muhammad al-Wezzani, known after his christening by Pope Leo X as Giovanni Leone or John Leo or Leo Africanus, who in 1518 wrote the first history of Africa in Arabic, which he translated into Italian in 1526).[9] The Anglo-Spanish connection led to a real but still relatively unnoticed

---

beginning decades of the sixteenth century. Lopes offers an important, considered corrective to the often repeated popular contemporary half-truth that Africans sold Africans into slavery, showing instead how King Alfonse of the Kongo (or Mvemba Nzinga, to use his African pre-Christian name) struggled unsuccessfully against Manuel of Portugal to stop the increasing Portuguese demands for importing Africans as slaves. The Antam Gonçalvez account of the bringing back of Africans from north Guinea in 1441 (in Zurara) also clearly describes the beginnings of the importation of Africans predominantly as illicit kidnappings and seizures rather than as trading. Manuel's marriage to Ferdinand and Isabella's eldest daughter, Isabelle of Aragon, in 1497 of course merges Spanish and Portuguese cultural life even more than the natural geographic proximity of the two countries had induced until then. For the direct connection between the enslavement of Spanish moors in the *reconquista* and the growth of the institution of Iberian slavery, see Hugh Thomas, who cites Ferdinand's enslavement of the moorish populations of Benemaquez and Malaga in 1487 and his distribution of them as presents (*The Slave Trade*, p. 83).

6 For brief accounts of the Italian slave trade in the fifteenth and sixteenth centuries see Minnich in Earle and Lowe, pp. 282–83, and Georgio Tognetti ibid., pp. 213–24.

7 Benjamin Braude, "The Sons of Noah," p. 104. For a similar position, see J. A. Williamson, *Sir John Hawkins*, p. 32.

8 Dieudonné Gnammankou, "The Past"; Robin Blackburn, "The Old World Background to European Colonial Slavery," pp. 81, 98. Paul Lovejoy's study (*Transformations in Slavery*) puts the numbers of Africans imported into Portugal by 1500 at 328,000 (Tables 1–2, p. xi, and pp. 24–41). From Portuguese archival sources, Saunders calculates the numbers of Africans imported as slaves into Lisbon alone between 1490 and 1530 to be between 300 and 2000 annually (p. 23). For a recent careful reassessment of the numbers of Africans in Portugal and Spain in the fifteenth and sixteenth centuries, see Jorge Fonseca, pp. 115–16, Annemarie Jordan, p. 157, and Deborah Blumenthal, p. 229, all in Earle and Lowe, eds., *Black Africans*.

9 Gnammankou, "The Part," p. 41. For Juan de Valladolid, see Hugh Thomas, *Slave Trade*, p. 74. See also Jeremy Lawrence, "Black Africans in Renaissance Spanish Literature," in Earle and Lowe, p. 70. For more accounts of the nature of the professions Africans had

result in 1501 when the Spanish princess arrived in England with her royal retinue that had several black people in it.

These first black arrivals, mentioned casually in a letter of Ferdinand and Isabella to De Puebla, their ambassador in England, in the detailed lists of the Spanish personnel that the Princess Catherine was taking with her to England as her household staff (Item 1), and shortly afterwards observed derisively by a youthful Thomas More watching the spectacle of the lavish city pageants put on to welcome what would be their new English queen and the proud, exotic train of her party, were innocuous figures, the objects of a mixed gaze. In the obtrusiveness of their unnamed mention in the Spanish royal letter, simply as "Two slaves to attend on the maids of honour," which is buried in the midst of a careful hierarchy of fifty-one waiting people and their specific assignments, above "servants," "officers," "chapel" staff, "pages," "equerries," and "gentleman in waiting," but at the very bottom of the list of "maids of honour," high female companions, and attendants, these black figures, who are for that reason in all probability female, are proud advertisements of an ambitious Christian Spain's recent imperial achievements. Those achievements are highlighted in Spain's triumphant conquest of the last Moorish stronghold of Granada just nine years earlier, in 1492.[10] This political history, which positions the two slaves as fitting accoutrements for a Spanish princess in her future foreign home, makes their black identity almost a certainty. This certainty is bolstered by the fact that since 1459 the word "slave" ("escravo") in common Portuguese usage primarily if not exclusively denotes a black African, an identification that will in fact be confirmed by More's description.[11] At the same time, appearing as they do in meticulous monarchic arrangements for a royal teenage daughter's future establishment, they are within their bondage, paradoxically, figures somewhat also of love. These black figures are arguably part of the fiercely protective love with which Catherine will try to look after her personal staff in the years of her pecuniary suffering both before and

---

in fifteenth- and sixteenth- century Spain, see Aurelia Martin Casares in Earle and Lowe, pp. 258–59. For Juan Latino's scholarly career, in addition to Gnammankou see Baltasar Fra-Molinero's essay "Juan Latino and Racial Difference," in Earle and Lowe, pp. 326–44, particularly p. 329. Fra-Molinero's essay, which is focused on a discussion of the *Austriad*, cites references to Latino in both Cervantes's *Don Quixote* and in a play by Lope de Vega called *La Dama Baba* (pp. 332–33). For a description of the professions Africans had in Portugal in the same period, see Jorge Fonseca, and Kate Lowe, in Earle and Lowe, pp. 116–19, and pp. 32–40, respectively. For the book that Africanus wrote, see *A Geographical Historie of Africa*. Much cited in its time, the work was first published by Giovanni Battista Ramusio in his *Navigations and Voyages of the Sixteenth Century* in 1588 and later translated into English by John Pory in 1600. For two recent studies of Africanus, see Dietrich Rauchenberger, *Johannes Leo der Afrikaner*, and Pekka Masonen, *The Negroland Revisited*, pp. 167–75.

[10] That is also the year that their financing of Christopher Columbus gains Spain the American continent. For an account of the scale of Spanish enslavement of its domestic moors in the *reconquista* and after, see Thomas, *The Slave Trade*, p. 83.

[11] For the developing late fifteenth-century Portuguese metonymy between "mouro" (moor), "escravo" (slave), and black people, see Saunders, *Social History*, p. xiii.

after each of her two marriages to Henry VII's two sons.[12] Catherine's passionate generosity will be so marked in future years that it will prompt some historians even to dub the age as the "Age of Catherine of Aragon."[13]

In contrast, More's English view cannot see them as anything more than ridiculous pomp (Item 5).[14] More's description, which is otherwise fulsome in its praise of the young Spanish princess, is significant in that it shows many of the codes that will operate in the naming and conceptualization of black people over the rest of the century. While the geographic identifier "Ethiopian" is onomastically typical in that it is geographically specific but not regionally precise—for More "Ethiopian" is a stand-in for African generally—it is one of the many such words that will be used to pejoratively designate black persons in England. Even if the identifier seems neutral, however, it already appears negatively marked with the trailing qualifier "pigmy," with which it is conversely linked, the resulting compound phrase itself being progressively arrived at from "ridiculous" to "barefooted." The negative marking in the geographic identification is visible now, but will not always be so in later decades.

---

[12] One example of Catherine's strong love for her servants is this passage from one of her letters to her father on 15 April 1507, six years after her arrival in England: "I also beseech your Highness to succour my servants, and to grant them some favours. If it is true that your highness considers services which I receive as services rendered to yourself, I think, there are no persons to whom your Highness is more indebted than to my servants. ... From the day that I arrived in this kingdom, ... they have always served me in the hope that things would be mended ... they serve me still with the same good will as though I granted them every day new favours." (*Supplement to Volume I and II of Calendar of Letters, Despatches, and State Papers* (CSP), ed. Bergenroth, p. 102. Catherine is writing in the years of her financial distress following Arthur's death shortly after her arrival, and before she was married to Henry VII's second son. In the letter the phrase "things would be mended" refers to Henry's ambivalent attitude toward her, and his consequently fluctuating financial support of her at this time.

[13] See Betty S. Travitsky, "Reprinting Tudor History," p. 165.

[14] My translation, from the original passage in *The Correspondence of Sir Thomas More*, ed. Rogers, p. 4. The letter, dated November 1501, is addressed to More's Oxford tutor, John Holt. After leaving Oxford, at this time More was living in London, in the area of Charterhouse, and was in spiritual training, and lecturing on St. Augustine (*Correspondence*, p. 4 n. 13). Roger's own translation of the passage, is in her *Selected Letters*: *St. Thomas More*, p. 2, and is as follows:

> But the Spanish escort—good heavens!—what a sight! If you had seen it, I am afraid you would have burst with laughter; they were so ludicrous. Except for three, or at the most four of them, they were just too much to look at: hunchbacked, undersized, barefoot Pygmies from Ethiopia. If you had been there, you would have thought they were refugees from hell.

Not only is Rogers somewhat liberal in her translation, she leaves out the word "laceri," meaning "tattered" or "torn," and adds "undersized," which is redundant. Rogers's translation is cited in part by Gordon Kipling, in his edition of *The Receyt of the Ladie Kateryne*, p. 139. Another translation of the passage, by R. W. Chambers, includes in its translation the word "laceri" but leaves out "curui," meaning "curved," "bent," and so "hunched, or hunch-backed": "You would have burst out laughing if you had seen them, for they looked so ridiculous, tattered, barefooted, pigmy Ethiopians, like devils out of Hell"; *Thomas More*, p. 81; cited by John Paul, *Catherine of Aragon and her Friends*, p. 9.

Thus, too, the catalog's openly negative tone is an abandonment of the acid sarcasm of the second clause of the opening sentence of the passage, in which More's horror at the very sight of the black figures in the princess's train is couched in the feigned politeness of an elite mockery, as a kind of polished inside joke between the smart divinity student and his tutor. This gives way quickly to an openly displayed, rising, movement, first of contempt ("burst with laughter"), then of ridicule ("ridiculous"), and finally of anger ("escapees from hell"). It is almost as if an instant anxiety fuels this catalogic growth, accelerating its series of invectives. The catalog comes to rest in an implicit note of spreading defilement, by the "escapees from hell," hinting at the instincts of separation and containment that will mark the Anglo-European response to black people in subsequent history. Furthermore, a visual refusal and cancellation is already in place, in the passage's exploitation of the fact that the letter's addressee hasn't seen these black people ("If you had seen them," "If present") which functions as a kind of wish fulfillment, and through the negative description signals a kind of subliminal discouragement of anyone seeing them because they are "ridiculous" to see. The trick of optical effacement of black people will accompany Anglo-European cultural sight, both at home and abroad in its future colonies.

What More is calling "pigmy" here may not be fully grown individuals of very short stature but in fact black female youths that Catherine has on her personal staff. Likewise, what he describes as "tattered" may be the trailing black lace that they may have worn. Young black male and female pages, and black Moorish lacework, will both become proud aristocratic fashions later in the century, taken up even by Henry VII's granddaughter, Elizabeth. Otherwise, it is inconceivable that members of a royal retinue would be turned out in torn clothes in their first public appearance in England. Curiously and ironically, More's contempt for black people as "barefooted" reflects the irrationality of racial construction, because the early modern English themselves do not seem to have much used proper shoes at this time, as is evident in the many portraits of Henry VIII both before and after he becomes king, most often showing him wearing sandals, and particularly in the well-preserved range of light footwear typical of Henry's reign that has been recovered from the wreck of the *Mary Rose*.[15] Overall, that this negative marking of black people comes from someone will become one of England's most famous Humanist philosophers is starkly indicative of how even European high philosophy will be complicit in the marking down of black people and the negative interpretation of blackness in early modern Anglo-European political and cultural history. Unsurprisingly, fifteen years after his denigration of black people, when More describes his ideal state he writes approvingly of slavery in it.[16]

The particular complexion of More's view of the black people he sees is clear if compared to the other descriptions of them in the two other eyewitness accounts of Catherine's entourage entering London. Identifying them as Catherine's maids in waiting, these accounts also describe the black individuals in negative terms albeit more restrainedly than More's. The first of these, in the third Vitellius chronicle,

---

15 See C. S. Knighton and David Loades, *Letters from the Mary Rose*, colored plate 6 ff., p. 70.

16 *Utopia*, chapter 2, "On Their Slaves, and Marriages,"opening paragraph.

has an almost polite character, mixing delight with discreet disapproval (Item 6). Likewise, the second, in *The Receyt of the Ladie Kateryne*, maintains a balance between civic interest and critique (Item 7). Although the persons being described here cannot be certainly identified as black since Catherine's entourage includes both Spanish and black maids, the fact that these figures make up the very end of the procession of her retinue in the chronicles' catalogs of people in that ceremonious street scene make it very likely that these are in fact black people that are being described. That is precisely the order in which they appeared in Ferdinand and Isabella's letter. They may even be the same figures that More describes, as the editor of one of these chronicles believes,[17] or, since these figures are described as being in a cart or "charys" rather than on foot, they may be additional black people in Catherine's entourage who are servants rather than "slaves."[18]

The politeness of language—which variably employs both a lack of "fair"-ness and Spanish as discreet euphemisms for black, in keeping with the insularity of a northern English consciousness untouched as yet by the already burgeoning internationalism of the Mediterranean basin in the south, and in this beginning moment of contact suspicious of it—is a useful clue to the identity of the authors of these descriptions. Both are probably the observations of city officials, possibly aldermen,[19] who are part of the local government charged with the arrangements of the pageants for the arrival in the city of Prince Arthur and Princess Catherine for their public marriage, and whose presence in the scene and their records of it involve in part at least their official duties. Their restrained language may thus be a reflection of the cautiousness that is a necessary part of their deferential public conduct at a royal event. In that, they provide a useful complement to More's more pronounced hostility. Taken together, More's description and those of the chroniclers could be said to make up a composite of the first reactions to black people in London, on the levels of private feeling and public notation, one frankly hostile and the other politely critical. The uncertainty of the identification of the individuals as black denotes that very invisibility of black people that will be a signal feature of their early modern English history. That invisibility is also a strong function of their namelessness in the initial British and Spanish-Portuguese experience of the black person, who is literally un-seeable and un-nameable to an early modern Christian cultural consciousness, and whose eventual christening will be an illumination that will be a permanent effacement of his or her African identity. The black person, like the unnamed and uncertainly identified black figures in Catherine's train, is invisible both before and after Anglo-European Christian thought sees her or him.

---

[17] See, in Gordon Kipling's commentary on the *Receyt*, his gloss to these lines: "Sir Thomas More provides a less circumspect description of the plainness of the Spanish escort" (p. 139). Kipling is citing directly from the very translation of the More passage in Rogers's *Selected Letters*, p. 2.

[18] The variable status of black people is a common feature of such populations in the Iberian peninsula in the sixteenth century, and one that will be quickly replicated in England, albeit in a much more obscure and confused fashion.

[19] C. L. Kingsford, *Chronicles of London*, "General Introduction," p. xliv.

More's description of the black people in Catherine of Aragon's entourage is also significant in the fact that, even as it lays out some of the basic patterns of the English responses to black people over the rest of the century, it is not exclusively denotative of all of the attitudes to blacks in its own moment. Generally, the arrival in England of the black people in Catherine's retinue coincides with the arrivals of other peoples of color in Britain at that same moment, and thus with the first close English encounter with physical and cultural difference, as for instance in the three Americans "like to bruite beaste" that Sebastian Cabot brings back for Henry VII in 1502 from his second voyage to Newfoundland, who are kept by the king at court at his expense (Item 8, and see Chapter 5). More importantly, in the first three or four decades of the sixteenth century several dozen black people are documented to be living in Scotland. Between 1500/01 and 1549, there are 92 references in the Scottish treasury records to at least six black people. These individuals, first noted by Peter Fryer, James Walvin, and Paul Edwards, and also mentioned by me elsewhere, include a royal personal attendant, a drummer, two black women, and two friars.[20] There is also a soldier or a soldier's aide. These persons are variably described in the records as "more[s]," "morien," "moryen," "moris," all of which in early modern Scottish usage refer to a black individual.[21] As several sets of multiple references to nearly all of these individuals extending chronologically over four decades sketch a documentary life for them, these references in fact constitute a unique set of black records. Although these references are Scottish, their proximity in temporal, geographic, and political terms to early modern English racial records make them a logical and valuable part of the documentary racial history tracked in this work.

III

An African cited as Petir Morien and as Petir the More first appears in the *Accounts of the High Treasurer of Scotland* in the year 1500/01 (Item 2). This black man's Scottish presence is probably connected to the privateering activities of the Barton brothers Andrew and Robert in Leith (Edinburgh's port and Scotland's most important and active seaport until the first decade of the sixteenth century), who were encouraged by the letter of reprisal against the Portuguese issued in their favor by James III following the seizure of the ship, crew, and cargo of their father John Barton by the Portuguese and his death in captivity in Lisbon in 1476. Even if this marque was not actually released either by James III at the time of his death in 1488 or by his successor until 1505, its openly publicized threat allowed the Barton brothers to exploit the favorable climate that it created for Scottish attacks on Portuguese freighters loaded with human and material cargo from West Africa. Such initiatives were pursued most actively by Andrew and Robert Barton, as well as possibly by the several other merchant sea captains based at Leith in the closing decade of the fifteenth century and the opening

[20] Peter Fryer, *Staying Power*, p. 4; Paul Edwards, "The Early African Presence in Britain," pp. 15–23; Imtiaz Habib, "Reading Black Women Characters of the English Renaissance," pp. 72–74.

[21] *Dictionary of the Scottish Language* (*DSL*), relevant entries.

one of the sixteenth.[22] Petir Morien or Petir the More is probably the first of such Portuguese human booty brought back by Scottish privateers to Edinburgh, and he appears in the records evidently after he has been christened.[23]

Irrespective of his exact origins, Petir the More immediately acquired permanent royal service, since on his first appearance on 13 February 1500/01 he was paid "xxviij s.," and then on 12 March "xv s. iij d." (Items 2 and 3), both amounts typified throughout the Treasury records as the compensations of a salaried employment. That he equally quickly proved of value in monarchic personal service is evident from the fact that on 2 May he was sent to France at the King's expense, presumably on a monarchic errand, even if that is unspecified (Item 4). When he reappears in the records two years later, he is a "pensoun[er]" receiving, on 12 January 1503/04, 14 shillings (Item 9), which he continues to receive regularly (Item 13), with his February pension possibly being paid in advance in January or misrecorded in that month or mistranscribed (Item 10), and his April pension being paid in arrears together with his pension in May (Item 16).[24] On 31 January 1503/04 a measure of an exotic imported Eastern dress fabric, "ane steik chamelot," was bought for him, and on 24 February he and his horse were taken to Dumfries at the cost of "vij s." (Items 11 and 12). If these are expenses for James's royal accompaniments during his frequent, typically energetic countrywide tours,[25] similar expenses of "ix s." each are recorded for the African on 19 and 21 May 1504 (Items 17 and 18), and again for 21 June, but this time for an amount equal to his pension (Item 20). Since on 4 and 27 July of that year he was paid "iij s. iiij d." and "vij s." (Items 21 and 23), these too are probably royal expenses for his maintenance during the king's travels. Peter the More's royal service ended in August 1504 when on the first of the month he was handsomely paid (Item 24). Still neglected in early modern British scholarship, this black man was clearly a favorite companion of the monarch, and well accepted in

22 Norman Macdougall, *James IV*, pp. 238–42; Edwards, "Early African Presence," pp. 16–17, and p. 18 n. 34; Patrick F. Tytler, *Lives of Scottish Worthies*, p. 331. Both Edwards and Tytler cite the *AHTS* records incorrectly, the former on p. 18 n. 34 where (a) for the record of 4 July 1505 in which black women are cited he attributes a ship to "William Wod," whereas no such ship is mentioned, and (b) he cites it as vol. 2, whereas it should be vol. 3; and the latter in his citation of the record of 7 Nov. 1504 as 8 Nov. 1504.

23 Two years earlier than the first reference to Petir the moryen, there are three references in the first volume of the *AHTS* to a servant of the king who is cited simply as "Blak." Described as being of the "chamire" (presumably the king's chambers), on 1 January 1497/98 he was paid ij shillings to "grast" [furnish] the king's "chamiris" at Elgin (1: 375); sometime after 6 February 1497/98 he was paid to take the king's dogs to Strivelin (1: 376); and, on 12 May 1498, he was given 15 shillings 6 pence to look after the king's dogs (1: 390). He does not appear any further in the records. Since the Scottish Treasurer's accounts are missing for the two years between 1498 and 1500, what happens to him and whether he has any connection to Petir the more who appears afterwards (could he be the pre-baptized Petir more?) is a tempting puzzle that must remain unresolved.

24 His earlier cited payment of 13 February 1501 is thus probably also a double payment made in arrears.

25 For a description of James's restless movements see Macdougall, *James IV*, p. 304.

the early sixteenth-century court of this culturally sophisticated Scottish king, even if his origins and subsequent fortunes are unrecorded.

Among James IV's personal staff is also an African drummer, the "morien taubronar," who is first recorded on 12 April 1504 as receiving "v Franche crounis" (Item 14). Although undocumented in the records, this African's origins can be plausibly tied to the same history as Peter the More's. He was part of the human booty arriving in Edinburgh in the late fifteenth and early sixteenth centuries as a result of Scottish privateering attacks on Portuguese shipping in the North Atlantic, and represents probably the second wave of such influxes. As Kate Lowe has detailed, Africans were frequently employed in the Iberian peninsula as musicians, and drummers in particular.[26] In the month after his arrival, on 3 May, he was paid "vij France crounis," for "expens, maid be the Morienis" (Item 15). These two large payments would seem to indicate the initial costs for setting him up at court, since the following month, on 13 June, he is given the more typical compensation of "xiiij s." (Item 19). That from this point he quickly becomes a permanent member of the king's personal entertainers—which James is documented to like carrying around with him—is reflected in royal expenses incurred for him on 4 July for transporting him and his horse to Striveling and for putting him up at Linlithgow, presumably en route (Item 22), and on 7 August and 11 September for transporting him and his horse to Eskdale and Dumfries respectively, and accommodating them there, this time together with the "four Italien menstrales," with whom he will be mentioned frequently from now on (Items 25 and 26). Two days later on 13 September, even a fresh horse is expensively procured for him from another member of the royal staff (Item 27). On that day he and the "Italien menstrales" are taken to "Peblis" [Peebles] at the cost of "xxviij s." (Item 28), while two weeks afterwards, on 26 September, he is given "v s. x d." to compensate ("red") him for "his lugeing and expens in Faukland," albeit here without his colleagues (Item 29). On 7 October he and the Italian musicians are paid "xiiij s." for "thair hors met [i.e. provisions], to pas to the Month with the King" (Item 30), and on 15 and 29 October they are given "xiiij s." each time for their services and upkeep in "Brechin" and in "Strethbogy" (Items 31 and 32). He continues to provide this obviously valued personal service to the king for the next two years, both by himself and with his Italian colleagues, being paid his due compensations on 1 February 1504/05 (Item 38), 5 May 1505 (Item 42), 1 October 1505 (Item 45), 11 November 1505 (Item 46), 1 January 1505/06 (Item 48), 12 February 1505/06 (Item 50), 14 April 1506 (Item 53), and 1 May 1506 (Item 54). 1 August 1506 (Item 59) is the last time his wages are mentioned in the records.

The standing and support that this black man has at the Scottish court is reflected in the range of payments made to him or for him, beyond his compensation for services rendered. Unlike Peter the More, this African has a family, and when he is away on service to the king his family is provided for, as on 14 November 1504, when 14 shillings are paid to him (Item 35), a payment that is repeated two years later on 24 March 1506/07 (Item 67), and on 22 May 1506/07 (Item 69). Not only is his musical expertise prized enough by the king for the drummer to be entrusted to put on a show

[26] Lowe in Earle and Lowe, pp. 32–40. Lowe points out that throughout Europe Africans were also prized as trumpeters.

for him on "Fasteringis Evin" (Shrove Tuesday eve) on 3 February 1504/05, but the unstintingly appreciative monarchic support for his expensive creations is evident in the substantial dress accessories that are provided for his 12 dancers at royal expense on that occasion (Item 39). In a similar vein, on 23 March 1504/05, 28 shillings are awarded for the painting of his drum (Item 41). On 26 November 1505 and on 9 July 1506 colorful dresses—in brown ("tanne") and yellow—are made for him, the latter when he is with the king on one of the monarch's sailing trips (Items 47 and 57, respectively). Remarkably, when the African drummer is assaulted sometime before 6 June 1506, full compensation is promptly made to him (Item 56).[27] This is followed up by medical care for him, when on 19 July and 10 August of that year, "ix s." and "xxxiv s." are paid to him and his "leich" (physician) respectively, the latter occasion being described as "quhen he was hurt" (Items 58 and 61). This injury may signal the end of this black musician's professional life, because he disappears from documentary sight after this point. Given the fact that he has a family, it is a logical speculation that he was absorbed into the historical anonymity of an assimilated early modern Scottish existence somewhere near the haunts of his courtly career.

Perhaps the most remarkable, and hence the most historically noted of these black people in early modern Scotland, are the women in this group. These women first appear in the Scottish High Treasurer's records on 7 November 1504, when two separate payments in connection with them are made on the same day (Items 33 and 34). Since Inverketh or Inverkethin (Inverkeithing), located directly north of Edinburgh across the Firth of Forth in Fife and on the route to the royal residence at Dunfermline, is one of the many excellent sea landing points on the Scottish east coast,[28] and since James, together with his new English bride, Margaret Tudor, is present in Dunfermline, and generally in Inverkeithing, on 7 November as well as throughout the month,[29] what the record describes is the transportation of the African women to James's palace in Dunfermline, after their arrival in Leith, by the Portuguese managing the transaction, presumably at the monarch's own stipulation. These women may be the same women mentioned in the Treasury records eight months later on 3 July 1505 as having been transported by a "William Wod" (Item 43), rather than those being an additional group of later black female arrivals, as Paul Edwards believes.[30] They may either have been entered here retrospectively by the new Treasurer, James Beaton, to correct a lapse in the accounts of his brother and predecessor David, or mistranscribed by James Beaton at this later date.[31] The

[27] Because "mendis" in early modern Scottish means compensation or satisfaction for injuries suffered (*DSL*), and "hurting: carries the sense of a. Injuring (bodily), wounding. Also, a bodily injury, a wound. b. Harming generally; wronging; causing detriment. c. Being damaged" (*DSL*), the incident seems to have involved injuries suffered unnaturally, such as in an assaulting of the black drummer by unspecified parties, rather than any sustained by accident.

[28] The Queensferry (Queen's Ferry) on the Edinburgh side, is the closest and most convenient point to cross the Forth estuary on to the north shore.

[29] See the comments of the *AHTS* editor, James Balfour Paul, in the "preface" to vol. 2 (p. li), and see the entries on 2: 266.

[30] "The Early African Presence," p. 17.

[31] *AHTS* editorial preface, 3: xiv ff.

contents of the November records and the July one seem to point to the same event, with the latter being fuller and more detailed than the earlier two (with the "bestis" of the first two enumerated as the horse, the cat, and the jennet in the latter, and the ship captain named in the latter citation instead of only the Portuguese escort of the earlier ones, which together may make up the "folkis with thaim" in the second of the first two references).[32] Even if William Wod's exact identity is uncertain, his involvement in this merchandizing of seized Africans points to his location within the merchant captain community of Leith that is at the forefront of such activity at this time.[33] As such, these black women are a part of the same history of forced relocation as are Petir the More and the black drummer, and constitute the continuing wave of black people's arrival in early modern Scotland.

While being a part of James IV's scrupulous treatment of his subjects overall, the costly meticulousness of the black women's transportation arrangement in these records—which include ferry *and* lodging charges in Inverkeithing—is notable, and hints at the nature of the care they will receive in James's court.[34] Immediately invoking the monarch's interest, the black women are taken back from Dunfermline to Edinburgh two weeks later on 27 December (Item 36), and two weeks following that, on 11 December 1504, the ritually immaculate christening of one of them is recorded (Item 37).[35] Although unrecorded in the treasury accounts, the other black women is also christened around this time, because they both appear later in the records as Margaret More and Elen More or Helenor, the one possibly after the name of James's English queen, Margaret Tudor, and the other after the name of her principal lady-in-waiting, Eleanor Pole;[36] they will eventually be cited directly as the Queen's maids.[37] They will be frequently billeted, however, with James's daughter

---

32 The "bestis" may also be named in a record of 22 November 1504 (see note to Item 36) which documents payment to "the man that brocht the Portugall hors with the rede tale and the must cat."

33 William Wod (Wood) could be (i) a lesser member of the family of the celebrated admiral Andrew Wood, who is a close associate of the Barton brothers, or (ii) another lesser-known merchant sea captain of Leith, or (iii) he may not be a sea captain at all but simply a merchant of Leith. His several other appearances in the *Accounts*—viz. 2: 84, 3: 368, 4: 45, 271, 306—support all of these identities, as also do his appearances in some legal documents of the time (3 August 1508, National Archives of Scotland MS GD16/41/5; 8 November 1512, National Archives of Scotland MS GD124/1/189).

34 For James's kindly disposition see the *AHTS* editor's Prefatory comments in vol. 1 (p. cclxxv): "It is impossible to peruse the Accounts without being struck with the many indications they afford of the easy intercourse which prevailed between the king and his servants, especially in the case of James IV; and the kindly and attractive bearing which encouraged even the humblest of his subjects to approach him with freedom." The treasury records contain numerous instances of James IV's random acts of kindness to poor strangers that he meets in his repeated travels through his kingdom. See, for instance, *AHTS*, Preface, 3: xvi, xxvi, liv; Preface, 4: xxiv, xxv, xxxi, xxxiv–xxxv, lxxxii.

35 According to Paul Edwards, the description of the event refers to "the old custom at the christening ceremony of placing a donation in the flame of a candle" ("The Early African Presence," p. 17).

36 *AHTS* Editor's Preface, 3: xcv.

37 See Item 93, discussed below.

by Margaret Drummond, Margaret Stewart (Lady Margaret), in Edinburgh castle under the guardianship of the castle captain, Sir Patrick Crichton and his wife,[38] with whom they will often be mentioned in the treasury records, this double resonance of the name Margaret connecting the black women to the same affection that the monarch has for his daughter. It is therefore unsurprising that their visibly pampered life at court starts immediately, detailed as it is in the numerous expenses busily recorded for their dresses and accessories from shortly after their arrival in 1504 to at least 1507/08, and then occasionally beyond. Items 40, 44, 49, 52, 55, 60, 62, 66, 68, 71, 72, 73, 74, 75, 77, 78, 79 list the brightly colored gowns of thick wool ("russait," "carsay"), the collars of linen ("lynyn"), and the belts, collars, and hose to accompany them, as well as a variety of boots and shoes ("butis," "schone") to wear with them, that the black women are repeatedly provided at no small expense, including board and lodging with Patrick Crichton and his wife in Edinburgh castle at the cost of a hundred pounds per year (Items 63, 64). In this time the nature of the black women's personal life is unknown, however, because even if the records document the birth of a child to one of them in February 1505/06, by whom and in what circumstances is unrecorded (Item 51). If this event leaves open the possibility of their sexual exploitation, that possibility coexists with a monarchic vigilance over, support for, and protection of them.[39]

The increasing recognition of these black women's social presence may be indicated in their eventual citation by their given Christian names, and even in one instance in the description of their official role. On 15 December 1511, when one of the black women receives a colorful brown gown of Flemish wool ("rissilis") as her Christmas present ("Yule"), she is for the first time cited by her name, "Elen More" (Item 87), which is also what she is called on 1 January, 1511/12, when she gets "V Franche crounis" as her New Year's present (Item 88), as well as the following year on 2 February 1512/13, when she gets new shoes and boots (Item 95). She appears with that name again in the treasury records on 31 May 1513 (Item 96), and even as late as 22 August 1527, although now in the slightly corrupt version of "Helenor" (Item 99). In similar fashion, the other black woman also becomes, by 1512, "Margaret Moire," when at Linlithgow castle on 5 April she is given "xiiij s." (Item 91), the same name being used to cite her the following year on 19 July 1513 to record the procurement of some "fyne russet" for "ane goune" for her (Item 97). Although for a while in 1512/13 the African women slip into a nameless plurality, as for instance in the New Year gift list of 1512/13, when as "the twa blak ladeis" they get "X Franche crounis" (Item 94), one of them in that same season is for the first time described as the "Quenis blak madin" when she gets a French woolen gown on 2 December 1512 (Item 93).

---

[38] *AHTS* Editor's Preface, 3: lxxxv.

[39] Of course, given both James's own busy sexual life and his conscientious support of his many illegitimate offspring, he could very well have fathered the baby himself. But if this is the case—and no historical sources or their studies have ever suggested that it is—that baby would represent a unique instance of cross-racial union at the monarchic level. The other possibility is that the black women, like the black drummer earlier, have their own black families, in which case there are more black people in and around James's court than what the treasury records indicate.

The most striking public prominence that the African women received, however, and what has been the most remarked aspect of their history, was the enthronement of one of them by the king as the object of knightly jousting.[40] Advertised elaborately and expensively in Scotland and abroad from early 1506/07, in specially commissioned documents (Item 65), and designed to extend for three days for 12 hours daily, this was a public extravaganza in which the king himself, disguised as the "blak knicht," was the black lady's champion.[41] Carried in a "chaire triumphale" decorated in Flanders taffeta, the blak lady had two squires to follow her (Item 70), and, on the repetition of this successful tournament the following year, dressed in a bright green serge girdle, she had maids ("madinnis") to attend on her (Item 82 Notes). In the tournament of that year, on 28 March 1508, the black lady was carried by 12 men to and from the tournament at the cost of "xxviij s." (Item 83), while the following month on 27 June she and her horse were carefully prepared for the tournament banquet at the cost of "xiij s." (Item 84). Five years later, on 1 January 1512/13, the black lady phenomenon was still alive, albeit now plurally to include both black women, when the "twa blak ladeis" get as their New Year's gifts "x Franche crounis" (Item 94). James IV's death in the battle at Flodden later this year marks the end of the celebrity careers of the African women as the black lady, although, as mentioned earlier, one of them is cited as late as 1527.

---

40 Historical comment on the phenomenon first appears contemporaneously in William Dunbar's venomous poem "Ane Blake Moir" in 1507/08, which was written for the occasion (*Poems of Dunbar*, ed. James Kinsey, p. 106), and then a few decades later in the sixteenth century in Robert Lindesay (Lindsay) of Pitscottie's neutrally toned account in *The Historie and Cronicles of Scotland* (pp. 242–44). Three centuries later it was mentioned without sarcasm or innuendo by the Victorian antiquary Patrick Tytler in his *Lives of the Scottish Worthies* in 1855 (pp. 330–40), but discussed derisively by the *AHTS* Victorian editor, James Balfour Paul (Preface, 3: xlv–lii), and its poetic description by Dunbar is commented on by David Laing in his *Poems of William Dunbar* (2: 306–7). In the twentieth century, Dunbar's shocking description of the event was attacked by Tom Scott in his *Dunbar: A Critical Exposition* (pp. 67–69), minimized by Robert Fleissner in his essay "Wiliam Dunbar's Sultry Pre-Shakespearean Dark Lady" (pp. 88–96), noted by Kinsey in his edition of Dunbar's poems (p. 308 n. 33), diffused by Paul Edwards in his essay "Early African Presence" (pp. 18–20), and in 2005 cited for its historical significance by Sue Niebrzydowski, in her essay "The Sultana and Her Sisters" (pp. 187–210), and by Oumani deSonghai in an electronic essay of the same title. Although the Scottish treasury records do not explicitly name either Elen More or Margaret More in connection with the black lady tournaments or include any other information that the figure is in fact a black person, no one has seriously doubted that one of them is the black figure in that pageant, except Paul Edwards. Even he, while believing that the figure is some one other than the "More lassis," implies that it is another unnamed black woman (pp. 18–20). That it could be another unnamed black woman, however, is an unlikely explanation, since no other black women are mentioned in the records, and no doubt in that direction is expressed by the *AHTS* editor, James Balfour Paul, in his otherwise hostile discussion of the subject.

41 Lindsay, *Cronicles*, pp. 242, 244. Lindsay mistakenly dates the original tournament in 1505, which the *Accounts* editor, James Balfour Paul, using the evidence of the records themselves, corrects as 1506/07 (*AHTS*, Preface, 3: xlvi–lii).

The extraordinary careers of these early modern Scottish black women might not represent a simple achievement of social success, since for them to be on public display in a ritual tournament marks them as a spectacle, but even for them to be the agents of a monarchic satire of an "exaggerated pursuit of whiteness," as Edwards suggests,[42] is to be the exemplars of a progressive social agenda, however ineffective, and that is historically significant. James IV's knowledge and acquaintance of them, and his apprehension of their possible oppression by society at large, may be precisely what induces him to project them lavishly in his glittering public pageants to make a bold point as it were, and his experience of them may be what makes him speak for other disadvantaged ethnic groups in general, as he did in April 1505 when he wrote to his uncle the King of Denmark recommending the passage of itinerant gypsies from Scotland into Denmark and asking for the latter's consideration of their welfare in their "afflic[tion]," helpless[ness]," and "calamities."[43] A case in point is the snarling vitriol of the Scottish poet William Dunbar in his description of them in the poem he wrote on the occasion:

My ladye with the mekkle lippis.
Quhon scho is tute mowitt lyk an aep
And lyk a gangarell unto graep
… Quhen scho is clad in reche apparel
Scho blinkis as brycht as ane tar barrel

My lady with the thick lips.
Who is double mouthed like an ape
and with hands that wander [flutter] loosely
… When she is dressed in rich clothes
She blinks as brightly as a tar barrel.

This is not just a reflection of the Scottish flyting tradition's language of mock sarcasm, as Edwards has defensively argued,[44] but also another aspect of their historical impact on mainstream early modern European popular culture, including Scottish, particularly the pervasively ingrained propensity of such cultures to violently other human difference, and for which they act as a kind of touchstone. Their impact is arguably evident even three centuries later, in the contemptuous astonishment of the *AHTS*'s Victorian editor at the "fantastic elevation" of "an absolute negress … a full blooded negress" at a tournament "whose excellencies were to be defended at the sword's point", and even in Edwards's apologetic diffusion of the viciousness of Dunbar's poem.[45]

There is a small, assorted group of references to black people in the Scottish archives that are briefer and more enigmatic than those considered so far but that should nevertheless be considered. The most intriguing in this group are the three pertaining to what seem to be two African friars or "more freris." These individuals first appear in the treasury records on 28 March 1508 when white woolen smocks or

---

42 "Early African Presence," p. 19.

43 The letter is transcribed and reproduced in Tytler's *Scottish Worthies*, pp. 338–40.

44 For both the Dunbar quotation and Edwards's argument, see "The Early African Presence," pp. 21–23). The translation of the Dunbar quotation is mine.

45 *AHTS*, Preface, 3: xlviii–xlix.

girdles are procured for them (Item 80). They are cited again in the following month on 25 April when "vj Franche crounis" are paid to the "more freris" (Item 81). On 5 August they are named again in the treasury records when John Knoxe is reimbursed 14 pounds for "the expens of the More freris quhen tha wer heir" (Item 85). They are again paid "xiij s" on 9 November of that year (Item 86) and "xviij s" on 10 August 1512 (Item 92). Given that (a) the treasury records offer no other information on these individuals, and (b) the *AHTS* editor makes no comment about them, as could have been otherwise expected given the singular phenomenon that African Christian clergy in early modern Scotland represent, and (c) "kirtles" sounds like the scapular knee-length tunic that Dominican friars wear under a black cape, and (d) the association of the Scottish Presbyterian reformer John Knox with any African friars may be anomalous in light of his documented closeness to the Dominican order, it may be temptingly obvious to assume that these references are not about Africans but about the European Dominican order of the black friars who are present in Scotland at this time. Several difficulties in this hypothesis, however, point to a different and surprising explanation. First, the Dominican order of the Blackfriars are cited separately in the *AHTS* and indexed somewhat separately by the *AHTS* editor as well,[46] and they are cited consistently as the "Blak freris," and not as the "more freris." Second, the very first time that the "more freris" are mentioned they are described explicitly as "blak more freris." Third, the *AHTS* editor's silence about the "more freris" may mean nothing, because he is also silent about Peter the More. In other words, there is nothing in the records themselves that inherently precludes these figures from being African clerics.

As a matter of fact, Ethiopian Christians date from the time of the Crusades, and though neglected in contemporary European scholarship, there are African clerics in late medieval and early modern Europe, such as in the numerous Abyssinian (Ethiopian) embassies and pilgrimages to Italy and Lisbon in 1402, 1408, 1427, 1452, and 1481,[47] including Henrique (Ndoadidiki Ne Kinu a Mumemba) [1494–1531], son of Alphonse of Congo, who was appointed Bishop of Africa in 1518; and Aba Cietro Tesfa Sion Malhezo of Ethiopia, who was ordained a priest in 1540.[48] Some Ethiopian clergy were even of the Dominican order, such as Tekla Haymanot.[49] Furthermore, Ethiopian clerics were not only known in fifteenth-century Portugal, but may have entered Europe through the Portuguese mass importation of Africans from the fourteenth century onwards. The "blak more freris" may thus be a rare example of such a group, and may even be of the Dominican order. The association of John Knox with these "more freris" may also therefore be perfectly consistent not only because of his affinity to that order but also because other Scottish clerics as well were associated with Africans, as

---

46 For the separate indexing of "Blak friars" by the *AHTS* editor, of first "Blackfriars (More Freris, Blak Freris), ... payments to ..." followed below that in a subheading, "—— in Edinburgh, payments to ...", see 4: 570.

47 Arthur Percival Newton, ed., *Travel and Travellers of the Middle Ages*, p. 193. Also see John Leo Africanus, *The History and Description of Africa*, p. 195 n. 6.

48 Earle and Lowe, pp. 294–95.

49 Newton, *Travel and Travellers of the Middle Ages*, pp. 192–93. For Ethiopians in the Dominican order see Minnich, in Earle and Lowe, p. 298.

was the Bishop of Murray, who in 1512 had a "more" who on 28 March is cited in the treasury records as receiving 14 shillings because he "brocht ane present to the king" (Item 90), although whether he was a cleric is not stated.

In their brevity, the "blak more freris" records reveal the existence of Africans in early modern Scotland, not just as monarchic personal attendants and possessions, but also as public professionals who are recognized as such by the ambient social order. Such recognition is also implicit in the sole record of a military man or soldier's aide three decades later, in the reign of Mary of Guise, in the recommendation of Lady Hume on 28 March 1549 of a "Mour" who is "als scharp ane man as rydis," and who deserves the Queen Dowager "to be gud prenssis unto him" (Item 113). Besieged by attacking English forces, who have killed her husband George, the fourth Lord Home, Warden of the East Marches, two years earlier in the Battle of Pinkie Cleugh in 1547, and desperately dependent on any military personnel that she can receive, Mary of Guise probably regarded the African as a mercenary like the "Spanygyarttis" with whom he is mentioned, and part of the kind of military specialists that had helped the Scottish aristocracy on the English border in the past and who were being asked for again now: "lat tham cum again." That these mercenaries, who will appear in the English archives as well, thus fight on both the Scottish and English sides merely underlines the great demand there is for their battle skills. This special request therefore marks the distinction of the African's professional reputation, visible here even in the chaos of a protracted, confusing war.[50] The phrase "to be gud prenssis unto him" may be a conventional imploration of royal patronage, but that it includes the African within its grace underlines the normalcy of his acceptance as a public figure of valuable skill in a time of dire need.

The Scottish records of black people provide a symptomatic template of the documentary history of black people in England in several fundamental ways. They predict the naming of black people in terms of an improvised surname that serves an ethnic or geographic descriptor of them such as the Petir the More, and a generic Christian name as a baptismal marker that is also often an advertisement of their precise or associative ownership, such as Elene or Margaret Moire after Eleanor Pole and Margaret Stewert, this latter feature following the Portuguese naming practice for slaves.[51] Baptism is the foundation of the naming act, what for an early modern British-European worldview is the generous progressing of the black from a pre- or non-recognizable status into the civic sightlines of a Christian humanity.[52]

[50] At the moment of this letter, one of Marion Home's sons has just recovered Home castle from the English after she had to surrender it to them when, in their earlier siege, the English had killed another of her sons.

[51] Saunders, *Social History*, p. 90. For the popularity of the name Peter in medieval European usage, particularly from the fourteen century, see the entry for that name in E. G. Withycombe's *Oxford Dictionary of English Christian Names*, pp. 231–32.

[52] Slavery becomes the European destiny of Africans from the time of Nicholas V's bull *Romanex Pontifex* in 1436, which specifies Portugal's right "to conquer and enslave all peoples south of Cape Bojador" (cited and paraphrased in Sweet, "Spanish and Portuguese Influences," p. 6), and the bull *Dum Diverses* in 1452, which grants "Portugal the right to reduce to perpetual slavery all Saracens and pagans, and other Infidel and enemies of Christ in West Africa." For a summary of papal rulings on slavery also see Minnich in Earle and Lowe (p. 281), and Saunders,

As this transformation is the beginning of the public history of the Christianized black individual, prior origins disappear in the silence of his or her community record, which does not know, because it cannot, anything more than the fact of the person's new identity and its context—where he or she lives and/or what he or she does. If the illumination of a baptized name is for some reason unavailable, ethnic/geographic descriptors and vocational markers provide some social sight, such as the more "taubronar" or the black "freiris." The social intelligibility of early modern British black identity is thus Christian arrival and communal utility. If the necessary sobriety of official record masks the community's racial animosities toward the black subject, such animosities break out in popular media, as happens in Dunbar's poem "Ane Black Moire." If economic competition more often than not fuels such animosities, as in Dunbar's case his satiric ire toward the Black Lady in particular is the perfect vehicle for the venting of his career-long resentment at being denied the full monarchic rewards that he felt he deserved,[53] that same motive arguably drives the violence that such animosities sometimes produce, as in the assaulting of the black drummer by parties that the records are unable to name.

Whereas the Scottish black records' prognostic features fit and are confirmed by More's account of Catherine of Aragon's African servants, what distinguishes these records is their perceptible neutrality of tone, and their contribution to the chronology of black presence in the early Tudor period. Even if the relative civility of the Scottish mentions of black people is due in part to the effect of James IV's markedly progressive cultural piety, and to the necessary sobriety of official record, they are indicative of a social politics in which the black subject's racial marking is as yet unexceptionable overall. There is little that is exclusionistic in the Scottish black person's local habitation, even if it is an indubitably xenophilic one. But if these black people are exotics, they not for the most part cultural transgressors that are resented, even if they can be on occasion the objects of the financial jealousy of others. The Scottish records, in short, see black people with a kind of ontological sight rather than with a racial epistemology already in process. Irrespective of whether this appearance of black people in Scotland is the result of James's English marriage, or whether the appearance of black people in England and Scotland at nearly the same moment (James had a favorite black attendant in 1500/01 and blacks arrived in England with Catherine in 1501) are independent and parallel phenomena or whether they are connected, since the Spanish court has contact with that of James IV from 1489,[54] these reasonably described black individuals mark the first decade of the sixteenth century as the tentative beginnings of a black population in the British Isles in the early modern period.

Social History, who also discusses at length how these papal permissions of Portuguese attacks on Africa were constructed by writers such as Alvarus Pelagius, Egidio Colonna, and Zurara into a circular justificatory philosophy of enslavement of Africans because their barbarism is sinful and their sinfulness—deriving from their descent from Canaan—makes them bestial, and condemns them to a natural Christian servility (pp. 38–40).

[53] For an account of the financial disappointments that lie behind and accompany Dunbar's satiric writings, see Macdougall, *James V*, pp. 288–89.

[54] Ibid., p. 285.

IV

The black presence in early sixteenth-century Scotland is, then, a useful backdrop against which to consider the dispersion of the black people in Catherine of Aragon's retinue in England in the same period. Despite the 52 people named in Ferdinand and Isabella's list as accompanying their daughter to England, the actual number may be as high as 150.[55] Among these, how many are black people is uncertain. Although More does not specify the number of black people he saw, he says of the total only three or four are for him "tolerable" to look at, which is to say none of the rest are fair, that is, are colored to some degree in his view. Thus, even though at least two black people (the two "slaves") are officially recorded in the Spanish list and described by More, there may have been more, such as the two who were "not the fairest" in the London chroniclers' accounts, assuming here that these are figures additional to those that More describes. Some may have been musicians, among the numerous "sakbotes," "trumpettes," "shalmewes," and "mynstrels" that both London chroniclers describe as being in Catherine's triumphal entry procession at Cheapside.[56] There is also the fool/acrobat mentioned as being part of the entertainment that Catherine had her staff put on for Henry VII and Prince Arthur.[57] Several of these were rewarded by Henry VII.[58] The severe reduction of Catherine's personal staff, as a result of her father-in-law's several excisions of her personnel in his wrangling over the remainder of her dowry that he claimed was payable to him,[59] may have meant the absorption of some

---

55 This is the number that one of the most respected biographers of Catherine of Aragon believes she had with her (Francesca Claremont, *Catherine of Aragon*, p. 83). Garrett Mattingly, however, believes the number was closer to 60 persons (*Catherine of Aragon*, p. 21), which tallies with the estimate of the author of the *Receyt* (p. 7, fol. 31ʳ, ll. 122–25).

56 "and aftir them such trumpettes, shalmewes, and sakbotes to a great nombre as came with the Princes owte of Spayne, and aftir theim straungers of Spayne ...," *Receyt*, ed. Kipling, fol. 42ʳ, ll. 675–83, p. 31; "Then a band of Spanish musicians ...," *Chronicles*, ed. Kingsford, "Notes" to fol. 193ʳ, l. 22, p. 335.

57 Mattingly, p. 42.

58 *Receyt*, ed. Kipling, "Notes" p. 138; see gloss to lines 675–76. Kipling quotes payments from the King's Household Accounts (E 101/415/3), to the Princess's "stylmynstrels" and trumpet players on 4 December 1501; to nine trumpets of Spain on 4 December 1501; to two Spanish minstrels on 7 December 1502; to "My Lady Princess mynstrells" on 20 May 1502; to the Earl of Spain's trumpets on 4 December 1502.

59 Claremont, *Catherine of Aragon*, pp. 106–7. See De Puebla's letter to Ferdinand and Isabella, 27 Dec. 1500, in which he mentions Henry VII's desire for the limitation of the number of Spanish staff to accompany Catherine of Aragon to England, and for the use of English personnel instead (*Calendar of State Papers*, ed. Bergenroth, 1: 251, Item 292, "Household of the Princess of Wales, S.E.T. c.1 L4. F.2"); Ferdinand and Isabella's reply to De Puebla of 23 March 1501, in which Isabella contests Henry and adds on the names of some more attendants that Catherine is to have, asserting that it is better that her daughter have Spanish rather than English personnel with her (*Calendar of State Papers*, ed. Bergenroth, 1: 253–54, Item 293); the letter of the Ambassador of Spain to England, Don Pedro de Ayala, to Queen Isabella in December 1501, in which Ayala reports Henry's refusal to support Catherine's personal staff (*Supplement to Vol. I and II of Calendar of State Papers*, ed. Bergenroth, p. 7); and Ferdinand and Isabella's letter to De Puebla of 6 January 1502 in which they communicate

of these people by the English, including at court. As Fiona Kisby has shown, the foreign musicians in the courts of the first and second Tudors usually settled in the city, in areas adjacent to their work places in the court.[60] Those taken up by Henry VIII may have included "Guyot, the spear," "Blewmantell, … Windsor herald," and "Cornelius, Our cordiner."[61]

The strongest confirmation, however, of the probability of Catherine of Aragon's retinue containing more black people than are mentioned in her parents' letter and who are absorbed by the English court, is the black man who was taken up in honor and respect by both Catherine's father-in-law and her second husband. Documented in the reigns of Henry VII and Henry VIII is a black trumpeter named John Blancke/Blak, whose surname is most likely an affectionate pun on his skin color.[62] Black trumpeters were valued throughout Europe, and as Kate Lowe has recently suggested, he was very likely a surviving member of the Spanish princess's entourage.[63] He appears on the Westminster Tournament Roll commissioned by Henry VIII in 1511 to mark the birth of his male child (Fig. 1.1 (and cover)).[64] This illuminated manuscript, depicting in a pictorial narrative the beginning, middle, and end of the two-day event, shows a black trumpeter, who according to the historian Sydney Anglo is almost certainly John Blanke, seated on a gray courser dressed

---

their indignation at Henry's dismissal of one of Catherine's gentleman ushers (*Calendar of State Papers*, ed. Bergenroth, 1: 265, Item no. 313).

60 "Royal Minstrels in the City and Suburbs of Early Tudor London: Professional Activities and Private Interests," pp. 199–200, 208.

61 *Letters & Papers of the Reign of Henry VIII*, 1 pt. 1, p. 303, Item 516, 30 June 1510; p. 358, Item 632, "Grants in November 1510" #79 24 November 2 Henry VIII; p. 465, Item 887, 3 Octoctober 1511, respectively. Since in late medieval English usage the word "bloman" or "blewemen" denotes a black person (A. L. Mayhew and Walter W. Skeat, *A Concise Dictionary of Middle English*, p. 69.), there is some possibility of the word "blewmantell" referring to a black man. Likewise, "Cornelius" sounds like one of the *faux* Roman classical names that some black English servants are typically given later in the century and in the next. See James Walvin, *Black and White: The Negro and English Society 1553–1945*, p. 166; K. L. Little, *Negroes in Britain: A Study of Racial Relations in English Society*, p. 168; Fryer, *Staying Power*, p. 24. Both these names, as well "Guyot," hint at black identities precisely because of the form in which they are cited, only by their single names, a form most common in the naming of seized and assimilated black people throughout Europe.

62 According to the BBC's web page statement, "Blanke, meaning white, is not believed to have been his real name, but given to him as a joke by the royal court … as a result, his exact origins aren't known, but he may have come from Africa or the Iberian Peninsula" <http://www.bbc.co.uk/london/yourlondon/unitedcolours/events/atoz_blackhistory.shtml> 6.22.05. Support for this reading of the name appears in Aurelia Casares's essay, in the record of a Spanish black slave named "Juan Blanco (John White)," which Casares says "may be a joke in bad taste since his owner's surname was not white" (in Earle and Lowe, p. 252). The record, incidentally, affords a sly connection with Shakespeare's *Othello*, as Blanco was accused of having stolen, among other things, "an embroidered handkerchief" (p. 232 n. 23).

63 Lowe in Earle and Lowe, p. 39.

64 Westminster Tournament Roll, College of Arms, London (see Fig. 1.1). A scanned image of a part of the roll—showing the black trumpeter—is available on the www at http://www.nationalarchives.gov.uk/pathways/blackhistory/early_times/blanke.htm [seen on 4.28.05].

richly in yellow and gray, and—uniquely among the other trumpeters—wearing an elaborate turban.[65] Musicians' payments in the accounts of the Treasurer of the Chamber record several payments to him of 8d a day, going back to the reign of Henry VII. He is named, for instance, in the Exchequer roll of 1507 as having been paid on 7 November 20 shillings or £430 in today's currency (Item 76). That he was chosen to perform in costly royal public spectacles, and that he appears continuously in the royal treasury records of two monarchs over more than a decade, clearly indicate the stable esteem in which he is held by court and city. Marking the degree of his acceptance and social assimilation is the fact of his marriage in 1512, which is recorded in the Exchequer Accounts of Henry VIII because the monarch sent him rich clothes as a gift on that occasion (Item 89). Whom he married, and what happened to his family, is not archivally visible, and that he himself is visible—luckily for him literally in a painting, which is one of the very few historical images of early modern English black people to have survived—is the accident of the lavishness of the royal occasion which enveloped him. The much-awaited (but ill-fated) birth of an heir of the Tudor dynasty illuminates in its happy largesse the otherwise un-seeable figure of a professional black man called upon to proudly embellish the event. Such is the fortuitous circumstance needed to unveil the obscured identity of black people in the early modern English archives, for many of whom their names—like John Blanke's—will reveal little of who they are, and by default pass for white.

Fig. 1.1 Great Tournament Roll of Henry VIII, 1511. Royal College of Arms, London

As I have pointed out elsewhere, in the closing years of Henry VIII's reign and the beginning of Edward VI's, there is a black military man by the name of Peter Negro

[65] Sydney Anglo, ed. *The Great Tournament Roll of Westminster*, p. 82.

who is mentioned repeatedly in official Tudor archives.[66] He is part of the group of Spanish mercenaries operating in England in the fourth decade of the sixteenth century that Gilbert Millar has studied in detail,[67] of which a possible minor example from the Scottish archives of this same moment was cited earlier (Item 113). He enters military service in the English acquisitions of Italian and Spanish mercenaries during and after the siege of Boulogne in 1544, a sizeable number of whom are brought into service in England after 1545 for protection against the threat of a cross-Channel invasion and in the campaign against the Scots.[68] He first appears in the English government records in 1545 when on 4 July in the company of several Spanish mercenaries he is paid 25 pounds (Item 103, 1 and 2). Even though the records here and later, and Millar, cite Peter Negro as a Spaniard, he is almost certainly a second-generation assimilated black man, since in early modern Spanish-Portuguese usage the name "Negro" always signifies either an African or someone with a lineal connection to one.[69] It is important to iterate that given the history of ethnic mixing in the Iberian peninsula, no Caucasian could have a name such as "negro" without in fact being one—in whatever hue.[70] Furthermore, as has been pointed out earlier, in the later medieval and early modern ages there were assimilated Africans in military service not just in the Iberian peninsula but also elsewhere in Europe.[71] Peter Negro's black identity is acknowledged in one of these two records (Item 103.2) in its choice of naming him as Peter Mogo, the surname appropriating a traditional African name as a typically generalized early modern British-European ethnic descriptor, exactly in the manner seen in the Scottish records.[72] That his blackness goes without comment in the rest of the records, including in a later instance by Peter Negro himself, and that

---

66 See my essay, "Othello, Sir Peter Negro, and the Blacks of Early Modern England."

67 Gilbert John Millar, *Tudor Mercenaries and Auxiliaries 1485–1547*; for the acute English dependence on mercenaries in the 1540s, see pp. 43–44, 173–77.

68 Ibid., p. 44, 132–33, and 174, respectively.

69 See Kate Lowe, "Notes to the Text," in Earle and Lowe, p. xvi; Saunders, *Social History*, p. xii, and James Sweet, "Spanish and Portuguese Influences on Racial Slavery," p. 7.

70 This is true even if the reverse is possible, as in the case of Alessandro de' Medici; see John Brackett's essay "Race and Rulership: Alessandro Medici, the first Medici Duke of Florence 1529–1537," in Earle and Lowe, pp. 303–25.

71 See Earle and Lowe, p. 33. Employing Africans in specialist military capacities is a trend that two centuries later will culminate in Russia in the celebrated example of Peter the great's Ethiopian general, (Ibrahim Petrovich) Hannibal, who not only had a distinguished military and diplomatic career, but also settled in Russia and founded a line of descendents that includes the celebrated poet Alexander Pushkin as well as important figures in the current royal family of England. See the essays by Albert Perry, "Abram Hannibal, the Favorite of Peter the Great"; Anne Lounsbery, "Russia's Literary Genius: The Great Grandson of an African Slave"; and Mario de Valdes y Cocom, "The Blurred Racial Lines of Famous Families: Pushkin Genealogy" (electronic essay).

72 For instances of "mogo" as an African name, see Julia Stewert, *African Names*, p. 92; Leo Frobenius, *The Voices of Africa*, p. 508; and Robert Dick Douglas, *Three Boy Scouts in Africa*, pp. 57, 60, 100.

his historical documentation is slight overall, might explain the curious invisibility of this remarkable black man in current historical knowledge of the period.[73]

Irrespective of when and how he acquired his fighting skills, from the beginning of his career with the English Peter Negro is as much of a prized military professional as his colleagues; this is evident in the considerable compensation he was offered by the English for his services. In the very next month after his first citations in the records, on 8 August 1546, his disbursement jumped to £75 (Item 105. 1 and 2), which becomes an annuity of £100 on 4 October (Item 106. 1 and 2). As Millar has revealed, these rewards are all part of the Tudor government's gratitude for the steadfastness of service shown by those Spanish mercenaries in their employ, who confronted and summarily punished defections in their ranks, such as that of Antonio de Mora, when he defected to the French.[74] They are also reflective in general of that government's desperate dependence on its specialist foreign officers for maintaining an effective fighting readiness that it could not maintain with its own dispirited English troops.[75] Both of these contexts signal, however, an unimpeachable dedication and integrity that distinguish Peter Negro and predict the even greater honor that he willl subsequently get from the English. As the lead officer of the three mounted infantry units headed by Colonel Pedro Gamboa accompanying Edward Seymour the Lord Protector in his successful Scottish campaign of Pinkie Cleugh in September 1547, Peter Negro led a charge of unbelievable bravery that secured for the English the besieged town of Haddington. Described in the eyewitness accounts of several European sources,[76] the exploit earned him a summary battlefield knighthood at Roxburgh on 28 September, as described by the high English official and subsequent adjudicator in the court of the Provost Marshall for the conquered territories who was present at the ceremony, William Patten (Item 107).[77] If the knighthood carried a cash award as one of the

[73] This scholarly blindness extends even to the newest attempt to study black people in early modern Europe, that of Earle and Lowe, who do not mention Peter Negro, presumably because they are unsure whether to regard him as black. So also Gustav Ungerer, who also "can't help concluding" that Peter Negro is not a black man, simply because no one "mentions he is black" ("Recovering a Black African's Voice in an English Lawsuit," p. 267 n. 4). As multiple examples in this book show, that is a dangerously unreliable assumption on which to base such a conclusion, because explicit identification of an individual as black is often an accidental and unpredictable phenomenon (as are, for instance, the record of John Blanke, and as will be seen later, that of Martin Frances, Item 384). Ungerer also does not pause to reflect on the possible history of Peter Negro's surname, and is unaware of the implications of such naming. In fact, in one of the instances cited above, the Tudor archives do allude to his African origins in the surname "Mogo" with which they cite him.

[74] For an account of the defection, see Millar, *Tudor Mercenaries*, p. 170. There were other Spanish defections as well, such as those of Arze and Juan de Haro; see Millar, p. 134.

[75] For references to the poor condition of English troops see Millar, pp. x, 44, 168.

[76] For the eyewitness accounts of the event, see Jean de Beaugue, *The History of the Campagnes 1548 and 1549*, p. 84, and the anonymous *Chronicle of King Henry VIII, Being a Contemporary Record of Some of the Principal Events in the Reigns of King Henry VIII and Edward VI*, ed. M. A. S. Hume, ch. 88, pp. 203–6.

[77] Other mentions of the event are in William Shaw's *The Knights of England*, p. 62, and in Millar, p. 175 n. 30 and "Index C," p. 191.

eyewitness accounts seems to suggest,[78] it may also have included other privileges such as an instant denization and land grants, since that is what accompanies such honors given to others.[79] This event marks the highest level achieved by a black person in early modern England in the entire range of this book's study.

If, paid more than his English counterparts, and rewarded and honored publicly over them, Peter Negro is to some degree the subject of the same resentment that Millar has described as facing his colleagues as a whole,[80] a part of this animosity is present in the deliberate or inadvertent archival disregard of his title for all of the subsequent times that he is named (Items 109, 110, 112, 115, 116, 117), except one (Item 114). Common, nonetheless, in all of these citations is the consistency of his discharge of his responsibilities, in keeping his men in tight control and movement through the chaotic and variable military campaign in the north. Item 110 in particular explicitly records the award of a £100 annuity "for life." Yet, unlike his colleagues such as Gamboa or de Mora, who become mired in scandal, he remained untouched by acrimony or controversy.[81] If this is the character of his English public service between 1546 and 1550, it is also that of the will that shortly before his death he scripted on 4 August 1551 in London in the prerogative court of the Archbishop of Canterbury, which, according to the Elizabethan urban chronicler John Stow, was in Ivy Lane in Farringdon Ward Within, even if Stow is describing London in 1598 (Item 119).[82] Within the pro-forma probity of the document's genre as a terminal legal document, the will's contents describe a sober reckoning of a life of fortune, whose bounty ("a chayur of gold," "five hundrith ducatts") afforded the rudiments of a familial experience albeit dispersed (in an implied but absent partner, a "house, and a minor "sonne" here, but a yet "to be approved" "doughter" in "Ittaly"), and the dispensation of whose frankly acknowledged future obligations both public and private can only depend on the honesty of those left behind, such as a close associate and friend ("I require Capitayn Cristofer Dyaz as my friende," "to restore and discharge my consyceince in those things"). There is here thus the dual impress, of a roaming soldier's years stretching across Spain, Italy, and England (in the English will's linkage to one of his closest Spanish associates, Cristofer Dyaz, and to an uncertain Italian daughter), and of the struggle for survival of a marginalized existence lost in a welter of origins geographic and ethnic in which an African identity however distant is no longer tenable. Only the surname "Negro" remains, a fossilized telltale of that lost history.

If death is the ultimate "settlement," Peter Negro's sudden illness and quick death is his "settling" into the oblivion of an absorbed early modern English history.

---

78 The *Chronicle* also cites a cash reward of £200 being recommended for Peter Negro (p. 206), although the veracity of the *Chronicle*'s details is doubted by Hume.

79 See the details of what is given both a Breton adventurer named Philbert De Chandee in 1486, as well as Pedro Gamboa in 1547 (Millar, pp. 30–31 and 170–71, respectively). Gamboa appears knighted in 1546 (*L&P* 1: 85, item 199. 490, and 2: 156 item 332.18).

80 Millar, pp. 134, 177.

81 In addition to De Mora's scandalous desertion mentioned earlier, others whose careers were clouded in disrepute include Arze and Juan De Haro (Millar, p. 134). For the reprehensible end of both Gamboa and Carlos de Guevarra, see *Chronicle*, pp. 201–14.

82 Stow, *A Survey of London*, 1: 342.

That his death, which occurred in London about a year after the drawing up of the will, is nevertheless a public event may partly be the effect of the continuing Spanish mercenary presence and of the survival of its perceived importance to the English authorities. Beyond that, however, it must be indicative of a certain degree of community recognition of an exemplary public service individual whose passing deserves the ceremony and dignity that its personal eyewitness account records (Item 120). Even though the original account is partly damaged by fire, and even if the transcription of the original by the seventeenth-century English antiquarian John Strype misdates the event by a year, the correct year of Peter Negro's death can be ascertained to be 1552 (see note to item). The description of Peter Negro's funeral by a London undertaker, Henry Machyn, on 14 July 1552 is identical in its details of ritual solemnity to those of other street pageants involving Tudor royals entered in Machyn's *Diary*. These include the "flut playng," the "flag," the "harold of armes," and the "mony morners" in the "stret honge with blake with ys armes." That Peter Negro's death inspires a grass-roots civic commemoration is signaled by Henry Machyn's identity as a simple London citizen with "no great scholarship or attainments" and "sufficiently prejudiced," so that, as the *Diary*'s editor puts it, "his opinions and sentiments would be shared by a large proportion of his fellow citizens."[83] In all, the narrative of Peter Negro is astonishing in the fact of its being almost totally unremarked in modern Euro-American historical scholarship.

In that same decade there is a "negro" needle maker who has a successful trade in the bustling business district of Cheapside in the early 1550s. William Harrison's casual memory of him in his magisterial account of the country as being jealously secretive about his needle-making technique because "he would never teach [it] to any," describes otherwise the professional respect in which he is commonly held (Item 121). Bounded on the east by St. Paul's church and on the West by the courts of the standard and Cornhill ward (in which will appear within the next decade Tudor London's first mall, the Royal Exchange), and close to Lombard street toward the south east where, according to the Tudor urban historian John Stow, gather "merchants, strangers of diverse nations … twice a day", Cheapside is the central concourse of early modern London, the city's chief boulevard, the proud site of all royal progresses from the time of Edward III through Henry VIII and Elizabeth, and the primary venue of all its shows and pageants, including possibly the funeral of Peter Negro. The city's most desirable shopping center, as East Cheap to its southeast is its principal food and perishable items market, Cheapside or Westcheap (the names of both East and West Cheap being derived from and literally indicative of a marketplace), is chiefly the upscale home of the drapery and mercery industry, and in 1553 the site of the city's best goldsmiths.[84] The location named in the reference is thus revealing. It identifies the black individual as a specialist craftsman at the peak

83 *Diary of Henry Machyn*, Preface, p. v.

84 The quotation about Lombard Street is from *A Survey of London*, 1: 201. For goldsmiths in Cheapside see 1: 81. For the upscale nature of Cheapside, see 1: 217, 345. Stow says Elizabeth led a procession into and from Cheapside in 1570 (1: 193). For the derivation of the name as a bargaining or market place, see the entry for "chepe" in Mahew and Skeat, *A Concise Dictionary of Middle English*.

of his career, situated successfully inside what is arguably one of the city's most elite and fiercely competitive business centers. That he appears, even as an incidental retrospective allusion in the detached view of a national survey, betokens the strength of his professional renown. At the same time, it is his skill that for the Tudor surveyor merits mention and not who he is. The generic identity of his blackness, which can nevertheless be somewhat excavated by connecting him to an Iberian background in terms of the Iberian Moorish skill in needlework, particularly that pertaining to black lace, much valued in Tudor England from the time of Catherine of Aragon,[85] offers some clue to the mixed nature of his metropolitan life that is both rewarding and pressured. That he is, evidently, an independent craftsman not discernibly bound to anyone is his singular achievement at this moment in time, and one that was presumably enabled by his rare expertise. Concomitantly, that he "would not teach his art to any" speaks of the resentment and animosity within and against which his valuable trade must have been plied.

Throughout this early Tudor period black people appear in the private sphere as well. One instance of this is in London in 1523. A black stable keeper and groom by the name of "Fraunces Negro" is employed at "The Stable" under the division of the "Queen's Chambour" at the wage of £10 20 shillings (Item 98). As in the case of the black Scottish drummer and John Blanke, salaried employment connotes a skill of repute, and one that merits his royal employer's willing anticipatory self-assessment in a tax document, aptly described as "Assessment of anticipation of Subsidy."[86] Attached to the Queen's household, he is almost certainly part of the Spanish black people in Catherine of Aragon's personal staff and a proud member of it. Employed at court, he is in all probability located in Westminster even if initially he may have been living in St. Martin Orgars parish in Canwicke street ward directly above London bridge (6R Agas Map, p. 25). Like John Blanke, he is a proud blazon of black Anglo-Spanish royal service. Another example of a beginning black population, deriving if not directly from Catherine of Aragon's retinue probably from the cordial Anglo–Spanish relations that the Spanish princess's English marriage generated, is the mention of "Dyego Negro servaunt with Thomas Bowyer" for whom an assessment of "4d" is made in a Tudor Subsidy Roll in the parish of St. Mary Woolnoth in Langborne ward in London in 1541 (Item 100). Located in what is one of the city's busiest merchant districts on Lombard street in east-central London as John Stow describes it, St. Mary Woolnoth offers one clue to Dyego's origins.[87] He is probably the procurement of a merchant trading in the Iberian peninsula, since there was a flourishing English merchant trade with Spain and Portugal in the first four decades of the sixteenth century, as the ledger of the early Tudor merchant Thomas Howell clearly demonstrates, and which may have brought back an occasional Iberian black person.[88] Merchants are frequently appointed city aldermen and, as will be seen fifty

---

85 M. Jourdain, "Lace as Worn in England until the Accession of James I," pp. 162–68.

86 For the Royal "Stable," see E. K. Chambers, *The Elizabethan Stage*, 1: 34.

87 See Stow's description of Lombard Street, cited above.

88 For the trade with Spain and Portugal see G. V. Scammell, "English Merchant Shipping at the End of the Middle Ages," p. 328, and "Shipowning in the Economy and Politics of Early Modern England," p. 386 n. 6. For Thomas Howell's ledger see the essay by Gordon Connell-

years later in the case of Alderman Paul Bannynge, they are heavily involved in the overseas commodity trading in the South Atlantic. Thomas Bowyer is prominent among the records of the city Aldermen in 1538 and 1542.[89] Like Peter or Pedro Negro in that his Iberian origin is more visible than is Fraunces's, Dyego's stature is like Fraunces's coded in the tax amount that he is recognized to be worth, the difference between the amounts mentioned for them being not just a matter of the two different kinds of tax data cited (salary versus tax due), but also that of royal service versus a private one. Although described here inhumanly in monetary terms, both amounts underscore the clear valuation of the skills and resources of Africans in the early modern moment.

What little illumination is present in the black records considered so far, however, may be the result of their location in prominent government documents. That minimal illumination is drastically reduced in black references in local parochial archives in the early Tudor reigns. These are also records of black people in the private sphere, but they are much harder to read. As was suggested at the beginning of this chapter, these are the records whose utter heuristic opacity compels only an intuitive consideration of their black content, and a method of analysis that can only be *sui generis.* One specimen of this kind of a record is the burial notice of "Alys Blackman" in the parish register of St. Margaret's Church in Westminster on 16 April 1543 (Item 101). The term "Blackman" is an expedient traditional ethnic descriptor from at least the previous century, as is evident from a late fifteenth-century Southampton record about a "blakman taboryn (drummer)" cited later in this chapter, and it is probably a successor to the earlier medieval term used for such purposes, "blewman," which appears for example in a household accounts book of the mid-fifteenth century.[90] "Blackman" as the designator of a black man occurs in English parish registers regularly in the sixteenth and the next two centuries and is cited by Victorian colonial ethnographers as well as by onomastics scholars in that capacity.[91] The record's lack of any explicit racial information, and of any punctuational marking of the individual's ethnicity, may weaken the authenticity of the record's black content, but it cannot disallow the historical possibility of a black individual in this place at this time. As a church parish located adjacent to the old

---

Smith, "The Ledger of Thomas Howell." W. Walton Claridge even cites two Englishmen named "John Tintam and "William Fabian," attempting to trade with Guinea as early as 1481; see *A History of the Gold Coast*, p. 54.

89 Alfred B. Beaven, *The Aldermen of the City of London*, pp. 110, 147, 181.

90 See the discussion of a Southampton beadle's fracas with "a blakman taboryn" in 1491, below. For the mid-fifteenth-century mention of "blewman" see "Richard Fyrthing, a blewman," in T. H. Turner, *Manners and Household Expenses in the Thirteenth and Fifteenth Centuries*, p. 578; cited by Edwards, *Early African Presence*, p. 15. For the medieval meaning of the term "blackman," see Mahew and Skeats, *Dictionary of Middle English*, p. 69, as cited earlier.

91 For an instance of the explanation of "blackman" as referring to an African by a colonial ethnographer see F. W. H. Migeod, "Personal Names among Some West African Tribes," p. 45. For explanations of the name Blackman as representing a black man by onomastics scholars, see Pine, *The Story of Surnames*, p. 90; Bardsley, *English Surnames*, pp. 445–46; Arthur, *Etymological Dictionary*, p. 36.

seat of monarchic power, Westminster palace, and close to the new one, Whitehall, that if officially absorbed by it two centuries later is even at this time frequently co-opted by it as its own, St. Margaret's parish is one of the most likely neighborhoods in which the remnants of Catherine of Aragon's black personnel might eventually appear.[92] Whether Alys (Alice) Blackman is a first-generation Iberian black transplant or the daughter of one, her ghostly allusion, with its mix of original and assimilated identities, may be a black life's only civic inscription of its existence, and that too only of the moment of its historical obliteration.

In any case, Alys Blackman may not be the only black woman in this parish because two years later an "Agnes Blackmore" was also buried here, on 5 October 1545 (Item 104). Evocative of the traditional English name for a moor dweller and a popular English place name, and proximate to the standard ethnic descriptor "blackamore" from which it misses only one letter, "blackmore" is one of the commonest, expediently derived, and ambiguous names for a black person in early modern England. Its blurred identity is the perfect representation of the silent masking of a black individual's ethnic history in the process of his or her English assimilation. The uncertainty of Agnes Blackmore's ethnic identity is, however, counteracted by the visibility of her gender, which together with that of Alys Blackman echoes the anonymity of the gendered racialization of Catherine of Aragon's two black female slaves four decades back who could only be both nameless and sexless in the official record. At the same time, the appearance of two women with probable ethnic descriptors as surnames, in the same west London parish, within a period of two years, creates unmistakably the sense of a growth of black people in and around the vicinity of monarchic presence in early Tudor London. Whether Alys Blackman and Agnes Blackmore know or are connected to John Blank, the monarch's black trumpeter, is a moot question, since the latter's residence must also have been close to the venue of his royal service, very likely in areas like St. Margaret's parish.

Another instance of this kind of black citation is that of the burial of "Jeames Blackemore" in St. Peter Cornhill on 13 August 1544 (Item 102). An ancient agricultural market close to Cheapside that will be fronted by the Royal Exchange two decades later, and that is at the corner where Cornhill street and Leadenhall are intersected by Gracious street coming up over London bridge from the river and Southwark (Agas map 4R, p. 12), Cornhill is a neighborhood of busy mercantile and foreign presence with many shops, where if John Stow is to be believed "merchandise brought in from beyond the seas" is weighed and sold.[93] As a prosperous ward that is assessed at the relatively high amount of £212 in the Tudor subsidy Roll of 1541,[94] it is a locale where personally imported and attached foreign metal workers and laborers, including black people, are liable to be employed. The proximity of the surname "Blackemore" to

---

92 See Fiona Kisby's discussion of St. Margaret's Church and the city of Westminster in early Tudor times, in her essay, "Music and Musicians in Early Westminster," esp. pp. 224, 225, 228.

93 *A Survey of London,* 1: 187–88.

94 "1541 London Subsidy Roll: Cornhill Ward," in R. G. Lang, ed., *Two Tudor Subsidy Rolls for the City of London 1541 and 1582*, pp. 54–56 (available at <http://www.british-history.ac.uk/source.asp?pubid=160>), seen 2.6.06.

"blackamore" signals an etymological relationship of the former to the latter in which the former is possibly an early orthographic mutation in the evolution of the latter name, exactly as the first name is relative to the modern form "James."

Yet another occurrence of this kind of citation is the burial notice of "Henry Blackemer, servant to Mr. Lordynge," in London in the parish registers of All Hallows, Bread street on 8 November 1548 (Item 111). If for this record as well as for the previous two, interpretative penetration is made difficult by the required clerical brevity of local government documentation, that difficulty is compounded by the uncertain format of a new government record-keeping promulgation for the local parish that, having being decreed by Cromwell in 1538, is just about a decade old. The precision of its descriptive contents, which will always be variably idiosyncratic, is indeterminate now and especially makeshift for ethnic newcomers to the parish. Since an early modern English orthographic culture in which non-uniform spelling is the standard will inevitably obfuscate the names that it is entrusted to inscribe, the surname "Blackemer" could be a refractive clerical improvisation. Some interpretative legibility is offered for the record by the Victorian editor who transcribed it for the Harleian Society's printing of this church's parish documents when he parenthetically suggests in the Index that the name in the record should be read as "Blakemore" (see note to item). If according to the editor "Blackemer" is the manuscript original of what he is suggesting should be understood as "Blakemore," could the original be a misrepresentation of "blackamore"? Could the word in the surname position be meant to represent "Blackamore," or in fact be "blackamore," especially since the "a" of the English secretarial hand could easily be mistaken by modern readers as an "e"?[95] That is, could "Blakemore" in the original manuscript mean "Blackamore," that is, be a variation of it? Thus, could the record be meant to be read as "Henry, Blackamore, servant to …"? This surmise is lent some credibility by the fact that "Blackemer" is not listed as an English name in any of the scholarly compilations of traditional English surnames. The difficulty presented to this identification by the suffix -mer, with its etymological connection to the Germanic root "mere" meaning lake, and therefore to a traditional Anglo-Saxon English toponym, is not an insurmountable one as toponyms merge indiscriminately with ethnonyms in the informality of early modern English naming practices, as will be seen in many of the names presented in this book, and as is strikingly evident, ironically enough, in the uncertainty about the origins of the surname of Thomas More himself.[96] This homonymic tendency, which is one of the major reasons for the historical undecipherability of black identities in early modern England, gives "Blackemer" as much of a probability of being a black name as of being an English one. So, even

[95] See Giles E. Dawson, and Laetitia Kennedy-Shipton, *Elizabethan Handwriting 1500–1650: A Manual*, pp. 30–31, and "English Handwriting 1500–1700: An Online Course" at <http://www.english.cam.ac.uk/ceres/ehoc/alphabets.html>.

[96] In his biography of Thomas More, Peter Ackroyd has pointed out that, while "the name Thomas was explicable … the origins of More's surname cannot be so easily discovered. If such names derive from some sense of place, then the great moors or marshes around London might find an echo here. It is also a name upon which a number of puns were constructed. 'More' could be the 'Moor' or black Ethiop and Desiderius Erasmus, the Dutch humanist who became his close companion, sometimes called him 'Niger'" (*The Life of Thomas More*, p. 7).

if the name is not preceded by syntactical markers such as "a" or "the" highlighting ethnic difference, there are credible reasons to think that the name "blackemer" has strong etymological connections to the ethnic descriptor "blackamore" and is an early version of it. The word "black a more" itself had appeared for the first time only a year earlier, in Andrew Boorde's *Introduction to the Book of Knowledge* in 1547.[97] If John Blanke can turn out to be a black man, it is much more probable that Henry Blackemer is one too.

The identification of the individual as "servant" strengthens the plausibility of this being a black person, since, as some of the records so far have shown, domestic service is what Africans brought into England initially or permanently often ended up in. That history gains credible relevance for this person, given his location, like those of the people in the previous two records, in a thriving merchant neighborhood in West Cheap, in south-central London, about three to four blocks due north of the Salt Wharf on the river, and directly across from Southwark, that is, reasonably close to the sea traffic coming into the city (Agas map 5M, p. 22).[98] According to John Stow, Bread Street was "wholly inhabited by rich merchants," and All Hallows Church was the burial place of many goldsmiths, aldermen, and mayors.[99] "Mr. Lordyng" is likely to be the merchant "Wylliam Lordyng" who was assessed £20 in the adjoining ward of Farringdon Without in 1541.[100] Given the proximity of Farringdon ward to that of Cornhill (both are near Cheapside), Henry Blackemer could share the probable Iberian origin of Jeames Blackemore. If, however, Henry Blackemer is not connected to the Iberian black people originating from Catherine of Aragon's personal staff, he could be the precursor of a new black influx, that illicitly stemming from the mid-sixteenth-century English African adventuring. The clear identification of the individual's employment status, together with the record's early date (before the West African forays of Elizabethan sea adventurers such as John Lok and John Hawkins had begun), however, make it an unusual entry, and point to the need for a reassessment of the range of Elizabethan seafaring history itself. A merchant named William Hawkins and several others were involved in an overseas commercial adventure in the 1530s and that trip brought back at least one black person, even if a kingly one who died of natural causes while being taken back.[101] Whether there were more is something of which this record should invite reconsideration. Even at the early date of the Henry Blackemer record London merchants may have been surreptitiously trafficking in Africans, because as Peter Ackroyd has pointed out, Thomas More's family coat of arms has the figure of an

---

[97] *OED*, 1: 223; cited by Mary Floyd-Wilson, *English Ethnicity and Race in Early Modern Drama*, p. 191 n. 33. In that same entry, the *OED* cites an earlier version of the word—"blacke moryan"—appearing for the first time in 1526.

[98] For the commercial character of the locale, and a derivation of its name, see *A Survey of London*, 1: 345–46.

[99] Ibid., 346.

[100] "1541 London Subsidy Roll-Farringdon Ward Without," in *Two Tudor Subsidy Rolls*, pp. 75–87 (available at <http://www.british-history.ac.uk/source.asp?pubid=160>), seen 2.6.06.

[101] Kenneth R. Andrews, Trade*, Plunder and Settlement: Maritime Enterprise and the Genesis of the British Empire 1480–1630*, p. 59.

African head on it, a feature common in the blazons of English slave-trading families throughout the early modern period.[102]

These documentational idiosyncrasies perhaps make the recording of the burial of "John A Moore" in St. Margaret's Church in Westminster on 6 January 1556 (Item 124) relatively easier to unpack. While corresponding to the etymological dubiety of the "A-" form in names such as "Black A Moore/More," and to the uncertainty of whether that is a surviving relic of the medieval patronymic derivative "Ap" or "Att," the name also strongly suggests an informal clerical orthography and punctuational personality that require neither a pause after the first name nor a lower case for the indefinite article as well as for the first letter of the name of the specific category that it is indicating. The latter possibility read into the citation makes it conform instantly to the commonest form of ethnic citation used in the early modern period: "John, a moore." As the surname metonymically obfuscates a traditional English origin with an African one, so the location and the date make two possible histories for John a Moore, one deriving from Catherine of Aragon and the other connecting either to Anglo-Iberian merchant trading or to initial English African adventuring, which symbiotically obfuscate each other. If a general onomastic typology and the possibility of two kinds of uncertain histories are the only indirect contexts of illumination of this black life, those in turn reflect precisely the defacing plurality and diffusive abstraction by which the human outlines of real black lives will be written out of the early modern English historical record. Even so, the burial of an adult baptized African in an elite Tudor metropolitan church betrays a civic support and acceptance for John A Moore that is important to recognize.

Taken together, the documentary record of black people examined thus far is both slight and significant. It is slight because notwithstanding its inevitably provisional nature (there may be more black identities in the records of the period than what has been proposed here), the total number of references to black people between 1500 and 1558 amounts to only a dozen people, if the multiple citations of the same individual are disregarded. The contents of such notations, in their brevity and linguistic indeterminacy, offer only a precarious heuristic access. The very idea of a black presence as such may appear difficult to validate, because the specificity of such a presence seems to be absent from or ignored in these archives. Yet, precisely that feature may be what makes these records significant despite their numerical slightness. The curiously casual or cryptic content of such references can be seen to confirm the evolving sense of early Tudor attitudes to black people, in the fact that such casualness or crypticity could mark a linguistic nonchalance about such a group that is indicative of a cultural space for them in the early Tudor social imaginary. That space, while not celebratory, may be an unspokenly tolerant one. This must follow from the lack of any visible rhetorical gesturing about the ethnicity of the people cited in these documents, which register black people's particularity in the most minimal of terms. "Blackamoor" or "Negro" in the surname position of an individual, and, without the syntactical underlining of a comma, can only be a

---

[102] *Life of Thomas More*, pp. 7–8. According to Ackroyd, More's official seal, when he is Henry VIII's under-treasurer, also has the same figure. There is a reproduction of this crest in J. A. Rogers, *Nature Knows No Color Line*, p. 76.

coherent practice in a community and in an historical moment in which black people are like everyone else and can be named just like them. Even when the distinctiveness of black people is noticed, as in the Scottish records in their frequent underlining of tribal specialty by the use of a "the" before an ethnically descriptive surname such as "Moryen" or "more," that notice is mostly not a negative pointing, although that may represent in part James's cultural interest rather than a response of the local populace as is Dunbar's nasty poem, despite its circumstantial context. Dunbar's hostile sentiments, like More's, are the exceptions in the overall emotional pattern of the black records. Indeed, the very numerical slightness of black people may be what contributes to their acceptance in the early Tudor period, where for the moment they exist somewhere between exoticism and resentment. This observation is strengthened if the symptomatic rather than literal value of the numbers of these early Tudor black records is kept in sight, by which they are taken to predict the phenomenology of a black presence rather than to demonstrate the exact volume of it.

V

Within the initial phase of black arrivals in England, however, the records show the seeds of a different trend in English perceptions of them than what has been described above. The hostility and sarcasm showed to Catherine of Aragon's black servants by More, the insulting of the black women by Dunbar, the assaulting of the black drummer, and the black needle maker's pressured practice may not be typical of the period, but they reflect a kind of local sentiment toward black people that is incipient still but that will emerge only in the pressure of particular situations later. As civil law is the inevitable arbiter of social conflicts, so legal records are an unfailing register of changing intra-communal relations that both describe the moment and foretell the future. A singular instance of a black person in an early Tudor lawsuit shows law as the particular and fundamental modality of the writing out of blackness in the larger early modern English political history. Such a record offers in all its different aspects one predictive explanation for the subsequent invisibility of the historical black subject in later sixteenth-century English national life.

On 8 February 1547/48 in a lawsuit heard before the High Court of the Admiralty in London, a 20-year-old black diver from Guinea by the name of Jacques Francis testified in support of his employer, Peter Paolo Corso, who had been hired by a consortium of Venetian merchants to recover valuable metal cargo from their ship, the *St. Mary and St. Edward,* which had sunk in a storm just off the sea coast (Item 108). The lawsuit, which was brought on by Dominico Erizo (Eryso), one of the Venetian merchant-owners of the ship, argues that the latter was raising the cargo to keep it and sell it himself. The black diver affirmed "of his own free will" that Corso had the previous year indeed found good amounts of tin and lead abandoned, but in another sunken ship and not the *St. Mary and St. Edward*, as it lay in the sea off Southampton at a point called "the Needles," and that having been commissioned by the Admiralty for extracting at his own cost and by his own efforts whatever precious cargo could be salvaged, he had rightfully claimed the materials in question. Erizo's arresting of Corso, according to Francis, was therefore wrongful, "false," and doubly so because his confinement had prevented all of the cargo from being salvaged. Francis's testimony was challenged by one of Erizo's witnesses, Anthony de Nicholao Rimero, a sailor who claimed common knowledge of all the parties concerned in frequent social interactions with them at the Dolphin tavern in Southampton, on the grounds that the former "ys a morisco born where they are not christenyd … and slave to the sayd peter Paulo… [and so] no Credite nor faithe ought to be geven to his Sayenges as in other Stranges Christian cuntryes hit ys to no suche slave geven."

Black people had been in use in European maritime projects since the beginning of the century, from the time of Columbus's probable use of a black pilot in his voyage to America.[103] In his discovery of pearls off the coasts of the West Indian islands and Venezuela, Columbus started a trend that in the next two decades would rapidly grow into a booming Spanish colonial trading venture that employed, after the exhaustion of Caribbean (Lucayan) divers traditionally expert in diving, African divers brought over from West Africa.[104] These human importations may mark the beginnings of the trans-Atlantic slave trade. Even in the earliest moments of Portuguese–African contacts in the fifteenth century, Zurara described the diving abilities of Africans to be like those of "cormorants[s]",[105] and throughout the sixteenth century and in the seventeenth, Spanish-Portuguese maritime personnel routinely maintained trained African divers for emergency salvage operations.[106] They were known for that skill elsewhere as well, as for instance in the Near East, as well as in California, as in the ill-fated gold expedition of Captain Cordone in 1611.[107] Thus, it is entirely unsurprising that in England in 1547 an African diver was employed in salvage work by the Tudor authorities, albeit through a Genoese salvage operator for whom he worked. As a matter of fact, the African diver may have been in England at least two years prior to 1547 and involved in more salvage operations than the one cited in the lawsuit because Peter Paolo was contracted by the Tudor authorities for another salvage job in 1545, in their unsuccessful attempt to recover Henry VIII's recently sunken warship *Mary Rose* in Portsmouth harbor close to Southampton.[108] As is pointed out in the note to the item, the two salvage operations are not the same ones, despite the closeness of their dates and locations, because the ships are involved are different: a warship vs. a merchant ship. Even though the notations of this earlier project do not specifically mention a black diver, it is credible to assume he is with

---

[103] Hugh Thomas, *The Slave Trade*, p. 87.

[104] Claridge, *History of the Gold Coast*, p. 80; Jennifer Watson et al., *Treasure Lost at Sea*, p. 9; Aldemaro Romero et al., "Cubagua's Pearl-Oyster Beds," p. 62; Daviken Studnicki-Gizbert, *Pearls* (electronic essay at <http://bell.lib.umn.edu/Products/pearls.html>, seen 2.12. 2006).

[105] Cited in Thomas, *Slave Trade*, p. 51.

[106] Kris Lane, *Pillaging the Empire*, p. 162; John Thornton, *Africa and Africans in the Making of the Atlantic World*, p. 135.

[107] On the use of African pearl divers in the Near East in the early modern period see Dirk Hoerder, *Cultures in Contact*, p. 158. For the African pearl divers with Captain Cordone, see Alton Pryor, *Classic Tales in California History*, pp. 55–56, and the electronic essays by Ken Weinman (*Treasure Galleon of the Mohave Desert*), and Al Maesters (*Amazing Treasure Ship of the California Desert*).

[108] See Knighton and Loades, *Letters*, pp. 122, 132, 133.

Paolo in this job as well, his compliant, that is silent, performance of his duties perhaps ensuring his invisibility in the records.

Beyond the obscurities of the two testimonies in the case (were there several sunken ships in the same vicinity? Was Corso still working for Erizo and his colleagues or had he become independent?), and irrespective of the case's outcome,[109] Rimero's argument here is notable for two reasons, one obvious and the other less so. To take the obvious one first, the exclusionary disallowance of the black diver's testimony (and it is exactly that, a disallowance, rather than a refutation of the latter's evidentiary contents) is a rare instance of othering based on non-visible stigmata (that is, ideology or living practice), and a striking example of the earlier kind of "racism without race" or religious racism that Etienne Balibar has described as the ancestor of modern racism based on physical stigmata that will emerge in this century.[110] The absolute denial of Francis's humanity is implicit in Rimero's insistence that Corso himself in September and October of 1547 at the Dolphin tavern "hathe in this deponentes presens offeryd hym to sell [i.e. Francis] to any that wold have bought hym." The logic of the disallowance of Francis's testimony turns on the reduction of the black diver from being a credible witness with a bona fide professional standing to a legally worthless chattel slave. This pointed denigration of a black person that is

---

[109] Although it has not been possible in this study to obtain the complete documents of this case, and thereby to verify its outcome, Gustave Ungerer, who has examined the case documents in considerable detail, has recently revealed that Erizo did win the case. See "Recovering a Black African's Voice in An English Lawsuit," p. 260. That Erizo won the suit is also indicated by another lawsuit shortly after this one in 1550 in which "sentence against lead of Erizo's" was issued "for necessaries supplied to Erizo's ship, which he had carried off" (*Select Pleas in the Court of the Admiralty*, ed. Marsden, 2: lxvi, file 18 A.D. 1550, Item 14, "Herdson c. Erizo"). If the lead that Erizo is being made to forfeit as compensation here is what was now in his possession, it could be the lead that came into his possession when he won the case against Corso in 1548. The phrasing of Marsden's mention of the 1548 case also seems to suggest a judgment in favor of Erizo: "Lead stolen by divers employed to salve" (*Select Pleas*, 1: lxvi, file 16 A.D. 1548, Item 66). Ungerer's assertions, however, that the "The admiralty judges were ready to acknowledge the humanity and selfhood of the black diver," and "All these objections were ultimately of no consequence, for the court of admiralty had made up its mind to grant Francis the status of a legal witness. It brushed aside all the attempts … to denounce Francis as the religious and racial other" (pp. 256, 264), are somewhat forced readings on his part and made more on good faith than anything else, because he is unable to cite or document the judges' precise response to the prosecution's attempt to disallow Jacques Francis's testimony. That Rimero's objections were made after Francis's testimony does not demonstrate that the testimony was accepted. The judges may very well have sustained the prosecution's objections and disallowed Francis's testimony after the fact. Thus, Ungerer's definitive pronouncement, "The High Court of the Admiralty's decision to admit a black witness has to be seen as an instance of pragmatic tolerance," and the entire paragraph that follows it (pp. 264–65), are conclusions that are more optimistic than compelling. The political implications of the very *fact* of the prosecution's attempt to disallow Francis's testimony on racial grounds in itself is what is of significance here. Ungerer is also clearly unaware of the perils of "recovering" reported voices, some of which are discussed later in this book in Chapter 4.

[110] Etienne Balibar and Immanuel Wallerstein, *Race, Nation, Class*, pp. 23–24.

implicit in the Peter Paolo case is not, as far as most archival notices of the first half of the sixteenth century described earlier would seem to suggest, typical of the period.

Of course the entire subject of early modern English slavery, just like the subject of a demographically significant black presence with which such a practice comes to be predominantly associated, is inevitably (to a degree that the terms "slave" and "blackamore" almost become synonymous, as Saunders suggests happens in Portugal) a shadowy terrain, denied in contemporary accounts, contradictorily treated in legal rulings of the time, and, in consequence, uncertainly regarded in current historical scholarship.[111] If the better-known official denials of English slavery—fed by an anxious national English Protestant culture straining to differentiate itself from what it holds to be corrupt Catholic cultural practices—are those of William Harrison, and following him that of Thomas Smith,[112] the lesser-known instances are those of Thomas Roe in the court of the Mughal emperor Jahangir in India,[113] and Richard Jobson in Gambia in 1620–21.[114] If the legal rulings against English slavery across the sixteenth and seventeenth centuries—derived from occasional papal edicts against slaving practices,[115] and corroborated in English common law

---

111 For the homonymy between slave and black in early modern Portuguese usage see Saunders, *Social History*, p. xiii. For this synonymous linkage in seventeenth-century Anglo-American Massachusetts, see Robert C. Twombly and Robert H. Moore, "Black Puritan: The Negro in Seventeenth-Century Massachusetts," p. 225 n. 3. For the only too easily assumed uncertainty of the size of early modern English black populations see the earlier cited cautious and apologetic admissions of Peter Erickson on p. 35 of his essay "The Moment of Race in Renaissance Studies," , pp. 27–36, and Kim Hall on p. 13 of her book *Things of Darkness*, about the lack of scholarly knowledge about the actual numbers of black people in early modern England. For a rather strenuous attempt to deny early modern English involvement in, and knowledge of, black people in England, see P. E. H. Hair's essay "Attitudes to Africans in English Primary Sources on Guinea up to 1650," p. 46. The essay's conviction is unsurprising given its exclusive reliance on published Elizabethan travel accounts such as those of Richard Eden, Richard Hakluyt, and Samuel Purchas.

112 *Harrison's Description of England in Shakespere's Youth*, 2: 124; Thomas Smith, *De Republica Anglorum*, 2: 24: "Certaine Orders Peculiar to England, Touching Punishment of Malefactors."

113 *The Embassy of Sir Thomas Roe*, journal entries of 23 March 1616 (p. 150): "The king condemned a Mogull on suspicion of felony, and being loth to execute him … hee sent him to me by the Officers in Irons for a Slave … for which I returned thancks: that in England we had no slaves, neyther was it lawfull to make the Image of God fellow to a beast"; and 6 November 1617 (p. 445): "he [the Mughal emperor] sent to me to buy three Abbassines [Ethiopians] … I answered: I could not buy men as Slaues, as others did, and so had profit for their momney" respectively.

114 On being offered slaves by an African merchant, Jobson said "We [English] were a people who did not deale in any such commodities, neither did wee buy or sell one another, or any that had our owne shape." Earlier cited, and in Hair, "Attitudes to Africans in English Primary Sources," pp. 51–52.

115 Such as the *Sicut Dudum* of Pope Eugene IV in 1453 condemning the enslavement of peoples in the newly colonized Canary Islands; Pope Pius II's letter in 1462 gravely warning against the enslaving of baptized Africans; and the *Sublimis Deus* of Pope Paul III in 1537 describing the enslavers of the West and South "Indies" as allies of the devil and

deriving from the Magna Carta[116]—are reflected in judgments such as those of the court case of 1569 ("Matter of Cartwright," 11 Elizabeth 2),[117] such rulings are contradicted by the expedient slavery propounded by the foremost Elizabethan jurist Sir Edward Coke in Calvin's Case in 1608, in which he proposes that "all infidels are in law perpetual enemies,"[118] and by the complex philosophical explanations of slavery of the political philosopher John Locke in 1679 as the justifiable product of a just war: "a state of war continued between a lawful conqueror and a captive."[119] The ambiguity of English slavery is exacerbated by its uncertain distinction from the medieval serfdom of *villeinage* derived from Roman civil law that is in an advanced state of decay by the sixteenth century in England,[120] and as that confusion is reflected in the Netheway vs. Gorge case in 1534, which fails to distinguish between serf and slave.[121] Within this contradictory legal history of English slavery, Rimero's demand seems to represent a particular moment of transition.

It is also instructive to remember—although Rimero might not have known this, since he was invoking the practice of other countries—that in the very year in which the events contested in the lawsuit took place slavery of a sort is trying to be introduced into England, in the Vagrancy Act of 1547 [1 Edw. VI c3 (1547)], which makes the "enslavement" of vagabonds or "masterless" people legal.[122] Although the act was repealed two years later, there was an attempt, albeit unsuccessful, to revive it in 1559,[123] suggesting that the 1547 act was not an isolated anomalous development. As Bradley Nicholson has pointed out, "Other features of this law, however, were commonplace in Tudor social legislation" (such as a pass system, branding the offender with the letter of the offense, "hue and cry," i.e. a "posse" to hunt for them, the transportation of vagabonds or runaway apprentices from constable to constable and the imposition on them of arbitrary mileage fines and summary judgments, etc). Thus, as Nicholson put it, "a preexisting set of rules … existed to govern the ownership, selling and buying of slaves. The common law concepts of property applied easily to slavery: as easily as they would apply to any chattel or real

---

declaring attempts to justify such slavery as "null and void." See Parker Pillsbury, *Acts of the Anti-Slavery Apostles*, pp. 830–31. This pattern exists, however, within contrary papal rulings as well, as in Pope Nicholas V's infamous *Romanus Pontifex*, of 1455 which expressly sanctioned the "perpetual slavery" of non-Christians; for a reproduction of the original text and its translation, see Frances Gardiner Davenport, ed., *European Treaties Bearing on the History of the United States and Its Dependencies to 1648*, pp. 13–20, and 20–26 respectively. For a brief summary of the contradictory papal rulings regarding slavery see Minnich in Earle and Lowe, pp. 281–82.

116 William P. Quigley, "Five Hundred Years of English Poor Laws," p. 76.

117 John Rushworth, *Historical Collections of Private Passages of State*, p. 468.

118 Thomas Bayly Howell et al., ed., *A Complete Collection of State Trials*, 2: 559.

119 *The Second Treatise on Civil Government*, 2: 4. Also see 2: 24.

120 Sir John Baker, "Human Rights and the Rule of Law in Renaissance England."

121 Cited by C. S. L. Davies, "Slavery and Protector Somerset: The Vagrancy Act of 1547," p. 542.

122 See Ibid., pp. 533–34; and Bradley Nicholson, "Legal Borrowing and the Origins of Slave Law in the British Colonies," p. 42, and p. 42 n. 1.

123 Davies, pp. 544–45.

estate."[124] That official accounts of the time are silent on the law is unsurprising, since, as C. S. L. Davies put it in his careful study of the law, "To admit to slavery was bad for national prestige."[125] Thus, even if the 1547 Vagrancy Act is not connected to black people specifically, it illuminates an important historical moment within which the sentiments of Rimero's charge are directly resonant. It is also telling perhaps to recall that, as has been pointed out earlier, the first recorded use of the word "blackamore" (blak e More) to signify an African ("born in Barbary") occurs in 1547. This echoes the earlier cited origination of the Portuguese homonymy between "black" and "slave."

Thus, Kate Lowe's explanation, in her citation of the case, that Romero is correctly citing the Roman law of slavery that is probably in effect in the Venetian state and that prohibits testimony from slaves except under torture,[126] is unhelpful for several reasons. For one thing, the Roman law of slavery is itself inconsistent, as is all law, since notionally no practice of law can be applied on the "one size fits all principle" given the infinite diversity of human situations. Furthermore, in sixteenth-century Sicily and Naples slaves could and did "sue their masters in a court of law," as two black slaves named Giovanni and Caterina did in Naples in 1565.[127] Even further, irrespective of the precise stipulation of Roman law regarding slave testimony, and irrespective of how consistently and clearly it is used in the Tudor legal system, with

---

124 Nicholson, "Legal Borrowing," pp. 42, 53.

125 "Slavery and Protector Somerset," p 547.

126 Earle and Lowe, p. 35.

127 For the inconsistencies of Roman slave law allowing slave testimony see Ronald J. Mellor's signed article in Encarta Online, which states the following: "Roman law was inconsistent on slavery. Slaves were considered property; they had no rights and were subject to their owners' whims. *However, they had legal standing as witnesses in courtroom proceedings*" (emphasis added). This statement, which I have not been able to confirm but which seems to refer to the wise and beneficent administration of the first five years of Nero's reign under the advice and influence of Seneca and the praetorian prefect Sextus Afranius Burrhus, known as the "Quinquennium Neronis," seems to be corroborated by three other sources: Sanderson Beck, *Ethics of Civilization*, who says "Nero reduced taxes and gave slaves permission to file civil complaints against unjust masters" (*Roman Empire 30 BC to 610*, vol. 5); Joseph McCabe, who says "Stoics such as Seneca certainly championed the rights of slaves. Seneca induced Nero, in his early years, to grant slaves the right to appeal to the Roman courts against cruelty" (*A Rationalist Encyclopaedia*, p. 96); and J. A. Farrer, *Paganism and Christianity*, who says: "In addition to generalised comments urging people to treat their slaves 'gently' and 'kindly,' in documents such as the Epist. 47 … Seneca induced Nero to appoint magistrates to hear complaints of cruelty" (pp. 82–83). For a law very similar to this see Justinian's *Digest* 40. 1. 5, ed. Watson, which stipulates the right of the slave to complain if the master refuses to manumit him after being paid an agreed sum. Among the instances that Watson elsewhere lists (in his "Roman Slave Law and Romanist Ideology") in which slave testimony is allowed, namely, commercial contracts, manumission, castration, and treason charges, the last three do not seem to require the evidence to be obtained under torture (pp. 57–65). For sixteenth-century Sicilian and Neapolitan slave laws permitting slave lawsuits against their masters, and for the case exemplifying this, see Minnich's essay in Earle and Lowe, p. 291. In all of these instances, whether the case prevailed is not the point (most of them did not). But such examples do suggest that the disallowance of slave testimony in Roman law is not as clear-cut a matter as it may seem.

its conflation of Roman with Anglo-Saxon law on the one hand and canonic law on the other, the invocation of Roman slave law can only be a very dubious business in a country in which slavery is not yet a stable, legally sanctioned social practice, as the preceding paragraphs have tried to demonstrate. The deeply contradictory and confusing Tudor attitude to slavery is clearly evident in sixteenth-century English law cases in addition to the one cited above, in which slave testimony is not only allowed but actively procured to enable a conviction against the slave owner, albeit through an interrogatory and against a Jew.[128] If Roman law "was fundamentally non-racist in the sense that it did not depend on the ideology of a superior race subjugating an inferior one," as some modern commentators of Roman slave law have argued,[129] Rimero's denigratory assessment of the worth of Jacques Francis's testimony depends on precisely such a mentality of moral superiority. Rimero's real concern seems to be about accepting a black man's words against that of a white and not just "that non-Christians should be allowed to give evidence," as Lowe believes.[130]

Of course, if the ground of early modern English law is Christian philosophy, Rimero's denial of Francis's christening is also revealing in that it cancels the latter's Christian identity manifest in his name. Baptism functions here as both moral hygiene and regional pathology, the first in the sense that those who are unchristened are morally unclean, and the second in the sense that being not christened, i.e. being morally unclean, is the incurable condition of a geographic locale. If therefore baptism is a civic badge of arrival and acceptance, a kind of ID card of legal rights, Rimero's charge of Francis's unchristened state is a retrospective abrogation of that credential and privilege in favor of an originary impurity in the latter that is impervious to the sanctification of Christian conversion. Admittedly, the social acceptance of the christening of blacks is in direct proportion to the need for a suitably assimilated labor force in a particular phase of colonial history, as Sue Peabody has shown in her study of the politics of French colonial evangelism in the Antilles in the first half of the seventeenth century, when missionaries such as Jacques Bouton and Pierre Pelliprat could serenely explain that conversion could "whiten" enslaved Africans and make them more attractive to their masters.[131] But that may have been an expedient French experience a hundred years after the Peter Corso case, and it is not matched by the English colonial experience in seventeenth-century Virginia for instance, when a christened English black slave named Fernando imported from England unsuccessfully sued for his freedom on the grounds of his natural human rights as a Christian. If a decade earlier the similar suit of a locally born black female slave in Virginia named Elizabeth Key *was* successful, it was, however, followed by the promulgation of an ordinance by the Virginia Assembly in 1667 that "the conferring of baptism doth not alter the condition of a person as to his bondage or freedom," and which probably explains the result of Fernando's

128 See the Hector Nones case, discussed in the next chapter.

129 Alan Watson, quoted in Bruce W. Frier, "Roman Slave Law," p. 1026.

130 Earle and Lowe, p. 35.

131 Sue Peabody, "'A Nation Born to Slavery': Missionaries and Racial Discourse in Seventeenth-Century French Antilles," p. 120.

case.[132] That christening can be a civic loophole through which blackness could pass into the socius is the kind of fear against which Rimero's abrogation of Jacques Francis's testimony seems to signal a containment instinct, and it is that instinct which enables the moral logic of the denial of christened black people's freedom in the interests of preventing the loss of desperately needed labor in European colonial history a century later. Thus, within the converging narratives of both early modern English slavery and slave baptisms, the Peter Corso case marks the emergence of a significant new pattern of legal definition for black people in England.

The location of the case's dispute in Southampton is in itself revealing in two ways. First, since the second half of the fifteenth century, as a prosperous port importing Italian wines, silks, and perfumes and exporting wool, the city had a relatively stable international enclave made up of visiting and resident Venetians, Genoese, and Spanish merchants.[133] At one point, it was the only English port to have the legal right to export tin and lead, even though it had lost that monopoly by the time of the Erizo lawsuit. But, secondly, by the end of the fifteenth century it was registering rising anxieties about foreign labor and trade competition, including xenophobic/racial insecurities: the black presence is mentioned only once, when in 1491 "Richard Hortensell, beadle of Godshouse [has] a fray with 'a blakman that was a taboryn in the galey of Hampton' and was fined for his misdeeds."[134] As a visiting shipboard drummer the black man was part of the city's traditionally respected foreign professionals and merchants, and the assaulting of him (irrespective of the latter's misdemeanor, and even if by a minor official of the city) is at this date still a punishable offense. The very occurrence of the violence, however, symptomizes the seeds of a particular somatic animosity that in 1547 will find stronger expression in the response to the black diver's testimony. If in 1491 the force of the law can include the black man in its protections, fifty years later that inclusion is under civic challenge. If legal practice is by its very nature a performance that builds on itself through the principle of precedence, one legal conversation becomes the cue and justification for the next. Rimero's demand to the High Court of the Admiralty to review and debar the black diver's human worth in law ["no Credite nor faithe *ought* to be geven to his Sayenges as in other Strange Christian cuntryes hit ys to no suche slave geven" (emphasis added)] arguably thus has the import of a juridical turning point in the legal history of blacks in early modern England. It is surely interesting that the Erizo case occurred just a year after a black man, Peter Negro, was rewarded for distinguished heroic service to the Tudor state, where the latter could be read as a causative factor in the phenomenology of the former.

---

132 William Billings, "The Cases of Fernando and Elizabeth Key: A Note on the Status of Blacks in Seventeenth-Century Virginia," pp. 467-70.

133 Alwyn A. Ruddock, "Alien Merchants in Southampton in the Later Middle Ages," pp. 7–10.

134 Southampton Municipal MSS, Book of Fines 1491/2. Cited by Ruddock, p. 12. Gustav Ungerer has cited the record of another black individual in Southampton two decades earlier. This is "Maria Moriana, the Moorish servant of the Italian merchant Filippo Cinni who had hatched a base plot to sell the manumitted Maria in Southampton in the 1470s" ("Recovering a Black African's Voice in an English Lawsuit," p. 261). Clearly, there were occasional black people in Southampton in the second half of the fifteenth century.

Notwithstanding the fact that whether the Peter Paolo case had a direct or immediate racial impact on London or elsewhere in the country is unknowable, the case symptomizes a development that anticipates the exclusionary construction of the black subject in England, particularly in London, later in the century. Within the limitations of the data, this argument offers one way of charting the origins of the social history of the black in Tudor England. The intrinsic fragmentariness of archives in general and of Tudor legal records in particular, and the obscurities of Tudor legal practice together with its inconsistencies, are merely reminders of the invariable pastness of the past and of our consequent duty to make it speak to the present. To have too great a fidelity to historical exactitude (to, for instance, the precise jurisdictional distribution of Tudor courts, and to the relationship between them and between the laws they enact or contest) is to make a fetish out of the archives, in effect to convert archives to some kind of holy grail of absolute truth. Archival memory, like all human memory, is inexact and the transmission of archival record even more so. It is their recoverable human import that must be important, particularly in its amenability to contemporary cultural reconstruction. Archives cannot only be the grounds of complacent scholarly self-exercises no matter how stimulating, insulated from the urgent needs of the moment of their re-reading and immune to the obligations of material intervention that all knowledge must carry. The legal disenfranchisement of blacks and their effacement from sixteenth-century English social history is the phenomenological precursor of the English enslavement of blacks in the next three hundred years, without the retracing of the social experience and memory of which the full understanding of that later history will always be incomplete.

There are significant changes afoot in the middle of the fourth decade of the sixteenth century in England. The mid-1540s sees at least one crop failure,[135] and a general tightening of the economy.[136] As A. F. Pollard describes this moment, "the social discontent which troubled England throughout the Tudor period, [comes] to a head."[137] Preceded by the bloody Pilgrimage of Grace in 1536, and followed by Thomas Wyatt's dangerous rebellion in 1554, two serious rebellions—the "Western" or "Prayer book" rebellion, and Kett's southern rebellion—broke out in 1549. Furthermore, as Michael Braddick has pointed out, the seeds of the modernization of the Tudor state, together with the implications that has for the legal reconstructions of the state's political life, were taking root in the closing years of Henry VIII's reign.[138] Generally, there was tighter government legislation against poor and indigent people, as in the Vagrancy Act of 1547. As the Reformation plunged Anglo–Spanish relations into crisis, so things associated with Spain and Portugal, including black people, were beginning to become suspect. If resentment against foreign mercenaries peaked

135 In 1546, although it was followed by good harvests the next two years; cited by Davies, "Slavery and Protector Somerset," p. 538.

136 For the government's increasing financial difficulties in this decade see S. J. Gunn, *Early Tudor Government 1485–1558*, pp. 111–13. According to some estimates, the government's taxation rates in this decade were the highest they would be for the entire century; see Ian Archer, *The Pursuit of Stability*, p. 12.

137 Pollard, *Tudor Tracts*, p. xx.

138 Braddick, *State Formation in Early Modern England c. 1550–1700*, p. 4.

between 1545 and 1549, as Millar has shown, popular attitudes toward all strangers, national and ethnic, cannot have been very different.[139] The word "blak e more," with all the restrictive connotations that it will begin to carry subsequently, first appears in the English lexicon in 1547. This confirms the beliefs of Alden Vaughan and Virginia Vaughan that negative connotations of English black people date from "the 1540s or earlier."[140] The growing awareness of black people only increases their vulnerability in this time of turbulence. The historical moment of the Peter Corso case does therefore have palpable ethnic resonances that are not useful to ignore.

VI

To sum up, the early Tudor period covering 1500 to 1558, and including English and connected Scottish records, has a total of 124 records. The overall frequency ratio of this data group is 2.1 records per year. Of these records, seven are burials, one a baptism, one a marriage, and seven are government notations and personal allusions. Of the 16 individuals of color named, three are women and 13 are men. Also, of the total number of individuals named, 11 are mentioned in professional capacities, with the range of professions including musician, soldier, religious cleric, personal companion, equerry, soldier's aide, instrument maker, deep sea diver. Two of the 11 appear in socially iconic public roles. This is to say that twice as many of these records describe black people in professional capacities as those that list them as menials or cite them in unspecified situations. While the great majority of these records are Scottish, the same proportion of black professional appearance is present within it and the smaller English group. There are three negative citations in this total data set. The high frequency ratio of the citations, the larger number of black individuals in professional or public roles, and the preponderance of positive or neutrally toned notations in these records suggest a steady Anglo-Scottish response to black people that is largely restrained even within the unnamed, directly or indirectly, violent history of their arrival in the British Isles. At the same time, the three negative citations describe the germs of a hostile ethnology that while predictive of a future social phenomenon is as yet unlinked to mass economic exploitation.

The records presented in this chapter might be described as the black hieroglyphics of the English archives, the crypticity of the notations registering the uncertain social epistemology of these lives. As the records flicker on the edge of analytical intelligibility, so the lives that left these signs glimmer on the backslope of historical knowability. Bleached out of all signs of an African identity by given Christian names and by the sedimentary acculturation of Anglo-European assimilation (John Blanke, Peter Negro), and ethically debarred when their ethnic identity is visible (Jacques Francis), Rimero's response to Francis's testimony, made of "his own free will," marks the beginning of the outlawing of blackness that will become the racism of physical difference in the reign of Elizabeth. Rimero's de-legitimizing of blackness describes the marking of the black subject in the state that will enable her and his violent importation into England

[139] Millar, *Tudor Mercenaries*, pp. 134–35, 171–77, especially pp. 134–35 and 177.

[140] "Before *Othello*," p. 28.

in the next five decades, beginning in the West African abductions of John Lok, John Hawkins and others in middle of the sixteenth century. If in the later Tudor years blacks become illegal shadows politically, Elizabeth's orders at the end of the century will make them legal outlaws and exiles, converting unofficial and ambiguous black presence into official black absence.

Chapter Two

Elizabethan London Black Records

The Writing of Absence

"a natural infection ..." "Those Kinds of People"

I

The growth of a regional community toward the idea of a nation, for a variety of political and economic factors, has a reflexive demographic signature. The increased inter-regional activities and contacts of such a community both spur and are spurred by a growth of its population. This in turn necessitates more complex administrative procedures for nourishing the material prosperities of the region's peoples and for sustaining the ideology of their distinctness from others that is the emerging morphology of their nation-ism. This is a paradoxically exclusionist phenomenon that is fueled by the instability of economic and ideological boundaries in which the marking of the other is symbiotically also the absorption of the other as the silent excess of the proto-nation's sameness of itself. The particular performance of this historical movement toward nation-ism in late Tudor England is marked by the growth of a black population whose numbers are not a part of the nation kingdom's conscious body, whose facts of existence are not the subject of deliberate historical record, and whose historical presence is an ontology of absence that must eventually be formally inscribed. To look at the black people in England in the second half of the sixteenth century is to understand both the volume and the nature of their absent presence.

If black people in early Tudor England are the result of two processes—first their introduction to England through the Africans in Catherine of Aragon's retinue and, under the aegis of cordial Anglo–Spanish relations that it both reflected and ushered in, work relocations of skilled black people to England (such as Pedro Negro or the black needle maker), and second, the small trickle of Africans brought back by English merchants trading with the Iberian peninsula—black people in the later sixteenth century arrived exclusively as a result of England's expeditionary forays to Africa and the Western Atlantic in search of new commodities and markets. This may be partly the result of worsening Anglo–Spanish relations following the Supremacy Act of 1543, and of deepening English economic problems resulting from the collapse of English wool and cloth exports by the middle of the century, but its effect on the English was to transform the African into a menial subject suitable for commercial exploitation through enslavement. This effect, which functioned as the beginnings of the English cancellation of the black person, perfectly satisfied growing English insular animosities about people of color and apprehensions about allowing them competitive space in the workplace, and was reflected in the sentiments of the plaintiffs in the Southampton court case in 1547 who denied the defense's black witness any legal standing as a human being. Thus, humanly barred and economically denied, Elizabethan black people not only existed only in the private sphere, they did so as menial chattels in a shadow population that did not exist officially in a Protestant English state that disavowed slavery, and whose default unnamed presence was eventually transmuted into their official absence by their legal expulsion from England at the turn of the century. This is to say, the Elizabethan black subject is both a consequence of the history of black people in the previous period, and a divergence from it.

Between 1558 and 1603 records of black people are comparatively much greater than in the previous period. The larger documentary volume does not, however, make the illumination of these lives substantially easier. The historical and local contexts may be a bit more visible for a portion of these notations than in those of the first half of the century, but many of them represent the traces of lives flecking the impenetrable silence of their early modern English existence. It is the records' greater volume itself that allows for some prognostic insights into the meaning of a growing early modern English black presence in the second half of the sixteenth century.

Even as the black citations between 1558 and 1603 naturally define these records as Elizabethan, the overall increase in the citational volume from 1558 onwards necessitates a consideration of records pertaining to Elizabethan London separately from those of London in the seventeenth century and elsewhere in the kingdom. This exclusive consideration is also mandated by London's growth from a city of about 40,000 in 1500 to one of 120,000 in 1550, and by the consequent emergence of its national predominance in the second half of the sixteenth century.[1] As the Swiss traveler in England Thomas Platter observed in 1599, "London is not said to be in England but rather England to be in London."[2] Just as these facts also make the Elizabethan a more zealous documentary age than the previous one, the decades of legitimacy and succession struggles that the age inherited nationally and the repeated religious and political pressures it faced internationally make its documentational character secretive, incriminatory, and for that reason fulsome. Paradoxically, what this fulsomeness produces, while not being liminal is accidental, in that the black content that it captures is in excess of what it is meant to reveal and is therefore a kind of out-of-focus, spectral supersight, that nonetheless, with the natural authority of its recording gaze, stamps the black subject of its seeing into new but specific currencies of meaning. To recognize this fulsome yet accidental but authoritative character of the later sixteenth-century English black records is to understand the peculiarly iterated spectrality of the black subject in the Elizabethan period.

---

1 The two figures are taken from David Harris Sacks, "London's Dominion," p. 22, and Roger Finlay and Beatrice Shearer, "Population Growth and Suburban Expansion," in A. L. Beier and Roger Finlay, eds., *London 1500–1700*, p. 39, respectively. For a discussion of London's impact on the country as a whole see the introductory chapter in the same book, "The Significance of the Metropolis," pp. 1–34, and Sacks's entire essay.

2 Thomas Platter, *Travels in England*, p. 153; cited in Orlin, *Material London*, "Introduction," p. 3.

The five categories of Elizabethan London citations, namely, royal and aristocratic household accounts, government proclamations and legal records, parish entries, medical notations, and personal accounts, extending across five decades, require a discussion of the records of each category in systematic succession while following a roughly chronological progression though each of them. This will yield an overlapping typological and cross-diachronic-synchronic perspective for the entirety of the records of the period, which will map their class hierarchies, frequency ratio, and geographic spread over a progressive temporal grid.

As in the previous chapter, the records here will be read in their projective and reactive modes. They will be considered in terms of what they say as well as what they are unable or unwilling to say. As tools of historical optics they will be made to illuminate the black subjects of their notation in themselves and by their contextual ambience, both of which in turn will be made to illuminate the historical culture that speaks through these records. The records will thus be used as the simultaneous agents and mirrors of Elizabethan urban communal vision, revealing at once the hardening image of the black subject and the political nature of that vision.

II

The accession to the English throne of Elizabeth Tudor in 1558 marks the beginning of a period that sees a radical increase in the numbers of black people in England. This was less the result of any monarchic action, as was the case with black people in the reigns of Henry VII and his son Henry VIII, and of their Scottish counterpart James IV, than of the private seafaring enterprises of merchants and mariners whose results were eventually co-opted tacitly by the monarch into a profitable trading initiative whose human booty though aimed at the Spanish colonial markets of the Caribbean start incrementally accruing at home. As the achievements and wisdom of Elizabeth's 45-year reign through one of the most dangerous periods in English national history are reflected not so much in things she did than in her resistance to the disastrous things she was incessantly pressured to do, so the growth of black people in her rule happened not because her government wanted their importation but because its support of such an activity was expedient and evasive. Thus, unlike that of the earlier period, the history of black people in Elizabeth's reign is unconnected to affairs of state and proceeds in the penumbra of such great matters, neither affirmed nor forsworn, and despite and contrary to the professed public character of the newly (re)formed, Protestant, English nation. In consequence, black people in the second half of the sixteenth century were seen but denied, known but unacknowledged, and more present than before but just as invisible.

The single most important context for the history of black people in the Elizabethan period is the rise of merchant seafaring and what might be described as opportunistic overseas venture capital trading through the emergence of joint stock companies. As has been well studied, this is the product of the collapse of English wool and cloth export to Europe around the middle of the sixteenth century. An accelerated adventuristic sea trading, north to Russia, west to the Spanish colonies in the Western Atlantic, east to the Levant and to south and east Asia, and south to the African coast, became one of mid and late Tudor England's hopes of economic recovery.[3] If all but the last of these developments have traditionally received more attention in studies of early modern English economic and political history, particularly those in the eastern and western directions because they produce the most tangible results, the African sector has tended to be downplayed because its economic dividends are sporadic and uncertain. This disregard corresponds exactly to the lack of scholarly knowledge about the history of black people in sixteenth- and seventeenth-century England. The African voyages are significant not only because they are inextricably linked to the western Atlantic forays, but also because they are the source for the hitherto ignored black presence in Elizabethan England and after.

Starting with Henry VIII's principal sea captain, William Hawkins of Plymouth, and his sons, between 1531 and 1567 there were sixteen trips either to the west African coast itself or to that coast en route to America. These were by William Hawkins himself in 1530, 1531, and 1532, Thomas Wyndham in 1551, 1552, and 1553, John Lok in 1554, William Towerson in 1555, 1556, and 1558, by the Company of Merchant Adventurers consisting of William Winter, Benjamin Gonson (secretary of the Navy board), and others in 1562, thrice by Hawkins's son, John, in 1562, 1564, and 1567, by Laurence Rondel and Robert Revel in 1563, and by George Fenner in 1566.[4] These voyages continued periodically over the next four decades. Examples include Thomas Stukely's voyage to Barbary in the 1570s (Hakluyt 9: 195–97), William Hawkins junior's trip to the Cape Verde islands in 1582, John Newton and John Bird's first voyage to Benin in 1588 (Hakluyt 11: 318–20), and both Richard Rainolds's and Thomas Dassel's voyage to Guinea and John Newton and John Bird's second voyage to Benin in the 1590s (Hakluyt 11: 331–38, 321–25 respectively).[5]

Furthermore, as G. V. Scammell's analysis of Tudor ship-owning shows, the three main ship-owning classes, aristocracy and landed gentry, merchant traders,

---

[3] George Unwin, "The Merchant Adventurers' Company in the Reign of Elizabeth," p. 41; K. R. Andrews, *Trade, Plunder and Settlement*, pp. 7–9; Pollit, "The Troublesome Voyages of John Hawkins," p. 40.

[4] For William Hawkins see Richard Hakluyt's *Principal Navigations and Voyages*, ed. Goldsmid, 14: 250–51 (all citations from Hakluyt, unless otherwise noted, are from this edition, and will henceforth be referenced parenthetically in my text itself); Hawkins, *The Hawkins' Voyages*, ed. Markham, pp. 3–4; and James Williamson, *Hawkins of Plymouth*, pp. 3–19. For Thomas Windham, see Hakluyt 11: 69–73, and for John Lok, see ibid., 84–101, and Claridge, *History of the Gold Coast*, 62–64. For Towerson, see Hakluyt 11: 102–29, 130–44, 146–63, and Claridge, pp. 64–73. For the trip sponsored by the Merchant Adventurers in 1562 see Claridge, p. 73. For John Hawkins see Hakluyt 16: 123–180; Williamson, *Sir John Hawkins*, pp. 78–116, 142–65; Markham, pp. 3–81; Pollit, "The Troublesome Voyages of John Hawkins," pp. 28–29. For Rondel's and Revel's trip see Claridge, pp. 75–78, and for George Fenner see Hakluyt 11: 173–87. Hugh Thomas also cites the slaving trip of Captain John Lovell of Plymouth to the Cape Verde islands off the African coast in 1564, where he seizes Africans off a Portuguese ship and tries unsuccessfully to sell them in the Western Atlantic (*Slave Trade*, p. 157). His failure to sell them has the consequence of his bringing some 50 of them back to England; Nick Hazlewood, *The Queen's Slave Trader*, p. 308. This is the hitherto ignored kind of product of these voyages that I point out below.

[5] William Hawkins's 1582 voyage is described by J. Williamson in *Hawkins of Plymouth*, pp. 218–21.

and seamen including naval sea captains, are all interchangeably overseas traders of opportunity.[6] As Theodore Rabb has shown, "between 31 and 34 percent" of members of parliament were members of overseas trading companies in the period 1584 to 1597, and "57 percent of all [parliamentary] admissions to [trading] companies … were recorded" between 1575 to 1630.[7] Concomitantly, in this kind of experimental and expedient oceanic commercial project in the African theater, seized and easily procured black people became as much of a tradeable commodity as gold, ivory, or pepper, despite the ambiguity of their inclusion in such a category. This is why all the African trading voyages cited above are also slave-trading ones. This can clearly be seen in Elizabeth's awarding of a patent to a company for trading to Africa in the very first year of her reign in 1558, her regularization of all English voyages to Guinea in 1561 implicitly "legalizing the purchase of Africans," and the letters patent she thrice issues for such voyages, in 1585 for trading to "Barbarie" (Hakluyt 11: 94–99), in 1588 for trading to Senegal and Gambia in Guinea (Hakluyt 11: 306–11), and in 1592 for trading to Cape Nunez and Sierra Leone.[8]

A percentage of the Africans of the English slave trade, in both its official and in its earlier unofficial phases, began to arrive in England by two obscure unrecorded processes, because of which the numbers of their importation are uncertain. First, Africans started arriving initially as curiosities, then as translators, and finally as surplus goods, the residue of their function as market commodities, through which they became items of miscellaneous consumption in the English domestic market. Some of the Africans may have been taken for the purpose of training them as translators for future English voyages, as was the case with those taken on Lok's trip, a practice that continued into the seventeenth century (for an example see Item 238), and many of them may have been eventually returned. But all Africans taken away

---

6 G. V. Scammell, "Shipowning in Early Modern England," pp. 390–97.

7 *Enterprise and Empire*, pp. 95 and 100 respectively.

8 Elizabeth's 1558 patent to a company for trading to Africa for ten years is cited in a document titled "An Account of the Charters and Statutes under the Authority and Protection of which the African Trade first began and has continued to the Present time," which is included in a 1788 Privy Council report on the state of the African trade; House of Lords Records Office, London, *Parliamentary Papers Vol. 84 of the General Collection, Accounts and Papers*, vol. 26, 1789, No. 646a, Part I. This obscure patent mentioned officially 230 years after the fact, virtually unknown to modern historians, and cited by Joseph Inikori in "The Volume of the British Slave Trade 1655–1807," p. 645, is a precise example of the deliberate secretiveness of a great deal of the Elizabethans' African activities. Elizabeth's regularization of English voyages to Guinea, by ordering the Admiralty to standardize operating procedures for all such voyages, is cited and discussed by Williamson in *Sir John Hawkins*, pp. 54–55; he identifies the documentary source for the order as "Foreign Calendar, 1561–2, No. 157" (p. 54 n. 1). See also K. R. Andrews, *Trade, Plunder, and Settlement*, pp. 109–10, for a discussion of a related subsequent order containing instructions for reconnoitering a suitable terrain on the Guinea coast for building an English fort, which he attributes to "Cal. SPF (1562), no. 18," (p. 110 n. 19), which Hakluyt extracts in 11: 164. It is most probably the royal order cited by Williamson to which Claridge, without providing a documentary source, refers on p. 81, in the words quoted here concerning the purchase of Africans. The charter that was granted by Elizabeth in 1592 was to merchants of Exeter "to trade between Cape Nunez and Sierra Leone" and it is mentioned without a source document by Claridge on p. 79.

were not thus employed, and even of those that were, all were not returned or did not return. Thus if the Brazilian chief taken by William Hawkins senior as a curiosity for Henry VIII in 1531–32 who created a sensation at court was soon taken back (though he died on the way), the Africans taken by others were not.[9] The three Africans named "George," "Anthonie," and "Binnie" that Towerson brought into England from his trip were meant to be returned, but whether in fact they permanently returned is not known.[10] The four or five Africans that Robert Gainsh kidnapped on Lok's voyage were taken back to England(Hakluyt 11: 101).[11] On George Fenner's trip in 1566 five Africans were taken, and although on the way back there was an attempt to sell them, whether the sale was completed or whether they instead ended up in England is unclear (Hakluyt 11: 188). On that trip, Fenner's people were told by some hostile Africans that "three weeks before wee came, an English shippe … had taken away three Africans" (Hakluyt 11: 179). Of the 500 Africans that Hawkins took to sell in the Spanish colonies in Central and South America in 1567–68 (Hakluyt 14: 228; Markham, p. 72), he kept a dozen with him on the return trip across the Atlantic, of which an unspecified number landed in England with him.[12] These Africans deposited in England became, according to Hazlewood, "trophies of the rich [and were] sold into domestic servitude."[13]

Second, as Africans become a tradeable commodity, they also become the object of illicit trading by secondary and tertiary merchant sources, both English and Iberian.[14] Businessmen, then as now, have fluid and impermanent residences in locations of convenience, so that just as there are English traders residing occasionally in Spain and Portugal, as Pauline Croft has shown, so there are Iberian and Italian merchants living at times in England, as J. A. Williamson and Ronald Pollit have pointed out, the documentary tracks of whose lives are necessarily illegible and mysterious.[15] And also then as now, for such merchants their goods both material and human are counters in the fluid logic of tactical exchange, to be used both directly for financial profit as well as indirectly for strategic marketplace advantage with powerful individuals and institutions. If illicitly acquired Africans in Elizabethan London are barely recordable entities, as items of a contraband trade they are even more so when they become casual gifts of business or political facilitation. In general, the numbers of their location in London and in England as a whole are in direct proportion to

---

9 For the Brazilian chief brought back by William Hawkins to Henry VIII's court, see Williamson, *Hawkins of Plymouth*, p. 29.

10 Eldred Jones, "The Elizabethan Image of Africa," p. 16.

11 Aso cited by Claridge, p. 67.

12 Hazlewood, *The Queen's Slave Trader*, pp. 261–62, 273–74, and Job Hortop's account in Hakluyt 14: 234.

13 *Queen's Slave Trader*, p. 319.

14 For illicit but vigorous Anglo–Iberian trading contacts during the middle and late years of Elizabeth's reign, see Scammel, "Shipowning in Early Modern England," pp. 395–96.

15 For a detailed study of the extent of Anglo–Spanish trading contacts, including English merchants resident in the Iberian peninsula, even during embargo periods, see Pauline Croft's essay, "Trading with the Enemy," pp. 282–87. For Spanish merchants in England see Williamson, *Hawkins of Plymouth*, pp. 7, 44; Ronald Pollit, "'Refuge of Distressed Nations'," pp. D1011–12; and Scammel, "Shipowning in Early Modern England," p. 396.

the success of their sale in the Spanish slave markets of the western Atlantic, and is a small, personally retained, and unaccounted percentage of such an activity. The direction of inquiry that traditional scholarship has not deigned to follow, and that needs to be pursued, is the further history of these individuals in their unnoticed settlement in England.

At the same time, there are two obvious reasons why the English in the late Tudor and Stuart periods would be less than forthcoming about their African voyages and their products. The first is the Portuguese monopoly over African slave trading mandated by Papal bulls,[16] which was difficult for a shaky Elizabethan Tudor regime to openly contravene.[17] The second was the political awkwardness, mentioned in the last chapter, of a Protestant England advertising its own involvement in one of the very evils for which it publicly criticized Catholic Europe, namely slavery. As a result, the English trafficking in Africans between 1550 and 1650 was an activity in denial of itself as it were, and not only not the subject of clear or deliberate recordation but also of documentary suppression. The Earl of Essex's disastrous Cadiz expedition of 1596 was expunged from some copies of Hakluyt's *Divers Voyages Touching the English Nation.*[18] Similar phenomena may have accompanied the oral and written dissemination of the knowledge of the African voyages and particularly of some of their dividends, given the dangerous international contexts of these voyages for England. One instance of undocumented voyaging by the English is the earlier cited unrecorded English voyage to the Guinea coast that was described by local Africans to George Fenner's party in their trip to the same area in 1566, in which three Africans were taken away by the English.[19] A clear example of deliberate elisions in the accounts of the English voyages to Africa is Hakluyt's omission of William Hawkins junior's trip to the Cape Verde islands off the African coast in 1582, because, according to J. Williamson, "it was then not politic to record offences between the English and the Portuguese."[20] As Williamson put it, in the larger context of the entire English involvement in Africa in the sixteenth century, "These transactions, which all parties tried to keep secret, have left little or nothing in the form of detailed narrative, and for the most part only summaries and allusions in the official documents have survived."[21] This instinct of documentary suppression may have been a tendency learned from the Portuguese themselves. Both W. Walton Claridge and Williamson point out that even the Portuguese in the first half of the sixteenth century deliberately falsified or altogether suppressed precise accounts of their Gold Coast trade to prevent the knowledge of that trade from passing to

---

16 Claridge, pp. 59–60, 80.

17 See Williamson, *Sir John Hawkins*, pp. 53–54, 58–59. Williamson cites William Cecil in 1564 protesting to the Spanish ambassador to England that "The Pope had no right to partition the world and to give and take kingdoms to whomever he pleases" (p. 53).

18 Hakluyt's *Divers Voyages touching the Discovery of America*, ed. John Winter Jones, p. xxxvi, n. 1.

19 Hakluyt 1: 179, cited in note 3 above.

20 *Hawkins of Plymouth*, p. 220. Williamson's sources for the voyage are Spanish archives. See also George Unwin, "Merchant Adventurers," p. 41.

21 *Hawkins of Plymouth*," p. 7.

other possibly competing European nations.[22] Even by the end of Elizabeth's reign that such voyages in general are regarded as opprobrious activities by the involved parties themselves is directly illuminated in Robert Cecil's instruction to Walter Raleigh when he invested in the latter's trip to Guyana in 1603, "as much as be, to conceal our adventure."[23]

Many of the African voyagers were people with powerful connections. Hawkins senior was a favorite of Henry VIII; Lok's father was a London alderman; Winter was a member of the naval board and an investor in African trading voyages such as Lok's; and the voyages of Hawkins junior were backed not only by naval board members such as Benjamin Gonson and William Winter but also by Lords Pembroke, Leicester, and Clinton, and by William Cecil and the Queen herself, who gave him the flagship in which he sailed, the *Jesus of Lubeck*.[24] As Ronald Pollit pointed out, the actions of such figures have obvious historical impact.[25] The actions of these voyagers are in an important sense not defined by public law as much as they set the conditions for the expediency of the legal. Black people casually brought in by them were not legal in the sense that they were not the objects of law but the exceptions of it and irrelevant to it. This anomalous location, where the law cannot identify black people because it does not know how to see them, describes the particular compounded spectrality of black people in the Elizabethan period.

It will therefore suffice to say that within the first five years of Elizabeth's reign the persistence of the search for new material and human trade commodities in Africa ensured the conditions for an incremental if surreptitious influx of black people into England over the duration of her reign and beyond. Illicitly seized, secretly traded, the passage to or arrival in England uncertainly recorded if at all, and its status unrecognized by law, this black population may have been missed in the great volume of studies of English maritime exploration and commercial expansion in the sixteenth century as well as by the formidable mass of English local history studies. But the logical outcome of this obscure disconnected history, and the historical validation of the black population that it produced, is the incidental notations of that population in the various localities and conditions of its English habitation, in a range of miscellaneous records including in the ever vigilant parish archives.

That the taking of Africans was a clandestine feature of the English voyages from the very beginning is implicit in the fact that even though John Hawkins is not recorded as having seized Africans on his second voyage he may in fact have done so, because, according to Raynor Unwin, on his third voyage in 1567, he had with him on his flagship an African "negro" page named Samuel (Item 130). This is admittedly a speculative citation, but a probable one nonetheless. It is speculative because neither John Hawkins himself, nor Job Hortop, Hawkins's gunner who was one of the eyewitness sources for Hawkins's third trip, nor Hakluyt (14: 233),

---

22 *History of the Gold Coast*, p. 55; *Hawkins of Plymouth*, p. 7.

23 Robert Cecil's letter to Walter Raleigh, 12 January 1603; cited in P. M. Handover, *The Second Cecil*, p. 276.

24 Thomas, *Slave Trade*, p. 156; Pollit, "The Troublesome Voyages of John Hawkins," p. 28–29.

25 Pollit, "The Troublesome Voyages of John Hawkins," pp. 32, 35.

nor Williamson, identified Samuel as a "negro" page as such.[26] Notwithstanding, the citation points to a probability for three reasons. First, as explained earlier, the taking of Africans in the English voyages was a frequently casual, illicit activity, particularly in the earlier stages, and specifically so in the carrying back of some of them to England and in their subsequent dispersion among the organizers and participants of such voyages, most of which will be unrecorded. Second, if Hawkins did take some Africans in his first two voyages, he could have kept one of them, baptizing him and making him his personal page, and taking him with him on his third voyage to be used as an interpreter if needed. Africans expediently carried along in that capacity were a common feature in English and Spanish voyages in the Atlantic in that period. Third, that the Hawkins brothers had Africans as personal pages is documented in the case of William Hawkins, junior who had an African by the name of "Bastien" who was buried in Plymouth in 1583 (Item 152). Just as Hawkins carried some of his seized Africans back across the Atlantic with him as a kind of financial insurance for his return trip with desperately depleted supplies, he may have taken Samuel back with him for similarly expedient reasons.[27] Overall, in view of the Hawkins's family's long history of contact with Africa and Africans, the likelihood of their having domesticated Africans as personal servants is high. John Hawkins was living in Tower Ward on London's East side in 1589, because in that year he was assessed the amount of £20 in the London Subsidy Roll.[28] This may be the location of his London residence from some time earlier, in an area on the east side of Gracious Street coming up from the London bridge over the river, in which other London merchant adventurers and other personnel of the Navy board with their bonded Africans were also frequently located, as was William Winter, as will be seen later. Either before or after Hawkins's 1567 trip, Samuel therefore may have been in a London neighborhood in which other such bonded black people may also have been present.[29]

If Samuel was indeed a black African, that he is one of the details that Hortop chose to add to his account of Hawkins's trip underlines his historical value. Clearly, he was prized enough for Hawkins to take him on this dangerous voyage. At the

---

26 Neither John Hawkins in his own account of the third voyage (in Markham, pp. 70–81), nor Hortop in the first edition of his account of the trip, *The Rare Travails of Job Hortop*, even mention Samuel or the on-board, battle-scene-beer-serving episode in which Samuel is involved, in the scenario in which he appears in Unwin. That scenario is present in the second revised edition of Hortop's account that appears in Hakluyt 14: 233, and in Williamson, who follows Hakluyt in his citation of the episode (*Sir John Hawkins*, p. 192). But in these accounts Samuel is simply a page, not a negro page.

27 See Hortop in Hakluyt 14: 234.

28 *The Visitation of London*, p. 162.

29 Hawkins's much better known London residence, was of course in the Navy Treasurer's house in Deptford on the other side of the Thames, at least until 1594, when he wrote his last letter to Burghley asking to be relieved of his post as Treasurer of the Navy. Continuing to be with Hawkins for the next several decades after his return, Samuel could fit the Deptford location as well, with its dockside environment of sailors and ships, and the high-class atmosphere of the official seat of the Navy Treasurer with his family and household; see Willianson, *Sir John Hawkins: The Time and the Man*, p. 467.

same time, that he was thus co-opted to serve the enslaver of his own people in the latter's enslavement project itself exemplifies the plight of the effaced early modern black subject employed in his own effacement. This is to say, the very uncertainty of Samuel's documentary life is precisely what makes it notable. If the precariousness of his historical existence, based on an unsupported adjectival phrase of a modern scholar, fuels a conviction that there was no such person, that in itself demonstrates the palpable historical invisibility of early modern English Africans like Samuel, who are literally not meant to be documentarily seen and known. They are not meant to exist.

The involvement of the highest echelons of the Tudor government in the African voyages makes it unsurprising that Africans appear in the household of Queen Elizabeth herself. Two decades after the voyage of John Lok, and a decade after those of Hawkins, two African minors are listed in the household records of the Tudor queen in 1574 and 1577, one described as "a litell blak a More," and the other as "Thomasen a woman dwarf" (Items 139, 143). If it is uncertain which of the aristocratic merchant adventurers or their financiers brought these individuals to her—two strong possibilities being John Hawkins, given that the black people he brought back with him from his 1567 voyage constituted perfect gifts with which to assuage the monarch, and Robert Dudley, the Earl of Leicester, whose backing of the African voyages from the outset and whose personal closeness to Elizabeth makes him a very probable donor to her of the Africans he received from such investments, as an emotional gift—it is certain that someone from that group did this as a politic gesture required by courtly protocol. Furthermore, if it is unknown when this happened, what the queen did with them is not. Suitably acculturated after arrival and then given to the queen either as gifts or as compounds, these young black people became part of the royal Elizabethan household's public life, the one as a page and the other as a member of her entertainment staff.

One of these individuals may be seen as a part of Elizabeth's necessary replacements of some of the traditionally male personnel of the Tudor royal household with women.[30] Yet, if the first individual has the classic anonymity of the black subject whose particulars are irrelevant for the early modern English historical record, so too is the second individual, whose blackness is lost in the assimilated name in which she appears, and not apparent to earlier scholars like E. K. Chambers, even if it was detectable to later ones like Peter Fryer and Stephen Greenblatt.[31] Furthermore, if the lavish items of dress, which seem to be from the queen's "summer" liveries, "a gasken Coate … of white tapheta … with tyncell [and] golde and silver lined with buckeram … and fased with tapheta," and "gowns" of "counterfeit silver and silke," signal a loving possession (implicit in the coddling language of royal endearment that also finds its way into the accounting record, "a littel blak A more") that is also a proud item of display, the latter is a reflection of the Tudor monarchic practice of keeping as ornamental public exhibits people from localities and regions over

[30] Chambers, *The Elizabethan Stage*, 1: 44.

[31] Listed by Chambers (1: 48 n. 4) as "Thomasina, the dwarf," this individual is identified by Fryer as a blackamore (*Staying Power*, p. 9). Together with the black page listed in 1574, she makes up, according to Greenblatt, the two black people that the queen has on her personal entertainment staff; see the Introduction to the *Norton Shakespeare* (p. 23).

whom the kingdom has dominion or ambition, as a symbolic advertisement of its power.[32] This is a practice that was cued by what Elizabeth's father and Scottish uncle before her did with the black people in their courts, and that was accelerated by the pressures of international ambitions that beset the young Protestant Tudor regime. Constructed thus of an xenophilic impulse that describes the transformation of black people into human fetishes (and as entertaining "abnormalit[ies]"), and a political instinct that marks them as the kind of surplus life from and against which a cosmopolitan early modern English national subjecthood is to be fashioned, these royally possessed Africans exist as anamorphic beings whose ethnic pathology is a transgression that is as yet fascinating, not threatening.[33] The objects of royal sight, they exist to display the efficacy of that sight rather than anything in themselves, their historical achievement consisting in their having drawn that sight to use them as it does.

The ontological anonymity of Africans possessed by Elizabeth is paralleled by those of her prominent nobles, particularly the one closest to her, as the existence of Africans in the household of the Earl of Leicester at this same time indicates. These citations reveal the kind of unrecorded dispersion of Africans among Tudor aristocrats that is a consequence of the African voyages throughout the Elizabethan period. An investor in the second African voyage of John Hawkins in 1564, Robert Dudley's acquisition of one or two Africans is reflected in two entries in his household accounts on 7 April 1584 and 6 January 1585–86 (Items 154, 157). Within the previous decade, Leicester had built on a plot of land in St. Clement Danes in Westminster extending from the Strand to the Thames "measuring about 140 ft along the waterfront and 140 ft deep on the east side," a grand "two-storeyed banquetting house in the garden by the river" that, according to the inventory taken after his death, had "a hall, 42 chambers, [a] high gallery … lodge, chapel and vestry, armoury, and banquetting house."[34] Close to Whitehall and Westminster palace, this palatial mansion, which will subsequently become Essex House, and which Stow calls "first amongst other buildings memorable for greatness, on the river Thames," was a hub of high courtly life that occasionally included among its residents fellow aristocrats involved in Atlantic slave trading such as Lord Rich.[35] Given the culture of competitive conspicuous consumption that is the signal feature of Elizabethan aristocratic life at court, it is this location rather than Leicester's other lesser establishment at Cree Church in east central London that was the most likely venue for the displaying of the latest exotic human dividends of overseas adventuristic trading.[36] Irrespective of whether the records describe the same

---

32 Chambers, *The Elizabethan Stage*, 1: 46. For the gorgeousness of the summer liveries of Elizabeth's pages and grooms, see 1: 52.

33 Chambers says the use of human physical difference as entertainment by Tudor royalty was the survival of a "characteristic medieval interest in mental and physical abnormality" (*Elizabethan Stage*, 1: 48).

34 "St. Clement Danes: Manors and Other Estates," in *The Victoria History of the Counties of England: A History of the County of Middlesex.*

35 *A Survey of London*, 2: 92.

36 For an acute documentary analysis of the reckless prodigality of late Tudor aristocracy, see Lawrence Stone, "The Anatomy of Elizabethan Aristocracy." For Leicester's other London

individual twice or two separate individuals, and irrespective of his or their exact position in Leicester's household, the citations document "reward" for aristocratic pleasure at services rendered, either as ornamental human displays or for some more specific jobs performed. The indescribability of their life in Leicester's household parallels their literal namelessness, both features in turn reinforced by their solitary opaque appearance among the personal documentary miscellany of the lord's high life in the city. Constituting one point of correspondence between the life of the queen's household and that of her favorite noble, and reflecting perhaps a fanciful token of the emotional bond between them, and since situated nearby perhaps even being known to each other, these Africans become, then, the signs of an ethereal black community in Elizabethan London.

Given the rapid social emulation that a new cultural practice sets off, it is not surprising that Africans in personal bondage appear among other members of the Elizabethan ruling class in other areas of London. William Winter's association with the African enterprises, both in his presence on the navy board and in his financial investment in some of the Guinea voyages, make it inevitable that he would procure an African himself. Two decades after the Hawkins voyages, and a decade after Francis Drake's 1577 trip to the Caribbean that he had also backed, the African that is listed in Winter's household on 27 August 1587 in St. Botolph, Aldgate on the city's eastern boundary is an acculturated individual who was baptized and given a makeshift toponym "Domingo," and identified by a supplementary phrasal descriptor, "a ginny negar," that together with his given name tries crudely to remember the lost cross-Atlantic history of his origins as an African from Guinea who was taken from Spanish Dominica in the Caribbean (Item 163). He was also a black person who had won from his aristocratic possessor not just an emotional attachment but also a certain degree of financially marked social recognition, because the ritual details of his burial were arranged with care. Domingo's English arrival is announced by the distinction of "the black cloth" with which William Winter chooses to mark his death, because given the additional expense it entails it is a distinction of affection and respect. The expense of this distinction is matched by the high prestige of Domingo's life that the record is careful to convey, "dwellynge" as he has been as the servant of "the right worshipfull Sr William Wynter knight," in "the abbye place" that is "the manor house of East Smithfield." This area, the east side of London close to the river, it should be recalled, is also where John Hawkins was located in 1589, for at least some time prior to that and possibly with his African Samuel. How long Domingo had been with Winter is unknown, but that like Leicester's African(s) who become(s) visible four years before his death in 1588, he appears two years before Winter's demise in 1589, suggests beyond the accident of his death a late life English aristocratic re-estimation of the African lives so casually seized by them which is also conversely the Africans' forcing of their abductors' moral respect.

Signalling the virulence of the phenomenon, illicitly acquired Africans appear in the highest levels of Elizabethan society even at the end of Elizabeth's reign past the turn of the sixteenth century. That the habit is not the eccentricity of one generation

establishment, and the possibility that many of his surviving household papers may relate to that houschold, see the editor's comment in *Household Accounts*, p. 43 n. 28.

is implicit in the fact that it was smoothly taken up by the monarch's highest officers who succeed the earlier stalwarts of her reign. William Cecil, as in all things in his career, may be cautious of personal involvement in the trafficking of Africans and detached from it, but that is not the model followed by his son, who succeeds his high political life and exceeds it with the kingdom's highest appointments in the reigns of two successive monarchs, Elizabeth and James, being knighted in 1591 and appointed Privy Council member the same year, made Secretary of State in 1596, and Master of Wards in 1599, and finally Lord High Treasurer in 1608.[37] Like Leicester and Winter, he was involved in the slave trade, but unlike like them, very discreetly so.[38] Like them, nevertheless, at the peak of his career his household was possessed of an African sometime before 1602. This is the individual known as "Fortunatus," whose death is recorded in St. Clement Danes, Westminster on 21 January 1601 (Item 247). Precisely where this black person was located is difficult to ascertain, since where Cecil was staying at this time is not clear. He built a house on the south side of the Strand at the mouth of Ivy Bridge Lane in 1601, but even though John Stow refers to the house of "wood and timber" as already built in 1598, no documentary evidence establishes his residence in that house before 1602. Until then he may have been living "either in a Savoy apartment," in its "Duchy chambers" further east on the Strand, or in "a house which he may have built adjacent to Burghley House" on the north side of the Strand.[39] In any case, St. Clement Danes at the eastern end of the Strand was a central coordinate for his location at this time since that is the church where Cecil himself was baptized in 1563, and that is the neighborhood for which by his own declaration he had a permanent attachment: ""I have great love for that quarter where I had my birth and breeding."[40] It is therefore safe to say that Fortunatus was located in a Cecil residence somewhere along the eastern stretch of the Strand, in an area that had the highest Elizabethan luminaries such as Essex, Bedford, Somerset, and Arundel living in it, and that was close to the queen's residence in Whitehall.[41]

---

37 For the dates of Robert Cecil's appointments see Lynn Hulse, "The Musical Patronage of Sir Robert Cecil," p. 24. That William Cecil may also have had an African is suggested by a suspicious entry in the *Returns of Aliens* in 1567: "Bishopsgate Ward, 1567: Domyngo, with my Lord Tresorer. 20 years. French. No denizens" (ed. Kirk and Kirk, pt. 1, p. 323). The name looks very much like that of an enslaved African, and since the compiled data of these alien tax assessments were ordered by, and sent directly to, Cecil, he could very well have had the full details of Domyngo's identity expunged, or alternatively the compilers could have suppressed such details out of deference to their employer's discomfort about such attachments.

38 He dabbled in privateering voyages from the mid-1590s, and financed one of Walter Raleigh's trips to Guyana in 1603. His involvement in such activities was so discreet that Alan Haynes says it is "obscured" from subsequent historical knowledge; see his *Robert Cecil*, pp. 81–82. See also his earlier cited letter to Walter Raleigh asking him to keep his (Cecil's) involvement in Raleigh's Guyana voyage in 1603 "as much as may be a secret."

39 For Stow's comment on Cecil's house see *A Survey of London*, 2: 95. For Cecil's residences at this time see Haynes, p. 69, and Handover, p. 276.

40 For Cecil's own baptism location see Handover, p. 12. Cecil's declaration of his attachment to the area is in his statement to the parish council on 4 August 1601, cited by Handover, p. 12.

41 For the high-powered composition of this locale see *A Survey of London*, 2: 97.

Fortunatus's connection to St. Clement Danes may signal an unusual personal attachment between him and Cecil, but irrespective of any other specific functions he may have, to an inevitable degree he is like the named and nameless African(s) possessed by Elizabeth, Leicester, and William Winter, another exotic black presence in a high-powered Tudor setting objectified as a human fetish. If Cecil's secrecy about his human trafficking is mirrored in the vagueness of Fortunatus's exact physical location in Westminster, it may also be reflected in the cipher of Fortunatus's name, which unlike Domingo's name masks all clues of his historical origin. Surrounded as he probably was by the other Africans silently held by Cecil's colleagues and royal mistress, and plausibly acquainted with them, he is one more member of a spectral black community gathering in late Elizabethan London.

Each of these Africans is in a location of high visibility, and hence of high impact. Yet, each of their histories constitutes what might be described as a narrative of documentary disregard. This paradoxical phenomenon, corresponding to what Peter Laslett has described as "noumenal" behavior (that is, "non ethically weighted, internalized, perhaps not even articulated or conscious regulatory norms that influence behavior within what [can be] perceived as a matrix of free choices"), stamped into cultural currency by high Tudor aristocratic practice, extends across each decade of Elizabeth's 45-year reign.[42] It is therefore inevitable that Africans will appear in unspoken chattel bondage in this same time among other social classes as well, throughout the city. Some of these Africans enter the city's records, not for themselves but in the sweep of the Elizabethan government's apprehensive domestic surveillance over the majority of its tenure, resulting from, as Ronald Pollit and Linda Yungblut have shown, xenophobic business fears about the encroachments of aliens, predatory merchant protectionism against resident European competitors, and the government's own nervousness about foreigners in the city and kingdom because of the deteriorating relations with Spain.[43]

Of the repeated population surveys between 1563 and 1593 that characterize this surveillance, two London examinations, one in 1567 and one in 1593, find and record between them six Africans held by the residents of the city. The first of these, dated 15 December 1567 and called the *The Bishop of* LONDON'S *Certificate* and subtitled *Certificate of the Nombers of all Manner of Straungers within the Severall Wardes and Parishes of the Saide Citie*, summarily lists under St. Michael Paternoster parish in Vyntry Ward, "blackmor 1," and under St. Olave's parish in Coleman Street Ward, "Niger 1" (Item 129). The location of the first entry, also sometimes spelled as Vintry Ward, a riverside area in south-central London extending a few blocks up from the Three Cranes Wharf (Agas map 6N, p. 23) and that is the

[42] For the concept of noumenal behavior see Peter Laslett, "Demographic and Microstructural History in Relation to Human Adaptation," p. 354. The explanation of the term is from L. R. Poos's invocation of it in his "Historical Demography of Renaissance Europe," p. 809.

[43] Pollit, "'Refuge of Distressed Nations,'" p. D1003; Yungblut, *Strangers Settled here among Us*, pp. 18-25; For another discussion see Picard, *Elizabeth's London*, pp. 111–15. For a more detailed discussion see Irene Scouladi, ch. 5, "General Background Leading to the Return and Aborted Bill against Merchant Strangers of 1593: General Background and Industrial Unrest," in *Returns of Strangers in the Metropolis*, pp. 57–71.

traditional disembarkation point on the north bank of the Thames for wines imported from Europe, is a neighborhood of wine merchants. The "blacmor" in the search document's summary is in the actual entry the "Moore" described as "Robert Tego, a Morisco, servaunt with Thomas Castlyn," who is documented in Vintry Ward in 1567 (Item 129.1a). Notably, if Robert's background is partly obscured by the possible corruption of "Diego" as "Tego" in the record's transcriptional language, that is more than compensated by the pointed precision of his description twice as "moore" and "Morrisco." The entry's side margin comment of "Not denizens," identifying Robert and his employer Thomas Castlyn as aliens, and possibly transient residents in this ward, helps to picture the commonalty of foreign merchant ownership of chattel black people that this possibly Spanish wine merchant's possession of a bonded African in this prosperous wine merchants' neighborhood in central south London visibly models.[44] The second entry's location in Coleman Street, properly called St. Olave Upwell, on the city's north side near the old city wall in the now defunct area of Jewish settlement and hence called "Old Jurie" (Old Jewry), is a community predominantly of mercers and metalworkers, "possessed," in Stow's empirical testimony, "by founders that cast candlesticks, chafing-dishes, spice mortars, and such like copper or laton works."[45] The "niger" listed in the search's summary in this location is in the actual entry in the search results listed under "Busshopsgate Warde," Bishopsgate and Coleman Street being adjoining wards that are often named interchangeably, particularly for locations such as St. Olave and Old Jewry, which sit almost exactly on the boundary between them. In the actual entry the second African is identified as "Francys Fran," a "Moryon" (Item 129.2a) living in the house of the "Peter Fanall," named in the immediately preceding entry as a resident here for "29 yeres" and a "denizen," even if Francys, said to have been here only for "4 yeres," is not. What is singular about the recording of Francys's presence is the synonymous use of the words "niger" and "moryon" to identify him, the latter being a rare and corrupt variation of "moryan" for Moor.[46] The locations of both entries are neighborhoods of merchant craftsmen, enclaves of skilled professionals with variable European connections and mobility, and in Stow's words describing the inhabitants of Vintry Ward, made up "as well [of] Englishmen as [of] strangers born beyond the seas."[47]

The ambient nature of both locations points to Robert's and Fran's existence as the personal possessions of ambitious transnational tradesmen acquiring either cheap or skilled black people to boost their productivity, the latter not only because of the example of the black needle maker in Cheapside mentioned in the last chapter but

---

[44] J. A. Williamson, in his *Hawkins of Plymouth*, says that the "Castlyns of London, a merchant family prominent for three generations, may have been, by their name, of Spanish origin, for 'Castlyn', also spelt 'Castelin', looks suspiciously like 'Castilean' " (p. 44).

[45] For the character of both locations see Stow's *Survey*, 1: 238–39 (Vintry Ward), and 1: 277–78, 281–82 (Old Jurie). The quotation about "Laton works" is on 1: 277. "Laton" is "A mixed metal of yellow colour, either identical with, or closely resembling, brass; often hammered into thin sheets." Entry for "Latten" in the *OED*, 1: 100.

[46] Entry for "morian," in the *OED*, 1: 663.

[47] *A Survey of London*, 1: 240.

also because African metallurgical abilities are known in early modern Europe.[48] But if these entries thus suggest that Elizabethan Africans are not just unskilled menials but also possibly professionals, they also might signal that unlike their countrymen in the previous period such skills as they might possess do not now redeem their lives from being solely bonded ones. As will be evident over the course of this chapter, there is not a single record in the Elizabethan period that shows an African in an independent professional capacity. Notwithstanding the casual interchangeability of their black identification as "blackmor, "niger," and "Moryon," the sighting of these Africans within a mass of French, Dutch, Italian, Spanish, and Portuguese notations may be innocuous, but that they appear in a document that is the product of the government's anxiety about foreigners in the very first decade of Elizabeth's rule foreshadows the expurgatory program to which they will be subjected even in their desolate state by the end of her reign.

Nearly thirty years after the first census, the second examination, carried out according to the letter of the Lord Mayor to the city aldermen in the name of the queen, dated 1 March 1592/93 and ordering, with "as great secrecy as may be … [a] diligent search … within all parties within your warde what and how many foreigners are residing and be remaining within the same, of what nation, profession, trade or occupation every one of them are of … how long every one of them have been in the realm …" discovered and listed four Africans, three of whom are women.[49] The three women are listed under "Baning, Alderman Paul, lodging three maids, 'blackamores'" (Item 185) and the fourth African is recorded simply as "Leying, Mouea, a 'blackamoor' of 20 years", described as being "at Mistress Barkers" (Item 186). The location of the three maids is in the ward of Farringdon Without on the city's west side but east of Westminster since that is where Paul Baning (variously spelled "Banyng/e," "Banning") has been made alderman that year, and the other African is in the city's east side in St. Olave, Hart Street in Tower Ward because "Mistress Barker" as "Widow Barker" was assessed four years earlier the amount of "CI^{li}" in Tower Ward, and two years later in 1595 is named in the registers of St. Olave, Hart street in that ward, possessing as it so happens another African.[50] That despite the search being aimed at foreigners these Africans are found with English people points not just to the secret history of their arrival in England but also to the prospective permanency of their residence there, living intimately among its

---

48 This knowledge comes partly from the experience of the African voyagers; see Hakluyt. For an account of African metallurgy through the ages, see Michael S. Bisson et al., *Ancient African Metallurgy*, pp. 51–60, 83–91.

49 The search order is from the extract of it in Scouladi, *Returns of Strangers*, p. 58.

50 Note below entry in Scouladi reads: "Paul Banning (Bayning), grocer was sworn Alderman for the Ward of Farringdon Without in 1593. Beaven, vol. 1, p. 157." "Beaven" refers to Alfred B. Beaven's *The Aldermen of London*. Picard mistakenly cites the source for this record as the census of 1568 in *Visitation of London 1568*, ed. Rawlins. "Paul Bannynge" does appear in that volume, but under the "London Subsidy Roll of c. 1589" when, in Tower Ward, he was assessed the amount of "Cxx^{li}" (p. 162). At this date he is not listed as an alderman, and there is no mention of any blackamore maids. For Widow Barker see the "Tudor Subsidy Roll of 1589," in *Visitation of London*, p. 162. For her mention in St. Olave, Hart Street, see Item 186, which is discussed separately later.

metropolitan population. If "Mouea Leying" is a woman, she and the three African maids announce the presence of black working women in Elizabethan London in addition to the monarch's own black female entertainer, Thomasen. If Mrs. Barker is a business woman, as very likely she is because of her multiple mentions as an independent person in the tax assessment, survey, and parish register, even though her business is not specified as those of several other businesswomen appearing in the survey are (such businesswomen being a remarkable and as yet unnoticed historical feature of the period), Mouea Leying is a skilled tradeswoman rather than a domestic, probably a seamstress or a worker in the drapery or clothworking industry. That is the character of the inhabitants of Tower Ward according to Stow, and so that would be the kind of business Mrs. Barker might have.[51] Mouea is thus the first example of a skilled black female professional to appear in the black archives presented in this book.[52] Yet, the unreadability of Mouea Leying's name, beyond the first name's echo of Baie de Mouea or the Bay of Mouea in the Spanish coastal region of New Caledonia, and including the uncertainty of whether even the name is that of a woman, is like the impenetrable silence of the rest of this African's life, the only surviving signal of whose existence is that it is a black one. Similarly, the three black maids of Paul Baning invoke only the quietly self-serving interactions of the trans-national Anglo-Spanish merchant community of which as an alderman he is a typical member, the illicit human products of which can enter the documentary record but not the activities themselves. The black women themselves remain muted in a history that cannot speak. As will be seen shortly, these women are not the only Africans that Paul Baning will keep.

In the same time as these Elizabethan surveys of London, there are also tax assessments made of aliens that are ongoing from the time of Henry VIII, and these also find Africans living commonly in the city and its suburbs. The very next year after the first survey, in the tax records of 1568, a London grocer named "Gabriell Levesy" living in the suburban parish of St. Giles in the Fields was found to have as a "tenaunte," one "Lambert Waterson," who is described as a "denizen, barbaryen" (Item 131). Although Peter Fryer has regarded this as a "doubtful reference" because the person's "ethnic origin is not stated," the term "barbaryen" can at this time hardly refer to anyone except a black person, and certainly not to a white individual.[53]

---

51 *A Survey of London*, 1: 130–33. For two studies of early modern English working women, see Marjorie Keniston McIntosh, *Working Women in English Society, 1300–1620*, and Diane Willen, "Women in the Public Sphere in Early Modern England: The Case of the Urban Working Poor."

52 Businesswomen appearing in the 1593 search include "Widow Stedon" (starcher, with four employees), "Dionis Welfes" (starcher, with eight employees and nine servants), "Joyce Vanderowe" (silk throwater, with 17 employees), Mary Jeames, widow (brewer, with more than 33 employees), the wife of "Penson" (kersey dyer, who own a business different from the beer-brewing business of her husband), "Lute Gysling," wife of "Daniel Gislinge [*sic*]" (mercantile activities, has 13 employees), "Drewett widow" (shoemaker, with eight employees), "Margery Dorington" (cloth maker, with five employees); *Returns of 1593*, ed. Scouladi, pp. 82, 139–41. Note some of these listings are from the Returns of 1635, 1639 included in that volume.

53 *Staying Power*, p. 9 n. 19.

While the name does not yield much insight about his origins, beyond the echo of the Barbary coast of West Africa in the qualifying descriptor "barbaryen," it does suggest a baptized and assimilated (denizened, and so, naturalized) black individual, who under the expedient label of tenant is probably a worker in the grocery business of Gabriell Levesy. He is probably a skilled worker because he appears once earlier, in the tax assessments of 1541 in St. Mary Stayning parish, listed with a "Garet Shomaker," who may be one in fact.[54] An affluent West London neighborhood not far from the Strand to its south and Holborn to its east, and within the powerful economic and cultural pull of Westminster, and probably because of which it is a tax exempt zone for "strangers," St. Giles in the Fields is in an area that knows black people, from those possessed by the queen and Leicester. As John Patten has pointed out, Elizabethan grocers are also merchant traders, and Levesy may have acquired Lambert through his connections to African trading voyages.[55]

Fourteen years later, on the city's east side, a tax record of 1582 notes that living in "in the house of John Baptista Sambitores" in All Saints, Staining in Langbourne Ward is "Fardinando, a Blackamore" (Item 151). Located on the corner of Fenchuch street and Mark Lane, and round the corner from St. Olave, Hart Street, and distinctive as one of the earliest stone rather than wooden churches in the city, from which it gets its name, All Hallows Staining is in an area of populous alien settlement.[56] Listed with one maid and three male servants, each of whom like him is valued at 4d, Fardinando is part of an obviously prosperous merchant household, a fact reflected in the total tax assessment of Sambitores of £20. Sambitores may be of Italian or Iberian extraction, but judging from his given name, Fardinando is certainly an enslaved Iberian African brought over with Sambitores's household or acquired through merchant contacts in England or en route.[57] His declared worth as an item of his owner's material goods, and his clear designation as "servant," may be the only redemptive illuminations of his otherwise irrecoverable life. Irrespective of whether his presence is temporary or permanent, it contributes to the normalization of keeping Africans in bondage in Elizabeth's London.

The following year, in Aldersgate Ward on the city's west side, the census and tax assessment of strangers most unusually find a Dutch tradesman with an African name himself. This is the person listed as "Charles Negroe" who is described as a Dutch "scholm^r^," that is, a shoemaker (Item 153). The ward is a relatively prosperous one in Stow's account of it, and a rather cosmopolitan one, as the many Dutch and

---

54 *Returns of Aliens*, ed. Kirk and Kirk, pt. 1, p. 50.

55 John Patten, "Urban Occupations in Pre-Industrial England," pp. 302–3.

56 For the history of the area's alien demography see Sidney Maddocks, *Stepney in Other Days*. All Hallows Staining, adjoining the Tower of London, and directly opposite St. Katherine Coleman on the other side of Mark Lane, has the overall character of Stepney and its environs, and particularly of the neighborhood of St. Katherine Coleman, that Maddocks describes. For the history of the church's name see Stow's *Survey*, 1: 203.

57 In the same volume of *Returns of Aliens*, there is another entry for Sambitores in the same parish for 1581, which lists his entire family, as well as "Ferdinando Negro," and a "Gregory Negro. Merchaunt, estr." (Pt. II, p. 220).

French tradesmen listed with Charles Negroe as living there would suggest.[58] This social character may make the fact of a foreign possibly black tradesman less striking than it might otherwise seem and partly explain it. As in similar cases seen earlier, the surname "Negroe" cannot be disregarded as the sign of a black lineage, even if a largely assimilated one. If so, this is probably the only instance of a possibly black individual with an independent status in Elizabethan London, and reminiscent of the black needle maker in Cheapside two decades back that was mentioned in the last chapter. That he may be a visitor mitigates, though, the historical significance of that fact and makes his case an exception in the overall history of black people in Elizabeth's reign.[59]

Fifteen years later, the tax documents of 1598 and of 1599 each note in Tower ward, in the parish of All Hallows, Barking, also on the city's east side, three Africans in the possession of three different individuals. In 1598 these are "Clar', a Negra at Widdow Stokes, Maria, a Negra, at Olyver Skynnars, and Lewse, a Negro at M[r] Mitons" (Item 228). The 1599 listing repeats some of these names and adds some: "Clare, a Negra at Widdow Stokes (an Englishwoman)," "Mary, a Negra at Richard Woodes," and "A blackamore, servaunt to Jeronimo Lopez" (Item 233). All Hallows, Barking on Fenchurch street is immediately around the corner from Mynching Lane (6T and 5S respectively, Agas map, p. 25), where Stowe says "in old time dwelt divers strangers born of Genoa and those parts."[60] If a part of this characteristic survives into Elizabethan times, this is a locality of transient Italians who might be bringing with them and introducing into the neighborhood some of the enslaved black people that Genoese merchants had been importing from Africa from the beginning of the century.[61] Furthermore, as Hawkins's location in this same ward indicates, Tower Ward in general was an area that had in it mariners involved in the African voyages, and already contained the several Africans discussed earlier. "Olyver Skynnar" and "Richard Woode" could be two more such mariner-merchants, both being taxed as such sixteen and seventeen years earlier in the Tudor Subsidy Roll of 1582 in this same ward.[62] So too might be the carefully addressed "Mr. Miton." These overlapping locational implications and their ambient demographics make partly transparent the possible circumstantial history of these Africans in this place, while the presence of the Clothworkers Hall at the mouth of Minching Lane where it meets Fenchurch Street suggests that they, particularly the black women, and/or their captors, may be connected to the cloth manufacture or retail trades, just as those of Mrs. Barker's possibly are. The Clothworkers Company itself had merchants heavily involved in overseas trade, including, if the comment of one of its members two decades later is taken literally,

58 Its prosperity is mainly in the area of Maiden or Engaine Lane, where St. John Zachary and the Goldsmiths Hall are located. See *A Survey of London*, 1: 305–6.

59 The record does not list a citizenship status for Charles Negroe.

60 *A Survey of London*, 1: 132.

61 For the history of Genoese and Venetian involvement in the African slave trade see the earlier cited discussions in Saunders.

62 "1582 London Subsidy Roll: Tower Ward," in *Two Tudor Subsidy Rolls for the City of London: 1541 and 1582*.

in "the handy trade in slavery."[63] Like the African women with Mrs. Barker, Lewse (or Lucy), Clar (or Clare), and Maria or Mary are also among the first black working women in early modern London, and not only do they comprise a unique professional group, judging from the repeated mention of some of them they are a group that is in healthy demand. If Jeronimo Lopez's name shows he is a resident Spanish or Portuguese merchant, that illumination does not extend to the African he holds, whose namelessness and gender blankness invoke the more typical historical anonymity of this dispossessed black population. This, then, is another shadow community of black people, paralleling the one that is forming on the city's west side.

In general the Elizabethan government scrutinies cannot and do not find all that they seek, and perhaps are not intended to do so in the first place, because they are only imperfectly aimed and have a limited field of vision. Thus, for instance, the black people held by the queen herself and by her nobles are missed by these records, because they exist behind the lens of the official seeing eye, as it were. Also missed are the numerous Africans secretly acquired by the rest of the merchant-official class, to which Paul Baning and many of the search officials themselves belong, even if the transient nature of urban populations makes it difficult to track the locations of specific individuals with accuracy, particularly those of such an inherently unrecordable status as black people kept in chattel bondage. Beyond these automatic self-elisions and lapses of the search instrument itself are the fluctuating cooperation and outright refusals of many of those examined to be fully forthcoming about the people in their households.[64] So, more than what they contribute of themselves, what the substance and pattern of the data of the Elizabethan censuses, searches, and tax records do is to expand the implications of what the royal and aristocratic household documents reveal, and together with those documents predict more black presence in other documentary levels of the city over the same period.

III

In fact, the most penetrating and comprehensive "seeing" of the Africans living in late Tudor London occurs at a more intimate, "micro" documentary level, at the level of the Elizabethan "neighborhood watch," so to speak, the parochial church records. As cases in point, it is this level that sees the Africans kept by William Winter and Robert Cecil, discussed above. Initiated in 1538 by Archbishop Cromwell's order, parish record-keeping becomes altogether more serious at the beginning of Elizabeth's reign, when the Privy Council renewed and elaborated the earlier order with all earnestness, stipulating not only the strict enforcement of the original order but the additional requirements of each church needing to keep two copies of the registers, with one being kept and maintained by the church warden under

---

[63] G. D. Ramsay, "Clothworkers, Merchants Adventurers and Richard Hakluyt," pp. 505, 512; the comment on slavery is cited on p. 512. Ramsay points out that one of the most famous beneficiaries of the Clothworkers Company was none other than Richard Hakluyt himself (pp. 517–21).

[64] For an instance of outright refusal, albeit in a later survey, see *Returns of Aliens*, ed. Scouladi, p. 141.

lock and key.[65] The results of these instructions is a steady accumulation of not just valuable data about the births, marriages, and deaths, that is, the material lives, of a cross-section of the early modern London population in general at the micro level of the neighborhood, but also, at regular periodic intervals, of black people among them. While parish records generally have justly been heavily mined for a great variety of insights into the first subject, the latter subject surprisingly has been all but ignored, noticed fragmentarily in varying degrees by W. E. Millar, Eldred Jones, Thomas Forbes, Peter Fryer, James Walvin, Roslyn Knutson, and Virginia Mason Vaughan, but not systematically combed for the aggregate of black presence in them. This is another reason why the early modern English black presence has remained an unknown and mysterious subject. These black entries in the parish records capture what the government surveys and tax records miss, and while appearing by themselves to be occasional stray entries in each parish, taken together they amount to a significant London presence in geographical and numerical terms that grows in particular strength in the last decades of Elizabeth's reign.

In the volume, regularity, social class, and locational pattern that these parish records of black people reflect, they lend themselves particularly well to the kind of cross-diachronic-synchronic examination used so far. A consideration of these records not individually but in terms of the broad social groups and metropolitan areas that they reflect, while traversing a rough chronological grid up and down as needed within each group, and while noting what singularities of notational content and contextual history as are present in each record or in its group as a whole, can transform the otherwise inchoate content of these records into a historically specific and analytically coherent body of data. The event typology of each record—birth/christening, marriage, or death—can be ignored for the first subset of records to be considered because they are exclusively christening and burial notices, both of which event markings illuminate the records so similarly that they can be considered without distinction. Such event typology will be useful to consider for the second subset of parish entries later in this chapter. Four political events that reasonably frame all but one of these records and help to explain the main pattern of their frequency are the Elizabethan government act of 1562–63 legalizing the purchase of Africans, and the Privy Council's letters patents of 1585, 1588, and 1592 authorizing commercial excursions to Barbary, Guinea, and Sierra Leone respectively.

In ways suggested earlier, Tudor royalty, aristocracy, and high political personalities, both English and the locally resident foreign, are sometimes privileged exceptions to legal sight, and hence also anomalies in the methodology of historical analyses. Certain activities of their lives have to be considered in their own terms, and, on occasion, even a-chronologically, simply because such activities, due to the high political standing of their actors, become an index for the actions of others in their social group, both before, during, and after their own moment. One late Elizabethan black record that invites attention in this perspective is the burial notice in St. Stephen, Coleman Street, on 24 August 1594 of "Katherin the negar,

65 W. E. Tate, *The Parish Chest: A Study of the Parochial Administration in England*, pp. 44–45; J. Cox, *The Parish Registers of England*, pp. 1–2, 5–6; Thomas Forbes, *Chronicle from Aldgate*, pp. 39–40.

dwelling with the Prince of Portingall" (Item 198). The "Prince of Portingall" is Dom Antonio, the Portuguese claimant to the Spanish throne maintained in exile in London by Elizabeth for tactical advantage in dealing with Spain, as for example in Essex's disastrous Cadiz expedition to try and put Antonio on the Spanish throne. According to Arthur Dimock, Antonio is at this time living in Windsor, i.e. Windsor house, which is in Coleman Street ward in north central London near the city wall and close to Moorgate, and which is a block to the west of St. Stephen, Coleman Street in Farringdon ward Within (Agas Map in 3M, p. 8 and 4P, p. 9).[66] Windsor House is described by Stow as a "great house … of stone and timber," which is appropriate since Dom Antonio's residence is the natural gathering place of high-level Portuguese expatriates in London, such as the queen's physician, Roderigo Lopez, and others.[67]

Katherin's attributed connection to Dom Antonio's household is part of the history of expatriate Iberians maintaining in their European residences the enslaved black people they have in Portugal and Spain, and which recalls even in Katherin's name the trend started by Catherine of Aragon in England at the beginning of the century. The record's advertisement of Katherin's domestic service to Dom Antonio points in fact to other black presences in the Iberian community in London at this time, as was seen in Jeronimo Lopez's African earlier and that will be seen even more later in this chapter. It is worth pointing out that Katherin's possible status as a foreigner's servant does not disallow her historical significance as a black subject in early modern England, because like the other recorded black people considered in this book it is the English social experience of her presence and all that experience entails that should be included in a fresh reckoning of English social history. As a black servant of a foreign dignitary resident in London, she connects homologously to the black people held by Tudor royalty and aristocracy in the city at the same time, to naturalize the phenomenon of a persistent black presence in the highest levels of London life in the reign of Elizabeth. Yet, Katherin's burial in a locale a little distance away from the high place of her employment noted in her record suggests a exclusionistic gesture of segregation marking the lost black subject, carefully separated from the London high life that she was used to serve when alive. If it is the accident of her death that makes her enter the records—a consequence of the necessity of her interment that at the micro level of the neighborhood parish cannot be unknown—then it is her death that illuminates for a moment the fact of her otherwise disregarded and unrecordable life.

Expectedly, there are black people living with Dom Antonio's countrymen as well, in comparable if not identical social classes. As early as 1568 there are at least 100 Spanish merchants in Elizabethan London, and they briefly even have their own church in St. Mary Axe just off Bishopsgate street just below Bishopsgate itself on the city wall, and not very far from Aldgate, to the east (Agas Map 4R,

---

66 Arthur Dimock, "The Conspiracy of Dr. Lopez," pp. 452, 453.

67 *A Survey of London*, 1: 316. Stow describes the ambience and relative locations of Coleman Street Ward and St. Stephen, Coleman Street as well; see 1: 283–84. For the social atmosphere of Dom Antonio's house, see Dimock, p. 440, 442–43, 452.

p. 12).[68] The demographic affinity of Bishopsgate and Aldgate is reflected in the fact that in 1593 they are the two areas of London with the highest foreign populations, and these populations often have black people with them.[69] Entirely predictable therefore is the African woman "Mary" with "Dco-r Hector" who is buried in St. Olave, Hart Street in the vicinity of Aldgate on 28 January 1587 (Item 167). "Dco-r Hector" is Hector Nonnez (also spelled Nunes, Nunnez, Nones, etc.), a well-known Marrano Portuguese immigrant physician and part-time trader who is part of Dom Antonio's high-powered political and social circle, and who with Roderigo Lopez, the queen's personal physician, makes up a pair of the two most successful and prominent Portuguese figures in Elizabethan London.[70] Between 1564 and 1591 he was living in Mark Lane, St Olave, Hart Street, where several other physicians live as well.[71] His possession of Africans is simply explained by the fact that with Sir William Winter he was an investor "in voyages to Guinea in which blacks were taken aboard."[72] The record of Mary's burial is a part of his neighborhood life there, which includes a large extended family in the area. Mary is not the only black women in Hector Nonnez's possession, however, as the burial four years later on 13 July 1591 in the same parish, of "Grace, a nigra oute of Dcor Hector's" (Item 179), reveals. As a matter of fact, even his extended family has at least one African woman as a domestic living with them, as will be seen later. Living in one household in one place and being part of the same extended family in which there are other black women, and being part of an Iberian high social circle in which there are still more black women, Mary and Grace are uniquely members of a micro black female community living in Elizabethan London. The terse notations of Mary's and Grace's deaths describe only the presence of their muted, finally expendable, lives. Like Katherin's, those lives appear here merely in retrospect, with the casualness of only given Christian names, a frequent mark of the African female's greater obscurity in her effaced English life compared to the male's.

Given the fluid interchangeability of early modern professional categories, merchants are also on occasion artisans and vice versa, and they too have black people with them. Such are the black people of two expatriate Iberian artisans resident in London, also living on the city's eastern limits in Aldgate. Their presence is documented in the burial notices of St. Botolph's church on 8 and 10 August 1593: "Suzanna Pearis, a blackamoore," and "Symon Valencia, a blackamoore," the former described as a "[borned? bound?] servant to John Despinois [de Spinoza?]

---

68 See Paul J. Hauben, "A Spanish Calvinist Church in Elizabethan London, 1559–65," p. 50 n. 2, and p. 52.

69 For the areas of Elizabethan London with the highest foreign populations see Yungblut, "Strangers Settled Here amongst Us," Table 3, p. 27. For the preponderance of artisans and merchants among this population see p. 14.

70 For Nonnez's prosperity as a merchant, see Charles Meyers, "Lawsuits in Elizabethan Courts of Law: The Adventures of Dr. Hector Nunez, 1566–1591," p. 157. For a fuller discussion of the histories of both Nonnez and Lopez, see below.

71 His residence location is in "Hector Nones: Biography," in Pelling, *Physicians and Irregular Medical Practitioners in London 1550–1640*. For other physicians listed as residing here, see Thomas Forbes, *Chronicle from Aldgate*, p. 90.

72 Knutson, "A Caliban," p. 115.

a hat bandmaker," and the latter as a "servant to Stephen [illegible] a medalmaker" (Items 189, 190). The slight obscurity of the identity of Symon Valencia's owner that is created by the record's imperfect legibility does not prevent an identification of his origins, given the record's specification of his profession as one that is very similar to Suzanna Pearis's owner, whose name does reveal him to be an Iberian. If the hat-band maker John Despinois (or de Spinoza) is Spanish so in all likelihood is Stephen the medal maker, both located by natural affinity in the same neighborhood, and both imbibing the cultural practice of domesticated black service common to their national backgrounds.[73] The distinction between the greater transparency of Symon Valencia's name with its tell-tale surname identifying his origin as an Iberian black from Valencia and his clearly designated status as "servant" compared to that of Suzanna Pearis, with its ethnically opaque assimilated name and ambiguous status as a bound or bond servant, may be an ominous reflection of the greater vulnerability of the black woman in her enslaved early modern Anglo-European history in which even her human morphology will be obscured into linguistic and cultural unrepresentability.[74] The bleak desolation of both lives is chillingly evident in the fact that 1593 is a plague year, their death notices marking the quick destruction to which their chattel unrecognized existences are inevitably abandoned.

The unspoken inscrutability of black lives in this social group of expatriate Iberian personnel in London is a feature common even in the earlier years of Elizabeth's reign. Just as Spanish or Portuguese merchants or business people are frequently unreadable historically even with their name, so are the black people they have with them. An instance is the mention in Christchurch Newgate Street, on 18 February 1579, of the burial of "Thomas Blackmore, servant to Mr. Jucent" (Item 149). If the social standing of "Mr. Jucent" is deducible from the record's clear notation of his status as a gentleman, his profession can be extracted indirectly from the record's particular location in west central London. Christchurch Newgate Street, containing the church formerly known as Greyfriars Church in 1547, and otherwise known according to Stow as "Bladder street," or "Blow Bladder street," because it is for "selling bladders there," is a butchers' area, the Elizabethan butchers' quarters being in Eastcheap and around the "shambles" at Newgate.[75] In the Newgate area, "the shambles" running from the mouth of Bladder Street to Newgate market in front of Newgate itself (Agas map 4k, p. 8), is, as the medieval meaning of its name suggests, a slaughter yard, or as Stow puts it, a "flesh-market."[76] Thus, "Mr. Jucent" could be an Iberian businessman running a meat retail business in London. Foreign butchers were admitted to sell flesh in London in 1533, first in Lime street, and then in Leadenhall. Their first hall was in Butcher Hall Lane in St. Nicholas Shambles

---

[73] For patterns of early modern English immigrant settlements in close clusters, see Yungblut, "Strangers Settled Here," pp. 28–29.

[74] For the nature of this cultural phenomenon, see Lynda Boose's essay, "'The Getting of a Lawful Race': Racial Discourse in Early Modern England and the Unrepresentable Black Woman."

[75] For the former name of Christchurch see note for Christchurch, Newgate Street, in the "Place Name Index" in Prokter and Taylor, *A to Z*, p. 37; For "Bladder street" and what it is known for, see *Survey of London*, 1: 343. As the Agas map clearly shows, "Bladder street" is more a street corner or cul-de-sac on the corner of St. Martin-le-grand than a street *per se*.

[76] *OED*, 1: 2767; *Survey of London*, 1: 316.

(clearly visible in the Agas map reference for Newgate Street).[77] Alternatively, because, as Cheryl Fury has pointed out, butchers can also expediently be and are seamen, Mr. Jucent could have been on an African voyage or been an investor in one.[78] Either possibility can explain his possession of Thomas Blackmore, the rhetorically unmarked style of whose ethnic name conforms to the pattern of some of the names of assimilated Tudor Africans seen in the last chapter. The cipher of his name matches the ambiguity of his owner's precise identity to make his death the only trace of his otherwise untraceable existence.

The Elizabethan London phenomenon of keeping chattel Africans is not of course an exclusively Iberian one, because given the eventual pan-European involvement in the first phase of the African plunder in the fifteenth and sixteenth centuries that would be an impossibility. On occasion, in Elizabethan London there are Africans with people of other nationalities as well. "Constant Negrone, dau. of Gregori Negrone," who was baptized in St Dionis, Backchurch near St. Paul's on 3 July 1577 (Item 141), is part of an alien, possibly Italian, part-black family. Constant may not be as transparently a black person, and she may not be of the same status as those of the other black people in the parish registers, but that she is a person of color is unmistakable from her surname. This surmise is supported by the facts that Gregori Negrone (or Negron) is listed in the city's searches and tax assessments a year earlier as one of the "Straungers" living in nearby St. Dionis Backchurch, and four years later in All Hallows Staining on the city's east side as one of the foreign merchants in that parish, where in fact his surname is given as "Negro."[79] Constant and her family are thus further examples of a discreet alien black presence in the city.

A clearer instance of an African held by a non-Iberian alien merchant in the city is seen in the case of the Dutch beer brewer Peter Miller in Aldgate, whose African, described as "a negar named Frauncis," was buried in St. Botolph on 3 March 1596 (Item 209). That Peter Miller was a long-time resident Dutch merchant of the Dutch community in east London is understood from his listing in the Privy Council's search for London strangers thirty years earlier, in which he is recorded as living in All Hallows, Barking with other Dutch people in 1568.[80] Just as East Smithfield outside of Aldgate, where Thomas Forbes's longer citation of the record of Frauncis locates him, is farther east in the same general area as is St. Botolph on Aldgate street just outside Aldgate but south of it, so All Hallows, Barking on Tower Street just inside Postern gate is southwest of East Smithfield, and south of St. Botolph (Agas map 6T, p. 25). This triangular area made up of St. Botolph Aldgate, All Hallows Barking, and East Smithfield, straddling the city's east wall, is where both Peter Miller and many of the Dutch merchant community resided, his profession largely reflective of one of the trades for which the middle level of Elizabethan Dutch immigrants were well known.[81] The area adjoining the Tower was not only one of alien settlement, as has been pointed out earlier, but was also associated with

77 "Butchers," in *A Dictionary of London* (1918).

78 *Tides in the Affairs of Men: The Social History of Elizabethan Seamen, 1580–1603*, p. 21.

79 *Returns of Aliens*, ed. Kirk and Kirk, Part II, p. 168, 220.

80 Ibid., Part I, p. 391.

81 Yungblut, *Strangers Settled Here*, pp. 11–12; Maddocks, "Stepney in Other Days."

the beer-brewing industry. Corn is not only grown in the fields of East Smithfield around Whitechapel east of All Hallows, Barking, but the beer itself is brewed in the vicinity, such as in a brewery named "Hermitage" on Nightingale Lane leading from East Smithfield to the north bank of the Thames.[82] However Miller acquired Frauncis—by his direct or indirect involvement in the Dutch participation in the African trade and human trafficking, or by his emulation of the cultural practice of his English mercantile colleagues—like some of the instances seen earlier Frauncis was probably a shrewd business investment aimed at securing Miller a cheap labor advantage over his competitors. As Frauncis's life was cheaply appropriated so was it quickly abandoned, being as he almost certainly was a hapless and inconsequential plague casualty of that year.

Slightly more visible are the Africans with English merchants in London, missed by the Elizabethan government's searches and tax records but caught in the documentary minutiae of their possessors' local neighborhood lives. First among these, not in chronology but in familiarity because of his appearance once already in the government searches of 1592 discussed above, is Alderman Paul Baning, who in the very last year of Elizabethan's reign is revealed to have an African woman named "Julyane," because on 29 March 1601 she was baptized in St. Mary Bothaw and given the name "Mary" (Item 242). St. Mary Bothaw in the southern end of Walbrook Ward in south central London, just off the thoroughfare known as London Stone, and facing on its west Dowgate street leading south to the old boatyard on the Thames known as Dowgate (and from which St. Mary Bothaw, meaning, according to John Stow, near or adjoining a boat yard, gets its name), was in a busy manufacturing area. To its immediate west were located the tallow-chandlers, skinners, glaziers, cloak cutters, and little farther out south toward the river bank the vintners and the joiners; on to its south east were the dyers (Agas map 6P, p. 23).[83] Mary's history may have a connection to any of these surroundings. Supplementing that indirect ambient history is the fact that she is a reflection of one grim aspect of the career of her owner. A one-time grocer who was made alderman in 1592, Paul Baning was one of the most powerful London merchant aldermen in the reigns of both Elizabeth and James, one of only four merchants who between them in 1589 owned 94 percent of the imports of the Levant trade and who is named by Elizabeth as one of the directors of the newly reorganized Levant company that is set up at the end of the century, who was knighted by James sometime before 1624, and later made a viscount, and who was head of "a vast household made up of many retainers, clerks, and servants."[84]

---

82 *A Survey of London*, 2: 71; Maddocks, "Stepney in Other Days."

83 For the meaning of Dowgate, called by Stow "Downegate," see *A Survey of London*, 1: 229. For Stow's view of the busy mercantile character of Dowgate ward, which fronts Walbook ward on the south, see 1: 231–38.

84 For the reference to him as a grocer, see *Blackwoods Magazine*, January 1901, p. 630. For the reference to his knighting and viscountcy, see "House of Commons Journal Volume 2: 27 September 1642," in *Journal of the House of Commons*; for his role in the Levant trade see T. S. Willan, "Some Aspects of the English Trade with the Levant," p. 406. The quotation about his household is from Gustav Ungerer, "Prostitution in Elizabethan London," p. 159.

Whether Mary is one of three unnamed African women in Paul Baning's possession discussed previously, or an addition to them, as is more likely since their citation was eight years earlier, she constitutes with them a micro African community in one London household just as the earlier cited African women with Hector Nonnez do. The record thus points to Paul Baning's singular status as an individual English illicit procurer of multiple Africans in Elizabethan London.[85] His social standing and power accords the phenomenon of the surreptitious Elizabethan acquisition of Africans a potent social currency, connecting to and reinforcing the phenomenon's virulence among Elizabethan royalty and aristocracy. Like the Africans with the Elizabethan elite, Mary is an exotic display in a high-impact setting, the hub of influential business and administrative activity that is Paul Baning's residence. But remarkably unlike them, she is a twice-effaced black subject who is baptized anew despite her already Christianized identity as Julyan, even if her second christening might be her inculcation into a Anglican Protestant faith from a possibly earlier Iberian Catholic one. Registered in the history of Mary's double christening is Anglo-Europe's anxious re-making of the seized black subject into an image of itself, an anxiety fed by the unstable reflux between sameness and difference that is the intrinsic dynamic of all racialized othering.

The symptomatic nature of Paul Baning's possession of Africans is evident in the prevalence of such activity among others of his class across London, as far back as 1585. The burial of "Goodman Wilkenson"'s "servant," "Annes more," in St. Margaret Moses, Friday Street, on 11 July 1585 (Item 156) may in itself be a cryptic record. But the facts that Friday Street, extending north from Old Fish Street, was a south central London neighborhood of fishmongers, and Bread Street Ward in which it was situated, about a block south of Cheapside (Agas map 5M, p. 21), was in general a very prosperous merchant residence originally made up of bakers, and that St. Margaret Moses together with the adjacent churches of St. John the Evangelist and St. Matthew to its north made up a small enclave of powerful London merchants and city officials including several sheriffs and mayors, make it plausible that Wilkenson was an affluent fish retail merchant who like his business colleagues had an African as a domestic.[86] The cultural etymology of the name, with the surname functioning as a makeshift ethnic descriptor even as it silently coexists with an English toponymic surname, is of a type seen before, so that the record preserves Annes More's blackness with exactly the degree of obscurity typical of the Africans in England seen so far.

The black identities of the Africans held by other English merchants appear more transparently, though, as does that of "Robarte a negar servant to William Matthew a gentleman," when, nearly a decade after Annes More's death in the aftermath of

[85] Interestingly, Paul Baning's predatory nature may also be evident in James I's order of 18 February 1606 to "the Archbp. of Canterbury and Bishop of London. To require Paul Bayning to allow a maintenance suitable to a lady, to Susan his wife, separated from him at his own wish; he promised to do so, but fails to perform." "James I: Volume 18: January–February, 1606," *Calendar of State Papers Domestic*: *James I, 1603–1610 (1857)*, pp. 277–94.

[86] The details of the locale's ambient character are from *A Survey of London*, 1: 344, 346, 351–52.

a plague outbreak in 1593, he was buried on the city's eastern limit in Aldgate, St. Botolph's churchyard (Item 195). Even if who William Matthew is cannot be exactly determined, since his name does not appear in most of the expected places in the city's records, it is a safe assumption that he was a merchant or trader of sorts simply because of his careful designation as "a gentleman." That designation in early modern English usage almost always implies minimally a person of a recognized financial status, which if it does not come from titled landed wealth can only come from a prosperous trade or mercantile livelihood. This assumption, which a part of William Harrison's contemporary discussion of the term seems to support, also applies to Goodman Wilkenson, whose precise status is similarly untraceable in the city's records.[87] In any case, the meticulous protocol of Robarte's identification as the servant of "a gentleman" paradoxically lends a brazen justification to the condition of his Christianized but chattel life, "dwelling in a garden being behynd Mr. Quarles hys house and neare unto hogg lane in the libertie of East Smithfield," that is, adjoining the fields of East Smithfield in the space backing on to Hog Lane (Agas map 5W, p. 27) and directly behind the house of what is presumably William Matthew's neighbor, an overall area that is described by John Stow as "filthy," "unsavory and unseemly."[88] Robarte's owner's privileged status as "a gentleman" unspokenly normalizes the hideousness of his bonded condition, cast out as he is to an illicit tenement shed or hovel in someone's backyard.[89] While his bonded condition palliatively merits the honor of a distinctive church burial with "the second cloth and fower bearers," that burial must still be in "the owter church yeard," as must befit a presumably unredeemed non-Christian.

The spread of this practice of the casual keeping of Africans, sometimes severally, by London merchants located in the same area and possibly emulating each other, is clearly evident in multiple instances of it in Aldgate, as is exampled by "Cassangoe, A moore servant to Mr Barber a marchaunte," also described more helpfully as a "neager," who was buried in St. Botolph, Aldgate on 8 October 1593 (Item 192). Mr. Barber, who is "Thomas Barber," was an obviously prosperous merchant of this area who in St Mary the Hill parish in the adjacent ward of Billingsgate in the 1582 London Subsidy Roll was assessed the considerable amount of £30, and who four years later lived in an expensive property in Poultry, Cheapside that he eventually bought

[87] In Harrison's words, writing almost at this very moment, 1587:

"Citizens and burgesses have next place to gentlemen, who be those that are free within the cities, and are of some likely substance to bear office in the same. …

In this place also are our merchants to be installed as amongst the citizens (although they often change estate with gentlemen, as gentlemen do with them, by a mutual conversion of the one into the other), whose number is so increased in these our days that their only maintenance is the cause of the exceeding prices of foreign wares …" (*Description of England*, p. 115)

[88] *A Survey of London*, 2: 72.

[89] For an account of the endemic nature of such constructions in early modern London and its environs, see Vanessa Harding, "City, Capital, Metropolis: The Changing Shape of Seventeenth-Century London," pp. 129–33, particularly pp. 132–33. Although Harding is talking about a slightly later time than that of Robarte's record, what she describes applies to early modern London generally. Robarte's living quarters are merely an early example of what becomes even more more prolific in the next century.

for £100.[90] As it turns out, Cassangoe is only one of two Africans held by Thomas Barber, because five days later another African named "Easfanyo," described as "a negar servant of Mr. Thomas Barber a marchaunt," was also buried in St. Botolph, Aldgate (Item 193). The obvious Iberian pedigree of the names of both the Africans does not leave in doubt their origins as enslaved Spanish-Portuguese Africans purchased by the Elizabethan mercantile community in the manner suggested so far, even if the exact details of their acquisition cannot be readily demonstrated. Typically, both entries carefully note the pride of these enslavements in their mention of the esteemed place of service of these Africans when alive, "in his [i.e. Thomas Barber's] howse at the signe of the Redd Crosse in the libertie of East Smithfield," even as Easfanyo's record at least does not fail to clarify that the burial is to be in the "common ground … [and] not to be … having a black clothe." Not only do Easfanyo and Cassango, living in the same household, make up between themselves another micro African community, they do so with "Robarte" held by William Matthew, as well as with "Domingo," the earlier cited African held by William Winter in his manor in this very same location six years back.

The significance of the East London location of St. Botolph, Aldgate is highlighted by the fact that more Africans are located in this parish in the 1590s, held by English traders and trades people. Such is "Marye Phyllis A Blackamore," who was baptized in St. Botolph's church in Aldgate on 3 June 1597 (Item 224). Described as "beinge aboute Twentye yeres of age," she is noted as "dwellinge with millicen porter sempster." This record is notable for several reasons. First, if as a "sempster" or seamstress Millicen Porter is involved in the cloth manufacturing trade centering on the Clothworker's Hall in nearby Mincing Lane, Mary Phyllis may be a skilled worker in that trade, possibly an expert in black lace needle work that is the traditional forte of Iberian Moors. If so, she was another black working woman in Elizabethan London such as those seen earlier, and another member of both that group and the community of black people of east London at the end of the sixteenth century. Second, like many other black people discussed so far Mary Phyllis's name is another example of black identities hidden behind Christian names which obliterate all traces of ethnic origins, even if the longer description of Phyllis's baptism recorded in his daybook by the parish clerk conducting her baptism, Thomas Harridaunce, cited by Roslyn Knutson, does identify Phyllis as the daughter of a "Morroccan basket and a shovel maker" who "was desyrus to become a Christian."[91]

Third, Harridaunce's meticulous description of the event is unusual and worth noting because it clearly reveals the cultural politics of early modern English adult baptisms of black people. The parish clerk's account, and its *raison d'être*, is a celebratory record of the triumph of early modern English Christian conversion, seen in the public character of the event in Harridaunce's writing of it, and a precursor of a phenomenon that will recur increasingly in the seventeenth century. The celebratory note of the event is carefully underlined not just in Phyllis's seemingly voluntary

90 "1582 London Subsidy Roll: Billingsgate Ward," in *Two Tudor Subsidy Rolls for the City of London 1541 and 1582*, pp. 142–49.

91 This is the day book of the parish clerk Thomas Harridaunce, who conducts the baptism, and it describes the ritual in greater detail.

seeking out of the Protestant faith, but also in the knowledge she has already acquired of it because of the way she answers "very decently and well" the "certen questions" that Harridaunce puts to her as required by Protestant English conversion protocol. The improbability of this scenario lies in the fact of Phyllis's gender precluding her from being either a co-opted trainee translator and trade facilitator for the English, as were some of the Africans brought back earlier in the century, or an agent for her people as was the youth from Sierra Leone in 1611 cited by Roslyn Knutson, as will be seen later.[92] In fact, the racial agenda that writes the interested fiction of these details is noticeable in the reference later in Harridaunce's narrative, when in ritually asking "the Congregation" to join him in the conversion ceremony, he asks for divine dispensation "to grant her the one thing which by nature she could not have." This is the larger complexity of racial Christian conversions that exists in Europe as well as later in America across the early modern period in which Christian conversion of Africans paradoxically is predominantly not and increasingly will not be allowed to neutralize enslavement. At the same time, the note of English Christian cultural self-reassurance implicit in Harridaunce's account overwrites completely the coercive pressures on a young black woman to conform to the necessities of her displaced and disadvantaged English life. In those pressures, the white woman, Millicent Porter, with whom Phyllis is "dwellinge," and who is present at the baptism, may then be an ambiguous accessory, and an instance of the occasional complicity of white women in the oppression of women of color.

In this same east London area of Aldgate, in around the same years, i.e. mid to late 1590s, there are some more Africans in the possession of English tradespeople. The incidence of Africans held by affluent aliens in St. Olave, Hart Street and its immediate surroundings has already been seen in the case of the black servant of Baptista Sambitores, and the black maids with the Portuguese Marrano physician Hector Nonnez, and that feature of this locality is further reflected in the presence of Africans kept by two London citizens in 1595 and 1598, the first of whom, as discussed earlier, already has an African, namely Mrs. Barker. In addition to the African named Mouea Leying that this woman is listed as having in the government survey of 1592/93, she has in 1595 "George, a blackeamore," who was buried on 23 January 1595 in this parish church (Item 204). That Mrs. Barker has, like Hector Nonnez, Paul Baning, and Thomas Barber, multiple Africans with her, and about all of whose presence the city may or may not be cognizant, shows the extensiveness of the acquisition of Africans in the city, for which there is by now obviously an illicit mercantile or business network that can regularly supply Africans to interested parties like her. As it so happens, a "Georg Negro, s. of John" was baptized in St. Margaret's, Westminster ten years earlier on 13 February 1585/86 (Item 158), who could be the same African who ended up with Mrs. Barker in St. Olave, Hart Street and died there. Whether George was a replacement for her earlier noted African or an addition, he signals an increasing community of chattel Africans living in the same London household and in the same or connected neighborhoods who are surely aware of each other. Reinforcing this possibility is the fact there was a further black individual in this area who is described as "Domingo Blackmore" and

92 Knutson, "A Caliban in St. Mildred Poultry," pp. 110–14, 116–23.

who was buried nearby in St. Botolph, Bishopsgate on 27 June 1595 (Item 206). In that same locale is also recorded the burial of "Madelen, a blackeamore out of Bernard's house" three years later on 23 November 1598 (Item 229). The extreme casualness of the naming of Madelen's location disallows any possibility of her possessor's identity and through that of any clues about her origins and condition, except perhaps the suspicion that she was a plague victim from ("out of") the house of one "Bernard," and which is also therefore George's fate. Could Bernard himself be her merchant owner or is he merely the landlord of an unnamed merchant who had brought her there? Notwithstanding, her life, like George's, is not an item of documentary interest for the city or parish except in the awkward business of her body's disposal in death.

In these years elsewhere in London as well, there are Africans with English merchants. One such merchant prominently associated with Africans is John Davies in St. Mary Woolchurch Haw in north central London. Among several John Davies/Davis that exist in Elizabethan London city records, Rosalyn Knutson has identified this John Davies clearly enough as a haberdasher who was a well-established life-long resident of this parish, being twice married here, being church warden once, and eventually being buried here in 1627.[93] His location is explained by his trade, since St. Mary Woolchurch Haw is a wool merchants' community, "so called of a beam placed in the churchyard which was thereof called Woolchurch haw, of the tronage, or weighing of wool there used."[94] His historical prominence as an African owner comes from his being one of the sponsors ("surety") in the earlier cited public baptism of an African from Sierra Leone in nearby St. Mildred Poultry in 1611 that Rosalyn Knutson has studied, and that will be discussed later (Item 277). But it is Davies's prior involvement with Africans that makes him a sponsor in that later event, and that experience is manifest in his possession of an unnamed African described as "a blakmore belonging to Mr John Davies," who was buried in St. Mary Woolchurch Haw sometime between 24 April and 20 May 1597 (Item 222). Knutson's convincing demonstration that this John Davies is not the John Davies who arranged the baptism of the African from Sierra Leone, because the former is named separately as one of the persons that stood as "surety" for that baptism ceremony, does not, however, explain the oddity of the fact that the African whose death is being registered in St. Mary Woolchurch Haw actually expired elsewhere, "in White Chappel parishe." but who was "laied in the ground in this church yarde." He was clearly seen as a stranger here and buried as one: "sine frequentia populi et sine ceremoniis quia utrum christianus esset necne nesciebamus [without any company of people or ceremony, because we did not know whether he was a Christian]." Yet, the John Davies who is named as this African's owner, in the phrase "belonging to Mr John Davies," was clearly recognized as a resident here, and not in Whitechapel. Given the uncertainty of whether this John Davies ever lived in or had any dealings in the record's time frame, i.e. up to 1597 in Whitechapel on the city's east side, since there are no records that he did, how this unnamed African comes to be with him in St. Mary Woolnoth, and what he was to him, is difficult to determine. Was he a secret

93 Ibid., p. 115.

94 *A Survey of London*, 1: 226.

possession of Davies that the latter kept hidden away from his respectable place of residence in the city, Whitechapel being in the area of the liberties of the open fields north of Hogg Lane and East Smithfield, beyond the city's eastern boundary [Agas map 4W, p. 13]), and for whose death brought on by the uncontrollable calamity of the plague that year Davies was forced to take responsibility? As such, this African's literal anonymity reflects and reinforces the anonymous circumstances of his London presence to cloak all but the fact of his chattel life, that cannot be hidden at his cheap but damaging death.

The parish records of black people presented so far of course deal only with Africans whose specifically named or implied Elizabethan ownerships give their documentary citations some transparency. Such records do not account for Africans who appear in Elizabethan London's parochial archives incidentally and by themselves. These are the debris of the clandestine history of the Elizabethan enslavements of Africans, and they litter the pages of the city's parish registers almost continuously for the 45 years of Elizabeth's reign. This second subset of parish records, touching all areas of London, includes not just African christenings and burials, but marriages and births as well, the latter evident in both the christenings and burials of African children and infants. Some of the names appearing in these records are of the peculiar variety examined in the last chapter and earlier in this one, which is to say that they occasionally have unmarked ethnic descriptors such as "Blackmore" or "Blackman" in the surname position where they merge homologously with traditional English surnames. That very fact, however, gives them as much of a probability of being the names of black persons as of English, and merits their consideration as such. To reiterate a point made at the beginning of this work and variously in the last chapter, in the interests of bringing to light a traditionally occluded history of early modern English black people, and given the instability and informality of English naming practices, it is more productive to err on the side of an aggressive inclusiveness than the other way around. In their volume and range of contents these records are best examined chronologically while noting frequencies/patterns of location and event typology, to trace where possible the movements and life changes of individual Africans through the city in their Elizabethan existence. Given the increase in citations of Africans in the last decade of Elizabeth's reign, it may also be useful to consider this entire subset of parish records in two phases, namely 1558 to 1590, and 1591 to 1603.

In the first phase, comprising the first four decades of Elizabeth's reign, and beginning with the government decree of 1562/63 enabling the purchase of Africans, 17 black people of varying degrees of black ethnic explicitness are recorded across the full range of event markings in parishes located in all four compass quadrants of the city. "Jhon the Blackamoor," who was baptized on 6 May 1565 in St. Mary the Virgin, Aldermanbury in the city's north-west section, and buried next year on 23 May 1566 in the same parish (Items 127, 128), was clearly an abandoned African left to die on the streets, more instances of which appear elsewhere. In the next decade there are eight individuals with names clearly indicating or implicitly suggesting an African identity listed in parishes in the city's west, east, south, and central zones. Some, such as "Margareta a Moor" and "Wm. Blackmore," appear in their burial notices, as does the former on 27 September 1571 in St. Margaret's Westminster on the city's west side and the latter on 19 September 1573 on the south in St.

Mary Magdalene, Bermondsey in Southwark (Items 134, 138). If the former's ethnic identification, together with her location in a neighborhood seen repeatedly by now to contain Africans, makes plausible her bleak history of illicit enslavement and abandonment to the plague (1571 being a plague year), the latter's black background is lent credence by the marriage notice in the same parish church's records four months earlier of "Mr. Blackmor and Sarah ffyson" (Item 137). While the unusual title of the groom's name in the marriage notice—of which there is no other instance in the black records of this study—may suggest that this is not a black person and is a different individual from the one in the burial citation, the fact that both records are from the same church and close in time strengthens the probability that they refer to the same person and possibly a black one, with the form of the groom's name in the marriage record being perhaps the result of an inexplicable scribal eccentricity. Furthermore, the groom's quick demise in a non-plague year may indicate this to have been a hasty maneuver aimed at securing for the bride a social alias in an awkward situation with the most hapless individual available, such as an African held mutely in bondage. In that case, the unusual form of the groom's name may be a cooperative effort on the church curate's part to lend as much authenticity to the marriage as possible. That black people were involved in such arrangements willingly and otherwise is evident from some records appearing later in this work (see the record of Martin Francis, Item 384).

If the marriage record of Mr/William Blackmor/Blackmore opens the possibility of cross-racial marriages, either as hasty exigencies or as practicalities, that phenomena is reflected in four more marriage notations in this same decade. These are the marriages of "Georgius Chesworth & Dorothea Blackemo'r" on 3 May 1573 in St. Martin in the Fields, Middlesex, just outside Westminster; "Robert Platt and Sara Blackmore" on 3 July 1575 in St. Botolph, Bishopsgate; "Isaac Hollowaye, tayller, to Katheren Blackamore" on 17 August 1578 in St. Pancras, Soper Lane; and "John Blackmore & Eliz. Michael" on 25 January 1579 in St. Matthew, Friday Street (Items 136, 140, 146, 148, respectively). Of these, Katheren Blackamore's marriage transcript may offer a clue about the nature of these unions in its revelation of her husband as a tailor. Soper Lane, off the great merchant concourse of Cheapside, while not being a neighborhood of tailors *per se*, does occasionally have tailors living in the area, such as the tailor Robert Bogas in Hosier or Bow Lane in 1536, and Hubert Reynolds in 1583.[95] Notwithstanding the fact that tailor could mean "a great merchant tailor or [a] poor 'botchor' making a scarce living repairing and mending,"[96] if Isaac Holloway is a lesser tailor than a greater one (such as a "cutter"), his union with what is arguably a black woman could represent a simple practicality and gesture of solidarity among poor working people for mutual convenience. So too could be the other three marriages, all of which occur in relatively mixed economic communities, with Dorothea Blacke'mor's marriage in a relatively

[95] "St. Mary le Bow 104/6," and "St. Pancras Soper Lane 145/29" in *Historical Gazetteer of London before the Great Fire*.

[96] John Patten, "Urban Occupations in Pre-Industrial England," p. 301; Peter K. Newman also discusses the penury of most tailors in his essay "The Early London Clothing Trade," pp. 244–45.

affluent Westminster suburb merely indicating the prevalence of this phenomenon even among other social classes.[97] The four marriages, together with that of William Blackmor, describe the equal incidence of such cross-racial union across both sexes, and mark a historically unnoticed but significant assimilatory aspect of the history of black lives in Elizabethan London. At the same time as these cross-racial unions reflect a certain degree of inadvertent social mobility for the black subject, which will be discussed more fully in the next chapter, the natural masking of their black identities by homonymous English names, together with their co-optation into English bloodlines, complete their historical disappearance.

A preponderance of baptisms and burials of rootless/vagrant black people recurs in the parish registers of the 1580s, and if the latter is a sign of the increased virulence of the plague in this decade, the former is probably a function of the government's authorization of merchant trading forays to Guinea and Barbary in 1585 and 1588 that produced more seized Africans. These two factors do not just variably overwrite what is the most complex record of this decade, and of the records seen so far, but also help to explain that complexity. This is the record of the baptism of "Elizabeth, a negro child, born white, the mother a negro" on 23 September 1586 in St. Botolph's, Bishopsgate (Item 159), which while minimally confirming the continuing contraband importation of black people into their life of unspoken English bondage, more importantly declares the casual sexual exploitation that is now an inevitable additional dimension of that oppression, and a signal of its greater ferocity. If the baptized Elizabeth compensates somewhat for her mother's unassimilated anonymity, that compensation also erases her mother's very existence, whose only claim to documentary memory is relegated to the opprobrium of her having been impregnated by a white man. The ambiguity of the black woman is reflected nevertheless in the strained documentary identity of her daughter, whose whiteness cannot be allowed to hide the fact that she is a "negro." Less plangent but significant nonetheless is the christening of "Elizabethe d.[aughter of] John Moore" in St. Mary, Somerset on Old Fish Street directly above the Broken Wharf on the Thames (6M Agas map, p. 21), on an unspecified date in 1589 (Item 173). The other parish records of this decade register the equally casual snuffing out of seized black lives, such as in the burial notices of "Christopher Cappovert, a blackamoore who dyed in the whitbell of the high street" on 21 October 1586 in St. Botolph, Aldgate; "Domyngo a Blackmore" on 8 January 1587 in St. Ann's, Blackfriars; "Isabell, a blackamor" on 6 June 1588 in St. Olave, Hart Street; "Sebrina, a blackamore wench" on 30 January 1589/90 in St. Andrew Holborn; and "Francisco, a nigro" on 5 September 1590 again in St. Olave, Hart Street (Items 161, 166, 170, 175, 176). Within the relentless regularity of these black deaths, and more chilling in its anonymity than any of them, is the grim entry on 29 June 1588 in St. Olave, Hart Street of a cast-off African whose destitute death is recorded for posterity simply as "A man blackamoor laye in the street" (Item 171).

If these black deaths in south-central, west, and east London, which are all part of the plague statistics for these years, demonstrate the abject desolation into which

---

[97] For a discussion of the professional categories of tailors in the sixteenth century, see Newman, "The Early Modern Clothing Trade," pp. 244–45.

Elizabethan black lives are silently cast, they also underline the extensiveness of their spatial spread across the city. That extensiveness acquires a greater complexity, however, in the baptism notation of "Edward, the sonne of Resonabell Blackman silkweaver" on 19 February 1586/87 in St. Olave, Tooley Street across the river in Southwark, in the way it reveals the existence of an entire African family. First pointed out by Roslyn Knutson, this is a unique record because it is the only record of an early modern English black family known to exist (Item 162).[98] The identification of the named father, Resonabell, not just as a "blackman" but more explicitly as a "blackmor" in another record discussed below, and as a professional like Christopher Cappovert (a metal worker, in his association with the White Bell metal foundry on Aldgate High Street), may show the possibility of financial and emotional prosperity for the city's underclass of black people. St. Olave Tooley Street, also known as St. Olave Southwark, however, is a neighborhood of aliens and poor people according to Stow, and not a neighborhood of silk weavers *per se*, whose community as a whole will appear as an organized and recognized English entity much later in areas like Spitalfields.[99] Resonabell is obviously the latest arrival in this alien and indigent locality but an unusual one in that he carries a valuable new technology with him, which will eventually become an industry, silk until now being usually imported, and in that he is a historically unnoticed example of the introduction of silk-weaving to England by immigrants, claimed by some scholars.[100] His relative prosperity must in part be due to this remarkable fact. But a cold reminder of the price of such a life, which Roslyn Knutson associates optimistically with the word "independent,"[101] is the stiff pressure of compliance that his otherwise charming given name resonates, and that is consistently the unarticulated but discernible logic of the Anglo-European categorization of "good" versus "bad" Africans in the earlier cited travel accounts of the age. A direct parallel of this logic is the black needle maker in Cheapside in the 1550s who was mentioned in the last chapter, whose ignominious anonymity is the palpable correlative of his refusal to "teach his art to any." How precarious Resonabell's prosperity is may be seen shortly, not in the fortunes of Edward, whose subsequent life remains unknown, but in that of his other children.

What principally distinguishes the second phase of this sub-set of black parish records in the last decade of Elizabeth's reign is not a divergence from the features of the records of the first phase but an increase in frequency and volume. Between 1591 and 1603 twenty-five notations of black people of fluctuating transparency mark all but one of these years, plausibly attributable at least in part to the Privy Council's letters patent of 1592 approving commercial expeditions to Sierra Leone.

98 "A Caliban in St. Mildred Poultry," p. 116.

99 For the social character of the parish, see *A Survey of London*, 2: 64. For a few silk weavers residing in St. Olave, Southwark twenty years earlier, see *Returns of Aliens*, ed. Kirk and Kirk, Pt. 1, pp. 470–71. For a brief account of silk weavers in early modern London, see "Industries: Silk-weaving," in *History of the County of Middlesex.*

100 For the claim that silk-weaving was started in England by aliens, see C. G. A. Clay, *Economic Expansion and Social Change*, 2: 39; cited in Yungblut, *Strangers Settled Here*, p.107 n. 9. Yungblut discusses nonetheless the contributions of aliens in developing and accelerating the English silk-weaving craft that existed in minuscule fashion until then.

101 "A Caliban in St. Mildred Poultry," p. 116.

Here too, the preponderance of burials and baptisms continues, the first point of interest in which being the recordings of the deaths of Resonabell's other children, "Jaine, d. of Reasonable, Blackmor" on 13 October 1592 and "Edmund, s. of Reasonable, blackmor" three days later on 16 October, both in St. Olave, Tooley Street (Items 182, 183). The loss of Resonabell's two children within three days of each other, even if to the plague, cannot but be a savage exposure of the fragility of a black man's prosperity struggling for survival in the wildest of the city's suburban liberties, described by a modern commentator as being from Roman times "a kind of satrapy … a relatively undeveloped and ill-regarded place … a boundary zone to which London could consign its dirt and rubbish."[102] In ironic contrast perhaps is the other distinction of this record, in the clarity with which it points out the black identity of the man whose devastation this is, not just with the ambiguity of the term "Blackman" as earlier but with the explicitness of the identification "blacmor." This, it should be noted, is a confirmation of what has been surmised so far in this study, that the term "blac(k)man" in early modern English usage can and does in fact refer to a black person. At the same time, the location of Resonabell and his family in St. Olave Tooley Street, just a few blocks directly east from the Rose playhouse, on whose boards in these very years roaring London crowds are watching villainous metaphors of black lives in plays like *Titus Andronicus*, should be a connection of not inconsiderable significance, as will be stressed later.[103]

Of related interest are the burials of "Emmanuel Backamore" on 22 October 1591 and "Elizabeth Moore" on 31 August 1593, both in St. Mary Mounthaw in central London, and "Elizabeth Blackmore" on 7 June 1593 in St. Dunstan in the East (Items 178, 191, 188). All three entries lack in lesser or greater degree the decisiveness of Resonabell's African identification but they have enough clues in them to connect these individuals to his ethnicity, comprising in the first case a likely transcriptional omission of a letter in the surname Blackamore and in the second and third cases of the natural merging of an African name with an English one in ways seen before. Seven individuals with the surname "Blackman" appear in a mix of baptisms and burials across this decade in the city's west side. They are "John s. of John Blackman," who was christened on 6 August 1591 in St. James, Clerkenwell (also spelled Clarkenwell); "Margeria Blackman," who was baptized on 1 August 1594 in St. Martin in the Fields; "Anne Blackman, d of William," who was baptized on 20 July 1596 and buried on 7 April 1597 in St. Margaret's, Westminster; "Maria Blackema," who was baptized on 7 April 1597 in St. Martin in the Fields; "Marye d. John Blackeman," who was christened on 28 March 1599 in St. Mary, Somerset; and "Elizabeth Blackman, d of Johan," who was christened on 18 January 1600/01 in St. Margaret's, Westminster (Items 180, 203, 216, 220, 221, 234, 241). Ambivalent in the faintness of their ethnic identity, including in the one unique variation or orthographic corruption of the

102 Peter Ackroyd, *London: The Biography*, pp. 678–79.

103 See the receipts for the playhouse for February 1591/2 to June 1592, December 1592 to February 1593, and December 1593 to February 1593/4 recorded in the diary of the playhouse's owner, Philip Henslowe, in *Documents of the Rose Playhouse*, ed. Rutter, pp. 58–60, 68–69, and 77–79, respectively.

name "Blackman" to "Blackema," these people may represent, like Resonabell's children, one large connected black and assimilated black family spread across the same area.

More black deaths recorded in this decade, but of yet another kind of African intelligibility, are those of "Jone Moros" on 15 October 15 1593 and "Rebecca A Lucressa Morro" on 2 November 1594, both in St. Margaret's, Westminster (Items 194, 199), the surnames "Moros" and "Morro" clearly designating black backgrounds, albeit of indeterminable Portuguese or Italian contexts and possibly prosperous social classes. Similarly diluted in their African pedigree are the parish notices of, "Ales Moore et filius Siluster," who was buried in St. Margaret's Westminster on 7 June 1597; "Edward Blakemore," who married "An Strinfellowe" on 8 July 1601 in St. Margaret's, Westminster; and "Constantia Negrea," who married "John Cathman" on 15 February 1598 in St. Olave, Hart Street (Items 225, 243, 226), the latter belonging to the same category as Rebecca Morro and Jone Moros, and the former two to the kind of corrupted and mixed English-African name groups represented by Elizabeth Moore and Elizabeth Blackmore.[104] Of greater ethnic perspicuity, however, are the black demises of "Cornelius Blacke a more," who was buried on 2 March 1593 in St Margaret's Lee, Lewisham, and "Peter Marley a blacamore, dire vira house [i.e. from the fearfully diseased house]," who was interred on 8 November 1594 in St. Olave, Hart Street (Items 186, 184, 200), worth noting in which are, in the case of Cornelius, the incidence of a *faux* classical name for a domesticated African that will become a frequent feature of early modern English black history, and in the case of Peter Marley the use of a completely English or European name in which no traces of his African origins remain. The starkest of these records of pathetic black lives leveled by the plague is the undated mention of an unnamed black person's anonymously charitable burial noted simply as "Received for the burial of a blak more" in 1596 in All Hallows, Staining (Item 210). The predominant plague deaths here, in a range of ethnic transparencies and social classes and extending to all directions of the city, including in one case beyond its eastern limits to the adjoining county of Kent, sketch conceivably the particular desolation of destitute and unprotected

---

[104] Boyd's Marriage Index, the source for Constantia Negrea's record here, and for several more records in this book, is an index of marriage entries copied down by Percival Boyd. The following statement appearing on a genealogy website offers a summary of information about this source:

> Boyd's Marriage Index is an index to English marriage taken from copies of parish marriage registers, Bishops Transcripts and marriage licences, for the period 1538 to 1840 (when statutory registration began). It was principally the work of Percival Boyd, MA, FSA, FSG (1866–1955) and his staff. It was made at his expense between 1925 and 1955, and has since been expanded. Copies of the original typescript index are with the Society of Genealogists, the College of Arms, the Genealogical Society of Utah and some county records offices and libraries have copies of segments of the Index.

Available at <http://www.originsnetwork.com/help/popup-helpbo-bmi.htm>. Seen 5.21.05. Because the BMI is only an Index, it does not include month and day details of the records it contains.

black lives by the ravages of a natural calamity that was also striking down the natural-born citizens of the metropolis.

Four records in the last decade of Elizabeth reflect an amplification of an ominous trend seen in the first four years of her reign. These are the burial of "William Harris 'blackamoor baseborn'," who was laid to rest on 7 August 1595 in St. Margaret's, Westminster; and the christenings of "Susan, A Black mores Childe" on 7 September 1595 from "Haliwel Street" in St. Leonard's, Shoreditch, and "Christian Ethiopia borne of a Blackmore" on 18 March 1602 in St. Dunstan and All Saints, Stepney Tower Hamlets (Items 207, 208, 249). Common to both entries is the sexual vulnerability of black women that they indicate. William Harris's "Baseborn" designation marks this as another chilling case of the casual sexual exploitation of black women who in this instance cannot even merit naming, even if her offspring is presumably given her English predator's name as a gesture of his retrospective generosity. Even that generosity, which may be a function of the power and affluence of this central Westminster parish, is not available to either Susan in a poor northern suburb of the city and or to Christian in its far eastern dockside perimeter, whose only commendations are the markings of an ignominious birth, "a black mores Childe," and "borne of a Blackmore."[105] Moreover, such dubious commendations cannot extend to the black parent of each infant, who must remain unseen and unknown. Such births may or may not be the products of illicit English sexual predation, but they mark the helplessness of black women confined to a silent chattel existence bereft of the protective structures of a normal civic life.

---

[105] Haliwel Street, also known as Halliwell Street, so named from the now defunct "Holy well" in the high street in Shoreditch coming up from Bishopsgate (Agas map 1R, 2R, p. 11), is in fact Shoreditch high street. It is at this time in Stow's testimony a built-up area of "base tenements" surrounded by fields on both sides (*A Survey of London*, 2: 73), within which are the *Theatre* and the *Curtain* playhouses. Kingsford explains further that these "base tenements" are in fact "gambling houses, brothels and other disreputable places that made the district notorious" (*A Survey of London*, 2: 369, "Notes," gloss to p. 74, line 25). St. Leonard's is partly, like St. Dunstan, under the jurisdiction of Stepney ("Stepney: Local Government," in *A History of the County of Middlesex*, vol. 11: *Stepney, Bethnal Green* [1998], pp. 63–70). Stow says the right side of Shoreditch, "beyond the … church … belong to the parish of Stebunhith [Stepney]," whereas the parish itself is "always" under the "Archdeacon of London" (*A Survey of London*, 2: 74, 75). St. Dunstan, which is in the hamlet of Ratcliff in Stepney and one of the Tower Hamlets a ways east of the Tower, is a busy maritime mercantile and industrial community on the Thames's north bank in east London, whose social character includes the presence of seized Africans brought back by its resident merchant mariners from their overseas commercial and maritime voyages. Among its residents was George Best, whose discourse on blackness is discussed later in this chapter. (For more on the social character of St. Dunstan and its environs, see the discussions of "Charity Lucanea" and "Mary a negro servant of Ann Isaac" in Ch. 3). Halliwell Street is, like Turnbull or Turnmill Street in Clerkenwell and Southwark, one of the prostitution districts of London (see Thomas Nashe's listing of the brothels of London in 1592 in his *Pierce Penniless*, cited in W. J. Pinks, *The History of Clerkenwell*, p. 538, and the map of "London Bawdy Houses" in Archer, *Pursuit of Stability*, p. 212). Both sites are thus locations of casual and formal black exploitation, more instances of the latter of which will be seen later.

This secret black population, in the households of monarch, aristocrats, foreign nobility, aldermen, foreign and English merchants, and private citizens alike, spread across London and its environs but concentrated in its eastern and western suburbs, constitutes a shadow historical community, known to its Elizabethan contemporaries but little recognized by them as one. That by the end of the century their surreptitious importation reached possibly mass volumes is indicated in a fragmentary reference in the records of the High Court of the Admiralty in 1600 that mentions in a bottomry case "A cargo of negroes" (Item 239). As a bottomry case the dispute involves wrangling over a shipload of black people who are being brought into England on a ship that has not been paid for. Such briefly named but otherwise invisible black people can only be creatures of miscellaneous drudgery for their owners, gagged by their linguistic and cultural alienation into lives of permanent and inconsequential silence. The very fact that Elizabethan Africans are an illegal population, contraband entities bereft of any civic mandates and human recognition, ensures that they live at the mercy of their captors in a way that even domesticated animals do not, in the sense that the latter's living space is guaranteed by their consumable functions. Images of their distorted lives in these conditions, variously the objects of their English keepers' curiosity, awe, and ire, are also caught in personal accounts of them by individuals, and in medical and legal records, in which what comes across is both their simultaneous submersion in and exclusion from the urban Elizabethan socius, and through that, their synchronic consideration in and exclusion from the genus of the English species.

IV

The most spontaneous account of black people in Elizabethan London is also the best-known one. This is the much discussed description of a black person in an inter-racial union in London that George Best digressively included in 1578 in his account of his journey with Martin Frobisher in search of the northwest passage titled "A True Discourse of a Voyage to Cathaya" (Item 145).[106] The overall popular contemporary appeal of the account is evident in Hakluyt's reprinting of it eleven years later in the *Principal Navigations* in 1589 (12: 113–41). Best's extensive narrative is an advocation of the suitability or "habitability" of what is the northern zones of North America for profitable English settlement and exploitation, which is the reason for its natural inclusion in the larger work by Hakluyt, otherwise early modern England's most indefatigable proponent of overseas English occupation and settlement. However, tucked within the many details that Best includes of the climate, flora and fauna, and peoples of that region, which he calls "Meta Incognita," is his sudden general comparative allusion to "black Moores" and "Aethiopians"

[106] Relevant critical discussions of the passage include, Karen Newman, "'And Wash the Ethiop White': Femininity and the Monstrous in *Othello*," pp. 78–80; Michael Neill, *Putting History to the Question: Power, Politics, and Society in English Renaissance Drama*, pp. 272, 276, 471, 474, 475, 482; Kim Hall, *Things of Darkness*, pp. 11–12; Lynda Boose, "'The Getting of a Lawful Race'," pp. 45–46; Mary Floyd-Wilson, *English Ethnicity and Race in Early Modern Drama*, pp. 8–9.

that "[w]e also among us in England have, which after a small continuance, can well endure the cold of our countrey."

Best's allusion is a direct contemporary testimony of the black presence in Elizabethan England, and which is of the first order of importance in a reconstructive history of early modern English black people because, as Kim Hall puts it, "There are no first hand accounts from the black Tudor population," even if the effects of Hall's claim are by the data of the present work necessarily subject to some qualification.[107] Also obliquely present in Best's portrayal, buried within a linked exhortation of English people to withstand the hardship of living in foreign lands, is the struggle of African people to survive in England. More significant still is Best's specific invocation, in direct exemplification as it were of the previous statement, of one particular African that he has seen in London, married to a white English woman with whom he has fathered a male black child: "I my selfe have seene an Ethiopian as blacke as a cole brought into England, who taking a faire English woman to wife, begat a sonne in all respects as blacke as the father was, although England were his native countrey, and an English woman his mother." Best himself was living in Ratcliff where, as was seen earlier, Africans were already present, and he could in fact be referring to one of them.[108] This constitutes a revealing comment on the mixed marriages of Africans and English people seen in the previous section of this chapter. What makes both of Best's references to black people in England especially valuable is the fact that they are tangential outgrowths of the natural flow of his thoughts, as he focuses on describing the land and peoples of the Meta Incognita, "(of whom and for whom this discourse is taken in hand)," as he emphatically puts it. What they illuminate is not therefore part of the rehearsed public rhetoric of the Elizabethan early colonial project, but something more intimate. They describe English social attitudes about historical black people in England that are developing in the second half of the sixteenth century. In that, they recall the English responses to both the Brazilian people brought to England earlier, to the court of Henry VII in 1501 (Item 8) and to that of Henry VIII in 1531–32,[109] and they provide a contrast to those experiences. Where those earlier cross-cultural exposures provoked an amazed curiosity, Best's remarks seven decades after the first event and four decades after the second one convey markedly negative social attitudes. The negativism of Best's view of black people also constitutes an unfavorable counterpoint to the history of John Blanke, Henry VIII's proudly showcased and happily assimilated black trumpeter, and of Fraunces Negro, the well-paid black stable keeper of Henry's queen, both discussed in the last chapter.

Best's negative social attitudes have been analyzed along a phalanx of important modern critical axes. Karen Newman has shown how "Best's account … textualizes the problem of social mobility in early modern England … [and] challenges the definitions of social identity based on birth," and which "is a disquieted fear of the social changes taking place … of 'masterless men' and of challenges to traditional

[107] *Things of Darkness*, p. 11.

[108] Best's residence in Ratcliff is cited by Sidney Maddox in his essay "Ratcliff."

[109] The latter Brazilian is the earlier cited tribal chief presented by Hawkins senior to Henry VIII in 1531–32, described in his *Hawkins of Plymouth*, p. 29.

notions of order and degree."[110] In contrast, Kim Hall has highlighted how what comes through in Best is "its articulation of cultural anxieties—about complexion, miscegenation, control of women ... —brought on by the presence of blacks."[111] Supplementing this, Michael Neill has connected Best's discourse to the Elizabethan struggle to keep distinct its particular racial taxonomies, citing as illustration the fact that Best's original description of American and East Indians "as being 'not black, but white'" is changed by Hakluyt to "'tawny and white'," "a distinction that other observers typically aligned with gender."[112] More sharply, Linda Boose has pointed out that what is contained in Best's conversation about a black man fathering a black child with a white woman are the suppressed fears of a white English patriarchy about the enduring power of blackness to overwrite whiteness, implicit in a story that [Best] does "not tell," that of black women bearing black children to white men. This is the mark of the "unrepresentability" of the black woman.[113] Recently, Mary Floyd-Wilson has insisted that Best's sketch is meant to allay the English fears of physical disfiguration in living in inhospitable foreign climates that was a subject of concern to English traders, and that even as Best embraces "the basic principles" of ancient geohumoral ethnic taxonomy that assigns skin color to climate, "he recognizes that the English people's fears of their own vulnerability may be assuaged by interpreting blackness as anomalous and peculiar."[114]

While these kinds of analyses have enduring critical brilliance, what also needs to be iterated is the penetrating ubiquity, and urgently needed cancellation, of blackness as an emerging English social category. The rhetorical randomness of Best's recollection of black people in England is a direct semiotic of the pervasiveness of black people in Elizabethan London, whom he has run into in life just as casually as his prose runs into them in his recollection of them, amidst his careful documentation of pleasing data that his trip is required to bring back for his patron, Christopher Hatton, who has sent him on that trip for that precise reason.[115] The mutually reinforcing unexpectedness of these mental and physical collisions with black people have for Best an unsettling quality, which is precisely the cue for the excursus of Newman and the other scholars. This note of discomfiture is betrayed in Best's abrupt shift of the frame of reference of his discussion twice from the exotic peoples of northern North America to the black people that "we among us have in England," the repeated distraction caught in his own admission the second time, "Therefore to returne againe to the blacke Moores ... ." This loss of composure is also paralleled exactly by the tonal difference between the relative calmness and detachment of his catalog of the "men, women, children, and sundry ... beasts in great plenty" that he has seen in Meta Incognita and the consternation of his

---

110 "'And Wash the Ethiop White,'" p. 79.

111 Hall, *Things of Darkness*, p. 11.

112 *Putting History to the Question*, p. 276.

113 "'The Getting of a Lawful Race,' " pp. 45–46.

114 *English Ethnicity and Race*, p. 9.

115 In his mini biography of George Best, Alan Cook points out that "Best's dedication to Hatton of his account of the Frobisher voyages suggests that Best undertook to join Frobisher's second voyage at Hatton's behest, 'to make a true reporte of al Occurrents'" ("Beste [Beste], George"). Even Hakluyt indicates as much, in the title he gives Best's narrative, which states that Best was "a Gentleman employed in the same voyages."

report of a black man having from "a faire English woman" "a sonne in all respects as blacke as the father."

Fueled by what for Best is the inexplicability of the origins and virulence of blackness, and reflective of all of the kinds of socially hierarchic, ethnographic, and patriarchal early modern English anxieties that Newman and the others describe, that consternation is equally importantly supported not just by an underlying assumption about blackness as an aberrant physiological condition but also as one that must be understood and marked as such. This assumption, in being asserted twice, once at the end of his presentation of his cameo of the black and white produced black child, "And the most probable cause in my judgment is, that this blacknesse proceedeth of some naturall infection," and again triumphantly at the end of his prognosis of that peculiarity, "Thus you see, that the cause of the Ethiopians blacknesse the curse and naturall infection of the blood," in fact frames his report-within-a-report of miscegenic black people in England. The compulsive insistence of this twice-asserted assumption can only come from what for Best is the urgency of recognizing the pollutive danger that the incidence of blackness in England represents, a danger that can only be contained by recognizing it as a social disease to be discouraged. This is the exclusion of blackness from English normativeness, in effect its outlawing.

At the same time, the precisionism of Best's observations overall gives both his description and his analysis more than an anecdotal or symbolic weight. It gives them the semblance of a reasoned, learned knowledge, precisely what even today in the reckoning of some like Alan Cooke' appears to be "sound scholarship" and "judicious conclusions."[116] In light of his patronage by Christopher Hatton, who by 1578 was the queen's Vice-Chamberlain and one of her most closely attached counselors, Best's attitude toward black people and the defiling effect of their assimilatory marriages has even more serious implications. By the 1580s Christopher Hatton was living in Ely House in Holborn, the Bishop of Ely's manor that he acquired with the queen's help, and which is located on the city's northwest side near Westminster and Whitehall, the government's seat of residence. Best's attachment to Hatton therefore also connects him to the physical locale of governmental deliberations and activity. Furthermore, given the fact of Elizabeth's direct involvement in Frobisher's project overall, including her personal attendance at the departure of the ships of his first voyage,[117] what Best is verbalizing is arguably compatible with, and has the stamp of, high Elizabethan authority. The prohibition of blackness as an acceptable English human physiognomy in Best's critique of African–English unions is thus potentially coterminous with seeds of Elizabethan government thought, and the germ of something that will eventually become official policy. It is perhaps therefore not a coincidence that when such a policy does in fact emerge at the end of the century, it does so shortly after the re-issuance of Best's chronicle by Hakluyt.

116 "Best (Beste), George."

117 Elizabeth apparently saw off the ship as it set sail, according to an eyewitness on board one of the ships: "Her Majesty beholding the same commended it, and bade us farewell by shaking her hand at us out of the windowe"; cited by A. B. Becher, "The Voyages of Martin Frobisher," p. 3.

Comparable responses to historical Elizabethan black people also occur in medical records and proverbial discourse, as in slightly different ways they too convey an assumption of blackness as an ailment with characteristic symptoms and virulent traits to be carefully treated. The best instance of this is in the medical casebooks of the ill-reputed Elizabethan physician Simon Forman, in which he entered on 5 May 1597 his diagnosis of a young African maidservant who was brought to him for treatment: "Polonia the blackmor maid at Mr Peirs of 12 yeare old" (Item 223).[118] Forman was living at this time either in the "Stone House" that is the re-vestry of St. Botolph's, Billingsgate, or in another stone house close by in Philpot Lane off Thames Street, since he himself sometimes mentions living in Philpot Lane.[119] This location, on the right of Gracious Street and New Fish Street coming up from London bridge, and adjoining East cheap to its immediate left (Agas map 5R, p. 25), is a poor neighborhood that is in Stow's unflattering description "no great thing" and filled with "diverse strangers" who "are there harbored," and who according to an unnamed city census that he cites numbers 30 households.[120] This demographic profile fits and connects with the general character of east London, seen earlier to have numerous black people in it, Billingsgate Ward being immediately adjacent to Tower Ward to its right, and Langbourn and Aldgate Wards above it to its northeast. The "Mr. Peirs," who is not listed in the *Returns of Aliens* of 1593, is a possibly English merchant living in this locality, who like his English or alien colleagues in East London has an African that he has either acquired himself or procured from them. The young black girl is probably a maid to Peirs's wife, who has brought her to Forman for some consultations regarding her indisposed condition, as a protection of the investment that the black girl represents for her and her husband. Peirs's wife is thus the "Mrs. (mistress)" who is mentioned in the notation of the incident, her consultation of Forman being compatible with the predominance of female clients in the 8,000 entries in Forman's casebooks.[121]

Consistent with the wealth of information about the quotidian problems of average Elizabethan Londoners that both Lauren Kassel and Barbara Traister have found Forman's voluminous casebook entries to contain, despite their persistent illegibility, his obscurely readable notation of the young black girl's case offers some penetrating insights about both the untold physical conditions of black lives in the city and the kind of cultural constructions that were put on the consequences

118 I am indebted to Barbara Traister for bringing this record to my attention.

119 Barbara Traister, *The Notorious Astrological Physician of London*, n. 62, pp. 229–30. That Forman is living at this address in 1597 is indicated when three years earlier on 8 March 1594 in one of the several Censorial hearings of his illegal medical practice that extend over his adult life, he is listed as living at the Stone House, St Botolph's Billingsgate ("Simon Forman," in Margaret Pelling, *Physicians and Irregular Medical Practitioners of London*).

120 *Survey of London*, 1: 208.

121 Lauren Kassel, "How to Read Simon Forman's Casebooks," p. 5. Kassel also points out on the same page: "Forman's casebooks document that in addition to consulting him more often than men for cases of illness, women were also more inclined to consult him about non-medical cases, to come to him in person, and to ask him questions on behalf of other people … gender emerges, not only as a factor influencing who consulted Forman in the first place, but as an integral component in what happened in the consulting room."

of those physical conditions by the English to naturalize and perpetuate them. The "fainte harte full of melancholy and cold humors mixed with collar" that Forman finds in her is resonantly descriptive of the stark terror and extreme dispiritedness of an enslaved young 12-year-old black girl in her state of captivity, and particularly in the face of what to her presumably are unintelligible owners who demand instant work ability and compliance in satisfaction of their money's worth in her purchase. Her indisposition may therefore simply be a transparent response to her helpless historical situation, lost irretrievably in the multiple links of human trafficking that have brought her far from home to a strange and hostile land. To her owners of course that response is her ingrained recalcitrance, a temperamental and physiological trait typical both of her people and her class, as can be seen in the turgidly melancholic and treacherous personalities given to blackamoor maids in the popular drama of the time.[122] It is a trait that needs to be, and can be, manipulated into conformity, hopefully in the hands of someone like Forman, who was popularly known to be able to bring about such transformations in forgetful husbands, wayward wives, and ailing lovers.[123] To the quack healer, drawing on the hucksterism of his professional class and humoral medical practice, the African girl's therapeutic treatment involved choosing a propitious astrological moment in which the undesirable behavior's host fluids inside her must be "purg[ed]." This, like George Best's conviction about the natural infection of black people, is the branding of them with an undesirable essential pathology that in its purgative excision in Polonia is simultaneously marked for social prohibition. The virulence of blackness's disease may also be present in another entry on the previous page of the same volume of Forman's casebooks, in his cryptic notation of a woman named Martha Skelton, who while not having a specific ailment is said to have "loved one in her ferst yers a Blackman."[124]

That blackness's constructed virulence is a poison that can on occasion be an extreme cure for a deadly condition is also discernible in the popularity of the early modern recommendation for eradicating venereal disease: sexual intercourse with a black woman. Even if Italian medical sources such as Ercole Sassonia and Julius Caesar Scaliger are associated with this apocryphal belief, that the saying is known in Elizabethan England may be evident, in the opinion of some scholars, in Launcelot Gobbo's enigmatic reply to Lorenzo's accusation of his having impregnated an unnamed offstage black woman in Shakespeare's *The Merchant of Venice*: "It is much that the Moor should be more than reason" (3.5.34–35). Gobbo's reply could mean his acceptance of the charge and his explanation of it as his medical need to sleep with a black woman.[125] In any case, this apocryphal context could explain the

---

[122] See my essay, "'Hel's Perfect Character' or the Blackamoor Maid in Early Modern English Drama."

[123] Kassel, "How to Read," pp. 3–4.

[124] Forman's Casebooks, vol. 226, Ashmole Collection, Bodleian Library, Oxford.

[125] For the apocryphal saying see Winfried Schleiner, *Medical Ethics in the Renaissance*, 201 n. 38, who locates it in Sassonia's *Luis venereae perfectissimus tractatus*, c. 37, fol. 40 (Padua, 1597); cited in Martin Japtok and Winfried Schleiner, "Genetics and 'Race' in *The Merchant of Venice*," 24 n. 67. Japtok and Schleiner add that while not widely published because of its controversial nature, the proverbial cure is listed in Theodor Zwinger's encyclopedic commonplace book (p. 168). The reference is to the *Theatrum vitæ humanæ*,

inevitable formal sexual exploitation of black women as prostitutes in Elizabethan London that Peter Fryer has said is one of three destinies of English black people at that time, and that is noticeable in the letter of Dennis Edwards to Thomas Lankford, the Earl of Hartford's secretary, on 28 May 1599, asking him to "Pray enquire and secure my negress; she is certainly at the Swan, at the Dane's beershop, Turnbull Street, Clerkenwell" (Item 235). The "stews" of Clerkenwell in northwest London, diagonally northwest beyond Aldersgate, was at this time one of the most notorious brothels of the city, particularly along Turnbull or Turnmill street, as it is sometimes called. Added to this is the fact that, as both A. L. Beier and Roger Finlay, and Johannes Fabricius in his study of syphilis in Elizabethan England, have explained, Elizabethan beer shops or alehouses were the equivalent of modern social clubs in which all manner of sexual liaisons were arranged and conducted.[126] If the "negress" is not the infamous prostitute Lucy Negro that I have elsewhere proposed she is, she is certainly one of her colleagues, and Dennis Edwards's proprietary addressing of her illuminates the sexual bondage within she is cast.[127] Her sexual exploitation as a prostitute is the most vicious form of the performance of a negative pathology for black people, particularly young black women, in which the only use that destitute enslaved black females can have is as casual sexual conveniences for the male public at large. Muted by her linguistic and cultural alienation, and incarcerated within economic and physical bonds, her compliance in her use as a sexual consumable is the ultimate cancellation of her black humanity and her final exclusion from the normative life of the English socius.

The marking of blackness as a prohibited social pathology in its deployment in the sexual commodification of black women is manifest at this same time in two Bridewell court records of 10 and 13 February 1598, about a black woman named Barbary Moore who was procured as a prostitute for Robert Everett by Alice Morise, "fishwife" (Items 231, 232). Several details in the two records spell out this scenario. First, Barbary Moore's blackness is self-evident from both her names, each of which is identical to informal ethnic descriptors seen many times in this book, although unusually she has two of them, of which the first may be a deliberate punning conflation of the Christian English name of Barbara with the African coastal place name of Barbary. Her black identity is also circumstantially suggested by the fact that Chick Lane in Tower Ward, running past All Hallows Barking, is in the immediate vicinity of locations already seen to contain numerous black people—

published in Paris in 1571. For the connection of this saying to the scene in Shakespeare's play, see Japtok and Schleiner's essay, p. 167.

[126] For the stews of Clarkenwell see Pinks, *The History of Clerkenwell*, pp. 338–39, 342–43, esp. p. 343, and pp. 695–96 for a list of brothels there, and Ian Archer, *Pursuit of Stability*, p. 213. There may be an allusion to a brown, i.e. black, prostitute in Clerkenwell in John Donne's *Polydoron*: "Things proffered and easie come by diminish themselves in reputation and price; for how full of pange and dotage is a wayling lover for it may be some browne Bessie? But let a beautie fall weeping overpressed with the sick passions, she savours in our thoughts of Turnbull"; cited by Pinks, p. 343. For the social character of Elizabethan drinking houses, see A. L. Beier and Roger Finlay, *London 1500–1700*, "Introduction," pp. 21–23, and Johan Fabricius, *Syphilis in Shakespeare's England*, pp. 98–99.

[127] See my book, *Shakespeare and Race*, pp. 13, 25, 30, 78.

such as St. Olave, Hart Street, All Hallows Staining, and St. Botolph Billingsgate (Agas map 6T, p. 25). Second, within the typically early modern ambiguity of the term "fishwife"—which could designate the traditional medieval European raucous street fish seller or the more socially elevated wife of a fish merchant—it is more probably the latter identity that is Alice Morise's since the record locates her in the fixed residence of a house in Chick Lane. It is that social ability, rather than the much more limited resources and credibility of a street side fish hawker, that can more plausibly enable the sexual assignation that the record describes her to have arranged, as well as explain her class access to an African in bondage. Third, that the event is a sexual assignment for Barbary Moore is apparent from the lack of any mention in the records of any prior attachment between her and Everett, their coming together in Alice's house seeming to be solely for the purpose of a sexual transaction. Finally, that the sexual assignment is an induced one is strongly evident from Alice Morise's personal supervision of its completion, as she "suffer[s] them to lye both together in one bedd having but one rome and did sitt upp in the rome all night having a candell lighted all night whilest the sayd Everett had the use of the body of the sayd Barbary." Notable here is the watchfulness and longevity of the supervision, stressed in the repetition of it having lasted "all night," and which clearly hints at the possibility of Barbary's recalcitrance and of Alice's continuous expensive coercion.

That Barbary was nevertheless punished together with the others points merely to the historical incommunicability of her people, unable, on arrival and long after, to perform the language and the culture of the land in which they are incarcerated. This is the incommunicability that exists beneath Barbary's spoken-over reported speech in her interrogation (when she is "exaied"), which is part of what William Hamlyn and Chandra de Silva in different ways have shown is the imaginary self-interested interpretation of non-European speech by European interlocutors in their encounters with non-Europeans in the early modern era, and which is still universally an unrecognized problem in critical scholarship.[128] More importantly, the indifferent callousness of Barbary's sentencing is the recognition by the Bridewell Court authorities, who in their function of social rehabilitation represent the government's moral values and civic codes, of the valuelessness of her social being and in that, an official validation of the dismissal of her black life to a nameless chattel sexual existence.

This emergence of blackness as a dismissible social pathology in the Elizabethan period can be sensed as well in other civic hearings and several law cases in London extending over the last three decades of the sixteenth century. The first of these, which also involves a prostitution case, is manifest in an earlier record of Bridewell court in London in 1577, in the legal charges brought against two prostitutes, Elizabeth Kirkham and Rose Brown, in which the former testified that "Rose Browne is a bawd and a whore to the saide Elizabeth Kirkham and others Elizabeth sayeth that the same Rose had dyvers & many blackamores and other persons resort to her

[128] William Hamlin, "Imagined Apotheosis: Drake, Harriot, and Raleigh in the Americas," pp. 409–410; Çhandra de Silva, "Beyond the Cape: The Portuguese Encounter with the Peoples of South Asia," pp. 308–22. Also see Charles Meyers's comments about the veracity of testimony supposedly acquired from non-English speaking black people in the Hector Nonnez case discussed below.

house whilst this Elizabeth dwelt there" (Item 144). The details of this case, as explained by Duncan Salkeld in his study of the case, include the facts that Elizabeth Kirkham was one of the many prostitutes of Gilbert East who was running a large prostitution ring in Turnmill street in Clerkenwell in tandem with Black Lucy, who had her own brothel. The members of this ring are those whom the Bridewell court authorities, engaged as they are with rehabilitative rather than penal prosecution of socially deviant individuals, are interrogating after they have been brought in by the beadles and constables of the city when they broke up the ring. Elizabeth Kirkham's testimony, like those of East and several others appearing before the court and in the typical culture of criminal confessions, is aimed at incriminating her co-sex workers in an attempt to lighten her own culpability.[129] What is of interest here is the casual mention of multiple black people among the alleged clients of Rose Brown, who herself could be an African.[130]

In the visible landscape of the case's proceedings, the location of the black individuals is revealing in the way it shows the surreal existence of black people in the eyes of the law. Situated below and beyond the level of legal examination, and hence of visibility, the blacks are only momentary backdrops to the scene, the desiderata of the actions of the scene's principal players. Invoked in the vague nameless plurality of "dyvers & many," they are not formed legal entities, just elements in the legal construction of the criminality of others. Not even criminals, they are the substance of which criminality is made and the attributes of it. Required for the substantiation of Rose Browne's venality (either as instances of the dubiety of her customers or as exemplifications of the opprobrious traffic being generated by her close colleague, Black Lucy, who as Lucy Baynham may be a black woman according to Salkeld),[131] they are the signs of a moral baseness and not the possessors of it. They are not asked to appear, as they otherwise might have been, because they have no legal form or shape in themselves.[132] Authorized by the historical reality of their numbers across London at this time, their use in law is nevertheless a fiction that can magically give them the quadruple agencies of financial ability, leisure time, free movement within the city, and sexual consumerism (the "many & diverse" who "resort" to Rose Browne's house) which their material experience need never provide. They are, in short, what they are required to be, evidentiary human simulacra rather than independent agents in the confirmation or contestation of phenomena. Unlike the initially defined legal humanity of Jacques Francis in the Admiralty case of 1547–48 discussed in the last chapter, Elizabethan blacks in law, such as those in the Elizabeth Kirkham and Rose Browne hearing, are the fictional exceptions of their legal non-being.

Exactly a decade later, in 1587 in a Court of Requests hearing in London, a Portuguese physician by the name of Hector Novimeis complained that his newly

129 Duncan Salkeld, "Black Lucy and the 'Curtizans' of Shakespeare's London," p. 13.

130 This, from her surname, and judging from John Donne's earlier cited allusion to "brown" women in Clerkenwell (see discussion of Dennis Edwards's letter above).

131 Salkeld, "Black Lucy," p. 13.

132 As I point out below in connection with another case, their proxy testimony cannot be simply said to be a matter of their illiteracy or of their linguistic inability, because the same factors did not preclude the black diver's appearance in court in 1548.

purchased black Ethiopian slave "vtterly refuseth to tarry and serve" him. Since he "hath not any ordinarye remedie at and by the corse of the comon Lawes" of the country, his appeal to the court is either to "compel the sayde Ethiopian to serve him during his liffe" or to "recover his sayd ffowre poundes Tenne shillings" from the English sailor who sold him the slave (Item 165).[133] Contrary to what Roslyn Knutson proposed in her study of the incident,[134] the case's particulars cannot be said to describe the legal prohibition of slavery in England at this time, since the hearing's results and the court's final disposition are unknown. Even if eighteen years earlier in the very similar case cited in the last chapter the court did decide against the plaintiff on precisely the grounds that Knutson infers, that case involved not a black individual but a Russian.[135] Rather, and more importantly, the case shows the anamorphism of the black person's legal existence.

The pressure on the Portuguese physician's contractual rights here stems from the obscurity of the black person's human definition in law. Neither a servant (according to the history of his relationship to the physician), nor a slave (according to existing statutory laws, since Novimeis "hath not any ordinarye remedie at and by the corse of the comon Lawes"), the black person is removed from legal sight, and, by analogy, from court appearance. What he is humanly, and what he might have to say, has no meaning or consequence in these proceedings. His "vtter refus[al] … to serve" is a negative agency that facilitates his legal obliteration, because his mandate to act comes from no communal epistemology that the socius's laws can reflect. As he cannot be what the higher Chancery courts of equity that have already turned down Novimeis insist on making him out to be—a servant with specific human rights, and as he cannot be what Novimeis wants this lower appellate court to make him be—a slave (either compelled or returned), he exists neither in the high road nor in the margins of the law. As he has no specific legal habitation, so he has no marked legal existence. From the palpably defined legal space that he or she had until 1547–48, the early modern English black has now become an always-already-lost legal subject.

The very next year in March 1587/88, in a piece of prolonged litigation in London, the Court of Queen's Bench heard a lawsuit for outstanding debts against the same Portuguese Marrano physician Hector Nonnez discussed earlier (Item 169). The lawsuit, initially against Nonnez and subsequently his widow, was brought on by his chief creditor Andrew Broome, and by Mrs. Mary May, the widow of Nonnez's other chief creditor, Richard May. The object of the suit, which went on to the Court of Chancery and dragged on till 1599 beyond the death of Nonnez himself in September 1591, was to extract from the prosperous physician and his survivors financial satisfaction for the unpaid obligations incurred by him in his many venture capital trading enterprises in the Iberian peninsula and the Low Countries, from what is felt to be his still considerable assets despite the family's assertions of economic distress. The prosecution's case includes the testimony by proxy of two blackamoor maids in the employ of the Nonnez's kinsman Ferdinando Alvarez. The black maids'

---

[133] Gustav Ungerer assumes without explanation that Novimeis is Nonnez ("Recovering a Black African's Voice in an English Lawsuit," p. 264).

[134] "A Caliban in St. Mildred Poultry," p. 116.

[135] *Matter of Cartwright* 11 Elizabeth; 2.

testimony is a part of the prosecution's attempt to reveal, through an exposure of the family's allegedly typical Jewish secretiveness and ingrained duplicity, its long-established but now hidden wealth. The case's outcome, which is recorded as being partly in favor of the plaintiff,[136] is irrelevant here, but not its details.[137]

Hector Nonnez's individual and community history yields a very useful perspective for understanding the history and nature of a significant part of early modern English black life. His particular background provides an important reminder of one of the most important sources for the entry of black people into England throughout the sixteenth century. These sources are Spanish, Portuguese contacts, extending from Anglo-Spanish monarchic entourages at the beginning of the century that included black personnel, to both kidnapped and domesticated blacks purchased either from Spanish Portuguese merchants resident in London or bartered or seized by English privateers such as Francis Drake and John Hawkins from Spanish and Portuguese galleys and carracks on the high seas, and including black arrivals in England in the household staff of successful and upwardly mobile expatriate Marrano professionals such as Nonnez and his close friend and colleague, Roderigo Lopez, fleeing from Catholic persecution of Jews in Spain and Portugal.[138] Even though both Nonnez and Lopez shot to the top of the London medical practice scene—with Lopez ending up as the queen's personal physician in little more than a decade after his arrival in the 1570s—their lives reflect the double pressures under which they are lived, first as perennially suspicious Jewish converts and potential Spanish Catholic spies (the latter costing Lopez his life in 1594), and secondly as disadvantaged non-native English immigrants, always subject to linguistic mistranslation and cultural offense.[139] As this double suppression extends compoundedly to the black people in their households, it becomes a cogent context for the civic and legal disembodiment of the black subject.

As in the previous two cases considered, the black presence in the Nonnez suit is the mythic anomaly of the real norm of its erasure in law. Spoken through a white servant of Alvarez named Thomas Wilson, and functioning as his free memories of the maids' many observations of alleged Jewish rituals practiced in that household,[140] the black maids' testimony, who in their exclusion from court are effectively gagged and spoken for, is the made-over speech of evidence without speakers, which is to say, the free-floating testimony of virtual witnesses. Their very virtuality is their

---

136 National Archives, Kew, C 33/94, p. 822, 14 June 1599; cited by Meyers, "Lawsuits in Elizabethan Courts of Law," p. 163.

137 Equally irrelevant is the other parallel lawsuit against Nonnez's widow that Broome started in the Court of Requests in 1591, after Nonnez died, and continued till 1597, demanding payment for a fly-boat purchase that Nonnez had secured with Broome's backing in 1590 while simultaneously reclaiming a wool export patent that according to Broome Nonnez had sold to him in 1591 in a desperate effort to clear his debts (National Archives, Kew, Req 2/64/22/F.1 1591). The outcome of this suit is unknown.

138 As I have pointed out earlier, and as most of the examples cited above show, the majority of the records of Elizabethan black people seem to indicate a Spanish-Portuguese origin for this population.

139 For discussions of both these figures see David Katz, *Jews in the History of England*, pp. 104–7, and James Shapiro, *Shakespeare and the Jews*, pp. 248–51.

140 Charles Meyers, "Elizabethan Marranos Unmasked".

usefulness in law since they can provide examples of human action without needing the space of human actors themselves. Their virtuality is the blank of their legal being on which any law and any transgression can be demonstrated and for which their linguistic and cultural alienness are both mandate and exception. Thus what Charles Meyers in his study of the case's documents regards as the problems of the black maids' evidence,[141] is in this view the identifying signature of their only kind of legal existence. Unseen, unnamed, and verbally possessed, they are the enablers of the law's expedient performance, their legal spectrality the pliant grounds on which its limits can be tested and reset.

V

If, together with the deployment of blackness as a condemnable pathology in the attitudes of George Best and Dennis Edwards, the Bridewell hearings, and the Court of Request and the Queen's bench and Chancery cases have served to exemplify the progressive debarment of the black subject from the human domain of Tudor legal performance compared to his legal status until 1547–48, Elizabeth I's three decrees in 1596 and 1601 expelling blacks altogether from England may be seen as the logical outcome of this development, as the formal outlawing of the black. Issued first on 11 July 1596, and repeated a week later on 18 July 1596, and finally reissued on 16 January 1601, the orders explain the deportation of blacks first as a necessity for recompensing a Dutch merchant named Casper van Senden for his rescue and transportation to England of several Englishmen languishing in Spanish jails, secondly to regulate an over-numerous black population, and thirdly to relieve economic pressure in the country in trying times:

> … Her Ma[jes]tie understanding that there are of late divers Blackmoores brought into the Realme, of which kinde of people there are all ready here to manie, consideringe howe God hath blessed this land w[i]th great increase of people of our owne Nation as anie Countrie in the world, wherof manie for want of Service and meanes to sett them on worck fall to Idlenesse and to great extremytie; Her Ma[jesty']s pleasure therefore ys, that those kinde of people should be sent forthe of the lande … to the nomber of Tenn …. (Item 214)

In the interests of keeping the exchange financially equitable for van Senden, the second order increases the numbers of deported blacks from the 10 mentioned in the first order to 89, which would match the number of Englishmen brought back:

> Whereas Casper van Senden a merchant of Lubeck did by his labor and travell procure 89 of her Ma[jesty's] subiectes that were detayned prisoners in Spaine and Portugall to be released, and brought them hither into this Realme at his owne cost and charges, for the w[hi]ch his expences and declaration of his honest minde towardes those prizoners, he only desireth to have lycense to take up so many Blackamoores here in this Realme and to transport them into Spaine and Portugall. Her Ma[jes]ty in regard of the charitable affection the supli[ant] hathe shewed … doth thincke yt a very good exchange and that those kinde of people may be well spared in this Realme being so populous and nombers

141 Ibid.

> of hable persons the subiects of the land and xpian [*Christian*] people that perishe for want of service, whereby through their labor they might be mayntained. (Item 215)

It may be worth noting that the use of the word "populous" in the line in which it occurs does not signify the second order's scope applying literally to a limited number of black people, as has recently been suggested by Emily Bartels. Bartels's assertion, which is made within a circuitous defensive argument that attempts to explain the first two orders primarily as compulsions of continuing tense Anglo–Spanish relations at the end of the century, reads "populous" as qualifying "those kinds of people" to assert that Elizabeth "may also be hinting that there will still be plenty of "blackamoors" to go around after the deportation. Indeed, her first pronouncement (in 1596) that "'there are allready here to manie' may itself imply that there will always be enough."[142] Given the informality and imprecision of early modern English linguistic usage, Bartels's misreading may be understandable, especially in light of the specific number of 89 mentioned earlier in the order, and in the context of the first order's description of black people in England as "there are all ready here to manie." But, *in context*, "populous" cannot refer to "those kinds of people," since the word's closest preceding syntactical referent is not "those kinds of people" but "this realm." Furthermore, "populous" leads directly to the reassertion of numerous, available poor English people who are able but unemployed because of black people: "nombers of hable persons the subiects of the land and xpian [*Christian*] people that perishe for want of service, whereby through their labor they might be maintained." The "sparing" of black people can only make sense in the context of a "populous" English "realm" that has enough of an able and available labor force to meet its needs. The "populous"-ness of the "realm" has already been highlighted in the first order's reminder of the "great increase of people of our owne Nation as anie Countrie in the world, wherof manie for want of Service and meanes to sett them on worck fall to Idlenesse and to great extremytie." Propelled by the pliable instincts of racial debarment, the "nombers" of black people have in the purview of the first and the second orders a magical elasticity, being few enough to be "89" and large enough to threaten local employment conditions, and constitute thus a kind of verbal shorthand for any and all black people.

Four years later, while keeping all the arguments the same the order removes all limits from the number of blacks to be deported:

> Whereas the Queen's Majesty, tendering the good and welfare of her own naturall subjects, greatly distressed in these hard times of dearth, is highly discontented to understand the great numbers of Negroes and Blackamoors, which (as she is informed) are crepte into this realme … who are fostered and powered here to the great annoyance of her own leige people that which covet the relief which these people consume, as also for that the most of them are infidels, having no understanding of Christ or the gospels … hath given a special commandment that the said kind of people shall be with all speed be avoided and discharged out of her majesty's realms. (Item 246)[143]

---

142 Bartels, "Too Many Blackamoors: Deportation, Discrimination, and Elizabeth I," p. 315.

143 Hughes and Larkin's transcription of this order (*Tudor Royal Proclamations*, 3: 221–22), which is the version frequently cited in scholarship, and which is based on John Roche Dasent's

Notably, this third order adds religious deficiency as a further justification for the deportation. As the numbers of blacks to be expelled increases, together with the justifications, so does the compulsiveness and desperation of the orders, becoming in the last instance a flat command with chilling consequences for non-compliance:

> These therefore be to will and require you and everyone of you … and if there shall be any person or persons which be possessed of such blackamoors that refuse to deliver them, then we require you to call them before you and to advise and persuade them with all good means to satisfy her majesty's pleasure therein; which if they shall eftsoone willfully and obstinately refuse, we pray you, to certify their names to us … .

Taken together, the three orders seem to describe three progressive phases in the legal effacement of black people in the Elizabethan period. The first two orders, in their semi-apologetic tone ("consideringe howe God hath blessed this land," and "to worke the delivery of our contrymen … could not be don w[i]thout great expence and also considering the reasonablenes of his requestes"), and their evasive conditionality ("take of those Blackmoores that in this last voyage under Sir Thomas Baskervile, were brought into this Realme to the nomber of Tenn" and "take up suche Blackamores … w[i]th consent of their masters"), seem to reflect the awkwardness and tentativeness of the resolve, while the third increases its confidence, total scope, and absolute finality ("hath given a special commandment," "these therefore to require … and if there be any person or persons which … willfully and obstinately refuse … certify their names to us …."). Whereas the first order is addressed to a typical catalog of officials ("the L[ord] Maiour of London and th'alermen his brethren, And to all other Maiours, Sheryfes, &c"), the second adds an insistently open range ("the L[ord] Maiour of London and to all other vyceadmyralles, Maiours and other publicke officers whatsoever to whom yt may appertaine"), which the third makes absolute in its address simply to "you and every of you." In all three orders, the restless movement between different justifications for the removal of black people—their excessive numbers, the country's food scarcities, rising unemployment pressures, and finally, their religious, i.e. cultural incompatibility—describes the inevitable expedience of legal performance that seizes the prohibited being of the unprocessed black human subject to mark the limits of the English socius's political corpus. In the manner of what Michael Hardt and Antonio Negri have termed the "negative dialectics of recognition,"[144] the three orders identify black people only to mark them for legal exclusion. If in the later Tudor years blacks are illegal shadows politically, Elizabeth's orders make them legal outlaws and exiles, converting unofficial and ambiguous black presence into official black absence.

---

frequently incorrect transcription of the MS (*Acts of the Privy Council*, 30: 733), is wrong in, among other things, the use of the words "carried over" since the original has "crepte." My citation here and in the "Chronological Record Index" is from the facsimile copy of the original MS that Eldred Jones provided in his *The Elizabethan Image of Africa* on p. 19. The date of the order is January 1601.

[144] Michael Hardt and Antonio Negri, *Empire*, p. 128.

VI

For the mass of data presented in this chapter, it might be useful to observe some patterns in it despite its necessarily provisional nature. Over the 45 years of Elizabeth's reign there are 89 citations of black people, with at least 95 black individuals of variable ethnic transparency appearing in them. Of these 89 records, seven are from royal and aristocratic household accounts, 16 from Census and Tax records, 56 from the parish registers, two from personal descriptions, one from medical literature, four from legal records, with three royal proclamations about black people completing the tally. Within the largest group, that of the parish registers, 32 occur in the 32 years between 1558 and 1590, while 24 appear in the last dozen years alone, between 1591 and 1603. At the same time, of the 89 total Elizabethan black citations 41 are of attached black people, of which 17 occur in the first four decades of Elizabeth's reign combined, whereas there are 24 such citations in the last decade alone (see Table 2.1). Within the group of records of destitute black people, the greatest frequencies of citation are, in an ascending order, in the first, middle, and last decade of Elizabeth's reign, which coincides roughly with the three government encouragements of trading forays to Africa in 1562–63, 1585, and 1592.

Table 2.1 Frequency of Elizabethan black citations

Type	**Number of citations**	**Period**	**Frequency of occurrence**
All	89	45 years (Total)	1.97
Attached	17	32 years (1558–90)	1 in 1.88 years
Attached	24	13 years (1590–1603)	1.8 per year

Locational patterns indicated by the records point to the city's west and east sides as the zones of greatest black presence, followed by the central areas of the city, with few black people being mentioned in the city's northern or southern suburbs. This corresponds to the patterns of alien settlement noted by Linda Yungblut in her study of the Elizabethan alien censuses and surveys, and to the areas of immigrant settlement listed by A. L. Beier.[145] The ratio of black men to women, which is a more viable statistic in the Elizabethan period than earlier, is 47 male citations to 49 female for the totality of the Elizabethan records, double-counting entries that either cite both men and women or include them implicitly. Among the records of abandoned Africans the breakdown is 26 women to 15 men, double-counting both the unnamed black women involved in the base-born births as well as their male offspring. Of these numbers, between 1565 and 1590 there are only eight black women, whereas for the years 1591 to 1603 that number goes up to 18. For the men

[145] Yungblut, *Strangers Settled Here*, pp. 25–29; Beier, "Social Problems in Elizabethan London," p. 208.

the converse is true, with nine black men recorded between 1565 and 1590 and only six in the 1591–1603 period (see Table 2.2).

Table 2.2 Gender breakdown of Elizabethan black citations

Type	Period	Male	Female
All	1558–1603	47	49
Unattached (abandoned, destitute)	1558–1603	26	15
Unattached (abandoned, destitute)	1565–90	9	8
Unattached (abandoned, destitute)	1591–1603	6	18

Other patterns are also discernible in the Elizabethan record data. With a few exceptions, the living situations of black people revealed in the data span a range from menial work, albeit with skills, to chattel existence, including prostitution, with the last two categories constituting the clear majority. Among the different kinds of work black people clearly or implicitly appear to be performing in the records even in their disregarded lives are metal goods production, cloth manufacturing and retail, beer production and retail, sexual service, ceremonial (decorative) household service, and menial domestic labor either as servants or as unspecified chattel possessions of their owners. If destitute Africans first appear in 1565 and sporadically thereafter, possession of multiple Africans by single foreign and English individuals such as Hector Nonnez, Paul Baning, Mrs. Barker, and formations of micro communities of Africans in the same neighborhoods or city areas including groups of black working women, as well as occurrences of inter-racial unions, begin to be visible toward the middle decades. It is at this same point too that instances of the sexual oppression of black women in the citations of "base born" births begin to emerge in the records.

Some important conclusions flow naturally from these statistical overviews. 89 black citations in 45 years means that on average 1.97, or nearly two, black records appear in each year of the last Tudor's reign.[146] Of these, records of black people appear continuously from 1582 every year until Elizabeth's death. This is to say that black people are a pervasive, repetitive, and accelerating presence in Elizabethan London, and unavoidably therefore a part of the city's collective social consciousness. Furthermore, contributing as they do to the city's manufacturing, trade, and service industries, they are part of the metropolis's growing resources and strengths. Additionally, if the adjusted total number of records is multiplied by a factor of 10 to estimate the real value of the symptomatic total number of black

[146] This ratio is calculated by dividing the total number of the Elizabethan records by the total years for the regime rather than by the number of years between the dates of the first and last records in it, in order to see these records against the totality of their particular political and historical epoch rather than as a part of them. If the total number of Elizabethan records is juxtaposed only against the range of the specific years of their occurrence, i.e. 89 records in 36 years, the ratio is much higher—2.47.

people mentioned in the records (that is, to include black individuals not documented, or missed by this study), that produces a possible real figure of nearly 900 black people in Elizabethan London.[147] Even that is a conservative projection because, as the records of this chapter show, one record can cite several black individuals. Still, out of a possible total London population of 200,000 in 1600, close to 900 black people might seem to constitute a minuscule percentage, less than 1 percent.[148] But that minuscule percentage is approximately 18 percent to 15 percent of the estimated 5,000–6,000 immigrants in Elizabethan London at the end of the sixteenth century.[149] If the "suburbs, with their population of casual laborers and unassimilated artisans, immigrants and paupers, [are] outstripping the city of London in growth," that is precisely where the largest numbers of black people are located.[150] If immigrants are the city's fresh lifeblood, what the city "need[s] to sustain its population growth," if they are what helps to "shape the path of England's future economic development," if in short they are the vital impetus toward the growing international capital that London is well on the way to becoming by the time of Elizabeth's death, the city's black population has to be regarded as a credible part of that emergence.[151]

Yet, the contributions of black people and their expanding numerical footprint are in inverse proportion to the social repugnance and cultural expungement they inspire. It is significant that in all of the Elizabethan records there is not a single instance of an African in a discernibly independent recognized public role as there was in the early Tudor period. While this may be in part due to the particular history of Elizabethan Africans, that fact should also make clear the political nature of this history. At the end of the first decade of their arrival in steady numbers and their settlement struggle, George Best's description of them as "a naturall infection" in 1578 denotes the beginning of their concomitant historical denigration and excision. This is a process that appears sporadically in the civic hearings and court papers, in which the legal construction of blackness as an illicit pathology starts to take shape. Physically needed but culturally forbidden, black people come to occupy an ambiguous zone in the penumbra of legal and historical sight, present but unseen. The culmination of this process is Elizabeth's

---

[147] For a statement of the necessity of inflating primary population data of the early modern English period by as much as 10 percent to get a true estimate, see Finlay and Shearer, "Population Growth and Suburban Expansion in Beier and Finlay, eds., *London*, p. 54.

[148] For the standard estimate of London's population in 1600, see Beier and Finlay, eds., *London*, p. 42. Also see David Harris Sacks, "London's Dominion," p. 22; Harding, "City, Capital, and Metropolis," p. 117; Archer, "Material Londoners?," p. 176.

[149] Beier, "Social Problems in Elizabethan London," p. 205; Archer, *Pursuit of Stability*, pp. 132, 150; Sacks, "London's Dominion," p. 23; Yungblut, *Strangers Settled Here*, pp. 19–21. The latest estimated figure of 6,000 is from Keith Wrightson, *Earthly Necessities: Economic Lives in Early Modern Britain*, p. 165.

[150] Lawrence Manley, *Literature and Culture in Early Modern London*, p. 125.

[151] For the palpable necessity of immigrants in Elizabethan London, see Archer, *Pursuit of Stability*, pp. 132–34, and Yungblut, *Strangers Settled Here*, pp. 95–96, 102–3, 106–11, 113, and Beier, "Social Problems in Elizabethan London," p. 205. Yungblut's discussion while not confined exclusively to the alien impact on London, includes it. The two quotations about immigrants are from Ian Archer's essay, "Material Londoners?" in Orlin, ed., *Material London*, p. 176, and from Yungblut, p. 113, respectively.

deportation of Africans from England, whose visible ineffectuality, reflected in its incrementally expansive triple repetition and its final grim reference to those "who willfully and obstinately" refuse to comply, profiles the aporetic space within which black people come to exist in London at the end of the sixteenth century—disliked but valued, politically debarred but quietly retained, legally non-existent but historically permanent. To put it in another way, as the physical habitation of black people in and across the Elizabethan metropolis is their possession of English material space, so their documentary occupancy in the city's records is their tenuring in English history, even if a political silence shrouds both appropriations.

This scenario of continuous surreptitious importation of Africans into London, together with their numerical spread across the city and their simultaneous cultural suppression and political and legal effacement, fits a number of analytical perspectives on Elizabeth's reign. Increasingly intransigent and expensive political (religious) and economic problems with the Low Countries and Spain, including tense military stand-offs in the 1580s, coupled with a fourfold increase in the national population between 1500 and 1600, resulted in rising prices of essentials, food scarcities, popular dissension and riots, an increase in the proportion of the London poor greater than that of the city's population, collective xenophobia about aliens, and the "obsessional" surveillance that was the response of the government to perceived challenges to its authority and to fears about alien infiltration and corruption of its national life. These connected perspectives sketched by a variety of standard historical studies plausibly characterize the near half-century of England under Elizabeth.[152] Within this complex interwoven history, the enslaved Africans that arrived in London as a result, as was proposed at the beginning of this chapter, of the mid-century collapse of the cloth export trade and the drive toward an import trade with, among other regions, Africa, are an obviously disadvantaged and victimized group. They are a subaltern population whose cultural rejection and legal debarment are the instant unseen outriders of the civic resentment and expedient government surveillance of and regulations against foreigners that, as was discussed earlier, erupt repeatedly in the last four decades of the century.[153] Furthermore, if Elizabeth's reign is conceived in terms of the two-part schema proposed by some historians, in which the first extending to 1585 is a phase of personal monarchic decisiveness and authority and the second up till Elizabeth's death on 24 March 1603 a period of increasing monarchic debilitation, inactivity, and consequently rulership by default,[154] with the hawkishness of the latter reversing the circumspect and balanced ruling style of the former, the two phases roughly complement the increasing appearance and repression of black people in London before and after 1578.

---

[152] Penry Williams, *The Later Tudors*, pp. 21–30; Alan G. R. Smith, *The Emergence of a Nation State*, pp. 236–41; Jim Sharpe, "Social Strain and Social Dislocation, 1585–1603." For a careful summary of histories of Elizabethan London and England, as well as a considered synthesis, see Ian Archer, *Pursuit of Stability*, pp. 1–14; for statistics on the growth of the poor, see ibid., pp. 152–54.

[153] See the discussions by Ronald Pollit, Linda Yungblut, and Irene Scouladi, cited earlier. For another extended discussion, especially of the waves of anti-alien animosities in Elizabethan London, see Archer, *Pursuit of Stability*, pp. 4–5, 134–35.

[154] John Guy, in Guy, ed., *Reign of Elizabeth I*, "Introduction," pp. 1–19.

If the "crisis" character of the end of the sixteenth century symmetrically recalls that of the mid-century five decades earlier, as two moments in which the cultural and political subjugation of the black subject reaches the level of legal scripting, that parallelism should not elide the greater racial prophylaxis of the Elizabethan moment. Notwithstanding the different administrative purposes of the several kinds of records in the two moments, if the earlier documentations are typically the product of government deliberateness in which the black subject is the object of a proud monarchic exhibition, as is John Blank or Peter Negro, the latter ones are mostly the results of a defensive governmental surveillance in which black people are negligible entities beneath the sweep of its attention and extraneous to it. This is true even for the Elizabethan local parish records, which, while possessing a greater regularity and meticulousness than comparable record-keeping earlier, note black people without particularity and therefore see them without remembering. This is to say, that if earlier the documentary sightline sees the black subject before it has politically processed it, the Elizabethan one sees it as a subject processed out of political sight. What precedes that earlier racial debarment is a curious processing of the black as a liminal, anamorphic political subject, whereas what leads to the attempted deportation of the black at the end of the century is a discontinuous but persistent scripting of it as an already formed illicit pathology marked for the outside of English cultural and political life. If the earlier recording optic culminates in the first prohibitive marking of the black, the latter continues and concludes that marking in its legal cancellation and expulsion of the black subject. It is this incremental but irreversible finalization of the processing of the Elizabethan black person as the detritus of the English socius that is the signal feature of the documentary sightline of this period, and one that has important consequences for the history of English black people in the seventeenth century.

Chapter Three

Black Records of Seventeenth-Century London

A Benign Neglect and the Legislation of Enslavement

"then comes Negers" "not excluded from beauty" "a black handsome wench" "there might be a Property in them"

I

The negative marking of a population is in certain conditions an irreversible process. Bolstered by changing economic necessities, and scripted directly or indirectly into legal thought, it becomes a virulent social infection that perpetuates itself by normalizing the particular conditions that give rise to it in the first place. Thus the racialized effacement of black people at the end of Elizabeth's reign enables a demand for the economic practices that extend that racialization into the next century. Seized expediently as human goods in the mid-sixteenth-century English forays for material goods in Africa, and over the remainder of the century deployed profitably in the emergent slave economies internationally and consolidated gradually as such in English domestic usage, black people become their own justification for their continued trafficking in the regimes of Elizabeth's successors. This is both a social practice and a political phenomenon that lie beneath the major events of seventeenth-century England, and that become visible only when the English slave trade emerges openly in the last quarter of the century. That eventual visibility is paradoxically the completion of the historical denuding of the early modern English black subject, who then appears fully processed as the legally mandated bare object of English colonial enslavement.

Black history from 1603 to 1676 does not follow the mainstream narratives of that century, which is the main reason for its invisibility. The usual topics of seventeenth-century English history, namely the financial and political problems of the reigns of the first Stuarts, the English Revolution, the Puritan government, and the Restoration, do not relate transparently to the black citations in the seventeenth century. As Hugh Thomas has put it, "The eclipse of the monarchy of Charles I, and the coming of a Puritan administration, had no effect on the City of London's desire to make money from slaves; nor did the change in regime after the Restoration of 1660 alter that ambition."[1]

---

1 *The Slave Trade*, p. 197.

The intense debates that have surrounded these topics, and that have characterized modern seventeenth-century English historiography as a whole, may be contextualized by the fact that some aspects of the history of the seventeenth century in England are determined by those of the sixteenth century, discussed in the previous chapter.[2] The economic depression of the seventeenth century, much noted by scholars, produced a population expansion reminiscent of the earlier epoch, as London's population doubled in the first half of the century, going from 200,000 in 1600 to between 375,000 to 400,000 in 1650.[3] If to Thomas Platter in 1599 it was self-evident that "London is not said to be in England but rather England to be in London," to King James I in 1603 it was imminent that "soon London will be all England." To many scholars, London's national impact in the seventeenth century is an extension of its national impact in the sixteenth.[4]

---

[2] For a lucid, even if inevitably judgmental, summary of the historiographic debates about seventeenth-century England, see David Underdown, *A Freeeborn People: Politics and Nation in Seventeenth Century England*, pp. 1–18. Eschewing the Whig view of history focused on a struggle over constitutional principles reflected in J. R. Tanner; the Marxist perspective of historians like R. H. Tawney (and Keith Wrightson, even if Underdown does not mention him) aimed at economic and social change but amounting, in Underdown's casual reckoning, to "no more" than a study of "class struggle"; the Freudian approach of Lewis Namier, Romney Sedgwick, and others interested in "prosopography … and interest or clientage groups"; and what might be construed as the deconstructive methods of Conrad Russell, John Morill, and Kevin Sharpe, proposing a narrow selective focus on the Stuarts' financial problems and the century's religious struggles rather than any grand narratives, Underdown instead advocates a people-centered history concerned with "the experience of the ordinary, non-genteel population," as demonstrated, in his opinion, by Christopher Hill. Despite his disavowal, Underdown's affinity with the interests of the Marxist approach should be obvious. Needless to say, no one mentions a need for an early modern black history of England. Comparable historiographic surveys, one from the standpoint of historical sociology and another from that of Marxist economic history, are also offered by Jack Goldstone, "State Breakdown in the English Revolution," pp. 257–70, and Keith Wrightson, *Earthly Necessities: Economic Lives in Early Modern Britain*, pp. 1–22, respectively.

[3] For views of early seventeenth-century England's troubled condition, see J. P. Kenyon, *Stuart England*, pp. 20–22; Christopher Hill, *A Nation of Novelty and Change: Radical Politics, Religion and Literature in Seventeenth-Century England*, pp. 6–9; Roger Lockyear, *The Early Stuarts*, p. 8; Underdown, p. 18; Keith Wrightson, *Earthly Necessities*, pp. 197–201. The latter figures are taken from Roger Finlay and Beatrice Shearer's essay, "Population Growth and Suburban Expansion," p. 39, and Goldstone, "State Breakdown," p. 106, respectively. Also see Vanessa Harding, "City, Capital, and Metropolis," p. 117.

[4] Thomas Platter, "Travels in England," cited earlier. The quotation from James I is in E. A. Wrigley's "A Simple Model of the Importance of London in the Changing English Economy and Society 1650–1750," p. 44. Wrigley's entire essay is on the national impact of London in the seventeenth century; see esp. pp. 54–55, 58–63, 65–69. See also Derek Keene, "Material London in Time and Space," in Lena Cowen Orlin, ed. *Material London: Ca. 1600*, p. 57. Additionally, see Wrightson, *Earthly Necessities*, who not only sketches, like Wrigley and Keene, London's dominance (pp. 164, 165), but also offers a balanced interpretation of the "seamlessness" of the sixteenth and seventeenth centuries in England as being necessarily inclusive of both continuity and change (p. 2).

Analogously, the records of black people in seventeenth-century London can for the most part be said to be a continuation of those of the Elizabethan period. Once cast in a particular mold, a minority population can only develop along that line. This is why, despite the attempt to expel black people at the end of the sixteenth century, they continue to appear in the English records in the following one in equal if not greater numbers and frequencies. Of direct consequence for the continuing proliferation of black records in the seventeenth century is the development and acceleration of all of the overseas trading projects started in the previous period, which in the African sector continue to produce enslaved black people in England, even if they do so in conjunction with the people of color that also start accruing from the American and Indian projects at this same time, as will be seen in the later chapters. Complementing this effect is the cessation of English hostilities with Spain in 1604, which while not modifying the English perception of Iberian black people coming into the country through Anglo–Spanish mercantile networks, facilitates the volume of such importations.

Initially, over the first half of the century, this accumulating black population occupies a transient temporal and cultural space, the first as the physical residue of the increasingly organized collective transportation of enslaved Africans to the American colonies and as the concurrent products of increased Anglo–Spanish mercantile interaction, and the second in its mixed social pedigree, which, while increasingly hardened from its Elizabethan marking as an object of menial use, has not yet within England reached the universally recognized status of slave. This in-between position, where the black subject's chattel meniality becomes increasingly established in common practice but still not yet articulated in social ideology, and which is a thus a progression of degree if not in kind of its Elizabethan history, is a temporary cultural locus that facilitates the growth of black people in London, by a kind of benevolent neglect as it were, in the first five decades of the seventeenth century. If what guarantees this locus are the continuing fortunes of English trafficking in Africans, those fortunes are also what eventually impel the transformation of the African into official slave with the monarchic legitimizing of English slave trading in mid-century. The third quarter of the century, framed at one end by the successively expansive re-formations of the Africa trading company in the 1650s and 1660s, and at the other by the first London court ruling in 1677 declaring Africans in England to be slaves, thus completes the 100-year journey of the black subject's urban obliteration beginning in the middle of the sixteenth century.

The considerable volume of these records, that are the greatest in aggregate though not in frequency of any chapter in this book, may partly be a reflection of the seven decades that they unbrokenly cover from Elizabeth's death. A more problematic distinction of these records, however, is the natural asymmetry created in them by the creation of the official African slave-trading companies in mid-century, which is reflected in the appellation of a black man as a "slave" for the first time in the entirety of the London records of this book in 1662, and which therefore constitutes a new theme for the last quarter century of the records of this chapter. This disproportion can be partly compensated, first by considering the seventeenth-century London black notations in two numerically unequal datasets, one covering 1603 to 1651, and the other extending from 1652 to 1676, and second by organizing the first dataset into two subsets of 25 years each. If the first dataset will track the continuing hybrid construction of Africans as menial chattels before and up to the setting up of the slave-trading companies, the second will examine the transformations in these hybrid constructions of Africans after their English trafficking officially begins. Breaking up the first dataset into two quarter-century units will afford some coherence to what would otherwise be an unmanageable volume of records and enable a progressive analysis of them over the five decades they cover. Within the two sets, including the subsets of the first one, the records can be examined by their different categories—parish records, personal accounts, government papers, medical records, and so on—while maintaining a systematic geographical movement through them that can also asynchronously traverse the periodic range of their occurrences as needed.

II

Over the first half of the seventeenth century, there is indirect evidence of English commodity and slave-trading in West Africa. The English parliament, the monarchs themselves, the Privy Council, and private traders are all involved in such activities. As Christopher Hill has put it,

> In early seventeenth-century parliaments, a third of the members of the House of Commons held investments in overseas trading companies. Even more interesting, more than half of these invested in trading companies *after* becoming MPs. Parliament acted as a sort of recruiting ground for business investment from the gentry.

As Hill further points out, such lucrative involvements are an insider secret, as is revealed in the comment of the Puritan John Preston (albeit about his Indian and not African investments) of how he was "willinger" to invest in such overseas enterprises "because the estates there were invisible."[5] In general, 57 percent of all enrollments in the trading companies between 1575 and 1630 occur between 1604 and 1620. Of the 498 members of parliament that is the average recorded number of sitting MPs with commercial investments between 1604 and 1628, 79 percent invest in African commerce between 1600 and 1614, which is the sixth highest of all MP investments for those years.[6]

These African trading projects unspokenly involve slave trafficking. In 1618 James I grants a charter to the Company of Adventurers to Guinea and Benin according Robert Rich and many others exclusive right to trade in Africa.[7] While the scale and nature of this company's activities are little recorded, there is an otherwise unexplained English map of 1623 that shows the navigation routes of the English "Adventurers" into Africa.[8] That the Privy Council supported such activities can be

---

5 *Nation of Novelty and Change*, p. 7, and 7 n. 2.

6 The figures are from Theodore Rabb's invaluable analyses of English parliamentary commercial activity between 1565 and 1630 in his *Enterprise and Empire*, pp. 93–96. The average numbers cited are computed from Table 3.10 on p. 94; the percentages are from p. 96 and 100.

7 R. Porter, "The Crispe Family and the African Trade," pp. 57–58; Thomas, *Slave Trade*, p. 174.

8 Cited by Rawley, *Transatlantic Slave Trade*, p. 152.

seen in 1626.[9] In that year a London merchant named Maurice Thompson traded 60 Africans in St. Kitts in the Caribbean. In that same year as well, not only did the Privy Council give the Gold Coast trader Richard Crisp a ship to take "niggers, and to carry them to foreign parts," but in 1629–30, Crisp sued the French for their seizure of 180 of his slaves from his ship, the *Benediction*.[10] As Joseph Inikori observes, Crisp's loss, amounting to £20,000, was reported by the Company of Adventurers to which he was attached through his brother Nicholas, without the company ever "mention[ing] slaving as one of its concerns."[11] A year earlier, in 1628, an English ship named the *Fortune* is casually mentioned as carrying "many negroes" to Virginia.[12] Around this time, an English fort at Cormantin on the Gold Coast functioned as the main staging area for English activities in the African coast until 1661.[13]

In 1630 Charles I granted an exclusive license to a syndicate of private traders to trade in Guinea, Benin, and Angola for 31 years, which also traded in Africans.[14] The rivalry of these private traders with the chartered companies makes slaving such a competitive business that, according to Dutch sources in Africa, between 1645 and 1647 19 English ships were buying slaves on the Gold Coast, increasing to 84 between 1652 and 1657.[15] These shadowy enterprises become a formal state activity in the setting up of the Guinea company in 1651, the Company of the Royal Adventurers into Africa in 1660, and the Royal African company in 1672. Although the named objective of the Guinea company is gold, its brisk work is in buying Africans, seen in its instructions to its ship captains to "to buy as many good lusty negers as shee can well carry."[16] Twelve years later African trafficking becomes an official objective for the first time in the charter of the Royal Adventurers into Africa: "the buying and selling, bartering and exchanging of for or with any negroes, slaves, goods … ."[17] By 1660, as Christopher Hill puts it, "wars for markets were conducted by the state: the plunder raids of Elizabethan sea dogs … gave place to state-sponsored colonial wars."[18]

These seminal developments of mid-century, all to officially conduct slave-trading voyages to Africa, are thus merely extensions of English instincts of the previous five decades, and of those of the five decades of the Elizabethan period, and which therefore represent steadier and more deliberate and irreversible intentions

---

9 For the letters patent for trading to Cape Ninez and Sierra Leone see Claridge, *History of the Gold Coast*, p. 79; Claridge also cites the other letters patent.

10 Cited by Rawley, p. 152.

11 *Africans and the Industrial Revolution*, p. 217. Inikori's source is Porter, "The Crispe Famile," pp. 60–61.

12 Thomas, *Slave Trade*, p. 175.

13 Ibid., pp. 174–76, and Hazlewood, *The Queen's Slave Trader*, p. 313.

14 Thomas, p. 176.

15 Inikori, pp. 217–18.

16 "The Guinea Company to James Pope, the 9 of December, 1651," in Elizabeth Donnan, ed., *Documents Illustrative of the History of the Slave Trade*, 1: 131; Thomas, p. 198.

17 Donnan, 1: 88 n. 70; Rawley, p. 152; K. G. Davies, *The Royal African Company*, p. 41.

18 *Continuity and Change*, p. 12.

than what is sometimes claimed in current scholarship.[19] The volume of the traffic involved is greater than the desultory accounts and fragmentary records suggest. Even in the most skeptical estimate of negative English treatment of Africans and of English slave-trading in Africa, namely that of P. E. H. Hair, there are 100 English voyages to Guinea between 1600 and 1650, by the latter date one hundred more than the total number by 1600. Yet, as Hair points out, these events are still little studied; the extant accounts deal with only a quarter of these voyages, and do not exist in published critical editions, Samuel Purchas's narratives being overwhelmingly reprints of those in Hakluyt, and of European, not English, voyages.[20] According to Joseph Inikori's recent probing re-examinations of the documents pertaining to seventeenth-century English slaving activities in Africa, using not just English shipping figures to Africa but also collating them with the recorded numbers of Africans arriving in the British Caribbean colonies as well as with the colonies' annual population data, the evidence suggests that no fewer than 100,000 Africans were taken from Africa up to 1662, perhaps more but not exclusively after 1650. Between 1662 and 1666 the Royal Adventurers trading to Africa deployed a total of 75 ships to carry Africans to the Caribbean, at an average of 6,000 per year. If to this the trafficking of the private traders in the same period is added, the total annual average of Africans taken between 1662 and 1671 becomes 10,000. These statistics are, to borrow a phrase from Inikori, an indication of "the order of magnitude" of seventeenth-century English trafficking in Africans.[21]

To reiterate a point made earlier, the history of English trade relations with Africa up to 1650 is usually ignored and dismissed in studies of early modern English transoceanic commercial expansion because of its supposedly marginal profits and consequent discontinuity. But as has been shown so far, it is a more substantial, continuous, and deliberate activity than has been assumed, and even that assumption is usually based more on a too easily invoked documentary uncertainty than on anything else.[22] It is not the fragmentary documentation of the English trade with Africa in itself that is questionable, but what is disappointing is the disinterest of scholars to ask what that means and to persistently probe the topic beyond its archival obfuscations in new ways and with different even if indirect data, as Joseph Inikori does. Documentary imperfection should be not a limit but a point of departure for scholarly investigation, particularly for topics with significant political repercussions such as the one under consideration. For the present study the

---

19 For such a view, see Emily Bartels, "Postcolonialism Reconsidered," pp. 53, 57–59. P. E. H. Hair's earlier cited essay, "Attitudes to Africans in English Primary Sources up to 1650," is another particularly desperate example. This kind of argument is both reflective of, and instrumental in propagating, the common scholarly mistruth that black people were not directly known in England until the second half of the seventeenth century.

20 "Attitudes to Africans in English Primary Sources," pp. 46, 51 n. 30, and 53.

21 *Africans and the Industrial Revolution*, pp. 219–21. While Inikori's earlier computations have sometimes been challenged (see Paul Lovejoy, "The Volume of the Atlantic Trade," p. 476, and George Zook, "The Royal Adventurers in England," p. 207), these figures appear to be his latest, revised estimates.

22 For examples of such dismissals as a habitual scholarly recitation, see Rawley, p. 152; K. G. Davies, p. 42; and D. B. Quinn and A. N. Ryan, *England's Sea Empire*, p. 163.

importance of sixteenth- and seventeenth-century English trading projects in Africa, however erratically conducted and desultorily documented compared to other areas, is its effect in supplementarily producing a black population *within* England. In a neat consequential fit, the dismissal of the first topic has enabled the obscurity of the second.[23]

As some of the instructions of the directors of the Royal Adventurers to its ship captains at mid-century make clear, a proportion of the Africans taken are for England, not the Caribbean colony: "We pray you buy 15 or 20 lusty Negers of about 15 yeares of age, bring them home with you for London," "to buy and put aboard … so many negers as yo'r ship can carry."[24] The open statement of such intentions in mid-century can only be an incremental development of what is unstated in the previous decades, when such activities were less controlled. The unrecorded numbers and continuity of this diverted African traffic to London cannot negate the fact of that importation. Even if Inikori's figures for the total numbers of Africans trafficked by the English up to 1662, as well as their estimated annual averages, are conservatively reduced by 50 percent, that still leaves a significant number for the proportion brought into England. What matters is not that these accruing Africans are a large population, but that they are a population at all, precisely because the very existence of such population in the first half of the century has been denied or ignored in scholarship of the period, which has seen black people in England only at the century's end.[25] That the transparency of their ethnic identities in the records spans a range from the obvious to the obscure is a part of the historical difficulty of their visibility, as was shown in the records of the previous periods, and constitutes a confirmation and not a denial of their black documentary character. Furthermore, if after 1650, when the English transatlantic slave trade begins, enslaved Africans become more profitable than gold,[26] then the English commercial ventures in Africa in the first half of the seventeenth century as well as in the previous six decades, which first make evident the value of Africans, have to be regarded as having a long-term economic impact, and therefore a crucial significance, for the overall history of early modern England.

---

23 The classic example of this is P. E. H. Hair's above-cited essay, "Attitudes to Africans in English Primary Sources up to 1650," p. 47.

24 "The Guinea Company to James Pope, the 17 September, 1651," and "The Guinea Company to Bartholomew Howard, 9 of December, 1651" in Donnan, 1: 128, 129, respectively; Thomas, *Slave Trade*, p. 198. According to Thomas, the implied destination of the latter instruction is also London.

25 James Walvin, in *Black and White*, Peter Fryer, and Gretchen Gerzina in her book, *Black London*, all show this tendency.

26 Richard Bean, "A Note on the Relative Importance of Slaves and Gold in West African Exports," pp. 351–56. Ernst Van Den Boogaart, "The Trade between Western Africa and the Atlantic World 1600–90: Estimates of Trends in Composition and Value," however, challenges this claim, asserting instead that for European nations generally slave-trading was more profitable than gold-trading by 1600 (pp. 370, 380). For related studies see Philip D. Curtin, *The Atlantic Slave Trade: A Consensus*, and Paul E. Lovejoy, "The Volume of the Atlantic Slave Trade: A Synthesis."

Just as these earlier seventeenth-century London Africans are the most visible of those in England at the time because of the city's national prominence, and just as they help to extend the historical visibility of the English black people known later, so they are in themselves not so much denizens of a repressed London life like their Elizabethan predecessors as they are the products of a kind of political inattention. This may be partly the result of their Elizabethan history, which makes Africans in Stuart London an already known group, and of the relaxation of Anglo–Spanish hostilities from 1604, which presumably produced increased interaction between English and Spanish merchants in the international European trading ports if not on the high seas. Of such interactions, and of the African trading voyages as well, black people in London are now a socially expected dividend. This is less a matter of any specific descriptive features in their notations as it is an intuitive implication of the uninterrupted frequency, and periodic range and political atmosphere, of their citations up to mid-century. Jamesian London is, for instance, as Kim Hall has observed, in intention at least a reflection of the incipiently pluralist culture of the monarch's blazon of *rex pacificus* or royal peacemaker (as compared with the studied singleness of Elizabeth's motto of *semper eadem* or always the same).[27] That kingly cultural ambition is particularly resonant with James's ostentatious scripting of a ceremonial public union of England and Scotland in his accession to the throne in 1603 (two months *before* his official coronation), with his conscious use of the term "Great Britain" to describe his kingdom to parliament in 1604, and with his own experience of black people in Scotland, reflected famously in his employment of two African pages in his marriage to Anne of Denmark in Oslo in 1589 (Item 174.1 and 2).[28] Concurrently, that expansive monarchic desire can be said to indent by default an oblique and contingent social space for the progressively accumulating black subject in the English capital. This is a space in which the negative Elizabethan marking of the black subject is assumed and not pursued further because it is already fixed, and in that is, paradoxically, a momentarily benign communal location within which the black subject drifts politically unattended. The black people of seventeenth-century London visible in the records of this chapter thus grow by a kind of inertia of motion that the phenomenon acquires in Elizabeth's reign, and because of which her attempt to deport them had little effect on their increasing presence.

In the first of the two subsets of 25 years each that comprise, according to the plan proposed at the beginning of this chapter, the London black records of the first five decades of the century, it is best to begin with parish records because they comprise

---

27 Hall, *Things of Darkness*, p. 126.

28 "Proclamation for the Union of England and Scotland." May 19, 1603, Greenwich, London, *Proc. Bk., p.* 18, in 'James I: Volume 1: March–May, 1603', *Calendar of State Papers Domestic: James I, 1603–1610*, pp. 1–13. See also his speech to parliament, "Speech of 1603," in *Political Works of James I*, ed. McIlwain, pp. 271–72. For his use of the phrase "Great Britain" see his "A proclamation concerning the Kings Majesties Stile, of King of Great Britaine, &c." issued on 24 October 1604 at Westminster, in *Stuart Royal Proclamations*, ed. Larkin, vol. 1. The Africans used and killed in James's wedding festivities are treated separately in Chapter 4. What is worth noting is the possible effect of James's project of Anglo-Scottish union, even though it failed to win support from the English parliament and was abandoned by 1608.

an overwhelming category. Although anxiety about aliens in London continues in the Stuart era, producing repeated searches for them, their documented results do not find black people.[29] In contrast, the volume of the city's parish entries of black people in those years makes them predominate in the documentary landscape. In their thematic content, ambient historical context, and geographical characteristics, they recall directly those of the Elizabethan period, although their social hierarchies are less varied. The parish records of the first subset can thus be examined on an expediently asynchronous periodic grid simply by their incidence across the different London neighborhoods, while noting the patterns of their event typologies to reconstruct as much of a virtual history of the black lives encased in them as their contents allow. The natural historical frame for this quarter century of parish records is James I's reign from 24 March 1603 to 27 March 1625, even though his reign does not affect the London black presence in anything more than its indulgence of an imperial mood conducive to an incidental social space for an ongoing captive black presence as described above, and even though the quarter-century range of the records carries them into the first three years of the reign of the next monarch.

A persistent feature of the Jacobean black parish notations, and perhaps a reflection of the age's imperial tone, is their frequent mention of black people by themselves. Thus in the records of the city's west side, the black individuals that are often noted are not just of fluctuating ethnic clarity as by now should be regarded as inevitable, but also of uncertain social situation. The first instance of this is Margery Blackman, an individual whose brief life spans the transition between the reigns of Elizabeth and James. Named Margeria Blackman in the Elizabethan parish records examined in the last chapter and noted as being baptized in St. Martin in the Fields, Middlesex on 1 January 1594, her burial as Margery Blackman is recorded in St. Margaret's, Westminster on 1 October 1603 (Items 203, 256). A child of nine at her death, she is part of a group of individuals with the same last name mentioned in the Elizabethan records of both parishes. Corresponding to the class of black citations seen earlier, in which the surname is an improvised ethnic descriptor of an assimilated black individual with a given Christian forename, the plausibility of Margery Blackman's black identity is strengthened by the overall Tudor history of a discreet black presence in the powerful London suburb of Westminster throughout the last century, as seen earlier. According to the latest study of Westminster, the city that contains "the royal palace of Whitehall in its midst" is in the early Jacobean years "a dynamic place" that sees "an increased gentry and aristocratic presence," highlighted by the residence here of James's most powerful minister, Robert Cecil, together with his client network of aristocrats seeking favor at court. St. Margaret's parishioners in particular are involved in the city's government, trade, and livery companies.[30] Given this strengthening of what might be described from the discussions of the last chapter as the constituent elements of the area's high fashion of a captive

---

29 See the "Returns of 1627, 1635, 1639," in Scouladi, *Returns of Strangers*, pp. 237–367. Generally, existing scholarly knowledge is not aware of black citations in the Hearth and Poll Tax returns of the seventeenth century either.

30 J. F. Merritt, *The Social World of Early Modern Westminster*, pp. 92, 154, 119–20, 124–29.

black presence, tellingly symbolized among others by Cecil's own possession of an African in Westminster just two years earlier, Margery Blackman's blackness becomes a plausible identification. That identification is unavoidably helped by the residence of the new monarch in this very area, the proximate impact of whose international ambitions is accelerating the keeping of domesticated Africans as a mark of the court's and the gentry's upward social mobility. Such identification is helped even further by the documented expediencies of the recording practices of Westminster parishes, by which if Mr. Portington the King's carpenter can be entered as "Mr. Carpenter," Margery the daughter of a black man can be written as Margery Blackman.[31]

But if Margery's African background is hinted at by the circumstantial character of this neighborhood of high court and government personalities with an already established habit of possessing black people, the identity of her keeper if any, and therefore her particular status, is not. She could have been in the possession or service of any one of the Exchequer or livery company officials, or bakers, grocers, and brewers, that J. F. Merritt has identified as making up the parish neighborhood, but her record's notation that she is a plague casualty of that year ("pl.") is only a default indication of a poor, possibly captive, black girl's' stark material vulnerability to a natural devastation.[32] This unspecified status, of which there are several instances in the Elizabethan period as well, is of greater significance for the Jacobean phase because it is the norm rather than the exception for its black parish records. Situated minimally in the plurality of Westminster's gathering poor, Margery's status as a black person hovers temporarily between denial and disregard and marks an unnamed political space that in ignoring the black subject enables its early modern English historical continuance.

The fertility of this political neglect can be seen in part in the several other "Blackman"s and in a similarly named person who appear in the Jacobean parish records, some of whom like Margery are Elizabethan individuals reappearing here. These are, all in St. Margaret's, Westminster, "Edward Blackman, s[on] of Thomas," who was christened on 24 August 1609, and buried the next day; "Elizabeth Blackman d[aughter] of John," who was christened on 31October 1618, the listed father here clearly being the John Blackman who was baptized on 16 August 1591 in St. James, Clerkenwell; and the "John Blackman" who was married to "Elizabeth Cornish" on 28 October 1620, who may or may not be the father of Elizabeth (Items 273, 274, 303 [180 for Elizabeth's father, John], 311). The innocuous black growth represented by the Blackmans is not confined to St. Margaret's, though. Within Westminster, in the adjacent parish of St. Martin in the Fields, the baptism of "Fran. Blaky" on 19 December 1615 and burial (as "Franciscus Blaky") on 4 April 1616 (Items 289, 292), is a variation of the Blackman records in that first, "Blaky" corresponds to an informal abbreviation of surnames such as "Blackman," and "Blackamore," and is an early instance of what will become a common derogatory English racial epithet. Second, St. Martin in the Fields at this time is even more of a populous, wealthy, and powerfully connected parish than St. Margaret's, being the locality of

31 The Portington reference is noted by Merritt, ibid., p. 116.

32 Ibid., pp. 125–26.

choice for high-powered aristocracy and gentry of court and parliament, who, as has already been said above, partake of the practice of African possession as a sign of competitive social eminence.[33] These onomastic and locative factors strongly point to Fran Blaky's black identity in ways identical to Margery Blackman, whose minority she exceeds in her infant death. These individuals may be biologically related to Margery Blackman or they may be simply her historical kindred. Their common last name, and the compatible dates of their Elizabethan and Jacobean parish citations, might suggest the ongoing assimilation history of one or several growing black families in early modern west London. Yet, the absence of any mention of parents in Margery Blackman's Elizabethan baptism citation, which is typical of initially arriving black people listed in English parish records, might indicate a black history for her different from theirs. In either case, together with her they describe a kind of unnoticed black proliferation in Westminster.

The quietly spreading black presence personified by the Westminster "Blackman" entries appears in other London environs as well. These include "Katherine d[aughter] of Allexander [Alexander] Blackman"; "Elizabeth, wife of Thomas Blackman"; "Thomas s. of Henry Blackman"; and "Thomas s[on] of Andrewe Blackman & Mary [his wife]," who were all buried in St. James, Clerkenwell on 31 July 1610, 15 June 1621, and 27 June and 27 July 1623, respectively (Items 275, 313, 317, 218); and "Lancelott Blackman," who was married to "Mary Bragg" in St. Mary Mounthaw on 26 September 1619 (Item 307). Some or all of these persons, of whom Lancelott and Thomas Blackman, together with the John Blackman of St. Margaret's cited above, will be mentioned again later with other inter-racial marriages, may be connected by blood to the Elizabethan Blackmans of St. James Clerkenwell of three decades back, as well as to the Blackmans of Westminster. They may thus describe the growth of a black family community in a proximate area on the city's west side, since Clerkenwell, located outside the London wall gate of Aldersgate and to its northwest, is close to Westminster and hard by its northeast.

Clerkenwell was a liberty, traditionally at variance in its political and religious character from the city, being the scene of one of Wat Tyler's most ferocious sackings of the city's monuments in 1381, and the seat of the long-standing Catholic priory of St. John that was to be seized by Henry VIII in the Reformation, and being physically unconnected to Westminster and therefore removed from its immediate effects, and on which the government's infrequent touch was a physical, literally defacing one, as in 1603 when a new path is cut through the fields around it to welcome James to London. Clerkenwell is perhaps an unsurprising settlement choice of a drifting black population temporarily unmoored from white attachment.[34] If Clerkenwell's unregulated atmosphere also draws in the naturally unprotected black people into its sex industry located in Turnmill or Turnbull Street on the south side of the parish, as is evident from the Elizabethan records of the black prostitutes cited there in the last chapter, that atmosphere enabled as well for them economic liaisons with

---

33 For the social make-up of St. Martin the Fields see ibid., pp. 18–27.

34 Peter Ackroyd, *London*, p. 458; Stow, *Survey*, 2: 83–84. The reference to James's entry into London through Clerkenwell is extracted from *The National Gazetteer of Great Britain and Ireland*, by Colin Hinson, in his electronic essay "History of Clerkenwell."

poor white people along the common axis of a disempowered life, as the inter-racial marriages suggest. Similar are the facilitating vacuities of St. Mary, Mounthaw for black people, despite its location within the city, on the south side of Old Fish Street Hill, and directly above the Broken Crane Wharf on the Thames in central London [Agas map 6M, p. 21]. A small church, according to Stow, and unassuming parish whose economic worth in 1638 amounted to the very modest sum of £392, St. Mary Mounthaw's riverfront wharf-side community was a sufficiently disconnected and undeveloped one to allow by default integrated black settlement, as the one Blackman marriage here demonstrates.[35] Overall, the black identities of these Blackman records, which recur in the century's later decades, may be of a barely detectable quality, but their unencumbered social appearance, even if of comparably faint visibility, introduces one aspect of the distinction of the early seventeenth-century black records.

This quality is reinforced by the records of stronger black transparency in London's west side in the later years of James's reign and in the early ones of his successor. Thus, "Nicholas," who was baptized in St. Margaret's on 19 March 1619, and described directly as "a negro" (Item 309), has neither parental nor social belonging. If he is a decorative black acquisition of a local aristocrat or court official, that connection is clearly not strong enough to merit archival documentation, even if some such connection in all probability is sponsoring his baptism. The invisibility of the other details of Nicholas's life, including his age, is conversely the ontological visibility of his bare presence outside of any specific social location, except that of his racialized description as "a negro." Precisely the same occupational blankness accompanies the record of "Cattelina," clearly identified as "a blackamoor," who was buried in the same parish on 6 October 1624 (Item 322). That she is a plague casualty is indirectly visible from the fact of this being one of the more dangerous years of that devastation, as is through that the material vulnerability of her disempowered life in this powerful neighborhood. Her blackness's clarity, which retains in her name a trace of her Iberian background, however, profiles by contrast the blankness of her communal status that in being unnamed points to a benign social space she may have inhabited unseen. Two other records of slightly lesser black clarity than those of Nicholas and Cattelina sketch the same obscure phenomenon that they do. These are the burials of "Elizabeth Moore" and "Andrew Blackamoore" in St. Margaret's, Westminster on 19 April and 28 May 1628 (Items 332, 333). Possessing the recognizable class of homonymous African-English surnames frequently seen in the parish records earlier, including in particular this Elizabeth Moore's Elizabethan namesake, Andrew's and Elizabeth's black identities are reinforced by the multiple black presence in this parish discussed already, which their notations therefore show to be continuing in the reign of Charles 1. While their records' lack of an ownership specification for them may be accidental, the uniformity of such a lack in the black archives of the early seventeenth century would point to it being a characteristic of the inadvertent political detachment of the black lives of the period that they are exemplifying.

---

[35] *Survey of London*, 2: 4–5: "Inhabitants of London in 1638: St. Mary Mounthaw," in *The Inhabitants of London in 1638 (1931)*, pp. 116–17.

That the attachment of black people is a rare phenomenon in the early seventeenth-century parish records is evident from the fact that there is only one black citation in London's west side that mentions it. This is the record of "Peter a blackamore," who was buried in St. Dunstan in the West on 2 August 1616, and who is described as being "from Mrs. Locksmithe's" (Item 293). Located on the eastern fringes of Westminster, just above the Temple Bars, and just outside the London wall due west of Ludgate (Agas map 5G, p. 19), St. Dunstan is a rich neighborhood of powerful resident aristocrats. Mrs. Locksmith is a resident merchant woman of this neighborhood, of the sort seen in the Elizabethan records, but probably of a predatory nature, since 22 years later in 1638 she was a tenement renter in St. Andrew, Holborn, which being northeast of St. Dunstan and on the west side of Clerkenwell (Agas map 4H, p. 5), shares with the latter early modern London's sex industry, albeit at the higher end of it.[36] As her location in affluent Holborn in 1638 signifies that she is an upscale procuress for that industry, just as in the Elizabethan records Elizabeth Kirkham is a lower-order one in the city's east side, her presence in St. Dunstan earlier in 1616 means that she is a supplier of Africans to the powerful Westminster community, St. Dunstan and Holborn in general being among the richest neighborhoods in seventeenth-century London.[37] Peter is then one item of her black human merchandise that does not survive her handling. The clarity of this record's revelation of African fettering is, however, reminiscent of the Elizabethan black archives, and not typical of those of the early seventeenth century. That it occurs is a reminder more of the untidy overlap and continuities of historical epochs than of anything else, and that it appears in the earlier decades of the century rather than later is also something that will appear to be symptomatic shortly.

The innocuously free-floating condition of black people is predominant in the records of the city's east side as well, otherwise the second largest group in the first of the two subsets that make up the records of black people up till 1654. The first example is from St. Dunstan, All Saints Stepney, Tower Hamlets, about a mile east of the Tower in the dockyard area of Ratcliff and in the vicinity of Limehouse. Located on the river's north bank as the Thames loops upward at this point, this area had been from Elizabethan times a busy maritime and manufacturing community, the latter from Limehouse's lime production industry based on the burning of chalk that is abundantly available from the red chalk cliffs of Ratcliff, from which Ratcliff gets its name.[38] St. Dunstan and its environs is for these reasons the residence of a prosperous and well-connected business community as Stow describes it, many of whom are actively involved in overseas maritime and commercial ventures, such as

36 "Inhabitants of St. Andrew, Middlesex," in *Inhabitants of London*, pp. 192–97. For prostitution in Holborn see Archer, *Pursuit of Stability*, p. 232; for St. Andrew's bawdy-house reputation see Tim Harris, "The Bawdy House Riots of 1668," p. 538.

37 Vanessa Harding locates the axis of affluence of seventeenth-century London on an east–west grid that on the western end includes Holborn; see her *The Dead and the Living in Paris and London, 1500–1670*, p. 40.

38 For Ratcliff's distance from the Tower, see Stow's *Survey*, 2: 71. For the history and character of Ratcliff and the derivation of its name, see Sydney Maddocks's essay, "Ratcliff."

the George Best whose discourse on blackness was discussed in the last chapter.[39] This ambient character explains the baptism here on 29 July 1603 of "Charity Lucanea a blackamore" from "Ratcliff" (Item 255). Charity's penurious birth, marked indelibly by the prefix of her name, and by the documentation in her record, probably of the almshouse in Ratcliff described by John Stow from which she comes, is preceded, it will be recalled, by the similarly ignoble one of "Christian Ethiopia" in this same parish just a year earlier in 1602.[40] The black people in the Ratcliff almshouse may be a product of the involvement in African slave-trading of the merchants in Ratcliffe as early as 1569, given the detailed knowledge of Caribbean slave categories, prices, and markets that William Fowler of Ratcliffe exhibited in a deposition at the High Court of the Admiralty in that year.[41]

But their similarities notwithstanding, where Christian's unspoken-for condition is not the predominant feature of the Elizabethan black records, Charity's is for the early seventeenth-century ones. This difference is present in the subtly differing qualities of their ownerlessness. In contrast to the preserved visibility of Christian's African origins in her surname, and the transparent cultural proprietorship of her naming as an Ethiopian who has been Christianized, which together in the Elizabethan moment equate to a kind of common public claim on her servile status, Charity's family name, while containing the trace of either a sexual ownership or an assimilatory history, carries no advertisements of bondage. Unlike the political baggage of Christian's birth record, in which the combination of "Ethiopia" and "borne of a blakamoore" describes a compulsive fixing of opprobrium on her, the simpler details of Charity's baptism note convey an indifferent attitude toward her birth. These differences suggest that the account of Charity's poor but unclaimed birth is reflective of the changing responses to black people that are beginning to appear in the age into which she was born.

Likewise in nearby St. Olave, Hart Street, the baptism notice of "Mark Antonio, a Negro" on 25 January 1616, and his burial as "Mark Anthonie, a negro Christian," three days later on 28 January, represent both familiar and unfamiliar phenomena (Items 290, 291). The explicitness of his African identification, and his location in a neighborhood containing other Africans from the Elizabethan period, are both reminiscent of the records of the last chapter. So too are the quick desolation of his life caught in the brevity of his documentary mention, and the implicitly negative cultural possessiveness of his description as an African who has been Christianized. But the fact that none of the foreign or English African-possessing merchants resident in this area from the earlier decades to whom he could have been connected are mentioned in his citation, recalls the condition of black destitution frequently seen in the Elizabethan records without suggesting an exact replication of it in his case,

39 *A Survey of London*, 2: 72. For George Best's residence here see Maddocks, "Ratcliff." For a general description of the area of Stepney parish and its connections to English maritime history see *Memorials of Stepney Parish*, pp. iii–ix, and William Ingram's *The Business of Playing*, pp. 105–6.

40 For the almshouse here see *A Survey of London*, 1: 116, 2: 71–72; "Stepney: Charities for the Poor," in T. F. T., *A History of the County of Middlesex*, vol. 11.

41 Donnan, *Documents*, 1: 72; cited in Hall, *Things of Darkness*, p. 21.

because of the perceptible social élan of his *faux* classical name. Symptomatic of the naming of Africans inculcated into upscale decorative domestic service chiefly in the seventeenth century (although one or two instances occur in the earlier black records), Mark Antonie's/Anthony's name betrays a degree of personal mobility that is a default of high-powered bonded ownership. If his location in St. Olave, Hart Street in a virtual community of other Africans is the end point of a life spent elsewhere in London, and if his self-sponsored, untypical black baptism is his attempt, albeit at the last stage of his life, at English assimilation, that trajectory of movement was enabled not so much by a social sanction as by a social disinterest in his life. This quietly untethered existence may be a sign of the unintentionally fecund, gathering political ennui about black people in early seventeenth-century England.

Nine months after the burial of Mark Anthonie the same laxity of attention to black people is indicated in the burial record of "Isabell [illeg. Peters (?)], a blacke-Moore lodging in blew Anchor Alley" in the parish of St. Botolph, Aldgate on 26 September 1616 (Item 294). Blue Anchor Alley, also known in later times as Red Gate, and Crown and Sheers Place, is at this time a site of tenement housing at the north end of the pathway going east-southeast out of the Minories past Little Tower Hill towards Upper East Smithfield (Agas Map 5U, 5V, p. 27).[42] Surrounded by black people, in Hogg Lane and East Smithfield to its east and south east, in St. Botolph Aldgate church itself to its north west, in St. Olave, Hart Street and St. Dunstan in the East on its west and south west on the other side of the Tower and London wall, this is a predictable location for Isabell. Yet, the assimilated quality of her name, and the material sufficiency of her singular "lodger"-ship, combined with the lack of a mention of any English possessors of her, all indicate an incidentally ignored social space within which her later if not earlier English life has been lived. If unlike the unspecified status of Mark Antonie/Anthonie's interment, Isabell's burial hierarchy "In our new churchyard" is casually distinctive, and if that distinctiveness hints at the unseen support of a past English or foreign captor in this area (such as the extended family of the Nunez's in St. Olave, Hart Street, who therefore may have been connected to Mark Antonie/Anthony as well), that such a connection is like Mark Antonie's/Anthony's case not a part of her record means that it is now a distant and inactive one and not directly relevant for her communal history. The discreetly polite parish account of Isabell's death may even posit for her life a modicum of self-agency enabled by the distraction of an English culture unconcerned for the moment about the black subject in its midst.

In this same parish a revealing example of such a minimalist self-agency, and of the kind of unconscious social integration within which it is operating and that it is engendering, is provided two years later by the burial notice of "Ane Vause a

---

42 See the entries for "Red Gate Court" and "Crown and Sheers Place, Royal Mint Street" in *A Dictionary of London*. For the tenements here see "St. Botolph Aldgate" in *The Inhabitants of London in 1638*; although the number of tenements cited in this source is from 1638, the number in 1616 could not have been too different. Blue Anchor Alley is not marked as such in the Agas map, although the Minories, Little Tower Hill, and the beginning of East Smithfield are; the approximate location of Blue Anchor Alley can be plotted from these coordinating points in the Agas map reference cited here.

Blak-more wife to Anthonie Vause trompeter," on 27 April 1618 (Item 301). Given the history of black people's connection to the profession of pubic musicians in early modern Europe described by Kate Lowe, and personified particularly in England by Henry VIII's black drummer, John Blanke, Anne Vause's marriage to a trumpeter may not be unexpected. She may even be descended from an unknown black English drummer herself. But what is striking about her record is that she is the first and only openly identified black woman in the early modern English black archives covered in this book to appear in the socially sanctioned role of someone's *wife*. Furthermore, irrespective of her genealogy, and given the fact of the handsome earnings of trumpeters in the reign of James, which is higher than that of their Elizabethan predecessors, and given their pervasive deployment in court, parliament, and in the city's pageants, most notably in the Lord Mayor's festive street procession in October of each year, Anne's life as the wife of such a familiar public professional involves a certain degree of communal currency if not of prominence. If Anthonie like other Jacobean musicians is a protected individual who may "not be arrested," nor "be chosen into any office nor warned to attend at assizes nor be impaneled on juries, not to be charged with any contributions, taxes or payments but in courts only as other of his majesty's servants," then his wife must share in some measure some of these franchisements.[43] One recorded instance, albeit Elizabethan, of the kind of social standing Anne may have been privy to is the baptism record of "Roose Raman" in All Hallows-in-the-Wall in 1585, in which one of the witnesses is "Martha Smyth, the wife of Richard Smyth one of her majesties trumpets."[44] In all of these aspects Anne may be an exception, but she is a telling instance of the incremental social consolidation of black people that the complacency of a Jacobean culture about its racial inscriptions is facilitating.

Even the east London records of lesser ethnic clarity at this time display a similar degree of casual personal space, be it in the reported character of their birth or in life choices such as marriage. An instance of the first, also in the same parish as that of Isabell and Anne Vause, is the christening of "William, son of Edward Blackamoore" in St. Botolph, Aldgate on 6 February 1608, and of the second is the marriage of "Joan Mure" to "Philip Upton" in St. Botolph Bishopsgate in 1613 (Items 271, 285). If William's African black ethnicity is identifiable through the location of his surname in the class of names that mix English with African backgrounds seen severally earlier, Joan's is as well, with "Mure" being very probably an orthographic corruption of "Moor/Moore." Within their probable black identities, William's and Joan's records point to comparable if not identical elements of social growth and assimilation. If Edward's genealogically consistent birth reflects the consolidation or the emergence of an African family in this known neighborhood of Africans, Joan's cross-racial marriage in a parish of diverse aliens traces the opportune mobility of

43 The information on Jacobean musicians, including the quotation of the royal dispensation regarding musicians, comes from G. A. Phillips, "Crown Musical Patronage from Elizabeth to Charles I," pp. 30–37; the dispensation quoted is for a particular musician, but as Phillips shows, it is common to the profession. For the date of the Lord Mayor's annual procession, see David M. Bergeron, "The Elizabethan Lord Mayor's Show," p. 269.

44 Cited in J. Charles Cox, *The Parish Registers of England*, p. 51.

naturally contracted affiliations across implicit cultural hierarchies that such now-accepted black lives are being afforded. The slim interpretative access of their records notwithstanding, William's and Joan's life notations acquire a cumulative effect if considered with the other East London records of fortuitous black growth discussed above.

All the documentations of black people in Jacobean London's east side do not of course show them in such discreetly unencumbered social situations, or to the same degree. One case in point is the burial record of "the blackamore gerle from Mr. Pintoe's," in St. Olave, Hart Street on 14 March 1610 (Item 279). Identified in his own unusual burial in the same parish eight years later on 30 December 1618 as "Francis Pinto a Portugal" who is "carried out to sea to be buried," this obviously wealthy Iberian merchant's ownership of the African girl is documentarily visible because it is a social commonplace, in part because of the Elizabethan residences here of African-owning Portuguese figures such as John Baptista Sambitores and Hector Nonnez.[45] An easy casualty of the plague that year in this crowded parish, this black girl's encumbered life is a reminder of the occasional persistence of the material conditions of Elizabethan black people in the reign of James. Likewise, the burial notice of "John Matthews a black-moore lodging in the precinct next to the Tower servant to one Mr. Kellet in Market lane," that is recorded in St. Botolph Aldgate on 24 July 1614 (Item 288) makes clear his bondage in a manner identical to that of the Elizabethan black records. The "precinct next to the Tower" is St. Katherine by the Tower, originally a fourteenth-century hospital in Portsoken Ward located adjacent to the Tower's east side, which was later made into a precinct or liberty because of the large assorted population that grew around it, and that served informally as a church until it was later formally united with St. Botolph.[46] Market Lane is in all probability a corrupt elaboration of the Mart Lane that is the original name of Mark Lane, "so called," as Stow explains, "of a privilege sometime enjoined to keep a mart there, long since discontinued … and that [is now] corruptly termed Marke Lane," and which runs north from Tower street inside the city wall in the Tower's west side (Agas Map 5S, 5T, p. 25), and is on the opposite side of Tower hill from St. Katherine's (Agas map 6W, p. 27).[47] Located across the corner from St. Olave, Hart Street (on the same page in the Agas map as Mark Lane), this is an area of frequent bonded African habitation in the houses of foreign and English merchants, of which Kellet is presumably one. Like the Elizabethan black records, Matthews's negative marking is visible in the record of his burial, which while noting that it has the distinction of the "black cloth" and is "coffin'd" does not fail to mention its expurgatory location "in the common ground" befitting a non-Christian. Yet, within the familiar negativity of this African's life, the disparity between his location, "lodging in the precinct next to the Tower," and his owner's in Market

[45] For Francis Pinto(e)'s burial see *The Registers of St. Olave, Hart Street*, p. 150.

[46] See *Stow's Survey*, 2: 138; Maddocks, "Stepney in Other Days.

[47] *A Survey of London*, 1: 149–50; see also entry for "Mark Lane" in *Dictionary of London*, and entry for "mart" in the *Early Modern English Dictionaries Database*, the latter as a counter to the *Dictionary of London*'s skepticism about Stow's derivation of the name on the grounds of what it claims is the relatively recent meaning of "market" for mart.

Lane, indicates a perceptible looseness in the political and cultural incarceration that otherwise ensnares him.

In contrast, the burial citation of "'John Come Quicke,' a blacke-moore so named, servant to Thomas Love, a Captaine," in St. Botolph Aldgate on 26 November 1623 (Item 321) shows, like Francis Pinto's black girl, a more directly restrictive condition for the black subject. The unique jingling given name, which not only blocks the individual's African identity but substitutes it with a jocular catchy phrase that nevertheless describes the menial serving function that is the sum of his existence and the instantaneous discipline with which it is to be performed, is an undisguised announcement of his bondage. The name also reflects the military background of the African's owner, who may be connected to parliament because he was rewarded by it 25 years later in 1648 for his provisioning of Puritan armies in the civil war, a service that is partly explained by his experience in procuring black labor like John at this time.[48] He may even have acquired such experience and John himself through his involvement in the African trading voyages authorized by James in 1618 mentioned earlier. If so, that constitutes further proof of the unrecorded importation of Africans into England in the reign of James. At the same time, if Love himself, like John Matthews's owner Mr. Kellet, resides somewhere else (since the record does not specify *his* residence), that would suggest a certain flexibility and autonomy in the conditions of John Come Quick's menial servitude.[49]

Comparable possibilities of a different sort are visible in the baptism record of "Mary a Negro maid … out of the house of Anne Isaac of Limehouse widow by license from the Lo: 2BP of London" in St. Dunstan, Stepney on 26 October 1627 (Item 331). Limehouse (whose name according to Stow is a corruption of "Lime Hurst," or "Lime Host")[50] is two miles east of the Tower on the Thames's north bank. Like Stepney itself, which it adjoins, it is part of the Tower Hamlets and under the division of Stepney. As was said earlier, it was a manufacturing area of lime production, as well as of beer brewing, baking, and ship repairing and provisioning. It has citizens with high city connections, as is confirmed by the reference to the baptism's licensing by the "Lo: 2BP of London," which, if it is the Archbishop of York, is at this time Tobias Matthew, and therefore a possible reflection of what

48 "House of Commons Journal Volume 5: 24 February 1648," in *Journal of the House of Commons*.

49 The relative autonomy of Johnny Come Quick as well as of William Matthews, suggested by their residences separately from their masters, may seem contradictory to the similarly separate Whitechapel residence of the Elizabethan African owned by John Davis in St. Mary Woolchurch Haw, who was buried there in 1597 that was discussed in the last chapter, but is not really so since the anonymity of the latter's burial notation indicates a more socially undeveloped and disenfranchised existence than the relative visibility of the communal lives of William Matthews and Johnny Come Quick present in their records. This, as has been reiterated so far, is a marginal distinction and one that is naturally so given the inevitable overlap between the Elizabethan and Jacobean regimes, but one that nonetheless is significant in terms of the changes in black people's social history that will appear later in the century.

50 *A Survey of London*, 2: 71.

historians have regarded as his tolerant enforcement of religious conformity.[51] If so, this high ecclesiastical involvement in the baptism of a possessed African, however remotely operative, and of which more instances from this time will be seen in a later chapter, demonstrates the same incidental permissiveness of attitude toward the English black subject that has been evident so far.

Some African destitutions like those of the Elizabethan period are still occurring, but on a much lesser scale, as the sole record of this type in the East London Jacobean parish registers suggests. This is the burial of "a blackamoore woman that died in the street, named Marie" on 4 November 1623 in St. Botolph, Aldgate (Item 320). The desolation of this stranger African death, which points not just to an ownerless condition but to a cast-off one, beyond the largesse of any parish poor relief, is partly mitigated by its exceptionality, occurring as it does in a neighborhood of other Africans who have not as yet met, and who may or may not meet, the same fate. The notation of Mary's indigent extinction is thus a reminder of the anomalous nature of the black growth occurring quietly in the Jacobean years.

The story spelled out by the Jacobean church records of the city's central, southern, and northern zones replicates the pattern of disjunctive black growth of the eastern and western sides. Inside the walls, in the city's central areas, a high incidence of cross-racial marriages of variable black clarity confirms the gradual social merging of black people seen in the city's west side. To begin with the most perspicuously black example, if the marriage of "James Curres a Moore Christian, and Margaret Pearson a maid" in Holy Trinity the Less on 24 December 1617 (Item 299) bears the familiar identificatory underlining of a Moor who has been converted seen earlier, here the stressed marking is implicitly self-congratulatory, emphasizing as it were the double English success of having achieved a black's cultural inculcation as well as a kinship tie for him. This subtly triumphant note resonates in part with the civic character of this location on the northeastern side of Trinity Lane where it meets Old Fish Street in Queenhithe Ward just above Thames street and Queenhithe wharf itself on the Thames (Agas map 5M, p. 21), "so called" according to Stow, "of a water gate or harborow for boates, lighters, and barges," that in "old time" was "for shippes" a "principal strand for landing and vnlanding against the middest and hart of the Citie." Even if the church of Holy Trinity the Less itself was at the time of Stow's writing "small, very old, and in danger of down falling," it was handsomely rebuilt in 1606–8 with contributions from the Merchant Tailors and Vintners, and the southern end of Trinity Lane till Thames Street and up to the south end of Bread Street paralleling Trinity Lane on its west side, was an area of "diuers faire houses inhabited by Fishmongers, Cheesemongers, and Marchantes of diuers trades."[52] James Curres's location and marriage in this central waterside area that is also prosperous is thus not incompatible with a possible narrative of his imported

[51] See "Stepney: Early Stepney," and "Stepney: Economic History" (for Limehouse), in *A History of the County of Middlesex*, vol. 11: *Stepney, Bethnal Green*. For Tobias Matthew's tolerant policies see Marc L. Schwarz, "James I And the Historians: Towards a Reconsideration," p. 121.

[52] The citations from *A Survey of London* are in 2: 1, 2, 4; also see 2: 6, where he says that "Queene hithe [is] a large receptacle for ships, lighters, barges, and such vessels." The

arrival and assimilation, the latter particularly congruent in the reign of James. The record's faintly celebratory instinct, traceable in its careful identification not just of the groom but also of the bride—as "a maid"—also resonates indirectly with the imperial quality of the Jacobean moment, under whose aegis several proud public inductions of colored people will occur, as will be seen later. The event described by the record is also of course projective of a measure of independent standing for James. Worth noting is the fact that this is the first record of an explicitly identified African male in an inter-racial marriage in the early modern English archives, and in that constitutes a parallel to the signal one of Anne Vause, discussed above.

Whereas the other black marriage records of central London are of weaker ethnic identity, they too describe the spread of anomalous black social development. The records note the marriage of "John Brabye of St. Brides, haberdasher, and Alles Moren, W. [widow?] Lic. Fac.," in St. Peter, Paul's Wharf on 24 June 1611 (Item 280). "Moren" is probably a variation of "morren," or a corruption of "moryen," "morien," or "moryon," meaning in either case, as has been pointed out earlier, a Moor or black person.[53] About four blocks west of Trinity Lane, St. Peter, Paul's Wharf on Thames Street is another riverside area a block north of Paul's Wharf on the Thames in central London (Agas map 6L, p. 21). Unlike Holy Trinity the Less, this was not, in Stow's time at least, a prosperous parish, even if in 1638 it was assessed for the not unhandsome amount of £1,184 sterling.[54] Yet, as a haberdasher from the wealthy parish of St. Bride's in Westminster, northeast of St. Paul's, John Brabye is an individual of some financial means, and his marriage to Alles (Alice) Moren indicates correspondingly some material substance in her for her to be an attractive proposition for him, something that is signaled by her respectfully marked designation as "widow."[55] If Alice had some assets inherited from her deceased husband, that in turn would point to her already established standing in this parish, a perception reinforced by the careful legality of this marriage conducted by license. The modest social status that this scenario suggests for Alice is remarkable for a black woman, and if indeed she is one offers another instance of the unnoticed progress of black people in early seventeenth-century London.

Three other marriages of this type occur in this same part of London. These are the marriages of "Randall Blackmore & Elizabeth Seagood" and "John Steele & Francis Blackmore" on 1 April 1619 and 31 October 1622 respectively in St.

---

church's renovation history is from the entry for "Trinity (Holy) the Less," in the *Dictionary of London*.

[53] See the entries for these words in the *Dictionary of the Scottish Language*; see also the record for "Francis Fran" described synonymously as a "moryon" and "niger," cited in Chapter 1.

[54] Stow describes it as "a small parish church" in which "no monuments do remain," adjacent to a "cook's house called the Blue Boar," and numerous wharves like Puddle Wharf, "a water gate into the Thames, where horses vsed to be watered, & therefore being filed with their trampeling, and made puddle," *A Survey of London*, 2: 6, 2, 13, respectively. For its assessment, see "Inhabitants of London in 1638: St. Peter, Paul's Wharf," in *Inhabitants of London.*

[55] For a relevant discussion of the financial attractions of early modern English widow marriages, see Vivian Brodsky's essay, "Widows in Late Elizabethan London: Remarriage, Economic Opportunity, and Family Orientations," pp. 127, 132–34, 137–41.

Benet, Paul's Wharf, and of "John Gibson with An Blackamore" in St. Nicholas Cole Abbey on an unspecified day in 1627 (Items 305, 315, 330). The first location is adjacent to St. Peter, Paul's Wharf on its west on Thames Street, whereas the second is on Old Fish Street, a very short distance west of Holy Trinity the Less on Trinity Lane as it runs north from Thames Street to meet Old Fish Street (Agas Map 6L and 5M, p. 21). Both churches, which Stow approvingly describes as "proper," are in a location of mixed character.[56] On the one hand they had some prominence due to the nearness on their west of Baynard's Castle, with its connections to royalty, the familial roots here of people like Inigo Jones, who is James's principal pageant and masque architect, and the fame of St. Benet's bells that are invoked in the popular stage fare of the playhouses directly across them on the south side of the river.[57] On the other hand, the presence of almshouses to their northwest, and the wharf on the river to their immediate south, makes them a locality of working-class people as well, including laborers of English and non-English origins.[58] Analogously, the marriages of Randall Blackmore and An Blackamore are also mixed, in their social pedigree as well as in their ethnic clarity, that compound indeterminacy being arguably a feature of this closely bounded area between Holy Trinity the Less and St. Nicholas Cole Abbey on Old Fish Street in the north and St Peter, Paul's Wharf and St. Benet, Paul's Wharf on Thames Street to the south. It will be remembered that Lancelot Blackman's marriage to Mary Bragg in 1619 in St. Mary Mounthaw just above St Peter, Paul's Wharf and St. Benet, Paul's Wharf on Thames Street is also in this same zone. Altogether, these communally and ethnically hybrid marriages could be said to be an echo of the unguided and unformed growth by default of black people in Jacobean London's central districts.

The imperceptibly relaxed Jacobean attitude toward black people that lies behind the casual social development reflected in their cross-racial marriages in central London is perhaps most lucidly evident in a particular kind of public baptism of colored peoples, including Africans, that appears at this time in the city's center. The baptism of "Dederj Iaquoah, a king's sonne in Guinnye" on 1 January 1611 in St. Mildred Poultry (Item 277) is one record that is an icon of the morphology of this phenomenon. As Roslyn Knutson's detailed discussion of this record reveals, John is a Guinean African king's son sent by his father with the English merchant trading there, John Davis, to become Christianized and Anglicized in order to learn the ways of the English and have better trade relations with them. Beyond the language of the parish record, however, the project's predatory instincts are buried in the identity of its participants. Edmund Towers and Isaac Kilburn were shareholding participants in the *Abigail*'s voyage,[59] and John Davies was a patent holder of the trade in Guinea and

[56] *Survey of London*, 2: 2, 15 (St. Benet, which Stow calls "St. Benet Hude [or Hithe]").

[57] Shakespeare alludes to the bells of St. Benet in 1602 in his *Twelfth Night*: "The triplex, sir, is a good tripping measure, or the bells of St. Bennet, sir, may put you in mind—one, two, three" (5.1.36–39); in *The Riverside Shakespeare*.

[58] According to Stow, an almshouse was located on St. Bennet Hill (*Survey of London*, 2: 16). Ian Archer also refers to the almshouse here (*Pursuit of Stability*, p. 91).

[59] "A Caliban in St. Mildred Poultry," p. 122.

Sierra Leone.[60] There are other sinister English designs in this event as well, because, as Knutson points out, although Davies's ship that brought back Dederj, the *Abigail*, took hats, cloths, silks, and velvets to trade for rice, pepper, and elephant tusks, it also trafficked in Africans, an exchange that Dederj was meant to facilitate.[61] This is precisely what Kim Hall has explained is religious conversion's deadly program of erasing difference while producing commercial profit that underlies the ideology of seventeenth-century Protestant English travel writing such as Samuel Purchas's *Hakluytus Posthumous, or Purchas His Pilgrimes.*[62] The narrative of the *Abigail*'s voyage and its bringing back of Dederj is another instance of the historically under-reported English trade with Africa in the first half of the seventeenth century and of its inevitable trafficking in black people. How far the project of the Christianizing and Anglicizing of Dederj is a coerced one, and what its pressures are on Dederj and his father (which are queries obligated by the history of Portuguese coercions of the Congolese King in the fifteenth century discussed in the first chapter), the record does not reveal. Consequently, how far this project succeeded is unclear, implicit unsurprisingly in Dederj's disappearance from the records when pirates attacked the *Abigail* on its return voyage to Guinea six months later.[63]

Nevertheless, in London at least and at the time, that Dederj's baptism is regarded as the auspicious beginning of the training of an international African diplomat is indicated by the careful assemblage of important community citizens as witnesses of the event, by the record's separate paragraph-long prominent entry, by the bold lettering of Dederj's name in that entry, and by the briefer repetition of the event in the list of other christenings for that day.[64] The signature of the event's public ambition is in its location in St. Mildred Poultry, just off what is London's grandest central thoroughfare and proudest mercantile concourse, Cheapside.[65] In many of the details of the event that the record carefully enumerates—namely its location of the origins of Dederj's English journey and its purpose in his father's desire for the same, and in which Davies is only a facilitator, and its notation of Dederj's interest and volition in the event itself ("He shewed his opinion concerning Iesus Christ … [and] repeated the Lords prayer in english") and which, while being possibly a part of the required protocol of early modern English adult baptisms, also betrays unmistakably the pride of an English cultural conquest—the record may recall the similar baptism of Mary Phyllis in 1597 discussed in the previous chapter (Item 224), and in that may provide another reminder of the expected degree of continuity and overlap between the cultural features of the Elizabethan and Jacobean

---

[60] Quinn and Ryan, *England's Sea Empire*, p. 163. See also Andrews, *Trade, Plunder, and Settlement*, p. 113.

[61] Knutson, "A Caliban," p. 120.

[62] *Things of Darkness*, pp. 53–58.

[63] Knutson, 122. Knutson speculates that Dederj abandons his English arrangement and goes back to Guinea (p. 23). This is a probability given the same ending of the narrative of another similarly co-opted African named Coree (Item 238), discussed in the next chapter.

[64] Noted by Knutson, p. 121.

[65] Schofield, "The Topography and Buildings of London," in Orlin, ed., *Material London*, p. 303; M. J. Power, "The Social Topography of Restoration London," in Beier and Finlay, eds., *London 1500–1700*, p. 208.

epochs. But the differences between the two are important. First, unlike Dederj, not only is Mary an attached individual, being named as "a bound servant to Millicent Porter," hers is not a sponsored baptism since no sponsors are named. Secondly, in contrast to the smooth progress of Dederj's baptism ceremony, Mary's was marked by the troublesome qualification of that "which she by nature could not have," for which a particular congregation-wide prayer for God's "Bownteous mercie" had to be invoked. These differences point to Dederj's baptism as being much more of an orchestrated and desirable civic event than Mary's. It is in this aspect that the record is part of the different, permissive Jacobean attitude to black people inhering in the seventeenth-century black records discussed so far. The event's location, while being a little above St. Peter, Paul's Wharf, St. Bennet, Paul's Wharf, and St. Nicholas Abbey, is also a central London one and even more so than they are, and in that reinforces the cultural characteristics of the black records of those areas. The symptomatic nature of Dederej's baptism account is borne out by another record of this sort in a different part of London at this same time that will be seen shortly, as well as by several baptism records of East Indians discussed in a later chapter.

There are two other Jacobean black baptisms in central London, but their demonstration of the pattern observed so far is less unified and defined. These are the baptisms of "a man child called John borne of a blackamoor woman & supposed to be the sonne of Edwarde a borrder in the howse of William Conrados" on 2 June 1606 in St. Benet Fink, and "Andrew, son of Henry Blackmore" on 10 December 1626 in St. Mary Woolnoth (Items 266, 327). Whereas the second record is of the less ethnically transparent category of black citations identified before, the first is an infant baptism and a record of an exploitative sexual union of the sort seen in the Elizabethan period. Furthermore, where the first is an early Jacobean record, the second is an early Caroline one. Yet, both are very prosperous central London locations, the first just above Cheapside and to the right of the Royal Exchange (Agas map 4Q, p. 10), and the second just below it to the southeast where Lombard street meets it (Agas map 5Q, p. 23). Both are wealthy communities of drapers and wool merchants, alien and English,[66] and therefore of a class with a propensity for casual possession of Africans well shown in the archives by now. Most importantly, not only do the two records not cite any attachments for the black individuals whose baptisms they document, they are both careful to include paternity information for them. If the latter feature denotes a dignity of language, that is especially noticeable in the first record, since it shows some responsible generosity on the part either of the white man who fathered the child or those who know of the incident in allowing the perpetrator to be named, and in that offsets to some extent the sexual oppression of the black woman even though she herself still remains unnamed. The distinction of the second record is that Henry Blackmore is a goldsmith, which would suggest that black people may be connecting to the goldsmith's trade at this time.[67] It is the

[66] *Survey of London*, 1: 225, 164 for St. Benet Fink. The character of St. Mary Woolnoth is identical to that of its sister church nearby, St. Mary Woolchurch Haw (identified next to each other on the Agas map); for the character of the latter see *Survey of London*, 1: 226.

[67] In the same register Henry Blackmore is identified in several baptism entries for his other children as a goldsmith. As the early Tudor black needle maker in Cheapside showed,

incipient civic probity toward black people projected by the first record, and the incidental black material well-being probably indicated by the second, that connect them to the transitory racial nonchalance of early seventeenth-century London. One trace of this probity may also be present in the sole central London burial record at this time, which is that of "Barbaree, servant to Mr. Smith" on 27 April 1623 in St. Peter, Paul's Wharf (Item 316). The appreciation of the service of this likely black individual with an obviously given nickname resonant of West Africa is manifest in his employer's expensive "coffined" interment of him.

The Jacobean black records of London's northern and southern areas are fewer than those of the central districts and show both similarities to and differences from them. The ones in the north have the kind of formal civic content that the central London ones have, including in one case another putative community celebration of a black baptism like the Dederj Iaquoah entry. This is the baptism of "Walter Anberey the sonne of Nosser Anberey borne in the kingdom of Dungala in Africa" on 3 February 1610 in All Hallows Tottenham, Harringay (Item 278). Tottenham is in the ward of Harringay, which is in the south end of the borough of Haringey just above Islington and Hackney, and northeast of Westminster and Clerkenwell. It was a fashionable resort area and watering-place that was long used for hunting, fishing, and pleasure walking by prosperous upper middle-class Londoners including royalty, since in the sixteenth century Henry VIII hunted here and in the seventeenth century not only did the fashionable leisure historian Izaak Walton recommend its fishing attractions,[68] playwrights such as Thomas Nabbes and Thomas Shadwell depicted its reputation as a favorite suburban London excursion destination.[69] Its upscale character is also indicated by the presence in it from medieval times of a vicarage.[70] Such a setting is congruent with the decorous description of this record, that while not as detailed as the Dederj one, displays in its discernible festivity and ritual flourish a comparably commemorative public design. The pointed association of the event's date, in the recording clerk's identification of it, with the sacred joyousness of "Shrove Sundaie" and with the royal aura of "the Eight yeare of Kinge James" frames the African's baptism as an iconic neighborhood event, even if formal citizen involvement is not listed by the record. Whereas the record fails to name a sponsor for the baptism, its elaborate notation of

---

for black people to be connected to specialist trades such as that of goldsmiths is not an altogether improbable development, and one whose plausibility is reinforced, as will be seen later, by a black record of 1675 (Item 442).

[68] Izaak Walton, *The Compleat Angler*. The book's entire conversation about the art and attractions of fishing begins and ends in Tottenham (pp. 33, 236, 245), the natural beauties of which are celebrated in pastoral style in between (pp. 137–40, 223–24).

[69] Thomas Nabbes, *Tottenham Court*, 1.1.1–21; see also Thomas Shadwell's *The Virtuoso*, which has this passage: "The Foolish World is never to be mended. For all this, your Glass-Coache will to Hyde Park for Air. The Suburb-fools trudge to Lambs Conduit or Totnam; your sprucer sort of Citizens gallop to Epsom; your Mechanick gross Fellows, showing much conjugal affection, strut before their wives, each with a child in his Arms, to Islington or Hogsden" (5.1.); quoted in Richard Perkinson, "Topographical Comedy in the Seventeenth Century, p. 271. For discussions, see also Theodore Miles, "Place Realism in a Group of Caroline Plays," pp. 433–34; and Perkinson, pp. 272, 280–81.

[70] "Tottenham: Churches," in *A History of the County of Middlesex*, 5: 348–55.

Walter's history as the "sonne of Nosser Anberey borne in the kingdom of Dungala in Africa" becomes an advertisement for the inspection of credentials of an individual whose initiation into English Christian fellowship is being offered as a triumphant note for the community. These incompletely visible social intentions anticipate and find credence in the more developed script of Dederj's public conversion the following year. The full extent of the political phenomenon represented by the kind of public baptisms that Dederj and Anberey underwent is reflected in a range of such baptisms of east Indians that also occurred at this time in various places in London. The two baptism entries together constitute a template for a kind of imperial Jacobean racial diversity in England that marks the apogee of the mood of indifferent inclusiveness of black people suggested by the other records of James's reign.

This formal racially expansive mood may be reflected less strongly but still usefully in the other London record of this time on the city's northern perimeter, five years prior to Walter Anberey's baptism. This is the marriage notice of "John Faggot with Margaret Morin" sometime in 1606 in All Hallows, London Wall (Item 265). Located flush against the London Wall, due north from the Royal Exchange and a short distance to the right of Moorgate, this Broad Street Ward parish, "So called of standing close to the wal of the Citie," and variously known as All Hallows by the Wall, All Hallows near the Wall, All Hallows under the Wall, All Hallows atte Walle, All Hallows Within the gate of Bishopsgate, and St. Augustine in the Wall or St. Agustine's Papey,[71] is both a reclusive neighborhood associated in the past with hermits and anchorites, and one of the poorest ones in the city.[72] The parish's past also includes the presence of a few beer brewers,[73] who, if still present, may like others of their class seen in the last chapter have Africans in their possession. If Margaret Morin's black identity is obscurely identifiable because of its possible belonging to the class of names that are a variation of the ethnic descriptor More, her presence and marriage in this parish may be connected to the few beer merchants either still resident or associated with the area. The very fact of the marriage, which, if Margaret is black, is another inter-racial one, contributes to the growing numbers of such marriages that the Jacobean black records have shown to be a sign of their times.

As stated earlier, the Jacobean south London black records slightly contrast and resemble those of the rest of the city. In illustration is the burial of "Constantyn, a negar oute of ye pilgrime at portsmouth …" on 5 December 1605 in St. Olave, Tooley Street, Southwark (Item 263). "[Y]e pilgrim," i.e. the *Pilgrim*, was a small warship owned by Walter Raleigh, commanded variously by Raleigh's principal sea captain Jacob Whiddon, in the capture of valuable Spanish booty on the Brazilian coast in 1590, and in Richard Granville's fatal raid on the Azores in 1591, in which the latter, on the *Revenge*, was ambushed and killed by a Spanish squadron, and by Richard

---

71 "All Hallows London Wall," in *A Dictionary of London.*

72 *A Survey of London*, 1: 161–63, 145–48; Vanessa Harding, *The Dead and the Living in London and Paris*, p. 40; Lawrence I. Conrad, Michael Neve, Vivian Nutton, Roy Porter, Andrew Wear, *The Western Medical Tradition: 800 BC–1800 A.D.*, p. 218.

73 "All Hallows London Wall," *A Dictionary of London.*

Boyle in the English campaign in county Kerry in Ireland in 1599.[74] Irrespective of its probable participation in predatory African voyages earlier, sometime in the next several years, just before or during Raleigh's years of imprisonment, the *Pilgrim* was deployed in some African trafficking trips, either by Raleigh himself (since he involved Robert Cecil in such projects and because of which the latter had the African named Fortunatus in 1601 discussed in the last chapter) or by its new owners, the visible trace of which is Constantyn's burial record in the rough dockside area of St. Olave, Tooley Street in Southwark on the Thames's south bank. Constantyn is clearly a freshly arriving seized African who did not survive the rigors of his kidnapping in this non-plague year. In the details of this inferential history, Constantyn's notation thus may appear to recall many of the Elizabethan rather than the Jacobean black citations. What is different, though, and a feature of this particular record, is the nature of the identification of his origins, as being "oute of ye pilgrime at Portsmouth," which shows a precision of documentary protocol that instead of abandoning an insignificant imported bonded black individual like him simply to the default anonymity of a terse description such as "a negar" or to the ignominy of a named ownership for him as the records of the previous decades commonly do, connects him to the ship that has brought him to England and in that leaves visible even if implicitly the possibility of a history for this black life elsewhere. This propriety of identification, and the equity of rhetorical address that it employs, connects Constantyn's burial notice to the easy English consciousness of black people variably present in the other records of this time.

The distinctiveness of Constantyn's citation is clearly visible if compared to the other record of this area four years later, namely the baptism notice of "Richard a Blackmore, 12 years old" on 19 February 1609 in St. George the Martyr in Southwark (Item 272). Located south of both St. Saviour's and St. Olave, Tooley Street, bounded by Lambeth on its west, Newington to its south, and Bermondsey to its east, and made up of a welter of streets and alleys, prisons, and cheap hostelries for laborers like the Mint, this is a rough parish that is as loosely composed as it is neglectfully documented. Its boundaries meander lazily and loop down over the top of Newington into both Lambeth on the west and Bermondsey on the east, and its record-keeping starts half a century after those of the rest of the city in 1602, only seven years prior to the date of Richard Blackmore's record. Correspondingly, its social character draws from even the meticulous Stow no more than a few brief passing sentences.[75] Unquestionably sharing the ambient riverside atmosphere of Southwark, this was a

---

74 Jacob Whiddon's connection to the *Pilgrim* is described in Jan Rogozinski, *Pirates!: Brigands, Buccaneers, and Privateers in Fact, Fiction, and Legend*, p. 365; The *Pilgrim*'s presence at the demise of the *Revenge* is in Hakluyt 7: 87. According to his own account, Boyle takes fresh ammunition and supplies to help George Carew, the Lord President of Munster, in his siege of Carrigfoyle in Kerry in July 1599, in the *Pilgrim* which he "bought of Sir Walter Raleigh"; cited in Dorothea Baker Townshend, *The Life and Letters of the Great Earl of Cork*, p. 19.

75 For its overhanging layout see "Illustrative map of London parishes," in *The Commissions for Building Fifty New Churches* (based on an eighteenth-century map, but helpful nonetheless). See George Wright, "Statistics of the Parish of St. George the Martyr, Southwark," p. 50 (for the parish's irregular shape), and p. 54 (for the late start date of its

parish of predominantly poor people, living for the most part on the farther side of the law, more so than those of both St. Olave and St. Saviour's to its north. That may be in part the reason that Richard's notation lacks the descriptive frills of the rest of the city's records, including those of other Southwark parishes, and echoes the Elizabethan records. Still, even in this rough location, the stamp of the Jacobean moment may be perceivable in Richard's citation in its lack of any English attachment or ownership connection for him. Implicit in that lack is that equanimity of reference to black people common to the early seventeenth-century archives.

The last three south London Jacobean records, which are from a location on Southwark's east side, in an area now known as Wandsworth, are equally mixed in their character. The first two of these comprise a Vestry minute notation and a Churchwardens' account entry of 1625 and 1626 respectively about the black maid of "Dame Ann Bromley" in St. Mary, Putney (Items 324, 329). Located on the south bank of the Thames, and bordered by it on the north, and by Beverley Brook on the west and Putney Heath to the south, Putney was at this time a peculiar of the see of Canterbury and St. Mary a relatively well-off parish that was occasionally visited by the king himself.[76] This social complexion is reflected in the affluence of the two records' principal participants. The first record, dated 27 March 1625, is a description of Dame Anne Bromley's bequest of £20 to the parish for the help of the parish poor, "to be imployed as a stocke for the releefe and comfort of the said poore in bread or otherwise," and an acknowledgment by the curate of the vestry's agreement to use the donation "according to [the] good intendment and purpose of the said Ladies charitable mind." Beneath the list of signatures of "the inhabitants there of the vestrie" that follow this text, however, is the curate's separate note clarifying that "within the £20 above mentioned is contayned £10 a legacie of a Christian negro servannt unto the sayd Ladie Bromley, and the other £10 is the guift of the sayd Ladie" (in Item 324). The second record, dated 20 March 20 1626, constitutes a Churchwarden's receipt of the "£21.10 shillings being so much put into Mr Angells hand to paie use for being the guift of the Lady Bromblie and a negro maid servant of hirs to the poore of this parish" (in Item 329).

Anne Bromley was originally Anne Beswick, the daughter of Thomas Beswick, a London alderman, who first married a London merchant named Offley, her marriage being typical of the marital alliances within the merchant class that Robert Brenner has shown occurs throughout the early modern period.[77] Sometime before 1603 she was widowed, which explains a later allusion in the 1625 Churchwarden Accounts', pointed out by Dorian Gerhold, who originally found both these records, to "the guift of Dame Lady Ane Bromblie and a negro maid-servant of Mr Offlies that died

records of births, marriages, and deaths). For Stow's casual treatment of the parish see the desultory mentions he makes in *Survey of London*, 2: 52–53, 67, 68.

[76] "Parishes: Putney," in *A History of the County of Surrey*, pp. 78–83.

[77] Brenner, *Merchants and Revolution*, p. 72 n. 58. The facts of Anne's early history are cited by William Retlaw Williams, *Kidderminster, Bromsgrove and Pershore, from the Earliest Times to the Present Day*, p. 35.

longe since."[78] In 1602 or 1603 Anne became the fourth wife of Sir Henry Bromley, a favorite of Elizabeth who fell from favor after the Essex rebellion because of his involvement in it and was imprisoned in 1602 before being restored by James in 1603.[79] At the time of the records she was again a widow, Henry Bromley having died in 1615, a fact not mentioned by the records. Even though the record 'does not say this either, and Gerhold ignores this possibility, the "William Offlie" that appears in the list of signatures beneath the text of the 1625 Vestry minutes could be Anne's son by her first husband who was present at the ceremonial investiture of honor on a member of his deceased father's household. Anne's overall personal history makes quite explainable her acquisition of an African maidservant through her previous paternal and marital affiliations with the merchant class, for whom such possessions are a cultural habit. As Gerhold puts it, "It can be assumed that the 'negro maid-servant' had belonged to Mr. Offley, the first husband of Lady Bromley, and it is he who had died 'longe since.' It is likely that upon his death, he left an amount of money to his maid-servant."[80] Although when Anne Bromley' became a resident of St. Mary's parish and if in fact she is one is not explained by the record, the neighborhood's social demographics and the various generous land gifts made to Henry Bromley by James's Privy Council in 1604[81] make plausible the existence of a Bromley estate in this area as well, which Anne inherited in her widowhood.

Its informational lapses notwithstanding, the record's contents are valuable for their illumination of the changing Jacobean history of black people. The clear visibility of the black woman's owned status reveals the underlying negative marking of black people persisting from Elizabethan times. In keeping with that negativity is her unexcepted anonymity, despite this commemoration of her good deed. What could follow then from both these conditions is a concomitant personal disempowerment, in which her supposed act of charity may be as induced as it was a volitional one. At the same time, the carefully documented coming together of high-powered aristocrat and her surviving extended family, together with local gentry, in the communal inscription of a black life's entry into the forms of a charitable English civility describes the social orchestration of a public event that is typical of the baptisms of Dederj and Anberey, seen earlier. Uniquely in the spectrum of black living conditions seen so far, the record represents the opposite end from that of Charity Lucanea, and is the first instance of a black person as a social benefactor.

---

[78] "Celebrating Black History in Wandsworth," p. 8. Dorian Gerhold supplies the historical information in the pamphlet, which was put out by Wandsworth area authorities. See also his essay, "Black People in 17th and 18th Century Putney." This allusion of course means that the Offley who was Anne's first husband cannot be the prominent London merchant Robert Offley mentioned by both Brenner and Gustav Ungerer ("Prostitution in Elizabethan London," p. 148), because that Offley married an Anne Osbourne (*Register Book of of St. Dionis Backchurch*, p. 11) and died in 1623 (George E. Cokayne, *Some Account of the Lord Mayors and Sheriffs of the City of London*, p. 22) which is too late for the 1625 record's reference to Offley's death as having happened "long since."

[79] William Retlaw Williams, *Kidderminster*, p. 35.

[80] "Celebrating Black History in Wandsworth," p. 8.

[81] See "James I: Volume 7: April, 1604," in *Calendar of State Papers Domestic: James I, 1603–1610*, pp. 90–103.

What is even more notable is the solid financial worth attributed to her, which in Gerhold's calculation amounts to £1,142 in modern British currency.[82] This substantial sum, which irrespective of whether it was a bequest or saved wages, is the first documentation of the capital accumulation of early modern English black people, as well as the collective effort to portray her in the role of social patron, however impurely motivated, and marks the understated changes in the English response to black people in the Jacobean period.

That the particular cultural phenomenon reflected in the citations of the unnamed charitable black woman is not unique for St. Mary's is evident in the record of another black woman in that same parish that constitutes the last south London record of this time. This is Black Joan, who again, according to Gerhold, "appears in the churchwardens' accounts receiving payment for menial tasks such as washing Sharpe's boy in 1626 and stripping and winding a poor man found dead in a barn in 1635" (Item 326). Gerhold also points out that in 1627 and 1628 she received "relief from the parish," and was later "awarded a place in the almshouse, whose accounts last record her in 1664."[83] What is notable here is not only the casual procedure of the naming of Black Joan's blackness, which confirms the typology of many names surmised to be black earlier in this and previous chapters, but also her unfettered status, which is unlike the specified servantship of the unnamed black woman. Also different is Black Joan's meniality, which appears to be at once more lowly and more unrestricted, even if the latter quality borders on a condition of indigence. But what is common to both black women is their communal recognition, in Black Joan's case not just in the payments to her for her acts of service that appear to be truly voluntary, but also in their careful documentation over nearly four decades. That recognition is also evident in the poor relief that she receives despite being in her blackness presumably a stranger in the parish, and in the publicly inscribed awarding to her of "a place in the almshouse," of which there are three at this time in Putney.[84]

To sum up, the inconspicuous phenomenon that the foregoing examination of the Jacobean records of black people has tried to identify is a default development of the already established negative construction of black people in the Elizabethan period and the expansive effect on that construction of the imperial instincts of James's reign. If the first factor makes black people in London known as a denigrated entity, the second formalizes that construction by assuming a social place for them in that denigrated capacity, including occasionally as the triumphant objects of the transformative civilizing power of a nascent English empire. Thus, for instance, Jacobean discourses on blackness are driven less by an anxiety about the threat of blackness's tribal defilement, as was George Best's in 1578, than by the need to celebrate the all-conquering majesty of English rule, as is Ben Jonson's *Masque of Blackness* in 1605.[85] The result is a kind of benign complacency about black people that borders on a casual tolerance of them and that continues to feed their

---

82 "Celebrating Black History in Wandsworth," p. 8.

83 Ibid., p. 7.

84 "Parishes: Putney," in *A History of the County of Surrey*, pp. 78–83.

85 See Kim Hall's discussion of this text in *Things of Darkness*, pp. 128–38, esp. pp. 135–37.

numbers across the city. Because this is a discrete development, the black living space it creates is a mixed, unstable, and transient one that is both like and unlike the condition of black people in the reign of Elizabeth.

III

Of the black citations in the first half of the seventeenth century, the second subset of records covering 1629 to 1653 consists of 26 records for that 24-year period. In this period, the features of English political history relevant to the history of black people in England include what Kevin Sharpe has shown is Charles I's essential replication of his father's principles of English monarchic rulership,[86] which produced a regime that was similar to its predecessor's but not identical to it. In place of the latter's imperial ambitions driving global English maritime oceanic expansion are expedient and incremental foreign-policy initiatives in African and Indian oceanic trade and American colonial settlements deriving from continental European developments. Chief among these developments are the breakdown of Anglo–Spanish relations in 1624, with the escalation of English involvement in the Thirty Years War, starting from its outbreak in 1618, the replacement of the Iberian trading presence in Africa by the Dutch as a result of that war, and connectedly, Charles I's assumption of the English sovereignty of the high seas.[87] Reflective of this, and within the imperfect documentation of seventeenth-century English African commodity and slave-trading, is the earlier cited patent of Charles I in 1630 for trading in Guinea that is different from, and supersedes, the one issued by his father in 1618. This patent, giving to a syndicate headed by Nicholas Crispe "exclusive right … to trade in Guinea, Benin, and Angola for thirty-one years," is one surviving sign of the English activity in African trafficking that continued to produce black people in Charles I's reign through the Civil War and up to the emergence of the Puritan government.[88] If as a result of the factors just cited English trade in general, including African forays, underwent a slight decline in Charles's reign, that is congruent with the smaller number of Africans recorded in London in this period. That smaller number may also be reflective of the beginnings of English migration to the new American colonies, which includes the accompaniment of black people with the migrants to that locale.[89]

Within their smaller numbers these records offer a useful panorama of the further development of the black presence in London up to the middle of the century. This was made possible by the slightly wider variety of these records, which include parish register entries, an ecclesiastical court account, a lawsuit, an anecdotal revelation, a newspaper report, and a philosophical discourse on blackness, as well as by their reasonable locational spread and chronological regularity. The records can be

---

86 Kevin Sharpe, "Private Conscience and Public Duty in the Writings of Charles I," pp. 644–45, 647.

87 For a succinct summation of these factors see Quinn and Ryan, *England's Sea Empire*, pp. 179–81. For Charles's assumption of English sovereignty of the high seas see Kenneth Andrews, *Ships, Money and Politics*, pp. 134–56.

88 Quinn, pp. 191–92. Also in Thomas, *Slave Trade*, p. 176, cited earlier.

89 Quinn, pp. 180–81.

examined in the descending order of their largest clusters, beginning with the parish entries and proceeding through them in the kind of diachronic-synchronic manner used with the Jacobean records. A large percentage of these parish records is of the ethnically uncertain variety seen many times before. That should not disqualify them from consideration, nor mitigate the usefulness of this dataset overall.

The predominant number of black records in the Caroline London parish registers are from the city's west side, and they also happen to contain most of the ethnically uncertain entries of this dataset. These are the records with the "Blackman" or "Blackmore"/"Blackamore" surnames, and the largest numbers among them are of burials. In St. James Clerkenwell they are of "Dorkas Blackman, a poor child" on 8 July 1632; "ffrancis Blackamore, a poor widow" on 19 October 1638; "Mary d. of Raph Blackamore" on 6 August 1639; "Eliz. Blackamore" on 3 March 1641; "Humphrye s. of widow Blackamore" on 4 September 1645; "Jone Blackamore, a poor woman" on 7 September 1645 (Items 343, 358, 360, 363, 369, 370). Concurrently, in St. Margaret's, Westminster is the burial of "Alice Blackman" on 9 March 1635 (Item 350). Dorkas in St. James, Clerkenwell and Alice in St. Margaret's, Westminster clearly recall the Jacobean and Elizabethan Blackman entries, many of them in these same parishes, and may reflect the continuing proliferation of this distinctly named and possibly blood-related group of black individuals on the city's west side over the sixteenth and seventeenth centuries. If the rhetorically unmarked and homonymously conflated condition of Alice's ethnically descriptive surname suggest for her an assimilated history rather than one of new arrival, that conjecture applies equally to ffrancis or Francis, Mary, Elizabeth, Humphrey, and Jone as well, whose variable economic status as "poor wom[e]n" locates them within the poor communities that Jane Merrit and Vanessa Harding have identified in both areas.[90] Whether they should thus be included in the high incidence of female poverty in early modern England noted by recent social historians of the period such as Marjorie McIntosh, Natasha Korda, and Bernard Capp, is also something worth considering.[91] At the same time, for some of these women (and their offspring) the designation "widow" indicates a certain amount of social recognition that is particularly striking for an area like Clerkenwell. A similar recognition may attend the listed parent of Mary, the person named as Raph Blackamore, since there are many entries for him over several decades in this parish, suggesting perhaps that he is the head of another black family such as the Elizabethan "Resonabel, blackman"/"Reasonable, blacmore" discussed in the last chapter.[92] Supported by the mixed ethnic complexion of St. James Clerkenwell (in the presence of Africans here seen earlier), the possible black identities of these individuals posits the casualness of black social integration that continues in London in the Caroline period.

---

90 Merritt, *Social World*, pp. 259–62; Harding, *The Dead and the Living*, p. 40.

91 Marjorie Keniston McIntosh, *Working Women in English Society*, p. 38; Natasha Korda, *Shakespeare's Domestic Economies: Gender and Property in Early Modern England*, p. 138; Bernard Capp, *When Gossips Meet*, p. 38.

92 For other Raph Blackamore entries see the *Registers of St James, Clerkenwell*, pp. 121, 126, 131.

Such innocuous assimilation is also of course indicated by the black inter-racial marriages in the city's west side in this period. In St. Margaret's, Westminster, the marriages of "Georg [*sic*] Hammond to Katherine Blackamoore" and "Zachary Blackman to Anne Rivett" on 2 May 1633 and 2 March 1645 respectively (Items 348, 366) display a civic propriety that is perhaps determined by the self-conscious formality of this high-powered neighborhood, but that propriety drives an assimilationist instinct that leaves black identity if visible at all politely ambiguous. Like Dorkas Blackman and Mary and Elizabeth Blackamore, for instance, Katherine Blackamoore and Zachary Blackman are ethnic ciphers that cannot demonstrate certitudes of black growth but only suggest the plausible inevitabilities of a surviving black existence within a white English population. Equally plausible outcomes of such discreetly merging black lives are the births in this same high-level west London parish, such as those of "Mary 'B B d of Christian Blackman'" on 6 January 1637 and "James Blackman, s of Robert and Ann" on an unspecified date in 1641 (Items 353, 364). Common to the "B B" or baseborn, i.e. illegitimate, birth of Mary and the proper one of James Blackman is the fruitfulness of both inter-racial unions. Whether they represent the growth of a particular "Blackman" family, or the proliferation of unrelated black individuals, such births, together with the marriages, symptomize even with their faint ethnicities the quietly continuing establishment of black people within the gathering turbulence of Charles I's reign. That there are only 11 records in the city's west side in the royal London suburb of Westminster during Charles's reign, and that too of weakly identifiable blackness, may be due in part to the increasing political frictions of this time preceding the civil war and including its early years in which English overseas commercial activities may have been slowed. The smaller number of black records and their uncertain ethnicities may also be due to Charles's fixation on decorousness and to his insistent aloofness from his lay subjects, and especially his injunctions to his high officials to keep poor people away from Westminster.[93]

The central London black records in this time are fewer still than the city's western ones but resemble them in the unobtrusiveness of their visible ethnicity. Only one record from this area displays an African identity openly, and in a manner evocative of the Elizabethan black citations. This is the baptism notice of "Timothy, a heathen Blackamoore" on 14 May 1629 in St. Mary Woolnoth (Item 335). The location's ambient social character as a prosperous wool merchant neighborhood bordering Cheapside, and its prior history of containing a bonded African presence, both seen in the discussions above and in the last chapter, combine to make Timothy's presence here not unexpected. What is somewhat notable is his description as "a heathen

93 Judith Richards, "'His Nowe Majesty' and the English Monarchy: The Kingship of Charles I before 1640," pp. 73, 75–78. The particular royal order that Richards cites on p. 77, titled "A Proclamation for restraint of disorderly and unnecessary resort to the Court" and issued at "Whitehall" on "17 May, 1625," restricts "the unlimited concourse of people of all sorts to His Court, or to the Townes or Parishes neere the same" up to a distance of "twelve miles." See also the order titled "A Proclamation concerning the Royal Household" dated 26 March 1625 expelling from the Court and its environs all "idle persons," "unnecessary attendants following the same" that "bring much dishonour to Our House" (*Stuart Royal Proclamations*, ed. Larkin, 2: 34–37).

blackamoore," a linguistic gesture that in the virulence of its negative marking makes this citation stand apart from the Stuart records as a whole, since the word "heathen" occurs only one other time in the entirety of the English archives considered in this book (see Item 312). This is a negativity that is all the more unusual if compared to the civic dignity of the Andrew Blackmore record in this same parish three years earlier (see Item 327). If this negativity is the sign of a new hostility toward black people, it is the forerunner of something that will become pronounced past mid-century. That this is an exception at this time, however, is seen in the racially restrained nature of the rest of the central London Caroline parish records, which include baptisms as well as marriages. These are the baptism of "Elizabeth d. of Winfeild Blackamore" on 11 February 1647/48 in St. Benet, Paul's Wharf; and the marriages of "Nich. Finch with An Blacky" on an unspecified date in 1637 in St. Gregory by St. Paul, "Phillip Hollybury and Grace Blackmure" and "Winfeild Blackamore and Elizabeth Benson" on 6 April and 27 December 1647 respectively in St. Benet Paul's Wharf, and "Henry Studfeuld [Studfeild], of All Hallowes the lessee, & Eliza. Blackmore of this parish" on 9 January 1653 in St. Stephen Walbrook (Items 375, 354, 372, 374, 378). Notwithstanding the possibility that in An Blaky's marriage notice the incipiently pejorative note of her surname—which is the ancestor of a modern slang for a racial slur—is another emerging negative racial sign in this period like the record of Timothy, all these records have a sobriety of racial content not unlike the city's western ones. They are noted as unexceptional events, occurring in locations that have been seen before to be either prosperous (as are St. Gregory's, located right next to St. Paul's on its south side, adjoining the Bishop of London's prison [Agas map 5L, p. 21], and St. Stephen Walbrook situated south of the Stocks on Cheapside, immediately south of St. Mary Woolchurch Haw [Agas 5P, p. 23])[94] or of a mixed character (as is St. Benet, Paul's Wharf). These features may be the result of the contiguous proximity of the city's center to Westminster on its west, and to the decorousness of urban behavior emanating from its royal court.

In the city's northern and eastern parish records black identities are more pronounced, but they too are cast in the softness of racial perception of the western and central records. In the sole Caroline black record in the northern parish of St. Leonard, Shoreditch, the baptism of "James Kelly s Halliwell Street 'an African Blackemoore'" on 25 April 1630 (Item 336) displays familiar characteristics. The particular, punctuational highlighting of James as "'an African Blackemoore'" evokes the denigratory markings of the Elizabethan black records, perhaps as a way of pointing to the unsavory part of the parish from which he comes. As has been described before, Halliwell Street in St. Leonard's, Shoreditch was a socially rough tenement neighborhood of gambling dens, bawdy houses, and riotous public theatres in the close vicinity, which from Elizabethan times had an African presence (see the discussion of "Susan" in Ch. 2). Like that Elizabethan African girl located here in 1595, James was probably the offspring of a black woman employed in one of the bawdy houses, possibly even hers. Unlike the negative description of her birth as "borne of a blackamoor," though, the notation of James's baptism is circumspect and matter of fact, confining his biological identity to the formulaic, simple coded

94 *Survey*, 1: 227–28.

letter "s." meaning son, despite the possibly similar circumstances of his birth. The practice of denoting a son with the letter "s," daughter with the letter "d," baseborn with the letters "BB," and so on may be a common formulaic convention of English parish register entries, but that convention usually cites parents, which is not the case here. That this is most likely not an accident of the parish clerk's ignorance of the identity of James's parents is borne out by the overall racial sobriety of the seventeenth-century black citations seen so far. In that aspect, the tone of James's baptism record suggests the prevalence, even in this predatory location, of the same relaxed attitude toward black people evident in the Caroline black archives of the city's western and central areas.

This unperturbed racial attitude is even more directly evident in the four Caroline black records of the city's east side. The first of these is the burial record of "Anthony a poore ould Negro aged 105 yeares" on 18 May 1630 in Hackney, in a medieval church known three decades later as St. John's but still dedicated at this time to St. Augustine (Item 337). This was a very large, affluent, and fashionable resort suburb extending northeast from the city walls at Bishopsgate, whose recent residents included luminaries like the king's great grandmother, the Countess of Lennox, and Edward De Vere, the Earl of Oxford, and a variety of other high-born and powerful people.[95] The locale's class demographics, which included aristocratic and lower-level merchants involved in maritime trading, would also make predictable the presence of Africans here, although not quite in the second romantic scenario or wholly in the third of the three currently proposed by the Hackney Archives department: "Antony … may have been a servant to a prosperous Hackney resident, a visiting nobleman, or … [he] may have retired to Hackney as a freeman after years of service."[96] It is clearly an area that could be expected share to some degree the muted racial attitudes seen at Westminster, a reflection of which is the sympathetic description of Anthony as "a poore ould Negro," even to the extent of exaggerating his age to the improbable figure of "105 yeares." Although unlikely to be "a freeman" as such, Anthony's appearance in the record as an unattached individual, and his advanced age irrespective of exactly how advanced that is, does point to a social ambience of racial benignity in which an elderly black individual can live out the remainder of his life without the strictures of a specific encumbrance or bondage. If such strictures are there, that they do not need to be documentarily visible can only mean they are no longer operative or relevant at this time.

The other three black records of the city's east side project a comparably gentle racial view as well, the first of which is more substantial than the rest. This is the baptism, in the same year as the burial record of Anthony, in a location southeast from his, in St. Dunstan, Stepney, of "James sonne of Grace – a blackmore servant of Mr Bromfield of Limehouse" on 9 February (Item 341). As was delineated earlier, Limehouse's social character included both a prosperous well-connected mercantile community and considerable maritime activity, the latter of which is reflected within

95 "Hackney: Settlement and Building to c.1800," in *A History of the County of Middlesex*, vol. 10: *Hackney*, pp. 10–14; also see "Hackney: Introduction," in the same volume, pp. 10–14.

96 See the web essay *Tudor Hackney: Local People: Black People in Tudor and Early Stuart Hackney*.

James's record in the mention of the "mariner," i.e. sailor "William Ward." That the area's black presence is of some duration at this time is made clear not just from the Africans here, and in Ratcliff and Limehouse discussed before (see Christian Ethiopia in Ch. 2, and Charity Lucanea, and Mary, Anne Isaac's "Negro maid" above) but also from the two generations of Africans appearing in the record itself, namely, in addition to James and his mother Grace, his deceased father, the "late" "James Diego," whose surname indicates an Iberian background. "Mr. Bromfield" is very probably the Richard Bromfield who was a Stepney parish vestryman and merchant with connections to the East India Company, to a Captain of which his daughter was married sometime before 1625–26.[97] That merchant mariners are also parish vestrymen in their neighborhoods is, as Cheryl Fury has shown, a sign of their prominent social standing.[98] Notwithstanding the bonds of ownership within which Grace's clearly inscribed "servant"-ship positions her, and irrespective of the uncertainties of whether James Diego is Bromfield's servant or William Ward's, or of why the birth otherwise took place "in the house of William Ward," that two socially prominent merchant mariners are visibly connected to the baptism of this black couple's child signifies the normalcy of a community involvement in black people that is unspokenly inclusive rather than exclusionistic. What Bromfield and Ward are indirectly overseeing by their publicly inscribed links to this event is in fact the social establishment of a black family. The difference of this tendency, and which connects to the racial moderation of the rest of the Caroline and early seventeenth-century London records, is evident if this record is compared with that of Christian Ethiopia in this same parish in the Elizabethan period.

Three years and five years later, the other two east-side parish records of the Caroline years also show a racial discreetness, even if in not the same details. These are the baptisms of "Thomas Wood, a Blackmoore" and "Thomas Williams a blackamoor," on 4 December 1633 and 5 May 1638, respectively, in St. Olave, Hart Street, just inside the city's east walls (Items 349, 356). The lack of any ownership bonds for the two Africans, in this locality of frequent African captivity well known from the Elizabethan period, conforms to the pattern of such notations seen so far. At the same time, the lack of parental information about them could mean these are adult baptisms of recently imported black people that are being presented as social occurrences that do not now need any comment. As has been explained once earlier in this chapter, if some early seventeenth-century records such as these ones seem to resemble some of those of the Tudor period, that is a reminder of the asynchronous, unconscious, and imperceptible nature of the lax social attitude toward black people that develops in the Jacobean and Caroline periods. There are distinctions, but these will be in the best of circumstances fragile ones. For one thing, there are fewer black baptisms in the records of the previous century, which in itself should indicate a changing black social history. For another thing, the social scenarios of the black persons in the sixteenth-century records rarely have the racially equivocal quality

---

[97] *Memorials of Stepney Parish*, ed. George Hill and Walter Frere, pp. 104, 105, 107–14, 120–24; see esp. p. 105 n. 1. Also see the web essay *Stepney Folk Vestrymen*. The source for most of the information cited on this website is from *Memorials of Stepney Parish*.

[98] *Tides in the Affairs of Men*, p. 72.

that most of the pre-1650 black citations have. It is in fact the lack of descriptive detail in Thomas Wood's and Thomas Williams's baptism notations that make these records further exemplify the overall pattern of unexcited black notations of the last several decades.

That the racial relaxation of the Stuart regimes up to the mid-seventeenth century is a heterogeneous, informal development is seen not just in contrary citations such as those of Timothy mentioned above, but also in the fact that it does not appear in legal proceedings, be they of a civil or ecclesiastical variety. An instance of the latter sort is the presentation before the Commissary Court of London in April 1632 of "Grace—, a blackamoore for living incontinently with Walter Church, Stepney" (Item 342). This is a sexual immorality case typical of the charges of the Bishop of London's Commissary Court, which sits in the Doctors Commons, immediately south of St. Paul's churchyard, just off Knightrider Street on its south side (Agas map 5L, p. 21),[99] and the ex-officio status of the proceedings reflects the sweeping powers that the court typically uses, specifically for investigating lay improprieties outside of ecclesiastical administration. As Lindsay Bryan in her study of English ex-officio cases in the medieval English ecclesiastical courts has explained, "Ex-officio cases were more like modern criminal cases, which could come to court through public fame, with offenders being cited by churchwardens or other officials, although it is often next to impossible to trace the origins of such cases."[100] The site of the alleged misdemeanor, Stepney, and the black identity of the accused, are unsurprising given the presence of Africans here, and which in fact is a further confirmation of that population in this area.

Within the cryptic details of the record, what is familiar is the negative marking of the African woman, implicit in her exclusive prosecution rather than of her partner as well. As L. R. Poos points out, "'many ostensibly *ex officio* actions' resulted from 'complaints to officials by victims or other interested parties.'"[101] The record's language precludes Grace from being the complainant in the case. Even though the record does not indicate if Walter Church was also charged, it is likely that he was not, given the obvious pervasiveness of patriarchal ideology in the early modern period. As such, he, or others in the community who had come to know of the relationship, could be the "interested parties" here, he attempting to punish her for her reluctance to continue to submit to him in a relationship gone sour, or the others, driven by their inquisitorial male fervor in the salacious nature of the union, striving to prosecute a defenseless black woman on whom *they* themselves could not thus prey. These scenarios, which, while not directly demonstrable, are historically plausible, could describe the chilling double exploitation of black women, sexual and legal, in a cultural environment in which she was always already morally suspect. In these features, and in the record's inevitable lack of what Duncan Salkeld in the related context of a similar record discussed in the last chapter (see the record of Rose

---

99 *Survey*, 2: 17; David R. Chesnutt and C. James Taylor, eds., *The Papers of Henry Laurens*, p. 408 n. 5.

100 Lindsay Bryan, "Marriage and Morals in the Fourteenth Century: The Evidence of Bishop Hamo's Register," p. 488.

101 Cited by Bryan, ibid.

Brown) has called the "*Ipsissima vox* of the defendant," i.e. here the woman's own voice in her narrative, the record recalls the Elizabethan black archives, including some of the court cases involving black women. Since the case's ultimate disposition is unknown, it is only possible to observe of the record's revelations that whereas a single black woman's casual consensual cohabitation with a white man is now entering the arena of local social acceptance, such unions are still dangerous traps for her in the realm of existing English laws.

An anecdotal account of a possibly black prostitute in these years offers yet another picture of the slight but meaningful developments of the black social presence in the early and mid Stuart decades. This is the casual mention by the seventeenth-century antiquary John Aubrey, in his biography of the early Stuart poet laureate and theatrical impresario William Davenant, that "He [Davenant] gott a terrible clap of a Black handsome wench that lay in Axeyard Westminster" (Item 345). The incident to which Aubrey alludes is Davenant's infection by a sexually transmitted disease, specifically syphilis, and the woman who is "lay[ing] in Axeyard" is clearly a prostitute who either owns or is in a sex-working business establishment there. Axeyard, a cul-de-sac on the west side of King Street in Westminster opposite Whitehall, and the site of a ancient "masauge" or beer-house, contained at this time a mix of high- and medium-level inhabitants.[102] This event, which happened when Davenant was in Westminster seeking court patronage sometime between 1628 and 1630, resulted in a three year, mercury-based treatment program (from a doctor whose subsequent widow became Davenant's second wife) that caused the disfigurement of his nose, the staple feature of all subsequent biographies of him.[103] There are some reasons for thinking that this was not a black woman. For one thing, there are examples at this time of "black" being used to denote hair color rather than skin. For another thing, such a liaison between a connected member of the gentry and a black prostitute in this elite west London suburb does not evoke any comment or response from Aubrey that might be expected if the woman were a black person. These assumptions are typical of modern exegeses of Aubrey, such as that of A. H. Nethercot and Richard Barber, who therefore confidently parse Aubrey's "black" as "brunette" and "black-haired" respectively, the former in his study of Davenant's life, and the latter in his edition of the *Brief Lives*.[104]

Yet, there is cause for caution in making such easy assumptions. It is apt to remember here Kim Hall's comment that "To insist on reading blackness solely as hair color equally ignores the fact that modern Western notions of race were developing at the very moment of the first contact between 'white' Europeans and his dark others."[105] As this book's examination of early modern English black notations has shown

102 *The Diary of Samuel Pepys*, eds. Robert Latham and William Matthews, "Companion," 10: 15–16 ("Axe Yard"); "Westminster: King St, Great George St and the Broad Sanctuary," in *Old and New London: Volume 4* (1878), pp. 26–35.

103 Kevin Sharpe, *Criticism and Compliment*, p. 56; Anthony Powell, *Some Poets, Artists and 'a Reference for Mellors'*, pp. 30–31.

104 A. H. Nethercot, *William Davenant: Poet Laureate and Playwright Manager*, p. 92; *Brief Lives*, ed. Richard Barber, p. 91.

105 *Things of Darkness*, p. 71.

repeatedly, denotations of blackness are if anything non-uniform and contradictory, and frequently unspokenly so. Thus, while in this particular moment "black" can signify a black-haired individual, in this case a brunette, such a usage could also in silent catachresis refer to an African woman. In fact, when Aubrey himself referred to a brunette he described her not as "black" but as having "dark browne haire," as he did in his biography of Venetia Digby, Kenelm Digby's wife.[106] In the syntactical message of his phrase, that this is "a black woman that is handsome" rather than "a handsome woman that is black," Aubrey may also be paradoxically revealing the attractiveness of black appearance, which would constitute the only such instance in the records of this book. Aubrey's distinctive phrasing, which by eschewing the more normal sequence of "handsome black wench" gives "black" an unqualified initial syntactical position in it and thereby makes "black" the preeminent category of his description, may marginally indicate an attempt to signal an African identity.

This signaling may be borne out by what Aubrey adds, to further unpack the identity of the "black handsome wench." Aubrey says that she was, according to Nethercot on Davenant's "own authority,"[107] "whom he [Davenant] thought on when he speakes of Dalga in *Gondibert*," the heroic poem that Davenenat published in 1650. The relevant passages in the poem to which Aubrey refers occur in the Third book, Canto VI, between stanzas 31 and 75. Of these the two most revealing stanzas are 31 and 41. The first of these, in introducing Dalga, describes the character as a courtesan whom Gondibert and his friend Goltho see from the street:

> For a black Beauty did her pride display
> Through a large Window, and in Jewels shon,
> As if to please the World, weeping for day,
> Night had put all her Starry Jewels on.[108]

These presumably constitute what Nethercot says are "the circumstantial details of the incident," what he describes as "an encounter after a carousal at the Brew House, a rendezvous which D'avenant is supposed to have frequented."[109] What precisely the phrase "a black Beauty" means becomes clearer in stanza 41:

> They enter, and ascend, and enter then
> Where *Dalga* with black Eies does Sinners draw;
> And with her voice holds fast repenting Men;
> To whose warm Jett, light Goltha is but Straw.

"Jett," in that form, is, in the third of the *OED*'s listed meanings for the word, "a deep glossy black."[110] In the line's context in this stanza the word cannot be referring to Dalga's eyes, because they are not mentioned here as they are pointedly in stanzas 44 and 63. The word cannot be describing her voice either despite the proximity

---

106 *Aubrey's Brief Lives*, ed. Oliver Lawson Dick, p. 101.

107 Nethercot, p. 92.

108 William Davenant, *Sir William Davenant's Gondibert*, ed. David F. Gladfish, 3.6.31. Remaining citations are also from this edition.

109 Nethercot, p. 92.

110 *OED*, 1: 1507.

of its mention in the preceding line, first because that would be a meaningless qualification, and secondly because it is juxtaposed to "light Goltha," clearly implying a visual contrast between the ineffectuality of Gondibert's light-skinned friend's apprehensive remonstrance not to proceed and the seductive "warm[th]" of Dalga's exotic complexion drawing them into her parlor. These unmistakable poetic allusions, largely ignored in Davenant scholarship, cannot but amplify Aubrey's hint of the phenotypical blackness of his "Black handsome wench." If such a reading of Aubrey's phrase is a difficult one for most modern readers used to the entrenched academic tradition of regarding historical early modern English blackness as a chimerical metaphor, that is the hard cultural encrustation within which early modern black identities are buried.

Since some of the earlier records have suggested the possibility of black prostitutes in London's west side, in Clerkenwell and Holborn, it is plausible that the "black, handsome wench" of Axe-yard, Westminster is also one. Davenant's family history, with its close associations with the Merchant Adventurers Company, may have given him first-hand experience of domesticated Africans in England, and in turn drawn him to a black woman in Westminster.[111] Additionally, a black identity for the woman is compatible with her negative marking in Aubrey's automatic supposition that she rather than what Kevin Sharpe calls his "profligate life-style" is the source of Davenant's infection,[112] which is the always already diseased condition of blackness implicit in George Best's description of it as an "infection" seen in the last chapter. At the same time, the social resonances of such a liaison as Aubrey records underline again the emergence of black–white coupling in the early Stuart years that has already been seen in the discussions above. If the woman to whom Aubrey alludes is indeed a black prostitute, she could be one working by herself, since her "lay[ing] at Axe-yard" does not seem to include any co-workers. She is also an upscale one, judging from Dalga's description in Davenant's poem. If so, her situation is not devoid of a kind of successful self-agency, even if of the sex-working variety.

The social awareness of black people in the Caroline period is reflected as could be expected in the philosophical discourses on blackness of the time, and these show, not unsurprisingly, a like moderation and reasonableness toward their subjects as the other seventeenth-century records examined above. A rich instance of this are the three essays by the natural philosopher Thomas Browne of 1646 titled "On the Blackness of Negroes," "Of the same," and "A Digression concerning Blackness" (Item 371). Generally, in the essays of the volume titled *Pseudodoxia Epidemica*, in which the discussions of black people's skin color occur, and particularly in the three essays that contain those discussions, Browne is a iconoclastic rational philosopher on a project of systematically debunking popular misconceptions, exactly in the manner of the French skeptical thinker Michael de Montaigne half a century earlier. In the first essay, after patiently exposing the contradictions of theories positing for the blackness of Africans climatic causes ("the heat and scorch of the sun"), and

[111] For the Davenant family's links to the Merchant Adventurers, see Powell, *Some Poets*, p. 30.

[112] Sharpe, *Compliment and Criticism*, p. 55.

after briefly considering the effects of noxious African waters, of pre-natal maternal imagination, of tribal cosmetics, and of the accelerated congenital effects of "Black Jaundice" on African skin color, he concludes not only that the causes of African blackness are "great obscurities" that cannot be "reduce[d] unto a resolution," but also that such blackness is part of the myriad differences of nature, such as one-backed and two-backed camels, straight-backed and hunch-backed oxen, and hairless and hairy dogs. In the second essay, after likewise dismantling divine sources of African blackness ("the curse of God on Cham and his posterity"), he points out that to Africans their skin color is not "a Curse" but a "content[ment]," and that to them the anomalous human condition is a white one. He then reminds readers that not only is human beauty a matter of form and proportion, and inner grace, by which "the Moors also are not excluded, but hold a common share therein with all mankind," but that it is also a relative judgment that "seems to have no essence that holds one notion with all." In the third essay, which in keeping with its title is the most digressive of the three, he considers the universal effects of natural diets of sulfurous and vitriolic salts on blackness. His discussions, in exposing the fallacies of popular opinions about the supposed nature and origins of black people, also catalogs such opinions, and thereby documents the pervasiveness of social thinking about black people at this moment.

Notable in Browne's discourse is the mixed quality of its racialism. The negative elements involve first the underlying assumption that blackness is a biological curiosity that needs to be explained, even if his project is to correct the misperceptions of it, and that falls under the subtitle of his work "Enquiries into Very Many Received Tenents and Commonly Presumed Truths." In this his obligation is to the exposition of philosophical objectivity rather than to an understanding of black people in particular. Black people are for him part of the other oddities of nature. Secondly, he implies on and off, as when he briefly considers the effects of tribal cosmetics on blackness, that it may be an acquired artificiality that is subsequent to an originary pre-black or white human condition. This is why his debunking of what he considers incorrect or misconceived explanations of blackness includes some fresh and original ones of his own, however conditionally stated. In both of these fundamental attitudes Browne is complicit in the negative marking of black people emanating from the Elizabethan period. These negative elements are what led Kim Hall to conclude that even though he "shows a good deal more cultural relativism," his overall view of blackness is as unfavorably judgmental as was George Best's seventy years earlier.[113] Shared by others as well, this estimate of Browne's views has become a staple of the new critical interest in English racial formations of the last three decades.[114]

But what is important to note in Browne, and these comprise the positive elements of his discussions, is that his views of black people are a lot more generous and inclusive than are Best's. The first instance of this is his gracious description of Africans as "a mighty and considerable part of mankind" early in his essay, followed

[113] *Things of Darkness*, p. 13.

[114] An early example is James Walvin's *Black Presence*, p. 33, and a recent one is Mary Floyd-Wilson's *English Ethnicity and Race*, p. 61.

later by his two repeated assertions that "Moors are not excluded from beauty" by the esthetic standards of both Aristotelian proportion and Platonic grace (pp. 472–73). Even if there may be a discernible patronizing defensiveness in such formulations, they mark what might be described as the first normative English view of black people that is articulated in the public sphere in the early modern period. Secondly, in his disinclination to pursue the causes of blackness beyond the "great obscurities" that bind it, and in his justification of that disinclination by his strident invocation of the great natural diversity of species ("And if any will yet insist, and urge the question further still upon me … I shall demand how the Camels of Bactria …"), Browne not only attempts to correctly undermine the logic of the topic itself and thereby permanently dismantle it, but also hints at what is arguably the principle of cultural pluralism as a political practice:

> For whereas it is imputed unto Anthropophagy, or the eating of man's flesh; that cause hath been common unto many other Countries … And thus if the favorable pen of Moses had not revealed the confusion of tongues, and positively declared their division at Babel; our disputes concerning their beginnings had been without end … (p. 468)

Reinforcing such a hint are words such as "several," "different," and "varieties." Thirdly, and supplementing the above two aspects, Browne's deployment of cultural relativism to explode the notion of African blackness being a "Curse" only to the English leads to a reverse esthetic judgment of white English people, in his explanation that Africans "esteem deformity by other colours, describing the Devil, and other objects, white." The cultural relativism and the reverse judgment that it enables act as a political equalizer, by which black people have the same power of discriminatory marking as white people, with whom they coexist virtually with identical self-agency on the same perceptual plane. Taken together, these three connected implications of Browne's excursus on blackness project a racial perspective that is unspokenly civil, tentatively accommodating, and nascently egalitarian. In their combined effect they counteract the perceptible negativity of some of his assumptions noted by Kim Hall and the others.

The contrasts of Browne's discourse with that of the Elizabethan George Best, despite Hall's equating of the two, are instructive in revealing the former's particular character. Although Best is an averagely educated but well-traveled mariner and Browne is "a doctor of medicine with degrees from Leyden and Oxford, and an intellectual of international stature,"[115] both are reasonably representative spokesmen of their times who are responding to the phenomenon of black people, even if the former is talking more about them in England than is the latter. Yet, whereas for Best blackness is a puzzling peripheral phenomenon that distracts him from his account of the attractions of the "Newfoundland," for Browne it is a centrally focused, familiar phenomenon that is need of being demystified. Where Best's comments are driven by the instinct to track, identify, and isolate African difference, Browne's are driven by the desire to dispel the myths of such difference. Where in Best's analysis blackness ends up being an "infection," in Browne's examination it appears as a natural human physiology however derived and different from the English.

[115] Walvin, *Black Presence*, p. 33.

Where Best's is driven by the anxiety of difference, Browne is guided by the wonder of natural diversity. Where Best seeks to contain the difference of blackness and diffuse it within the familiarity of Englishness, Browne aims at accepting it in its own terms and joining it to the genus of the species. Where Best is mutedly alarmist and separative, Browne is comfortably educative and inclusive. Of course, how far Browne's ideas found lasting compatibility with his readers is difficult to gauge, because even though *Pseudodoxia Epidemica* went through several editions until 1672 it was rarely reprinted afterwards.[116] Nevertheless, in the totality of their contents, Browne's discussions amount to a complex social consideration of black people that clearly marks the particularity of English racial consciousness in the middle of the seventeenth century.

That Thomas Browne's nuanced public views of black people are not an elite exception is evident in the fact that they are more or less echoed, appropriately in a newspaper report about London black people, around the same time. This is the account in the *Moderate Intelligencer*, in its issue of 10–17 April 1645, about a festive community of black people that gathered near the Portuguese ambassador's house in London:

> It's a strange custome in *Lincolne's Inn-fields*, not far from the *Portugall* Ambasadours house, the practice we conceive every way as bad, as any that were used when the book of Recreations commanded or permitted maygames, and revellings: … There gathers many hundreds of men, women, maids, and boyes together, then comes Negers, and others of like rankes, these make sport with our English women and maids, offer in the *Venetian* manner, by way of introduction to that used in their *Stewes*: why these black men should use our English maids and women upon the Lords day, or any other, in that manner, we know no reason for: but the truth is, the fault is wholly in those loose people that come there, and in the Officers of those Parishes where it is done. (Item 368)

The Portuguese ambassador at this time was Antonio de Souza, who assumed the position in 1642, and according to some accounts stayed in London throughout the Civil War years. De Souza was a close friend of Charles I, and among other facilitations that he offered the king he acted as a via media in the latter's communications with his exiled French-born Catholic wife, Henrietta Maria, in his necessarily hurried and scattered movements in the accumulating political turmoil of those years. A Marrano, De Sousa's residence was the gathering place for other ranking Portuguese Jews resident in London chiefly for purposes of Catholic worship.[117] This was an activity that fell between diplomatic privilege and its excess, but seen increasingly as the

116 Keynes, *The Works of Thomas Browne*, "Editor's Preface," pp. vii–viii.

117 For the start of De Souza's ambassadorship in 1642, see "Secretary Nicholas's Letter, for the Ship to carry Home the Portuguese Ambassador," in "House of Lords Journal Volume 5: 4 July 1642," *Journal of the House of Lords: Volume 5: 1642–1643 (1802)*, pp. 176–81. For his ambassadorship in 1645, his Marrano identity, and the Marrano gatherings at his house, see Albert Montefiore Hyamson, *A History of the Jews in England*, p. 171. For De Souza's closeness to Charles, and his continued residence in England through the Civil War years, see *Charles I in 1646: Letters of King Charles the First to Queen Henrietta Maria*, ed. John Bruce, p. xxxiii; and Samuel Rawson Gardiner, *History of England from the Accession of James I, to the Outbreak of the Civil War 1603–1642*, pp. 348–49.

latter with the rise of the Puritans to parliamentary power, and because of which De Souza's residence and those of the other Catholic ambassadors, all of which have Catholic chapels, were repeatedly under local scrutiny and parliamentary inquiry.[118] The *Intelligencer*'s report might reflect in part this community apprehension about frequent congregations of foreigners with alternative religious persuasions at his house.

The Portuguese embassy, including De Souza's official residence, was at this time somewhere just south of Lincoln's Inn Field, on a street that will for that reason after the Restoration come to be called Portugal Row.[119] Hence the report's allusion to the "Portugull Ambasadour's house" being "not far" from "Lincolne's Inne-fields." This is a spot north of the Strand and not far from it, because in the year of the *Intelligencer*'s report his brother, who was arrested on murder charges for killing an innocent man in the heat of an affray in the vicinity of the new Exchange in the Strand, took refuge in De Souza's house, claiming the diplomatic immunity of extra-territoriality, even if that was a claim that did not ultimately prevail with the parliamentary authorities.[120] In that location south of Lincoln's Inn Field, as well as south on the other side of the Strand bordering the Thames, were stately houses, including in the latter case the mansion estates of Arundel Place, Somerset House, Savoy Palace, Bedford House, the Leicester–Essex House, as well as Cecil's own imposing home (Agas map 5D, p. 17). Close as well to Whitehall and high government offices, the neighborhood was clearly compatible with high diplomatic housing, and thus a very plausible site for De Souza's official residence.[121] Skirting the open meadows to its immediate north, this location would be naturally privy to, and an enabler of, the revelries cited in the report.

At the same time, the report itself is a reflection of the rise of the cultural idea of "news" as a general consumable item that, as both Joad Raymond and Thomas

---

118 William Raleigh Trimble, "The Embassy Chapel Question," pp. 97–101. For parliamentary records about this issue, see the item titled "A Complaint that the *Portugall* Ambassador caused *English* Papists to be rescued out of the Officers Hands, and cried, Kill them," in "House of Lords Journal Volume 5: 10 May 1642," *Journal of the House of Lords: Volume 5: 1642–1643* (1802), pp. 57–58, and the order titled "Harbouring ill-affected, Persons, &c.," in "House of Commons Journal Volume 3: 12 June 1643," *Journal of the House of Commons: Volume 3: 1643–1644* (1802), pp. 125–27.

119 Lady Ann Fanshawe, who took up residence here in 1660, calls it "Portugal Row"; see Ann, Lady Fanshawe, *The Memoirs of Ann, Lady Fanshawe*, p. 95.

120 For accounts of the incident see John Foster, *The Statesmen of the Commonwealth of England*, p. 572, and *Dictionary of National Biography*, ed. Sidney Lee and Leslie Stephen, p. 162 (under "Henry Rolle"). Henry Rolle was the judge who presided over the case. Also known as Britain's Burse, the new Exchange is the shopping concourse built by James I in 1609 on the Strand's south side in Westminster, in the yard of Durham House on the north end of Ivy Lane as it meets the Strand ("Book 4, Ch. 3: The parishes of the Liberty of Westminster," in *A New History of London: Including Westminster and Southwark (1773)*, pp. 717–38).

121 For the posh character and history of Lincoln's Inn Fields see "Lincoln's Inn Fields," in *Old and New London: Volume 3* (1878), and "Book 5, Ch. 1: The out-parishes of Westminster," in *A New History of London: Including Westminster and Southwark* (1773), pp. 739–47. For its status as a highly preferential neighborhood see Emrys Jones, "London in the Early Seventeenth Century," pp. 130–31, including the map on p. 131.

Cogswell in different ways have shown, occurred in the middle decades of the seventeenth century. Such a cultural idea was fueled in part by the need for loyalist and parliamentary Puritan groups progressively enmeshed in bitter and violent conflict to have public outlets for the dissemination of their causes, and by the general growth of interest in reliable information about public events fed in some measure by prolonged and confusing international events such as the Thirty Years War. As a cultural formation, weekly "newsbooks" such as *The Moderate Intelligencer* combine the twin functions of news as dialogue and news as special information or knowledge for a consciously curious lay public.[122] The most prolific of those that were quick to seize the commercial potential of "news," and a pioneer in that game, the *Intelligencer*'s author (who is in effect its one-man staff) was a clothing manufacturer named John Dillingham with good connections to both parliamentary Puritans and monarchic loyalists in the aristocracy and gentry (for both of whom he was a military outfitter), and already a prominent government journalist writing *The Parliament Scout* as well as contributing to several other publications when he started *The Moderate Intelligencer* for the publisher and printer Robert White in January 1645. Working within a rapidly growing and rancorous media industry, Dillingham's pieces are characterized by their concern for moderation and civility in an increasingly fragmented national community, as A. N. B. Cotton has shown in his study of Dillingham's career.[123] What is unusual about the item cited, however, is that it is an exception to Dillingham's usual coverage, as well as to those of his colleagues, devoted to military developments and political advocacy. Hence, the report's apology at its outset for straying from "Mars" to "Venus" and "Bacchus." What makes the report's contents "newsworthy" in that moment, of course, is what is of interest to the present inquiry.

These historical contexts and the location implied help to illuminate the black people mentioned in the report. Their presence is made predictable by the general history of their possession by Iberian expatriates all across London, as was seen in several examples in the last chapter. Their incidence in this location is also consistent with the royal and high Westminster fashion of keeping domesticated black people started in Elizabethan times and continuing into this century, as seen earlier. The black individuals appearing in the report thus are a commingling of Africans already resident in the area and those from the households of the Iberian personnel repairing to De Souza's house for Catholic worship and social interaction. The merrymaking described in the report may be inherited from familiar community rituals of "permitted maygames and revellings," which, coming down from its observance in the later Middle Mges often in connection with church-ales on the first day of May and at Whitsuntide, while prohibited in Elizabethan and early Jacobean times,

[122] Thomas Cogswell, "The Politics of Propaganda: Charles I and the People in the 1620s," pp. 189–209; Joad Raymond, "Introduction," in Joad Raymond, ed., *News Networks in Seventeenth-Century Britain and Europe*, p. 3.

[123] Dillingham's career is detailed by A. N. B. Cotton, in his essay "John Dillingham, Journalist of the Middle Group." See particularly pp. 817–19, 821–25.

were expressly reauthorized by James and Charles.[124] At the time of the record they were a continuing popular English folk entertainment despite disapproval by conservative groups in both Puritan and monarchist camps. Although it is unclear if the phenomenon was a one-time event or a recurrent occurrence over several weeks, the gathering was clearly part of a seasonal springtime activity in which the black people were now a happy part of the merrymaking crowd. They thus appear as an additionally mentionable part of a spontaneous street happening that in the *Intelligencer*'s concerned sight is cause for thought, a concern heightened by the traditional sobriety of the Sunday on which it is taking place. The scene's incredible felicity can easily be imagined from the anonymous Portuguese painting titled *Chafariz d'el Rei in the Alfama District*, done in Lisbon between 1560 and 1580 and depicting a convivial scene of urban cross-racial mingling that Kate Lowe and T. F. Earle reproduce in their book (see Fig. 3.1), the logic of the invocation lying in the fact that English experiences of black people emanated from and followed the cultural experiences of the Iberian peninsula, as this study has maintained throughout. Both peripheral and central to the scene in which they appear, the former because they are not the sole object of the *Moderate Intelligencer*'s report, and the latter because they are what give the report its sharpest news interest, these black people describe a social moment that captures the story of their seventeenth-century English history.

This can be seen in the report's verbal architecture. Preceded by an apology for their inclusion that makes them a digression, "Give us leave to insert somewhat this day, and pardon the digression to the day and also of the matter," the black people appear seven lines after the report begins. Their status as digressions is a double one because it is encased within the merrymaking incident itself, which is the primary digression for the newsbook's normal fare, "our business." At the report's end, their dismissal from culpability for the unauthorized revelry within which they are seen, "the fault lies wholly in the loose people that come here, and in the Officers of those parishes where it is done," is their trivialization in the cancellation of their self-agency. So, textually admitted reluctantly as in "but not to keep you from the matter any longer," and set aside quickly in two lines, with the hurried qualification of "but the truth is," black people are tangential to the report's admissible interests and outside its conscious gaze. This is their virtual absence from the report. At the same time, emerging in the seventh line of the 15-line report, the black people are located exactly in the report's center, not just in structural but in thematic terms as well. The latter aspect is made up of the unspoken attractiveness of the black people that drives the report's teleology, as it brushes compulsively past the "hundreds of men, women, maids, and boyes," to "then comes Negers," the subject of whose actions occupies the next six lines. This disproportion in the deployment of its verbal assets betrays the report's real concern and interests, namely its uneasiness at the "sport" that the black people are making with "our English women and maids," a familiar fear of miscegenic defilement that is accentuated by the reversal of the order of "women" and "maids" when the phrase is repeated in the next line: "why these

124 Annie Abram, *English Life and Manners in the Later Middle Ages*, p. 243; *Phillip Stubbes's Anatomy of the Abuses in England in Shakspere's Youth*, ed. Frederick James Furnivall, p. 306; Michael J. Colarucio, *The Province of Piety*, pp. 273–74.

Fig. 3.1 Artist Unknown, *Chafariz d'el Rei in the Alfama District, Lisbon*, ca. 1570–98. The Barardo Collection, Lisbon

black men should use our English maides and women … in this manner … ." This is the sensational appeal that lies beneath the report's modest language. Deepening that lurid appeal are the marking of blackness as a "ranke" in the casual reference of "like rankes," and the allusion not just to local "stewes" but to "Venetian" ones as the origins of the black people and their behavior, the xenophobic touch both increasing reflexively the corruption of English womanhood and marking a gestural semiotic of black expulsion.

The inadvertent way in which the black people edge into the center of Dillingham's concerns, despite their oblique location in his reporting gaze, replicates generally the English history of black people in the preceding century and half, and particularly the dynamics of black people's mixed history in the first five decades of the seventeenth. That replication is implicit in the fact that, whether consciously or not, in the report's experience black people are both undesirable and attractive, unseeable but present, the object of the kind of negative recognition that attaches to them in the sixteenth century. Cloaked in the nameless anonymity of a generalized plurality, distanced in the vague grouping of "and others," and described as a threat to English morals and sanctity that "use our … women upon the Lords day," the report's black people are also the principal actors in the joyousness and vivacity of this festive scene of voluntary cross-racial mingling of "hundreds of people." They are the graceful initiators of such mingling, in the "introduction[s]" they "offer in the Venetian manner … used in their Stewes," i.e. in their kisses, and which, judging from the report's silence about the results, delight the recipients and are welcomed by them. The report's uneasy concluding disapproval of the entire scene, as it quickly deflects judgment from them to a suddenly constructed "those loose people that come there," which could mean the white elements in the crowd, including the women, and to the local parochial authorities, "the officers of the parishes," while disempowering the Africans as suggested above also has the effect of preserving their innocence. The split attitude of Dillingham's report, between condemnation and condonation, disavowal and compulsive interest, between an official marginalizing and an inadvertent centralizing, delineates precisely the mixed atmosphere of benign neglect that is the locus of black growth in the first half the seventeenth century as seen in the records so far. That this attitude is reflected in a mid-century newsbook whose genre typically combines desirable information and dialog about it means that such an attitude is both reflective of public opinion and an advocation of it. In this way the *Moderate Intelligencer*'s report about black people becomes a mini index of the black history of the early modern moment.

The report also contains, as it so happens, the germs of the developments in English black history that are now imminent. In its criticism of the "Officers of the parishes" for allowing the kind of activity that it describes, the report also implicitly articulates a review of the black presence that it thinks has grown unbeknown to its readers, and which is partly the logic of its calculated appeal in the first place, suggesting that it has existed too long as an inexplicable thing: "we know no reason for." The throwaway nature of that remark belies the specificity of the charge that contains it, namely the query of why "the black men should use our English maids and women upon the Lords day," its real encompassing nature evident in the query's quickly sliding qualification that follows, "or any other," so that the phrase "we know no reason for" ultimately comes to bear on the insensibility of such black behavior at all times, and by implication on the impermissibility of black people in general. Overall, the report's disquiet about "Negers" is part of the alarmist concern sounded at the end of the preceding report, titled "From beyond seas thus," at the deterioration of life everywhere: "What an Age is this!" The reference is in part to the spectacle of European nations at each other's throats and involved in a relentless killing spree with the Turks, and in part to the scenario of rising urban alcoholism in the invocation of the "abundance of Drunkards" in the second digressive report that follows that of the "negers." The "negers" report is thus the middle of a three-part protest against global degeneracy, of which the instance of unfettered black people cavorting happily with white English women in public is the high point. The happy black scene unintentionally evident in Dillingham's report, accruing from a benign neglect that has nourished black people's survival over the previous five decades, is, in other words, under notice. It is about to pass.

1645 was a critical year. English national politics was evenly poised between alternative outcomes, an increasingly unpopular but familiar monarchic order, or a popular but radical and uncertain Puritan republicanism.[125] Charles, while expelled from London, was still successfully resisting the new Puritan army. Before the year was over, the national scene would begin to change, and new English policies, both carrying and being carried by international economic forces, would obliterate the bubble of a humane

[125] These choices are nicely described by Latham and Matthews in their edition of Samuel Pepys's *Diary*, 1: xxvi.

black English survival. The ominousness of the larger historical moment of Dillingham's news item lends a preciousness to the hopeful black scene inscribed in it.

The swelling climax of early seventeenth-century English black history made up of the *The Moderate Intelligencer*'s black citation and by those of Browne and Aubrey, and that is represented by the epigraphic quotations placed for expository convenience in that order in the heading of this chapter, constitute the point of critical mass, so to speak, of the temporary locus of black growth. The innocuousness of that growth is reflected in the fragility of this locus, which is a heterogeneous, indistinct, and default formation. It was shaped by the particularities of English political and social history in the reigns of James I and Charles I, and by the natural discursive divergences of black people's negative Elizabethan markings stemming from their continued presence in the next half century. This locus is not so much reflective of an increase in the numbers of black people, symptomatic or literal, as it is of a transitional mutation in English responses to the black subject in the early modern period. It is also partly thus a cumulative phenomenon in that it carries forward many of the aspects of the early and later Tudor periods. In fact, the locus's benignity might be a function of the relative numerical diminution of black people in the Jacobean and Caroline years, as is the similar benignity of the smaller black presence in the early Tudor regimes. If this linkage between the fortunes of black people in the first half of the sixteenth century and that of the seventeenth is one of progression, from fewer to greater numbers and from an English benignity fed by curiosity to one fed by familiarity, the same incremental parallelism between the later sixteenth century and that of the seventeenth predicts for the latter a like increase in numbers and a radical escalation of the captivity of black people from casual chattelhood to official mass slavery. Thus, existing as an interlude between the progressive negative black markings of the Elizabethan period and those of the later seventeenth century, that is, as a moment of respite in the history of its English oppression, as a brief moment of brightness between two enveloping epistemes of desolation, the locus of black growth in the first half of the seventeenth century could, at risk of straining a now unfashionable literary metaphor, be described as a renaissance of English black people in the early modern age. To be sure, this "renaissance" has no signal accomplishments of prominent personalities, no breakthrough developments in any branch of human learning or endeavor, not even any "events" as such, to herald its claim. What it does have is the dignity of survival of a violated people, which *is* an achievement in the enduring silence of their forgotten English history.

A precise reflection of the black peacefulness of the mid-1640s is provided in a pictorial representation of a black person in 1645. Done by Wencelaus Hollar, this is the portrait of a black woman dressed in the clothes of her service (see Fig.3.2). The image's poise, calmness, and character, which Kim Hall has commented on, is the only visual representation of a English black person in this demeanor that exists.[126] In that it seems to uncannily personify the black hopefulness of this moment.

---

[126] The possible English location of the portrait's subject is suggested by the fact that the portrait is situated in a private household in Kent. See Hall, "Object into Object," pp. 368–70.

Fig. 3.2 Wenceslaus Hollar, *Black Woman*, 1645. Folger Shakespeare Library, Washington, DC

A foretaste of what lies ahead is present in the citation of a legal record of 1658 that Margo Hendricks has pointed out. This is the entry in the Middlesex Sessions of the Peace of 21 October 1658, describing the suit of a black man against two young women for defrauding him of an amount of money with false promises of marriage, and for which he seeks compensation: "That Katherine Hutchins, and Elizabeth Simpson and Mary Biggins pretended to make a marriage between

Martin Francis (a blackamoore) and the said Elizabeth, thereby defrauding him of seventeen pounds in money" (Item 384). The propriety of considering this record at this point in this chapter's discussion can be seen in three immediately noticeable aspects of this record. The first is the relatively independent social standing of Martin Francis that is evident not just in the lack of any visible encumbrances for him but also in his obvious possession of financial means sufficient to make him a credible marriage prospect. Second, irrespective of exactly what transpires between the three individuals, the incident echoes the social atmosphere of inter-communal mixing seen in the *Mercurius Politicus*'s news item. As Margo Hendricks put it, "The brief entry serves as further proof of the presence and assimilation of people of African ancestry into early modern English culture."[127] That generally relaxed racial atmosphere is also implicit in Martin's ability to seek legal redress, even if how his suit turns out is not known. Yet, the details of the case point to strains in this setting. If true, Martin's suit underlines a cynical perception of the black man that assumes an emotional gullibility in him amenable to financial exploitation. Without putting too fine a point on this inference, it is possible to acknowledge that the record's contents show a degree of friction not present in newsbook's report thirteen years earlier. That difference may be a sign of the changed cultural politics that has appeared in the years following Dillingham's publication.

IV

Within a decade of the *Moderate Intelligencer*'s report, starting from the end of the very year in which it was published, the royalist forces lost the Civil War, Charles I was executed, and Oliver Cromwell's Puritan government officially assumed power in England in 1653. This rehearsal of the basic events of English Civil War history might seem to be little connected to a black English history were it not for a fact little noticed in traditional English historical scholarship of the period. As black historians have pointed out, one of Cromwell's earliest moves was to capture Jamaica from the Spaniards in 1655. This event signaled, as Follarin Shyllon put it, the "wholehearted participation in the slave trade," not just of Cromwell's England but also that of the later Stuart monarchy, restored to power in 1660.[128] Untouched by the vicissitudes of English national politics, English slaving activity in Africa continues from the 1630s onwards with Charles's renewal in 1631 of the African trading patent given out by his father in 1618, with the renewal of the Guinea company's monopoly in 1651, and also in the company's own testimony in 1686, in its dispute with a Swedish company over land near the Cape Coast, of its prior claim to that land from four decades earlier.[129] This continuing English investment is partly to be explained by the increasing involvement of parliamentary gentry in overseas trading, as was stated at the beginning of this chapter. The black people arriving residually in England from the African trade supplement the resident black population, which is also perhaps sustained by the favorable climate for black trading at the level of Anglo-Spanish

127 "Feminist Historiography," p. 372.

128 Shylonn, *Black Slaves*, p. 2.

129 Hugh Thomas, *Slave Trade*, p. 197; Davies, *Royal African Company*, pp. 40–41.

commercial contacts that may have been resurgent from Charles I's cessation of hostilities with Spain at the beginning of the 1540s, even if by that time Spain and Portugal are no longer the major players in the African theatre. But the difference of this modest activity from what follows is starkly evident in the fact that from just two years after Dillingham's report, English slave purchases in Africa over the next five years increased by nearly 300 percent, according to Joseph Inikori's calculations.[130] This jump was the product of the rising ascendancy of the plantation and joint stock company investing parliamentary gentry whose ascendancy brought Cromwell to power and propelled his interest in aggressive English pursuits of plantation economies, first in Barbados and then in Jamaica, and whose continuing influence guided the young king brought in to succeed Cromwell after his death in 1658 to make African slave-trading a mass commodity industry headed by the royal family itself.[131] Appropriately titled, when the Royal Adventurers into Africa was set up in 1660 in the very first year of Charles II's reign, its list of investors included the king himself, his two brothers and one sister, and "two dukes, a marquis, five earls, four barons, and seven knights." Joining this list in 1663, when the company's original charter of "a thousand years" was reissued, were the king's new queen, Catherine of Braganza, and the king's mother.[132] Among the assets contributed by the king to the Royal Adventurers in 1661 was a ship pointedly called *The Blackamoor*.[133] The company's broad social base is reflected in its inclusion of the political philosopher John Locke and the social diarist Samuel Pepys. Unsurprisingly, Charles II himself had an African in 1679.[134] If the slaving of black people is thus the point of commonalty between the otherwise bitterly divergent Puritan and monarchist groups, that is merely a pointed demonstration of the natural convergence of and collusion between the rise of early modern capitalism and its insatiable thirst for markets, and the global European colonial project that evolved partly as an attempt to slake that thirst.

As Hugh Thomas put it, "the profits that could be made from trading slaves" had by the middle of the century been learned by Puritans and royalist alike. Devoted to a quarter of its total volume from the outset, the new African trade's slaving business, which was now stated openly in its charter, returned some £100,000. Jamaica received three hundred slaves in 1663 alone, while Barbados acquired over 3,000 between 1663 and 1664. If by 1663 the profits coming back from the African trade in general produced an altogether new, and what will be an enduring, English coin called the "guinea," by 1667 they led to a demand for slaving in Guinea "as and when ... [the English slavers] liked." In 1668 the Royal Adventures begot another company, the Gambia Adventurers. Expectedly, the successor of the Royal Adventurers in 1672, the Royal African Company, also had a thousand years African trading charter, but it had more people

---

130 Based on Dutch accounts of English slave shipping in Africa between 1645 and 1647 (19 ships) and 1652 and 1657 (84 ships). Inikori, *Africans and the Industrial Revolution in England*, p. 218.

131 Ibid., p. 37; Davies, *Royal African Company*, pp. 32–38, 51–54.

132 Hugh Thomas, *Slave Trade*, pp. 198–99.

133 George Fredrick Zook, "The Royal Adventurers in England," p. 146.

134 *Moneys received and paid for secret services of Charles II and James II from 30th March, 1679, to 25th December, 1688*, p. 58, cited by J. A. Rogers, *Nature Knows No Color Line*, p. 161.

from the business class and an even more pronounced interest in slave-trading than its predecessor. A stark reflection of the increasing normalizing of the greed of slaving is the proud self-display of first the Royal Adventurers and then of the Royal African Company in an ostentatious building in London's Broad Street called the Africa House, the venue of what one of the company's principal defenders, the Restoration economist Charles Davenant (William Davenant's son), said was its performance as "an academy for training an indefinite number in the … knowledge of … the African trade."[135] The result was that "3000 merchants" used the Royal Exchange in the reign of Charles II," and "private banking" to handle "regular commercial investment," began.[136] The sterling profits of slave-trading between 1662 and 1660 alone were between £40,000 and £52,000.[137] This mushrooming culture of the astronomical profitability of slave-trading is what impelled the transformation of black people in England from what James Walvin has described as "humanity to commodity."[138]

This historical context of sweeping changes in the English perceptions of Africans inevitably frames the history of black people in mid-seventeenth-century London, although the effect of the former on the latter is not immediate or demonstrably direct. This is because there is always a disconnection and time lag between events at the macro level and the minutiae of local life. Even if the exact numbers of black people thus enslaved in Restoration London are inevitably impossible to ascertain, the evidence of the documentary records provide some indication of the scale and the nature of the radical change in black history that appears from the middle of the seventeenth century. Between 1654 and 1677 there are fifty records of assorted varieties that tell this story, which is a difference in frequency ratio between 2.17 records per year for this quarter century alone (50 records in 23 years) versus 1.4 per year for the entire previous half century (71 records in 50 years), and which is an increase of 54 percent. Already located on a chattel level of existence, even if the quality and substance of that life has been incrementally mutating in the century's first five decades, black people in mid-century London show the impact of the new historical forces bearing down on them only in subtle ways, such as, in addition to the increased volume of their appearance, their clearer identification as black people (in 37 out of 50 records, i.e. in more than half or 72 percent of them, they are clearly identified as negroes or blackamores), and in the resurgence of the naming of their encumbrances. Only in two instances in the records of this period is the new changed history of the black subject unambiguously apparent, in one of which a black person is for the first time clearly called "a slave," and in the other of which an unconditional English sovereignty over black people is asserted. Limited by the straining scope and length of this study, it will be possible here to provide only a cursory discussion of the contents of these black records of the third quarter of the seventeenth century.

The first group of black citations among these records is made up of the ambiguous "Blackman/Blackmoore/Moore" varieties and it occurs in the city's

135 Thomas, pp. 198–203.

136 Maurice Ashley, *Great Britain to 1688*, pp. 383, 386.

137 Inikori, *Africans and the Industrial Revolution*, p. 220.

138 See the chapter titled "Humanity to Commodity," in Walvin, *Black and White*, pp. 31–45.

west side, encompassing all three event categories of baptism, marriage, and burial. These entries consist of the burial of "Elizabeth Blackman" on 1 November 1655 in St. Margaret's, Westminster, and in the same parish the baptism and burial of "Eizabeth Blackmoore" on 22 February and 2 June of 1657, respectively, the burial of "Adam Moore" on 28 February 1659, the burial of "Sarah Blackmore" on 25 October 1659, the christening of "Martha Blackmore" on 1 August 1660, the burial of "Ed Blackmore" on 5 February 1663, and the marriage of "Jo. Johnson to Eliz. Blackmoore" on 12 December 1676 (Items 379, 381, 382, 389, 387, 390, 406, 447). In nearby St. Martin in the Fields, Westminster are the burials of "Georgius Blackmore" and "Samuell Blackmore" on 25 November 1662 and 23 April 1663, respectively (Items 399, 401), and in St. James Clerkenwell to the north-east is the marriage of "Phillip Waddleworth and Anne Nagar" and "John Blackmore and Ane Hartley" on 6 April 1666 and 26 September 1667, respectively (Items 413, 418). Finally, also in Westminster is the marriage of "Daniel Price and Jane Blackmore" on 25 April 1675 in Holy Trinity, Knightsbridge (Items 440).

Several brief summary observations came be made about these thirteen entries. First, these are all likely descendents of the similarly named individuals seen in these locations in the records of the earlier periods. The location of John Blackmore's and Anne Nagar's marriages in St. James, Clerkenwell, while having a somewhat different character from that of St. Magaret's, Westminster and St. Martin in the Fields, is neither entirely bereft of people of affluence nor unacquainted with Africans, even if in its stews. The other exception here is the site of Jane Blackmore's marriage in Holy Trinity, Knightsbridge, also known as Trinity Chapel, west of Charing Cross, which was a small poor chapel of ease set up by Bishop Laud in Charles I's reign and attached to what was at one time a leprosy hospital.[139] The impoverishment of the locale suggests that Jane's marriage to Daniel might be one of mutual convenience between similarly disempowered people. These marriages are identical to some of the other cross-racial marriages seen earlier in this place in Elizabethan and later decades. Third, this group may constitute the surviving vestiges of the innocuous growth and assimilation of black people of the previous Jacobean and Caroline reigns, partly enabled perhaps by the distracting political tumult of the changing regimes of the 1650s and 1660s. In any case, to a certain degree, here as well as in all the previous instances of their documentary appearances, these kinds of entries are cryptic anomalies that allow only for only the most uncertain and speculative of interpretations. The very ambiguity of their surnames invites a minimum consideration of the possibility of these individuals as black people.

Among the remaining 37 records of the Cromwellian, Restoration, and post-Restoration years that more pointedly identify black people are 25 more parish records of different London districts. Of these, 19 citations are of black people named without any encumbrances. On the west side these include the baptisms of "Francis Honey a Blackamoor" on 17 July 1660 at St. Giles in the Fields, "John Brant, a Neger" on 30 August 1663 at St. Mary, Putney, "John Paul a negro" and "Thomas Paul, a negro" both on 25 February 1668 at St. Giles in the Fields, "John

[139] *Survey of London*, 2: 146–47; "The western suburbs: Knightsbridge," in *Old and New London*, vol. 5 (1878), pp. 15–28.

the son of Abimelech Potter a blackamoor" on 4 April 1669 at St. Mary, Lambeth, and the burial of "Clemen, a blackamore" on 22 July of the same year in St. Paul, Covent Garden (Items 392, 403, 420, 421, 424, 426). In the 1670s occur the baptisms of "Thomas a blackmore" on 6 April 1672 at St. Paul, Covent Garden, "Joseph, a blackmore about 20 years of age" on 12 May 1672 at St. Botolph Aldersgate, "Thomas Springe, a blackemore supposed to bee about Eight yeares of age" on 29 March 1674 at St. Mary Lambeth, and "Charles, a black, his name Hercules" on 21 December 1675 at St. Clement Danes, Westminster (Items 431, 432, 438, 443). The last item, in the suggestion of extraordinary strength present in the given nickname, offers a clue to the hard labor in which this African will have been employed. In this decade are also the unusual simultaneous baptisms of "James Mooty, Henry Cushdy, John Bonock, David Assica, Moores" on 23 June 1672 at St. Giles in the Fields, and of "Thomas Dingley," "Hannah Botun," 'blackamores'" on 22 January 1675 (1676) in Christchurch, Newgate Street (Items 433, 444), which while being within the city is close to its western walls and adjoins Westminster.

Several features in this group of 12 records are worth noting. First, their locations are suggestive of the continuities of London black history in this century. St. Clement Danes Westminster, St. Giles in the Fields, and St. Mary Putney are locations seen earlier to have a black presence in them, so that for Africans to be named in these two sites is not unexpected. The two new locations are also compatible with a black presence. St. Paul, Covent Garden, the church for the parish of Covent Garden (originally spelled Convent Garden), just north of the Strand in Westminster, was like Holy Trinity, Knightsbridge a new church built in the reign of Charles I; it was made a parish church in 1660, all under the auspices of Francis Russell, the Earl of Bedford,[140] and associated with the new playhouse, the Theatre Royal in nearby Drury Lane on its east. Not only does the proximity of St. Paul, Covent Garden to locations all around it that had Africans from the beginning of the century predict the African named here now, so does the Earl of Bedford's own history, which even though he died in 1641 included privateering investments from as far back as 1625.[141] St. Botolph Aldersgate, immediately outside the city gate of Aldersgate and directly to its north, and situated on Little Britain Street on the west side of Aldersgate Street running north-west to St. Albans (Agas map 3L, p. 7), was "a proper parish" in Stow's

[140] Reginald Jacobs, *Covent Garden: Its Romance and History*, pp. 38–42; "1ª *vice lecta est Billa*, An Act for the Making of the Church and Inhabitants of *Convent-garden* parochial," in "House of Commons Journal Volume 2: 16 January 1643," *Journal of the House of Commons: volume 2: 1640–1643 (1802)*, pp. 928–30.

[141] See the listing of the Earl of Bedford as a backer of commercial privateering projects in Rabb, *Enterprise and Empire*, p. 369; see key to Rabb's listing procedures on pp. 231–32. For extended discussions of the nature, geographic scope, and profits, of early modern English privateering enterprises, see K. R. Andrews, *Trade, Plunder and Settlement*, pp. 245–55, and Rabb, pp. 61–62. Privateering projects, that by the beginning of the seventeenth century and by 1629 reached, according to the estimates of both these sources, 60% profit returns from outlays of £100,000 annually, were particularly profitable in the western Mediterranean and eastern Atlantic coastlines, including the African coast. They almost certainly included, with their other booty, seizures of Africans.

time.[142] In the vicinity of Cooks Hall and Windsor House, which faced the church on its east side, and Northumberland House which faced it on its south side just inside the city wall, and not far from the Halls of the Goldsmiths Haberdashers, and Chandlers, to its south-east, St. Botolph Aldersgate was a reasonably well-off parish conforming to the political and economic pull of Westminster.[143] Its well-connected mercantile and political character, the latter reflected partly by the residence here at this time of the Bishop of London,[144] was conducive to the importation of seized Africans, just as was the case with many London neighborhoods seen earlier.

Secondly, these new locations show the spread of the English cultural habit of possession of black people. In the way that the citations in St. Paul, Covent Garden, St. Botolph Aldersgate, and St. Mary Lambeth show fresh incidences of adult baptisms, they provide one reflection of the increasing influx of captured Africans into mid-seventeenth-century London. Thirdly, even if these records do not mention encumbrances for black people, the regularity of their black markings from the end of the 1650s seems to indicate a change, in that from the Restoration onwards clearly marked black records begin to appear each year. Such a change is particularly suggested by the baptisms in St. Mary, Lambeth of John the son of Abimelech Potter and Thomas Springe within five years of each other, which together signally mark the accelerated resurgence of the phenomenon of interested politically demonstrative English conversions of black people first seen in the case of Walter Anberey from Dungala in 1610 and repeated in that of Dederj Iaquoah from Sierra Leone in 1611. Located on the south bank of the Thames south-west of Westminster Palace, St. Mary, Lambeth was the church attached to Lambeth Palace on its east (Agas map 8C, p. 16), the residence of the Archbishop of Canterbury since several centuries earlier.[145] While unlike the earlier baptisms, John's and Thomas's were not publicly orchestrated events, their political character is unmistakably evident thus in their locations, which unavoidably connect them to the Archbishop of Canterbury or the involvement of his high office, and which together with Joseph's baptism in St. Botolph Aldersgate, where the Bishop of London is resident, mark the first time such an involvement is visible in the early modern English black records. This particular phenomenon is even more strongly evident in the repeated baptisms of East Indians, as will be mentioned later. Finally, the two entries of simultaneous multiple black baptisms point to the beginning of mass importations of Africans, an observation that the predominance of adult baptisms in these entries also supports.

The rest of the 19 citations of unambiguously named but unencumbered black people in mid-seventeenth-century London are from the city's east and south sides. Comprising a total of seven records, these include in the east the baptism of "Sara

---

142 *Survey of London*, 1: 304, 309.

143 "Book 2, Ch. 4: Aldersgate Ward', *A New History of London: Including Westminster and Southwark* (1773), pp. 543–45.

144 P. Griffiths, J. Landers, M. Pelling, R. Tyson, "Population and Disease, Estrangement and Belonging 1540–1700," p. 227. Griffiths et al. describe St. Botolph Aldersgate as an example of the maze of alleys and courts in many London neighborhoods shared by the rich and poor alike.

145 "Book 3, Ch. 2: Rotherhithe, Newington Butts and Lambeth," *A New History of London: Including Westminster and Southwark* (1773), pp. 690–94.

Reide of ye age of 27 years a Blackamore" on 31 March 1659 in St. Dunstan, Stepney, the burial of "Joseph Lisbone, a blackemore" on 1 February 1663 (1664) in St. Katherine by the Tower, following in the same parish the baptism of his son, "son of Joseph Lisbone and Martha Cradwell," on 31 January of that year, and his marriage, "Joseph Lisbone married Martha Cradwell" three years earlier on 19 January 1660 (Items 385, 405, 404, 388). In that same parish was also the marriage of "Paul Peache, a blackemore and Rosamond Key" on 26 September 1672 (Item 434). In the city's south side are the two baptism records of "Ralph Trunckett, a blackamoore aged 20 years" on 11 October 1668 in St. Saviour's, Southwark, and "Robert a blacke" on 24 July 1670 in St. Nicholas, Deptford (Items 422, 429). Aspects of this subset of black notations deserving comment include first the fact that the east-side entries are in unsurprising locations of black presence long established in the records of this book, including in the two parishes named, St. Dunstan Stepney and St. Katherine by the Tower. These notations are therefore part of the growing black importations documented in the city's west-side records in this time, and which is also seen in the new black location of St. Nicholas Deptford. Secondly, the black consolidation in family growth and cross-racial marriage seen in the Joseph Lisbone and Paul Peache citations, while being hopeful social signs in themselves, may be anomalous features, accruing from the particular benign neglect of these poor east-side liberties. That such developments are unusual for this time is seen in the fact that the contemporary south-side items of Southwark and Deptford do not show them, even if those areas have slightly rougher social characters. The exceptionality of the Lisbone and Peache entries is reinforced by that of the Sara Reide baptism record, which in its mention of a black woman marks a variation from the predominantly male black citations of the Restoration and post-Restoration period overall. Thirdly, that black people are appearing in the dockside area of Deptford, itself situated east of Southwark on the Thames's south bank, since the beginning of the century was the chief point of disembarkation for the returning ships of the English cross-oceanic trading projects, is a small sign of the escalation of their slave-trading activities by this time. The St. Nicholas Deptford citation is in fact one of several documentations of other black people, such as East Indians, occurring here, as will be shown in the book's concluding section.

Of the 25 parish records that directly identify black people, six plainly show their encumbered statuses. These are the baptism of "Daniel Thomas a Negro servant to Mr. Hutchinson of stepnie" on 24 September 1661 in St. Dunstan, Stepney; the burial of "Emanuell Feinande, Mr Adams' friend's slave, a blackmore" on 20 November 1662 in St. Benet Fink inside the city; the burial of "A negro man servant of Mr. John Newton's, from Mr. Raworthe" on 29 July 1665 in St. Olave, Hart Street; the baptism of "Edward Dedford, a black at John Turner's" on 10 September 1665 in St. Mary Putney; the burial of "Theophilus Cock, a Blackamore, Sr john Thorowgoods foot-boy" on 26 March 1674 in Kensington, Middlesex; and the burial of "A blackamore boy of Mr. John Temple, Goldsmith" on 25 April 1675 in St. Mary Woolnoth inside the city (Items 396, 398, 410, 412, 437, 442). What is of immediate interest here are the locations, owner identities, and revelatory wording of the records. To start with the first point of interest, all the locations here are again demonstrative of the connectedness and continuity of the geographical pattern of black importation in early modern London seen earlier. Whereas each of these locations has a more or less marked prior history of domesticated black presences, the appearance here of locations within the city walls and in the city center (St. Olave, Hart Street, St. Benet Fink, St. Mary Woolnoth), compared to the mostly suburban neighborhoods in the immediately preceding subgroup of records, points symptomatically to a gradual intensification of the phenomenon of black possession between 1660 and 1675.

The identities of the owners are even more instructive. The "Mr. Hutchinson" of the baptism record of Daniel Thomas is almost certainly the Richard Hutchinson who appears in the vestry minutes of St Dunstan All Saints, Stepney in October 1655 and April 1658, in the same role of a disburser of public funds in which he was first mentioned in 1644 when he and two other London citizens were appointed by parliament to disburse relief money to wounded soldiers, a role that eventually made him secretary of the Navy in 1650.[146] He was either from Stepney, its maritime connections facilitating his appointment as Navy Treasurer, or by the middle 1650s he was living in Stepney, presumably retired, which is why his name appears in the Stepney parish vestry minutes. This history, if correct, would explain his acquisition of the African Daniel Thomas. While in the Emanuel Feinande record the friend of "Mr. Adams" may be ultimately unknowable, the latter may be the Scottish merchant of that name who was licensed by parliament in August 1642 to "go beyond seas", and who was a provisioner for the army in Ireland in November 1642.[147] He may be the "Richard Adams" who had privateering involvements in 1625, whom Theodore Rabb lists in his catalog of English parliamentary figures with mercantile investments.[148] He may have had connections to St. Andrew Hubbard in Eastcheap from his possible residence there in 1638, which could explain the record's location in St. Benet Fink, which is not too far to the east from the former location.[149] If the identification is correct, this history is compatible with Adams either himself possessing an African or being close to colleagues who did so, and of his offering his good offices to them regarding such a possession, or even vice versa (if by the record's date he is dead), these possibilities being suggested by the curiously extended relationship within which Emanuell is described.

While it is difficult to know precisely who John Newton was, he may be the merchant MP of that name who had investments in the Spanish Company.[150] That possible identification would make his "negro man servant" an easy product of his

---

146 *Memorials of Stepney Parish*, pp. 214, 225, 228; "Ordinance for a Collection on the Thanksgiving-day, for Relief of maimed Soldiers," in "House of Lords Journal Volume 7: 4 November 1644," *Journal of the House of Lords: volume 7: 1644* (1802), pp. 45–48; ("Navy Victualling" in "House of Commons Journal Volume 6: 10 October 1650," *Journal of the House of Commons: volume 6: 1648–1651* (1802), pp. 481–82).

147 "Licence to Adams," in "House of Commons Journal Volume 2: 17 August 1642," *Journal of the House of Commons: volume 2: 1640–1643* (1802), pp. 723–25; "Irish Affairs" in "House of Commons Journal Volume 2: 01 November 1642," *Journal of the House of Commons: volume 2: 1640–1643* (1802), pp. 828–30.

148 Rabb, *Enterprise and Empire*, p. 233.

149 "Inhabitants of London in 1638: St. Andrew Hubbert, East Cheap," in *The Inhabitants of London in 1638* (1931), pp. 22–23 (a Mr. Adams is assessed here the sum of £10 in 1638).

150 Rabb, *Enterprise and Empire*, p. 349.

business career. Sir John Thorowgood was a parliamentarian who in 1647 was part of the officers escorting the defeated King Charles to his imprisonment, and who in 1649 was one of those appointed to try the defeated Earl of Cambridge for conspiracy.[151] His lineage makes his possession of a captive African a by now well-established, decorative social necessity. St. Mary Putney, and Putney itself, is in Surrey county, for which John Turner was a member of parliament, and among those entrusted to raise money for the army in Surrey in 1643, and charged to raise civil defense measures in Surrey county in 1645.[152] His possession of the African named Edward may be part of the black possessions seen in Putney before, and to which it has now become habituated. Finally, listed in the record as a goldsmith, John Temple's class affiliations make transparent, from the tendencies of merchants seen throughout the records of this book, his proclivity for acquiring a seized African. That five of the six owners of the Africans listed in this record subgroup were thus either MPs or very closely connected with parliament and government demonstrates the ascendancy of English parliamentary mercantile investment that was fueling the importation of Africans into mid-seventeenth-century London, as was mentioned above.

The wording of the records is still more significantly revelatory, not just in the consistent clarity of their black markings but also in the appearance among them of the word "slave" for the first time. The descriptive phrasing in evidence here, "a Negro servant to," "A negro man servant of," "a black at," "a Blackamore … Thorowgoods foot-boy," "A blackamore boy of," in its lack of ambiguity, suggests a uniformity of address of the black person and analogously, a hardening of black disempowerment that approaches a social standard. This can be seen in the evenness of the incidence of such phrasing in the city proper and in the suburbs, and in merchant and aristocratic attachments. Within the small sample that this particular subgroup of records represents, such phrasing symptomizes the regularization of what was a casual, sporadic, and inconsistent English instinct of black possession into a comfortable and transparently pursued cultural behavior. If this constitutes the ultimate maturation of early modern English black possession, that high point is clearly profiled in the emphatic description of Emanuel Feinande as a "slave, a blackmore." The singularity of the appearance of the word "slave" here, compulsively qualifying "a blackmore," while not necessarily predictive of its constant use henceforth in such contexts, does betray the underlying evolution of the morphology of social slavery into which the black person is now cast. That it occurs in a record

151 "Committee for receiving the King," in "House of Commons Journal Volume 5: 12 January 1647," *Journal of the House of Commons: volume 5: 1646–1648* (1802), pp. 50–51. ["That this House doth approve of Sir *John Thorowgood* of *Kensington*, to be one of the Persons that shall attend the King in his Journey to *Holdenby*."]; "Trying E. of Cambridge, &c.," in "House of Commons Journal Volume 6: 5 February 1649," *Journal of the House of Commons: volume 6: 1648–1651* (1802), pp. 131–32.

152 "Names added to Committees for the several Counties, for a Weekly Assessment," in "House of Lords Journal Volume 5: 21 March 1643," *Journal of the House of Lords: volume 5: 1642–1643* (1802), pp. 656–58; "Ordinance to put the County of Surrey in a Posture of Defence," in "House of Lords Journal Volume 7: 2 July 1645," *Journal of the House of Lords: volume 7: 1644* (1802), pp. 470–73.

in the city's heart suggests the centrality of this development in the life of later seventeenth-century London.

The remainder of the 37 mid-seventeenth-century records that clearly name black people display this new material and discursive incarceration of Africans, albeit in varying degrees of luminosity. The single largest group among them, and which in itself forms a kind of micro subset of data about black people in Restoration London, is provided by the references to them in the diary of Samuel Pepys in his movements through the city between 1660 and 1669. On 9 October 1660, in a afternoon tavern conversation over lunch in the midst of a day-long walking trip to Deptford dock with Sir William Penn, he mentions "one Damford, that, being a black man, did scald his beard with mince-pie and it came up again all white in that place and continued to his dying day" (Item 393). In 27 March of the following year, in the dinner for a business acquaintance in an upscale tavern called the Dolphin, he includes in his account of the after-dinner festivities with two of his immediate colleagues, Sir William Penn and Sir William Batten, a description of Penn's and Batten's two black servants that are made to dance: "At last we made Mingo, Sir W. Batten's black, and Jack, Sir W. Pen's, dance, and it was strange how the first did dance with a great deal of seeming skill ..." (Item 394). On 30 May 1662, in narrating his trip on the river to see Montague's secretary on the former's flagship, the *Royal James*, he cites seeing the secretary bringing back with him "a little Turk and a negro" that Montague has purchased for his daughters (Item 397). On 7 September 1665, in his account of a dinner conversation with a rich banker named Sir Robert Viner at the latter's house, he recounts Viner's attempt to entertain him with the sight of a "a black boy that he had that died of a consumption; and being dead, he caused him to be dried in a Oven, and lies there entire in a box" (Item 411).[153] On 13 April 1666, while on a quick errand to pick up some inexpensive stationery from an old woman in Pannier Alley in Newgate street, he confesses to being attracted by her "very comely black mayde ... servant" (Item 414).[154] On 30 March 1667, on a trip to Arundell House on the Strand's south side to attend a meeting of the Royal Society, he details his sight of the Duchess of Newcastle's black waiting-woman, one "Ferrabosco ... [who] is indeed black, and hath good black little eyes, but otherwise but a very ordinary woman, I do think; but they say sings well." He also mentions having seen in Arundell House "a very pretty black boy that run up and down the room, somebody's child in Arundell-house" (Items 415, 416). On 5 April 1669, he praises "A black-moore of Mr. Belcher's (Doll), who dresses our meat mighty well and we mightily pleased with her" (Item 425).

Points to be made about these citations should begin with a clarification of the blackness of some of the people mentioned by Pepys. Notwithstanding the persistent modern critical tradition of assuming seventeenth-century English uses of the word

[153] For Robert Viner (Vyner), see "Ickenham: Manors," in *A History of the County of Middlesex: Volume 4*, pp. 102–4.

[154] This black woman, who is later said by Pepys to be named Nan (7I: 101), appears several more times in the *Diary*, as Pepys is drawn into an extended relationship with her, despite his wife's discovery of the affair; see the entries for 18 and 23 April, 2 May, and 25 July, all in 1666.

"black" in the context of human appearance to refer to hair color, as was mentioned in the discussion of Davenant and the Axe-yard black prostitute earlier, and which the *Diary*'s editors demonstrate in their cautious gloss of "black" in Pepys's *Diary* as meaning "dark in hair or complexion",[155] and despite Pepys's own deployment of the word "nigro" to refer to an African in a later diary entry, there are strong reasons to think that the persons mentioned by Pepys are in fact black. On the one hand, that early modern English human color signifiers are inconsistent is evident in the records of this book. Added to this is the fact that Pepys's own methods of composition are cheerfully heterogeneous.[156] On the other hand, there are the particular contexts of the entries, such as Penn's and Batten's servants being used as bizarre spectacular entertainment and the black boy being grotesquely dried in Robert Viner's oven, common to all of which is the note of extreme disempowerment applicable historically to the captive English African. Likewise, the piquancy of the anecdote about Damford's scalded beard turning white acquires greater strength than otherwise if he was a black-skinned person whose facial hair was not expected to be white. As it so happens, Mr. Prin, the source of the Damford story who appears in the paragraph preceding the anecdote and elsewhere in the *Diary*, is William Prynne, the lawyer, Puritan pamphleteer, and MP from Bath, who in 1625 was a privateering investor. An almost certain product of that privateering involvement was his acquisition of an African, who is very probably the Damford that he talks about, and who he implies is now dead.[157] As it also happens, Mingo too is identified as a "negroe" by William Batten himself in his will (a record that is discussed in the next chapter) (Item 419). Furthermore, aside from Belcher's servant, who is unambiguously called a "black-moore," and the young people Montague gets for his daughters who are specifically described as "Turke" and "nigro," even some of the names of the other individuals, such as Ferrabosco, suggest domesticated African backgrounds. For the people associated with them, such as William Penn, William Batten, Robert Viner, the Duchess of Newcastle, possession of African servants was now a cultural inevitability of their social class. Finally, there is Pepys's faint angst at the impressive dancing skill of William Batten's servant, which can only stem from his assumption of the lack of such skill in an African. Even if Pepys is unaware of this, the two servants' dancing skills are typical of the convivial reputations of Africans in early modern Europe,[158] as the Dillingham report also attests.

The second point to be made about these black citations is that their usefulness lies in the very casualness of the anecdotal cameos within which they appear. Attached to Lord Montague in his service career across the regimes of Cromwell and Charles II and James II, Pepys was a government and naval bureaucrat whose ordered professional recording habit became in his *Diary* a careful man's informal personal account of each day, in which the principal of selection of its contents was an ontological one. People, places, events that figure in them do so by chance, caught in the path of Pepys's daily working and leisure movements and cast in the unique

---

155 *Diary*, "Companion," 10: 570 (gloss for "black").

156 *Diary*, "Introduction," i: lviii, cvi, cxviii.

157 *Diary*, i: 62 n. 3, and Rabb, *Enterprise and Empire*, p. 362.

158 *Black Africans in Renaissance Europe*, p. 35.

objectivity of his whimsical fancy. The random presence of the black figures in the *Diary*'s varied micro-narratives therefore provides a good measure of the fixity of their deep embeddedness across Restoration London society. Thus, Damford, for instance, is self-evidently "a black man," an entity that is a known absorbed element in the general social landscape of the conversation. He is as unspokenly familiar to William Prynne who has owned him as he is to William Penn, who knows black people from his service in the capture of Jamaica in 1654–55 and has a black servant himself, and to Pepys as well, who in the 1680s will employ in his residence at York Buildings what the *Diary*'s editors themselves describe simply as "a black boy."[159] It is the accepted triple level of Damford's unspecified discursive location, behind Prynne's anecdote and Pepys's private recounting of it, that is a sign of the stability of the incarcerated social status he had when alive. Like him, Mingo, Jack, Ferrabosco, the little black boy in Arundell House, the comely black maid, Belcher's black-moore, in being background figures deeply buried in the narrative fabric of Pepys's diary entries, are examples of the extent of the English normalization of African domestication. They are all emblems of the silent pervasiveness of enforced African servility processed into the smoothness of London high fashion, what Kim Hall has called "meta-objects," invisible in their performance of "necessary tasks," but visible in their symbolization of their owners' "accumulation of profitable foreign goods."[160] These twin aspects constitute the English socialization of the captive African as unofficial slave by the end of the Restoration period.

Also useful to note is the gender disproportion in the black persons Pepys sees. Of the total number of such people that he mentions only three are women. While this might be a result of the limited sample range represented by his citations, paucity of black women is a feature of the mid-seventeenth-century records as a whole. The dearth of black women might be the reflection of an English preference for labor-capable black males in the African trafficking process itself, guided by the demand for such labor in the fledgling American colonies at this time. If so, that is another sign of the increasing maturation of the English shackling of Africans in the years of Pepys's *Diary*.

Pepys's nonchalant bureaucratic instincts of recordation are of course neither interested in nor capable of registering the response of the black subject to the progressive standardization of its social and material incarceration. But while solitary in number, there are some documentary items that do so. These include a newspaper advertisement and a personal journal entry of a German visitor to London. The first, which is only the earliest of many such advertisements later in the century, is the announcement in the *Mercurious Politicus* in its issue of 4–11

---

159 For William Penn see *Diary*, 10: 312 ("Penn, Sir William"), and for Pepys's own "black boy," 10: 194 ("Household: Domestic Servants").

160 *Things of Darkness*, p. 212. The second of the three quotations here is from Yi-Fu Tuan, *Dominance and Affection*, pp. 137–38, cited by Hall. Hall's point, and those of Tuan and Chandra Mukerji ("the growth of the trading system depended on cultural innovation: the development of social meanings for the new consumer good," which led not just to "a good deal of social strain and conceptual discomfort" but also "cultural confusion"; *From Graven Images*, p. 13), whom she cites, are actually most applicable to this precise moment, the mid-seventeenth century, rather than generally to the early modern period as a whole, though Mukerji's formulation has resonances with what happens in the Elizabethan period.

August 1659 of a reward for information about a runaway African: "A Negro boy about nine years of age, in a grey serge suit, his hair cut close to his head, was lost on Tuesday last August 9, at night in S. Nicholas Lane, London. If anyone can give notice of him to Mr. Tho. Barker, at the Sugar Loaf in that lane, they shall be well rewarded for their pains" (Item 386). Thomas Barker was a London merchant with a history of privateering investments from several decades earlier,[161] who may or may not be related to the Mrs. Barker who was seen earlier to be involved in the illicit procurement of Africans in the Elizabethan years, a connection made probable by the proximity of Thomas Barker's current location in Nicholas Lane on the opposite side of Gracious Street from St. Olave, Hart Street in the east, where Mrs. Barker was located. St. Nicholas Lane is off Lombard Street to its north, and hence in the heart of London's business district, just a block south of the Royal Exchange itself (Agas map 5Q, p. 23). The Sugar Loaf Inn mentioned in the record was probably a popular business meeting place for local merchants.[162] This history and location may explain the presence of the African boy and his owner, who may either have just purchased him or brought him there for an upscale re-sale, the financial investment of either scenario explaining the reward he offers for information leading to the boy's recapture. Instantly notable here is the socialized state of the captive African boy in his smart English clothes and trimmed hair. The use of the word "lost" is probably a necessary euphemism for covering the embarrassment of the successful flight of a seized African, and a minor one at that, and to prevent the event from being an emulative model for other held black people. The notice of the boy's flight, if that is what it is, is the first documented instance of the resistance of black people to their captivity in England. The advertisement also captures the fact that the enticements of enslavement—the fine attire and grooming—are not enough to prevent the Africans' rejections of such a life. Although whether the boy was recovered is unknown, the prospects of the success of such resistance were bleak. English xenophobia, his linguistic disability, and what was very likely for him the unfamiliar terrain of the now huge city, predict a grim outcome for his flight. The boy's flight itself is perhaps a signal of the pressures now bearing down on black people.

The black subject's vulnerability, generally, and particularly at this time of its increasingly formal social encumbrance, is what is starkly apparent in the journal notation of William Schellinks, a Dutch visitor to London in March 1663. Writing down all that he saw and did each day in England, somewhat like Pepys but with an even greater circumspection than him, he dryly records the public hanging of a black woman in London: "On the 7th we saw at Tyburn eleven people being hanged, three of the King's bodyguard, two women, and one negress or coloured woman" (Item 400). This is the first documented execution of a black person, and of a black woman, in early modern England. Surrounded by the predatory sightseeing throngs that traditionally gather to watch Tyburn Tree's busy work in human gore and blood, and that has also brought Schellink and his party there, and obscured

[161] Rabb, *Enterprise and Empire*, p. 240.

[162] There was of course more than one Sugar Loaf Inn in London in the sixteenth and seventeenth centuries, and like most such establishments, of transient lives. This one in St. Nicholas Lane is not mentioned by Stow.

by the more familiar English figures of those accompanying her to the scaffold, this unnamed African woman and her "crime" are lost to her world and to history, as legally unprotected as she is historically unredeemable, even her ethnic identity undecidable in Schellink's verbal stumble between "negress or coloured woman." Caught probably in a royalist purge of suspected Cromwellian collaborators, with whom her association may not have been volitional, she could speak to or for no one. Her "crime" was not one of non-compliance but of conflicting compliances equally helplessly borne, her "punishment" serving only to facilitate English state power's redefinition of itself. Her human legality is the blankness of her status as simply, "a negress, or coloured woman." Although the actual details of this black woman's arraignment, if in fact there was one, are unavailable, the speculative scenarios offered here are fair surmises of the historical possibilities of her hanging. These scenarios are not identical to that of the runaway African boy in the newspaper advertisement, but they help to outline the futility of the resistance of black people to the irreversible hardening of their bound status in English society.

A somewhat removed but similarly resonant instance of the vulnerability of the black subject in the increasingly legalistic binding of its captive servitude to the English is the certificate issued by the English consul in Lisbon, Thomas Maynard, on 5 October 1671, protesting the Portuguese inquisition's seizure of an English-owned black youth: "about the Middle of the Month of Sept last, the officers of the Inquisicon Seized a Negro boy called John Adue of about the age of Seventeen years, belonging to Richard Borthwick of London; wch Negro Boy was carried prisoner to the Inquisicon, upon the pretence that if he remained with his Master that he would make him a Heretick" (Item 430). Richard Borthwick was an English sea captain in the 1670s and 1680s commanding cargo ships plying in the Mediterranean and eastern Atlantic,[163] who, docked in Lisbon at the time of the document, was an English citizen dependent on the English Consul for prosecution of any grievances he may have against the Portuguese authorities. John Adue was presumably his onboard English black page who had been seized by Portuguese officials while on shore for the reasons mentioned in Maynard's complaint to them: "of which the said Richard Borthwick complaining to me, I drew up a Memoriall wch I delivered to the Inquisito.^rs^" Phrased as all such diplomatic protests are to make their case impeccably meritorious, the English behavior here seems certainly more reasonable that that of the Portuguese, particularly in light of the Portuguese obduracy in refusing to release the boy despite Maynard's affirmation of his English birth: "Especiall the afore said John Ague being borne a Subject of his Ma^ts^. as I have been informed by the said Richard Borthwick … Notwithtanding … they still retaine him in their power without giving any satisfactory answer." But the competing claims of the English and Portuguese for possession of the African serves merely to deepen his possessed status, now as a "Roman Catholic" servant in Portugal and formerly as a Protestant one in England. What is in question is not whether he should be possessed but to whom that possession belongs. Maynard's generous affirmation of the black youth's Englishness also discreetly normalizes the state of his captivity by Richard

163 Peter Lefevre and Joseph K. Lange, *Precursors of Nelson: British Admirals of the Eighteenth Century*, pp. 129–30.

Borthwick. "[B]eing borne a Subject of his Ma^{ts}," John Adue's captivity is multi-generational, passed from his parent to him in an unspoken practice that is now almost institutional. Irrespective of the visible obscurities of the matter, such as the reasons for the unconditional Portuguese claim that "all Blacks, are within their Jurisdiction," even if that is how Maynard reports it, and the precise purpose of the document that Maynard draws up, the certificate thus displays the firmness of the black subject's commodified condition. It has now become something that can be assumed civilly without particular explanation, as much by England's traditional rival as by itself, a kind of European *lingua franca* of commerce whose material or spiritual "value" is an item of seizure and recompense between them. Unlike the arch denials of English slavery of Thomas Rowe in India in 1616 and Richard Jobson in Africa in 1620,[164] Maynard's public "affirm[ation]" in Portugal fifty years later of English possession and domestication of black people amounts to an international announcement of their *de facto* legalization of the practice.

The formal legalization of English possession of Africans occurred in 1677 in the King's Bench case titled "Butts v. Penny," which ruled that Africans are merchandise:

> Trover for 100 Negroes, and upon *Non Culp* it was found by special Verdict, that the Negroes were Infidels, and the Subjects of an Infidel Prince. and are usually bought and sold in America as Merchandise. by the Custom of Merchants, and that the Plaintiff bought these. and was in possession of them until the Defendant took them. And Thompson argued, there could be no Property in the Person of a Man sufficient to maintain Trover. and cited Co. Lit. 116. That no Property could be in Villains but by Compact or Conquest. But the Court held, that Negroes being usually bought and sold among Merchants, and so Merchandise, and also being Infidels, there might be a Property in them sufficient to maintain Trover, and gave Judgment for the Plaintiff, *nisi Causa*, this Term. (Item 448)

The dispute centers on whether trover, a common law action to recover goods wrongly appropriated by somebody else, can apply to the hundred black people that the plaintiff claims are its commodity that has been seized by the other party, and for which it seeks redress. In its case, the prosecution is invoking European Papal law that England has followed, despite its break with Roman Catholicism in 1534.[165] As has been explained earlier, that law allows for territorial dispossession and enslavement of those non-Christian peoples whose supposedly primitive living practices are in violation of natural law, typically including "cannibalism, sodomy, incest, bestiality," that is, people who live "like beasts in ignorance of European customs."[166] The best-known official statement of this law is Pope Nicholas V's *Romanus Pontifex* Bull of 8 January 1455 allowing Christian princes and their officers to "invade, search out, capture, vanquish, and subdue all Saracens and pagans whatsoever, and other enemies of Christ wheresoever placed, and the kingdoms, dukedoms, principalities, dominions, possessions, and all movable and immovable goods whatsoever held and

---

[164] Cited earlier in the "Introduction."

[165] Patricia Seed, "Taking Possession and Reading Texts: The Authority of Overseas Empires," pp. 201, 209.

[166] Saunders, *Social History of Black Slaves*, p. 37.

possessed by them and to reduce their persons to perpetual slavery."[167] This is the law used by Portugal for its ferocious attacks on Africa in the fifteenth and sixteenth centuries, and by other European nations subsequently for their activities in Africa and America. For its part, the defendant is invoking the defunct medieval peasant bondage of *villeinage* to claim that the black people in question were people like serfs in whom no property can reside. Notwithstanding the disingenuousness of both arguments, the court's ruling in favor of the plaintiff, which while being prescriptive rather than definitive, allows for the existence of property in black people.

Two sources of possible confusion in the modern understanding of the case perhaps need to be clarified here. First, although there is some question about whether the disputed event occurred in the Caribbean colonies and whether it was part of the jurisdictional wrangling that broke out between English courts and those of the colonies,[168] the ruling's effect cannot be excluded from England proper, particularly since it is being argued in one of the highest courts in the country, the King's Bench. The court's opinion that there may be monetary value in the possession of Africans because "Negroes … [are] usually bought and sold among Merchants" cannot be applicable only to the English plantation economies overseas, as the records of this book extending over the last hundred years have made evident. Secondly, contrary to Leon Higginbotham's warning that "one cannot … be too certain of the true social and legal ramifications attending the use of the term 'slave' when used in cases" such as *Butts v. Penny* and others of the period (p. 324), the legal briefs of the time, both for and against the *Butts v. Penny* ruling, do show particular attention to the word in its negative connotations, as this extract from the court's opinion in *Smith v Gould* in 1705–06 attests:

> A Man may have a Speciall Property in his Captive to Get his Ransom. So a Man may have the Like in his Villein … But our Law takes notice of Negroes nor knows Such Slaves … Negroes are Inheritances in Barbados. And Bringing 'em into England don't make Chattels …[169]

The same exactness of terminological usage is observed by William Wiecek in his study of the Mansfield case and those leading up to it, including Butts v. Penny: "The distinction [of Judge Holt in his flat assertion in the *Chamberlain v Harvey* case in 1697 that neither trover nor trespass would be applicable in the seizure of a slave] was more than technical. Trover would treat the slave as a chattel, a thing so utterly unfree that it was vendible; trespass … would liken the slave to a bound or apprenticed laborer, a slavish servant,' a human being whose freedom was restricted but not annihilated."[170] The semantic precisionism of these legal conversations can only be necessitated by the implications of the *Butts v. Penny* ruling for England itself.

What the ruling does is to clear the way for officially validating what until then was a pervasive but informal convention encompassing liveried servantship, bonded labor, and chattel enslavement of black people in England and in its American

---

[167] The citation is from the reproduction of the Bull in Frances Gardiner Davenport, ed. *European Treaties*, p. 23.

[168] A. Leon Higginbotham, *In the Matter of Colour*, p. 322.

[169] Cited by James Oldham, "New Light on Mansfield and Slavery," p. 49.

[170] "Somerset: Lord Mansfield and the Legitimacy of Slavery," pp. 90–91.

colonies. Suggestive of an effect of facilitation if not one of direct consequence, the case's historical moment coincides with the growing practice of separating enslaved black people from poor whites in English slaving ships and fron indentured white servants in the American colonies.[171] This is also the time when proposals about the disenfranchisement of black baptisms appear, as for instance in the earlier cited declaration of the Virginia legislature in 1667. That declaration, which denied the suit of an African servant brought to Virginia from England claiming freedom on the grounds of his prior English baptism, was in response, it should be remembered, to the success of another such suit a decade earlier.[172] The *Butts v. Penny* ruling is the culminating expression of such growing sentiments, and an attempt to bridge what William Wiecek has described as the "paradox[ical]" gap between the "iron structure" of "the clear and specific 'thou-shalts' and 'thou-shalt-nots' regulating the minutiae of behavior of whites and blacks alike" and the "uncertain jurisprudential foundation" on which that structure rested, that is between the "statutes governing slaves" and "the case law of slavery."[173] It is entirely unsurprising, then, that *Butts v. Penny* was immediately followed by *Noel v. Robinson* in 1687, *Chambers v. Warkhouse* in 1693, and *Gelly v. Cleve* in 1694, all of which uphold the legality of property in black people, the second classifying black people with imported animals.[174] The ruling's complicated long-term aftermath also shows its lasting effect. Even though Justice Holt rejects it in the *Chamberlain v. Harvey* case in 1697, Attorney General Phillip Yorke, later to become Lord Hardwicke, reasserted it in 1729 and 1749. In 1762 Lord Chancellor Henley again partially denied Hardwicke's reassertion of it, before Lord Mansfield finally dismissed it in the famous *Somerset* case in 1772.[175]

This back-and-forth history, which James Walvin calls a "legal see-saw,"[176] describes, however, not the struggle to abolish English slavery but to legally establish it. The rulings of both Holt and Mansfield, as modern commentators have pointed out, were the product of their attempts, not to deny slavery but of their failure to avoid the issue.[177] Mansfield's ruling did not stop English domestic and colonial slavery.[178] James Walvin's comment about these seeming "reversals" is apt: "in reality the judgment[s] made not the slightest impact on the daily practice of

---

[171] For an instance of each, see two parliamentary documents of 1675 and 1670 in *Documents Illustrative of the History of the Slave Trade*, ed. Donnan, 1: 201, 174. Also see Walvin, who cites an order of the Privy Council for the Plantations to the effect that servants should be classed "under two heads, blacks and whites. The blacks bought by way of trade [are] … perpetual servants" (*Black and White*, p. 38).

[172] William Billings, "The Cases of Fernando and Elizabeth Key: A Note on the Status of Blacks in Seventeenth-Century Virginia," pp. 467–70, cited in Chapter 1.

[173] "Somerset," p. 87.

[174] Higginbotham, p. 324, Wiecek, p. 93. The second case is cited by Peter Fryer, *Staying Power*, p. 113, and by Anthony Lester and Geoffrey Bindman, *Race and Law in Great Britain*, p. 28.

[175] Oldham, pp. 48–51.

[176] See the chapter titled "The Legal See-Saw: Slavery and the Law to 1772," in *Black and White*, pp. 105–16.

[177] Shyllon, *Black Servants*, p. 80; Wiecek, pp. 89, 92–93, 105; Oldham, pp. 46–64.

[178] Wiecek, pp. 107–8, 118; Oldham, pp. 62, 68.

slavery in England."[179] As Benjamin Franklin, the American Ambassador to Britain at the time of the Somerset case, put it in his disgust of English deceptiveness in this matter, "the hypocrisy of this country, which encourages such a detestable commerce by laws for promoting the Guinea trade; while it piqued itself on its virtue, love of liberty, and the equity of its courts, setting free a single negro."[180] The real effect of the 1677 court ruling, in other words, was that for the English boom in African ownership it acted instantly as a legal precedent, despite the case technically not being a precedent-setting proceeding, since its judgment was a deferred one. The patterns of its argument were replicated in the slavery cases that followed it.[181] By 1770, according to William Wiecek, "it was distinctly possible that English courts would legitimate slavery in England, especially in light of the baneful influence of … the scattered dicta about trover lying for a Negro." If the *Somerset* case's decision had a far-reaching effect,[182] the case's context itself was a consequence of *Butts v. Penny*. Such was the landmark legacy of the *Butts v. Penny* ruling as the first English legal articulation of the status of captive English Africans in general. In ruling that black people may be considered as property, a clear reversal of the rulings of the previous hundred years, such as the Matter of Cartwright in 1569 and the Hector Novimeis case in the 1580s cited in the last chapter, the court was in effect initiating the legalizing of their slavery and thereby promulgating, however informally, what would become an infamous English institution over the next two centuries.

V

As a seminal moment for a new episteme, the *Butts v. Penny* case marks the *terminus quo* for the documentary history of black people in seventeenth-century London. The high volume of the records presented in this chapter, obligates, in the interests of providing coherence and transparency to their meaning, an outlining of the major patterns of the data and a summarizing of their significance, while keeping in mind the data's unavoidably conditional nature overall as well as the expository purpose of the analysis that follows. There are 121 London records of black people of assorted ethnic clarity in the 74 years between 1603, the first year of James's reign, and 1677, the year in which English legal opinion affirmed their status as commodity. The average frequency of black citations for this entire period comes to 1.6 citations per year. Of the total number of seventeenth-century black records, 45 are from the years 1603 to 1628, coinciding predominantly with the reign of James I, 26 are from the years 1629 to 1653, extending over the reign of Charles I and the Civil War up to the beginning of the Cromwellian regime, and 50 are from the years 1654 to 1677, spanning the Puritan government years and those of the Restoration up till the *Butts v. Penny case* in 1677. The variable volume of each these three quarter-century breakdowns of data that have been necessitated by the unwieldy total number of the seventeenth-century

179 *Black and White*, p. 111.

180 Cited by Wiecek, p. 88.

181 Wiecek, p. 90 and p. 93, for the case's lack of precedent-setting ability, and pp. 91–92 for replication of the pattern of the case's arguments in *Chamberlain v. Harvey*.

182 "Somerset," p. 101 (for the quotation), pp. 114–41.

records that this chapter has sampled, reflect a frequency-of-occurrence ratio of black citations as follows: 1.8 for the period 1603–28, 1.08 for 1629–53, and 2.17 for 1654–77. This curve in the frequency ratios shows a steady accumulation of black people in the Jacobean and early Caroline years, succeeded by a drop in the century's middle years, followed by a sharp, greater than 100 percent increase across the Cromwellian and Restoration decades (see Table 3.1). As pointed out earlier, the increase in the frequency ratios between the entire first half of the century and its third quarter is 54 percent, going from 1.4 (71 records in 50 years) to 2.17.

Table 3.1 Frequency of seventeenth-century black citations (1603–77)

Number of citations	Periods	Frequency of occurrence
121	74 years (total)	1.6 per year
45	25 years (Jacobean)	1.8 per year
26	24 years (Caroline and Civil War)	1.08 per year
50	23 years (Cromwellian Regime and Restoration years)	2.17 per year

Black location patterns show a predominance of west London sites, with 16 out of 43, 12 out of 26, and 31 out of 50 citations for each of the three data units, or a total of 59 out of 121 records coming from that zone of the city. Next in numerical strength are east-side citations, with 12, 4, and 7 for each of the data sections, or a total of 23 out of the 121 records. The central and north zones combined contribute 10, 10, and 6 mentions for each data period, or 26 out of the overall record volume, while the city's south side has 5, 0, and 2 notations, or an aggregate of 7 in the totality of the century's data. The high number of citations from the city's west and east sides, amounting to 82 out of 121 records or 67 percent of the total, confirms the black settlement pattern of the Elizabethan period, as well as the conclusions of most early modern London historians such as M. J. Power, A. L. Beier and Roger Finlay, and Vanessa Harding, about the economic character and demographic make-up of these two suburban regions of the metropolis.[183] As poor aliens typically gathered in those locales, in the service of the wealthy in the west side and to fend for themselves in the poorer areas of the east, so did black people. The distinction of the seventeenth-century data is its revelation that in the seventeenth century it is the city's western rather than its eastern precincts that have the most black people in them. This trait is a probable pointer of the ascendancy of parliamentary gentry with overseas trading involvements resident in Westminster and its environs, generally over the century and particularly from its mid-point.[184]

The gender ratio evident in the black records also displays divergences, although not in as marked a degree as the locational patterns. Double-counting both named black

---

183 See the essays cited earlier.

184 See Beier and Finlay, eds., *London*, "Introduction," for an enumeration of the increase in this kind of a population in Westminster by 1630 (pp. 12, 14).

females as well as unnamed ones only whose children are cited at birth, in the first data unit there are 23 males and 20 females mentioned, in the second 17 males and 10 females, and in the third 37 males and 14 females. The greatest gender equity in the first data unit and the greatest gender disproportion in the third describe the difference between the inadvertent English disregard of the black presence in the Jacobean years, which facilitates an innocuous black settlement and integration, and the purposeful importation of black people for organized commercial slave supply to the American plantations from the middle of the Civil War years and in which black males are a preferred category.[185] The start of the latter phenomenon can be seen in the slight widening of the gender ratio in the second dataset. At the same time, examples of cross-racial unions both legal and illicit, including black people in named unions and those deducible from the birth of their children, comprise 18 instances in the first data unit, 13 in the second, and 8 in the third. This steady decline in black and white pairings over the seven decades of the seventeenth century spells the changing progress of black assimilation and integration, climbing from 41 percent of the total number of black mentions in the reign of James, to 50 percent in that of Charles and the Civil War years, and then dropping to 16 percent in that of the Restoration regimes (see Table 3.2). Yet, probable cases of gender oppression and economic destitution of black women occur in a total of only four times in the seventeenth-century records overall. These are the unnamed black woman impregnated by William Conrados's boarder in St. Benet Fink, the black woman named Marie who died in the street in Aldgate, the black woman named Grace who was reported to be living incontinently in Stepney, and the black woman hanged in Tyburn. Whether this relatively low incidence of black sexual exploitation is the product of the relative benignity of the periods of the first two record units must remain a matter of some consideration.

Table 3.2 Gender ratios in the seventeenth-century english black records (includes double counts)

	Jacobean	**Caroline and Civil War**	**Cromwellian and Restoration**
Males	23	17	37
Females	20	10	14
Cross-racial unions	18	13	8

Other trends noticeable in the data concern the fluctuating ownership status of black people. In the three data periods examined in this chapter, black people are clearly named as having owners in 11 of the 45 Jacobean records, in only one of the 26 Caroline and early Civil War records, and in as many as 14 of the 50 Puritan and

185 Greater and lesser gender disproportion in the context of the English black presence can, of course, be both positive and negative indicators, depending on the overall social atmosphere. Generally, the low gender imbalance in the black records of the first several decades of the seventeenth century parallels the muted racialism of those years. The opposite is true of the gender numbers of the Elizabethan period.

Restoration records. This pattern shows the general laxity of English attitudes to black people in the first half of the seventeenth century, with the greatest moment of relaxation occurring in the later years of Charles I's reign, followed by a steep acceleration of black disenfranchisement in the years of Cromwell and Charles II. The figures strongly suggest a changing history of black people in the seventeenth century, between an initial phase of benign neglect conducive to black settlement and integration and a subsequent one of possession and enslavement. These two phases correspond to the informal African trafficking of English privateers up to the third and fourth decades and the organized mass pursuit of that objective by successive English trading companies from the century's middle decades, fed by matching increases in demands for slave labor in the American colonies across those years.

In all of the data patterns outlined above, there is clearly a point of change in the middle decades of the seventeenth century. Whether more marked in some data trends, as in the percentage drop from 50 to 16 in cross-racial unions, and the percentage increase from 3.8 to 24 in ownership citations, or less marked, as in the widening gap between 17 males to 10 females and 37 males to 13 females in the gender ratio of the records, the closing decade of the first half of the century occupies a transitional moment separating two contrasting data tendencies. This moment is both an apotheosis of what comes before as well as a harbinger of what lies ahead. Constituting a culmination of long-term developments, such as the end of a 100-year period extending from the Reformation and the start of parish register recording in the 1530s to the steady disruption of that practice with the onset of the Civil War in the 1640s (leading to its collapse altogether in the fire of 1666, after which London's parochial administration itself will be reorganized), and of short-term developments such as the high point of the 60-year stretch of the city's aggressive expansion from the 1580s[186] and the replacement of one merchant class obeisant to and patronized by the monarchy by another that overthrew that order and heavily controlled the new one that it ushered in, the 1640s is the last and brightest moment when things growing until then will be visible. Chief among such profiled developments is, for the interests of this book, the fruition of innocuous black English assimilation and settlement that is pictured in the *Mercurius Politicus*'s "news" report in 1645. The statistical data, in other words, supports the idea of the first half of the seventeenth century producing a locus of inadvertent black survival on the eve of the slave trade.

The 1640s is in fact the only, evanescent moment of visibility of the black subject in its human outlines, a spectral temporal point when that subject flickers into sight between its demonization in the previous century and its dehumanization in the next two, starting with the immediately following quarter century. It is a spectral point because it has nothing else to supplement its materialization, except this conjectural observation about what the data implies but does not overtly articulate. Although helped by Thomas Browne's balanced discourse about black humanity, and by Aubrey's anecdote about the high-class sex professional with whom Davenant has a tryst, the scarcity of other kinds of inscriptions such as that of the *Mercurius Politicus* in being part of the general irregularity of public records in the turbulence of the Civil War and Puritan years mentioned above, points merely to the elusiveness

[186] Finlay and Shearer, "Population Growth and Suburban Expansion," pp. 42, 46, 48, 54.

of the survival of black humanity, not to its impossibility. This is to say that the locus of black existence's humanity in the English early modern period is a rare, brief thing, understood retrospectively as a contingent comparative suspicion of a possibility rather than as a demonstrable fact, a possibility of what happens between the early marking of the black subject in the Elizabethan regime and its later more organized one in the years of the Restoration and after. This hypothetical nature of black humanity's survival, which is another reason for the black subject's invisibility in early modern English history, ironically makes it as phenomenologically unreal as its denigrated and enslaved state before and after, its visibility in this moment issuing only from the difference of its phenomenology as something positive.

If the visibility of the black subject's humanity is fleeting and ephemeral, that of its slavehood is palpable. The proliferation of black citations in the third quarter of the century is only one contributory factor of this effect. The palpability of the black person's changed status accrues not just from the sharply different gender ratios of the Restoration records, which hints at the profiling of black persons as male slave labour, nor only from the increased mentions of their ownership, and neither exclusively from the stability of the unspoken assumptions of their bondage, but also and most plangently from the emergence of far-reaching English legal opinion defining them as merchandise to be traded. These traits, which in objectifying the black person totally occlude its humanity, initiate its fading into the public light of the state-sponsored activity that is the slave trade. Its presence in private households and other social locations is as an after-image of that public exposure. The black person's appearance as slave is conversely its disappearance from English history. If the legalization of the black person as slave in the ruling of *Butts v. Penny* is a perfect parallel to its lawful national expurgation in Elizabeth's deportation orders 80 years earlier, its emergence in the later Stuart regimes as the visibly objectified slave in which the human being is invisible completes the vanishing circle of English black history that began with the arrival of the black person in England a 177 years earlier as a being whose humanity was unrecognizable.

Chapter Four

Black People outside London, 1558–1677

The Provincial Backdrop

"Cooree home goe, Saldania goe, home goe …" "I am often tempted against my life …" "I am not as others are. I do not look so as others do …"

I

The same fundamental historical development that created a black presence in early Tudor and Elizabethan London predictably produced a scattered black population across England over the sixteenth and seventeenth centuries. Indeed, for this not to happen would have been surprising. That fundamental historical development is quite simply the emergence of overseas trading initiatives by merchant mariners backed by powerful aristocrats, both in conjunction with and independent of local and London-based trading collectives over the 177 years of this study's range. As Lawrence Stone put it,

> In the sixteenth century, thanks to the growing strength of the Crown, there was a decline in the political authority of peers; in the seventeenth century, thanks to the growing power of Parliament, there was a decline in the political influence of courtiers.… [Concomitantly] there was a marked increase in the influence of the merchant community over English policy—especially foreign policy—thanks to the leverage it could exercise over any government by the offer or withholding of its facilities for credit.

This is probably why, Stone suggests, Gregory King's pioneering estimate of the English population in 1688 includes a figure of "10,000 merchants by land and sea,"[1] some of whom could even and did bankroll the government when needed, as did the merchant syndicate that loaned Elizabeth £30,000 at 10 percent interest at the very outset of her reign.[2] The black presence that this boom in mercantilism produced is documented in 85 black records dispersed across the different counties of England between 1558 and 1677, including two in Scotland, one in Norway, one in Paris, one in South Africa, and two on the high seas.

While providing an overall backdrop for the London black records, the notations of black people outside London do not simply replicate the thematic patterns

---

1 Lawrence Stone, "Social Mobility in England 1500–1676," pp. 28–29. The quotation is from p. 28.

2 The syndicate includes aristocrats such as Leicester, Clinton, and Pembroke, and business figures powerful in London administration such as Thomas Lodge, William Garrard, Rowland Heyward. See Ronald Pollit, "Troublesome Voyages," p. 37.

of the London data. With the exception of the Southampton black diver who appeared in the Admiralty case of 1547 discussed in the first chapter, there are no mentions of black people outside London until the beginning of Elizabeth's reign. Furthermore, the socio-political phenomena that the outside London records reflect, while corresponding in many ways to those of the London black archives, are not identical to them. Nor should they be expected to be. In these aspects, the records of black people in the English provinces offer important confirmations as well as modifications of the black history of the London citations.

There are two tracks in the history of the early modern English black presence outside London. The first is that merchant traders and their powerful associates in the aristocracy and landed gentry bring black people to their country residences. As has been suggested before, the virulent attraction of overseas trading with its lure of astronomical profits, including the material and human booty of Africa, was something from which few Tudor aristocrats and gentry, royal councilors, and city merchant aldermen alike were immune. Elizabethan luminaries such as William Cecil, Leicester, Pembroke, and Clinton, naval administrators such as Benjamin Gonson and William Winter, and aldermen merchants such as Thomas Lodge, William Gerard, Lionel Duckett, William Chester, and Paul Baning were *all* direct or indirect investors in African trading voyages, including ones involving slaving. There is a direct connection between the rapid cash profits of this class from such investments and their purchase of English provincial lands for speculation and possession, in their home counties as well as in others. Examples include Thomas Lodge's purchase of property in Wales and Lincolnshire, William Garrard's in Buckinghamshire, Surrey, and Kent, and Rowland Heyward's in Gloucestershire and Somersetshire, the last in the substantial amount of more than £2,000. Pembroke and Winter acquired land holdings in Gloucestershire. The aristocracy's wealth had of course already been fattened by the crown distribution of lands in the monastic dissolution of 1538, even if prodigal living had started to diminish some of that in the Elizaberhan period, as Lawrence Stone has shown.[3] Individually, and in a merchant syndicate that included aristocrats, this class made repeated mass purchases of land for speculative profit and prestigious possession, the latter for conversion into competitively conspicuous country estates.[4] This is confirmed in the great burst of country house construction that occurred, in the reckoning of one historian, between 1575 and 1625.[5] Accompanying such advertisements of material pomp in the English countryside, and sometimes adorning them, were the captive black people regularly being brought back from the overseas business projects.

The second track is that of rival business groups, such as outport traders, who also brought back and kept black people in their own rural localities outside London. The traditional monopoly of the London-based Merchant Adventurers over foreign

---

3 "Anatomy of Elizabethan Aristocracy," pp. 2–3.

4 For detailed discussions of the late Tudor and early Stuart history outlined here, see Pollit, "Troublesome Voyage," pp. 33–34, 36–37, and Stone, "Anatomy of Elizabethan Aristocracy," pp. 7–8, 10.

5 Stone, "Social Mobility," p. 26. Also see W. G. Hoskins, "The Rebuilding of Rural England 1570–1649."

trade, which was relaxed in 1497 and reinforced at the beginning of the Elizabethan period in 1564–65, was successfully contested by provincial businessmen through their parliamentary representatives at the beginning of the reign of James. The growth of restrictive branches of the Merchant Adventurers in Newcastle, Chester, Exeter, York, and Bristol in the second half of the sixteenth century was paralleled by the simultaneous rise of regional craftsmen eager to officially enter, and already transgressing into, lucrative English overseas trading, the turning point of which is the passage of the Free Trade Bill in 1604 and especially the related statute of 1606, ordaining the entry of provincial businessmen into England's foreign trade.[6] The resultant combined proliferation across the countryside of small merchants with big ones, that is, of dilettantish "pedlar-like traders" as well as professional "mere merchants," is reflected in Gregory King's grandiose overall figure of "10,000 merchants by land and sea" cited above.[7] That proliferation is part of the changes in the power hierarchy of the counties outside London over the sixteenth and seventeenth centuries by which the income of merchants became as great as that of the propertied aristocracy.[8] This history of a competitive relationship between small merchant traders in the countryside and the elitist, numerically larger, London-based merchants, including their provincial representatives, includes inevitably the former's emulation of the latter's business practices and living habits. That emulation includes the acquisition of black people.

The 85 records of this chapter are best examined in three overlapping arcs. First, they can be discussed in a movement from areas of greater to lesser volumes of citation. Secondly, the discussion can proceed from records of greater completeness of documentation to those of lesser. Both of these trajectories of discussion will simultaneously track a geographic pattern, moving from black citations of the coastal southwest to the southeast and then to the rest of the country. Third, both discussion schemes can each traverse within their data a simple linear chronology, beginning with the earliest and ending with the latest dates in their respective groups. This composite plan, while not unduly flattening the complex changing contexts of the records over the 177 years of their range, will contribute a certain cogency to their otherwise unmanageable geographic spread, great temporal range, and variable substance and transparency.

---

6 George Unwin, "The Merchant Adventurers' Company in the Reign of Elizabeth," pp. 34–39; Robert Ashton, "The Parliamentary Agitation for Free Trade in the Opening Years of the Reign of James I," pp. 40–46.

7 The members of the Spanish company in London used this phrase in 1606 to derisively refer to their mainly provincial competitors, who were trying to break into their trade monopoly; cited in Ashton, p. 42; David Harris Sacks defines "mere merchants" as those "for whom long distance wholesale trade is the foundation of business" (*The Widening Gate*, p. 62), as opposed to other working folk for whom overseas trading is a contingent and opportunistic activity.

8 Stone, "Social Mobility," pp. 27, 29.

II

To a large extent, the pattern of the black presence outside London is a function of geography. Because of their great ease of access to the southern and western Atlantic, locations on England's southwestern coastline became natural points of origin for naval, expeditionary, and commercial projects alike throughout the reigns of the last Tudor and that of the Stuarts. Port cities such as Bristol and Plymouth, in particular, long active in England's seaborne trades with the European continent, emerged as the staging grounds of choice for maritime enterprises to Africa and America whenever such enterprises originated, and were in fact causative factors in their origination.[9] As Kenneth Andrews pointed out, Plymouth and Bristol, together with Weymouth and Southampton, were in the forefront of the privateering activities, in which provincial merchants were the most aggressive participants.[10] In J. A. Williamson's words, Plymouth was the "home port of adventurers and … the forward base of the Navy in the new oceanic operations that distinguish the Tudor century."[11] A sample of Plymouth ships, for instance, specifically involved in African and Caribbean voyages in the late Elizabethan period includes in 1596 the *Prudence* and the *Adventure*, in 1600 the *Scorn*, the *Prudence*, and the *Pearl*, and in 1601 the *James*.[12] Between 1625 and 1629 as many as 78 privateering ships were licensed in Plymouth and its immediate environs.[13] As was mentioned in an earlier chapter, merchants in nearby Exeter were twice awarded charters by Elizabeth in 1588 and 1592 to trade in Senegal, Gambia, and Sierra Leone.[14] It is therefore not a coincidence that powerful sea-faring families such as those of the Hawkins, Walter Raleigh, Humphrey Gilbert, Thomas Cavendish, Francis Drake, and John Young took root in Plymouth and Bristol from the very beginning of England's early modern cross-oceanic out-thrust, and they derived a significant portion of their wealth from their maritime involvements, including privateering.[15] Correspondingly, the first retail trade activities in the English provinces appeared in the counties near the southern coastline, as Bristol, Exeter, Plymouth became the first provincial mercantile centers.[16] As Williamson described it,

> the privateering, begun by old William Hawkins in the 1540s and continued by his sons throughout the century, pour[ed] rich goods into Plymouth … stimulating the town and

[9] Henry Woolcombe, "Statistics of the Three Towns, Plymouth, Stonehouse, and Davenport," pp. 179–80.

[10] *Trade, Plunder and Settlement*, p. 21.

[11] *Hawkins of Plymouth*, p. 38.

[12] K. R. Andrews, "English Voyages to the Caribbean, 1596 to 1604: An Annotated List," p. 246, 249–50.

[13] Richard Nicholls Worth, *History of Plymouth: From the Earliest Period to the Present Time*, p. 91.

[14] W. Walton Claridge, *History of the Gold Coast*, p. 79; earlier cited in Chapter 2.

[15] Walter Raleigh's name is also frequently spelled as "Ralegh." In this work the former version will be used.

[16] Roland M. Berger, "The Development of Retail Trade in Provincial England ca 1550–1700," p. 125.

> its hinterland to supply the victuals and drink, the clothes and the weapons, and all the chandlery for the upkeep of ships that were built from the forest and the forge and handled by stick and string. To the same end worked the ocean voyages of the 60's, and their successors … of the 70's, collecting men, multiplying wants, bringing home lavishly the means to pay for them ….[17]

This well-known history makes it entirely predictable that the single largest group of citations of black people outside London will be from southwest counties such as Devonshire and Gloucestershire.

There are thirty-three black citations from Devonshire, or Devon as the county is often commonly called. Of these about half, or seventeen citations, are from St. Andrew's, Plymouth alone. There is a strikingly resonant logic in this fact, since Plymouth was where the first black people in England in the period of this study arrived in 1501, in the retinue of Catherine of Aragon, and St. Andrew's was the first church at which that troupe paused, to enable the Spanish princess's prompt prayers of thanks for her safe landing. That more than five decades later, more black people were brought into this same venue by the English, arguably suggests a delayed effect of the earlier event on the latter, by which the importation of black people in chattel bondage emerged as a desensitized even if surreptitious and casual English social practice. The track of that desensitization follows not just the spill-over effects of the English presence in the England of the first Tudor monarch of Catherine's multi-colored entourage, and of the Americans brought to back to Henry VII's court from Newfoundland by Sebastian Cabot in 1502, cited in Chapter 1, but also of the projects of aggressive seafarers in Plymouth in the third and fourth decades of the sixteenth century to investigate the maritime commercial enterprises of the Portuguese in Africa and the western Atlantic with an aim of emulating their rich financial dividends.[18] If such exploratory forays by William Hawkins senior occasionally brought Americans back from Brazil as diplomatic facilitators of prospective English trade with those regions, three or four decades later, in the more purposive English commercial forays into Africa in the early years of Elizabeth's reign from this same southwestern English port, that practice was remembered and revived, including the practice's inevitable spin-off of seizing black people anyway, simply as chattel goods. The revival and development of that practice was not just by the descendants of William Hawkins, such as his sons John and William, but also by others of that social group, as well as by their business rivals. Plymouth's developing sixteenth-century black history contains, in other words, the originary moment of early modern contact between English and African peoples, as the natural geographic venue for pursuing such accidental and deliberate interests across the seas, and the available local human and material resources (in the maritime interests and abilities, and financial strengths of families such as the Hawkins, and their

---

17 *Hawkins of Plymouth*, p. 196.

18 Williamson, in his *Hawkins of Plymouth*, has a probing discussion of the phenomenon of the first English seafarers trying to learn the secrets of the west Atlantic voyaging and trading of the Spanish and Portuguese, specifically in the case of William Hawkins senior; see pp. 26–28.

competitive business emulators), making it the foremost locale for the appearance of black people outside London.

To start with citations of Africans in a visibly encumbered state, and with burial notices, which together comprise the largest group in the St. Andrew's black notations, there is the burial of "Bastien, a Blackmoore of Mr Willm. Hawkins, Plymouth" on 10 December 1583 (Item 152), which is notable for the transparency of the history it encodes. William Hawkins is the oldest son of William Hawkins senior or "old Master William Hawkins,"[19] and the older brother of John Hawkins the first slave trader. As is well known, William Hawkins was at this time a powerful Plymouth resident, already elected mayor in 1578–79 (and who will be mayor again in the Armada years of 1587–88),[20] a "magnate" of Plymouth who was privy councilor of the borough, a de facto "governor of Plymouth" and prominent ship owner whose cruisers were the "terror of Spain,"[21] an African and western Atlantic expeditionary leader,[22] and a privateering investor.[23] Whether Bastien was a gift to William Hawkins from his brother John, from the Africans the latter may have brought back from his third voyage more than a decade earlier, as was suggested in Chapter 2, or whether he was a product of William Hawkins's own 1582 expedition to the African coast and the western Atlantic, which returned to Plymouth in November of that year heavily loaded with booty,[24] is uncertain. If the latter was the source of Bastien's English arrival, which seems probable since there is no record of his baptism, his death notation would mark the quick end of a casually seized life, the notice itself with its clear marking of his African origin in conjunction with the careful naming of his owner serving merely to advertise the social stature of William Hawkins, "magnate" of Plymouth. One clear demonstration, in a citation that is not a burial record, of the function of captured black people to display their owner's social pomp is that pertaining to James Bagge, Plymouth shipowner, mayor, vice-admiral of Devonshire, and member of parliament, in his order in 1628 that his "negrowe" be "handsomely clothed" (Item 334). This is an African that was almost certainly connected to Bagge's privateering investments of 1625.[25] The recording of the order in the official papers of Charles I's government reflects the pervasiveness of the

---

19 For the sixteenth-century currency of the phrase "old Master William Hawkins" as applying to William Hawkins senior, see Williamson, *Hawkins of Plymouth*, p. 37.

20 Worth, *History of Plymouth*, pp. 213–14.

21 According to the family history written by the family's nineteenth-century descendent, Mary W. S. Hawkins, *The Hawkins Family* (1888), chapter 2.

22 Williamson, *Hawkins of Plymouth*, pp. 57, 300, 219–25 (for the 1582 trip to the African coast and western Atlantic). The reference to William Hawkins being privy councilor for the borough is also from Williamson.

23 Theodore Rabb, *Enterprise and Empire*, p. 310. For the Hawkins family, the privateering career began with Henry VIII's issuance to William Hawkins senior the "letters of marque" in 1544 to prey on French shipping to offset the danger of a French invasion; see Williamson, *Hawkins of Plymouth*, p. 34.

24 Ibid., p. 224.

25 For information on Bagge's political offices see Worth, *History of Plymouth*, pp. 169, 214, and R. G. Marsden, "The Vice Admirals of the Coast," p. 740; for his privateering and other investments see Rabb, *Enterprise and Empire*, p. 238.

normalcy of deploying seized Africans for the social advertisement of their English captors at the highest English levels, and particularly for provincial gentry competing with current fashions in Westminster. Like Bastien's, the citation of James Bagge's unnamed "negrowe" is not about him but about his owner. These features will be basic aspects of the majority of the outside London black notations.

In exemplification, as it were, are three other encumbered black notations in St. Andrew's, Plymouth. These are the burials of "a Blackmore at Capt. Sparks" on 30 November 1601; "a Blackmore at Mr. Stallenge" on 6 December 1601; and "a neager who was employed by Mr Abraham Jennings" on 8 August 1640 (Items 244, 245, 362). Captain Sparks is most likely the John Sparks who was also a mayor of Plymouth in 1591–92,[26] and a prominent promoter of the Virginia colony who was mentioned in the second charter issued to the colony on 23 May 1609.[27] More importantly, he was a member of John Hawkins's crew on his first and second African slaving voyages, and one of the chroniclers of the second voyage.[28] Mr. Stallenge is William Stallenge, likewise another Plymouth government administrator, who in 1596–97 was the government's commissioner for the shipyard at Plymouth and involved in the preparations for the Earl of Essex's Cadiz campaign against Spain,[29] and who was a burgess of the city and MP in 1601.[30] Abraham Jennings was an even more visible Plymouth personality who as an industrious coastal, Atlantic, and transatlantic trader was one of the largest individual ship owners in Plymouth at the beginning of the seventeenth century was cited by the Privy Council as one of the four "Western traders" who were "fitt and indifferent persons," and who by the time of his death was a wealthy man of considerable standing in the local community, a close associate of the Earl of Warwick, and owned considerable property in Plymouth and its environs, leaving a bequest of over a thousand pounds.[31] The direct or indirect African trading connections of all three figures over the course of their careers, more obvious in the cases of Sparks and Jennings' than in that of Stallenge, make their possession of Africans inevitabilities of their class behavior. The validity of such an assumption is not undermined by the lack of direct evidence, since as Williamson put it regarding casual slave-trading voyages from Plymouth in the early Elizabethan decades, "The survival of evidence is a matter of chance, and it does not follow that the voyages of which little is known were unimportant, or that there were not a number of voyages." Such activity, he insists, "must have been of the clandestine kind."[32] In contrast to the luminous historical identities of Sparks, Stallenge, and Jennings, the anonymity of the three Africans are reflections of their bestial captivity that is accountable only as the loss of propertied goods in their deaths. These three

26 Worth, p. 214.

27 "Second Virginia Charter," in "The Virginia Charters."

28 Williamson, *Hawkins of Plymouth*, pp. 70–81.

29 L. W. Henry, "The Earl of Essex as Strategist," p. 382.

30 "Members of Both Houses of Parliament 1601," in *History of Collections: Or an Exact Account of the Proceedings of the Four Last Parliaments of Q. Elizabeth* (1680), pp. 337–50; Worth, p. 162.

31 John C. Appleby, "Abraham Jennings of Plymouth: The Commercial Career of a 'Western' Trader, c. 1602–1649," pp. 24–38.

32 *Hawkins of Plymouth*, pp. 198–99.

spare black citations offer some indication of the primitivism and tracelessness that characterizes the beginnings of the black presence in the early modern English provinces. At the same time, in the four decades that the records span that some changes begin to appear may be implicit in the relatively greater clarity of the third record and in its designation of "employed" to describe the condition of Jennings's African, which while still cryptic conveys more of a sense of normative social location for the African than do the blunt possessiveness of the "at" phrases used to designate the black people with Sparks and Stallenge.

If in the logic of early modern Christian culture black baptisms are assimilatory instincts of inclusion, however historically damaging in their effects, as has been argued earlier in this book, those of St. Andrew's, Plymouth, like many of the London records, extend those inclusive instincts only to black births and not to the parents. Thus, the three baptisms of encumbered Africans in St. Andrew's, those of "Helene, d[aughter] of Cristian the negro s[er]vant to Richerd Sheere, the supposed father binge Cuthbert Holman" on 2 May 1593; "Cristien, d[aughter] of Mary, a negro of John Whites and the supposed d[aughter] of John Kinge, a Dutchman" on 17 November 1594; "Fortunatus, s[on] of a negro of Thomas Kegwins the supposed father being a Portugall" on 24 December 1594 (Items 187, 201, 202), serve the function only of recording the increase of the black people's owner's chattel goods rather than any civic occasion marking the birth of human beings. By the same logic, the burial notice of "Cristian, d[aughter] of Cristian, Richard Sheers' blackmoore" on 14 April 1593 (Item 197) serves more to note the loss of Sheers's assets than to lament the loss of Christian's daughter, the record also reflecting possibly the "farming" of seized black people in Sheers's house. If in three of these cases, the mother's name is recorded, namely Cristian and Mary, even that recognition is not awarded to the mother of Fortunatus, who remains lost in the generalized sexless descriptor of her peoples, simply as "a negro." Instead, what is prominent in all three notations is the studiously recorded identity of the owners of these Africans by which such human possessions clearly become signs of their social and financial substance. While aside from John White, who was a trader from Dorchester in the adjoining county of Dorset actively involved in the Plymouth company and presumably resident now in the latter city and a shipowner there,[33] the precise identities of Richard Sheere and Thomas Kegwins are unknown, it is a safe surmise that they were merchant mariners of Plymouth whose incidental dabbling in African slave seizures or whose tacit subscription to such activities by their colleagues was part of the social life of their business careers.

Two features worth noting in these records are their paternity citations, and their frequence of occurrence. First, in each of the three cases, the insistence of a paternal attribution of the birth, together with the concomitant qualification of the named attribution as "supposed," points to the simultaneous civic attempt and failure to "normalize" what is patently the exposed consequence of the illicit sexual exploitation of a black women held in chattel bondage. Irrespective of whether the sexual coercion occurred before or during the black women's tenure with their Plymouth owners, the naming of Portuguese, French, and Dutch men as the possible perpetrators offerred a

[33] A. L. Rowse "Tudor Expansion: The Transition from Medieval to Modern History," p. 315; Worth, p. 91.

measure of protection to the women's English captors, who could by that rhetorical deflection appear to be more humane. If this tendency appears in the London records as well, it is much less frequent, so that it is possible to speculate that the sexual exploitation of black women in the countryside, where the pressure of distant urban civic constraints if any were likely to have a weaker impress and be adulterated by local power structures, was a commoner phenomenon that it was in the metropolis. Secondly, that four citations of near identical content occur within a range of two years suggests a growing volume of black importation into Plymouth in these years, particularly of women, and of their sexual exploitation, as well as of the increased presence of alien traders in the English west country ports at this time. That last aspect further multiplies the possibilities of a black presence in Plymouth.

Familiar patterns are also present in the citations of unencumbered black people in St. Andrew's. The burial notices of "Anthony, John, a Neyger" on 18 March 1587; "Carbew, Lazia, a negro" on 11 March 1591; and "White, Cristian, d[aughter] of John, Negro" on 10 March 1594 (Items 168, 177, 196) are distinguished on the one hand by their unambiguous African identifications—which has been a feature of the outside London black citations so far and will continue to be so—and on the other by their conspicuous silence about the particular attachments if any of these Africans. If the first feature is a sign of the relative lack of integration of black peoples in the English countryside at these dates, so that the ambiguity of assimilated and unmarked black names will not appear here, unlike the data of the London records, the second feature is almost certainly a sign of their destitute state in which their lives, abandoned to a hostile cultural and meteorological environment, were quickly extinguished from natural or unnatural causes, and which *is* like many of the Elizabethan London records even if not the seventeenth-century ones. Even if their Christian names point to an assimilated past for them, their unattached status at their deaths signal not their independent standing, which would be historically implausible in this conservative west country outport with limited support even for European aliens, but their indigent ends. This is credible even in the case of Cristian White, the motherless citation of whose death can only be a pointer to the penury of her father John. The clustered dates of these records within a seven-year period from 1587 to 1594, again underlines an intensification of the black presence in Plymouth in the closing decades of Elizabeth's reign.

If Christian White's motherless burial mention hints also at the lugubriousness of black chattel lives, several unencumbered baptism notices in St. Andrew's expand this note, each with unmistakable traces of the sexual oppression of held black women. These are the baptisms of "Susan, d[aughter] of a Blackmoore" on 1 July 1596; "Pedro, Katheren, d[aughter] of don Pedro a basterd Neger" on 4 October 1596; "Ric, son of Marye a Neger, base, ye reputed father Rog[er] Hoggett" on 23 June 23 1603; "Katherin d[aughter] of a Blackamore" on 17 January 1630; and "Elizabeth, d.[aughter] of Angell, A Blackmoore, the reputed father a fleming" on 11 January 1633 (Items 213, 217, 254, 336 338, 346). These records echo those of the encumbered black baptisms discussed above with the exception that the black parents involved here were spoken for by no one. Two of these parents are nameless, and two of the offspring have no fathers, while of the three that do two are of uncertain, "reputed," authenticity, with one being of illicit paternity himself, "a basterd Neger." Unlike the St. Andrew's encumbered black citations, only two aliens are cited here as having possibly fathered a black child. Significantly, all the five unions involve black women, even if only two, Marye and Angell, are clearly identified as such and the other three implied. That Katherin and Susan were also the products of a black woman impregnated by a white man is a likelihood mandated by the historical implausibility of a bonded black man in this place at this time having the social empowerment and sexual agency to have an illicit sexual relationship with a white woman. So, too, Don Pedro's "basterd"[y] includes the possibility of the name itself being a hurriedly chosen conveniently Iberian pseudonym for a violated black woman, deployed to mask her captive English sexual oppression, as was earlier suggested could be the case for some of the encumbered black baptisms in St. Andrew's. Arguably, the same design could underlie the documentary attribution of Elizabeth's paternity to "a fleming." Within this grim racial scenario in the English provinces, that benevolent cross-racial unions are a rarity at this time is reflected in the sole record in St. Andrew's of such a coupling, that of "Blackmore alias Hellier, John and Anstice Light, wid.," on 30 October 1599 (Item 236).

Next in prominence among Devon citations of black people, and in the one locale that most shares Plymouth's character, is Barnstaple, on the other, north, end of Devon, on the southeast bank of the Taw river as it faces southward to the Atlantic. Like Plymouth heavily involved in English maritime Atlantic history because of its location, it was another site of the emergence of powerful seafaring trading families, foremost among which is that of Richard Dodderidge. A merchant trader, who rose to considerable wealth, and consequently to political prominence, in Barnstaple in the later decades of Elizabeth's reign, he was a prominent shipbuilder, owner, and, following the Armada's defeat in 1588, an active privateer and investor in the Senegal company and in trade to Barbary, with several riverfront holdings in the town.[34] The "sumptuous" living style of English west country merchants is exemplified by the elaborately designed and fitted residence of the Dodderidge's in Barnstaple in the late 1590s.[35] This is the historical context for the baptism of "Grace,

[34] For references to Dodderidge as a shipowner and builder, see *Calendar of State Papers, Domestic Series, of the Reign of Elizabeth, 1591–94*, p. 530. For Dodderidge's privateering investments see Rabb, *Enterprise and Empire*, p. 281. For a sensational instance of the kind of privateering loot acquired by Dodderidge, see the eyewitness account of the thousand pounds of gold seized by his ship, *Prudence*, from a Spanish vessel and brought back to Barnstaple in 1590, recorded by Barnstaple's town clerk, Philip Wyot, in his diary; cited in J. R. Chanter, *Sketches of the Literary History of Barnstaple*, p. 96. For his trading to Africa, see K. R. Andrews, "Christopher Newport of Limehouse," p. 34. According to a web article titled "Richard Doddridge," in a genealogical website (Family Tree Legends at <http://www.familytreelegends.com/trees/patlowe/1/data/613>, seen 9.12.06), the records of Dodderidge's extensive property holdings in Barnstaple are at the North Devon Record Office, Barnstaple, Item #1142 b/T38/14-16, 18; and at the Devon Record Office, Exeter, Item #96 M/Box 83/13. For an instance of the Dodderidge's prominent standing in Barnstaple, see Catherine Patterson, "Conflict Resolution and Patronage in Provincial Towns, 1590–1640," pp. 12–14.

[35] See the description of the house of Dodderidge's son, Pentecost, in Herbert Crescinsky, "An Oak-Panelled Room in Barnstaple," pp. 298–303. For a sketch of the house, see Alison Grant, "Breaking the Mould: North Devon Maritime Enterprise," p. 125.

a neiger servant of Mr Richard Dodderidge" on 6 April 1596 (Item 211). As the date connects to Dodderidge's West African trading of eight years past documented by Theodore Rabb, that connection is transparently the origins of Grace's English presence. Implicitly coded in the subtext of the entry is the civic celebration, not of Grace the black woman, but of the pomp of "Mr Richard Dodderidge," who has now added a "neiger" to his many fine possessions. The dignity of Grace's condition as a "servant" rather than as unspecified chattel is the dividend of the record's language, as it pays homage to the high standing of a dignitary of the town.

All but one of the other Barnstaple black notations are overwritten by the same class characteristics, and these may therefore be discussed as a group. These include, among the encumbered records, the baptisms of "Elizabeth, a nigor with Mrs Ayer" on 10 April 1598; "Mary, base daughter of Elizabeth, a nyger, with Mrs Ayer" on 22 May 1605; "Chaterin, a nygor with Mr Lanyon" on 2 February 1605 (1606) (Items 227, 261, 264), and the burial of "Peter Mingus, negor servant of Mr Norrishe" on 22 May 1596 (Item 212). The only unencumbered black mention is that of the baptism notation of "Elizabeth, daughter of Susannah, a nygor" on 10 November 1606 (Item 269). Mrs. Ayer is most likely the wife of John Ayre, who like "Mr. Norrishe" was a merchant of Barnstaple prominent enough to be named in the same trading charter issued by Elizabeth in 1577 that also names the Richard Dodderidge discussed above.[36] The identity of "Mr. Lanyon" may be less readily traceable, but that merely suggests that the practice of chattel African possession in the English countryside is a phenomenon involving better- as well as lesser-known members of the provincial English merchant class. At the same time, despite the very similar social identities of Ayer, Lanyon, and Norris, why Elizabeth and Mary and Chaterin should be casually described as simply being "with" their English owners and Peter Mingus more precisely noted as a "servant" is something that remains unresolved. Within the common class character of these records, those of Elizabeth and of her daughter Mary kept by Mrs. Ayer are unusual, in that they are the first records in this book to directly show the extension of a black individual's captive condition to that of its progeny. Elizabeth and Mary's records are also notable for the distinctness with which they show the sexual exploitation of black woman in the countryside, since Elizabeth's illicit impregnation (with her "base daughter," Mary) during her possession by Mrs. Ayer points indubitably to her casual sexual usage by English parties unknown. That sexual vulnerability is more obvious in the case of the single-parent birth of Susannah's daughter, Elizabeth, the mother's unattached status being probably both the cause and the consequence of her personal desolation. For the early modern English black subject, particularly in the provinces, it is an abiding paradox worth observing that the ownerless state is a condition more malignant than the captive one, the slow living death of the civilly rationalized incarceration of the

[36] Cecil T. Carr, *Select Charters of Trading Companies 1530–1707* (1913), p. 67. Norris (sometimes spelled Norrys) was also a privateering investor (Rabb, *Enterprise and Empire*, p. 349), who in 1606 petitioned Robert Cecil for compensation for losses suffered in the now-concluded Anglo–Spanish wars ("James I: Volume 24: December, 1606," *Calendar of State Papers Domestic: James I, 1603–1610*, pp. 336–42). Norris is also mentioned by the Barnstaple town clerk Philip Wyot in his diary; see Chanter, *Literary History of Barnstaple*, p. 102.

latter being replaced by the inevitably catastrophic, terminal physical, linguistic, and cultural expurgation of the former. If the English countryside's local civic structures had no room for the indigent and the masterless, it had no means for even seeing or knowing humanly the stray black person for whom no one could speak.

Among these citations, the mention of "Anthonye, my negarre" in the will of Nicholas Wichehalse on 28 August 1570 (Item 133) is deceptive. Nicholas Wichehalse was a prosperous merchant who in 1558 and 1563 was church warden of St. Peter Church in Barnstaple, in 1560 a burgess of the city, and who that same year acquired the Lordship and Manor of Barnstaple for the price of £200.[37] First mentioned by Peter Fryer, this citation of a kept black man within a wealthy Devonian's extensive listing of property for his successors is not simply the record of a gift to the former that it might seem to be. Such an impression might be communicated by the confusing syntax and vocabulary of the will, which seems to say that Nicholas Wichehalse is leaving "all … [his] lands in the Towns and pisshes [parishes] of Lynton and Counseberye, Peracombe, Loxforde and Berynarber," etc., jointly to all the people that it lists before this catalog of property, as well as to his wife, Marye, "for life." Anthonye's mention at the end of that list of people, and immediately before the catalog of property, makes it appear as if Wichehalse was also making the African servant a joint owner of "all … [my] lands", which while being immensely appealing emotionally to modern readers is highly implausible historically and simply illogical. Such a will would be an irresponsible one, since Wichehalse's English heirs would almost certainly be unwilling to share their valuable inheritance indivisibly with a black servant, even if they learned how to share their inheritance commonly between themselves.

What is much more likely is that Anthonye was part of the catalog of property that syntactically begins with him in the will's text, and that is being passed on to the wife to whom the catalog leads and with whom it ends, for judicious and equitable disbursement: "for sattisfacon [satisfaction] of my debtes and legacyes." Even if some benefit for Anthonye is intended in the will, it is likely to be of a qualitatively and quantitatively different order from that intended for the others mentioned in the document. How Marye Wichehalse discharged the entirety of the charges entrusted to her by her husband is not known, except for one instance that is evident in her own will of 24 September 1584, in which she carefully sets out apart inheritances of her daughter and her husband, and that of her son.[38] But if Anthonye was included in the rest of Mary Wichehalse's disbursements of her husband's will, in however small a fashion and in whatever kind (perhaps in relaxed terms of bondage as a preferred menial gifted to someone within the family or without, and in secure habitation for him during his remaining years of service and after), he was both the recipient of largesse and the symbol of it. This mixed denotation of Anthonye, as a human agent and a material token, which makes his record distinct from the ones seen so far, is symptomatic of one kind of historical obfuscation of the provincial English black subject and a precursor of a phenomenon that will occasionally be seen in the next century.

---

[37] J. R. Chanter and Thos. Wainwright, *Reprint of the Barnstaple Records*, 1: 200, 211, 222, 239–40.

[38] *Report and Transactions of the Devonshire Association*, p. 240, Item "No. 13." The will itself is in the National Archives,MS PROB 11/68 dated 25 September 1585.

The remaining Devonshire records are from a variety of even more rural locations across the county's middle and southern latitudes. Of these, the encumbered citations include from East Allington the baptism of "the blackmoor of Mr John Ffortescue of ffallapytt named George" on 20 August 1577; and from Colyton the burial of "Katheren, a blackamoor servant of Sir William Pole" on 1 June 1619 (Items 142, 306). "ffallapytt" is Fallapit, the country seat of one of the branches of the prolific and influential Fortescue family, which included Sir John Fortescue, the fifteenth-century jurist cited earlier in this book. Fallapit became the residence of the branch of the family headed by Henry Fortescue, Chief Justice of Common Pleas in Ireland, from the time of his second marriage to an heiress of the Fallapit family in the first half of the sixteenth century. The John Fortescue of the record is Hugh Fortescue's grandson.[39] This history explains the class affiliation of John Fortescue, by which he may have acquired an African, almost certainly for his country residence, even if the exact nature and scale of his mercantile investments are uncertain.[40] Furthermore, the Buckinghamshire branch of his family was connected by marriage to William Pole,[41] which may help to further explain the presence of an African in bondage in both families in Devon. If George's record, like that of Anthonye, is worth noticing for the relatively earliness of its date, Katherin's citation is as well, for the comparative circumspection of its language describing her as "a servant," and in that recalling the probity of the language of many of the Jacobean London black records.

The unencumbered notations are from Bishops Nympton the burial of "Anthony Blackmore" on 2 February 1588; from Hatherleigh the baptisms of "Grace, a blackamore" on 13 May 1604 and of "Rebecca, base daughter of Grace, a Negro" on 10 August 1606; from Ottery St. Mary the marriage of "blackemore," "joan" and "pynsent", "edw." on an unknown date in 1605; and from Chulmleigh the burial of "Luce the Blackamoor" on 1 June 1658 (Items 172, 260, 262, 267, 383). Each of these records has its own singularity. Anthony's record is the first one of an uncertain ethnicity to be seen so far in the outside London records, due to its use of an unmarked ethnic descriptor in the surname position. Grace and Rebecca's records reflect the spreading incidence of the sexual abuse of black women in the Devon countryside. Luce's notation, with its curious use of the definite article, "the blackamoor," signals the social familiarity of the black subject whereby she was now known in the community but nevertheless an oddity. In this group, Joan Blackemore's marriage record, while also displaying like the citation of Anthony an unmarked ethnic identifier as a surname, is of different kind in that the cross-racial union described in it signals a certain amount of black integration occurring in the Devon countryside. But the record's rural location in a small hilly town in east Devon does not say much about the prevalence of this phenomenon in the county, recalling as it does only the marriage of the equally doubtfully named Hellier Blackmore in Plymouth six years earlier. These five citations, conveniently tracking across the late Tudor, early Stuart,

---

39 Bernard Burke, *A Genealogical History of the Dormant Abeyant, Forfeited, and Extinct Peerages of the British Empire*, p. 221.

40 Rabb lists the Fortescues as investors in overseas trade, but does not specify the companies with which they were involved (p. 203).

41 Michael C. Questier, *Catholicism and Community in Early Modern England*, p. 75.

and Restoration decades, reflect most of the changing characteristics of the black records across the sixteenth and seventeenth centuries seen in the earlier chapters.

Of the three other records from Devon, two are from the city records of Exeter, one registering the appointment of "William Moore lute Servaunte of Sir Ames Bampfild" as "one of the Waites of this Cittie … so longe as he shalbe of gu(...) [good] behavior" on 10 August 1606, and the other from St Mary Major noting the burial of "Thomas, the son of a Blackamoor" on 4 February 1631 (Items 268, 340). "Sir Ames Bampfild" is Amias Bampfield, an Exeter lord, who was a close associate of Francis Drake and joined to Drake's family in marriage, a member of parliament and an advocate of the English militia in Ireland, and himself involved in predatory colonial trading in that region.[42] This contextual background credibly identifies William Moore's English presence to be a result of Drake's seizure of him on any one of the latter's warring piratical voyages and passed on to a member of his social circle in Devon, while his employment as a waite or city piper connects him to the cultural history of Africans employed as musicians in early modern Europe mentioned in the first chapter. Additionally, the record's surviving visible threat of violence for any non-compliance exposes the violent coercion involved in the so-called employment of seized Africans, even as such employment awards them a measure of protection and dignity. These clues credibly remove the ambiguity of William Moore's black identity despite the ethnic dilution of his assimilated name, which like those of Anthony Blackmore or Joan Blackemore also uses an unmarked ethnic descriptor as a surname. Concomitantly, the mention of "Thomas"'s burial in a church in Exeter reveals the multiplicity of the casual black importations of Drake and his circle in this seaport town, including the growth of such a group after arrival, within the squalor of their bonded lives. That such importations lead inevitably to some assimilation is spelled by the third Exeter record, which is from Tiverton further inland, and comprises a note in the account books of Blundell's School to the effect that in 1619 the trustees sent a black boy to London on an errand (Item 304). Founded fifteen years earlier by a £2,400 bequest from Peter Blundell, a wealthy and well-connected west country clothier and close friend of the high Elizabethan and Jacobean government figure Sir John Popham, the school was a charitable institution intended to provide free education to its locality.[43] That aspect of the school's history may perhaps explain the presence of the African youth here, who was nonetheless not fortunate enough to be a student, and the rest of whose history is unrecorded. The quality of the black youth's assimilated state, which enabled a more than hundred mile journey to London by himself without confusion or fear of harassment if not persecution, is undermined, however, by the anonymity of his documentary citation, which while broadcasting the unusual trust placed in him in the errand in which he is cited cannot give him a name.

---

[42] For information on Amias Bampfield see Russell Trevillian, *The Rearview Mirror*, p. 36, and Charles Wareing Bardsley, *A Dictionary of English and Welsh Surnames*, p. 75. For Bampfield as an MP, see Micheline White, "Women Writers and Literary-Religious Circles in the Elizabethan West Country," p. 191 n. 7, and for his trading investments see Rabb, p. 239.

[43] Douglas Walthew Rice, *The Life and Achievements of Sir John Popham*, 1531–1607, pp. 152–55, 158.

Several black entries are from Gloucestershire, northeast of Devon, with thirteen notations occurring in four different locales of that county. These include nine entries from the port city of Bristol, which while being uniquely a county in its own right straddles the northern borders of Gloucestershire and Somerset. Connected to three rivers, and bounded by two, on the edge of the Bristol channel flowing southwestwards toward the Atlantic, Bristol is arguably one of the most naturally endowed and important English ports, well established as that in medieval times, and accelerated into a greater capacity in that role in the sixteenth century. It was not only the home port for Sebastian Cabot's voyage to Newfoundland at the end of the fifteenth century and of Martin Pring's at the beginning of the seventeenth, but also the residence of that indefatigable advocate of colonialism and colonial ethnographer Richard Hakluyt, who as a young man was a prebendiary there.[44] More than any other port city, Bristol's early modern life history was directly dependent on sea trade and, in the sixteenth century, to the pursuit of the wealth that such trade with newer regions such as Africa and America brought, so much so that already by the middle of the sixteenth century 70 percent of the city's taxable population lived in the city's portside area itself.[45] Dominated as the city was by the Merchant Venturers of Bristol, licensed in 1552,[46] by the beginning of the seventeenth century 50 percent of the city's administrators were members of the company, a figure that jumped to more than 60 percent in the next several decades.[47] As elsewhere, competing with them were aggressive smaller traders of opportunity. More than other English towns, Bristol was a direct beneficiary of the slave trade from the closing Elizabethan decades and, after of the seizure of Jamaica in 1655, of the sugar industry.[48] Bristol's maritime history and social character is thus in total compatibility with, and fully predictive of, the cluster of black citations that appear here.

One of these is a legal reference to a black man with Sir John Young of Bristol in a Star Chamber case in London in 1560: "[Young] did appointe a blacke moore to keep possession of his garden" (Item 126).[49] Even though the case is heard in London, the record's substance pertains to Bristol. John Young was an especially powerful Bristolian, described variously by modern historians as "arguably Bristol's wealthiest and most influential citizen," and as "a prominent gentleman resident of Bristol" connected to the Earl of Pembroke, and leader and spokesperson for "Bristol retailers."[50] His private residence, which he constructed *after* 1560, was an "impressive new" one in one of the port city's wealthiest neighborhoods on Horse Street, adjacent to St. Austin's or St. Augustine's church on the city's west side on the site of an old Catholic friary, which was traditionally one of the most

---

[44] "Attempts towards Colonization," p. 687; Hakluyt, *Diverse Voyages Touching America*, ed. Jones, title page's author description.

[45] David Harris Sacks, *Widening Gate*, pp. 46–50, 147–49.

[46] S. J. Jones, "The Growth of Bristol," p. 75.

[47] David Harris Sacks, "Corporate Town and English State, p. 91.

[48] S. J. Jones, "Growth of Bristol," p. 71.

[49] The record's documentary source could be either National Archives STAC 5/S14/26 or STAC 5/C81/29.

[50] The first quotation is from Mark C. Pilkinton, *Bristol*, p. 284, the last two from Sacks, *The Widening Gate*, p. 198.

privileged areas of the city. The sumptuousness of this house, which had a beautiful garden, is evident from the fact that Queen Elizabeth herself visited John Young here in 1574, and was in fact so well taken care of in it that she knighted him.[51] According to the Bristol chronicler John Latimer, at the time of the record's date, 1560, Young was living on the premises of the old Friary, which may already have included the garden.[52] That the African is a man of some skill is implicit from the ornate Elizabethan "knot garden"[53] of which he is charged to "keep possession," the expression possibly denoting his responsibility in guarding and maintaining what Young obviously regarded as a valuable material asset, and to which he would shortly add the befitting mansion that will become his "Great House." This, then, is the entirely appropriate personal history and physical locale for the black man cited in the record. Buried deep in the backdrop of Young's swelling political career and wealth, a part of the latter deriving arguably from his privateering investments,[54] it is wholly unsurprising that the black man that he keeps is barely visible in the record and appears anonymously, even though he is himself as much of a social distinction for Young as the garden the latter placed in his care. The overall documentary silence about the circumstances of this black person's English presence, or more precisely, of the details of John Young's acquisition of him, vindicates the assertions made in Chapters 2 and 3 that a lack of documentation of English trafficking in Africans at any given point in the sixteenth and seventeenth centuries cannot be taken to mean an absence of such activities. The record's date of 1560 points to the early Elizabethan years as being one moment particularly prone to such hidden phenomena.

Bristol's other encumbered black citations show the spread of the habit of African possession among its other social classes over the next half century. William Hayman

---

[51] For the Queen's visit, see Pilkinton pp. 284, 285, and Tudor Edwards, *Bristol*, p. 22. For the demography of Bristol see Sacks, *Widening Gate*, pp. 146–47. Also see the web page of Port Cities Bristol, which has this statement: "The first reference to a black person, or a 'blackmore' as they were then often called, in the city's records is in the 1590s. It is to a black man who worked as a gardener in the Great House owned by the Young family. The house stood on the site of what later became the Colston Hall (which still exists today as a venue for performances). The Red Lodge, now a museum, is the last remaining building from the Young's estate. A picture of the Great House is shown here. It is taken from a detailed map drawn in 1673. In 1653 the house became the second sugar processing house in Bristol. Sugar from the Caribbean plantations would have arrived 'raw'. It required processing to make it into the white refined sugar which people used to sweeten their tea and coffee." <http://www.discoveringbristol.org.uk/showNarrative.php?narId=471&nacId=474>. Seen 07.02.04. The 1590s dating of the reference on this site is incorrect.

[52] Pointed out by Margaret McGregor, Archivist, Bristol Record Office, in a personal communication to the author. Thus, Madge Dresser's querying of the date of the record (see the note in *Slavery Obscured*, p. 10), is mistaken.

[53] For a description and a picture of the current reconstruction of John Young's knot garden, see the website <http://www.timetravel-britain.com/06/March/lodge.shtml>, seen 06.06.06.

[54] It is credible that the "John Young" that Rabb lists as a privateering investor (*Enterprise and Empire*, p. 410) is this John Young of Bristol. Although Rabb dates his privateering investments in 1581, it is also plausible that such investments started much earlier, perhaps clandestinely, and consequently with little documentation.

was "a mariner" who, as part of the city's "upper class" that was adjudged by the King's commission to receive knighthood, was fined £10 in 1631 for refusing the same.[55] His stated profession, even if untraceable in its career details, quite plausibly explains the African in his possession, a "blakman" named Solomon who was baptized on 4 February 1631 in St. Augustine's Church, Bristol (Item 339). This is the same location as the record of John Young's black gardener from several decades back, which shows the growing practice of black possession in Bristol's city center. Similarly, even if "Willyam Edmondes," i.e. William Edmonds, whose servant "Mary a Blackmore & Servant" was buried in St. Philip and Jacob's church on 12 September 1632 (Item 344), may not be fully identifiable, the likelihood is that he was a merchant or small trader. As Madge Dresser points out, St. Philip and Jacob's Church is in the old "market area" of the city, on the north bank of the river Avon on the opposite side of the city from St Augustine's, and at this time "a commercial and manufacturing center. This in itself suggests a link between merchants and African servants that pre-dates any formal entry of Bristol into the African slave trade."[56] If the origins of Mary's English presence are not fully traceable, that untraceability is another pointed example of the historical ghostliness of black people in early modern England.

In contrast, such a tracklessness of origin does not surround the woman appearing in what is perhaps the most revealing of Bristol's black records, and possibly the most important one in the entire provincial English group. This is the mention of "Dinah the Moor," a black woman who on 31 May 1647 visited a celebrated Baptist spiritualist named Sarah Wight in London for advice and consolation, which the latter's amanuensis, the Baptist preacher Henry Jessey, recorded in 1647 in his account of Sarah Wight's life of spiritual ministrations (Item 373).[57] Dinah's grimmer subsequent history is that of the woman called "Dinah the Black," which the nineteenth century antiquarian Bristol chronicler John Latimer pieced together from the July 1667 minutes of the Aldermen's Court in Bristol. That history includes her service for the five preceding years as a servant to a Dorothy Smith in Bristol, when she was baptized, after which she was sold by her mistress without her knowledge to a man who wanted to take her to America. Dinah's resistance to her sale and exportation to America—she wanted to live as a Baptist Christian in England—and the commotion it caused, prevented her departure, but since her mistress was unwilling to take her back, the matter came before the Aldermen's court, which decided temporarily at least to let Dinah earn her own living. According to Latimer, "From the peculiar way in which she is described, it may be assumed Dinah was a negro woman captured on the African coast, and had lived as a slave in Bristol," which is "A curious example of the practice of kidnapping human beings."[58] That Dinah was the woman in the 1647 conversation of Sarah Wight recorded by Henry Jessey is plausibly suggested by his description of her as "a Moor" in his introduction to the episode, and by his

---

55 John Latimer, *Annals of Bristol*, p. 10.

56 Dresser, *Slavery Obscured*, p. 11.

57 For a brief contextual introduction to Henry Jessey, see Suzanne Trill, Kate Chedzgoy, and Melanie Osborne, eds., *Lay by Your Needles Ladies, Take the Pen*, pp. 155–58.

58 John Latimer, *Annals of Bristol*, p. 344.

naming of her in the list of Sarah Wight's visitors as "Dinah the Black," both of which he added to the 1658 edition of his book.[59]

The composite record of Dinah Black is extraordinary for many reasons. First, it is one of the few records in this book that clearly displays the complete trajectory of black lives seized from Africa and inducted into casual chattel English slavery before the slave trade began. In that it confirms the history of early modern English black people that is only fragmentarily and intuitively present in the majority of the black citations collected in this book. Secondly, the record reflects two historically problematic aspects of the assimilation process seen earlier, namely the unmarked deployment of an ethnic descriptor as a surname, which renders more ambivalent the already occluded seized black subject, and the ultimate irrelevance of baptism for the legal standing of the black subject, who despite being a Christian can, as in this case, be again sold as a slave. Third, and what is invaluable, is the record's inscription of what may, as in an earlier instance in the last chapter, be described as the black subject's *ipsissima vox*, that is, her own voice,[60] despite the overwriting of it by Henry Jessey. That Dinah's words are overwritten by Jessey is made explicit by his parenthetical explanatory interjection in his introduction to the episode, that "her [i.e. Dinah's] words were better understood by Mrs. Sarah, than by the Writer, and sometimes were guessed at, from the Answers given to her, viz." By "Answers" is meant the replies made by Wight to Dinah's expressions of distress, which were then being used by Jessey to reconstruct that to which they were a response. But this prominent visibility of the transcription's corruption also directs attention to that which is being corrupted, and therefore to the presence of Dinah's authentic speech, however unintelligible and untranscribable. In other words, Jessey's "guess[ing] at" the meaning of Dinah's speech preserves that speech phenomenologically and opens an intuitive access to its contents. Jesse's interested "guess[ing]," and inside that, Wight's, of what they *think* Dinah is saying, that is, what they *expect* Dinah to be saying, in the manner seen earlier in some of the Elizabethan records, serve as limiting markers for what Dinah is *not* saying, and therefore as inverse guides to the psychic space of her actual speech. In these ways, it is possible to see Dinah as one of the first living black subjects in the records of this book.

Fourthly, and what is most invaluable of all, within that faint voicing what is discernible, to a degree not available in any of the records of this book, is the plight of the racialized black subject trapped historically in a color-conscious English society in which she will be negatively marked forever. The discreet racial undertone of Jessey's and Wight's readings of Dinah's spiritual distress, noted by Barbara Dailey and by Peter Linebaugh and Marcus Rediker, can be seen in the way Dinah's series of supposed statements of affliction—that she is "sore assaulted by Satan," that even though she "desires him [Christ]" Christ "shall not" save her even though "he is able

---

59 In the "Table of Contents" Jessey describes the woman as "a blakmor"; noted by Peter Linebaugh and Marcus Buford Rediker, *The Many-Headed Hydra*, p. 368 n. 60. That Jessey names her as Dinah Black is pointed out by Barbara Ritter Dailey, "The Visitation of Sarah Wight" p. 449.

60 Salkeld, "Black Lucy and the 'Curtizans' of Shakespeare's London," ch. 6.

to," and even though "he may do this for some, but not for [her]"—are centered on her climactic sequential confessions:

> I am a filthy wretched creature …
> I am tempted against my life …
> I am not as others are, I do not look so as others do.

This, it will be recalled, is the precise early modern English Protestant doctrinal position about the divinely mandated excludability of the naturally foul-because-sinful black subject articulated in the notations of Thomas Harridaunce in his baptism of Mary Phyllis in 1597 in St. Botolph, Aldgate discussed in Chapter 2. In the logic of Jessey's text of the conversation, this is the malaise to which Wight's words of consolation address themselves: "When Christ comes and manifests himself to the Soul, it is black in it self and uncomely, but he is faire and ruddy and he clothes the Soul with his comeliness … and makes it comely therein," and "He doth not this to one only, for as many Nations must be blessed in Him … ." That this comforting is to be taken as a successful one is underlined by Jessey's concluding note that "The Relator spake afterwards with this afflicted Maid, She told him the Lord had given some support and refreshings to her, since that Conference," in which Dinah's previously unintelligible words are apparently now by an equal miracle totally intelligible to him.

The design of Jessey's rendition of the conversation rests on Dinah's unhappiness about her blackness and on Wight's consolation of her about her blackness, both of which table blackness as a problem. That is, in comforting the black subject about its blackness, Jessey and Wight confirm the black subject's racial marking. Thus, the real substance of Dinah's words may lie lost within the relentlessly closed circle of the conversation that Jesse produces. Barbara Dailey's summation of this purported conversation of the black woman is succinct:

> There is a … poignant irony in this dialogue. It is the communication of that "comfort" wherein lies the root cause of this woman's distress. To say that Christ would clothe her in his "faire and ruddy complexion" confirmed the fact that in the eyes of the English and their God she was "black" and "uncomely." Are we to believe that this comforted stranger never experienced the double take of delayed realization?[61]

It may be useful to add that Dinah's "double take" "realization," instead of being a "delayed" one, could be the very substance of what she was trying to say. At the same time, the very incommunicability of the racialized subject's despair to its English captors about the solipsism of its always-already alien condition is precisely what will be rewritten by its addressees in the accents of their own benevolence, in their "comforting" of the black person lost to the denigration to which they have fated it. The unreadability of Dinah's words, which is its most intrinsic message, is the indescribability of the endless repressions of the early modern English black life.

Fifthly, that in her ability to independently seek out Sarah Wight Dinah shows a degree of self-agency, confirms Chapter 3's examination of the laxity of English attitudes toward the black subject in the first half of the seventeenth century, and

[61] Dailey, "The Visitation of Sarah Wight," p. 450.

most pointedly in the Civil War decade of the 1640s. A reflection of this laxity could, not implausibly, be seen in Dinah's singleness and generally in the lack of sexual harassment in her life, at least in the parts of it that can be read from the records. Dinah's subsequent history of being again sold as a slave in the 1660s also demonstrates, as was suggested in the preceding chapter, the instability that such a moment of English racial laxity inevitably has, as the discursive and material incarceration of the black subject quickly resumeed with the onrush of the official mass English slave trafficking of Africans in the Restoration years. Taken in all these five dimensions, Dinah the More's or Dinah Black's composite record constitutes a striking template of the records of black people outside London, revealing and articulating by itself what is only implicit and fragmentary in most of them. Most importantly, while many of its features will be echoed in several black documentations in the remainder of this chapter, in its struggle to articulate the inexpressible, to describe the searing anguish of racial incarceration that is the primary note of the seized black subject's historical consciousness, Dinah's reported words form a pair with another possible voice of black captivity occurring three decades earlier that is discussed below (Cooree, Item 238), and with which it uniquely completes a chronological verbalization of the struggle and despair of the seized African subject in the early modern English provinces.

Unencumbered black citations appearing in the Bristol records are those of the burial notices of "Joane smyth the wyfe of Thomas smyth beinge a blackamoore," on 14 December 1603, and "Peeter a Blackmoore" on 14 December 1610, both in St. Philip and Jacob's church (Items 258, 276). Common to both of these records is the complete opacity of the origins of the Africans named in them, which, as has been seen convincingly, is emblematic of the tracklessness of the early modern English seizures of Africans. The vulnerability of these black individuals is suggested by the strong likelihood of both of their deaths being from the plague despite the infestation being mentioned only in the first citation, because 1603/04 was the first of the two deadliest plague years in Bristol, which eached kill between 2,500 and 3,000 people or about 17 percent of the city's population.[62] The first record's contents have the additional uncertainty of whether the black person is the husband or the wife, even if the syntactical logic of the record's phrasing does point in the direction of Joane Smyth being the African, since the record begins with her and hence probably is about her. What is transparent here, however, and worth noticing, is not just the cross-racial union involved (since only one partner is indicated as black), but also the correctness of Joan Smyth's description as "wife," both of which are untypically positive social signs in the black records of this area, with Joan's wifely social acknowledgment being a unique recognition for a black woman in the provincial English records as a whole. Yet, the social hopefulness of Joan Smyth's record must remain somewhat circumstantially inexplicable for its location and historical moment in Bristol in the first decade of the seventeenth century, for which the rest of the records suggest on the whole a rather different picture.

---

[62] The percentage is derived from population figures cited by Sacks, *Widening Gate*, p. 353, as also is the plague information.

The remaining black citations from Bristol include the burial notice of "Katherine a blacke negra servante at the horshed" in Christchurch on 4 January 1612, and "a Blackymore maide named Francis" in the Church of Christ in Broadmead on an unspecified day in 1640 (Items 281, 361). The distinction of Katherine's citation is that she was a single black working woman, employed in a public tavern, the Horsehead. The tavern sat on what at this time is Christmas Street, a steep narrow path extending upwards from the bridge over the River Frome outside the city wall to the city gate at St. John's.[63] While the consequential wide range of the social knowledge of her in a public place might seem to betoken a broad acceptance and support for her life as an independent black woman, the record's careful insertion of the additional qualifier "servante" sets down the limits of such an acceptance. Additionally, the tavern's riverfront location keeps visible an inferential history of her arrival sometime in the past as chattel merchandise from beyond the sea. If the Horsehead, like many such riverside establishments, is also a brothel, Katherine's "working life" may have included demands other than those of menial drudgery. In that, her record may recall that of the "negress" at the Swan tavern in Elizabethan London, about which Dennis Edwards wrote to his friend in 1599.

Whereas what Francis's working conditions as a "maide" may have included is not as deducible, her life is illuminated by the history of the church with which she is associated. The Church of Christ in Broadmead was the center of the Baptist movement that came to prominence in Bristol in the Civil War years, and her record was enthusiastically authored by one of its most ardent proponents, Edward Terrill, as a triumph of the movement's egalitarian ideology. The background, however, of this record, which has started to receive some critical attention recently, profiles Francis's record deceptively as a triumph of black integration in white society, and of black womanly leadership in a time of rising women's social organization and reassertion. Taking Terrill's praise of Francis's piety and devotion at face value, modern commentators have seen Francis's citation in the congratulatory accents of a revisionist early modern English women's history or of a new revolutionary account of the English Civil War. Aside from the fact that such perspectives either ignore or consider cursorily the perspective of a black history,[64] such readings miss the

---

63 Electronic Statement at Port Cities Bristol web page.

64 Linebaugh and Rediker, pp. 71–102. Although their chapter-length discussion of Francis (in which they also reproduce Terrill's account of Francis in its entirety and provide a transcription of it) contains frequent interrogations of Terrill's agenda, and sharp awareness of Francis's racialized and disempowered position vis-à-vis Terrill's (as when they observe, "She was black; he was white. She was a woman; he was a man. She was a sister in the congregation; he was an elder of the church. She was a servant; he was a master," p. 72) and the compelling possibilities of her history (as when they point out that the "Back of Bristol" where Francis was a servant when alive, was a wharfside area on the Avon's edge where "deep-water vessels—slave ships included—moored," an "interface of the triangular trade" where Francis could not but have agonized daily over the English enslavement that bound her and was binding the others she must have been seeing freshly brought in; p. 77), their overall focus is on the revolutionary nature of 1640s movements such as the Baptist one in which Terrill was involved, which were "silenced" in the Cromwellian and Restoration years (pp. 92–93, 96), without also being critically invested in a developing history of black people

important phenomenon seen in the Dinah Black document and also strongly present here, which is the complex ventriloquism of the English voicing of a disempowered black woman.

What frames Terrill's praise of Francis, for the "humble"-ness of her "walk"-ing and the "blameless"-ness of her "Conversation," and for the "precious"-ness of her Christianity in her deathbed exhortation to "ye whole Congregation" to "let The glory of God be dear unto them" and to keep it in "their families, neighborhoods or places where God places them," and which is "fit for a White heart to store," is his ominous repetitive underlining of Francis's identity as "a Blackymore maide" and a "poor Aethiopian" whose natural ability to "be truly Convinced of Sin" and to be "truly Converted" is doubtful. That is why, in Terrill's view, Francis's presence in their community is "memorable" and worth broadcasting, for it shows "Scripture made good" and proves "God is no respecter of faces." In other words, what qualifies Francis for inclusion in Terrill's memoirs of the Broadmead congregation is not her Christianity but her blackness, which is useful because it is deferential and pliable. Terrill's account represents a seizure of a compliant, because disempowered, black woman for exemplary proselytizing, beneath which her own voice remains silenced. Terrill's voicing of her is in effect her permanent gagging. Following Henry Jessey's telling confession of "guess"-ing Dinah Black's words from Sarah Wight's utterances to her, modern readers of Francis's record can only "guess" what she can be historically saying through Terrill's speaking for her. What is also worth registering is that Francis's record is in that same decade of the 1640s as Dinah's, and in that cumulative but brief historical moment of English laxity toward the black subject in which the latter approaches a natural visibility, including extraordinarily, as in these two cases, an indirect audibility. Whether such a development is a reflection of the "revolutionary" nature of the 1640s, as Peter Linebaugh and Marcus Rediker propose, is an idea that must remain under some consideration.

The other citations of black people are from Bristol's environs in Gloucestershire. These brief notices, which therefore can be treated a group, comprise from Shipton Moyne the will of "Agnes Blackamoore or Blackamore" on 2 July 1582; from Bisley the burial notice of "John Davies 'ye black'" on 22 November 1603; from Almondsbury the burial record of "Catellena a single Negro woman" on an unspecified date in 1625; and from Arlingham the baptism notation of "Hannah, daughter of Thomas Liston, a Barbados merchant," on 4 December 1668 (Items 150, 257, 325, 423). Even if John Davies "ye black" does not have the ethnic ambiguity of Agnes Blackamoore, he shares with her an opacity of origins, with only the two-decade range of the dates of their records hinting at the connection of their English presence to the multifarious illicit west country African trafficking that was vigorous in those years. The financial stability of Agnes that is implicit in her will is partly illuminated by Catellena's history because of the bequest of £6 9s. 6d. that the latter left behind. Although this suggests some personal consolidation, it is unlikely to be

as such. They also seem overall to take Francis's "speech" in Terrill's text literally, despite their own acute understanding of the refractory impress of his own position and interests on his account of Francis.

indicative of a literally unencumbered state, as some have suggested.[65] Her history may be similar to that of Anne Bromley's black maid in St. Mary Putney in London at this same time that was mentioned in Chapter 3, who also left a bequest of £10 in 1626 even if the latter's was specifically directed to church charity, whether freely or induced to do so. Hannah's record is revealing in the silence of its ethnicity, because if she was a black woman, as the Gloucestershire local historian James Tuttle believes (see note to Item), then she was the offspring of an illicit or legitimate cross-racial union in the English West Indian plantations, the social pressures against which on the parent's return to England with his child is conveyed by the record's discreet omission of her ethnicity, and which could also therefore be a measure of the English father's attempt to protect his child. The consequent ethnic masking of this black child is then another instance of the spectrality of the black subject in early modern England, who is present but obfuscated if not abandoned altogether, as is Hannah's unmentioned black mother.[66]

Two other black records in the southwest are from the immediate east of Gloucestershire and Devon, in Wiltshire county. The altogether more extraordinary of these two notations is the documentation in Savernake, which describes the drawing out on an unspecified date in 1673 a deed between "John, Duke of Somerset and Alice Long (daughter of a blackamore, Britannia, a daughter of the King of Morocco), making provision for her descendants" (Item 436). This badly damaged record refers to John Seymour, who from 1646 till his death in 1675 was the fourth Duke of Somerset, whose family had owned the forest and the parish in neighboring Wiltshire since 1553.[67] According to the Wiltshire and Swindon Record Office, all that is known of this record's contents is that "Britannia with her entourage was

[65] See the statement on the web page of Port Cities Bristol: "Another black woman was Catellena, who lived in Almondsbury in Gloucestershire. She seems to have been a freewoman because she had a small amount of property [Dresser: "an estate worth over £6.00"] to leave in her will. A slave would have would have been unlikely to own property so this suggests that she might have been free." Pip Jones and Rita Youseph specify the exact amount she left behind as "£6–9–6."

[66] Some more black citations from Gloucestershire have been pointed out to the author in a personal communication from Margaret Mcgregor of the Bristol Record Office. These are:

> In the parish of Dyrham [near Bath] 1575: A negro of the age of xxx [30] yeres was here bap[ti]sed the 15 day of August and was called to nam[e] Gylman Ivie.
>
> In the parish of Olveston 23 March 1655 was baptised: Jonathan Jarwell a Neger borne at Geney (Guinea) in Barbery being betwixt 18 and 19 yeares of age, Baptised March 23rd being Captain Heans servant.
>
> In the parish of Mangotsfield 01 January 1672 was baptised: a Niger servant to John Meredith esq by the name of John and Nevis assumed as his surname.

Regrettably, these records were received too late to be included in the main body of this work.

[67] "Savernake," in *A History of the County of Wiltshire*, vol. 16, pp. 207–15.

captured at sea first by the Dutch, then the English and came to England."[68] This is an extraordinary record for several reasons. First, this is the only record among those presented in this book that directly connects the highest level of English aristocracy with a north African. Secondly, whereas it is striking enough if the record is describing the adoption of a stranded African woman and her child by the duke, the fact that the deed involves Alice Long, Britannia's daughter, complicates matters considerably because it raises questions about the nature of the duke's relationship with her. If the duke has a blood connection with Alice, that is, if she is the product of his illicit relationship with Britannia, which would not only explain the deed as his attempt to provide for the child but also Britannia's and Alice's names as typical given and baptized names, then the record becomes one of the sexual exploitation of a black woman directly by a member of the English nobility itself.

Thirdly, if Alice is indeed the duke's illegitimate daughter, his attempt to take some responsibility for her future and ensure it legally, while encouraging and while partly explainable in terms of the childlessness of his own marriage with Sarah Alston,[69] notably does not include his inclusion of Alice within his own family name, titles, and privileges. Fourthly, the deed's effect is then to effectively make permanent the obscuring of the black identities of both Alice and her mother Britannia already started by their assimilatory naming, i.e. to complete their historical expurgation. Even if within the deed itself the mother and child's African origins are kept visible, that carefulness is possibly intended as a hint of the necessity of such a deed—namely to explain the duke's action as a charitable gesture toward two black women. Fifthly, if the above reading of Alice as possibly the duke's own illegitimate daughter is correct, that would suggest that for the early modern English sexual oppression of black women the social or political identities of such women are irrelevant: a commoner black woman and a black king's daughter are equally sexual chattel. Sixthly, in its careful naming of Britannia as a "blackamore" the record also incidentally offers a useful clarification of a confusion persistent in modern academic scholarship about the supposed non-blackness of north African Moors. The presence of seized Africans in the Seymour family is probably also helpfully contextualized by the family's investment in African trading from the time of Edward Seymour, and by Francis Seymour's ownership of lands also in Savernake, the latter allowing for a possible but improbable alternative history for Alice Long.[70] Finally, Alice Long's record also helps to illuminate retrospectively the other Wiltshire black citation, that of "Matthias the Morian" in Salisbury Cathedral on 22 February 1601/03 (Item 248), in that it points to the possibility of an earlier history of a seized African presence in the county, which sharing as it does a seacoast location with Devon and Gloucestershire also probably shares their African slaving histories, with Matthias's naming as a "morian" reflecting the earlier late medieval English naming practice for Africans seen in the first chapter.

---

[68] Steven Hobbs, Archivist, Wiltshire and Swindon Record Office, in personal communication to the author.

[69] John Debrett, *The Peerage of the United Kingdom of Great Britain and Ireland*, 1: 7.

[70] For Edward Seymour's African investments see Rabb, *Enterprise and Empire*, p. 374; for Francis Seymour's land ownership in Savernake see "Savernake," in *A History of the County of Wiltshire*, vol. 16, pp. 207–15.

III

In the country's southeast, on the opposite side from Devon and Gloucester, there are a dozen black notations in Kent. The contexts of these records are slightly different from those of the southwest, because Kent's connection to African slave trading was not like those of Bristol' or Plymouth'. Southern Kent ports such as Dover were not bases for long-distance maritime voyages of exploration or trade, including trafficking; they were historically engaged more in cross-channel shipping trade with northern Europe, and in the activities of the Cinque Ports scheme.[71] Instead, Kent's involvement in the history of black people is first through its traditional shipyard on its northeast border on the Thames, Deptford, and through the industry based on that shipyard, ship building. From the time of the commissioning of the Royal Dockyard in Deptford by Henry VIII in 1513,[72] it was the major origination and disembarkation point for serious transoceanic traffic throughout the Tudor and Stuart reigns, which is why some of the black records of the earlier chapters have connections with it, as also will many of those of the next one. Secondly, as Deptford, sitting on the Thames's south bank and adjoining Southwark to its immediate west and Stepney, Ratcliff, Limehouse to its north on the opposite bank of the Thames, was invariably pulled in to the activities of London, so the context for the county's black records is to a small extent the history of prominent London merchants and shipbuilders resident in Kent as well as occasionally rural magnates in the county, both in locations close to London on the county's northeast border, and elsewhere in it. Such figures include for instance Maurice Thompson, William Pett, the Sidneys of Penshurst, and the Sackvilles of Knole. Similar is the context of Gravesend, also on the south bank of the Thames though farther east from Deptford, and which too was a part of London life in the traffic to and from it of people, goods, and services from the metropolis.

Thirdly, the documentations of black people in Kent may also to a degree be the result of Dutch and French aliens in the county, traditionally resident here from the close links of Kentish ports, especially Dover, to Calais, from late medieval times.[73] This small alien European population could and on instance did have black

---

[71] The Cinque Ports were ports granted certain privileges such as pillaging foreign shipping, freedom from tolls and taxes, and the right to have their own courts (i.e. to "soc and sac, tol and team, bloowit and fledwit, pillory tumbril infangentheof, outfangentheof, mundbryce waives and strays, flotsam and jetsam and ligan," in the famous statement of the original charter of 1155, cited at <http://www.digiserve.com/peter/cinque.htm>, seen 5.10.2005), in return for supplying the King with ships and men when needed. The Cinque Ports were Hastings, Sandwich, Dover, New Romney, Hythe including Rye and Winchelsea, and Seaford, Pevensey, Folkestone, Faversham, Lydd, Tenterten, Deal, Margate, and Fordwich. For an explanation of the Cinque Ports scheme, see Samuel Pepys, and Mynors Bright et al., *The Diary of Samuel Pepys: For the First Time Fully Transcribed from the Shorthand Manuscript in the Pepysian Library, Magdalen College, Cambridge*, 9: 144–45; W. H. Smyth, *Chapman the Sailor's Lexicon*, pp. 186–87.

[72] Charles E. Orser, *Encyclopedia of Historical Archaeology*, p. 149.

[73] For an overview of the early modern character of Kentish ports, see Peter Clark, *English Provincial Society from the Reformation to the Revolution: Religion, Politics and Society in Kent 1500–1640*, pp. 11–12.

people with them. Fourthly, the sea-pillaging activities of Kentish Cinque Ports also conceivably brought in some black people seized from enemy merchant ships in the English Channel. Overall, if Kentish ports ever had direct connections to cross-oceanic maritime activity, such connections were probably sporadic occurrences too marginal to be a context *per se* for the black people appearing in the county's records. Thus, Kent's seacoast location does have a bearing on the black presence in the county, but not in exactly the same way as in the English west country. The heterogeneous contexts of Kent's black records, while not enabling as substantial a discussion of them as the Devon and Gloucestershire citations, do help in illuminating them in some measure.

A consistent feature of Kent's history is the relative thinness of the aristocratic presence here.[74] This feature may help to explain the fact that only two of the county's encumbered black records have aristocratic connections. The first of these is the reference in Knole, to "Grace Robinson, a blackamoor" and "John Morockoe," who were employed in the Earl of Dorset's household between 1613 and 1624, the former as a washing woman, who is remembered by Lady Anne Clifford in her *Diary* (Items 283, 284). Anne Clifford was the wife of Richard Sackville, the third Earl of Dorset, in whose family, as Peter Fryer and Kim Hall have pointed out, there was traditionally an African by the name of John Morrocco. While the history of this tradition, which Kim Hall has described as a "hundred-year" old Dorset family habit, is difficult to decipher, the presence of the two black people in the Dorset manor in the early decades of the seventeenth century is not, because both Anne's husband Richard Sackville himself, as well as her father George Clifford, had privateering involvements in those years. Knole was an imperial country mansion, described by Peter Fryer as "huge," and corresponding exactly to the kind of English aristocratic locale in which seized black people could by now in this book's experience be expected to appear.[75] In appearing casually only in the list of household *personae* that Anne compiled for her time at Knole and not in the main entries of her *Diary*, Grace Robinson, as well as John Morrocco, performed what Kim Hall has called the "symbolic" function of black people in early modern England. John and Grace's cryptic listing, at the very bottom of the hierarchic arrangement of the household staff, by their mistress, who was herself alienated and detached from the family culture of the Dorsets as well as of the Pembrokes, with whom she was later joined in her second marriage,[76] may not much illuminate the two Africans *per se* beyond

[74] Ibid., p. 6; Alan Armstrong, ed. *The Economy of Kent*, "Introduction," pp. 6–7. The Kent County Council website states in its web essay, "The History of Kent": "Unlike many parts of England, Kent had no single, powerful and owning family," although "by the sixteenth century a number of significant landed families began to emerge."

[75] For Peter Fryer's reference to the Dorset's family habit see *Staying Power*, p. 24, and for Hall's see *Things of Darkness*, p. 13. For George Clifford and Richard Sackville's privateering involvements see the list in Rabb, *Enterprise and Empire*, 370, and 62, 266, and K. R. Andrews, "Robert Cecil and the Mediterranean Plunder," (for Richard Sackville). For a description of Knole and a history of the Sackvilles, see Edward Hasted, *The History and Topographical Survey of the County of Kent*, 3: 72–82.

[76] Anne's alienation in her married life is obliquely caught in one of her autobiographical comments many years later: "the marbe pillars of Knole and Wilton were to mee oftentimes

confirming their menial usefulness, but it connects them to an English black presence whose variable visibility is its historical footprint.

Very similar is the baptism citation in Chepsted in Chevening, probably on 12 February 1664 rather than 1564, of "John an Ethiopian a blackamoor Servant to the Lady Katharine Strode of Chepsted being 18 years of age or thereabouts as is supposed" (Item 409). The record, which was found by Marika Sherwood from a source now misplaced, is probably of the year 1664 rather than 1564, because whereas there is no reference in any document to a Strode in Chepsted, Kent in the latter year, there is documentation of a Strode family there at the former date. The record's original document, currently untraceable, is almost certainly part of the gap in the 1663/64 entries of the Chevening Parish registers at the Center for Kentish Studies.[77] Ancillary documentation indicates nonetheless that "Katharine Strode" is Katherine Strode, the second wife of Nicholas Strode, a royalist supporter of Charles I who after Charles's defeat and execution in the Civil War, died in exile in Europe in 1663.[78] Chepsted (also spelled Chipstead), which was the residence known as Chepsted Place or Chepsted-House, and distinct from the manor of Chepsted, of which it was once a part, is described in a survey of the property in the 1690s prior to its sale by Katherine Strode as an elaborate "substantial" mansion of reasonable social elegance,[79] befitting the decorative employment there of a seized African youth. Whether John was part of Nicholas Strode's property that his widow inherited at her husband's demise, or he was an acquisition of hers is unknown, but his baptism by her may be a part of her putting her house and possessions in order. Even if exactly how he came into the Strode's' possession is also unknowable, his location and ostensible situation fit the profile of fashionable English aristocratic African possession seen numerous times in this book's records, and precisely compatible with the acceleration of English slaving from the middle of the seventeenth century. His reiterative identification as an "Ethiopian" and a "blackamoor" displays the renewed negative marking of the black subject that is symptomatic of the Restoration decades, as was discussed in the last chapter.

Citations of unattached black people in Kent occur in a variety of mostly less prominent locations across the county. These include from All Saints Church in Staplehurst the baptism of "George A blackman S[on] of George" on 13 February

---

but the gay Arbours of Anguish … inasmuch as … I lived in those of my Lordes great families as the River Rone runs through the lake of Geneva, without mingling any part of its streams with that Lake, for I gave myself wholly to Retyredness as much as I could …"; *The Diaries of Lady Anne Clifford*, ed. Clifford, p. 94.

77 Personal communication from Michael Carter, archivist at the Center for Kentish Studies.

78 M. G. S., "Strode of Chepsted," p. 331; Peter Le Neve and George W. Marshall, *Neve's Pedigrees of the Knights Made by King Charles II, King James II …* , p. 83.

79 H. C. Wright's survey and valuation of the property for the Marquess of Conyngham, dated 31 December 1827, East Kent Archives Center, MS EK-R-U438/E36. Conygham expressed an interest in purchasing the property from the Polhills, who had acquired it in the early eighteenth century. According to the survey's report, William Emerton of the Temple bought the old mansion at Chipstead from the widow of Sir Nicholas Strode in July 1693. For accounts of "The Manor of Chepsted" and "Chepsted-House," see Hasted, 3: 116–20.

1619, and of his daughter "Elizabeth blackamore D of George 'the Blackamore'" on 19 May 1622. Earlier in that same church "George a blackmore [and] Marie Smith" were married on 16 October 1616 (Items 308, 314, 295). A small woodland location in the large forested area straddling west Kent, Surrey, and East Sussex known as the Weald (Staplehurst's name literally deriving from the Saxon words for post and forest), Staplehurst was at this time a wealthy wool- and broadcloth-producing enclave south of Maidstone on the old Roman road leading from Beauport to Rochester, with many Flemish woolweavers traditionally settled in it and in nearby Cranbrook.[80] While the origins of the Africans named here are probably connected to this population, what the citations specifically describe is the settling and integration of one black individual named George into this community. The relative independence and wellbeing of George, in his cross-racial marriage to Marie Smith in 1616 and in the birth of their son George and daughter Elizabeth three years and six years later, are again aspects of the laxity of the English attitudes toward blacks in the Jacobean period noted in Chapter 3. Of comparable note here is the gradual clarification across the three records of the identity of George the Blackman as an African, which is another confirmation of the early modern English use of that word to denote a black person, surmised earlier in this book.

Other single citations of unattached possibly and clearly black individuals in Kent appear in Boughton-under-Blean, where "Rose Blackamoor" was buried on 26 July 1558, and in Chislehurst, where "Cristofer Adam a blackamore … a man growne" was baptized on 22 April 1595 (Items 125, 205). If the opacity of Rose Blackamoor's history is compounded by the uncertain ethnicity of her name and by the obscurity of her location in a small north Kent village "under," i.e. south of the old forest of Blean on the ancient Roman road of Watling Street, Cristofer Adam's enslaved origin is somewhat lit up by the prominence of his foregrounded blackness and perhaps indirectly by the context of his location in Chislehurst. While this was also a small rural north Kent site in a forest clearing in the county's east side, in the late Tudor years it was not only a well-off town with "handsomely built houses" inhabited by merchants but more particularly it was connected to the Elizabethan shipbuilder Peter Pett and his sons Joseph and Phineas, whose Deptford-built vessels used in English adventuring and slaving trips in the south and west Atlantic were built of the timber from this area.[81] That Cristofer was a casual by-product of these two aspects of Chislehurst's history is an unavoidable possibility. Also in the north, in Dartford in the county's west side, is the burial notation of "Iferdynando a blackmore svannte to Alexander Neuby" on 19 January 1597; in Gravesend, also in the northwest, the burial mention of "Frances the Mullato" on 19 February 1603; and in Herne, in northeast Kent, the birth citation of "Grace negres" in 1635 (Items 218, 253, 351). The proximity of Dartford and Gravesend to London, both close to the Thames or on it as it flows out eastwards, the former a "principal market town" of the county and the latter a borough on the river on the western edge of the metropolis's urban

[80] James Gibson, *Kent*, p. xvi.

[81] D. B. Quinn and Alan Ryan, *England's Sea Empire*, pp. 213–19; Jess Steele, *Turning the Tide: The History of Everyday Deptford*, p. 22. The quotation is from Alan Armstrong, ed., *The Economy of Kent 1640–1914*, p. 9.

sprawl that is a routine provisioning stop for merchant ships heading out to sea,[82] makes transparent their origins as illicit mercantile imports in the English provinces. Such an inference is reinforced by Iferdynando's visibly Iberian origins and Frances's description as the "Mullato", the latter emerging in English lexical currency only eight years prior to the date of Francis's record in connection with the description of Drake's African and South American adventures in Hakluyt.[83] The location of Grace's citation, in the small fishing village of Herne in northeast Kent, supports, for reasons comparable to those of Iferdynando and Cristofer Adams, the probability of it being another ethnic record, albeit with a greater degree of opacity and uncertainty.

In Kent's southeast side, in Dover, a different kind of record is that of an African youth named John Anthony, who in March 1620 petitioned the city Mayor for the full payment of his unpaid wages for his service on board the *Silver Falcon*, which, while initially held in abeyance, was fully granted on the 20th of that month (Item 310). The *Silver Falcon* was a Dover-based vessel that made cargo runs to the Iberian and American coasts and particularly to the Virginia plantation, connected to whose trips were powerful London merchant backers and investors such as Phineas Pett and John Zouche.[84] Just as the ship's service history puts into view John's origins as a casually seized African domesticated into shipboard service sometime in the immediate past, the ship's powerful connections help to make visible why the Mayor of Dover was not initially allowed to grant Anthony's suit. The satisfaction of the suit, which was not the only one in which the ship was named at this time,[85] makes this an unusual record, and the only one in this book in which a black man is a plaintiff in an early modern English court, and a successful one at that. It is difficult to fully gauge what enables this sign of racial equity, a sign that should recall in contrast the denial of Jacques Francis's legal humanity even as a witness nine decades earlier in Southampton. Two possible contextual clues to John Anthony's legal standing and the success of his suit might be the special jurisdiction of the Cinque Ports of which Dover was a part, and generally the inadvertent English racial relaxation of the Jacobean period that was seen earlier in the seventeenth-century London records.

Still more black citations from counties on the English southern coastline are from Essex. These are from Leyton, the baptisms of "Joseph, the sonne of Master George Swanley gentleman and Barbare his wife" on 2 October 1656, and of "Robert poppogunde blackeomore … baptized the same day" (i.e. as "Mickele sonne to Sir William Hicks" on 19 June 1667), and the burial of "Anne daughter of Robert the Black from Mile End" on 30 July 1676 (Items 380, 417, 445). Located "5 miles north-east of London," Leyton, so called because it lies on "the 'tun' on the river Lea," was a small parish that in the middle of the seventeenth century was

---

82 Christopher Chalklin, "Towns," in Armstrong, ed., *Economy of Kent*, pp. 208–9; Clark, *English Provincial Society*, p. 10.

83 *OED*, 2: 1872.

84 Francis Burton Harrison, "Footnotes on Some XVII Century Virginians," pp. 31–35; Henry Mainwaring, *The Life and Works of Sir Henry Mainwaring*, p. 32. For Zouche as a powerful investor, see Rabb, *Enterprise and Empire*, pp. 102 n. 1, 420.

85 For another case concerning the *Silver Falcon* see the National Archives, MS E 134/22Jas1/Mich38.

"increasingly a 'pretty retiring place from London' for wealthy merchants, bankers, and professional men," with extensive households living in large, freshly constructed or rebuilt houses. "Master George Swanleye" is Captain George Swanley, a Leyton sea captain variously involved in the Civil War years in maritime voyages and military missions in the Atlantic and in India. Since 1650 Swanley was one-third owner of the manor house of Leyton, sometimes known as Leyton Grange. William Hicks was a descendent of Burleigh's secretary Michael Hicks, who acquired his country house, known as Ruckholt Hall, from the son of the Michael Hicks's widow from her first marriage to Henry Parvish, i.e. from his step-brother. Ruckholt Hall was an extensive manor house, although by the end of the 1660s it was slightly run down because of William Hicks's losses in the defeat in the Civil War of the royalist forces with whom he had sided. Robert can plausibly be assumed to be Hicks's possession, acquired by him from his overseas trading investments and from the habits of his class.[86] Even though George Swanley's wife is treated in modern sources as Barbara, and consequently white,[87] the record's spelling of her name leaves open the possibility of her being an assimilated African, and hence of her citation being an unusual instance of an inter-racial union. The maritime careers of George Swanley, as well of William Hicks, who almost certainly was a overseas trade investor like others of his class in parliament,[88] make very probable their contact with Africans. The location of Anne's record in Mile End, which in adjoining areas such as Ratcliff and Limehouse, with their communities of seamen and the black people they bring back, points also to merchant mariner connections for her and her father, indicates as well another instance of the growth of black life even within its bonded condition. Beyond these incidental and tenuous contexts, these records may have little to illuminate them except perhaps the reminder that these are the vigorous opening years of official English slave-trading in Africa. Altogether, the three citations describe the fluctuating legibility of the provincial English black presence that is an ineluctable feature of its history.

One black record in Essex that is transparent, however, is that of the black person named Mingoe encountered earlier in the seventeenth-century London records, in Pepys's *Diary*. Named as "Mingoee, a negro that now dwelleth with me," this black man is cited in William Batten's will in 1667 as being left by the latter a handsomely paid guardianship of Batten's lighthouses in Harwich, Essex (Item 419).[89] Located on the Essex's eastern seaboard, Harwich was a strategically important port for

---

86 For information on Leyton, and on George Swanley and William Hicks, see "Leyton: Introduction," in *A History of the County of Essex: Volume 6* (1973), pp. 174–84, and "Leyton: Manors and Estates," ibid., pp. 184–97. Also see, for Ruckholts and William Hicks, W. G. Hammock, *Leytonstone and Its History*, pp. 5–6, and for Swanley, Samuel Rawson Gardiner, ed., *Letters and Papers Relating to the First Dutch War*, p. 153; and April Lee Hatfield, *Atlantic Virginia: Intercolonial Relations in the Seventeenth Century*, p. 255 n. 70.

87 As for instance in "Leyton: Manors and Estates," in *A History of the County of Essex: Volume 6*.

88 Rabb lists William Hicks as an overseas trading investor, but does not name the companies involved (p. 314).

89 The National Archives web page transcription of the will cites the date as 24 December 1667, whereas the National Archives catalog dates the document as 22 November 1667. The

the English from which to monitor and control merchant shipping to and from the Continent. Constructed in 1665, the lighthouses mentioned in the will consisted of two structures, one a 90-foot tall tower with "a coal fire in a chamber" in the town and the other with "a lantern in a timber hut on the foreshore," which were meant to provide a navigation beacon for incoming ships.[90] The construction, operation, and ownership of the lighthouses, together with the privilege of collecting tolls and taxes on merchant shipping to and from the harbor, are what Batten, who had been a naval commander throughout the Civil War years, procured at the end of his career.[91] His acquisition of Mingo probably occurred at some point of, and in connection with, his life at sea. The will leaves Mingoe the "somme of Twenty pounds a yeare of lawfull money of England" that he is to receive "during the Terme of his naturall life" for "his paines" in looking after the lighthouse, which Batten specifies should be in Mingoe's "custody and keeping." These "paines" include keeping the lighthouse light burning continuously, as stipulated in the king's letters patent mentioned at the bottom of the will, which gave the charge of the lighthouse to Batten originally.[92] Given the vital part played by the lighthouses in Harwich's strategic posture, and given the financial value they have for Batten's heirs, the entrusting of them to Mingoe constitutes a vital public and personal trust in him. Additionally, Mingoe is to receive "Tenne pounds" as a legacy within a year of Batten's death. Mingoe's naming at the beginning of the list of servants mentioned in the will indicates clearly his preferred position, as also does the amount to be given him, which equals that left to some other family members cited in it.

Mingoe is more visible here than he is in his London citation, due largely to Batten's generous bequest, which seems to recognize his abilities and reward them. However, to the extent that the normalization of racialized slavery is what perpetuates it, gestures of decency and seeming compassion to racialized and enslaved people are inducements to them to accept their condition as normal, and by extension what allow subsequent ages to argue that some slavery is benevolent. They do nothing to address and reverse the phenomena of racialization and enslavement themselves. It is instructive to ask what exactly Batten's bequest does to change the ruling conditions of Mingoe's life. It gives him material security but does not affect his discursive marking as a once racialized and enslaved individual. Those markings are the fixed limits within which Mingoe will have to lead his subsequent life, no matter how materially secured. Given only a catchy nickname with tropical allusions, Mingoe

---

will itself was signed 6 July 1665. Since the document is keyed to the catalog date, that is the one used here.

90 E. A. Labrum, *Civil Engineering Heritage: Eastern and Central England*, p. 148.

91 For Batten's career, see Joseph F. Callo and Alastair Wilson, *Who's Who in Naval History*, p. 16; the entry for Batten under "Biography; B" in the web article by David Plant, "British Civil Wars and Commonwealth"; and the web essay by John Rickard "Admiral Sir William Batten."

92 The original patent was given on 24 December 1664, and allowed him to construct the lighthouses and for him and his heirs to "secure," i.e. keep, the revenues from them, i.e. tolls and taxes on shipping, for 61 years (National Archives MS C 66/3062/part 12, 15 Charles II). See *Diary of Samuel Pepys*, ed. Latham and Matthews, 6: 3 n. 4. These therefore constitute Batten's profitable assets, which he assigns in his will to his wife.

remains an exotic pet, albeit one with useful skills. To the extent that Batten's will makes Mingoe visible as a freed black slave, it distorts and obscures the essential humanity of his blackness forever. Contrariwise, what Batten's bequest does do is to advertise *his* human largesse and nobility, and by doing so elides his complicity in the inhumanity of the slaving practice itself. In these ways, instances of the seeming benignity of early modern English enslavement are also in fact subtle consolidations of the practice as an acceptable social institution. Such a reading is consistent with the date of the record, which is in that moment when English slavery as a declared national policy was accelerating to a mass industry, and therefore in need of construction as a civil aspect of English domestic life.

These numerous black citations in points along England's southern coastline, stretching from Gloucestershire in the west to Kent and Essex in the east, can only be a natural consequence of the English mercantile involvements in Africa over the sixteenth and seventeenth centuries, whether such black people were initially brought in illicitly or later transported openly, with the initiation of the English slave trade. That conclusion follows credibly, both from the proximity of the locale of these citations to some of the major or active English trading ports of the time, such as Bristol, Plymouth, Exeter, Dover, and Gravesend, and from some of the names mentioned in the citations, such as William Hawkins (the early Tudor sea captain), John Young (a pioneering Bristol slave merchant and investor in the sugar business), Richard Dodderidge (a prominent Devonshire merchant financer), James Bagge, the Dorset family, William Batten, William Hicks, and so on. These black records extend and clarify further the black presence revealed in the London documents examined over the course of this book.

IV

What might be less expected, though, are the black citations farther inland in places as central as Northamptonshire and as far north as Lancashire. In their geographic spread, these English midlands and northern black citations, while fewer in number, also invite consideration.

Such citations include in Northamptonshire, in Paulespury, the personal diary entry of Arthur Throckmorton sometime between 1587 and 1591, mentioning his acquisition of "Anthony, a blackamoor from Guinea" (Item 164).[93] Paulespury

---

93 I am indebted to Nikki Taylor of the Northamptonshire Local History Research Council for this record. Because A. L. Rowse does not mention dates systematically for the diary entries that he discusses, the actual date for the entry could be sometime in the summer of 1590 for two reasons. First, he begins the section following the one where he cites the entry about Anthony with the specification that the year was 1590 (*Ralegh and the Throckmortons*, p. 122). Secondly, right after the point where he mentions Anthony, he discusses Arthur Throckmorton's correspondence with the English envoy to James VI's court, William Ashby, in which he mentions Ashby's reports to Throckmorton about James's enamorment with his newly married bride Anne of Denmark (p. 122). Since that marriage occurred in November 1589, the year of Throckmorton's entry could be 1590. Exactly where Throckmorton takes this African into his service is unclear, because even though the family seat was in Paulespury, Northamptonshire,

(sometimes also spelled Paulerspury) was an estate acquired by the formidable Elizabethan figure and rival of William Cecil, Nicholas Throckmorton,[94] which his son Arthur inherited on his father's death in 1571, and on which he constructed his family's manorial residence between 1595 and 1600. This elaborate country house, which contained French wainscot paneling, marble and alabaster chimneypieces, and was outfitted with "barns, stables, coach-houses, outhouses" and sprawling gardens and lush orchards, was Arthur Throckmorton's official residence from sometime after 1593 until his death in 1626.[95] Arthur's acquisition of Anthony was very probably as a gift from Walter Raleigh, his brother-in-law, who aside from his other projects mentioned in the earlier chapters was involved in privateering ventures in 1581 and was an investor in the Guinea company at least by 1594 and possibly earlier.[96] The likelihood of Raleigh's gift to Arthur of a seized African from one of his ventures is made stronger if it is seen as a kind of house-warming present to the latter befitting the ostentatious country mansion that he will soon construct and in which he will set up aristocratic residence. In short, and irrespective of whether the locale of Anthony's keeping is Paulespury, Northamptonshire in the later 1590s or Colchester, Essex earlier (where Arthur Throckmorton's residence in his in-laws' home in St. John's was, according to Rowse, also spacious[97]), he was largely situated within the context of English aristocratic decorative possession of Africans seen so numerously in this book. It was probably the pride of such a possession that impelled the mention of Anthony in Arthur's diary.

Also in Northamptonshire, in Gretton sometime between 1663 and 1730, there was an African connected to the aristocratic family of the Hattons who is mentioned in the will of Christopher Hatton as "my servant James Chapell" on 7 May 1695 (Item 402.2). Despite the will being of a date later than that of the records covered in this book, its substance pertains to an earlier time. The African James Chappell was a black man in Hatton's service who saved the latter's life when one night in 1672, while

---

he did not settle down there till later in the decade. According to Rowse, in the years following his marriage to Ana Lucas he was living with his in-laws in Colchester, Essex (p. 108), where he was elected a burgess at the same time as he mentions Anthony, Rowse mentioning both events in the same paragraph. According to Nikki Taylor, "Arthur Thockmorton inherited land at Paulespury on which he started to build his house in 1593. By 1598 he had settled down there. His sister Elisabeth married Sir Walter Ralegh in 1592." This information is corroborated in the history of "Paulerspury," described in *A History of the County of Northamptonshire: Volume 5*, pp. 245–89, which also indicates that the diary itself is in the Canterbury Cathedral Archives (n. 12). Thus, even though there is also some question about whether Anthony was acquired in Paulespury, Northamptonshire or in Colchester, Essex, it is the latter that will be assumed as the locale for this discussion on the logic that it was the Throckmorton's manorial family seat for which Anthony's service must have been originally intended and where it must have properly been performed rather than in Colchester, where Arthur is living with his in-laws. Alternatively, Anthony may have been acquired after 1591, in the closing years of the decade, when Arthur Throckmorton was in residence at Paulespury.

94 Rowse, *Raleigh and the Throckmortons*, p. vi.

95 *A History of the County of Northamptonshire: Volume 5*, pp. 245–89.

96 Rabb, *Enterprise and Empire*, p. 233.

97 *Raleigh and the Throckmortons*, p. 108.

resident at Castle Cornet, Guernsey in the Cannel Islands, as governor of Guernsey, the castle blew up as a result of a lightning strike on the castle's powder magazine. Hatton's bequest is partly a reflection of his gratitude to Chappell for this act and generally an appreciation of his service. Chappell was with Hatton purportedly from the age of 15, in Gretton, London, and Guernsey, and over the course of his service to Hatton till the latter's death was baptized, married, and settled in Gretton, near the four-generation-long Hatton country seat of Kirby Hall where he had served.

This record, and its black history, present considerable difficulties for elucidation, beyond that of its date just explained above. For one thing, records of Chappell's baptism, marriage, and the birth of his daughter are scattered uncertainly between St. Martin in the Fields, Westminster (London) and Gretton, Northamptonshire (Item 402.1, 435, 446).[98] For another thing, the details of Chappell's black identity, and his saving of Christopher Hatton, are located in apocryphal local sources. Among the

---

[98] This record was supplied by Nikki Taylor at the Northamptonshire Local History Research Council, who adds: "The Hattons lived at Holdenby originally. Sir Christopher Hatton (d.1591) was a favourite of Elizabeth I and her Lord Chancellor. He built a palace at Holdenby but nearly bankrupted his family. His cousin, another Christopher, who succeeded in 1597, sold it to the King and settled at Kirby Hall, a mansion Sir Christopher had bought from the Staffords of Blatherwycke. Hatton entertained James I several times at Kirby and was also knighted. He died in 1619 and was succeeded by his son Christopher, who became the third Sir Christopher, and also played host to the King at Kirby. He was Controller of the King's Household and was made Lord Hatton in 1643. Hatton was an antiquarian and friend of Sir William Dugdale. He exiled himself to France during the first years of the Commonwealth leaving Lady Hatton to run the estates. Between 1662 and 1665 he was Governor of Guernsey. His son Christopher succeeded as 2nd Lord Hatton in 1670. He took over his father's Governorship and was in Guernsey between 1670 and 1680. James Chappell was a negro servant of Christopher, second Lord Hatton, when Lord Hatton was Governor of Guernsey based at Castle Cornet. James Chappell was taken in to service with the Hattons in 1663 when he was 15 years old. One night in 1672 there was a massive explosion when lightning set fire to the magazine at the Castle. [Although] His wife and mother were both killed, Lord Hatton and several members of his family were rescued by James Chappell who was rewarded with a pension of £20 per year [Lord Hatton's will of 1695]. Gretton is in Northamptonshire. Kirby Hall near Gretton was one of the main family homes of the Hattons. It was here that Sir Christopher came back to after the explosion at Castle Cornet. Castle Cornet is in Guernsey which is in the Channel Isles. [There is] a record … in the parish register of St Martin, Westminster [St. Martin in the Fields, Westminster/Middlesex, in London] of the marriage of "[a] Jacobi Chappell" to Elizabeth in 1672. [Although this record is present *not* in the Registers of St. Martin in the Fields but in the International Genealogical Index, this is very probably the same individual—which means he first came to live with the Hattons in London, and then was taken by Christopher Hatton to Castle Cornet, and eventually—that is, after a brief stay in London also in 1672, when he must have returned there with Hatton when the latter came back to his city residence after the explosion in Castle Cornet, which is also when and where he must have married—to Kirby Hall near Gretton, still later (i.e. settling himself in familias in Gretton)]. James Chappell … later came to live at Gretton [in Northamptonshire]. Local legend has it that he became the landlord of The Hatton Arms, however there is no documentation to prove this. However parish records show that after the death of Elizabeth Chappell (daughter, baptised 1676 [Gretton Parish registers at Northamptonshire Record Office show 'Elizabeth the daughter of James Chapell baptised Sept 10 1676,' buried 1679], and Elizabeth wife, buried 1704). James married Mercy

documentation of such apocrypha by Gretton local historians, one is a ballad written by George William Finch Hatton, Lord Winchelsea, whose family inherited Kirby Hall after the Hatton line became extinct and therefore inherited its legends as well, which not only describe Chappel's rescue of Christopher Hatton in the explosion at Castle Cornet, Guernsey in 1672, but also identify the former as "James Chappell, the Negro." Another partly apocryphal narrative is the autobiographical account of James Chappell's life as recorded by Joshua Lankert in 1727 when Chappell was 82 years old, the text of which has been preserved from a surviving copy of the lost original by Daniell Heneage Finch Hatton, the Rector of Great and Little Weldon, in 1872. This account includes Chappell's own words, and his statement that he began his life with Christopher Hatton in 1663 at the age of 15.[99]

The very difficulties of this record constitute, however, its usefulness and importance. That James Chappell's black historical existence, as well his heroic service, are apocryphal, is a pointed example of the ethereality of early modern English black people, whose unimportance to, and denial by, traditional history confines them to the desiderata of legend where they flutter uncertainly between cold fact and exotic fiction. Rendered unverifiable by an English documentary culture that disdains to consider them deserving of inscription, they cease to exist in the historical record. If they do appear, they do so shorn of their blackness, as James Chappell does in Hatton's will, as an individual the vacuity of whose identity supports the default assumption that he is a white servant. As his ethnicity is masked, and his heroism obscured, so the origins of his enslavement are removed from direct sight, leaving behind only speculative probabilities about Christopher Hatton's investments in overseas trading as the overriding compulsion of his time and his possession of a black menial as the inevitable fashion of his class.[100] If James by his own testimony began his enslaved life with Hatton in 1663, that is in the same decade that Mingo was in William Batten's keeping, the perfect congruence of Batten's and Hatton's class identities unavoidably indicates a like congruence of black identity between their two servants. Furthermore, the textual similarities between Hatton's will and those of Batten's discussed above include the correspondence between them of the manner of their respective citations of Mingo and James, the latter mentioned in the same position in the list of household beneficiaries as the former. This correspondence by analogy reinforces the probability of James being black. As such inferences provide the only access to James Chappell's life, they describe the occlusion that is the reality of the provincial English black subject's historical existence.

Less can perhaps be said about the other Northamptonshire record, the burial citation of "A Guinean boy" who was William Craven's servant, "baptized ye summer

---

Peach in 1705. They went on to have a daughter Amey. Thomas Peach (father or brother) was the licensee at the Hatton Arms in this period."

[99] See the articles by Andrew Butterworth, "'Kit' Hatton and the Weird Old Woman..." and "How Sir Kit Was Rescued from the Rubble." Both these written sources were supplied by Nikki Taylor, Northamptonshire Local History Research Council, in a personal communication to the author.

[100] That there were Hattons who were overseas investors is indicated by the appearance of several Christopher Hattons on Rabb's list (*Enterprise and Empire*, p. 310).

before and named Winiwick," on 17 December 1674 in Winiwick, Northampton (Item 439). William Craven is Sir William Craven, nephew of the Earl of Craven, both Royalist supporters of Charles I and his son, the latter of whom they join in exile. Shortly after the restoration of Charles II to the throne, on William Craven's marriage, the Earl of Craven gave William Craven the manor of Winwick (i.e. Winiwick), where William subsequently resided with his wife. The manor was a large dwelling with "a highly decorated archway." Not only did William Craven himself serve in the navy in the Dutch wars, the Earl of Craven, who died in 1697, is mentioned in Charles II's second Carolina charter of 30 June 1677.[101] The record's date, like those of the black people with Batten, Hicks, and Hatton, falls within those same post-Restoration decades when official English mass trafficking in Africans is in full sway. Most important of all, Lord Craven was a principal investor in the company of the Royal Adventurers into Africa in 1660.[102] This history, particularly the last-named aspect of it, while not revealing the details of Winiwick's possession by William Craven, certainly establishes its context. The one feature that does stand out in this record is the name given to the African, which is a unique instance of an English place name used to designate a seized black subject. In a way, Winiwick's naming is a symbolic advertisement of the collective possession of the African by this Northampton community as a whole, and, by implication, by the country itself. If his baptism the previous year marked, as such events in the experience of many of this book's records have marked, the approximate time of his arrival, his death underlines the starkness of his English captivity, which killed him in the space of a year, whether from a natural devastation or other causes.

The remaining provincial black citations are mostly sparer entries, sometimes even of uncertain documentary integrity. These can therefore be considered cursorily in regional groups. In Bedfordshire's Cardington parish the christening of what is probably a black person, "Philip Blackamore," is recorded on 18 January 1599; and the baptism of "Robart the blake more servant of Sr George Blundell" is noted in 14 July 1661, while in Shelton a "Grace Negar Or negus" may have been born on 5 January 1603 (Items 230, 395, 252). While Philip Blackamore and Grace Negar's citations do not allow much insight into their black histories, beyond what is suggested by their names, and despite the unverifiability of the latter's record, Robert's record does, in that George Blundell was a prominent royalist aristocrat with seaborne military service in the Cadiz campaign of 1625, in which he was Knight Quartermaster General,[103] and with family connections to the Africa Company in which Francis Blundell his brother and heir was an investor.[104] Unmistakably an acquisition of that latter involvement, Robart was, like Mingo, James Chappell, and Winiwick, almost certainly a decorative menial at Cardington Manor house,

---

[101] W. J. Stavert, "Note on the Cravens of Appletreewick," pp. 451, 452, 461, 462 (quotation); "The second charter Granted by King Charles II: to the proprietors of Carolina," in John Lawson, *A New Voyage to Carolina*, pp. 209–12.

[102] Hugh Thomas, *The Slave Trade*, p. 198.

[103] John Glanville, *A Voyage to Cadiz*, p. 37.

[104] Catherine Wilhelmina Powlett Cleveland, *The Battle Abbey Roll*, p. 111; Rabb, p. 248.

which came to George Blundell from his wife's inheritance, and which remained the Blundell's family country seat over the next hundred years.[105] Assorted and more impenetrable reports of black people occur in Buckinghamshire's Hedgerley parish, where a "Mary Negro" may have been christened on 15 December 1607, and in Hertfordshire's Hemel Hempstead, where a "Susan ethuop" may have been married on 16 June 1600 (Items 270, 240).

Up north in Cheshire's Chester, a postmortem was conducted on "Blackamore, George" on an unspecified day in 1617 (Item 298). Notwithstanding the uncertain black identity of the name, with its use of an unmarked ethnic descriptor in the surname position, the fact that this is a Court of Wards and Liveries document may mean that the postmortem was a legal investigation into the death of a black servant possibly of Chester's gentry or aristocracy. On the immediate north of Cheshire, in Lancashire, in Lathom Hall, black slaves are mentioned in the household books of the estate of Edward Stanley, the third Earl of Derby, on 12 February 1568. An aristocratic household instruction sheet like that which mentions Grace Robinson in the Earl of Dorset's house in Knole, Kent discussed earlier, and probably pertaining to the Derby estate in Lathom, the document details Stanley's instructions to his staff about their daily stations and seating protocol: "No Slaves nor boyes shall sitt in the Hall but in place therefore to be appoynted convenient" and that "The Yeman of Horses and Gromes of the Stable shall not suffre anie boyes or Slaves to abyde about the Stables nor lie in theym nor in any place aboute theym" (Item 132). Contrary to Peter Fryer's hesitation in regarding this record as necessarily referring to black people, based on the instinctively defensive and unsupported assertion of the document source's Victorian editor F. R. Raines to the effect that that these "slaves" were simply "the villeins regardant of the manor" whose "manumission … was effected soon after the Reformation," the likelihood of "slaves" in fact referring to black people, which scholars such as C. S. L. Davies have felt,[106] is supported by the details of the citation itself.

In the document's invocation of the elaborate hierarchy and specifically appointed places of the "Yeman of horses and Grooms of the stable," the only personnel that are likely to be unspecifically appointed and placeless on ordinary days would be black pages employed flexibly as household ornamentation on special occasions. Hence, the document's repeated linkage of "slaves" and "boyes," which cannot be relevant to "villeins" as such, even if one discounts the fact that the practice of villeinage was largely extinct by the middle of the sixteenth century, as was explained earlier. Given Edward Stanley's penchant for a "great retinue" and "splendor of living,"[107] it is highly plausible that he had seized Africans as pages, and that these are in fact the "slaves" mentioned in the household book. If the foregoing assumption is correct, it is a pungent revelation of the true human valuelessness of Stanley's enslaved Africans

---

[105] "Parishes: Cardington with Eastcotts," *A History of the County of Bedford*, pp. 233–38.

[106] Peter Fryer, *Staying Power*, p. 9 n. 19; William ffarington, *The Derby Household Books*, ed. F. R. Raines, pp. 94–95; C. S. L. Davies, "Slavery and Protector Somerset: The Vagrancy Act of 1547," p. 548 n. 3.

[107] "Townships: Knowsley," in *A History of the County of Lancashire: Volume 3*, pp. 157–68.

who when not deployed in their decorative capacities can "abyde" not even where his horses do but in "appointed places" that like them remain nameless, which is to say out of both documentary and human sight. If the black people in Stanley's possession exist as nameless hints, elsewhere in Lancashire their historical existence becomes a little stronger four decades later, as is the case in St. Mary, Lancaster where "Richard nigroe" was christened on 12 November 1602 (Item 251). A bit more ethnically visible in the details of his name than is George Blackamore, Richard's history is nonetheless more opaque than his, his parish register baptism entry allowing only the indication of a black presence developing in Cheshire and Lancashire by the turn of the century and that may be a continuation of the phenomenon represented by the Earl of Derby's unnamed "slaves."

Even further north, but in the east, in Durham's Sedgefield parish, an "Ana Negros" may have been christened on 12 February 1649, and a "Mariana Negro" on June 27 of the following year (Items 376, 377). These mentions, like those of Richard Nigroe, as well as of Matthias the Morian, Grace Negar/Negus, Mary Negro, and "Susan Ethuop" in Wiltshire, Bedfordshire, Buckinghamshire, and Hertfordshire, respectively, reflect in the opacity of their content and specific context, and in the possible weakness of their documentary integrity, merely the relative obscurity of the provincial English black records compared to the London archives. That obscurity is probably a sign of the greater tracklessness of the desolation of the black subject in the countryside, where paradoxically the metropolis's intricate structures of documentary surveillance are weak if not altogether inoperative and cannot therefore even imperfectly illuminate it. They can only be the irrecoverable fossilized traces of the same black history spelled out by the other more accessible records.

Finally, this same group of northern provincial black records logically includes those in Scotland. These records should be reminders, of course, of the history of the black presence in Scotland examined in Chapter 1. As those earlier records connected to and helped provide a backdrop for the early Tudor black citations, so these contextualize and confirm the features of the provincial black presence in the Elizabethan and Stuart regimes. As those Scottish records were in part connected to the English ones through the marital alliance of the Henry VII with James IV, so these records are joined to English national history through the union of England and Scotland in the Scottish James VI's accession to the English throne as James I in 1603. As such, the features they show correspond multifariously to those of the English records. Such Scottish records comprise the description in Edinburgh, on 17 May 1589, of "a colorfully dressed blackamore holding a sword" who appeared in the welcoming party for James VI's Danish bride, Anne of Denmark (Item 174.2). At the wedding itself in Oslo the previous November, two naked African youths were part of James's wedding festivities, even though they died in the extreme cold (Item 174.1). In 1591, the burial of an African in Falkland is recorded in the burial expenses disbursed by the Scottish royal exchequer for that purpose (Item 181), who may not be one of the individuals who died in Oslo earlier, but who may serve to further exemplify the frequent price of black decorative service common to both Scotland and England.

Equally logical to consider with the provincial English black records at this point are those in an international setting. Such records include the case of Diego, an enslaved black man, who, defecting from his Spanish captors, joined Francis Drake during the latter's raid on Nombre de Dios in 1573, and who was used by Drake as one of his most trusted and able personal pilots and guide to Spanish treasure on the high seas (Item 135). Whereas the two sources of Diego's record both describe his service with Drake, they do so differently. Although the English account, compiled from the testimony of Drake's crewmen by a "preacher," who was possibly the fleet chaplain and overseen by Drake himself, tries to defensively underline Diego's voluntary joining with the English ("willingly came unto us") (Item 135.1), the Spanish record, which is a deposition in a Spanish Inquisition court, plainly details Diego's seizure by Drake from an enemy ship earlier ("whom he had taken prisoner from a frigate") (Item 135.2).[108] Even if Diego's history is lost between the admittedly interested agendas of these two sources, it is plausible to assume that his service with Drake was under the pressure of competing and unresolveable choices of two equally predatory European colonial powers. A grimmer account is that of the black woman named Maria who was captured by Drake from a Spanish ship in 1578/79 and made by him into an onboard sexual chattel for himself and his crew, and who was eventually abandoned in a pregnant condition on an uninhabited island in the Indian ocean (Item 147. 1 and 2). The original account, appearing within the voyage's journal kept by the fleet's shipboard chaplain, Francis Fletcher, preserves the details of Maria's sexual abuse by Drake and his crew (Item 147.1), silently edited out in the transcription of the record produced at the end of the nineteenth century, which however adds that the black women was left with two other African males and some "rice, seeds and means of making a fire" (Item 147.2).[109] These inversely related elisions have prompted the recent call of the black feminist historian Margo Hendricks for critical scholarship to step back "into the archives."[110] The contrasting narratives of the two records neatly serve to illustrate the fundamentally exploitative instincts of the early modern English toward black people, in which the fates of Diego and Maria are direct functions of the kinds of use that Drake perceives in each of them. That Maria was useful only as an onboard sexual chattel, to be consumed and discarded when physically spent, demonstrates the extreme vulnerability of the early modern English black woman seen periodically in the London records earlier.

Two further instances involving seized Africans abroad include, first, the record of "Cooree," the African kidnapped by an East India Company ship crew off the Cape of Good Hope sometime before 1614 (Item 238).[111] He was brought back to the house of Thomas Smith, the company governor in London, whereupon because

---

[108] For the identification of the English account's author, see the title page of *Sir Francis Drake Revived,* which states: "Faithfully taken out of the report of Master | Christopher Ceely, Ellis Hixom and others, who| were in the same voyage with him | By Philip Nichols Preacher | Reviewed by Sir Francis Drake himself | Set forth by Sir Francis Drake Baronet (his nephew)."

[109] The author of the original account is identified as "Francis Fletcher: Chaplain of the Expedition," on the title page of its published version, *The World Encompassed.*

[110] "Feminist Historiography," p. 367.

[111] Given the fact that the record's chief source, Edward Terry's account, was published in 1655, which is long after the events in question, and given that independent documentary corroboration of the exact dates of Cooree's arrival and stay in London have proved difficult

of his continued resistance to captivity he was taken back to Africa at that date in the hope that he would aid the company to trade with his tribe, a hope disappointed in his immediate cooperation with his people in their hostility to the English. Best considered as an international record, since it encompasses London and Africa, its main account was written by Edward Terry, a shipboard chaplain like Philip Nichols and Francis Fletcher, and one of the East India company's most enthusiastic evangelicals, who unlike other shipboard chaplains earlier, provideed the company with the ideological justifications of its predatory cross-oceanic trading activities. The kidnapping occurred on the return voyage from India of the *Hector* when it stopped, like other ships of the company, at this victualling point on the southern tip of the African continent, and it was the sudden idea of the ship captain Gabriel Towerson, who thought of it as a way of showing his enterprising spirit to the company directors in London. Despite the occasional accents of sympathy in Terry's narrative, implicit in it and in the company reports of those who took Cooree back is the assumption of ingrained barbarity of black people like Cooree, who are "ungrateful dogs … not better to be expected," that prevents them from availing of their civilized English possession, which is, "compared with his former condition, an Heaven," even when they receive that "Heaven" unasked.

Cooree's narrative recalls and differs from that of Diego, because like Diego he was a prospective black facilitator of the English but unlike him he was an unwilling and ultimately failed one. If Diego was the good, as in compliant, black subject, Cooree was the evil, as in uncompliant, one. If the former's goodness has to be seen in the careful notation of his voluntary submission to the English, the latter's devilry has to be projected in his refusal to be owned by them. He is like Dederj Joqouah in the Elizabethan records, who resisted the English inducements of guided cooperation and returned to his people. Even though Cooree does not in the end survive the brute force of the predatory European trading project, being hanged by the Dutch sometime after his return home,[112] it is the strength of his resistance that distinguishes his history. Cooree's record is singular in that it is one of the few records in this chapter and book in which the indentation of a black voice may have survived its inscription. His plaintive cries for freedom while a captive in Thomas Smith's house, however corrupted by the very act of their recordation, speak virtually for all the black lives appearing in the citations of this book. His, and Dinah Black's intuitively perceivable responses cited above, together complete a sequential vocalization of struggle against captivity followed by despair, and could be said to sum up the foundational experience of the English black subject. At the same time, the Jacobean date of his narrative exemplifies again the innocuous change in English attitudes to the black subject at the beginning of the seventeenth century observed before, what in the words of one commentator of this record is the "fondness for such curiosities" of "English people in the time of 'our James.'"[113]

to obtain, the date for his record has been expediently described simply as sometime in the early 1600s but no later than 1614.

112 Ian Duncan Colvin, *South Africa*, p. 78.

113 Ibid., p. 77.

The other record is the allusion sometime before 1670 to "a poor Ignorant Lad just come from Guinea" in the possession of George Villiers, the second Duke of Buckingham, who is so intelligent that the duke mentions him proudly in a conversation with a Jesuit priest who recorded it (Item 428). The duke, who gave the boy the name Tom, took him with him to Paris when he was appointed by Charles II as ambassador in 1670. There, he was so struck by the boy's response to a Catholic Mass at Notre Dame cathedral that the latter saw, that he cited it subsequently in his argument with Father Fitzgerald about the unsensibility of the Catholic doctrine of eucharistic transubstantiation, when much later Fitzgerald came to him at the behest of James II to convert him in his retired years to the Catholic faith.[114] Tom's refusal of the miraculous logic of God being an entity that can make "people [fall] upon their knees and beat their brests" and also something that they can "put into their mouths and [swallow]" is one of the main counters in Villiers's demonstration to Fitzgerald of the transubstantiation doctrine's inefficacy and by implication the Catholic faith itself. To Villiers, the obviousness of this inefficacy is manifest in the fact that it is a "reflection" that even "a poor ignorant lad just come from Guinea" can make "by himself." Villiers's deployment of Tom's "reflection" as a counter in an intellectual debate clearly betrays the pride of his possession of an African. If Villiers, who was a lifelong friend of Charles II and who shortly after the Restoration was "one of the richest men in England," had this conversation shortly before his death in 1687,[115] and if Tom was with him nearly two decades earlier, that would put his acquisition of Tom squarely within the peak English slave-trafficking years. This was an acquisition that is made transparent in the fact of his being after Charles II himself the most important investor in the company of the Royal Adventurers into Africa in 1660 and in its successors afterwards.[116]

Beyond the fact of Tom's obvious mental versatility in engaging with the intellectual preoccupations of his English captors and furthering them, all the more remarkable for someone "just come," and which Villiers is quick to deploy strategically, two aspects of this record are clearly valuable. The first is the way the record offers another instance of the possible psychic space of the voice of an early modern English black subject of the sort seen several times in this chapter. The way that Tom's words, as narrated by Villiers and reproduced by Fitzgerald, echo the urbanity and sophisticated wit for which Villiers himself was known, may make self-evident its twice overwritten and hence unreliable nature, but what obtrudes through that distortion is the impress of the auditory event itself that is being overwritten. What enables Villiers random deployment of Tom's made-over words in his argument with Fitzgerald is some verbal response from Tom, however originally inarticulate and undecipherable, about matters relevant to their debate, which mandates its credible effect. What remain in the manipulated version of his words are the intuitive possibilities of the substance, intention, and context of what Tom could have said. Tom's "words" are the end products of the now irrecoverable speech acts of the

114 A. T. Thomson and Philip Wharton, *The Wits and Beaux of Society*, p. 45.

115 Juliet Gardiner and Neil Weinborn, *The Columbia Companion to British History*, p. 782, quotation included.

116 Hugh Thomas, *The Slave Trade*, pp. 198–99.

black subject in a history in which such acts can neither be performed nor processed. In the surviving visibility of the phenomenology of those acts, Tom's "words" allow him to historically "speak."

Second, what Tom may be saying may have more to do with the duke himself than with the rituals of Catholicism that the latter is interested in dismembering, and in ways that the latter may not understand. In the dangerously allusive affinity that Tom's "words" have, in the implicit homology they suggest between the figure in "party coloured" "fine cloaths" that both invokes God and offers him up to the congregation to eat and the "Devil" and "his cubs" that "pinches" and is "plaguy mischievous," to what is to his lightly clothed people the waves of strangely decked predatory English merchant mariners that are enslaving his people, Tom could be slyly articulating the historical plight of his land. The latter is almost directly visible in his cleverly worded wish to have "a hundred or two of these fine men in our Country to eat the devil for us." At the same time, since he can "just make a shift to be understood in English," the real rhetorical direction of his locution remains obscured, and his "words" stay helpfully open to the reconstruction that "a poor ignorant lad just arrived from Guinea" will need. Occasioned by the irrationality of Christian worship, Tom's "words," like those of Dinah Black, may be inscrutably addressing the inexplicability of the black subject's human condition. While such a deconstruction of Tom's reported speech cannot recover his authentic voice, it can encourage an intuitive consideration of the devastating historical experience from which such a voice can arise.

V

The geographic, temporal, and thematic heterogeneity of the provincial English black records especially necessitate a statistical breakdown of the patterns and trends within it. As in the case of the previous chapters, a reminder is necessary that such statistical analyses as follow are most useful if regarded as approximate and expository and not absolute derivations, mandated by the axiomatically provisional nature of the data. There are a total of 85 records of black people in the 119 years between 1558 and 1677 across the Elizabethan, Jacobean, Caroline, and Restoration regimes. Of these, 41 are from the Elizabethan period, 33 from the Jacobean and Caroline regimes, including the Civil War years, and 11 from the Restoration decades up to 1677. The records are spread over 12 counties, and occur also in Scotland, Paris, South Africa, and the high seas. Among these are 60 parish records, five wills, including one deed, three aristocratic household accounts, three marine chaplain accounts, two aristocratic diary entries, two court records, two city records, two pastor's observations, one royal wedding account, one royal disbursement, one parliamentary order, one postmortem, one memoir, and one school board accounts record.

The roughly equal distribution of 41 and 44 citations over the sixteenth and the seventeenth centuries points to the regularity of the black provincial presence over the temporal range of this chapter's records. 85 citations in 119 years suggests a frequency ratio of one citation in 1.4 years. The frequency ratios of each sub-period, however, reveal a different phenomenon. With one record in just over a year for the

Elizabethan decades, one record in 1.72 years for the Jacobean, Caroline, and Civil War years, and one record in 1.5 years in the Restoration era and after,[117] the greatest volume of the importation of black people clearly appears to be in the Elizabethan period, with a drop in the century's first half followed by the beginning of a climb from the Restoration onwards (see Table 4.1). The significance of the high density of the Elizabethan black notations is reflected in the perceptible impact their frequency ratio of one citation in just over a year has on the quotient of one mention in 1.4 years for the black provincial English records overall.

Table 4.1 Frequency of black provincial English citations (1558–1677)

Number of citations	**Period**	**Frequency of occurrence**
85	119 years (total)	1 in 1.4 years
41	45 years (Elizabethan)	1 in 1.09 years
33	57 years (Jacobean, Caroline, and Civil War)	1 in 1.72 years
11	17 years (Restoration and after)	1 in 1.5 years

The locational patterns of the notations of black people in the English countryside, and of the situations of black people in them, have mutually complementary ratios. The geographic spread of the black citations outside London extends over the 12 counties of Gloucestershire, Devonshire, Wiltshire, Kent, Essex, Northamptonshire, Bedfordshire, Hertfordshire, Buckinghamshire, Cheshire, Lancashire, and Durham. The majority of the locations are in the southern seacoast counties, with the heaviest concentrations occurring, as has already been suggested, in the southwestern counties, with 34 citations from Devon, 13 from Gloucester, and two from Wiltshire, followed by 12 from Kent and four from Essex in the southeast. In the Midlands there are four mentions in Northamptonshire, three in Bedfordshire, and one each from Buckinghamshire and Hertfordshire. Cheshire and Lancashire in the northwest each have two records and Durham in the northeast has one. The two provincial cities with the highest citations are Plymouth, Devonshire with 18, and Bristol, Gloucestershire with nine. Of the 85 English provincial records, including those in an international context, 45 are of encumbered black people, which is 52.94 percent of the total for this dataset. The majority of the encumbered notations are from households of the aristocracy and nobility, with black possessors including, in addition to the Scottish king, 2 dukes, 7 earls (either in direct

[117] This ratio is derived by projecting the total number of records of each period against the total years for each regime rather than against the years between the dates of the first and last records in it, in order to see each subset of records within the totality of its particular political and historical epochs rather than in a part of them. If the total number of records of each period is juxtaposed only against the range of the specific years of their occurrence, the ratios for each sub-period will be different, Notably, the Elizabethan ratio will be much higher and will then be 2.05.

involvement or indirect association), and 13 knights (also either in direct involvement or indirect association), who together figure in 51 percent of the total numbers of black encumbered citations and in 27 percent of the total number of the provincial records. The remaining black owners include 19 merchants, who are named in 42 percent of the encumbered black citations, and in 22 percent of the total number of black records outside London. 40 citations of black people representing 47.05 percent of the provincial dataset do not specify their encumbrances. All but one of these (the exception being the record of Katherine working at the Horsehead Tavern in Bristol), are, however, best regarded as encumbered citations as well even if their encumbrances are not visible, simply because of the extreme historical unlikelihood of "free" black people existing in the English countryside in such numbers in these centuries. The nonvisibility of their attachments is unavoidably a revelation of their abandoned or destitute status.

Overall, the majority of the notations of encumbered black people with aristocrats and with merchants are in the seacoast counties, the only exceptions being those of James Chappell with Christopher Hatton in Gretton, Northamptonshire, and of Robart with George Blundell in Cardington, Bedfordshire. This pattern describes two kinds of phenomena. The first is mostly the illicit importation of black people by provincial seacoast county magnates and their chattel use of them in their estates and manors in those locations. The second is more or less the acquisition of black people by that class in London and their removal of them to their country estates in counties around the metropolis. The latter accounts for the black records of the inland counties of Northamptonshire, Bedfordshire, Buckinghamshire, and Hertfordshire, the exception here being Kent, which despite being a seacoast county is part of this phenomenon. In sum, the predominant phenomenon of the possession of seized Africans as decorative self-advertisements by the provincial English aristocracy and its client class of merchants, from as early as Elizabeth's reign, indicates that contrary to the argument of Kari McBride, empire comes to the English countryside not late but early.[118]

The gender breakdown of the data, double counting for purposes of inclusiveness gender-unspecific citations as both male and female, and including in birth notations both the mothers and their offspring, comes to 49 males and 47 females. Of these, 24 black males and 22 black females are recorded in the Elizabethan period, 13 males and 11 females in the Jacobean, four males and 11 females up to the Restoration, and eight males and three females in the post-Restoration years. The greatest gender proportion in the Elizabethan data is indicative of the intensity of black importation in the period, a fact also signaled by the significantly greater combined volume of that data subset compared with those of the other three (see Table 4.2).

Table 4.2 Gender ratios of black provincial English citations (includes double counts)

	Elizabethan	**Jacobean**	**Caroline and Civil War**	**Restoration and after**
Males	24	13	4	8
Females	22	11	11	3

118 *Country House Discourse*, pp. 130–36; see particularly p. 130 and p. 136.

The increasing number of black females in the second and third data subsets, a variation of the pattern in the corresponding data of the seventeenth-century London records, is offset by the gradual increase in the gender disproportion of these data units. That is probably also suggestive of the slackening of black importation in the first half of the seventeenth century in the English provinces, which is compatible with a like tendency in the London records of that half century. The sharp drop in the number of female citations, and the concomitant increase in male notations in the provincial black records in the Restoration and post-Restoration years, is, however, exactly congruent with the pattern of the London records for that time, both reflecting the pressure on African male importations for the labor market of the American colonies that is a sign of the virulent inauguration of official English slaving on a mass scale at mid-century.

If the trough in the first half of the seventeenth century constituted by the declining figures of black notations in each of its two sub-periods (33 in the Jacobean and the Caroline and civil war decades, compared to 41 in the Elizabethan; Table 4.1) is one sign of a change in early modern English black history in that century, another sign is that of the bequests to black people that appear in the last quarter century of this study's range, and which could be said to explain and develop the implications of that trough. If the trough is taken to be reflective of the slackening of English enslavement of Africans, and analogously of an inadvertent relaxation of the racialization of black people brought into and present in England, the greatest point of which is in the 1640s, as has been argued in the previous chapter, the particular social corollary of this is the gradual English desensitization to the black presence in its midst. The consequences of that desensitization can plausibly be seen in the acknowledgment of black people and of their service in the wills and deeds of Christopher Hatton, Willian Batten, and the Duke of Somerset in the Restoration and post-Restoration years, however self-interested such acknowledgments also invariably are. Nicholas Wichehalse's citation of Anthony in his will in 1570 may be an untypical early instance of the same development, which is to say that such acknowledgments are more numerous and clearer in the seventeenth century than in the sixteenth. Anthony's, James Chappell's, and Mingo's casual appearances in the wills of their owners, on the same syntactical level, and hence on the same plane of documentary consciousness, as the other members of their households including kin, clearly show the entry of the black person into a civic English consciousness, albeit with captive racial markings.

The most revealing reflection of this development is the six incidences of purported black voices of varying audibility and directness that appear in the seventeenth-century provincial English records between the beginning of the century and the closing year of this study. These include the reported speech of Cooree, John Anthony, Dinah Black, Francis, James Chappell, and Tom. Of these John Anthony's "voice" may be present not in the form of his reported words but only inferentially, in the petition he filed with the Mayor of Dover for uncompensated services on board the *Silver Falcon*, but like the others it constitutes an articulated response of the black subject to its situation. Undoubtedly, the inevitable corruption of such "voices" in the very act of their inscription, and the myriad intractable and competing difficulties identified in modern critical excursus as surrounding the phenomenon of voice,[119] preclude any attempt to regard them as authentic speech. But each of these instances of reported black speech represents a value to their reporters, which is why they are being invoked. Thus, if the subaltern cannot speak, as Gayatri Spivak has seminally explained,[120] the very attempt to make it speak signals the emergence of the black subject as a speaking, and hence a political and history-bearing, entity. Such "speeches" could therefore be said to mark the rise to consciousness of the black subject in early modern English history.

This development cannot, however, be simply seen as a neatly celebratory moment in the inevitable forward movement of a progressivist history. For one thing, the appearance of purported black speech is not a teleologically symmetrical event, occurring as it does both within the early seventeenth-century decades when English attitudes toward the black subject have temporarily and distractedly improved as well as after those decades have passed in the century's second half. In fact, half of these instances occur in the resurgent boom of the slave trade during the Restoration and after. For another thing, many of these recorded voices convey the anguish of captivity and racial denigration, as do those of Cooree and Dinah Black. Others, like those of James Chappell and Tom, while seemingly articulating a sovereignty of consciousness, do so under the aegis of a bonded life. Most crucially, the values that these reported speeches have for their reporters are a reification of the black subject's racialized disempowerment if not of its official slavehood. The rise to audibility and consciousness of the black subject is thus inversely coterminous with the disappearance of its humanity into the history of its institutionalized mass enchainment over the next few centuries. The emergence of black "speech" in the English province in the seventeenth century is thus the cry of the black historical self at the moment of its final permanent incarceration, a nativity that is also its apocalypse. This simultaneously progressive–regressive function of black speech can be said to define the appearance–disappearance character of the black subject represented by the outside London records as a whole, both echoing those of the London records and extending them uniquely.

119 For a good summary see Bernadette Baker's essay, "What is Voice? Issues of Identity and Representation in the Framing of Reviews."

120 See the essay "Can the Subaltern Speak?"

Chapter Five

Indians and Others

The Protocolonial Dream

"the first-Fruits of India"

I

Although this study's focus has been on documentary records of black people, that is not meant to suggest that the historical colored people of early modern England are all from Africa. To imply either would be a patent historical absurdity. The same fundamental historical development that created a black presence in early Tudor and Elizabethan London predictably produced a variously colored population across England over the sixteenth and seventeenth centuries. Its presence is documented in 32 records of Indians, Americans, and others in different parts of the country, including the capital. Whereas the black records of London and the countryside examined so far contribute significant, irreversible, and hitherto unavailable materialities to the current understanding of racial/colonial formations in sixteenth- and seventeenth-century England, this latter dataset of citations of other people of color breaks relatively newer ground in making analytically visible a subject previously unthinkable and unknown—East Indians and Americans in early modern England.

In the opaque taxonomy of an anxiously self-referential early modern English white cultural optics, "Indian" is merely a generalized category of the non-white, synonymous with "negar" and "blackamoor/blackamore." But ancillary indicators such as the known typology of regional names and allusions to the English overseas trading companies that began their forays to particular global destinations in the Tudor and Stuart eras, enable the identification in these records of documentations of people from the Indian sub-continent and from the Americas. These identifications are proposed here with the reminder that there is a historical propriety in the coexistence of the two subgroups of East and West Indians in the English black archives and in this study, since from the late Middle Ages "India" was the original destination of Europe's ferocious expedition for wealth, an imagined physical locale that was the focus of a desperate dream of economic treasure. In this early modern narrative, Indians—of the west and of the east—cannot but cohabit the same English political imagination. These two archival subgroups are thus discussed not with regard to any essential geographic ethnicities of the individuals cited in them but in terms of the particular politics of their naming and the specific nature of their material consequences.

Among other people of color present in the archives, East Indians are the largest group, and they are cited in a few instances outside London but mostly within. They will therefore be considered first, followed by Americans, with the very few citations of colored people from other regions making up the concluding category. Conforming to the discussion pattern of the previous chapters, the East Indian records will be considered in two sequences, beginning with those from London and succeeded by ones from elsewhere in the country. Because the American citations lack a distinctive regional concentration, they will be taken up simply by the chronology of their dates.

II

In 1614 an Indian youth was transported to England, taught English and Latin, and in December 1616, in a busy commercial district of East London, baptized with the name Peter Pope. The terse record of the incident, which is dated the 22nd of the month, reads: "An East Indian was Christened by the name of Peter" (Item 296). The location is St. Dionis (or Denis, as it sometimes spelled) Backchurch, in Jacobean London's terms just across from the intersection of Lombard Street and Gracious (or Grace church) Street, and north of Eastcheap, and directly north from London bridge (Agas map 5R, p. 25). A site mentioned often in the Elizabethan London records discussed in Chapter 2, this is a great mercantile concourse, particularly Lombard Street, which, according to John Stow in 1598, traditionally was a gathering place of "merchants, strangers of diverse nations assembling thee twice a day", before the Royal Exchange was built in the adjoining ward of Cornhill in 1568. Even afterwards, respectable city officials and professionals continued to live here, as is clearly evident from the list of important individuals buried in St. Dionis Backchurch that Stow lists.[1] This setting is a clue to the public importance and meaning that this seemingly casually recorded event has for both those who organized it and those who saw it.

The ceremony was, in fact, a carefully orchestrated, demonstrative public spectacle, put together by the merchant company that brought the youth to England. This was the "Company of Merchants of London" that on 31 December 1600 was incorporated by Elizabeth with the exclusive charter for "the honour of this Our Realme of England, as for the increase of Our Navigation, and advancement of trade of Merchandise within Our said Realmes," to "adventure, set forth one, or more Voyages … by way of traffique and merchandise to the East-Indians, in the country and parts of Asia and Africa, and to as many of the Ilands, and Cities, Townes, and places thereabout,"[2] and that would thereafter be known as the infamous East India Company. The youth was brought to England by Patrick Copland, a young, newly-ordained, and enthusiastic chaplain of the company, who was the embodiment of the instincts of many of the directors of the newly-formed company, who felt the need of keeping this new English trading project always in close proximity to, and in conformity with, Christian preaching,[3] otherwise a clear instance of the evangelical zeal that will be one of the earliest and most enduring justifications for the later English colonial project's global pillage. Copeland's petitioning of the company, from Masulipatam on the Coromondel coast where he is stationed, for shipping the

1 *Survey of London*, 1: 201, 202.

2 Extracted in Samuel Purchas's *Hakluytus Posthumus, or Purchas His Pilgrimes*, 2: 368.

3 See the remarks of Patrick Copland, a chaplain of the East India Company, in *Memoir of Reverend Patrick Copland*, ed. Edward D. Neill, p. 9.

boy back to England and teaching him English and Latin, was based on the argument that Anglicizing and Latinizing the youth (who was judged by Copeland to be a quick learner, "talented"[4]) would make him an instrument of the company's work in India in the sense that he "could proselytise his own people,"[5] here evangelical persuasion being discernibly perceived to be intimate with, and facilitative of, commercial penetration. The company's investment in the youth—his shipping costs, and the "20 markes per annum" that they voted as the expenses for the youth's conversion[6]—was rewarded when Copeland declared in another petition to the company in little more than "the space of a yeare" after the boy's arrival that he had learned "to speake, to reade and write the English and Latin tongues and hand, both Roman and Secretary," and that his immersion in Christianity had reached a level that called for his public baptism, as "the first-fruites of India."[7]

The account of Peter Pope's publicly celebrated baptism, which is to say the joyous, government-orchestrated "Englishing" of an Indian, recalls and demonstrates fully a phenomenon seen variably several times in the late Elizabethan and early seventeenth-century London black records. Those records, which include the largely assembled neighborhood baptism of Mary Phyllis in St. Botolph, Aldgate on 2 June 1597 that was so carefully recorded by the church clerk Thomas Harridaunce (Item 224), Walter Anberey's decorously described baptism in All Hallows, Tottenham on 3 February 1610 (Item 278), and most pointedly the elaborately noted community christening of Dederj Iaquoah in St. Botolph, Aldgate on 1 January 1611 (Item 277), occurring within the same two decades, describe a phenomenon that could be called the first manifestation of early English colonialism, or protocolonialism. This is a phenomenon much felt by contemporary critical analyses of the English early modern period but still not formally identified. Protocolonialism is the forerunner of colonialism, and something that occurs without colonization or before full colonization has formally emerged. It can be described as the collective communitarian desire to possess and remake the other that has both a predictive and substitutive relation to the material manifestation of that act in colonization proper, and, together with the popular commonality of its occurrence, can be said to be bound to formal colonization in a double linkage of invisibility or secondary theoretical visibility.[8] No less devastating in its material consequences than colonialism proper, it is a more dangerous phenomenon in that it is an insidious collective social mindset that is undetectable in analyses of economic history.

---

4 Ibid., p. 10.

5 Cited by Rozina Visram, *Asians in Britain: 400 Years of History*, p. 1.

6 India Office Records, cited ibid.

7 Copland, *Memoir*, p. 11; Patrick Copland and Peter Pope, *Virginia's God Be Thanked, or a Sermon of Thanksgiving for the Happie Successe of the Affayres in Virginia This Late Yeare. Preached by Patrick Copland at Bow-Church in Cheapside before The ... Virginia Company ... 18 of April, 1622 ... Hereunto Are Adjoyned Some Epistles Written First in Latine (and Now Englished) in the East Indies by Peter Pope, an Indian Youth ... Who Was ... Baptised ... In London, December 22, 1616.*

8 For my earlier derivation of the notion of protocoloniality as colonialism before coloniality analogously from Etienne Balibar's notion of racism without and before race (*Race, Nation, Class*, pp. 23–24), see my essay, "Shakespeare's Spectral Turks," p. 2.

Corresponding to the phenomenon of racism without or before the notion of race, and partly helping to explain it, protocolonialism sees the colored subject not in its humanity but as part of the material prospects of the lands that it inhabits, which must be refashioned as the facilitator of the colonizer's exploitation of the resources of that land for his benefit and profit, that is, as a prospective colonized subject. For the protocolonial mind, the colored individual's existence outside this view is its savagery, primitivism, treachery, and malevolence, the degree to which the colored subject can be refashioned describing for the colonizer the extent to which its tribe is "good," or "intelligent." The public baptisms of Peter Pope, Walter Anberey, Dederj Iaquoah, and Mary Phyllis mark the moment of completion of the colored subject's refashioning, the point at which the latter is expected to have become the fully trained agent of the colonizer, in fact his clone or surrogate. Hence, the variably celebratory tone of these events evident in their records, which reflect and advertise the material and cultural ambitions of Jacobean England. This is the expansive political character of James's reign that was pointed out in the previous chapters.

The charged political script that underwrites this entire episode is reflected in the personalities and parties that are involved in it, for that list includes King James himself, the Archbishop of Canterbury, members of the Privy Council, the city Aldermen, and the directors of both the East India Company *and* the Virginia Company. Once the baptism proposal had been vetted, as it had to be, by George Abbot, who had assumed the primacy of the Archbishopric of Canterbury just five years earlier, the monarch himself chose the name, the full form of which is "Petrus Papa" or "Peter Pope".[9] If James's choice of the surname is intriguing, since England's Protestantism now, unlike half a century earlier, was unmistakably visible (so, does the naming of a seized Indian youth as "Pope" signify sanctity or insult for him?), that uncertainty could be the obscurity of the protocolonial drive's love–hate symbiosis in the object of its possession. For the carried-over Indian youth to be given an English name and made into a Christian was for the English to confusedly reproduce themselves in the youth, otherwise the conflicted self-replication that is historically Anglo-European colonialism's fundamental instinct. This is why one unknown Indian youth's conversion drew *all* the chief symbolic icons of the early English colonial body politic. If the monarch's interest in the conversion mandated the Privy Council's attendance at the ceremony, that in turn ensured the Alderman's presence. Officials from both trading companies were present because the evangelical ideology of the event was crucial to the success of both. In the conjoining of the executive apparatus of the state (the monarch, the Privy Council, the Aldermen) with the missionary and the merchant, is the coming together of the three elements that will fuel colonialism's rapacity: brute force (state power), cultural ideology that will justify that power (here evangelization), and the benefit that these two elements are to produce in combination—economic profit. The conversion of an obscure Indian youth is thus a protocolonial English political imaginary's symbolic seizure of India. Understandably, this triumph has to be produced as a busily attended public spectacle, caught in Copland's language, in his happy memory of the event, as "the

9 As will be evident later, the Archbishop of Canterbury will continue to be associated with the conversion of Indians in early modern England.

sea of upturned faces" in the church, and reproduced by Copland's Victorian editor two centuries later as the "curious" women and "astonish[ed]" children in the street, and the "densely packed congregation inside."[10]

Within two weeks of his baptism, the Christianized youth was sent back to India with his trainer and presumably as an *Indian* chaplain or "missionary" of the East India Company.[11] Appropriately, the vessel that carried the pair back to India was the *Royal James*,[12] at 1,000 tons one of the biggest ships ever built by the EIC.[13] His success in that role is evident in the three surviving Latin epistles that he wrote to the Governor of the East India Company in 1620, and to the captain of the *Royal James*, Martin Pring. This incident, just a decade and a half after the setting up of the company, marks early modern England's colonial instincts from the beginning of its global adventures, and is one of the clearest instances of the subaltern deployed in his own extinction. For, beyond the brief moment of his Anglicization and Christianization, Peter Pope is lost to history; of his own people and the precise location of his origin nothing is known except that he was from the "Bay of Bengala".[14]

In its other aspects, Peter Pope's record is not a unique one, as there are others like it, elsewhere in London and its liberties. For instance, more than six decades earlier there is the burial mention of "Salamon Nurr" on 22 March 1550 in St. Margaret's, Westminster, in which the spelling of the name sounds exactly like an Anglicized corruption of the Muslim name of Suleman Noor that is possibly Near Eastern but more probably Indian (Item 118). Closer to Peter Pope's record but three years earlier, on 28 December 1613 in St. Nicholas church in Deptford, near Greenwich, on the Thames's south bank, a Jane Johnson is recorded as marrying a "Samuel Munsur," who is described simply as a "blackamore." There is a fragmentary and partly legible baptism record of 28 November 1613 in the same church that reads "…unser, a blackamour that came in one of …erne [illegible] shyppes baptized" (Items 286, 287). Taking into account the notorious inaccuracy and non-standard orthography of early modern English record-keeping that produced the slight variation of the spelling of the surname in the baptism record, that record very probably refers to the same individual mentioned in the marriage notice, and to the fact of his being baptized on arrival in England and just before his marriage to Jane Johnson. The surname "…unser/ Munsur" is almost certainly Indian (and possibly Muslim), for the following reasons. First, Deptford (or "deep ford," as it was known from Roman times because the Romans used to ford nearby Ravensbourne Creek on the road from Dover to London) is just west of Southwark and part of London's south bank.[15] This area, as was seen in the earlier chapters, had numerous black people recorded in the archives as living here for several decades before this time.[16] In other words, as part of a busy riverfront/dockside area,

10 Copland, *Memoir*, p. 11.

11 Visram, *Asians in Britain*, p. 1.

12 Copland, p. 13.

13 Jean Sutton, *Lords of the East*, p. 42.

14 East India Company Court Minutes, cited by Visram, p. 7.

15 See Robert Adams's map of 1588 in P. D. Harvey's *Maps in Tudor England*, p. 52.

16 Some earlier cited examples include "Mary, a blackamore from Dcor Hector's," "the blackamore gerle from Mr. Pintoe's"; "Edward, the sonne of Resonabell Blackman silkweaver," "Constantyn, a negar oute of ye pilgrime at portsmouth," "Richard a Blackmore, 12 years old." According to a web essay by a London local historian named Steve Martin, in

new transported human contraband such as seized colored peoples from Africa, Guyana, and elsewhere, as well as cargo, coming in from the sea, would more than likely appear here, before dispersing northwards across the Thames into the city. Secondly, when such populations began to include Indians specifically, such Indians would also appear here, since Deptford was where the East India Company's ships to India and the Far East sailed from, and to which they returned.[17] Serving as the East India Company's shipyard from 1608/9, Deptford was seventeenth-century London's Indian port at home throughout the century.[18] That the record appears in the archives of St. Nicholas, Deptford, is predictable since St. Nicholas was, and had been for several centuries, the preferred patron saint for mariners, and a familiar icon for East India Company personnel in particular.[19] Both of these contexts are reflected in the baptism record's notation of the history of the man's arrival here in one of the "shyppes," the allusion incidentally echoing a like allusion in the seventeenth-century London black records of the last chapter, in the burial citation of "Constantyn" in St. Olave, Tooley Street, Southwark, on 5 December 1605 who is described as having coming "oute of ye pilgrime at portsmouth" (Item 263).

Third, the fact that the name "…unser/Munsur" occurs in the position of the surname confirms the person's Indian pedigree. This is because, as has been seen in the course of this book, in English civic records in the early modern period a frequent naming practice for people of color, in cases where the person is not given a Christian first name *and* a surname or a *faux* classical name such as Scipio or Pompey, was to use the person's known or perceived place of origin as the surname to follow the person's given Christian name, as in the case of the individuals named Christopher Cappovert or Symon Valencia in the Elizabethan records, indicating individuals from the Cape Verde islands and Valencia, Spain, respectively. As an ethnic indicator this practice more commonly—and in cases where presumably the person's place of origin was not known—was replaced by one in which terms such as "Negro" or "Blackamoor/blackamore" became the surname. Given the blissfully irrational conflation of peoples from disparate geographic regions that marks the early modern English constructions of the racial other (which even that industrious early modern English ethnographer Samuel Purchas himself admits[20]), Indians were also "Negroes" and "blackamores," although in most cases with the descriptor "Indian" or "East Indian" before either term.

---

the yard of St. Nicholas, Deptford itself is buried "Sarika, a black woman," and "John Kaffey," with the year "1620" marked on the gravestone ("Revealing London's Black History: A Case Study"). It is also possible, of course, that given the Muslim name the individual "…unser/Munsur" could also have been North African, although Deptford's connection with the EIC in this moment makes it more probable that he was East Indian.

17 Kristen Wilson, "Deptford, England, the East India Company and the Global Economy in Geography"; Anim-Addo, *Sugar, Spices, and Human Cargo*, p. 27.

18 H. V. Bowen, Margarette Lincoln, and Nigel Rigby, *The Worlds of the East India Company*, pp. 1, 7; Anthony Wild, *The East India Company, Trade and Conquest from 1600*, p. 67.

19 "East India Company," Encyclopedia entry.

20 Purchas explains: "This confusion of names, I think, did first grow from the confusion of nations. For as before observed out of Eusebius, the Ethiopians arose from the river Indus, & settled their habitation neere Egypt. Perhaps, they brought the Indian name also to these parts. Or else the ignorance of these remote parts might doe it; in which respect not only a third part of the olde world, but another new found world it named India. Therefore *Acosta*

In the present case, for some reason the name "…unser/Munsur" was itself felt to be sufficient as an ethnic descriptor of the individual.

As such, "Samuel "…unser/Munsur" is both a typical case and an exception, the former in that its joint Christian/non-Christian construction conforms to and confirms the naming codes for colored people in early modern England, and the latter in that the discernible trace of an Indian surname has against all odds survived the deadly erasure of the conversion process, and in the fact that it has done so without any other supplementary geographic indicators or even any orthographic modifications, since the name's spelling is identical to its contemporary usage.[21] The record is also of exceptional interest because of its nature, which is a marriage record, and the only one of its kind in the records of Indians in early modern England currently uncovered. Otherwise, it is a part of the numerous records of cross-racial unions between black/colored and white people that exist in the early modern English archives. As in all such cases in which the violence of cultural arrival and assimilation produces what Jan Mohammed has called colonialism's traumatic cultural catalepsy,[22] Samuel Munsur/unser's marriage, like his conversion, while probably being a necessity of his survival in Jacobean London, is also part of the very process that will subsequently efface him in history.

If Samuel …unser/Munsur's obscure baptism and marriage in one of the city's rough liberties, Deptford, was the unformalized precursor of the English political ambition reflected in Peter Pope's officially emblazoned public baptism in the heart of the city proper, the legacy of both events is, arguably, reflected in several records of Indians in the city's archives. These include the baptisms of "Thomas Mamoto, an Indian" in St. Nicholas, Deptford on 25 December 1617; the burial of "James (an Indian) servant to Mr. James Duppa Beerebrewer" in St. Botolph, Aldgate on 8 September 1618; "Phillip, an Indian blackmore, borne in the East Indies at Zarat [Surat]" on 20 August 1623 in St Katherine by the Tower; the baptism of "Sonday Anthony, an Indian aboute the age of sixteene yeres" on 30 January 1624/25 in St. Peter's Cornhill; and the public baptism of "George Horsan, an Indian dwelling with ye Archbishop of Canterbury" who on 31 December 1626 "being presented at the ffount [fount] by Dcor Harns & Dcor Jefreys Chaplaines in House & after the Indian had made his confession of ffaith & Craving to be Baptised, was by Dcor ffeatly then Rector named Georg" (Items 300, 302, 319, 323, 328). As the records of Thomas, James, and Phillip signal by their east side riverfront locations, the history of these individuals' casual seizures by the East India company's earliest traders, so also that of "Sonday Anthony," by the jingle of his name, announces like that of some other individuals seen in Chapter 3 (such as "John Come Quick," Item 321) the demeaning jocularism within which their deadly servitude will be enacted. In the last record, the Indian's supposed enthusiasm to be Christianized that is so proudly underlined is directly reminiscent of Peter Pope's

esteemed India to be a generall name to all countries which are far-off, and strange to vs, although it be properly attributed to the East Indies …"; *Purchas His Pilgrimage*, p. 559.

21 Of course, the name's future represents no threat to protocolonial English conformity, as in its subsequent Christian English genealogical journey it will undoubtedly move increasingly toward a comfortable, even if unusual, English sound.

22 Abdul R. JanMohammed, *Manichean Aesthetics*, pp. 5, 273.

pointedly recorded gratitude to Patrick Copland in the Latin letters he wrote to him and to the captain of the *Royal James*, Martin Pring, from India.[23] That the record is careful to document the willingness of the *convertee* in his conversion is of course an Anglican doctrinal requirement of the procedure, and has little to do with the inevitable pressures of the experience for George, which go unrecorded as they must, as also do the circumstances of his arrival in England. That this baptism, like that of Peter Pope, is connected to people of the highest stature, such as the Archbishop of Canterbury, again registers the symbolic protocolonial significance that these Indians and their conversions held for the English political imaginary at the very highest levels.

The process also continued, of course, as is shown by the burial of "Thomas a[n] Indian, out of the Lord Brooke's house, [who] was layed in the Church as Catumelant" in St. Andrew, Holborn on 17 April 1633;[24] and of the baptisms of "Abraham Thornburye, an Indian" in St. Olave, Hart Street on 15 January 1638; and of an Indian male, "a National & Natural Indian about ye age 15 years by the name James Robert(s)," in St. Mary, Stratford Bow on 24 July 1638 (Items 347, 355, 357). The fully Christianized names in both records represent the commonest process of the effacement of the historical identity of all people of color in early modern England, a phenomenon through which such a population's ethnicity will become invisible to, and impossible to determine in, subsequent historical inquiry, unless the vagaries of individual parish clerical notations include some additional identificatory information, as are the cases here.

More notable perhaps is the baptism of a 16-year-old female "Indian Chirugeon [surgeon]" who is named "Loreto," in the church of St. Olave, Hart Street in 1638 (Item 359). In all the cases of Indian teenagers cited so far, including this one, the details of their appearances are unrecorded, but that very silence, and their youth, inscribe nonetheless the inevitable violence of their removal from India. The record of "Loreto" is unique in the way it shows not just the assimilation of the Indians brought to England but also the skill and resourcefulness that ironically marked them for their fateful colonial destiny. If female surgeons were a fragile minority in the patriarchal Tudor–Stuart medical landscape,[25] how astonishingly singular can a *16-year-old female colored, Indian surgeon* be? Do the pressures of forced transplantation and assimilation mark this young Indian woman as the double colonized subject in terms of both her ethnicity and gender, the ultimate subaltern?

There are more citations of Indians in London. There is the description of "a youth in an Indian habit, attended by two blackamoors" who were part of the welcoming ceremony put on near the East India Company offices for Charles II's entry into London on 22 May 1661, the location and the sponsors pointing almost certainly to all three figures being Indian (Item 391). The arrangement recalls somewhat the details of Charles's grandfather's wedding in Norway and Scotland more than half a century earlier that was discussed in the last chapter, when blackamoors were deployed in James VI/I's wedding to Anne (one of then frozen to death in Oslo) (Item 174, 1

---

23 Patrick Copland and Peter Pope, *Virginia's God Be Thanked.*

24 "Catumelant" is probably an indication that the individual was a *catechumen*, a Christian convert being prepared for baptism, but not yet baptized.

25 Charles Webster, ed., *Health, Medicine and Mortality in the Sixteenth Century* (New York: Cambridge University Press, 1979), p. 79.

and 2), and was perhaps inspired by it as a family tradition, with captured East Indians substituting the Africans of the earlier event. Yet more Indian citations mention the baptism of "Hannah Foster, and [*sic*] Indian" on 11 July 1664 in St. Vedast, Foster Lane, London; "Richard Indem a Blackamoor" (another Indian, judging from the malformed last name) on an unspecified day in October 1664 in Little Stanmore, London; and the public baptism of "George, an Indian servant of Mr. Robert Andrews, chirugeon, aged 16 yeares or thereabout" who is "Christened in ye publique congregation" on 29 April 29 1675 in St. Olave, Hart Street (Items 407, 408, 441). The public character of the event in the last record, in connecting with the like character of George Horsan's baptism in 1626 cited above, and in together recalling the heralded baptism of Peter Pope in 1616 and that of Dederj Iaquoah and the others earlier, shows the continuity of the phenomenon of triumphantly orchestrated conversions of seized Indians across the century, the continuity marking also the progression of English protocoloniality toward colonialism proper by the end of the century.

Cryptic mentions of Indians but without any allusion to the history of their arrival, which is the norm for the records presented in this chapter, appear in church documents outside London as well. These citations include the possible christening of "Peter Indine" in Reading, Berkshire on 12 March 1553; and the baptism of "Nich Bix 'an Indian Ethiopian youth now aged about 13,'" in Fordwich, Kent in 1635 (Items 123, 352). Each of these has a striking feature. Peter Indine's surname, which has every likelihood of being a corruption of the word Indian, comprises a unique instance of the use of Indian being used as an unmarked ethnic descriptor, and alludes probably though not certainly to his East Indian rather than American origin. As notable in the baptism of Nicholas Bix is the deployment of the word "Ethiopian," which is clearly functioning here as a color descriptor, much as the word "negar" is doing in the other records cited so far. The surname Bix is without parallel in the early modern English black archives. The baptism citation of "Gifferdandgorge" in St. Andrews, Plymouth, Devon on 22 October 1602, who is described simply as "an Indian" (Item 250), is equally noteworthy in the very unusual and totally opaque form of his name, which occurs in no other record in this book, and which partly destabilizes the authenticity of his East Indian origin.

A pictorial reference of what is probably an East Indian rather than an American or an African is the "liveried dark-skinned … male servant" who appears in the painting of *Lord Tichbourn Handing out the Dole in Front of his Country Estate* in Tichborne, Hampshire (Item 427) (see Fig. 5.1), to which Kari McBride has pointed, an item similar to the many pictorial representations of black people that Kim Hall has presented. The Tichborne dole of flour and bread is handed out traditionally to the poor of the village parish by the Tichborne lord from the steps of his manorial seat every year on the 25th of March. The painting, done by a Dutch artist and commissioned by Henry Tichborne,[26] describes this event with all the self-interested aristocratic solemnity that it has acquired by this time. A precise ethnic identification of the colored figure that

---

26 Tichborne's commissioning of the portrait is cited by John Trevor Cliffe, *The World of the Country House in Seventeenth-Century England*, p. 141. For the artist, Gilles Van Tillborough, see Richard Leppert, *The Sight of Sound: Music, Representation, and the History of the Body*, pp. 30–32.

appears innocuously at the very left edge of the portrait of the gathering of the Tichborne household in front of Tichborne House is, however, a difficult undertaking. Whereas the Hampshire location of the scene, adjoining Devonshire, points to an American or African connection for the individual, and whereas deployment as decorative aristocratic servant is more typical of the seized early modern English African, and even though the painting's seacoast location is untypical of the history of seized east Indians in England, the figure's appearance, as far as it can be made out in the overall dark tint of the painting, suggests an East Indian individual. If the figure is indeed an East Indian, this pictorial record would mark an early instance of the presence of transported Indians in gentry households in the English countryside that is generally more prominent later in the century and in the next. If, as one scholar has warned, "The picture should not be read as 'a straightforward depiction of gentry charity for the poorer sort,'" but "as a representation of social hierarchy" that "reflects an idealized view of the relationship between the 'respectable poor' and their betters, something the use of such charities was designed to achieve after the fright of the English Revolution,"[27] the politics of that intended message must also apply to the colored figure in the portrait's edge, whose deferential posture of holding out a basket of bread for the gathered poor projects its compliance in its own undocumented captivity.

Fig. 5.1 Gillis Van Tillborough, *Lord Tichbourn Handing out the Dole in Front of his Country Estate* (1670). English Heritage, London

[27] John S. Morrill, *The Oxford Illustrated History of Tudor and Stuart Britain*, p. 200.

III

What evidentiary acknowledgment there is in the East India Company's own papers of its traffic in colored, possibly Indian people, exists indirectly in private correspondence, something that merely indicates that the EIC's ships had black people on board—whether from India or elsewhere—in their voyages to the Far East. At least some of these were from India, as is visible in John Davies's cryptic mention in the account of his trip to India in the *Tiger* in 1599 of having seized 12 Indians somewhere on the Coromandel coast in southeast India: "we tooke with us twelve of the Indians of severall places" (Item 237).[28] It is possibly this same kind of human contraband that appears in John Gurney's private letter to Sir Thomas Smith on 28 July 1614, from Pattania [Siam?], referring to the two blacks with them who were both killed in fights that the ship had with the King of Sambas's men: "for one of our blacks being stepped ashore was slain ... and another black which was a slave leapt overboard for fear and they think he was also slain … ." Adam Denton, in his letter of 5 October 1614, also refers to their having a black: "Mr. Lucas sent Tho. Samuel and Tho. Driver with a Moor up to Zangomaye (Kiang-mai)."[29] The sole direct evidence of the East India Company's traffic in Indians at this time is in 1621, when William Bragge is recorded in the City of London's archives as claiming £6875 from the East India Company for assorted goods, including thirteen negroes or Indian people (Item 312). Since it is the East India Company that is named here—and not the Virginia company—these are probably East Indians and not native Americans, a distinction that is evident for a majority of these records in the way that they specify the person named as being "Indian" or "East Indian" rather than being from "Barbados," "Guinea," "Madagascar," and so on. The hidden context for the particular wording of Bragge's plea, and what underlies his seeming profession of Christian sympathy for the humanity of the "Indians" and his request for them "not to be vallewed," is probably his attempt to avoid paying taxes and duties for the "merchandise" that he has obviously transported on behalf of some importer. As such, an additional distinction of this record is the fact that it constitutes one of the earliest pieces of written evidence of black people being sold in early modern England. The only earlier instance would be the complaint in the Elizabethan records of Henry Novimeis in 1587 about his newly purchased black servant's recalcitrance, but that may involve an alien.

As such, it is significant that for all but two of the records of Indians in England cited so far (Peter Pope, and Samuel …unser/Munsur), there is very little directly corroborating evidence of such people and their history in the East India Company's own, more commonly available records. If official documentation detailing the seizure and transportation of Indians to England by the EIC is present in the company's papers, as for instance in the company's Court minutes, such records are incomplete since the company's books for several early decades of the seventeenth century are missing, and what portions of the Court minutes do exist have yet to become as freely

[28] In Purchas, *Hakluytus Posthumus*, 2: 325.

[29] *Letters Received by the East India Company from Its Servants in the East*, ed. Danvers and Foster, 2: 113.

available as the other transcribed materials of the company, held as they are solely by the British Library's India Office Records. Other documentary sources such as the Calendar of State Papers contain only scattered, infrequent, and opaque allusions to Indians in connection with the EIC in the first half of the seventeenth century. This is to say that the government's highest legislative and executive bodies seem to show little notice of, and connection to, the traffic in Indians, and are therefore insulated from its ethical charges. Freely available detailed acknowledgments (by the East India Company itself, and by the local archives, of the protocolonial transportation of such people) are more typical of both the English local church archives and the company's documentary records only in the closing decades of the seventeenth century and beyond, which cite Indians more commonly and describe a bit more fully the history of their passage.

Thus, overall, four kinds of overlapping erasures bind the topic of Indians in early modern England. First, despite the fact that the European world expansion in the early modern period—starting with Christopher Columbus's arrival in the West Indies in 1492—that has shaped world geopolitical history until now, began with a search not for any other region but specifically for *India*, topoi such as "India" and "Indians" in late Tudor England (which five years after Columbus, in the first Tudor's reign, tried deliberately to match his feat in Sebastian Cabot's trip to Newfoundland,[30] and which a century later in the last Tudor's reign set up the trading company that was to be the vehicle of the formal English seizure of India eventually) do not today have even the dignity of being the constitutive objects of a coherent research inquiry.[31] "India" is the metaphor of the early modern Western world's dream of wealth, in pursuit of which the European global colonial adventure set sail, and the ideological destination of its physical journey. But if for Columbus's voyage the landfall in the western Atlantic became the "*West* Indies," the qualifying gesture in that naming, describing the India found in the West, was soon silently dropped as the inhabitants of the West Indies and of the subsequently discovered American land mass all become simply "Indians." By a correspondingly astonishing occlusion at the beginning of the seventeenth century, the inhabitants of the Indian land mass encountered by James Manchester, William Hawkins, and Thomas Roe became merely "East Indians" as in Purchas (in the passage cited earlier), that is, a subspecies of the species of the original European colonial dream that is India.

A second, analogous effacement is evident in the fact that Indians brought back into England immediately—and directly in conformity with the dynamics of colonization—were Christianized, and thus slip at once into invisibility in common historical memory. Third, as the national English protocolonial instinct of the state-sponsored trading voyages that brought back Indians is, with the exception of the Peter Pope baptism, hidden in the obscurity of brief church records, so the political ambition of such acts is buried beneath the silence of the English executive and legislative bodies, which seem to know nothing about such events, and are therefore

---

[30] George Birdwood and William Foster, eds., *The Register of Letters &c. Of the Governour and Company of Merchants of London Trading into the East Indies, 1600–1619*, p. 192.

[31] One welcome exception in this regard is Shankar Raman's *Framing 'India': The Colonial Imaginary in Early Modern Culture*.

dissociated from them. So too, the implicit rapacity of both such seizures and such assimilative conversions is buried in the silence of official EIC records, which, with the exception of the Peter Pope case, do not record or mention all the Indians thus brought back to India, and who are therefore left to harmlessly ghost the city archives, safely shrouded in the obscurity of partly written-over names whose histories no one can fully uncover. The fourth erasure occurs as the lapse of historical memory becomes the felt "absence" of historical record, in which the written-over becomes the forgotten, which in turn becomes the non-existent, the growing assumptions of an erased memory becoming the dogma of a traditional historical consciousness and a popular scholarly view that does not know of Indians in early modern England. Thus, Victorian antiquarian scholars such as Edward Neill could serenely declare in 1871 that Indians were a rare sight in early modern England,[32] in which the complex implications of relative numerical scarcity are swept away by the force of an absolute statement. With this kind perspective, of course, goes the concomitant belief about the implausibility of ascribing colonialism to late Tudor and early Stuart England.

IV

A group of records present people of color from other regions. The first instance of this is the earlier cited description of Robert Fabian in Westminster in 1502, of three Americans brought back from Newfoundland by Sebastian Cabot who are "clothed in beastes skins, and ate raw fleshe, and spake suche speech that no man could understand them," but who two years later are so assimilated that Fabian cannot "discerne [them] from Englishemen" (Item 8). It is surely a telling fact that the very second English overseas expeditionary voyage in search of new lands and wealth, whose treasure Fabian describes in the headnote to his description, with compulsive repetition as an "Ilande … rich and replenished with riche commodities," instantly ended up in kidnapping colored people. It is also revealing that because, of the three items of the Americans' otherness that he underlines – dress, diet, and language – the first and last to satisfactorily disappear two years later, the Americans became no longer different from "Englishemen." Aside from whether there was an accompanying anxiety about the subversive disappearance of difference mixed in this approval, the experience of the three Americans outlines clearly the self-replicating instincts of the English seizure of people and their reconstruction of them in their own image that will fundamentally characterize the English drive to possess lands and their peoples over the next several centuries. There is as well a sharp and revealing irony in Fabian's comments about the otherness of the Americans, as Ronald Pollit has pointed out, given the fact that Fabian himself was a recent immigrant's descendent, albeit a white European one.[33]

The next series of American importations commence in the second decade of Elizabeth's reign. Starting in the 1580s with Walter Raleigh's American colonization projects, seven Americans, among many others, were taken to England, from Virginia

---

32 Copland, *Memoir*, p. 11.

33 Pollit, "'Refuge of the Distressed Nations,'" p. D 1011.

and North Carolina in 1584, and from Guyana in 1597, in the first decade of the seventeenth century, and in 1616. They were taken by ship captains undertaking voyages on Raleigh's behalf and acting on his instructions to that effect, and by Raleigh himself, both as part of his plan to train them as interpreters and use them to garner greater royal support for his project of English plantations in America.[34] The first of these, who were taken by Philip Amadas and Arthur Barlow from the Virginia and North Carolina coasts, and were called Manteo and Wanchese, were housed at Durham House on the Strand in Westminster, where they were described by a German visitor to Elizabeth's court as being like "white Moors … [with a] usual habit … of rudely tanned skins of wild animals, no shirts, and a pelt before their privy parts … [but] Now … clad in brown taffeta," who "No one … [could] understand … [and making] most childish and silly figure[s]" (Item 155).[35] In 1597, on the turning of Raleigh's attention to Guyana as an additional and better English plantation prospect, a boy named Charles was brought back sometime by 1597, for his death is recorded in St. Luke, Chelsea that year (Item 219). Sometime in the next decade, two more individuals by the names of Leonard Ragapo and Harry were acquired by Raleigh from Guyana (Item 259), and after being taught suitable language skills in England, were subsequently active in English negotiations with American tribes in the mid-Atlantic coast and in the Caribbean. Finally, yet two more men from Guyana by the name of Pedro and Christopher or Christobal Guayacunda were seized by Raleigh on his last Guyana trip and brought back to England in 1616 (Item 297), in his last attempt to bolster support for the Guyana plantation project with a new English monarch interested in cementing peace with a Spain that wanted a cessation of English activities in what it perceived to be its imperial American territories. Although Pedro died enroute, Christopher was present in London through Raleigh's downfall, imprisonment, and execution, supposedly testifying on his behalf about the truth of Guyana's riches, and witnessing at "close hand" his beheading in October 1618.[36]

Still more instances of the importation of Americans outside London include the five individuals brought back to Plymouth from Maine by George Weymouth in 1606, three of whom ended up in the house of the principal resident officer of the Merchant Adventurers in Bristol, Ferdinando Gorges.[37] One more Indian record that probably belongs to the same group of mid-Atlantic or Guyanian Americans brought back by Raleigh and his associates is the burial note of "John, an Indian of the forte" in 1613 in St. Andrews, Plymouth (Item 282). The "forte" is very likely the fort built by Francis Drake in Plymouth before the battle with the Spanish Armada in 1588 as part of the port's defensive battlements, and the "Indian" is plausibly therefore one of the numerous individuals brought back from Virginia, North Carolina, or Guyana

34 Alden T. Vaughan, "Sir Walter Raleigh's Indian Interpreters," p. 344.

35 Giles Milton's transcription is looser; *Big Chief Elizabeth*, p. 54.

36 Vaughan, "Sir Walter Ralegh's Indian Interpreters," p. 371. See also Robert Lacey, *Sir Walter Ralegh*, who also claims without documentation that the Americans regularly visited Raleigh in the Tower (p. 325).

37 See the antiquarian documentary report "Attempts towards Colonization: The Council for Colonization and the Merchant Venturers of Bristol", p. 683. These records were encountered too late to be included in the Chronological Index of this book.

in the several American voyages that either started from Plymouth or returned there. This probable identification is encouraged by Walter Raleigh's family connection to Drake, and by his pursuit of his American plantation project, either in person or through his ship captains. John's deployment at the "forte" may be a further sign of his origins, since that military outpost environment would be compatible with John's real or perceived fighting or scouting skills for the English. The first contemporary attempt to identify these seized Americans with any particular geographic accuracy, by using the name of the American landmass as an ethnic descriptor, and which is therefore the uniqueness of such a record, is the baptism mention of "John Americanus a 'blackamore'" on 30 March 1645 in Newark, Nottinghamshire (Item 367).

These mid-Atlantic and Guyanian Americans are actually part of an even larger multi-regional colored American population that was brought into England in the Elizabethan and Jacobean years. These other Americans include, in 1576/77 in Bristol, an Eskimo male who died of a vicious beating during his capture, given him by one of the sailors who wanted to teach him "a Cornish trick," and a mother and child whose canoeing and hunting skills drew a crowd of spectators on the banks of the river Avon, before the mother died of a skin infection a few days later. This population also included a Chesapeake American who was displayed in London in a makeshift zoological park with animals brought back from America, and three Americans from Virginia who weere displayed boating in the Thames in 1603.[38] Exactly how large a group the Americans brought to England altogether constitutes is uncertain, but for one scholar at least it was substantial enough to be described as "two score" i.e. forty in number, or more than "fifty."[39]

A significant aspect of these American records is the note of the friendly cooperation of the Americans with the English that is implicitly or explicitly present in them. According to the language of the original accounts, and of the modern popular descriptions that are based on those accounts, the Americans were all instantly agreeable to helping the English trade with them and eager to see their land and learn their language and ways. Thus, a member of Manteo's Algonquin tribe "paddles out" to Amadas and Barlow's ships and is "friendly" to them, and Manteo himself "behaves … toward us as a most faithfull English man".[40] Thus too, Ragapo "loveth our nation with all his heart," and entertains Raleigh's men "with all kindness," and with "much respect and love."[41] So as well, in Raleigh's own account of his Guyana trip, the tribal chief Topiawari "freely gave me his onelie son to take with me into England," and "the Indians [brought by the brother of Harry, an American formerly

---

[38] Alden T. Vaughan, "Trinculo's Indian: American Natives in Shakespeare's England," pp. 50–51, 56, and "Sir Walter Ralegh's Indian Interpreters," pp. 357–58. In the two essays Vaughan discusses multiple documentations of American Indians. All these references were also unfortunately encountered too late for them to be included in the already numbered Chronological Index.

[39] Alden Vaughan, "Trinculo's Indian," p. 50; "Sir Walter Ralegh's Indian Interpreters," p. 344.

[40] Arwin D. Smallwood, *Bertie County: An Eastern Carolina History*, p. 25; John White's account of his 1585–86 trip to Roanoke Island, quoted in Alden Vaughan, "Sir Walter Ralegh's Indian Interpreters," p. 354.

[41] *Hakluytus Posthumus*, 16: 368.

with Raleigh in the Tower] stayed with me all night, offering their services and all they had."[42] Even modern scholars, while sometimes being suspicious of the circumstances of the cooperation of the Americans, frequently fall back on this pattern, suggesting for instance that "the Indians may have been sent by [their] tribal superiors to gather information about England's resources," or that they were curious or hopeful about securing "a favorable connection to European merchandise."[43]

But that more often than otherwise the English–American contacts were pressured and the latter's co-optations by the former were violent, is revealed in French and Spanish eyewitness sources,[44] and in the American refusals and resistances and the punitive English reprisals against the Americans for the latter's minutest transgressions, which intersperse these same accounts and which cannot be hidden by them. Instances include the testimony of a French explorer by the name of John Mocquet about Raleigh's taking of Topiawari's son by "Subtillity,"[45] the Spanish ambassador's report to his government in the 1580s that the English were "teaching and training [the Indians] to say how good that country is for people to there and inhabit it,"[46] and Spanish eyewitness claims about Raleigh's carrying away Christopher Guayacunda to England on his third Guyana voyage under "duress."[47] This is therefore the reality behind the myth of Guayacunda's "service" to Raleigh unto his death in the Tower, a binding that in its terrifying absoluteness might recall the ancient Egyptian practice of living slave incarcerations in pharaonic tombs. The most visible instance of actual American resistance of the English is Wanchese's unhappiness in England and his refusal to help the English when he returned to America.[48] The best example of English reprisals against Indians for the slightest failures is Philip Amadas's fierce punishment, in Richard Granville's 1585 trip to the Carolina coast, of the entire American village of Aquascogoc for the supposed theft of a silver cup by "one of the savages,"[49] an overcompensation that would seem to exemplify the chilling formula outlined by the aristocratic colonial propagandist George Peckham for dealing with recalcitrant Americans, implying through the euphemism of the Englishmen's "right to defend themselves" the deadly prescription of "pursuing vengeance with force."[50] It may be pertinent to ask whether the beating of the Eskimo by Frobisher's man is part of this same violent English doctrination of compliance in the American. As such, what these American accounts do, in their stressing of the natural "friendliness" of the Americans, is in effect to program the American in mythic postures of natural

42 *The Discovery of Guiana*, p. 80, 180.

43 D. B. Quinn, quoted. by Alden Vaughan, and Vaughan himself, "Sir Walter Ralegh's Indian Interpreters," p. 346.

44 Alden Vaughan, ibid., p. 345 n. 8.

45 Cited ibid., p. 361.

46 Cited in Alden Vaughan, "Trinculo's Indians," p. 54.

47 Cited in Alden Vaughan, "Sir Walter Ralegh's Indian Interpreters," p. 370.

48 Ibid., pp. 349, 350.

49 Ibid., p. 350.

50 Cited in K. R. Andrews, *Trade, Plunder and Settlement*, p. 198.

subservience, to set up what will be the casting of the American in the early modern English political and popular imagination.[51]

There are two citations of other people of color that do not fit the mold of either the American or the East Indian records, both in terms of certainty of historical origins and transparency of thematic substance. They are therefore best regarded as *sui generis*. The first of these is the burial of "Anthoine an Egyptian" on 26 May 1553 (Item 122) in Gravesend, Kent, who may be a Gypsy or a Near Eastern person, but in either case is a person of a dark enough complexion to inspire the citation's particular description of him. There is also the possible christening record of "Jehan Vannaigre" on 13 July 1642 in London, in which the first name is possibly indicative of a Near Eastern Muslim name, and the surname suggestive of a corrupt ethnic descriptor of French lexical pedigree denoting in the root "naigre" a person of some color (Item 365). That this may be a Persian is suggested by the incidence of another individual of a similar name catalogued by E. K. Chambers in his listing of the personnel of the Elizabethan theatre industry, who is called "Jehan Sehais," the surname of which is compellingly suggestive of an Anglicization of the Persian name "Jehan Shah."[52] Listed euphemistically as a "player," he may be a gymnast and rope trick performer, and in that possessive of skills that Jehan Vannaigre might also have shared. The two Jehans may be part of two assimilated performers of Persian origin in early modern London, and of which Anthoine may also be a part albeit

[51] This phenomenon is almost perfectly evident in the case of the Powhatan chief's daughter, popularly known today as Pocahontas. Beneath the familiar story of her courageous saving of the governor of the Jamestown settlement of 1607, John Smith, from certain death at the hands of her tribe, and her conversion to Christianity, her romantic marriage to another English settler, John Rolfe, and her supposedly triumphant visit to England in great honor as the Lady Rebecca Rolfe, lies a very different set of details recorded by English sources themselves before the colonial propaganda about her takes hold. Matoaka, or Amonute, to use her American names, was in fact lured on board an English ship and held captive for a year, during which she was converted to Christianity and married to John Rolfe in an attempt to induce the Powhatan tribe to greater cooperation with the English. Her supposedly triumphant trip to England, which was in reality an attempt to display to the English public the success of English colonial efforts in Virginia, is belied by the barely concealed denigration of her, according to one observer, as "no fayre lady, yet with her tricking up and high stile and titles, you may thinke her … " and despite her wishes to see and know more the land of the English, the trip was is quickly brought to a close by their firm insistence that she leave. Some sense of her own feelings about her treatment by the English, while not committed to writing (because she was taught only to speak a smattering of English but not to write, in keeping with early modern English expectations about the desirable illiteracy of English women), is nevertheless obliquely evident in John Smith's accounts of both her captivity (in her "silence" and "pensiveness" during that time) and in the conversation he had with her at the inn in Brentford, England, where she was waiting for shipboard passage back to America just before she died. Her responses, both gestural and audible, recorded by John Smith, thus afford more instances of the possible speaking space of the black subject, such as those seen in the last chapter. For detailed examinations of these details of this unfortunate American's life, see the essays by Karen Robertson, "Pocahontas at the Masque," and Melanie Perreault, "'To Fear and to Love Us': Intercultural Violence in the English Atlantic."

[52] E. K. Chambers, *Elizabethan Stage*, 2: 338.

in the province, irrespective of whether his name is indicative of a Near Eastern person or simply of a Gypsy. If so, their unattached statuses would make them the exceptions among the records of people of color.

V

The complex heterogeneity of the records of Indians, Americans, and other peoples of color underlines their historical significance, despite their relative numerical leanness. That significance is best outlined in a statistical breakdown of the major trends and patterns in these records. As before, a necessary qualification that must preface such an analysis is that because it is based on the necessarily provisional character of the data it must be regarded as having a tentative and expository nature and containing values that can only be not absolute but approximate. Discounting the records mentioned but not listed in this book's index of records (such as the "two score" or "fifty" American records cited by Alden Vaughan), there are 32 references in 175 years of people of color other than black. Nine records are from the Elizabethan period, nine from the Jacobean years, and seven from the Caroline and Civil War years, including those of the Puritan government, and seven from the Restoration years. Of the total number of these records, 25 are from London, three from the western, southwestern, and southern counties, and three from the eastern or southeastern ones, with one record pertaining to an English ship on the Indian ocean. Among these records, there are 22 East Indians, eight Americans, and two individuals of possibly Near Eastern origins.

Observations that follow from this data include the following. Thirty-two records in 175 years reflect a citation frequency rate of one mention in 5.4 years. That ratio for the each of the political periods in the data amounts to one mention in 5 years for the Elizabethan records, one in 2.5 years for the Jacobean, one in 5 years for the Caroline and Puritan, and one in 2.42 years for the Restoration years between 1660 and 1677. The highest frequency ratios are those of the Restoration decades, followed by the Jacobean, while the lowest are those of the Elizabethan, and the Caroline and Puritan regimes (see Table 1). The two highest and near identical citation rates here are probably reflective of two different historical facts. First, the dominance of the Restoration ratios may be less surprising than it otherwise might appear if it is seen as a sign of the increased importation of people of color in general in those decades that is a spillover effect of the African slave trade's accelerating impetus. It may also be in part the result of the maturing of the activities of the East India Company in India, which, getting underway in the reign of James I, produced the Jacobean period's second highest rates for mentions of people of color other than black, within which it is East Indians who comprise the main category. For the same reason, the Elizabethan period has the lowest ratios of citations of non-African colored people, as the East Indian and American projects are just starting in roughly the second half of this regime, with the former at the very end of it. Secondly, the overall fall in the citation rates between the Jacobean and the Restoration years (to a level identical with that of the Elizabethan decades) parallels that phenomenon in the seventeenth-century London records and is caused by the same factor as in that dataset, namely the distractions caused by the political unrest of the king–parliament standoff and the uncertainty of the Civil War and of the regime change that it produced.

Table 5.1 Frequency of English citations of people of color (1502–1677)

Number of citations	Period	Frequency of occurrence
32	175 years (total)	1 in 5.4 years
9	45 years (Elizabethan)	1 in 5 years
9	23 years (Jacobean)	1 in 2.5 years
7	35 years (Caroline, Civil War, and Cromwellian Regimes)	1 in 5 years
7	17 years (Restoration and after)	1 in 2.42 years

The location pattern of these records also conforms to that of the black records. That 25 out of 32 citations or 78 percent of these records are from London parallels the predominance of London in the black records overall, which with 331 out of 448 records accounts for 73.8 percent of the total archives. As in the case of the black records outside London, the predominant sites are in the southwest and the southeast, which with three each constitute 9.37 percent of the total colored records. That ratio is roughly comparable to the 11.7 and 3.86 percent of the total black records from the southwestern and southeastern counties, respectively. This congruence of location patterns between the colored and black records not unsurprisingly confirms the topographic status of the southern English coastline as the natural staging area for the importation of black and colored people.

The gender and attached/unattached ratios of these notations (24 men to 8 women, and 8 attached for 24 unattached) are not particularly useful statistics because the records span three different ethnic groups. Still, the facts that women are mentioned only eight times, and individuals appear in clearly attached capacities only eight times, might point to an English political dynamic for the non-African citations that is different from the African ones; aside from the few enumerations of formal attachment the gender disproportion indicates a less comprehensive importation of people of color than would otherwise be the case if the gender numbers were more proportionate. But if that dynamic implies an English view of non-African people of color that is gentler than that toward Africans, that perception should be qualified by a reminder that twice as many of the records of this dataset are from the seventeenth century, with most from its first half, particularly those that depict these other people of color in seemingly lesser or non-menial situations. As was shown in Chapter 4, that is the time span during which there is a relaxation of racial attitudes toward black people as well. What strengthens this qualification is the fact the sole citation of a non-African specifically as a servant is from the Restoration decades, which is also the time when the denigration of the African intensifies in the mass black seizures of the slave trade. In the larger view, therefore, the records of East Indians, Americans, and others are a part of the history of black people in early modern England.

Of the two main ethnic groups in these records, the importance of the East Indian records is that they establish East Indians as an earlier English presence than has hitherto been known in scholarship of the period. The preponderance of baptisms in these notations of Indians, including several that were carefully organized public events in London, and the frequent allusions in them to high government officials, including those of the East India Company, shows that these unknown seized Indians weree a singular version of the bare life of the early modern English black in that their politicization as the racial subject—in the ceremonial staging of their conversion to Christianity—was English protocoloniality's formal exhibition of its reproduction of the black other as a simulacrum of itself. In that proud remaking such Indians became for the English civic imaginary the symbolic prize of commercial conquest and the human replica of the material bounty that such conquest holds—"the first fruits of India." Beginning to appear, as these baptisms in "ye publique congregation" do, in the first decades of the seventeenth century and shortly after the initiation of the initially exploratory and quickly institutionalized English voyages to India, these "willing[ly]" converted Indians became part of the demonstrative vindication of those enterprises themselves that was to continue through the century. The same politics constructs the others in this group whose less public conversions comprise the commonplace many that the visible few exemplify. Re-faced instantly by their symbolic representations in their conversions as proud specimens of Anglo-Christian triumph, these Indians also simultaneously engraved themselves into an aspiring English imperial metropolitanism that needed them even if as token cultural sacrifices to advertise its historical arrival.

Corresponding to the seizure and "willing" conversion of the Indian black is the American black's acquisition and happy compliance, archived in the postures of volitional obedience and resilient loyalty to the English state that makes up the kindness of its captivity. Less numerous than the African blacks, and less symbolically celebrated than the Indians, the American black occupies a minimal zone of luminescence in the English hierarchy of primitive life that defines the former's civility and sustains it. Its spectrality is the English fantasy of a natural ethnic subjection, echoed pointedly in Marlowe's *Dr. Faustus* in Valdes's explanation of the uses of the power that Faustus seeks: to "make all nations canonize us / As Indian moors obey their Spanish lords."[53] A like fantasy may write the sole instance of the Egyptian or Gypsy mentioned in these records, whose naming as "Anthonie" could reflect the subliminal longing for classical Roman imperial grandeur that typifies the Anglo-European protocolonial dream, a longing that is otherwise reflected in the noticeable incidence of *faux* classical names throughout the black archives as a whole. For both Indians and Americans the records faithfully tabulate the conversions that ready them for menial consumption, simultaneously illuminating and effacing them as a ghostly micro community that is and is not a distinct social group.

If the pattern of more common public documentation of the seizure and transportation of Indians to early modern England in the second half of the seventeenth century is revelatory of the later confidence of English colonialism's rapacity (and generally of the confidence of the European Atlantic slave trade which then is

[53] *Dr. Faustus*, ed. Michael Keefer, 1.2.122–23.

aggressively evident), does the relative silence in the East India Company's records in particular *before* 1650, about this nameless human traffic that it was conducting, silhouette the silent brutality of English colonialism's beginning moments, and the deliberate self-obliteration of early modern English culture's own troubling beginnings?[54] Furthermore, could the effect of the cultural differences of observed Indian culture, as in the accounts of Ralph Fitch and others,[55] and the lived English experience of the transported "Indians" in England presented here, together with those of Africa (as in Africanus, Hakluyt, and Purchas) and of seized Africans and native Americans in England (as recorded in local English archives), have produced in the late sixteenth and early seventeenth centuries what Etienne Balibar has described as the new racialism of the early modern period, that is, racialism based on tangible stigmata as distinct from the earlier, medieval religious racialism based on intangible difference?[56] And could the media of the popular English stage—which between 1550 and 1650 has nearly 300 representations of and references to Indians alone,[57] including the as yet unexplained Shakespearean references to the Indian boy stolen from his parents that Oberon and Titania fight over in *A Midsummer Night's Dream* (2.1.25, 2.1.123–37)[58] and to the "strange Indian with the great tool" that the porter suddenly invokes in *Henry VIII* (5.3.33–35)—have been the chief vehicle for the dissemination of this new racism that undergirded the rise of the Anglo-European cultural episteme that has produced the contemporary world? Were these, then, the real "first fruits of India?"

To conclude, these documentations of East Indians, Americans, and Near Easterners offer several points of confirmation of phenomena seen in the London records of this book. First, they demonstrate the same English behavior seen in the African theatre in which the search for trading commodities produced human beings casually included as material goods. The same predatory impulse and documentary reticence mark both spheres of activity, the latter in terms of the scarcity of the East India Company's written records about such activities. This contradicts in part the observation of some scholars about the inherent differences between the early modern English responses to Africa and to India.[59] Secondly, the conversion process resulted in the same naming pattern as in the case of Africans, in which

---

[54] Peter Stallybrass and Allon White, *The Politics and Poetics of Transgression*, p. 5.

[55] See John Courteney Locke, *The First Englishmen in India: Letters and Narratives of Sundry Elizabethans*. Fitch and two other Englishmen visited India in 1583, traveling incognito to reconnoiter India's resources and observe its peoples and their customs. Fitch returned five years later, and his enthusiastic advocacy of English trade penetration of India was instrumental in Elizabeth's first charter to set up the precursors of the East India Company in 1599; see esp. pp. 99–120.

[56] Etienne Balibar and Immanuel Wallerstein, *Race, Nation, Class*, p. 23.

[57] Figure compiled from a simple computer search of occurrences of characters designated as "Indian" in Chadwyck-Healey's electronic texts of Enbglish verse drama at the University of Virginia library.

[58] For a powerful theoretical discussion—but not a historical explanation—of the reference see Margo Hendricks's essay, "Obscured by Dreams: Race, Empire and Shakespeare's *A Midsummer Night's Dream*."

[59] Ania Loomba, "Shakespeare and Cultural Difference," pp. 176–77.

the surname acts as a crude ethnic descriptor, as in the case of Richard Indem or John Americanus, although other naming tendencies include the preservation of the original name, as in the case of Samuel Munsur. Thirdly, the morphology of religious conversion processed as an English political triumph and celebrated as a public event seen in the baptisms of several of the London Africans discussed in the book is replicated and confirmed in the treatment of Indians brought to England, explicitly in Peter Pope's case in the description of the event as the "first fruites of India."[60] Fourthly, as Africans of different regions are all negroes or blackamoors, so too are Africans, Indians, and Americans, indistinguishably. This is the historical grounding of Samuel Purchas's earlier cited cheerful conflation of people of different ethnicities and geographic origins, when he said "*India* [is] a generall name to all countries which are far-off and strange to us, although it be properly attributed to the East Indies." One distinction of the Indian records is that some of them seem to indicate an earlier date for the English importation of Indian people than that of Africans, the history of which must at this point remain unknown. Overall, both datasets significantly contextualize and expand the implications of the London black records explored in this book.

60 See Copland, *Memoir* for a full account.

Afterword

I

A statistical analysis of the black archives sampled in this study reveals several valuable patterns. But before embarking on such an analysis it is necessary to reiterate that the significance of the records lies not in their total number but in the predictive effect of their symptomatic nature. As has been implied throughout this book, the total volume of black records presented in this study constitutes only a symptomatic indicator of the black population in early modern England and not a representation of their actual numbers, which are liable to be higher. Several cogent factors mandate this understanding, and a summary enumeration of them may be helpful here, in this study's closing overview.

First, documentations of people, whether in government record, legal document, parochial notation, or personal observation, are imperfect activities in any age, and particularly so in the early modern period, when it is a relatively new cultural habit that is pursued unsystematically, incompletely, and whimsically by modern standards. The mobility of people even in the early modern age, and the inevitably imperfect mechanisms of their recordation, together with the variable responses that such mechanisms elicit from the very communities that are expected to subscribe to them, ensure a demographic picture that is partial at best. Furthermore, if the results of such incomplete demographic accounts survive at all they do so in what is best described as a state of greater or lesser obscurity, because of the illegibility of data unmoored from the cultural contexts of its archiving and the natural physical degeneration of documents over a period of time that exceeds the technological abilities of their preservation. Secondly, within this intractable incompleteness and precarious condition of the available demographic data, the recording of black people is an intrinsically accidental documentary event. Given the history of the illicit acquisition and possession of Africans in sixteenth- and seventeenth-century England, their recordation is anything but a purposive activity. Their appearance in the archives is the chance after-effect of a history that is not meant to be remembered. Thirdly, several complementary levels of erasure occlude the identity of black people as such. Without invoking an uncritical black essentialism, it is necessary to be aware of the defacement of African origins implicit in the processes of English assimilation, in formal baptisms as well as in the prolonged chattel domestication of Africans. Such processes immediately or eventually mask Africans irremovably under Christian names that are indistinguishable from those of the native English population. Compounding these obfuscatory effects is the informality of English naming practices that in silent homonymy combine English place names with ethnic descriptors as unmarked surnames, such as "moore" or "blackamore/blackmor." As a result, the black people in the English archives between 1500 and 1677 who can be seen and determined to be *such*, can only be the symptoms of a larger population that must now remain unavoidably invisible, but whose substance must be included however proportionately in any serious assessment of the historical black presence of the period.

The symptomatic nature of the records points, thus, to a larger population than that represented by the records cited here, who may not have been recorded, or whose recordation is yet to be discovered. As Philip Curtin and Ivan Elbl found in their studies of the early Portuguese Atlantic slave trade, subsequently visible archival data tends to be less than that known in contemporary accounts.[1] Although Curtin and Elbl use that phenomenon to adjust their final estimate downward, it is equally plausible to do the opposite—adjust the estimated tally upward, as Finlay and Shearer have done in their population studies, cited earlier. That upward adjustment may be additionally obligated by the fluctuation in the numerical contents of the black records, which can occasionally include more than one individual. In these considerations, the total volume of citations sampled here provides a reasonable range of data from which to draw some overall observations, even if of a necessarily tentative and prognostic nature. An important caveat applies to the number count used in the analysis that follows, and even for those used earlier in this book. Due to irresolvable ambiguities in some of the information of the records, such as black references in unspecified plurals, or in gender-indeterminate language, and because of possible variations in methods that can be used in computing total counts, including differences in subjective understanding of some of the criteria of the different count categories, such counts as are derived here cannot claim absolute accuracy. As a general rule collective or group references are counted as single citations, and where the gender is unspecified the reference is double-counted as both a male's and a female's. Double counting is also used to include an infant and its parent. By these procedures the numbers used in this book are expected to fall within a value of ±5 of counts derived by any computing method.

There are 448 records of black people between 1500 and 1677. That number is within an overall English population of between 1.4 million in 1500 to 5.6 in 1700.[2] Adjusting the total number of records upwards conservatively, by the same factor that Finlay and Shearer used, produces a possible black population that is .12 percent of the average English population in 1600.[3] That is not quite a numerically insignificant national ethnic group. Even taken as is, 448 records in 177 years yield an average frequency ratio of 2.5 per year. Even if the aggregate number of records is reduced by 10 percent, to filter out citations of ambiguous ethnicity, the frequency ratio is 2.3 per year. That means that minimally black people are occurring in the early modern English experiential knowledge that these records represent *more than twice every year* of the 177 years of this study's range. This would suggest that they cannot be anything less than a regular presence in the material landscape and the cultural consciousness of the period. However calculated, the numerical size of

---

1 Philip D. Curtin, *The Atlantic Slave Trade: A Consensus*, p. 17; Ivana Elbl, "The Volume of the Early Atlantic Slave Trade, 1450–1521," pp. 31–75, esp. pp. 31, 36).

2 David Sacks, "London's Dominion: The Metropolis, the Market Economy, the State," p. 23.

3 Finlay and Shearer use a factor of 10; see Beier and Finlay, *London 1500–1700*, p. 48. The figure for England's population in 1600 is taken from p. 39.

the black records relative to the total population cannot debar black people from historical consideration, since such consideration is given to other small alienated foreign groups resident in the country in this period, such as Hanseatic merchants and Huguenot and Dutch weavers. The significance of a small black population, however dispersed, is by that logic of as much value. At the same time, the histories of English xenophobic persecution of these groups cannot simply be equated with that of black people either, simply because what happened to the latter did not happen to them or to any other such groups—namely racialized mass slavery.[4]

The fluctuations within the overall frequency ratios of the black records reveal a picture that is both expected and surprising. The early Tudor black records extending from 1500 to 1557, and containing 124 notations in 57 years, show a yearly citation rate of 2.1. The Elizabethan records, going from 1558 to 1603, with 89 black notations in those 45 years, reflect an annual frequency figure of 1.97. Citations of black people in the seventeenth century, between 1603 and 1677, and numbering 121 records in that 74-year range, occur on the scale of 1.6 per year. Culling similar data from the mentions of black people outside London brings out a record frequency of one in 1.4 years. For Indians (Eastern and American), and people of other regions, the notation rate over the same period is one in 5.5 years (see Table 6.1).

Table 6.1 Breakdown of frequencies of English citations of black and colored people across different periods between 1500 and 1677

	Total number of records	**Total years**	**Frequency of occurrence**
Early Tudor records	124 (121)	58	2.1 per year
Elizabethan London records	89	45	1.97 per year
Seventeenth-century London Records	121	74	1.6 per year
Outside London (Provincial records)	85	119	1 in 1.4 years
Records of others of color	32	175	1 in 5.4 years

Two necessary qualifications in this data include first the fact that in the early Tudor period, the number of specifically black records is 121, three being of individuals of other backgrounds. Secondly, these 121 records are actually about 16 individuals. If that figure is used, as it more properly should be, the occurrence ratio of these records falls from 2.1 per year to one in 3.5 years. The lowest rates of occurrence then are for the early Tudor years, which confirms the assumptions of traditional English history. The Indian citations are of course lower still, and the outside London black records, while having an occurrence ratio that is higher than the early Tudor ones,

4 See, for instance, Linda Yungblut's discussion of such communities, *Strangers Settled Here amongst Us*, pp. 51–60.

is still low. Both of these data groups constitute a somewhat different, independent, category, given their more totalistic time range. The value of the Indian records is not in its numbers *per se* but in the fact that it breaks new historical ground in making analytically visible a subject previously unthinkable and unknown—East Indians, and in early modern England.[5] What should be equally startling is that the highest ratios are for the Elizabethan and the seventeenth-century records, with the single highest frequency figure occurring, not in the seventeenth century, as might have been conventionally suspected, but in the Elizabethan period. The highest ratios are also for mentions of London black people only, which at 1.27 per year for 226 instances in 177 years (sum of the top three columns in Table 1, and counting only 16 for the early Tudor group) is considerably more than the one in 1.4 years rate for citations of them elsewhere in the country. More narrowly, the highest reference ratio for black people, both elsewhere in the country and within London, is between 1558 and 1603, which for the former with 41 citations only in that period or about half the total number of records in that dataset has a frequency rate of 1.09 per year (see Table 4.1). That is roughly comparable with the 1.97 ratio of the Elizabethan London notations. What these multiple data patterns indicate is that the greatest number of black people in England's countryside and in its metropolis in fact occur in the very period traditionally assumed to be devoid of black people. As a matter of fact, 257 of the 448 records or 57 percent of the total records presented in this book are from the sixteenth century. That is, there are more black citations from the sixteenth than there are from the seventeenth century.

Patterns of black employment, service, and chattel exploitation in the different periods also contain important directions of developments in black history. Citations of black people in clearly independent professional capacities appear only in the early Tudor period, with 11 out of 16 records indicating such a scenario and representing 68 percent of that data set. In the other three record periods there are no instances of black people recorded in visibly independent professional lives. The question for the remainder of the records then becomes one of the relative proportions of the black people who are encumbered, i.e. attached, and unencumbered. In the 89 Elizabethan records 41 are of attached black individuals while 48 are of unattached ones, whereas in the seventeenth century records that ratio is 26 to 95, with more than half of the attached references (14) occurring in the Puritan and Restoration period alone. In the records of black people outside London, 45 out of the 85 notations are of encumbered individuals, with 25 of those occurring between 1558 and 1628, and only nine in its last twenty-four years. In the references to Indians there are eight described in an attached state of the 32 total references in that group (see Table 6.2).

[5] For an extended discussion of the Indian citations in the early modern English archives, see my essay, "East Indians in Early Modern England as 'The First Fruits of India': Colonial Effacement and Postcolonial Re-inscription."

Table 6.2 Breakdown of attached and unattached citations of black and colored people across different periods between 1500 and 1677

	Total number of records	**Attached**	**Unattached**	**Percentage of attached records**
Elizabethan London	89	41	48	46.06
Seventeenth-century London	121	26	95	21.48
Outside London (provincial records)	85	45	40	52.94
Records of Indians, Americans, and others	32	8	24	25

The highest rate of attachments is thus in the records of black people outside London, constituting 52.94 percent of the total of that dataset, while the lowest at 21.48 percent is in the seventeenth-century London archives. The Elizabethan citations of attached black people are the second highest, at 46.06 percent of its total data. Within these data streams, the combined highest frequencies of attached citations are those of the outside London black records between 1558 and 1628 (25 out of 85 attachments), and those of the Elizabethan London ones, with 55.55 and 46.06 percent, respectively. This homology of high percentages of citations of black possession within and without London over approximately the same period, i.e. during the Elizabethan and early Stuart years, is again inescapably descriptive of a peak of black incarceration in the precise decades usually thought of as being unaware of black people. What particularly profiles this striking conclusion is that the frequencies of attached black people in the Elizabethan decades and their immediate after years is that they are higher than even those of the century's last quarter, which amount to one in 1.5 years for 14 attached citations in 22 years for the seventeenth-century London records, and one in 2.6 years for nine attached black records in 24 years for the black provincial records.

The distribution of the black records' gender ratios is similarly instructive. The early Tudor records cite 13 men and three women, while the Elizabethan archives mention men 47 and women 49 times. For the seventeenth-century archives the breakdown is 77 male to 44 female citations, and for the records of black people outside London it is 49 male to 47 female notations. Of the 32 records of Indians and others, the figures are 29 male mentions to three women (see Table 6.3).

Table 6.3 Gender ratios in black citations across the different periods (* = includes double-counted figures).

	Total	**Men**	**Women**
Early Tudor	16 (in 124 [i.e. 121] citations)	13	3

	Total	Men	Women
Elizabethan London*	89	47	49
Seventeenth-century London	121	77	44
Outside London (provincial records)*	85	49	47
American, Indians, and others*	32	29	3

Notwithstanding the gender disproportion in all the data groups, the greatest congruence is between the first and the last dataset, with the numbers of the women in both representing a quarter and approximately a tenth of those of the men respectively. The middle three sets are both similar and dissimilar, the former in that they have the lowest ratios of the five, and the latter in that they all diverge from each other significantly. The lowest gender disparities, at 1.04, are those of the Elizabethan and the outside London figures, with the greatest at 1.75 in the seventeenth century.

Lower gender disproportions in this study's context are actually ominous signs, since they are indicative of the greater comprehensiveness of English importation of black people, and consequently of the greater degree of historical black captivity. Thus, the more telling figures here are those of the Elizabethan and outside London ratios, their numerical closeness yet again suggesting a link between Elizabethan London black history and that of the country at large. The greater difference of the black gender breakdowns of seventeenth-century London would then point in part to the relative racial relaxation of the metropolis in the century's first half and to the emphasis on black male importation in the third quarter of the century with the organization of the slave trade, and which would then quantitatively confirm what the examination of that data group showed in the book's third chapter. Confirming these conclusions are the facts that high proportions of the records of attached blacks are women in both the periods, and the highest incidence of sexual exploitation of black women in the totality of the records presented in this book occurs in the Elizabethan period within and outside London.

The range of baptisms or christenings, deaths, and marriages in the black records is just as revealing. Across the corpus of 168 London parish records, six are from the early Tudor period, 60 from the Elizabethan decades, and 102 from the seventeenth century. There are 81 deaths, 59 baptisms, and 28 marriages recorded. Whereas the early Tudor years have only five deaths, the Elizabethan period has 36 burials, accounting for 60 percent of its total parish records. Comparably, there are 40 deaths in the 77 years of the seventeenth century covered in this book, which comes to nearly 40 percent of the total records of that group. The highest number of christenings are in the seventeenth century, with 42 baptisms accounting for 41 percent of its total records, compared to only 17 baptisms comprising 28 percent of the Elizabethan notations. The same is true for marriages, with 20 marriages representing 19 percent of the seventeenth-century church archives, as against the seven marriages in the Elizabethan years making up 11 percent of its parish entries. Outside London, there are 71 church entries of black people, with 37 baptisms, 29 deaths, and five marriages cited in them. In the 23 Indian church records, 14 are baptisms, six are deaths, and three are marriages (see Table 6.4).

Table 6.4 Breakdown of black baptisms/christenings, marriages, and deaths across the different periods

	Total Parish entries	**Christenings/ baptisms**	**Marriages**	**Burials**
All periods combined	168	59	28	81
Early Tudor	6	—	1	5
Elizabethan London	60	17	7	36
Seventeenth-century London	102	42	20	40
Outside London (provincial records)	71	37	5	29
Indians, Americans, and others	23	14	3	6

That deaths are the highest of all the three categories of the early Tudor, Elizabethan, and seventeenth-century church records, comprising 81 out the 168 records of those data periods or 48 percent of their total, is, beyond the explanations of natural devastations like the plague and the great fire of 1666, grimly indicative of the desolation of black lives in the history of their English captivity. That the highest percentages of deaths are in the Elizabethan and the outside London or provincial data groups (36 out of 60 or 60 percent, and 29 out of 71 or 40 percent, respectively) is as before unavoidably indicative of the common politics that links these sets of records. That politics also explains the comparably high percentage of black deaths in the seventeenth-century London records (40 out of 102, or 39.2 percent). At the same time, the ascendancy of baptisms in the seventeenth-century London records, which while being a less bleak phenomenon registers the growth of an imperial English ideology that processes the possession of black and other people as its spiritual triumph, and that while providing the seized black subject a temporary respite will mutate into the mass devastations of the slave trade.

II

But perhaps what is most revealing in the data of the records is the geographic footprint of the black presence that it provides. Of the 448 citations sampled in this work nearly 350 of them, covering London entries of the sixteenth as well as the seventeenth centuries, show black people in 78 places, which includes nearly 70 percent of the over 100 parishes in the parochial administration of the city and its liberties that existed before its reorganization after the fire of 1666. This means that black people are present in almost every area of the city and its environs in every direction, at some point between 1500 and 1677. At the same time, the pattern of their location maps the history of their arrival as well as the conditions of their existence. One model of this are the 84 citations of them in the city's west side, describing their muted lives of decorative captivity in the mansions of the high and the wealthy, and the 46 notations of them in the crowded alleys of the eastern perimeters "pestered" up in the labyrinthine tenements of the small traders and middlemen whose chattel possession of them is the only means of their survival. Their spread across London's metropolitan sprawl can be clearly felt if their locations are plotted on a contemporary map, as Figure 6.1 does. Seen on such a map, the London black presence appears

Fig. 6.1 A partial representation of locations of black people in London between 1500 and 1677, as indicated by documentary citations. Map: Frans Hogenberg, "Londinum Feracissimi Angliae Regni Metropolis," 1572. Folger Shakespeare Library, Washington, DC. Key: triangle = early Tudor; star = Elizabethan; diamond = seventeenth century. All locations are approximate

ubiquitous. Outside London, the black geographic spread projected by the archives is just as comprehensive. Cited in Devonshire, Gloucestershire, Hampshire, Wiltshire, Kent, Essex, Northamptonshire, Hertfordshire, Bedfordshire, Buckinghamshire, Cheshire, Lancashire, Durham, and in Scotland, black people dot the English map, literally, as Figure 6.2 shows. They appear on English ships on the high seas, and in English consular offices abroad.

Most importantly, the locations of black people in London are coterminus with those of the personnel of what is early modern London's media industry, its public theatres, so that the black presence is inextricably intimate with the metropolitan cultural production of the age. The black presence is documentated in 90 percent of the neighborhoods dominated by the theatre industry, such as Southwark (The Rose, The Globe, The Swan), Bishopsgate and Cheapside (Cross Keys Inn, Mermaid Tavern), Aldgate (The Red Lion, The Boar's Head), Blackfriars (Blackfriars), Shoreditch/Hackney (The Theatre, The Curtain), and Clerkenwell (The Red Bull). As Roslyn Knutson has tellingly pointed out, players such as Robert Lee, Richard Darlowe, Thomas Goodale, Augustine Phillips, Robert Armin, Phillip Henslowe, Edward Alleyn, and William Sly, are living in Aldgate and Southwark in the very years during which black people like Suzanna, Symon Valencia, or Cassangoe

Fig. 6.2 A partial representation of the locations of black people in Britain between 1500 and 1677, as indicated by documentary citations. Map: Association of English Counties

are buried there.[6] James Burbage was buried in St. Saviour's, Southwark on 2 February 1595, within the same decade that "Edward, the sonne of Resonabell Blackman silkweaver" was christened there, while Nathan Field attended church in St. Mary, Overs (Overie) in Southwark in 1616, which he called "myne owne

6 "A Caliban in St. Mildred Poultry," p. 121.

parish Churche," because he had protested at being denied communion at that church sometime later.[7] William Shakespeare is recorded as living in Bishopsgate and Southwark in the 1590s, where black people such as those encountered in this book may also have been living, even if unrecorded.[8] The documented residences of black people in the very same neighborhoods in which English theatrical figures were present, and during the peak years of the English popular theatre, indubitably posit an empirical awareness in the latter of the former, with all the consequences that such an awareness obviously entails. Those consequences would constitute, then, the as yet unrecognized imprint of black people on the cultural life of the best-known period in Anglo-European history.

III

In order to bring to light a population that has been invisible not only to us but also to most of its contemporaries (slightly rephrasing here the question posed by Patricia Fumerton in *her* project),[9] there has to be a recursive linkage between "imprints" and "invisible" in the title of this study that radically qualifies both in a deliberately paradoxical double sense: even as what leaves imprints is no longer invisible, it is the imprints that are visible and not their imprinters. In this sense, "imprints" will have to work as both as noun and verb, as that which is visible will reveal by its very visibility that which is not. In Slavoj Žižek's terms, the imprint, while an immanent construct, is the virtual symbol of the racialized subject, the real of which remains the empty space vacated by the subject in its virtualization, to which the immanent imprint points and over which it dominates.[10] To appropriate Giorgio Agamben's terminology, the real of the racial is the excluded "bare life" of the pre-politicized natural man that will be the politicized exception of the black man included as the racial other of the socius symbolized by the imprint, an entity whose insideness is its outsideness, whose presence is its occlusion, and whose reality is its unreality.[11] The

---

7 For Burbage's burial see "Burials 1558–1699" in the Registers of St. Saviour's, Southwark, London Metropolitan Archives, MS X 094/096. Field's connection to St. Mary Overie is mentioned by Field himself in his letter, "Field the Players Letter to Mr. Sutton, Preacher at St. Mary Overs" in 1616, protesting what he implies is the preacher's attempt to "hinder the Sacrament and banish me from myne owne parishe Churche"; see Chambers *The Elizabethan Stage*, 4: 259. For more names, see Emma Marshall Denkinger, "Actor's Names in the Registers of St. Botolph Aldgate."

8 Samuel Schoenbaum, *William Shakespeare: A Documentary Life*, pp. 161–64.

9 "London's Vagrant Economy," p. 216; her question is, "How can we pretend to 'know' the vagrant subject when such a subject is virtually invisible and incomprehensible, not only to us but to many of his or her contemporaries?"

10 *Plague of Fantasies*, pp. 155, 163.

11 *Homo Sacer*, pp. 7–9, 11; see 97–101. esp. p. 99 for homo sacer as wax effigy. The term "socius" used here and throughout this work is drawn from Gilles Deleuze and Felix Guattari's invocation of the term (*Anti-Oedipus*, p. 10), and is meant to suggest the unarticulated but palpable sense of group identity that individuals invoke that is the subliminal impetus for the idea of a society, in which the ancient Greek idea of "oikos," meaning the naturally bonded relations of hearth and home, and the classical Latin idea of "socius," meaning the camaraderie of a

real of the racial is thus both the empty space vacated by the subject in its symbolic racialization and that racialized symbol itself, that is, a doubly virtual construct. The real of the racial as the unreal racial of the subject excluded from history is also the virulent taxonomy of the black archival imprint in its nominative range from "negroe" to "neager" to "negar" and "Ethiopian" to "Indian" to "Americanus," which is the tireless fixing of the infinite malleability of human difference against the self-sameness of the early modern English socius's morphology of itself.

In their macrological dimensions, the early modern English black records facilitate a responsible postcolonial critical perspective that illuminates both the consequences and the origins of the European colonial project, that is in the temporal modes of both colonialism's post- and pre-history, within the specificities of located histories of regional and temporal distinction. In such a perspective the black archival imprint is the virtual effigy of whiteness's alterity, the taxonomic mapping of which will be part of the colonial genome, and the bill of purchase for its possession, of the species. In this sense, the citational brevity, provisional lexicon, and variable syntax of the naming of the archives are the self-correcting gestational marks of the English colonial drive in its subliminal beginnings or the signatures of its protocoloniality. The virtual imprint as effigies of blackness encased in protective archives is, then, at once the etiolatory English protocoloniality's capture, transformation, and reproduction, that is, its seizure and mirroring, of the other in the likeness of itself, its translation of the *differend* of blackness into an acceptable simulacrum of difference that is neither the confidence of the stereotype nor the anamorphism of the unrecognized but that strives toward the former even as it issues from the latter. The discrete black archives are the first embodiments of this unstable knowledge construction that will become the virtual epistemology of English colonialism proper in its worldling of the world in the birthing of itself. That this protocolonial investment in the inscription of the visible stigmata of difference that is the archiving of the black signals the rise of what Etienne Balibar has called the new racism of the early modern period,[12] makes coherent the synchronicity and interdependence of the genesis of racism and colonialism in the history of modern Europe.

Imprint as stamping, however, is a bi-directional reflex—the convex force of an expurgatory defacement and the concave pressure of a cumulative in-growth—in which the protocolonial/colonial English socius's exclusionary gesture of differential stamping of the black subject is conversely the stamping of that socius's racialism by the black subject of its separation, otherwise the passing of Etienne Balibar's "prophylaxis" of exclusion into Michael Hardt and Antonio Negri's "negative dialectic of recognition."[13] This is the "blacking" of the white archives that in effect

---

freely chosen companion, are merged with the classical Greek notions of "politicos," meaning citizenry, and "politikon," meaning community to form the idea of a society (George Caffentzis, "On the Notion of a Crisis of Social Reproduction," p. 4), and that is both a "society-cause" and what the Marxist political philosopher Louis Althusser termed a "society-effect" (Jason Read, "A Universal History of Contingency," section 13), and that is the operational plane of a social consciousness that both directs and is directed by individual actions.

[12] Etienne Balibar and Immanuel Wallerstein, *Race, Nation, Class*, p. 23.

[13] Ibid., pp. 17, 24, 26; Michael Hardt and Antonio Negri, *Empire*, p. 128.

is the diffusion of the phenotype of early modern English cultural history, in Michel de Certeau's terms the return of the repressed to write itself on that which has read and written it,[14] and a resurgence of what Peter Stallybrass and Allon White have called the erased *ecriture* of that history's own beginnings.[15]

The documentary record is the plane of historical sight, the film of community vision on which is deposited the result of its collective seeing through the varied sightlines of government accounts, local ecclesiastical notations, and personal memory. As the product of a communal ocular memory, the documentary record is both formed by and reflective of the instrument of its recordation, displaying in its processed image that instrument's field of focus as well as its limitations. The documentary record is thus passive and active, registering the imprint of social sight while simultaneously penetrating the repertoire of that epistemology. It constitutes what might be described as the visibility sightline of the archives. As the visibility sightline, the archival document is the virtual machine of the prophylaxis of separation that imprints the cultural genetic code of the black subject's perpetual emergence-effacement in early modern English memory.

As part of the visibility sightline the arcane black documentary notation is the involuntary ocular reflex of the protocolonial/colonial English self as the shadow of the black other falls across it and obtrudes in its field of vision. Processed ocularly as cultural refusal, the black subject becomes protozoic debris in the corneal fluid of the English socius, not the object of its viewing but the imperfection in its vision. This is the black subject's marking of the eye of Anglo-European social seeing, even as in the extreme proximity of its location to the seeing instrument it is a supersight that does not just exceed that instrument's seeing and cognition but is also a distinct ontology for itself. These two symbiotic phenomena of black appearance-occlusion—the marking out of the black at both ends of its early modern English narrative as unrecognized life and as primitive life recognized as colonial prey, and the black's stamping in of itself on the resistant consciousness of a progressively imperial-colonial English sociopolitical life—comprise the invisible imprint of the black in the visible history of early modern England, the elided pre-history of its recorded history as the object of the slave trade. As the uninscribed English black individual arrives and disappears into a developing English protocolonialism, he/she emerges as the inscribed slave on which English colonial history constructs itself. The invisibility of the black is the visibility of early modern English material cultural achievement.

Perhaps as a final afterthought it needs to be stressed that what has been presented in this work is not the result of comprehensive and systematic searches of all available documentary databases. The Middlesex Quarter Sessions Rolls, the records of the Livery companies, or those of the High Court of the Admiralty, or even the Port books of London and the provincial ports, have not been combed. Much more, clearly, can be done. This work is thus a sample of what can be found, and in that it is an invitation to others to examine more early modern English databases for records of black people, perhaps in confirmation or qualification, or even contestation, of the historical scenarios sketched here. A fascinating and compelling untold story awaits.

---

14 *The Writing of History*, p. 14; *The Mystic Fable*, p. 9.

15 Peter Stallybrass and Allon White, *The Politics and Poetics of Transgression*, p. 5.

Chronological Index of Records of Black People, 1500–1677

Dating Procedures Used

To coordinate dates of the early modern calendrical system, in which the year ended on 25 March, with their modern equivalents, a split-year dating system has been used in which the second of the two dates in such entries refers to what would be the modern year for that date.

Item no.	Year	Location	Item	Document/ Source	Notes
1.	1500	Granada, Spain	3 October. Citation in Spanish royal correspondence (in the letter of Queen Isabella of Spain to De Pueblo, the Spanish ambassador to England, within the list of attendants to accompany her daughter, the Princess Catherine, on her impending journey to England and make up her household staff there): "Two slaves to attend on the maids of honour."	"Katharine Princess of Wales—List of Officers and Servants of her Household who are to remain with her in England." In *CSP/ Sp.* 1:246–47, Item 288, noted as S.E.T. c.1 L.2 1500 3 October.	Cited without source by: 1. Fraser, *Wives of Henry VIII*, p. 23, who describes then as "probably Moorish prisoners." 2. Sherwood, "Black People in Tudor England," p. 40. 3. NatArch, "Black Presence" Home Page, available at: <http://www.nationalarchives.gov.uk/pathways/blackhistory/early_times/settlers.htm> Seen 10. 15.04. Their page states: "In 1501, for example, we know that Catherine of Aragon landed at Deptford with a multinational and multicultural entourage of Moors, Muslims and Jews – descendants of those who had settled in Spain from the 8th century."
2.	1500/01	Edinburgh, Scotland	Royal disbursement. 13 February (under "the xiij day of Februar"): "Item to Petir the Moryen, the samyn day, be the Kingis command xxviij s."	*AHTS* 2: 96–97.	Editorial notation at the end of this item: "[And other similar entries]." The dates—for this and the next entry—should be 1500/01, to reflect the fact that even though in the pre-Gregorian calendric system in use at this time the year date will not change until March 25, by modern standards the year 1501 has already begun. The split year format is used predominantly in the rest of the *AHTS*.

3.	1500/01	Edinburgh, Scotland	Royal disbursement. 12 March: "Item, be the kingis command, to the Moryen, xv s. iij d."	*AHTS* 2: 99.	Editorial notation at the end of this item entry: "[And other similar entries]." "mor," "moryen," "morien," "more[s]," "moris," "Moriane"
4.	1501	Edinburgh, Scotland	Royal disbursement. 2 May: "Item the second day of Maij, giffin to Petir the Moryen, quhen he passit his way in France be the Kingis command, five French crounis summa. Iij. li. x. s."	*AHTS* 2: 106.	
5.	1501	London	Eyewitness account of Thomas More, while a student, watching the street scene of Catherine of Aragon's arrival in London with her royal train. November 1501: "At Hispanorum comitatus, proh deorum atque hominum fidem, qualis erat! Vereor ne si aspexisses ruptus ridendo fuisses, ita ridiculi erant; facies praeter tres aut ad summum quattuor vix tollerabiles; curui errant, laceri, nudipedes, pigmei Ethiopes; si affuisses ex inferis euasisse putauisses." ["But the Spanish retinue, alas, ye gods and men protect us, what they were! If you had seen them, you would surely have burst with laughter, they were so ridiculous. Scarcely three, at most four, of them were tolerable to look at. They were hunchbacked,	Original Latin text in More, *Correspondence*, ed. Rogers, p. 4. Translation by author.	

			tattered, barefooted, Ethiopian pygmies. If present you would have called them escapees from hell."]		
6.	1501	Cheapside, London	Eyewitness account of city official of Catherine of Aragon and her train arriving in the city. Friday, 12 November 1501: "The procession was concluded by Maids of Honour, ladies and gentlewoman in waiting (the Spanish women were marvelously dressed, but were not of the fairest) …"	"Third chronicle" in BL MS Vitellus A XVI , Book II, fol. 193^{r}, in *Chronicles of London*, ed. Kingsford, p. 334.	
7.	1501	Cheapside, London	Eyewitness account of city official, of Catherine of Aragon and her train, entering the city: "And aftir those v charys came ij other charys not so richely beseen, in which ij charys were Spanyssh women apparellyd aftir the Spanysshe fachion. Ther apparel was busteous and marvelous, and they were not the fairest women of the company."	"The Receyt of the Ladie Kataryne," fol. 42^{v} ,ll. 741–45, in *The Receyt of the Ladie Kataryne*, ed. Kipling, p. 33.	"busteous" = a variant form of "boistous," both late medieval/early modern English words meaning coarse, rough, rustic. *OED* 1: 302, 22.
8.	1502	Westminster, London	Eyewitness account of Robert Fabian of the transformation of three American men he meets, who in their dress and appearance seem perfectly assimilated into English society: "This yeere also were broughte vnto the king three men taken in the new founde Islande that before I spake of in William Purchas time being Maior. These were clothed in beastes skins,	"A Note of Sebastian Cabotes Voyage of Discouerie, taken out of an old Chronicle, written by Robert Fabian, sometime Alderman of London, which is in the custodie of John Stowe, Citizen, a diligent searcher and preseruer of Antiquities: Of three sauage men which he brought home and presented unto the king in the xvii yeere	Hakluyt is a prebendary of Bristol at this time, according to this volume's title page. Also advertised by the LMA on "Black and Asian Londoners" web page at <http://www.corpoflondon.gov.uk/Corporation/lma_learning/schoolmate/BAL/sm_bal_timeline.htm> Statement on page: "About this time … early explorers bring

			and ate raw fleshe, and spake suche speech that no man could understand them, and in their demeanour like to bruite beasts, whom the king kepte a time after. Of the which vpon two yeeres past I saw two appareled after the manner of Englishemen, which at that time I could not discerne from Englishemen, till I was learned what they were. But as for speeche, I heard none of them utter one word."	[1502] of his raigne"; Hakluyt, *Diverse Voyages Touching America*, ed. Jones, p. 23.	three American Indians, probably kidnapped, to Henry VII's court. An account at the time describes them as acting 'like to brute beasts'."
9.	1503/04	Edinburgh, Scotland	Royal disbursement. 12 January: "Item to Petir the More, in his pensoun, xiiij s."	*AHTS* 2: 415.	
10.	1503/04	Edinburgh, Scotland	Royal disbursement. 27 January (under "Item the xxvij day of Januar"): "Item to Peter Morien, in his pensoun, xiiij s."	*AHTS* 2: 417.	This could be a scribal error, since he couldn't have been paid his monthly pension twice in the same month. It could be his February pension, since no pension payment to him is otherwise recorded for February.
11.	1503/04	Edinburgh, Scotland	Royal disbursement. 30 January (under "Item the penult day of Januar") "Item, for ane steik chamlot, to Pete the More, V. ii."	*AHTS* 2: 318.	The items in these accounts are not always entered in a strict chronological order; see the *AHTS* editor's comment on 2: xiii. On the colloquial use of the name in this entry see Paul Edwards's comment ("Early African Presence," p. 17). "chamelot = a dress fabric of Eastern origin (*DSL*; also "Camelot"). Steik = a commercial measure of an item (*DSL*).

12.	1503/04	Edinburgh, Scotland	Royal disbursement. 24 February: "Item the xxiiij day of Februar, to Petir the Moryen, to fee him ane horse, to Dumfreis, vij s."	*AHTS* 2: 420.	
13.	1503/04	Edinburgh, Scotland	Royal disbursement. 9 March: "Item, the ix day of March, to Petir Moryen, in his pensoun, xiiij s."	*AHTS* 2: 422.	
14.	1504	Edinburgh, Scotland	Royal disbursement. 12 April (under "Item, the xij day of April"): "Item, be the Kingis command, to the Moryen taubronar, v Franche crounis, summa v li. xij s."	*AHTS* 2: 427.	"taubronar" = drummer (*DSL*).
15.	1504	Edinburgh, Scotland	Royal disbursement. 3 May: "Item, the thrid day of Maij, to the More taubronar, to his expens, maid be the Morienis, vij France crounis, summa vli xij s."	*AHTS* 2: 430.	
16.	1504	Edinburgh, Scotland	Royal disbursement. 9 May (under "ix day of Maij"): "Item, to Petir the More, in his pensoun, xxviij s.; and sa payit xj French crounis."	*AHTS* 2: 432.	This could be two month's pension—April and May—paid together, since no pension payment is recorded for April.
17.	1504	Edinburgh, Scotland	Royal disbursement. 19 May (under "xix day of Maij"): "Item, be the Kingis command, to Petir the Morien, ix s."	*AHTS* 2: 434.	
18.	1504	Edinburgh, Scotland	Royal disbursement. 21 May (under "the xxj day of Maij): "Item, to Petir the Morien, to fee him ane horse, and to pay for his lugeing in Striveling, ix s."	*AHTS* 2: 435.	

19.	1504	Edinburgh, Scotland	Royal disbursement. 13 June (under "Item, the xiij of Junij): "Item, to the Morien taubronar, xiiij s."	*AHTS* 2: 439.	
20.	1504	Edinburgh, Scotland	Royal disbursement. 21 June (under "the xxi day of Junij"): "Item, to Petir the Morien, to cum again fra the King fra Hammiltoun, xiiij s."	*AHTS* 2: 442.	
21.	1504	Edinburgh, Scotland	Royal disbursement. 4 July (under "the ferd day of Julij"): "Item, to Petir the More, be the Kingis command, iij s. iiij d."	*AHTS* 2: 444.	
22.	1504	Edinburgh, Scotland	Royal disbursement. 4 July: "Item, the ferd day of Julij, in Linlithgow, to the More taubronar, to fee him hors to Strivelin, and to pay for his lugeing in Linlithgow, xiiij s."	*AHTS* 2: 444.	
23.	1504	Edinburgh, Scotland	Royal disbursement. 27 July (under "the xxvij day of Julij"): "Item, to Petir the More, be the Kingis command, vij s."	*AHTS* 2: 449.	
24.	1504	Edinburgh, Scotland	Royal disbursement. 1 August (under "the first day of August"): "Item, to Petir the More, to pass his way for ever, be the Kingis command, iij ii."	*AHTS* 2: 450.	
25.	1504	Edinburgh, Scotland	Royal disbursement. 7 August: "Item, the vij day of August, to the four Italien menstrales, and the More taubronar, to fe theim hors in Eskdale, v Franche crounis; summa iij li. x s."	*AHTS* 2: 451.	
26.	1504	Edinburgh, Scotland	Royal disbursement. 11 September (under "Item, the xi day of September"): "Item, to the four	*AHTS* 2: 457.	

			Italien menstrales, and the More taubronar, to thair expens, and for thair expens in Dumfreis, vj France crounis; summa iiij li. iiij s."		
27.	1504	Edinburgh, Scotland	Royal disbursement. 13 September (under "Item, the xiij day of September"): "Item, for ane hors to the More taubronar, bocht fra Pete Johne, trumpet, be the Kingis command, vj Franche crounis; summa iiij li. Iij s."	*AHTS* 2: 458.	Edwards observes this is an expensive gift received by the African drummer ("Early African Presence," p. 18).
28.	1504	Edinburgh, Scotland	Royal disbursement. 13 September (under "Item, the xiij day of September"): "Item, to the Italien menstrales, and the More taubronar, to fee thaim hors to Peblis, xxviij s."	*AHTS* 2: 458.	
29.	1504	Edinburgh, Scotland	Royal disbursement. 26 September (under "Item, the xxvi day of September"): "be the kingis command, to the more taubronar, to red his lugeing and expens in Faukland, v s. x d."	*AHTS* 2: 459.	
30.	1504	Edinburgh, Scotland	Royal disbursement. 7 October (under "Item, the vij day of October"): "Item, to the four Italien menstrales, and the More taubronar, to thair hors met, to pas to the Month with the King, xliij s."	*AHTS* 2: 461.	The expression "hors met" which recurs in these accounts, refers to "provendar for horses" (*DSL*).
31.	1504	Edinburgh, Scotlans	Royal disbursement. 15 October: "Item, the xv day of October, in Brechin, to the four Italien menstrales, and the More taubronar, to thair hors met, xliij s."	*AHTS* 2: 462.	

32.	1504	Edinburgh, Scotland	Royal disbursement. 29 October (under "Item, the xxix day of October"): "Item, in Strethbogy, to the menstrales, and the More, to thair hors met, xiiij s."	*AHTS* 2: 464.	
33.	1504	Edinburgh, Scotland	Royal disbursement. 7 November (under "Item, vij day of November"): "Item, for hors to the More lasses and for carriage hors to the bestis to the Quenis Fery and syne to Inverkethin, and for their fraucht to the Fery, x s. viij d."	*AHTS* 2: 465.	
34.	1504	Edinburgh, Scotland	Royal disbursement. 7 November (under "Item, vij day of November"): "Item, to Mosman, Portingair, to red the Mores expens, the Portingall hors and bestis and folkis with thaim, in Inverketh, xxx s."	*AHTS* 2: 465.	"red" = to pay (*DSL*, 10a, b, c, d).
35.	1504	Edinburgh, Scotland	Royal disbursement. 14 November (under "Item, the xiiij day of November"): "Item, to the More taubronar, be the Kingis command, to his cheldis expens, the tyme the King was at the Month, xiiij s."	*AHTS* 2: 466.	This the first reference to the drummer's family.
36.	1504	Edinburgh, Scotland	Royal disbursement. 27 November: [the xxvij day of November]: "Item, to ane woman that tursit the More lasses fra Dumfermlyne to Edinburgh, iiij s."	*AHTS* 2: 468.	Five days earlier, on this page in the same volume of *AHTS*, a payment is recorded to "the man that brocht the Portugall hors with the rede tale and the must cat," which Edwards thinks were also taken from the captured Portuguese ship from which the two

					African women were seized ("The Early African Presence," p. 17 n. 34).
37.	1504	Edinburgh, Scotland	Royal disbursement. 11 December (under "Item the xj of December): "Item, quhen the More las was Cristinit, giffin to put in the candill, ix s."	*AHTS* 2: 469.	
38.	1504/05	Edinburgh, Scotland	Royal disbursement. 1 February (under "Februar," "Item, the first day of Februar"): "Item, to the More taubronar, xxviij s."	*AHTS* 2: 472.	
39.	1504/05	Edinburgh, Scotland	Royal disbursement. 3 February (under "Februar," "Item, the thrid day of Februar"): "Item, for xij cotis and xij pair hos half Scottis blak half quhit to xij dansaris be the More taubronaris devis agane Fasteringis Evin, be the Kingis command, xiij li. ij s. x d."	*AHTS* 2: 477.	
40.	1504/05	Edinburgh, Scotland	Royal disbursement. 13 February (under "Item, the xiij day of February"): "Item, foe ix 1/2 elne grene carsay to be tua gownis to the tua Moris; ilk elne iij s. vj d. summa xlvij s. 3d."	*AHTS* 3: 94.	
41.	1504/5	Edinburgh, Scotland	Royal disbursement. 23 March (under "Bursa Regis" [Miscellaneous expenses] (under "Item, the xiij day of March"): "Item, to the More taubronar, to pay for the paynting of his taubroun, xxviij s."	*AHTS* 3: 132.	
42.	1505	Edinburgh, Scotland	Royal disbursement. 5 May (under "Lie Wages: Item, the fift day of	*AHTS* 3: 118.	

			Maij"): "Item, to the More taubronar, his quarter fee, iiij li. vij s. vj d."		
43.	1505	Edinburgh, Scotland	Royal disbursement. 3 July (under "Item, the third day of Julij"): "Item, to William Wod, for the fraucht of the Portugall quhit hors, the must cat, and the jennet and the Moris, xii ii."	*AHTS* 3: 148	This item is probably a duplication of the record of the African women's seizure and arrival described in an entry of 22 November 1504 (see "Notes" to Item 36 above), and for some reason entered here on the wrong date, nine months later. The greater completeness of this record—it mentions the "Moris," whereas the earlier record left that out—suggests that this is perhaps a retrospective correction on the part of the the current Lord Treasurer, James Beaton, of the recording of his brother and predecessor, David Beaton, who does not appear to be Lord Treasurer after November 1504 (see the Edititor's comment on 3: xiv ff.). Edwards thinks this refers to a fresh group of Africans ("Early African Presence," p. 17).
44.	1505	Edinburgh, Scotland	Royal disbursement: 22 September: "Item, the xij day of September, for vij elne russait to the Moris; ilk elne, vj s. viij d.; summa xl s."	*AHTS* 3: 101.	On the same day, there are eight more items of payment for accessories for the dresses of the African women, such as collars, belts, girdles, etc.
45.	1505	Edinburgh, Scotland	Royal disbursement. 1 October (under "October"): "Item, the first day of October, to the Italien menstrales and the More taubronar,	*AHTS* 3: 163.	

			be the Kingis command, vj Franche crounis; summa iiij li. iij s."		
46.	1505	Edinburgh, Scotland	Royal disbursement. 11 November (under ("Lie Wages": Item, the first day of Januar"): "Item, to the More taubronar his quarter pensoun siclike, iiij li. vij s. vj d."	*AHTS* 3: 121.	
47.	1505	Edinburgh, Scotland	Royal disbursement. 26 November (under "Item, the xxvj day of November"): "Item, for v elne tanne to the More taubronar; ilke elne xiij s, iiij d.; summa iij li. vj s. viij d."	*AHTS* 3: 108.	
48.	1505/06		Royal disbursement. 1 January (under "Item, the third day of December): "Item, to the More taubronar siclike his quarter fee, iiij li. vij s. vj d."	*AHTS* 3: 122.	
49.	1505/06	Edinburgh, Scotland	Royal disbursement. 7 February: "Item, the vij day of Februar, for butis [and] schone, to Cristofer and Lady Mergret in the Castell, and the Moris, and to Curry Sen Alhallo day bipast, xxxj s."	*AHTS* 3: 182.	
50.	1505/06	Edinburgh, Scotland	Royal disbursement. 12 February: "Item, the xij day of Februar, to the More taubronar, be command, xxviij s."	*AHTS* 3: 182.	
51.	1505/06	Edinburgh, Scotland	Royal disbursement. 12 February: "Item, to the nuris that brocht the Moris barne to see, be the Kingis command, xxviij s."	*AHTS* 3: 182.	The notation leaves unclear whether the "barne" (baby) is the drummer's or one of the two black women's. Edwards thinks it belongs to some other Africans at court ("Early

					African Presence," p. 17). It is likely one of the two black women's.
52.	1506	Edinburgh, Scotland	Royal disbursement. 11 April (under "Item, the xj day of Aprile"): "Item, for ij pair grene carsay hos to the Moris lasses, vj s."	*AHTS* 3: 113.	
53.	1506	Edinburgh, Scotland	Royal disbursement. 14 April (under "Item, the xiiij day of Aprile"): "Item, to the More taubronar, Guilliam, taubronar, Adam Boyd, his son, Ansle, Guilliame's man, taubronaris, ilk man ix s; summa liiij s."	*AHTS* 3: 190.	
54.	1506	Edinburgh, Scotland	Royal disbursement. 1 May (under "Pensiones: Item, first day of Maij"): "Item, to the More taubronar, his quarter fee, to cum siclike, iiij li. Vij s. vj d."	*AHTS* 3: 124.	"cum" = to arise, to take source or origin *DSL* (entry #9), "siclike" = similarly (*DSL*). The sense of the combined phrase "cum siclike" is probably "to similarly begin," i.e. cyclically, with "similarly" referring to the immediately preceding entries of the same nature regarding other individuals.
55.	1506	Edinburgh, Scotland	Royal disbursement. 4 May (under "Item, the ferd day of Maij"): "Item, for vj paris schone to Marjory Lindesay, and the Moris with hir, viiij s."	*AHTS* 3: 114.	There is also a payment on the same day for "ane unce ribanes" for her.
56.	1506	Edinburgh, Scotland	Royal disbursement. 2 June: "Item, the secund day of Junij, to the More taubronar, to the mendis of the hurting of him, for the menstrales x Franche crounis; summa vij li."	*AHTS* 3: 197.	"mendis" = satisfaction or compensation for wrong done, loss or injury inflicted; recompense, reparation, redress; atonement, expiation (*DSL*).

57.	1506	Edinburgh, Scotland	Royal disbursement. 9 July: "Item, the ix day of Julij, agane the Kingis saling to Maij, for v elne yallow for ane cote to the More taubronar; ilke elne vj s.; summa xxx s."	*AHTS* 3: 115.	
58.	1506	Edinburgh, Scotland	Royal disbursement. 19 July: "Item, [thye xix day of julij], to [More taubronar] his leich, be the Kingis command, ix s."	*AHTS* 3: 206.	"leich" = physician (*DSL*). The item is probably connected to the medical care the More received when he was assaulted (entry for 2 June 1506)
59.	1506	Edinburgh, Scotland	Royal disbursement. 1 August (under "Item, the first day of August"): "Item, to the More taubronar, his wage of this moneth of August allanerly, xix s. li d."	*AHTS* 3: 126.	"allanerly" = solely, only (*DSL*)
60.	1506	Edinburgh, Scotland	Royal disbursement. 6 August (under "Item, the vj day of August"): "Item, to John Davidson, cordoner, for schone tane fra him to Lady Mergret the Kingis dochtir and Marjory Lindesay and the tua Moris fra Candilmis to this day, xvj s. ij d."	AHTTS 3: 155.	
61.	1506	Edinburgh, Scotland	Royal disbursement. 10 August: "Item, the x day of August, to the More taubronar and his leich, quhen he was hurt, xxxv s."	*AHTS* 3: 330.	
62.	1506	Edinburgh, Scotland	Royal disbursement. 27 November (under "Item, the xxvij day of Novembere"): "Item, for schone to La[d]y Margreit, the Kingis dochtir in the Castell, Marjory Lindesay, and the Moris, tane at divers tymes, xx s."	*AHTS* 3: 172.	

63.	1506	Edinburgh, Scotland	Royal disbursement. 7 December: “Item, the vij day of December, to Schir Patrik Crechtoun, capitane of Edinburgh [castell], for the barnis expens, and with her Marjory Lindesay and the Moris and servandis, for ane year, j^{c} li.”	*AHTS* 3: 175.	
64.	1506/07	Edinburgh, Scotland	Royal disbursement. 5 January (under “Item, the v day of Januar”): “Item, to the Capitane of Edinburghes wife for Lady Mergretis burd ane year, and with hir Marjory Lindesay and tua Moris, j^{c} li.”	*AHTS* 3: 361.	
65.	1506/07	Edinburgh, Scotland	Royal disbursement. 1 February (under “Item, the first day of Februar”): “Item, for tua quaris gold to illummyn the articules send in France for the justing of the wild knycht for the blak lady, x s.”	*AHTS* 3: 365.	This same document cost “xlij s.” to complete; see 3: 372 (“Item, the ix day of March, …”)
66.	1506/07	Edinburgh, Scotland	Royal disbursement. 26 February (under “Item, the xvj day of Februar”): “Item, to the said Johne [John Davidson, cordoner], for schone to the lady in the Castell, Marjory Lindesay and the Moris, Norne, and the Spanyart, at divers tymes, xxiiij s. iii d.”	*AHTS* 3: 370–71.	
67.	1506/07	Edinburgh, Scotland	Royal disbursement. 24 March: “Item, the xxiiij day of March, to the More taubronaris wif and his barne, xiiij s.”	*AHTS* 3: 377.	“barne” = child (*DSL*).
68.	1507	Edinburgh, Scotland	Royal disbursement. 15 May (under “Item, the xv day of Maij”):	*AHTS* 3: 387.	

			"Item, to the said Johne [John Davidson, cordoner], for schone and butis to Cristofer, Andro Home, the French boy, litil Martin, Norne, John Bute, the Moris, and Marjory Lindesay, Iij li x s."		
69.	1507	Edinburgh, Scotland	Royal disbursement. 22 May (under "Item, the xxij day of Maij"): "Item, to the moris wif and his barne, be command, xiiij s."	*AHTS* 3: 388.	This probably does refer to the black drummer.
70.	1507	Edinburgh, Scotland	Royal disbursement. 15 June (under "Item, the xv day of Junij"): 1. "Item, xxiiij elne taffeti for the chair triumphale for the blak lady, quhilk taffeti wes of the Flandrez taffeti befor writin." 2. "Item, xiiij elne j quarter quhit dames of Ingland to tua haf cotis to Maister William Ogilivy and Alexander Elphinstoun to be squeris to the blak lady, and sa all the quhit dames spendit."	*AHTS* 3: 258.	There are more than a dozen items of expenditures for details of the ceremonial dress of the blak woman on this date covering 3: 256–61. The "the Flandrez taffeti befor writin" refers to the item on 3: 256 (under "item, the xv day of Junii") "Item, bocht in Flandrez, be the Kingis command, j^{c}lx elne Flemys of taffeti, quhit, yallo, purpur, grene, and gray… ."]
71.	1507	Edinburgh, Scotland	Royal disbursement. 10 August (under "Item, the x day of August"): "Item, to the said Johne [John Davidson, cordoner], for schone and butis to Cristofer, Andro Home, litil Martin, the Spaniart, the French boy, Norne, John Bute, the Moris, and Marjory Lindesay, sen Beltane bipast, xliij s. iiij d."	*AHTS* 3: 409.	

72.	1507	Edinburgh, Scotland	Royal disbursement. 24 August (under "Item, the xxiiij day of August"): "Item, to Jhone Davidson, for schone to the Lady Mergreit in the Castell, the tua Moris, Marjory Lindesay, Litil Martin, John Bute and Norne, divers tymes, xxvij s. iii d."	*AHTS* 3: 336.	Either the records of this page are chronologically misplaced, or their transcription by the *AHTS* editor is misdated or misprinted, because between 3: 333 and this page, the date briefly jumps forward by a year from August 1506 to August 1507, before returning to 1506 in the subsequent pages.
73.	1507	Edinburgh, Scotland	Royal disbursement. 3 November (under "Item, the thrid day of November"): "Item, for schone to Marjory Lindesay and the Moris, iiij s."	*AHTS* 4: 82.	
74.	1507	Edinburgh, Scotland	Royal disbursement. 7 November: "Item, the vij of November, for iij pairis hos to Majory Lindesay and the tua Moris, viij s."	*AHTS* 4: 51.	
75.	1507	Edinburgh, Scotland	Royal disbursement. 3 December (under "Item iij December): "Item, for vij elne Scottis russet to the tua Moris; ilke elne vij s.; summa lvj s."	*AHTS* 4: 59.	
76.	1507	Westminster, London	Government payment record. 7 December: "Item to John blanke the blacke Trumpet for his moneth wages of Novembre last passed, at viij d the day –"	Exchequer Rolls of Henry VII, West.Arch E 36/214, f. 109 (7 Dec 1507).	Statement on City of Westminster web page at <www.westminster.gov.uk/archives/blackpresence/01.cfm>: "The first recorded presence of black people is that of the 'black trumpet' who was living in London in 1507. He was employed in the courts of Henry VII and later Henry VIII, and was twice portrayed on the painted parchment rolls of the

					1511 Westminster Tournament." *Westminster Tournament Roll* (1511). He was called "John Blancke." "It appears that John Blanke, a Black trumpeter, was a regular musician at the courts of both Henry VII and Henry VIII. Musicians' payments were noted in the accounts of the Treasurer of the Chamber, who was responsible for paying the wages. There are several payments recorded to a 'John Blanke, the blacke trumpeter'. This trumpeter was paid 8d a day, first by Henry VII and then from 1507 by Henry VIII."
77.	1507/08	Edinburgh, Scotland	Royal disbursement. 1 January (under "Item, the first day of Januar"): "Item, for iij elne lynyn to be collaris to Marjory Lindesay and the Moris; ilke elne iij s. summa vj s."	*AHTS* 4: 61.	
78.	1507/08	Edinburgh, Scotland	Royal disbursement. 7 February (under "Item, vij day of Februar"): "Item, iij pair hos to Marjory Lindesay and the Moris, viij s."	*AHTS* 4: 62.	
79.	1507/08	Edinburgh, Scotland	Royal disbursement. 8 February (under "Item, the viij day of Februar): "Item, to the Moris and Marjory Lindesay for schone the said tyme, vj s."	*AHTS* 4: 100.	
80.	1508	Edinburgh, Scotland	Royal disbursement. 28 March: "Item, the xxviij of March, for xvj elne quhit carsay to be tua kirtillis to the More freris' ilke elne, iiij s. vj d."	*AHTS* 4: 62.	"frer" = friar (*DSL*).

81.	1508	Edinburgh, Scotland	Royal disbursement. 25 April (under "Item, the xxv day of April"): "item, to the blak More freris, vj Franch crounis iiij li. iiij s."	*AHTS* 4: 112.	
82.	1508	Edinburgh, Scotland	Royal disbursement. 10 May (under "Item, the x day of Maij"): "Item, for vij elne demy Ostad grene to be ane kirtill to the blak lady; ilk elne iij s.; summa xxj s."	*AHTS* 4: 64.	On this same day, on the same page of the *Accounts*, mention is made of dress items for the black lady's "madinnis" (maiden, i.e. maids). Also, there are some unspecified payments to the two black women on 7 May 1508, who are cited by the editor simply as "the two Moors" (*AHTS* 4: 116).
83.	1508	Edinburgh, Scotland	Royal disbursement. 31 May "Item, the last day of Maij, to the xiiij men that bure the blak lady fra the Castell, to the barres and syne to the Abbay, xxviij s."	*AHTS* 4: 119.	
84.	1508	Edinburgh, Scotland	Royal disbursement. 27 June (under "Item, the xvij day of Junij"): "for bukkiling and grathing of Martin and the blak lady agane the bancat, xiiij s."	*AHTS* 4: 129.	
85.	1508	Edinburgh, Scotland	Royal Disbursement. 5 August: "Item, the v day of August, to John Knoxe for the expens of the More freris quhen tha wer heir, xiiij li."	*AHTS* 4: 139.	
86.	1508	Edinburgh, Scotland	Royal disbursement. 9 November (under "Item, the ix day of November"): "Item, to the blak freris in Elimose, xiiij s."	*AHTS* 4: 178.	
87.	1511	Edinburgh, Scotland	Royal disbursement. 15 December (under "Elen More"). "Item,	*AHTS* 4: 232.	This is the first time one of the black women is named, presumably

			the xv day of December, for hir leveray gonne agane Yule, iiij ½ elnis Rissillis broun; price elne xxvj s. viij d.; summa xxx s."		inspired by the festivity of the Christmas ("Yule") season, Christmas itself falling on 5 January (*DSL* entry for "Yule"). There are eight more payments for other accessories for her dress on this same date.
88.	1511/12	Edinburgh, Scotland	Royal disbursement. 1 January (under "Item, the first day of Januar, beand New Yeris day"): "Item, to Elen Moire, v Franche crounis iij li. x s."	*AHTS* 4: 324.	This item appears among a series of New Year's gifts to several court favorites. In the pre-Gregorian calendric system used in these records, January 1 was called New Year's Day even though the year date did not change until after 25 March.
89.	1511/12	London	Payment record. "John Blak's Marriage," 14 January: "Warrant to the Great Wardrobe to deliver John Blak 'our trompeter.' A gown of violet cloth, &c. including a bonnet and a hat, 'to be taken of our gift against his marriage.' Greenwich, 14 January 3 Henry VIII."	Exch, Accts. 417 (6), f. 50. R.O., in *L&P H VIII*, 1.1: 505 #1025.	
90.	1512	Edinburgh, Scotland	Royal disbursement. 28 March: "Item, the xxviij day of Marche, to the Bischop of Murrais more, at brocht ane present to the king efter his command, xiiij s."	*AHTS* 4: 338.	
91.	1512	Edinburgh, Scotland	Royal disbursement. 5 April (under "Item, the v day of April"): "Item, to Margaret Moire in Linlithgow, xiiij s."	*AHTS* 4: 339.	This is the other named black woman in these records. She and Elen could be the "tua Moris" of the previous entries, or the two names could be referring to the same individual.

92.	1512	Edinburgh, Scotland	Royal disbursement. 10 August (under "Item, the x day of August"): "Item, deliverit to the Maister Maxwell to the blak freris, ij Franche crounis, xxviij s."	*AHTS* 4: 191.	
93.	1512	Edinburgh, Scotland	Royal disbursement. 2 December: "Item, the second day of December, for iiij elnis ane quartar Franche russet to the Quenis blak madin, ilk elne xvij s.; summa iij li. xvj s. vj d."	*AHTS* 4: 428.	
94.	1512/13	Edinburgh, Scotland	Royal disbursement. 1 January (under "Item, the first day of Januar, viz. New Yere day"): "item, to the twa blak ladies, x Franche crounis summa vij li."	*AHTS* 4: 401.	The item appears among numerous New Year gift notices.
95.	1512/13	Edinburgh, Scotland	Royal disbursement. 3 February (under "Item, the third day of Februar"): "Item, pait to the said Johne Davidson [cordiner], for schone, butis, tane fra him to Schir James Hammiltoun, Watte Stewart, Barone, Symond, lutar, Mownis, the Baillie of Feris sone, and Johne of Bute; and to Marione Stewart, Maistress Musgrave, Elene Stewart, and blak Ellene, fra Lammes to Alhallo day bypast, the tyme the Bischop of Cathnes was Thesaurar, vli xij d."	*AHTS* 4: 404.	
96.	1513	Edinburgh, Scotland	Royal disbursement. 31 May: "Item, the last day of Maij, for v elne Franche russet be ane goun to Blak Elene; ilke elne xx^{tj} s.; summa v li."	*AHTS* 4: 434.	Two other items of expenditure are recorded on this day for accessories for her dress.

97.	1513	Edinburgh, Scotland	Royal disbursement. 19 July "Item, the xix day of Julij, for iiij elnes of fyne russet to blak Margaret ane goun; elke elne xij s.; summa xlviij s."	*AHTS* 4: 436.	
98.	1523 (1523–24)	1. London 2. St. Martins Parish, Canwickstreet Ward, London	Tax record. 1. (Under "Lay Subsidies Additional": "'Assessment of anticipation of Subsidy,' 15 Henry VIII (1523–24), on the Queen's Chamber": "The Queen's Chambour": "*The Stable*": "Straunger":) "Fraunces Negro, for fee and wages x.li … xxs." 2. "Francisco Vynegre."	1. *RA*, Lay Subsidies, Additional 1523–4. 3: 301. 2. *RA*, Lay Subsidies, Additional 1523–4, 1: 2.	
99.	1527	Edinburgh, Scotland	Royal disbursement. 22 August (under "Item, the xxij day of August"): "To Helenor, the blak moir, xl s."	*AHTS* 5: 328.	
100.	1541	St. Mary Woolnoth, (Langborne Ward), London	London subsidy roll (Tax assessment). "LANGBORNE WARDE: Petty collectors: Thomas Curtes of the parish of St. Edmund the King and Martyr, pewterer, and William Chester of the same parish, merchant taylor: Seynt Mary Wolneth perryshe: Dyego Negro servaunt with Thomas Bowyer [assessed] 4d."	"1541 London Subsidy Roll: Langbourn Ward," *Two Tudor Subsidy Rolls*, pp. 87–95; *RA*, 1: 46.	
101.	1543	St. Margaret's, Westminster (London)	Burial. 16 April: "Alys Blackman."	*Memorials of St. Margaret's Church*, p. 378.	
102.	1544	St. Peter Cornhill, London	Burial. 13 August: "Burying of Jeames Blackemore, the 13th of August."	*Registers of St. Peter Cornhill*, p. 107.	The first name is entered in the Index (p. 268) as "James," which is probably the editor's emendation of the original spelling of the name.

103.	1545	Greenwich, London	Privy Council payment record. 4 July: 1. (under "Att [*sic*] Grenewiche, the iij^{de} of July"): "Warrant was addressed to ____ … to captayne Negro, Spanyard, xxv^{li}; … ." 2. (under "Augmentations") "4 July, … Peter mogo, reward 25*l* … ."	1. *APC* 1: 207–8, fol. 73. 2. *L&P H VIII* 21.1: 313, Item 643 'Augmentations,' fol. 68.	
104.	1545	St. Margaret's, Westminster (London)	Burial. 5 October: "Agnes Blackmore."	*Memorials of St. Margaret's Church, Westminster*, p. 383.	
105.	1546	Westminster, London	Privy Council payment record. 8 August: 1. (under "At Westminster, the viijth of Auguste") "Warrant was addressed to Sir John Williams to paye by waye of rewarde unto sundry capitaynes, Spaniardes and others, as followeth … to Capitayne Petro Negro, lxxv^{li}… ." 2. (under "Meeting at Westminster 8 August") "Warrant to Williams for rewards as follows, to … Capt. Petro Negro *75l.*"	1. *APC* 1: 511, fol. 548. 2. *L&P H VIII* 21.1:718, Item 1433.	This handsome payment was specifically for loyalty: Peter Negro and his colleagues had accompanied one of their comrades, Julian Romero, to Fontainebleau in France a month earlier, in his confrontation and punishment by execution of one of their former colleagues, Antonio de Mora, for deserting his contractual service to the English in the siege of Boulogne. See *APC* 1: 501. For an account of the incident see Millar, *Tudor Mercenaries*, p. 170.
106.	1546	London	Privy Council payment. 4 October: 1. (under "Documents signed by Stamp") "51. Peter Negro. Annuity. *G* 4 October." 2. (under "Grants in October, 1546") "14. Peter Negro, Spaniard, the King's servant. Annuity of 100*l.* Windsor, 25 Sept. 38 Hen. VIII. *Del.* 4 October … ."	1. *L&P H VIII* 21.2: 85, Item 199.51. 2. *L&P H VIII* 21.2: 156, Item 332.14.	This annuity is also in reward for loyalty for the incident cited in the "Notes" to Item 102.

107.	1547	Roxburgh, Scotland	Accounts of royal award. 28 September (under "Wednesday, the 28th of September"): "My Lord's Grace, considering that of virtue and well doing the proper need is honour (as well therefore as reward to them that had afore done well, as for cause of encouragement to others, after, to do the like) did this day afternoon, adorn many Lords, Knights, and Gentlemen, with dignities as follow … [under "Knights"] Sir Peter Negroo."	Patten, *The Expedition into Scotland, 1547*, reproduced in *Tudor Tracts*, ed. Pollard, pp. 148–50.	
108.	1547/48	Southampton, Hampshire, and London	Court record. 8 February: "Mercurij viij° Februarij anno d[omi]ni second[um] computac[ione]m Anglicanum 1547 Reg[ni] supreme d[omi]ni n[ost]ri Edwardi sexti anno primo secondo. Petrus Paulo contra Dominicum Erizo: (*Wednesday 8th February in the year according to the English computation 1547 [modern year 1548] in the second year of the reign of our supreme lord Edward the Sixth: Peter Paulo against Dominico Erizo*) : Testimony of a black diver, Jacques/James Francis: "That the sayd Dominico Erizo dyd by force take waye from the sayd Peter Paulo one pece of tynne w[hi]ch the same Peter Paulo founde ij myles from Hampton (*Southampton*) in the see	NatArch HCA 13/93, fols. 275–76.	Also see: (a) "A Black Diver Gives Evidence: Papers relating to a suit (claim) and countersuit before the High Court of the Admiralty in 1547/8 give us a glimpse of one slave working in Tudor England. In November 1546, a merchant ship, the *St Mary and St Edward* of Southampton, caught fire and sank while riding at anchor two miles off Southampton. An Italian salvage operator, Pietro Paulo Corso, was hired to recover tin and lead from the ship, these being the only salvageable parts of a cargo valued at £6,000. Domenico Erizo, one of the consortium of Florentine and Venetian merchants who owned the cargo, subsequently claimed that Corso had secretly removed tin from the sunken ship and hidden it away

			and brought uppe the same and evey payd for the takyng thereof But sayd falsely that the same Peter had stolen hit to his hynderaunce … " Counter testimony of Anthony Rimero: "That in August and September and october 1547 this deponent beyng at Southe hampton dyd perfetly see perceave and knowe the same James Fraunces slave to the sayd paulo John Ik George Blake and ij other whoes names he knoweth not were by all the sayd tyme servauntes to the same paulo he payeng for ther meate and dryncke at the Dolphin in hampton where sondry tymes this deponent was present … That the sayd James Fraunces and thother wytnes before namyd be all poore laboryng men and sekyng ther levyng abowte in sondrye places where they maye gett hit having but letle of ther owne that his deponent did harde of … That the sayd James Fraunces ys a morisco born where they are not christenyd and slave to the sayd peter paulo who hathe in this deponentes presens offeryd hym to sell to any that wold have bought hym And therefore he beleavythe that no Credite nor faithe ought to be geven to his Sayenges as in other Strange Christian cuntryes		for his own benefit. One of Corso's divers in this salvage operation was a man called Jacques Francis, a slave from Guinea in West Africa. We know something about his role because he and other witnesses gave depositions (statements under oath) in support of Corso's claim against Erizo for damages and/or Erizo's countersuit. A number of these depositions display unfavourable attitudes towards slaves or Blacks as witnesses." NatArch "Black Presence" Home Page at: <http://www.pro.gov.uk/pathways/blackhistory/early_times/settlers.htm> (seen 11.19.04). This is an important instance of (i) black people in legal records and (ii) primary evidence of responses to black people. (b) Knighton and Loades, *Letters from the Mary Rose*, pp. 122, 132, 133, for earlier references to Peter Paolo in the unsuccessful salvage operations on the *Mary Rose* in Portsmouth harbor between 1545 to 1549. Francis must almost certainly have been with Paolo in this project as well, given the almost overlapping dates and locations of the

			hit ys to no suche slave geven … ." [Extract from NatArch transcription]		two jobs—which cannot, however, be regarded as one and the same, since the ships named are different: the warship, the *Mary Rose*, which keeled over and sank off Portsmouth in 1545, and the the merchant ship, the *St. Mary and St. Edward*, which caught fire and sank off Southampton in 1547.
109.	1548	Greenwich, London	Privy Council payment. 17 April (under "Sundaye, the xvth of April, 1548, at Grenewiche."): "*xvij^{o} Aprilis.* Theexcheaquier [*sic*] had two warrants to paye to the same Sir Christofer [Christofer Diaz] and to Pedro Negro, sent northwards, theyre half yeres pencion to be due at Mychelmas next."	*APC* 2: 183, fol. 303.	
110.	1548	Greenwich, London	Privy Council payment (Exchequer disbursement). 30 April (under item # "38 April 30. Declaration of fees paid by royal warrant out of the Exchequer to foreigners"): "Petro Nigro—£100, for life."	*CSP/D E VI*, p. 12.	
111.	1548	All Hallows, Bread Street, London	Burial. 8 November: "Henrye Blackemer, servant unto Mr. Lordynge."	*Registers of All Hallows, Bread Street and St. John the Evangelist, Friday Street*, p. 157.	In the Index of this volume on p. 247 the last name of this item is listed as "Blakemore (Blakemer)," which is the editor's indication that "Blackemer" should be regarded as "Blakemore." This probably is a black person.
112.	1548/49	Westminster, London	Privy Council payment. 2 March (under *ij^{o} Martij.*"): "Theexcheaquer [*sic*] had warrant for ciij^{c}lj^{li} v^{s} to … and to Petro Negro, by way of reward	*APC* 2: 261, fol. 492.	

			for his charges in keeping toguither of c souldiours Spanierdes."		
113.	1549	Edinburgh, Scotland	Scottish aristocratic correspondence [Maryon, Lady Hom[e]] to the Queen Dowager [Mary of Lorraine/Guise]. 28 March: "Home [estate of] 28th March [1549]: "Als sua I beseik your grace to be gud prenssis to the Spanygyarttis and lat tham cum again, for tha do lyk noble men, and als suay the Mour. He is als scharp ane man as rydis, beseking your grace to be gud prenssis unto him."	Cameron, ed. *Scottish Corr. Mary of Lorr.*, pp. 296–97.	"prenssis" = princess (*DSL*); "sua," "suay" = thus, in this fashion, in the manner just described (*DSL*).
114.	1549	Westminster, London	Privy Council payment. 7 April (under "Sunday, the vijth of April, 1549"): "The same Thresaurer ["The exchequer"] had like warrant for Sir Peter Negro for one half yeres pencion for his better furniture, being appointed the leading of ij ensignes of Spaniardes serving the North which ar now joined in oone."	*APC* 2: 275, fol. 510.	
115.	1549	Westminster, London	Privy Council payment. 25 April (under "*xxvº Aprils.*"): "Mr. William had warrant for … moreover to captein Petro Negro for xlli for one monethes wages afforehand to xl Spanyardes here mustred and appoynted to be joyned to the rest of his band in the Northe; to be paid of the sales."	*APC* 2: 279, fol. 515.	
116.	1550	Westminster, London	Privy Council payment. 27 March (under "At Westminster … Thursday,	*APC* 2: 419, fol. 129.	

			the xxvijth of Marche"): "Warrant to ___ viij^{eli} for Edward Grymston esquier, to be by him payd over to the bandes of Julian Romero, Pedro Negro, and John [*sic*] de Guevarra."		
117.	1550	Greenwich, London	Privy Council payment. 10 April (under "At Grenewich … Thursday, the xth of Aprell, 1550."): "Warrant to _____ for $^{ml\,n}$ to John Grymston, for the wages of John de Guevarra, Juiio Romero, Pedro Negro, and their bandes for one monethes wages, begyning the xixth of Marche and ending the xxvijth of this present, for a full contentacion of them all."	*APC* 2: 427–28, fol. 141.	
118.	1550/51	St. Margaret's, Westminster (London)	Burial. 22 March: "Salamon Nurr."	*Memorials of St. Margaret's Church*, p. 389.	Very likely, an Anglicization of a Muslim name: Suleiman Noor. On the same page of this register there is also a burial entry for 4 April for a "Collet Nurr," presumably his English wife.
119.	1551	Prerorogative Court of Canterbury, London	Recorded will. 4 August: "I Peter Negro saye that forasmoche as … I fele my self yll of bodye but hole of understanding and naturall judgment whiche yt pleased our lord god to give me/ … and considering that we be all mortall and that also at this present deathe mighth appear upon me as yt is naturall to men/ As a faithfull to pray I [commend] my soule to hym whiche made yt/ And I saye touchyng my	"Will of Peter Negro 04 Aug, 1551." NatArch PROB 11/34.	

			goods temporall I require Capitayn Cristofer Dyaz as my friende/ … that he take all my goods whome I make my executer wher of fyrst I requyre hym to paye my debts/ And of the rest … hand yt to my sonne … when he ys of age/ And yn the meane tyame to put them where they may be kept … and assured/ which goodes ar a chayur of gold that weyeth seven and seventie ounce of gold/ and more five hundrith ducatts … wher of I gave and [assign?]/ and all the movables of my house I will to be solde and to make money there of and to depose yt … for my childe likewise I requyere Capitayn Christofer Dyaz to restore and discharge my consyceince in those things … / and yf by fortune that a doughter that I have in Ittaly to be approved to be my doughter/ then I will she haue [fiftie?] ducats/ witnessed at the making of this testament … monthe of Auguste … Cristofer Dyaz."		
120.	1552	London	Diary entry. 14 July (Peter Negro's funeral): 1. [under "*The ensuing imperfect passage probably relates to the funeral of sir Peryn Negroo knt. (Strype, Mem. II. 279)*"] … targett, elmet, and sword … and apone the castyll a man with a shurt of … hand and with xij	Henry Machyn, *Diary*: 1. p. 8. 2. p. 320, Notes to p. 8.	Before Machyn's *Diary* was partly damaged by fire, particularly the pages of entries for the earlier years, John Strype had made copies of most of them. The relevant missing sections are provided by the *Diary*'s editor John Nichols, from Strype. Strype's transcriptions, however, contain

			staffes, torchys bornyng … flut playng, hoveles, and ys flag borne, and … in the grond, and the stret honge with blake with ys armes … ther dyd pryche the Doyttur Bartelet, and ther was the compeny [of Clarkes] and a harold of armes, and mony morners of capt. …. 2. "*Funeral of sir Peter Negro.* 'Sir Pyter Negro knight dysseased the xiiijth day of July in the yere of our Lord 1551, in the vth yere of the raigne of our soveraigne lord kyng Edward the 6. His crest is a castell broken, and upon the castell a man with a shert of male and a sword in hos hand.' (Harl. 897, fol. 14^{b}) He was one of the knights made by the Duke of Somerset after the taking of Leith, September 28, 1547."		numerous errors, as Nichols points out in a footnote on p. vi. Strype has evidently misdated the entry for 1551 whereas it must be 1552 since)a) according to his own transcription the "vth yere of the raigne" of Edward VI would be 1552, and (b) Peter Negro obviously could not have made his will in August 1552 if he died in July 1551.
121.	1553	Cheapside, London	Elizabethan antiquarian citation. n.d.: "… in Queene Maries time, there was a Negro made fine Spanish needles in Cheapside, but would neuer teach his Art to any."	Harrison, *Harrison's Description*, 2: 34; cited in Arnold, *Queen Elizabeth's Wardrobe*, p. 182.	In the Kraus reprint of Furnivall, this item is in the second volume—series 6, nos. 5, 8.
122.	1553	Gravesend, Kent	Burial. 26 May: "Anthoine an Egyptian."	Sherwood, *Faversham Society Newsletter*, 450 (October 2001).	
123.	1553/54	Reading, Berkshire	Christening. 12 March: "Peter Indine."	IGI.	
124.	1556/57	St. Margaret's, Westminster (London)	Burial. 6 January: "John A Moore."	*Memorials of St. Margaret's Church, Westminster*, p. 396.	
125.	1558	Boughton-under-Blean, Kent	Burial. 26 July: "Rose Blackamoor."	Registers of Boughton-under-Blean, Kent, Canterbury Register Office.	

126.	ca. 1560	Bristol (and London)	Court of Star Chamber testimony. 1. "He [Younge] 'did appointe a blacke moore to keep possession of his garden.'" 2. "a 'blackmore' gardener was employed in the merchant Sir John Young's 'Great House backing onto Bristol's quayside'."	1. Jones and Youseph, *Black Population*, p. 2. 2. Dresser, *Slavery Obscured*, p. 10	
127.	1565	St. Mary the Virgin, Aldermanbury, London	Baptism. 6 May: "Jhon the Blackamoor."	*Registers of St. Mary the Virgin, Aldermanbury*, p. 26.	
128.	1566	St. Mary the Virgin, Aldermanbury, London	Burial. 23 May: "Jhon a Blackamoor."	*Registers of St. Mary the Virgin, Aldermanbury*, p. 27.	This is probably the same person as in the preceding record.
129.	1567	St. Michael Paternoster, Vyntry Ward, and St. Olave, Old Jewry, Coleman Street Ward/Bishopsgate Ward, London	London census. 15 December: 1. (under "*VYNTRY* WARD") "St. *Michael Paternoster*: Blackmor 1." 1a. (under "VINTRY WARDE") "Moore: Robert Tego, a Morisco, servaunt with Thomas Castlyn Not denizens." 2. (under "*The* WARD *of COLMAN-STREETE*") "St. *Olives* Niger 1." 2a. (under "BUSSHOPSGATE WARD") "Moryon { Francys Fran', in the house of the said Peter Fanall } 4 yeres No denizen." 3. (above "*Sum Total of all the Strangers aforesaide*") "Blackmores —— 2."	1. *Coll/SP/E*, 1: 457. 1a. *RA*, 1:336. 2. *Coll/SP/E*. 1: 460. 2a. *RA*, 1: 323. 3. *Coll/SP/E*, 1: 461.	St. Olave, Old Jewry is on the border of Coleman Street Ward and Bishoposgate Ward, and is sometimes named interchangeably, as it is in the two extracts of the 1567 Returns in *Coll/SP/E* and in *RA*. The unnamed "niger" of 2 is the Moryon, Francys Fran, in 2a.
130.	1567	Tower Ward, London	Personal memoir. n.d: Samuel, a Negro page, owned by John Hawkins.	Job Hortop in Hakluyt, *PN* 14: 233; Williamson, *Sir John Hawkins*,	Does John Hawkins have a London residence in Tower Ward at this

				p. 192; R. Unwin, *The Defeat of John Hawkins*, p. 205.	time? He is assessed there in the London Subsidy Roll of 1589 (*Visitation of London*, p. 162).
131.	1568	St. Giles-in-the-Fields, London	Tax assessment. n.d.: "Lambert Waterson, denizen, barbaryen, tenaunte of Gabriell Levesy, grocer, and goeth to his parishe churche. Barbarien, j."	*RA*, 3: 407; cited in Sherwood, "Black People in Tudor England," p. 40.	Gabriell Levesey could have been living formerly in Shoreditch because there is a "Gabriell Lowey" listed there in 1540 in the Lay Subsidies of Middlesex (*RA* 1: 21), who could be the same individual. "Lambert Waterson" is assessed 8d in St. Botolph's, Aldgate in the Subsidy Roll of 1541 (*RA*, 1: 50). There he is listed with a "Garret Shomaker," but the relationship between them is not specified.
132.	1568/69	Lathom, Lancashire	Household records of Edward Stanley, third Earl of Derby (under "12 February 1568"). "No Slaves nor boyes shall sitt in the Hall but in place therefore to be appoynted convenyent' and 'The Yeman of Horses and Gromes of the Stable shall not suffre anie boyes or Slaves to abyde about the Stables nor lie in theym nor in any place aboute theym.'"	William ffarington, *The Derby Household Books*, p. 9; Walvin, *Black and White*, p. 7; Fryer, *Staying Power*, p. 9.	
133.	1570	Barnstaple, Devon	Will. 28 August: "No; 12.: ABSTRACT OF WILL Of NICHOLAS WICHEHALSE OF BARNSTAPLE: (D, 1570). P.C.C. (28 LYON).: 28 AUG, 1570. Nicholas Weichalsce of perfect memory and good remembrance. To be buried	*Report and Transactions of the Devonshire Association*, 38 (1906): 240, Item "No. 12"; cited Fryer, pp. 8–9.	

			in the Churche of Barnstaple. Unto the Vicar of Barnstaple for tythes forgotten, Unto Hunte the Clerke, unto John Wicchalse my kinsman, in consideration that he doe marrye with Katherine Salisburye, my wyfes daughter, to Johan Wicchalse, my daughter, To Nicholas Wichalse my sonne at 21, To Nicholas Wichalse my kinsman and svaunte, To Piers Wicchallsee my kynsmanne, To Anthonye my negarre, Bequeth all my lands in the Towns and pisshes of Lynton and Counseberye, Peracombe, Loxford, Berynarber, ffrementon and Barnstaple, to Marye my wyfe for life, and for the sattisfacon of my debtes and legacyes and pformaunce of this my wyll. I do make said Marye my hole Executrixe, And for overseers I ordaine Mr. Robert Appelye and my brother John Darte. Proved P.C.C. 23rd Sep., 1570 by procurator of Mary the relict."		
134.	1571	St Martin in the Fields, (Middlesex) London	Burial. 27 September: "Septes fuit Margareta a Moore."	*Registers of St. Martin in the Fields, Middlesex*, p. 116.	Also see West.Arch <http://www.westminster.gov.uk/archives/blackpresence/02.cfm>
135.	1573	High seas, south Atlantic, and Plymouth, Devon	Shipboard account. n.d.: 1. "We were no sooner returned to our strength, but there was a report brought by some of our men that our pinnaces were in danger to be taken	1. Nichols, *Sir Francis Drake Revived*, pp. 14, 26. 2. "Deposition by Nuno Da Silva as to how he was made prisoner by English Pirayes on his voyage from	

			… This report had his ground from one DIEGO a Negro, who, in the time of the first conflict, came and called to our pinnaces, to know 'whether they were Captain DRAKE'S?' And upon answer received, continued entreating to be taken aboard, though he had three or four shot made at him, until at length they fetched him, and learned by him, that, not past eight days before our arrival, the King had sent thither some 150 soldiers to guard the town against the Cimaroons … which we all the rather believed, because it agreed with the report of the Negroes, which we took before at the Isle of Pinos … ." "For in our absence, Captain John Drake, having one of our pinnaces, as was appointed, went in with the Main, and as he rowed aloof of the shore, where he was directed by DIEGO the Negro aforesaid, which willingly came unto us at Nombre de Dios, he espied certain of the Cimaroons, with whom he dealt so effectually, that in conclusion he left two of our men with their leader, and brought aboard two of theirs … ." pp. 14, 26. 2. "He also carried with him, from his country, a negro, named Diego, who spoke Spanish and English,	Oporto to Brazil 23rd May 1579," in *New Light on Drake* p. 302. Also cited by Sherwood, "Black People in Tudor England," p. 41.	

			and whom he had taken prisoner from a frigate in the North Sea near Nombre de Dios about seven or eight years previously … ."		
136.	1573	St. Martin-in-the-Fields, (Westminster, Middlesex), London	Marriage. 30 May: "May 30: Georgius Chesworth & Dorothea Blackemo'r."	*Register of St. Martin-in-the-Fields, Middlesex*, p. 66.	
137.	1573	St. Mary Magdalene, Bermondsey, London	Marriage. 9 June: "Maryed. Mr. Blackmor and Sarah ffyson (Dayes) June— 9"	*Registers of St. Mary Magdalene, Bermondsey*, p. 74.	
138.	1573	St. Mary Magdalene, Bermondsey, London	Burial. 19 September: "Buryed: Wm. Blackmore (Dayes) September—19."	*Registers of St. Mary Magdalene, Bermondsey*, p. 76.	
139.	1574	London	Queen Elizabeth's household documents. "14 April [given] "a gasken Coate for a litell blak a More of white tapheta cutt lined under with tyncell striped down with golde and silver lined with buckeram and bayes pointed with poyntinge Rebande and fased with tapheta."	BL, Egerton 2806, fol. 270, warrant dated 14 April 1574; cited Arnold, *Queen Elizabeth's Wardrobe*, p. 106.	The same black page is cited again in a warrant of 1575: BL, Egerton MS 2806, fol. 83, dated 13 April 1575.
140.	1575	St. Botolph, Bishopsgate, London	Marriage. 4 July: "Robert Platt and Sara Blackmore."	*Registers of St. Botolph, Bishopsgate*, p. 12.	
141.	1577	St. Dionis Backchurch, London	Baptism. 3 July: "Constant Negrone, dau. of Gregori Negrone."	*Register of St. Dionis Back Church*, p. 83.	
142.	1577	East Allington, South Devon	Baptism. 20 August: "The xx August was baptised the blackmoor of Mr John Ffortescue of ffallapytt named George."	Devon Record Office.	See also Devon Record Office web page, available at <http://www.devon.gov.uk/newsletter_may2000.pdf.> Seen 9.15.04.
143.	1577 (1577–1603)	(Westminster) London	Payment record. 12 October: Queen Elizabeth's household records: Dresses of "streighte bodied" gowns "layed	BL, Egerton 2806, fols. 145, 146, warrant dated 12 October 1579; NA $LC_{5/37}$, fols. 283, 284, warrant dated	Fryer, *Staying Power*, p. 9, and Greenblatt, "Introduction," *Norton Shakespeare*, p. 23),

			with lase of counterfeit silver and silke" given to "Thomasen, a woman dwarf," and (on May 21 1603) to "Tomasen the woman dwarf."	21 May 1603; both cited by Arnold, *Queen Elizabeth's Wardrobe*, p. 107.	believe this a black person.
144.	1577/78	(Westminster) London	Legal record. 15 January: Legal charge against Elizabeth Kirkham, and Rose Brown, prostitutes "for that Rose Browne is a bawd and and a whore to the saide Elizabeth Kirkham and others Elizabeth sayeth that the same Rose had dyvers & many blackamores and other persons resort to her house whilst this Elizabeth dwelt there."	BCB Books Vol. 3, fol. 280^{r}; cited by Salkeld, "Black Lucy."	Salkeld also says the prostitute Black Luce or Lucy Negro, who also appears in the B.C.B., was Lucy Baynham (or Bayntham), who "may indeed have been a black woman, since [citing Forbes] there were several 'blackamores' dwelling in Aldgate at this time'" (ch1.50). That "Lucy Negro" is the name of a black person is reinforced by Elizabethan naming practices.
145.	1578	(Westminster) London	Personal description. n.d.: George Best reports that "We also among us in England have blacke Moores, Aethiopians, which after a small continuance, can well endure the cold of our countrey … ." "Therefore to returne againe to the blacke Moors, I my selfe have seene an Ethiopian as blacke as a cole brought into England, who taking a faire English woman to wife, begat a sonne in all respects as blacke as the father was, although England were his native countrey, and an English woman his mother: whereby it seemeth this blacknes proceedeth rather of some natural infection of that man, which was so strong, that	Best, *A True Discourse*, pp. 34–37; Hakluyt, *PN*, 12: 115, 123–24; partly extracted in Walvin, *Black Presence*, pp. 33–37.	

			neither the nature of the Clime, neither the good complexion of the mother concurring, coulde any thing alter, and therefore, wee cannot impute it to the nature of the Clime … And the most probable cause to my judgement is, that this blackenesse proceedeth of some naturall infection of the first inhabitants of that Countrey, and so all the whole progenie of them descended, are still polluted with the same blot of infection … Thus you see, that the cause of the Ethiopians blackness is the curse and natuarall infection of blood … ."		
146.	1578	St. Pancras, Soper Lane, London	Marriage. 17 August: "Isaac Hollowaye, tayller, to Katheren Blackamore."	*Registers of St. Mary-le-Bow, Cheapside, All Hallows, Honey Lane, and St. Pancras, Soper Lane*, p. 418.	
147.	1578 (1578–79)	High seas, south Pacific Ocean off the Peruvian coastline of Lima, and, Malaccan Islands, Indian Ocean	Shipboard account. ca. 4 April–November: 1. "From hence sayling in toward the West he mett wth a ship, and the owner thereof, a Spanish Gentilman, in her; w[ch] ship was lade with lynen cloth and fine China silks … Drake tooke out of this ship a pilate to carry him into the haven of Gwatulco, and also a ppr negro wench called Maria, w[ch] was afterward gotten with child between the captaine and his men pirates, and sett on a small iland to take her adventure as shalbe hereafter shewed … in the latter ende of August	1. 'SHORT DISCOURSE OF THE PRESENT VOYAGE IN HAND-WRITING OF THE TIME": "A Discourse of Sir Francis Drakes iorney and exploytes after hee had past y[e] Straytes of Megellan into Mare de Sur, and throughe the rest of his voyage afterward till hee arrived in England. 1580 anno.," in Fletcher, *The World Encompassed*, pp. 182–84. 2. *New Light on Drake*, pp. 32–33. Also cited by Hendricks, "Feminist Historiography," pp. 367–69.	

			they set sayle … and had not the sight of land againe till ye the latter ende of November, at wch time they had sight of one of the Iles of Molucca, called Trenate … whereof they thoroughly furnished their ship. At their departure Drake left behinde him vppon this Island the twoo negrose wch he tooke at Agwatalca, and likewise the negro wench Maria, shee being gotten with childe in the ship, and now being very great, was left here on this Island … ." 2. "Thence they ran along the coast towards Guatulco, taking, on their way, a vessel bound for Lima, in which traveled a gentleman named Don Francisco de Zarate …Francis Drake showed much favour to Don Francisco … He took from Don Francisco a negress named Maria … They sailed out to sea … the whole of April and May until the middle of June, from Guatulco … thence they sailed to the Moluccas … reac[hing] it after … twenty days and remained there for eight days … From thence they went to an island … and, as it was uninhabited … there left the two negroes and the negress Maria, to found a settlement, leaving them rice, seeds, and means of making a fire … ."		

148.	1579/80	St. Matthew, Friday Street, London	Marriage. 25 January: "John Blackmore & Eliz. Michael."	*Registers of St. Matthew, Friday Street, London*, p. 48.	
149.	1579/80	Christ Church, Newgate Street, London	Burial. 18 February: "Thomas Blackmore, servant to Mr. Jucent."	*Registers of Christchurch, Newgate Street, London*, p. 276.	
150.	1582	Shipton Moyne, Gloucestershire	Will. 2 July: Will of Agnes Blackamoore or Blackamore of Shipton Moyne, Gloucestershire.	NatArch, Tirwhite, PROB 11/64.	
151.	1582	All Sayntes, Staynings parish, Langbourne Ward, London	City census and tax assessment. n.d.: "In the house of John Baptista Sambitores: Fardinando, a Blackamore … iiij d."	1. *RA*, 2: 235; "1582 London Subsidy Roll: Langbourne Ward', in *Two Tudor Subsidy Rolls*, pp. 259–69.	
152.	1583	St. Andrews, Plymouth	Burial. 10 December: "Bastien, a Blackmoore of Mr Willm. Hawkins, Plymouth."	*Register of Baptism, Marriage and Burial of the Parish of St. Andrew's, Plymouth*, p. 292.	
153.	1583	London	City census and tax assessment. n.d.: "Charles Negroe Dutch Scholm^{r}."	*RA*, 2: 333.	
154.	1584	Leicester House, (Westminster), London	Household records of the estate of the Earl of Leicestoer. 17 April: " xvijth of April: Gyven in reward the same day by your lordship's commandment to the blackmore vs [i.e. 5 shillings]."	Adams, ed., *Household Accounts and Disbursement Books of Robert Dudley, Earl of Leicester*, p. 178.	Marika Sherwood: "Was it this man who received the 'mattress given to the blackamore' in March 1583?" (*Leicestor House Inventories*, p. 178)," "Black People in Tudor England," p. 41, and personal correspondence with author. Sherwood is misquoting the title of the *Household Accounts*.
155.	1584	Chelsea, London	"Wanchese" and "Manteo," two Americans brought back by Philip Amadas and Arthur Barlow from Virginia and North Carolina for Walter Raleigh and trained as interpreters: 1. Travel report (1584): "We brought home also two of the savages,	1. "Amadas and Barlow's Voyage," in Hakluyt, *Voyages of the Elizabethan Seamen to America*, ed. Payne, p. 221. 2. Lupold von Wedel, "Journey," ed. Klariwill, p. 323; cited in Alden Vaughan, "Sir Walter Ralegh's Indian Interpreters," p. 347; Milton, p. 64.	Also see London Metropolitan Archives; Corporation of London web page, "Black Presence," available at: <http://www.corpoflondon.gov.uk/Corporation/lma_learning/schoolmate/Bal/s _bal_stories_detail.

			being lusty men, whose names were Wanchese and Manteo." 2. Personal description of German visitor Lupold von Wedel to Elizabeth's court15 October, 1584: "a ship had arrived that had found a land or an island which is said to be larger than England, and which had as yet been untrodden by Christians. A certain Master or Captain Rallegh had brought two men of this country with him and had them about his person … They were in countenance and stature like white Moors. Their usual habit was a mantle of rudely tanned skins of wild animals, no shirts, and a pelt before their privy parts. Now, however, they were clad in brown taffeta. No one was able to understand them, and they made a most childish and silly figure."		asp?ID=33>. Seen 8.30.04.
156.	1585	St. Margaret Moses, Friday Street, London	Burial. 11 July: "Annes More, servant to Goodman Wilkenson."	*Registers of St. Mildred, Bread Street and St. Margaret Moses, Friday Street*, p. 69.	Probably a black person.
157.	1585/86	Leicester House, (Westminster), London	Household records of the Estate of the Earl of Leicester. 6 January: "vjth January: Gyven in reward the same day by your lordship's commandment to Mr Rawles blackamoore, xxs [i.e. 20 shillings]."	Adams, ed., *Household Accounts and Disbursement Books of Robert Dudley, Earl of Leicester*, p. 210.	
158.	1585/86	St. Margaret's, Westminster (London)	Christening. 13 February: "Georg [*sic*] Negro s. of John."	*Memorials of St. Margaret's Church, Westminster*, p. 47.	

159.	1586	St. Botolph, Bishopsgate, London	Baptism. 25 September: "Elizabeth, a negro child, born white, the mother a negro."	Registers of St. Botolph Bishopsgate, GL 4515/1.	
160.	1586	St. Margaret's, Westminster (London)	Burial. 20 October: "Anthonye 'a man of the Indians.'"	*Memorials of St. Margaret's Church, Westminster*, p. 448.	
161.	1586	St. Botolph without Aldgate, London	Burial. 22 October: "Christopher Cappovert, a blackamoore who dyed in the whitbell of the high street was buryed the 22 October anno domini."	Registers of St. Botolph without Aldgate, GL 9222/1 Register General 1571–93.	Noted by Forbes, Chronicle, p. 4, Knutson, "A Caliban," p. 113. Remains of the "whitbell," which was an iron/metal foundry, still exist—in the form of a restored gate—in the current Whitechapel area, which is just down the street from St. Botolph church. There may have been more Africans buried on this day, because GL MS 3713/2A has the additional notation "(other negroes)."
162.	1586/87	St. Olave, Tooley Street, London	Christening. 19 February: "Edward, the sonne of Resonabell Blackman silkweaver."	Registers of St. Olave Tooley Street, LMA X097/233.	Noted by Knutson, "A Caliban,"p. 114.
163.	1587	St. Botolph without Aldgate, London	Burial. 27 August: "Domingo being a ginny negar and being servant to the right worshipfull Sr William Wynter knight dwellingye in the abbye place beinge the manor house of East Smithfield was buryied the xxvii daye of August in anno 1587… He had the black clothe."	Registers of St Botolph's Without Aldgate, Memoranda Books, GL 9234/1.	Noted by Knutson, p. 114.
164.	1587 (to 1591)	Paulespury, Northamptonshire, and Colchester, Essex	Personal diary entry. "He took took into his service Anthony, a blackamoor from Guinea."	Sir Arthur Throckmorton's Diary; cited by Rowse, *Ralegh and the Throckmortons*, p. 121.	
165.	1587	London	Legal record. Court of Requests lawsuit of a Portuguese physician	NatArch REQ 2/164/117; cited Knutson, "A Caliban,"p. 116.	Knutson also says: "Having assumed that the laws of England were like

			named Hector Novimies, complaining that the Ethiopian he has purchased from an English sailor for £4 10s "utterly refuseth to carry and serve him."		those of his native Portugal, the doctor finds—to his astonishment and dismay—that 'he hath not any ordinarye remedie at and by the course of the common Laws' of England unless the queen through her ministers in the Court of Requests will 'compel the sayde Ethiopian to serve him during his life; if the court will not so order, Novimeis asks that it 'Recover his sayd ffowre poundes Ten shillinges' from the mariner" (p. 116).
166.	1587/88	St. Ann, Blackfriars, London	Burial. 8 January: "Domyngo a Blackmore."	Registers of St. Ann, Blackfriars, GL 4510/1. Noted by Knutson, "A Caliban," p. 114.	
167.	1587/88	St. Olave, Hart Street, London	Burial. 28 January: "Mary, a blackamore from Dco~r Hector's."	*Registers of St. Olave, Hart Street*, p. 121; Vaughan and Vaughan, "Tales."	
168.	1587/88	St. Andrew's, Plymouth	Burial. 18 March: "Anthony, John, a Neyger."	*Register of Baptism, Marriage and Burial of the Parish of St. Andrew's Plymouth*, p. 305.	
169.	1587/88 (1588–99)	London	Legal record. 20 March: Testimony of William and Thomas Wilson in a Queen's Bench and Court of Chancery case against Hector Nonnes and his widow by his creditors about their secret Jewish ways, citing the testimony *by proxy* of two blackamoor maids in the employ of the Nonnes's kinsmen Alvarez in London.	NatArch KB 27/1331, N313, 20 March 1588; cited Meyers, in "Lawsuits," p. 157, 163, and in *Elizabethan Marranos*.	Meyers: (1) "[The late] Lucien Wolf considered Nunes, a prosperous merchant since his entourage consisted of servants, clerks, butlers, and two negresses" ("Lawsuits," p. 157). (2) "In 1588 Mrs. Mary May sued Dr. Hector Nunes, a Portuguese physician and merchant in the Court of Queen's Bench for debt. … The case was not decided until June 14, 1599 in the Court of Chancery, with Mrs. May prevailing. … Mary May's

					suit depended upon the testimony of William Wilson, a former Christian servant of Bernal Lewes, a brother-in-law of Nunes … who displayed his personal knowledge of the Nunes family … [and of] his brother Thomas, a servant of Ferdinando Alvarez, a Nunes kinsman by marriage …None of the testimony presented by the Wilson brothers in Chancery can be corroborated. Thomas told the court that his Passover testimony was derived from the observations of blackamoors (black slaves) in the Alvarez and Lyma [another kinsman of Nunes] households. Illiterate slaves and Christian servants were the sole transmitters of this vital religious data. I do not have to emphasize that the "transmission" of verbal information to others loses much of its validity in the process. How do we judge their observations and words?" (*Elizabethan Marranos Unmasked*, pp. 1–2).
170.	1588	St. Olave, Hart Street, London	Burial. 6 June: "Isabell, a blackamore."	*Registers of St. Olave, Hart Street*, p. 121.	Vaughan and Vaughan, in "Tales," cite a fuller description for a woman of this name, but without a complete reference.
171.	1588	St. Olave, Hart Street, London	Burial. 29 June: "A man blackamoor laye in the street."	*Registers of St. Olave, Hart Street*, p. 121.	
172.	1588/89	Bishops Nympton, Devon	Burial. 2 February: "Anthony Blackmore."	IGI.	

173.	1589	St. Mary, Somerset, London	Christening, n.d. " Elizabethe d. John Moore."	*Registers of St. Mary Somerset*, p. 21.	
174.	1589 (1589–90)	Oslo, Norway, and Holyrood House, Edinburgh, Scotland	Account of marriage entertainment of James VI and Anne of Denmark: 1. 23 November: [To entertain his Oslo hosts after his wedding] "at James's orders four naked blackamores danced in the snow in front of the royal carriage, but the cold was so intense that they died a little later of pnemonia." 2. 17 May: "At the celebrations for the marriage of James and Anne in Holyrood house in Edinburgh, after the couple arrived back in Scotland, the procession of the royal pair was led by a colorfully dressed blackamore holding a sword."	1. Ethel Carleton Williams, p. 21; cited by Hall, *Things of Darkness*, p. 128. 2. Stevens, *Scotland's Last Royal Wedding*, pp. 60, 109.	
175.	1589/90	St. Andrew Holborn, London	Burial. 30 January: "Sebrina, a blackamore wench."	Registers of St. Andrew Holborn, GL 6673/1.	
176.	1590	St. Olave, Hart Street, London	Burial. 5 September: "Francisco, a nigro."	Registers of St. Olave, Hart Street, GL 28867; cited by Knutson, "A Caliban," p. 114.	
177.	1590-91	St. Andrew's, Plymouth	Burial. 11 March: "Carbew, Lazia, a negro."	*Register of Baptisms, Marriages and Burials of the Parish of St. Andrew's, Plymouth*, p. 334.	
178.	1591	St. Mary Mounthaw, London	Burial. 22 April: "Emmanuel Backamore."	*Registers of St. Mary Mounthaw*, p. 61.	
179.	1591	St, Olave, Hart Street, London	Burial. 13 July: "Grace, a nigro oute of Dcor Hector's."	Registers of St. Olave, Hart Street, GL 28867; *Registers of St. Olave,*	

				Hart Street, p. 123; Knutson, "A Caliban," p. 114.	
180.	1591	St James, Clerkenwell, London	Christening. 16 August "John s. of John Blackman."	*True Register of St James, Clerkenwell*, p. 24.	"blackman" is probably a black person, since that is what "Resonable" is called and he is also describd as a "blackamor."
181.	1591	Edinburgh, Scotland	Royal disbursement. n.d.: "For the buriale of a Moir in Falkland … vij[ti] vj s. viij d."	*AHTS* 29 in MS. NAS E21.	
182.	1592	St. Olave, Tooley Street, London	Burial. 13 October: "Jaine, d. of Reasonable, Blackmor."	Registers of St. Olave, Tooley Street, LMA X097/233.	Noted by Knutson, "A Caliban," p. 114; Knutson also cites the christening of another son in this family in this register on 19 February 1586/87, which she documents as GLRO [LMA] MS R622.
183.	1592	St. Olave, Tooley Street, London	Burial. 16 October: Burial: "Edmund, s. of Reasonable, blackmor."	Registers of St. Olave, Tooley Street, LMA X097/233.	Noted by Knutson, p. 114.
184.	1592/93	St. Margaret's, Lee, Lewisham (London)	Burial. 2 March: "Cornelius Blacke a more buried ye second of marche.'"	Registers of St. Margaret's, Lee, Local Studies Centre, London Borough of Lewisham; Anim-Addo, *Sugar, Spices, and Human Cargo*, p. 6.	The church is currently in the diocese of Southwark.
185.	1593	Ward of Farringdon Without, London	Government city survey. "BANING, Alderman PAUL, in his house lodging three maids, 'blackamores.'"	"Returns of 1593," in *RSM*, p. 149; cited by Picard, *Elizabeth's London*, p. 110.	
186.	1593	St. Olave, Hart Street, Tower Ward, London.	London census. "MOUEA, LEYING, a 'blackamoor,' of 20 years; at Mistress Barkers."	"Returns of 1593," in *RSM*, p. 197; cited by Picard, *Elizabeth's London*, p. 118.	
187.	1593	St. Andrew's, Plymouth	Baptism. 2 May: "[Blank], Helene, d[aughter] of Cristian the negro s[er]vant to Richerd Sheere, the supposed father binge Cuthbert Holman, [illeg.]."	*Register of Baptism, Marriage and Burial of the Parish of St. Andrew's Plymouth*, p. 47.	

188.	1593	St. Dunstan in the East, London	Burial. 7 June: "Elizabeth Blackmore."	*Registers of St. Dunstan in the East, London*, p. 157.	
189.	1593	St. Botolph without Aldgate, London	Burial. 8 August: "Suzanna Pearis a blackamoore [borned? bound?] servant to John Despinois [de Spinoza?] a hat bandmaker was buryed the 8 daye of August Anno Domini."	Registers of St. Botolph, without Aldgate, GL 9222/1 Register General 1571–93.	John Despinois (de Spinosa) was himself buried on July 1594 (St Botolph without Aldgate Register).
190.	1593	St. Botolph without Aldgate, London	Burial. 20 August: "Symon Valencia a blackamoore servant to Stephen [illegible] a medalmaker was buryed the 20 daye of August in anno domini."	Registers of St. Botolph, without Aldgate, GL 9222/1 Register General 1571-93.	Noted by Forbes, *Chronicle*, p. 4, and Knutson, "A Caliban,".
191.	1593	St. Mary Mounthaw, London	Burial. 31 August: "Elizabeth Moore."	*Registers of St. Mary Mounthaw*, p. 62.	
192.	1593	St. Botolph without Aldgate, London	Burial. 8 October: 1. "Cassangoe a black A moore servant to Mr Barber a marchaunte was buried the 8 daye off October in Anno Domini." 2. "Cassangoe a neager servant to Mr. Thomas Barbor a marchaunte from his howse at the signe of the Redd Crosse in the libertie of East Smithfield."	1. Register of St. Botolph without Aldgate, GL 9222/1 Register General 1571–93, Burial 1593–1602. 2. Knutson cites this entry from the day-books, as: "(GL 9234/4)" (p. 114).	
193.	1593	St. Botolph without Aldgate, London	Burial. 13 October: "Easfanyo a negar servant of Mr. Thomas Barber a marchaunt … his house … at the signe of Rood/Flood (?) … in the liberties of East Smithfield was buried this xiii day of October ano 1593. … common ground … not to be … having a black clothe."	Register of St. Botolph without Aldgate, GL 9234/4 (Memoranda books).	Right margin comment has (as presumed cause of death) "plague." Noted by Knutson but as being in the "day books." Forbes has another entry for 8 October for a blackamoor named Easfanyo, which she documents as GHL MS 9223.
194.	1593	St. Margaret's, Westminster (London)	Burial. 15 October: "Jone Moros."	*Memorials of St. Margaret's Church, Westminster*, p. 462.	

195.	1593	St. Botolph without Aldgate, London	Burial. 29 November: "Robarte a negar servant to William Matthew a gentleman dwelling in a garden being behynd Mr. Quarles hys house and neare unto hogg lane in the libertie of East Smithfield was buried in the owter church yeard being without the cross wall before … this xxix day of November Anno 1593. He had the second cloth and fower bearers."	Registers of St. Botolph without Aldgate, GL 9234/4 (Memoranda Books).	Right margin comment has (as presumed cause of death) "plague"; left margin comment has "buryed in outer graveyard without crosse wall." A shorter version of this item, reading "Roberte, a blackamoor servant to William Mathew," is in register General book 9222/1.
196.	1593/94	St. Andrew's, Plymouth	Burial. 10 March: "White, Cristian, d[aughter] of John, Negro."	*Register of Baptisms, Marriages and Burials of the Parish of St. Andrew's Plymouth*, p. 349.	
197.	1594	St. Andrew's, Plymouth	Burial. 14 April: "Cristian, d[aughter] of Cristian, Richard Sheers' blackmoore."	*Register of Baptisms, Marriages and Burials of the Parish of St. Andrew's Plymouth*, p. 343.	
198.	1594	St. Stephen Coleman Street, London	Burial. 24 August: "Katherin the negar, dwelling with the Prince of Portingall."	Register of St. Stephen, Coleman Street, GL 4448.	
199.	1594	St. Margaret's, Westminster (London)	Burial. 2 November: "Rebecca A Lucressa Morro."	*Memorials of St. Margaret's Church, Westminster*, p. 463.	
200.	1594	St. Olave Hart Street, London	Burial. 9 November: "Peter Marley a blacamore, dire vira house."	*Registers of St. Olave, Hart Street*, p. 127.	
201.	1594	St. Andrew's, Plymouth	Baptism. 17 November: "Cristien, d[aughter] of Mary, a negro of John Whites and the supposed d[aughter] of John Kinge, a Dutchman, … (illeg)"	*Register of Baptisms, Marriages and Burials of the Parish of St. Andrew's Plymouth*, p. 57.	
202.	1594	St. Andrew's, Plymouth	Baptism. 24 December: "Fortunatus, s[on] of a negro of Thomas Kegwins the supposed father being a Portugall."	*Register of Baptisms, Marriages and Burials of the Parish of St. Andrew's Plymouth*, p. 58.	
203.	1594/95	St. Martin in the Fields, (Middlesex), London	Baptism. 1 January: "Margeria [*sic*] Blackman."	*Registers of St. Martin in the Fields*, p. 25.	

204.	1594/95	St. Olave, Hart Street, London	Burial. 23 January: "George, a blackeamore oute of Mrs. Barker's."	*Registers of St. Olave, Hart Street*, p. 128.	
205.	1595	Chislehurst parish, Bromley, Kent	Baptism. 22 April: "Cristofer Adam a blackamore christ[ened] on the 22 daie of April, a man growne."	Local Studies and Archives, Bromley Public Libraries, Bromley, Kent, Chislehurst parish Composite register: ref. P92/1/1- date: 1558–1681, p. 1.	
206.	1595	St. Botolph, Bishopsgate, London	Burial. 27 June: "Domingo Blackmore."	*Registers of St. Botolph, Bishopsgate, London*, p. 316.	
207.	1595	St. Margaret's, Westminster (London)	Christening. 7 August: "William Harris 'blackamoor baseborn.'"	*Memorials of St. Margaret's Church, Westminster*, p. 58.	
208.	1595	St. Leonard's, Shoreditch	Baptism. 7 September: "Susan, A Black mores Childe was baptised ye same daye [i.e. 7th September 1595]. Haliwel Street."	Registers of St. Leonard's Shoreditch, GL 7493.	
209.	1595/96	St. Botolph without Aldgate, London	Burial. 3 March: 1. "A Negar supposed to be named Frauncis, he was servant to Peter Miller a beare brewer, was buried the 3 day of March ano domini." 2. "A Negar whose name was supposed to be ffrauncis, he ws servant to Mr. Peter Miller a bearebrewer." 2. "A Negar whose name was supposed to be Frauncis, he was servant to Mr. Peter Miller a beare brewer dwelling at the signe of the hartes horne in the libertie of East Smithfield."	1. Registers of St. Botolph, without Aldgate, GL 9234/5 (Memoranda Books). 2. Knutson, "A Caliban," p. 14. 3. Forbes, *Chronicle*, p. 4.	
210.	1596	All Hallows, Staining, London	Burial. [n.d.]: "Received for the burial of a blak more—00-00-04."	Register of All Hallows, Staining, Vestry Minutes, GL 4956/2; cited by Knutson, "A Caliban," p. 114.	

211.	1596	Barnstaple, Devon	Baptism. 6 April: "Grace, a neiger servant of Mr Richard Dodderidge."	North Devon Record Office.	
212.	1596	Barnstaple, Devon	Burial. 22 May: "Peter Mingus, negor servant of Mr Norrishe."	North Devon Record Office.	
213.	1596	St. Andrew's, Plymouth	Baptism. 1 July: "Susan, d[aughter] of a Blackmoore."	*Register of Baptisms, Marriages and Burials of the Parish of St. Andrew's, Plymouth*, p. 67.	
214.	1596	London	Royal proclamation deporting blacks from kingdom. 11 July: "An open le[tt]re to the L[ord] Maiour of London and th'alermen his brethren, And to all other Maiours, Sheryfes, &c. Her Ma[jes]tie understanding that there are of late divers Blackmoores brought into the Realme, of which kinde of people there are all ready here to manie, consideringe howe God hath blessed this land w[i]th great increase of people of our owne Nation as anie Countrie in the world, wherof manie for want of Service and meanes to sett them on worck fall to Idlenesse and to great extremytie; Her Ma[jesty']s pleasure therefore ys, that those kinde of people should be sent forthe of the lande. And for that purpose there ys direction given to this bearer Edwarde Banes to take of those Blackmoores that in this last voyage under Sir Thomas Baskervile, were brought into this Realme to the nomber of Tenn, to be Transported	NatArch PC 2/21, fol. 304 (11 July 1596) (Cecil Papers 91/15).	Repeated twice more, as in entries of 18 July 1596 and 1601, below.

			by him out of the Realme. Wherein wee Req[uire] you to be aydinge & Assysting unto him as he shall have occacion, and thereof not to faile."		
215.	1596	London	Royal proclamation deporting blacks from kingdom. 18 July: "An open warrant to the L[ord] Maiour of London and to all other vyceadmyralles, Maiours and other publicke officers whatsoever to whom yt may appertaine. Whereas Casper van Senden a merchant of Lubeck did by his labor and travell procure 89 of her Ma[jest's] subiectes that were detayned prisoners in Spaine and Portugall to be released, and brought them hither into this Realme at his owne cost and charges, for the w[hi]ch his expences and declaration of his honest minde towards those prizoners, he only desireth to have lycense to take up so many Blackamoores here in this Realme and to transport them into Spaine and Portugall. Her Ma[jes]ty in regard of the charitable affection the supli[ant] hathe shewed being a stranger to worke the delivery of our contrymen that were there in great misery and thralldom and to bring them home to their native contry, and that the same could not be don w[i]thout great expence and also considering the reasonablenes	Nat.Arch PC 2/21, f. 306 (18 July 1596) (Cecil Papers 91/15).	

			of his requestes to transport so many Blackamoores from hence doth thincke yt a very good exchange and that those kinde of people may be well spared in this Realme being so populous and numbers of hable persons the subiects of the land and xpian [*Christian*] people that perishe for want of service, whereby through their labor they might be mayntained. They are therefore in their L[ordshi]ps' name req[ui]red to aide and assist him to take up suche Blackamores as he shall finde w[i]thin this Realme w[i]th consent of their masters, who we doubt not considering her Ma[jesty's] good pleasure to have those kindes of people sent out of the lande & the good deserving of the stranger towardes her Ma[jesty's] subiectes, and that they shall doe charitable and like Christians rather to be served b y their owne contrymen then with those kynde of people, will yilde those in their possession to him."		
216.	1596	St. Margaret's, Westminster (London)	Christening. 20 July: "Anne Blackman, *d* of William."	*Memorials of St. Margaret's Church, Westminster: Registers*, p. 58.	
217.	1596	St. Andrew's, Plymouth	Baptism. 4 October: "Pedro, Katheren, d[aughter] of don Pedro a basterd Neger."	*Register of Baptisms, Marriages and Burials of the Parish of St. Andrew's Plymouth*, p. 69.	
218.	1596/97	Dartford, Kent	Burial. 19 January: "Iferdynando a blackmore svannte to Alexander Neuby."	Sherwood, *Feversham Historical Society Newsletter*.	

219.	1596/97	St. Luke, Chelsea, London	Baptism. 13 February: "Charles, a boy by Estimacon x or xii yers olde brought by Sir Walter Raleigh from Guiana baptized"	Registers of St. Luke, Chelsea, LMA P74/LUK/161.	Also see LMA "Black and Asian Londoners 1536–1840 Final Report: Summary. Available at: <http://www.bl.uk/about/cooperation/pdf/report29.pdf. >. Seen 10.8.2004.
220.	1597	St. Margaret's, Westminster (London)	Burial. 8 April: "Anne Blackman."	*Memorials of St. Margaret's Church, Westminster: Registers*, p. 468.	Editorial footnote explains that part of the date for this entry is torn away.
221.	1597	St. Martin-in-the-Fields, Westminster (Middlesex), London	Baptism. 17 April: "Maria Blackema."	*Register of St. Martin-in-the-Fields*, p. 26.	The name is very likely a contraction, and another variation of "blackamore/blackamoor."
222.	1597	St. Mary Woolchurch Haw, London	Burial. n.d. (between entries for 24 April and 20 May): "a blakmore belonging to Mr John Davies, died in White Chappel parishe, was laied in the ground in this church yarde *sine frequentia populi et sine ceremoniis quia utrum christianus esset necne nesciebamus* [without any company of people and without ceremony, because we did not know whether he was a Christian or not]."	Registers of St. Mary Woolchurch Haw, GL 7644; cited by Knutson, "A Caliban," p. 116.	
223.	1597	London	Medical entry. 5 May: "Polonia the blackmor maid at Mr Peirs of 12 yeare old 1597 5 May Sunday am at 30 past 7 … disease the mrs. [mistress] for the servant … much pain syd, stam[ach]. Lyk to vomit/ a fever in her bones faint harte full of melancholy & cold humors mixed with collar/ purge her of [Saturn] in { } & full of wind."	Simon Forman's Casebooks. Ashmole Collection, Bodleian Library. Entry for 5 May 1597, vol. 234.	
224.	1597	St. Botolph, Aldgate, London	Baptism. 3 June: 1. "Marye Phyllis A Blackamore	Registers of St. Botolph, Aldgate, GL. 1. 9220; cited by Knutson,	

			beinge aboute Twentye yeres of age and dwellinge with millicen porter sempster." 2. "Mary Phyllis of Morisco being a blackamore she was of late servant with one Mr. Barber of Marke Lane a widower she said her father's name was Phyllis of Morisco a blackasmore being both a basket maker and shovel maker. This Marye Phyllis being about the age of xx yeares, and having been in England for the part of xii or xiii yeares and as yet was not christened now being bound (?) servant with one Millicent Porter a sempster dwelling in the liberties of east Smithfield and now taking part … of faith in Iesus Christ was desyrous to become a christian wherefore she made suit … to have sonme conversation with the curat of this the parish of st. buttolph without aldgate London … the curat named Christopher Threlkeld demanding of her certen questions concerning her fayth whereunto she answering him quite Christian like; and afterwards she being by the said Mr. Christopher Threlkeld … to say the lord's prayer and also to repeat the articles of her belief which she did both say and repeat both decently and well. Concerning her faith then the said curat demanded of her if she weare	"A Caliban," p. 113. 2. 9234/6. Both cited by Knutson, p. 116, and p. 120.	

			desyrous to be baptized in the said fayth (whereat?) shee said yes. Then the said curat did go with her unto the fonte and desiring the congregation with him to call upon god the father through our Lord Iesus Christ that of his Bownteous mercie he wold graunt to her that thing … by nature she could not have, that she may be baptized …"		
225.	1597	St. Margaret's, Westminster (London)	Burial. 7 June: "Ales Moore et filius Siluster."	*Memorials of St. Margaret's Church, Westminster*: *Registers*, p. 468.	
226.	1597-98	St. Olave, Hart Street, London	Marriage. 15 February: "John Cathman & Constantia Negrea, ancilla, p. licen."	*Registers of St. Olave, Hart Street*, p. 256. Also in *BMI*.	"negrea" is probably an early Modern French word (as in "negre"; *OED*) or a Latin word for negro.
227.	1598	Barnstaple, Devon	Baptism. 10 April: "Elizabeth, a nigor with Mrs Ayer."	Registers of Barnstaple, Devon, North Devon Record Office.	
228.	1598	Tower Ward, London	City census and tax assessment. 1 October 1598: "Clar', a Negra at Widdow Stokes, per poll … viij d. Maria, a Negra, at Olyver Skynnars, per poll viij d. Lewse, a Negro at Mr Mitons, per poll … viij d."	*RA*, 3: 28.	
229.	1598	St. Olave, Hart Street, London	Burial. 23 November: "Madelen, a Blackeamore out of Bernard's house."	*Registers of St. Olave, Hart Street*, p. 131.	
230.	1598/99	Cardington, Bedfordshire	Christening. 18 January: "Philip Blackamore."	IGI (Batch no. P003891, source file no. 0845460, printout call no. 6905932)	
231.	1598/99	London	Legal record. 10 February: "Robert Everett and Barbary Moore also Browne sent into this house by George Hart the constable of St. Andrewes The	BCB Books, IV Folio 60v, GL.	Reference provided by Cristine Varholy, Hampden-Sydney College, VA.

			sayd Barbary being exaied [examined] whether the sayd Everett hath not had thuse and carnall knowledge of her bodye she saieth that he hath had thuse and carnall knowledge of her bodye three severall tymes at the house of one Alice Morrise Fishwyf dwelling in Cheeke[?] Lane the sayd Everett being allso exaied [examined] confesseth that it is trew and that he hath the use and carnall knowledge of her bodye three or foure tymes whereuppon it was ordered that they shalbe both ponished and that the sayd Everett shall putt in suretyes to appeare on Saturday the fourtenth of Aprill which was done accordinglye."		
232.	1598/99	London	Legal record (under "the thirteenth of Februarie 1598"): "This daye Alice Morise Fishwyfe dwelling in Chicke[?] Lane brought into this house by warrant for harbouring Robert Everett and Barbary Moore also Browne and suffered them to lye both together in one bedd having but one rome and did sitt upp in the rome all night having a candell lighted all night whilest the sayd Everett had the use of the body of the sayd Barbary as by their former examinacion appeareth whereuppon the sayd Alice Morrise was ponished."	BCB Books, IV folio 61v, GL	"Moris" is probably a variant of "morrisco/morisco," i.e. moor as in a black person. Reference provided by Cristine Varholy, Hampden-Sydney College, VA.

233.	1599	All Hallows, Barking, St. Dunstan (in the East), St Olave (Hart Street), Tower Ward, London	City census and tax assessment. n.d.: "Clare a Negra at Widdow Stokes (an Englishwoman) … per poll … viij d.; Mary a Negra at Richard Woodes … per poll … viij d.; A blackamore, servaunt to Jeronimo Lopez … per poll … viij d."	*RA*, 3: 54, for the first two entries and 3: 55 for the last.	
234.	1599	St. Mary, Somerset, London	Christening. 28 March: "Marye d. John Blackeman."	*Registers of St. Mary Somerset*, p. 29.	
235.	1599	London	Private correspondence. 28 May, Denis Edwards to Thos. Lankford, Secretary of the Earl of Hartford: "Pray enquire and secure my negress; she is certainly at the Swan, at the Dane's beershop, Turnbull Street, Clerkenwell."	*Comp/SP/D*, 270:119; *CSP/D Edward VI 1547–1553*.	
236.	1599	St. Andrew's, Plymouth	Marriage. 30 October: "Blackmore alias Hellier, John and Anstice Light, wid."	*Register of Baptisms, Marriages and Burials of the Parish of St. Andrew's Plymouth*, p. 242.	
237.	1599	*HMS Tiger* (London)	John Davies's cryptic mention in the account of his trip to India in the *Tiger* in 1599 of having seized 12 Indians somewhere on the Coromandel coast in southeast India: "we tooke with us twelve of the Indians of severall places."	Purchas, *Hakluytus Posthumous*, 2: 325.	These individuals were probably carried carried back to England at some point. See the item about William Bragg below.
238.	Early 1600s (but not later than 1614)	Saldania or Table Bay, Cape of Good Hope, South Africa, and East India Company, London	Company memoirs and letters: 1. "About three years before I went to *India* … one of the Companie ships returning thence, and arriving at this barbour [*sic*], after a little stay, when	1. Terry, *Voyage*, pp. 20–24; cited Fryer, *Staying Power*, pp. 12–13. 2. *Voyage of Nicholas Downton*, p. 2. 3. "3: 251 Thomas Elkington to the East India Company, Laus	

			she was ready to set sayl for *England*, and having then two of these Salvages aboard, her Commander resolved to bring them both home with him, thinking that when they got some English here they might discover something of their country which we could not know before. These poor wretches being thus brought away, very much both against their minds, one of them (merely out of extreme sullenness, though he was very well used) died shortly after they put to sea, the other who called himself *Cooree* (whom I mentioned before) lived and was brought to London, and there kept, for the space of six monthes, in Sir Thomas Smith's house (then Governour of the *East India* Company) where he had good diet, good clothes, good lodging, with all other fitting accommodations; now one would think, that this wretch might have conceived his present, compared with his former condition, an Heaven upon earth, but he did not so, though he had to good entertainment made for him, a Chain of bright Brasse, an Armour, Brest, Back, and Head-Piece, with a Buckler all of Brasse, his beloved Metall, yet all this contented him not, for never seemed to be more weary of	Deo in Swally Road, aboard the *Solomon*, February 15, 1614 [1615]," in *Letters Received by the East India Company*, p. 2.	

			ill usage, than he was of Courtesies; For when he had learned a little of our Language, he would daily lye upon the ground, and cry very often thus in broken English, *Cooree home goe, Saldania goe, home goe*; And not long after when he had his desire and was returned home, he had no sooner set footing on his own shore, but presently he threw away his *Clothes*, his *Linnen*, with al other *Covering*, and got his sheeps skin upon his back, guts about his neck, and such a perfum'd cap … upon his head … After this fellow was returned it made the Natives most shie of us when we arrived there … it had been well if he had not seen England, for as he discovered nothing to us … he told his Country-men (having doubtless observ'd so much here) that *Brase* was but a base and cheap commoditie in *England* … that we had never after such a free Exchange of our Brase and Iron for their Cattell … ." 2. … 'When Gabriel Towerson, captain of the *Hector*, was leaving Table Bay for England in May 1613, he carried off two natives who had come aboard his ship. …" 3. "We landed there the Saldanian brought home by Captain Towerson but after he once got ashore with such things as your Worships bestowed on		

			him we could never see him more; so greatly do fear he mought be cause of our worser entertainment, for which he had no occasion given, being all the voyage more kindly used than he anywise could deserve, but being ungrateful dogs all of them, not better to be expected …"		
239.	1600	London	Court record. n.d.: "A cargo of negroes" [mentioned in a *bottomry* case of the High Court of the Admiralty].	*Select Pleas*, ed. Marsden, 2: xvi.	Since this was a bottomry case heard in the Admiralty court, it must have involved wrangling over a shipload of black people who were being brought into England on a ship that had not been paid for.
240.	1600/01	Hemel Hempstead, Hertford	Marriage. 16 January: "Susan ethuop."	IGI.	
241.	1600/01	St. Margaret's, Westminster (London)	Christening. 18 January: "Elizabeth Blackman, *d* of Johan."	*Memorials of St. Margaret's Church, Westminster*, p. 65.	
242.	1601	St. Mary Bothaw, London	Baptism. 29 March: "Anno 1601: March 29: Julyane, a blackamoore servant wyth Mr Alldermane Banynge of the age of 22 yeares was baptized and namyd Marye 29 daye of March 1601."	Registers of St. Mary Bothaw, London, GL 4310.	Probably one of the three black maids who were recorded at the Alderman's house in 1593. Paul Bayning, was Sheriff 1593–4, and Treasurer of the East India Company, 1600–1602.
243.	1601	St. Margaret's, Westminster (London)	Marriage. 8 July: "Edward Blakemore with An Strinfellowe."	*Memorials of St. Margaret's Church, Westminster*, p. 311.	
244.	1601	St. Andrew's, Plymouth	Burial. 30 November: "a Blackmore at Capt. Sparks."	*Register of Baptisms, Marriages and Burials of the Parish of St. Andrew's Plymouth*, p. 383.	Spark was with Hawkins on his slaving voyages. For Sparks see Williamson, *Hawkins of Plymouth*, p. 70.
245.	1601	St. Andrew's, Plymouth	Burial. 6 December: "a Blackmore at Mr. Stallenge."	*Register of Baptisms, Marriages and Burials of the Parish of St. Andrew's Plymouth*, p. 384.	

246.	1601/02	London	Royal proclamation deporting blacks from kingdom. January: "Whereas the Queen's Majesty, tendering the good and welfare of her own natural subjects, greatly distressed in these hard times of dearth, is highly discontented to understand the great Numbers of Negroes and blackamoors which (as she is informed) are carried into this realm since the troubles between her highness and the King of Spain; who are fostered and powered here, to the great annoyance of her own liege people that which co[vet] the relief which these people consume, as also for that the most of them are infidels having no understanding of Christ or his Gospels; hath given a special commandment that the said kind of people shall be with all speed avoided and discharged out of this her Majesty's realm; and to that end and purpose hath appointed Casper Van Senden, merchant of Lubeck for their speedy transportation, a man that hath somewhat deserved of this realm in respect that by his own labor and charge he hath relieved and brought from Spain divers of our English nation who otherwise would have perished there. These shall therefore be to will and	Proclamation 804.5-805 in *Tudor Royal Proclamations*, 3: 221–2 (ca. January 1601).	

			require you and every of you to aid and assist the said Casper Van Senden or his assignees to taking such Negroes and blackamoors to be transported as aforesaid he shall find within the realm of England … .”		
247.	1601/02	St. Clement Danes, Westminster, (Middlesex), London	Burial. 21 January: “Fortunatus a blackmoor seruant to Sr Robert Cicill”	Registers of St. Clement Danes, West.Arch.	
248.	1601/02	Salisbury Cathedral, Wiltshire	Burial. 22 February: “Matthias the Morian.”	Personal communication, Marika Sherwood.	
249.	1601/02	St. Dunstan and All Saints, Stepney Tower Hamlets, London	Baptism. 18 March: “Christian Ethiopia borne of a Blackmore baptised the xviii day.”	Registers of St. Dunstan and All Saints, Stepney Tower Hamlets, LMA P93/DUN/255; also in IGI.	Also see LMA “Black and Asian Londoners 1536–1840 Final Report”: “Summary.” Available at: <http://www.bl.uk/about/cooperation/pdf/report29.pdf>. Seen 10.8.2004>
250.	1602	St. Andrew’s, Plymouth	Baptism. 22 October: “Gifferdandgorge, an Indian.”	*Register of Baptisms, Marriages and Burials of the Parish of St. Andrew’s Plymouth*, p. 106.	
251.	1602	St. Mary, Lancaster, Lancashire	Christening: 1 November: “Richard nigroe.”	IGI.	
252.	1602/03	Shelton, Bedfordshire	Birth/christening. 5 January: “Grace Negar Or negus.”	IGI (AFN: 8WHK-CW and Compact Disc #18 Pin #494913)	
253.	1602/03	Gravesend, Kent	Burial. 19 February: “Frances the Mullato was buried.”	Personal Communication, Marika Sherwood.	
254.	1603	St. Andrew’s, Plymouth	Baptism. 23 June: “Ric, son of Marye a Neger, base, ye reputed father Rog[er] Hoggett.”	*Register of Baptisms, Marriages and Burials of the Parish of St. Andrew’s Plymouth*, p. 110.	
255.	1603	St. Dunstan and All Saints, Stepney Tower Hamlets, London	Baptism. 29 July: “Charity Lucanea a blackamore baptized the xxix day [no month] from Ratclif.”	Registers of St. Dunstan and All Saints, Stepney Tower Hamlets, LMA P93/DN/255.	Also see LMA “Black and Asian Londoners 1536–1840 Final Report”: “Summary,” available at: <http://

					www.bl.uk/about/cooperation/pdf/ report29.pdf>. Seen 10.8.2004>
256.	1603	St. Margaret's, Westminster (London)	Burial. 1 October: "Margery Blackman *pl*."	*Memorials of St. Margaret's Church, Westminster: Registers*, p. 480.	pl = plague
257.	1603	Bisley, Gloucestershire	Burial. 22 November: "John Davies 'y^{e} black' was buried."	Gloucestershire Archives, P47 IN 1/1.	
258.	1603	St. Philip and Jacob's Church, Bristol	Burial. 14 December: "Joane smyth the wyfe of Thomas smyth beinge a blackamoore was Buried also the xiiiith [14th] day of the plague."	Registers of St. Philip and Jacob's Church, Bristol, Bristol Record Office; cited Dresser, *Slavery Obscured*, p. 11.	
259.	1603 (to 1616)	Chelsea and Tower of London	1. "Leonard Ragapo" and "Harry," two Americans brought back by Walter Raleigh from Guyana and kept by him as servants: Travel account (1608): "To the north north west of which [i.e. Moroogа] therte falleth into the sea a river called Conawini … whereof an Indian named Leonard Ragapo is Chiefe … This Indian is Christened and hath been heretofore in England with Sir Walter Raleigh, to whom he beareth great affection; he can a little inderstand and spake our language, and loveth our Nation with all his heart …"	1. "Robert Harcourt's Journal," Purchas, *Hakluytus Posthumus*, p. 368.	Also see, Corporation of London web page, "Black Presence," available at: <http://www.corpoflondon.gov.uk/Corporation/lma_learning/schoolmate/Bal/sm_bal_stories_detail.asp?ID=32>. Seen 8.30.04.
260.	1604	Hatherleigh, Exmouth, Devon	Baptism. 13 May: "Grace, a blackamore."	Devon Record Office.	
261.	1605	Barnstaple, Devon	Baptism. 22 May: "Mary, base daughter of Elizabeth, a nyger, with Mrs Ayer."	Devon Record Office.	

262.	1605	Ottery St Mary, Devon	Marriage. n.d.: "blackemore," "joan" and "pynsent", "edw."	*BMI.*	
263.	1605	St. Olave, Tooley Street, London	Burial. 5 December: "Constantyn, a negar oute of ye pilgrime at portsmouth … ."	Registers of St. Olave, Tooley Street. LMA X097/233.	Noted by Knutson, "A Caliban".
264.	1605/06	Barnstaple, Devon	Baptism. 2 February: "Chaterin, a nygor with Mr Lanyon."	Devon Record Office.	
265.	1606	All Hallows, London Wall, London	Marriage. n.d.: "John Faggot with Margaret Morin."	*BMI.*	
266.	1606	St. Benet Fink, London	Baptism. 2 June: "was baptized a man child called John borne of a blackamoor woman & supposed to be the sonne of Edwarde a borrder in the howse of William Conrados."	Register of St Benet Fink, GL 4097; noted by Knutson, "A Caliban," p. 113.	
267.	1606	Hatherleigh, Exmouth, Devon	Baptism. 10 August: "Rebecca, base daughter of Grace, a Negro."	Devon Record Office.	
268.	1606	Devon city	City records. 10 August: "Who agree that William Moore lute Servaunte of Sir Ames Bampfild 30 r& Sir [Io Acland] Knightes & the rather at his requeste/& Sir Iohn Acland shalbe admitted to be one of the Waites of this Cittie in the place of Dodridge decessed so longe as he shalbe of gu(...) good behavior & that he shalbe admitted to the liberties of this Cittie gratis so longe as he keepes the place of a Wayte of this Cittie 35 And they agree that Sir Ames Bampfild & Sir Iohn Acland Knightes shalbe admitted to the Liberties of this Cittie	REED, Devon records, Receivers Account Rolls DRO, ECA mb 2d (Civic officials'fees) 1606–7 Council Chamber Act Book 6 t)ao, ECA: GI/B1/6 fol. 140 (10 August) [Item mor giuen to the pleayeres by mr mayors order 01-00-00 181 1606–7].	Transcribed text of item is available at: <http://ia300202.us.archive.org/2/items/devonREED00wassuoft/devonREED00wassuoft_djvu.txt.> Seen 10.16.05.

			in the Assias weeke nexte gratis And they agree that the now Receiuer shall deliuer vnto the said Moore a gownes Clothe of some better price then ordinarilie ys for 40."		
269.	1606	Barnstaple, Devon	Baptism. 10 November: "Elizabeth, daughter of Susannah, a nygor … ."	Devon Record Office.	
270.	1607	Hedgerley, Buckinghamshire	Christening. 15 December: "Mary Negro."	IGI (Batch no. C130202, source call no. 1042384, printout call no. 6900197).	
271.	1607/08	St. Botolph, Bishopsgate, London	Christening. 5 February: "William, son of Edward Blackamoore."	*Registers of St. Botolph, Bishopsgate*, p. 171.	
272.	1608/09	St. George the Martyr, Southwark, London	Baptism. 19 February: "Richard a Blackmore, 12 years old."	Register of St. George the Martyr, LMA P92/GEO/139.	Also see LMA "Black and Asian Londoners 1536–1840 Final Report": "Summary." Available at: <http://www.bl.uk/about/cooperation/pdf/report29.pdf>. Seen 10.8.2004.
273.	1609	St. Margaret's, Westminster (London)	Christening. 24 August: "Edward Blackman *s* of Thomas."	*Memorials of St. Margaret's Church, Westminster*, p. 73.	
274.	1609	St. Margaret's, Westminster (London)	Burial. 25 August: "Edward Blackman."	*Memorials of St. Margaret's Church, Westminster*, p. 492.	
275.	1610	St. James, Clerkenwell, London	Burial: 31 July: "Katherine d. of Allexander [*Alexander*] Blackman.	*True Register of St James, Clerkenwell*, p. 112.	
276.	1610	St. Philip and Jacob's Church, Bristol	Burial. 14 December: "Peeter a Blackmoore."	Register St. Philip and Jacob's Church, Bristol, Bristol Record Office; cited Dresser, *Slavery Observed*, p. 11.	
277.	1610/11	St. Mildred Poultry, London	Baptism. 1 January: "Dederj Iaquoah about ye age of 20 yeares, the sonne of Caddi-biah king of the river of Cetras or Cestus in the Countrey of Guinny,	GL 4429/1; cited by Knutson, "A Caliban," p. 111.	

			who was sent out of his cuntrey by his father in an english shipp called the Abigail of London, belonging to Mr John Davies of this parishe, to be baptized. At the request of the said Mr Davies, and at the desire of the said Dedery, and by allowance of authority, was by ye parson of this churche the first of Ianuarie, baptised and named John. His suerties were Iohn Davies haberdasher Isaac Kilburne Mercer, Robert Singleton Churchwarden, Edmund Towers Paul Gurgeny and Rebecca Hutchens. He shewed his opinion concerning Iesus Christ and his faith in him; he repeated the Lords prayer in english at ye fonte, and so was baptised and signed with the signe of the Crosse."		
278.	1610/11	All Hallows, Tottenham, Harringay, London	Baptism. 3 February: "Walter Anberey the sonne of Nosser Anberey borne in the kingdom of Dungala in Africa, was baptized upon the thirde day of February being Shrove Sundaie, in the Eight yeare of Kinge James, anno, 1610."	LMA, DRO/015/A/01/001.	Also see LMA "Black and Asian Londoners 1536–1840 Final Report": "Summary." Available at: <http://www.bl.uk/about/cooperation/pdf/report29.pdf>. Seen 2.2.06.
279.	1610/11	St. Olave, Hart Street, London	Burial. 14 March: "the blackamore gerle from Mr. Pintoe's."	*Registers of St. Olave, Hart Street*, p. 143.	
280.	1611	St. Peter, Paul's Wharf, London	Marriage. 24 June: "John Brabye of St. Brides, haberdasher, and Alles Moren, W. [widow?] Lic. Fac."	*Registers of St. Peter Paul's Wharf*, Book A, p. 207.	"Moren" is probably a corruption of "moryen," meaning "moore," possibly female.

281.	1612/13	Christchurch, Bristol	Burial. 4 January: “Katherine a blacke negra servante at the horshed was buryed.”	Registers of Christchurch parish, Bristol, Bristol Record Office; cited Dresser, *Slavery Observed*, p. 11.	
282.	1612/13	St. Andrew’s, Plymouth	Burial: 23 February: “John, an Indian of the forte.”	*Register of Baptisms, Marriages and Burials of the Parish of St. Andrew’s Plymouth*, p. 454.	There are several entries with the location “at the forte.”
283.	1613 (to 1624)	Knole, Kent	Household list and diary. n.d.: “Grace Robinson, a blackamoor.”	“The Laundry Maids,” Table, the Earl of Dorset’s 1613 to 1624 household list, in Williamson, *Lady Anne Clifford*, p. 478; *The Diary of Lady Anne Clifford*, p. lxi; cited Fryer, *Staying Power*, p. 24 n. 43; Hall, *Things of Darkness*, p. 13 n. 16.	
284.	1613 (to 1624)	Knole, Kent	Household list. n.d.: “John Morockoe a blackamoor.”	“Kitchen and Scullery: Earl of Dorset’s Household and Family 1613 to 1624, in Williamson, *Lady Anne Clifford*, p. 478; *The Diary of Lady Anne Clifford*, p. lxi; cited Fryer, *Staying Power*, p. 24; Hall, p. 13.	
285.	1613	St. Botolph without Bishopgate, London	Marriage. n.d.: “Philip Upton with Joan Mure.”	BMI.	
286.	1613	St. Nicholas (Deptford), London	Baptism. 28 November: “…unser a blackamour that came in one of … [illegible] erne shyppes baptizd.”	Registers of St. Nicholas, Deptford, LMA P78/NIC/001; cited by Visram, *Asians in Britain*, p. 7; Anim-Addo, *Sugar, Spices*, p. 61.	This is Samuel Munsur, the East Indian (below).
287.	1613	St. Nicholas (Deptford), London	Marriage. 26 December: “Samuel Munsur and Jane Johnson.”	Registers of St. Nicholas, Deptford, LMA P78/NIC/001; cited Visram, p. 7; Anim-Addo, p. 61.	
288.	1614	St. Katherine by the Tower, Portsoken Ward, and St. Botolph without Aldgate, London.	Burial. 24 July: “John Matthews a black-moore lodging in the precinct next to the Tower servant to one Mr. Kellet in Market lane, was buryed	Register of St. Katherine by the Tower, GL 9221/1 Register General 1593–1602.	

			in the common ground, the xxiii day of July, Anno Dom 1614, was coffined and had the black clothe."		
289.	1615	St. Martin in the Fields, Westminster	Baptism. 19 December: "Fran. Blaky."	*Registers of St. Martin in the Fields, Westminster*, p. 46.	BMI lists the marriage of a "fran. blacky" with "elz. Mickelborrow" in 1619.
290.	1615/16	St. Olave, Hart Street, London	Baptism. 25 January: "Mark Antonio, a Negro."	*Registers of St. Olave, Hart Street*, p. 30.	The *faux* classical names that Elizabethan blacks are typically given are noted by Fryer, *Staying Power*, p. 24; Walvin, *Black and White*, p. 66; K.L. Little, p. 168.
291.	1615/16	St. Olave, Hart Street, London	Burial. 28 January: "Mark Anthonie, a negro Christian."	Registers of St. Olave Hart Street, GL 28867; *Registers of St. Olave, Hart Street*, p. 149.	
292.	1616	St. Martin in the Fields, Westminster	Burial. 4 April: "Franciscus Blaky."	*Registers of St. Martin in the Fields, Westminster*, p. 172.	
293.	1616	St. Dunstan in the West, London	Burial. 2 August: "Peter, a blackamore … from Mrs. Locksmithes."	Registers of St. Dunstan in the West, GL 10342; cited by Knutson, "A Caliban," p. 114.	
294.	1616	St Botolph without Aldgate, London	Burial. 26 September: "Isabell [illeg. Peters (?)], a blacke-Moore lodgying in blew Anchor Alley was buried the xxvi day of September, Anno Dom 1616. In our new churchyard."	Registers of St Botolph without Aldgate, GL 9223.	
295.	1616	All Saints Church, Staplehurst Parish, Staplehurst, Kent	Marriage. 16 October: "George a blackmore [and] Marie Smith."	Registers of All Saints Parish, Centre for Kentish Studies, ms P347, ref. # 560.	
296.	1616	St. Dionis Back Church, London	Public baptism. 22 December: "An East Indian was Christened by the name of Peter."	Registers of St. Dionis Backchurch, GL 17602l; *Register Book of St. Dionis Back*	This individual's full given name is Peter Pope (Petras Papa).

				Church, p. 96; Cited by Visram, *Asians in Britain*, p. 1.	
297.	1617	Chelsea, London	"Pedro" and "Guayacunda," two more Guyanians brought back by Walter Raleigh from his last trip, although the latter is usually called Christoval or Christopher.	Alden Vaughan, "Ralegh's Indian Interpreters," pp. 369–70.	
298.	1617	Chester, Cheshire	Medical/Legal. Court of Wards postmortem: "Blackamore, George: Chester, 14 Jas I. [1617]."	NatArch WARD 7/51/27.	
299.	1617	Holy Trinity the Less	Marriage. 24 December: "James Curres, beinge a Moore Christian and Margaret Person, a maid."	Registers of Holy Trinity the Less, GL 9155.	
300.	1617	St. Nicholas, Deptford, London	Baptized. 25 December: "Thomas Mamoto an Indian."	Registers of St. Nicholas, Deptford, LMA P78/NIC/001.	
301.	1618	St. Botolph, Aldgate, London	Burial. 27 April: "Ane Vause a Blak-more wife to Anthonie Vause trompeter."	Registers of St. Botolph, Aldgate, GL 9222/1; cited by Knutson, "A Caliban," p. 113.	
302.	1618	St. Botolph, Aldgate, London	Burial. 8 September: "James (an Indian) servant to Mr. James Duppa Beerebrewer."	Registers of St. Botolph, Aldgate, GL 9222/1; Cited by Forbes, *Chronicle*, p. 4.	Probably East Indian, according to Forbes.
303.	1618	St. Margaret's, Westminster (London)	Christening. 31 October: "Elizabeth Blackman *d* of John."	*Memorials of St. Margaret's Church, Westminster: Registers*, p. 99.	
304.	1619	Tiverton, Devon	Miscellaneous mention. n.d.: "[From the] Account Book of Blundell's School we learn that in 1619 the trustees sent a black boy to London on an errand."	Devon Record Office.	See the Devon County Council web page statement of 25 May 2000 at <http://www.devon.gov.uk/newsletter_may2000.pdf>. Seen 9.15.04.
305.	1619	St. Benet, Paul's Wharf, London	Marriage. 1 April: "Randall Blackmore & Elizabeth Seagood."	*Registers of St. Benet and St. Peter, Paul's Wharf*, p. 1.	Listed in Index as "Blakmore (Blackmore)," the parenthehetical word indicating the editorial

					suggestion for the meaning of the original name.
306.	1619	Colyton, Devon	Burial. 1 June: "Katheren, a blackamoor servant of Sir William Pole."	Devon Record Office.	
307.	1619	St. Mary, Mounthaw, London	Marriage. 26 September: "Lancelott Blackman and Mary Bragg."	*Registers of St. Mary Mounthaw*, p. 13.	
308.	1619/20	All Saints Church, Staplehurst Parish, Kent	Baptism. 13 February: "George A blackman S of George."	Registers of All Saints Parish, Centre for Kentish Studies, P347, ref. # 717.	
309.	1619/20	St. Margaret's, Westminster (London)	Baptism. 19 March: "Nicholas a Negro of unknown parents was baptized at the age of 3 yeares or thereabouts."	*Memorials of St. Margaret's Church*, p. 103.	
310.	1619/20	Dover, Kent	Legal record: 1. n.d. March: Petition of John Anthony "for payment of £30 wages, due to him for services on board the ship Silver Falcon, which the Mayor is ordered not to pay without warrant." 2. 20 March: "Item: the Mayor has paid the black boy's money with interest."	1 and 2: *CSP/D (Edward VI, Mary, Elizabeth and James 1619–1622)*, "Petition of John Anthony," March 1620, p. 131; cited Edwards and Walvin, *Black Personalities*, p. 11.	
311.	1620	St. Margaret's, Westminster, (London)	Marriage. 28 October: "John Blackman to Elizabeth Cornish."	*Memorials of St. Margaret's Church*, p. 328.	
312.	1621	London	Petition to Sir Thomas Smith, Knight, East India Company: "Item, more, for thirteen Negroes or Indian people, six wommen, seaven men, and boyes, the price of them not to be vallewed, for why … Well, the Estimacion of these poore Soules, they are not be vallewed at anie price. The cause why, I will shewe you, because the Lord Jesus	1. Pinkerton, "Cats, Dogs," pp. 345–46; cited Shyllon, *Black People*, pp. 6–7. 2. Fryer, *Staying Power*, p. 8 n. 18.	

			hath suffered Death as well for them as for all of you, for in time the Lord may call them to be true Christians … And now for the Thirteen Heathens … So far now my most Worshipful Masters, I most humblie beseeche for my heavenlie God, I may not receive Rewards either of Gold or Silver for such as are created after the Image, Similitude, and Likenesse of God, … 2. "thirteen negroes or Indian people, six women, seaven men and boyes" whom William Bragge claims to have transported to England and for which he demands £6875 from the East India Company.		
313.	1621	St. James, Clerkenwell, London	Burial. 15 June: "Elizabeth, wife of Thomas Blackman."	*True Register of St James, Clerkenwell*, p. 152.	
314.	1622	All Saints Church, Staplehurst Parish, Kent	Baptism. 19 May: "Elizabeth blackamore D of George 'the Blackamore.'"	Registers of All Saints Parish, Centre for Kentish Studies, P347, ref. #800.	
315.	1622	St. Benet, Paul's Wharf, London	Marriage. 31 October: "John Steele & Francis Blackmore."	*Registers of St. Benet and St. Peter, Paul's Wharf*, p. 7.	
316.	1623	St. Peter Paul's Wharf, London	Burial. 27 April: "Barbaree, servant to Mr. Smith upon St. Peter's Hill, the churchyard, coffined."	*Registers of St. Peter Paul's Wharf*, p. 209.	
317.	1623	St. James, Clerkenwell, London	Christening. 27 June: Thomas s. of Henry Blackman."	*True Register of St. James, Clerkenwell*, p. 96.	

318.	1623	St. James, Clerkenwell, London	Christening. 27 July: "Thomas s. of Andrewe Blackman & Mary [*his wife*]"	*True Register of St. James, Clerkenwell*, p. 96.	
319.	1623	St. Katherine by the Tower, London	Baptism. 20 Aug: "Phillip, an Indian blackmore, borne in the East Indies at Zarat."	Registers of St. Katherine by the Tower, GL 9659/2.	"Zarat" = Surat, on the west coast of India.
320.	1623	St. Botolph, Aldgate, London	Burial. 4 November: "a blackamoore woman that died in the street, named Marie."	Registers of St. Botolph, Aldgate, GL 9222/1.	
321.	1623	St. Botolph, Aldgate, London	Burial. 26 November: "'John Come Quicke,' a blacke-moore so named, servant to Thomas Love, a Captaine."	Registers of St. Botolph, Aldgate, GL 9222/1.	
322.	1624	St. Margaret's, Westminster (London)	Burial. 6 October: "Cattelina, a blackamoor."	*Memorials of St. Margaret's Church, Westminster: Registers*, p. 531.	
323.	1624/25	St Peter's, Cornhill	Baptism. 20 January: "Sonday Anthony, an Indian aboute the age of sixteene yeres."	*Registers of St Peter's, Cornhill*, p. 75.	
324.	1625	St. Mary, Putney, London	Vestry minutes. 27 March: "Martii 27 1625 At a vestrie holden at Putney by the inhabitants there of the vestrie Whereas Dame Anne Bromley hath bestowed £10 uppon the poore of the parishe there, to be imployed as a stocke for the releefe and comfort of the said poore in bread, or otherwise at the discretion of the said vestrie men. We whose names are underwritten in the name of the parishe doe	St. Mary Putney, Vestry Minutes, LMA P95/MRY1/413, p. 15; cited by Gerhold, "Black People," p. 22 and extracted in "Celebrating Black History in Wandsworth," pp. 7–8.	

			intertaine and are willing to receave the sayd monies, and shall endevor accordingly to settle the sayd monies as a continued stocke and the benefitt thereof to accrue unto the poore of the said parishe according to [the] good intendement and purpose of the said Ladies charitable mind. Nicholas Lusher William Leo Thomas Clarke William Offlie Robbart Angell Abraham Dawes Thomas Wootton William White Richard Willett Churchwarden Henry White Robert Boughton John Starkey Richard Penner his X mark Memorandum. That within the £20 abovementioned is contayned £10 a legacie of a Christian negro servant unto the sayd Ladie Bromley, and the other £10 is the gift of the sayd Ladie. Ita testor Guiliel. Leo."		
325.	1625	Almondsbury, Gloucestershire	1. Burial inventory. n.d. May: "Catellena a single Negro woman." 2. Probate inventory for Cattelena of the parish of Almondsbury singlewoman a negro. Her goods were worth £6.	1. Almondsbury, Gloucestershire Registers; Dresser, *Slavery Obscured*, p. 11; Bristol Probate inventories no. 18, May 1625, cited Jones and Youseph, *Black Population*, p. 2. 2. Bristol Record Office, Inventory 1625/18.	

326.	1626 (to 1664)	St. Mary, Putney, London	Churchwarden's account summary: "One of the first black people mentioned in Putney was Black Joan, who appears in the churchwardens' accounts receiving payment for menial tasks such as washing Sharpe's boy in 1626 and stripping and winding a poor man found dead in a barn in 1635. In 1627 and 1628 she received relief from the parish, and she was later awarded a place in the almshouse, whose accounts last record her in 1664."	St. Mary Putney, Churchwardens' Accounts 1623–1693, LMA, P95/MRY1/413, pp. 36, 42, 48, 55, 58; BL Add. MS 34718. Cited by Gerhold, "Black People," p. 22.	
327.	1626	St. Mary Woolnoth, London	Baptism. 10 December: "Andrew, son of Henry Blackmore."	*Registers of St. Mary Woolnoth and St Mary Woolchurch*, p. 37.	
328.	1626	St. Mary, Lewisham, London	Public baptism. 31 December: "George Horsan an Indian dwelling wth ye Lo: Arch Bp of Cant his Grace being presented at the ffount by Dcor Harns & Dcor Jefreys Chaplaines in House & after the Indian had made his confession of ffaith & Craving to be Baptised, was by Dcor ffeatly then Rector named Georg."	Registers of St. Mary, Lewisham, LMA P85/MRY1/342.	
329.	1626/27	St. Mary, Putney, London	Churchwardens' accounts. 20 March: "Henry White and Dunstone Duck Churchwardens: their accoumpts of monies receaved and paid out for the Church this yeare 1626: More receaved: of Mr Robart Angell the 2 of Maie 1626 by order of the Vestrie the some of £21.10 shillings being so much put into Mr Angells	St. Mary Putney, Churchwardens' Accounts 1623-1693. LMA P95/MRY1/413, p. 35. Cited by Gerhold, "Black People," p. 22, and extracted in "Celebrating Black History in Wandsworth," pp. 6–7.	

			hand to paie use for being the guift of the Lady Bromblie and a negro maid servant of hirs to the poore of this parish. And ordered by vestrie the daie above to be paid in to the churchwarden Henrie Whit to put out to use for the poor. £ 21.10 shillings"		
330.	1627	St. Nicolas Cole Abbey	Marriage. n.d.: "John Gibson with An Blackamore."	BMI.	
331.	1627	St. Dunstan, Stepney, London	Baptism. 26 October: "Mary a Negro maid bapt by that name out of the house of Anne Isaac of Limehouse widow by license from the Lo: 2BP of London the xxvi day of Octob 1627 Friday."	Registers of St. Dunstan, Stepney, LMA P93/DUN/256.	
332.	1628	St. Margaret's, Westminster (London)	Burial. 19 April: "Elizabeth Moore."	*Memorials of St. Margaret's Church*: *Registers*, p. 549.	
333.	1628	St. Margaret's, Westminster, (London)	Burial. 28 May: "Andrew Blackmoore."	*Memorials of St. Margaret's Church*: *Registers*, p. 549.	
334.	1628	Saltram Hall, Plymouth	Order. That Sir James Bagge's "negrowe" should be "handsomely clothed."	*CSP/D* (Charles I 1627–28), p. 521; cited Fryer, *Staying Power*, p. 25.	
335.	1629	St. Mary, Woolnoth, London	Baptism. 14 May: "Timothy, a heathen Blackamoore."	*Registers of St. Mary Woolnoth and St Mary Woolwich*, p. 38.	In the index this item is entered as: "Blackamoore, A."
336.	1630	St. Leonard's, Shoreditch	Baptism. 25 April: "James Kelly, an African Blackemoore, was baptised the 25th [of April 1630]: Hallywell Street."	Registers of St. Leonard's Shoreditch, GL 7493.	

337.	1630	St. Augustine (St. John), Hackney, London	Burial. 18 May: "Anthony a poore ould Negro aged 105 yeares was buried."	Registers of St. John, Hackney, LMA P79/JN1/021.	Mentioned (transcribed and actual entry displayed as a gif file), at <http://www.learningcurve.gov.uk/tudorhackney/localhistory/lochlp.asp> on 3 July 2004. [Site states: "We have no other record of Antony, who may have been a servant to a prosperous Hackney resident, a visiting nobleman, or who may have retired to Hackney as a freeman after years of service."]
338.	1630/31	St. Andrew's, Plymouth	Baptism. 17 January: "[Blank], Katherin d[aughter] of a Blackamore."	*Register of Baptism, Marriage and Burial of the Parish of St. Andrew's Plymouth*, p. 562.	
339.	1630/31	St. Augustine's Church, Bristol	Baptism. 4 February: "Solomon, a blakman of Mr. William. Haymans."	Registers of St. Augustine's Church, Bristol Record Office; cited Dresser, *Slavery Obscured*, p. 11.	
340.	1630/31	St. Mary Major, Exeter, Devon	Burial. 4 February: "Thomas, the son of a Blackamoor."	Devon Record Office.	
341.	1630/31	St. Dunstan, Stepney, London	Baptism. 9 February: "James sonne of Grace – a blackmore servant of Mr Bromfield of Limehouse begotten as she affirmeth by James Diego a Negro late servant to Mr Bromfield born in the house of William Ward of Limehouse mariner at 4 days old."	Registers of St. Dunstan, Stepney, LMA P93/DUN/256.	
342.	1632	Stepney, London, and Comissary Court, London	Church court record. April (n.d): "Grace—, a blackamoore presented by churchwardens for living incontinently with Walter Church, Stepney."	Commissary Court 'Ex Officio' Book, GL 9065E/1 fol .81.	
343.	1632	St. James, Clerkenwell, London	Burial. 8 July: "Dorkas Blackman, a poor child."	*True Register of St. James, Clerkenwell*, p. 205.	

344.	1632	St. Philip and Jacob's Church, Bristol	Burial. 12 September: "Mary a Blackmore & Servant to Willyam Edmondes."	Registers of St. Philip and Jacob's Church, Bristol Record Office; Dresser, *Slavery Obscured*, p. 11.	
345.	1632 (1630>)	Axeyard, Westminster, London	Personal anecdote. "He gott a terrible clap of a Black handsome wench that lay in Axeyard Westminster."	*Aubrey's Brief Lives*, p. 86.	
346.	1632/33	St. Andrew's, Plymouth	Baptism. 11 January: "[Blank], Elizabeth, d.[aughter] of Angell, A Blackmoore, the reputed father a fleming."	*Register of Baptisms, Marriages and Burials of the Parish of St. Andrew's, Plymouth*, p. 587; cited Fryer, *Staying Power*, p. 32 n. 33.	
347.	1633	St. Andrew Holborn, London	Burial. 17 April: "Thomas a[n] Indian, out of the Lord's house, was layed in the Church as Catumelant."	Registers of St. Andrew, Holborn, GL 6673/2.	
348.	1633	St. Margaret's, Westminster (London)	Marriage. 2 May: "Georg [*sic*] Hammond to Katherine Blackmoore."	*Memorials of St. Margaret's Church, Westminster: Registers*, p. 341.	
349.	1633	St. Olave, Hart Street, London	Baptism. 4 December: "Thomas Wood, a Blackmoore."	*Registers of St. Olave, Hart Street*, p. 43.	
350.	1635	St. Margaret's, Westminster (London)	Burial. 9 March: "Alice Blackman."	*Memorials of St. Margaret's Church, Westminster*, p. 569.	
351.	1635	Herne, Kent	Birth. n.d.: "Grace negres."	IGI.	
352.	1635	Fordwich, Kent	Baptism. n.d.: "Nich Bix 'an Indian Ethiopian youth now aged about 13' was baptised at Fordwich in 1635."	Sherwood, *Feversham Society Newsletter*.	An East Indian. "Ethiopian" here functions as a color descriptor, such as the word "negar" would.
353.	1636/37	St. Margaret's, Westminster (London)	Christening. 6 January: "Mary 'B B *d* of Christian Blackman.'"	*Memorials of St. Margaret's Church, Westminster*, p. 153.	B B = base born, i.e. born out of wedlock.
354.	1637	St. Gregory by St. Paul, London	Marriage. n.d.: "Nich. Finch with An Blacky."	BMI.	
355.	1637/38	St. Olave, Hart Street, London	Baptism. 13 January: "Abraham Thornburye, an Indian."	*Registers of St. Olave, Hart Street*, p. 48.	

356.	1638	St. Olave Hart Street, London	Baptism. 5 May: “Thomas Williams a blackamoor.”	*Registers of St. Olave, Hart Street*, p. 48.	
357.	1638	St. Mary, Stratford Bow, London	Baptism. 24 July: “Baptized a national & Natural Indian about ye age of 15 years by the name of James Robert(s) 24 Jul 1638 15 years old.”	Registers of St. Mary, Stratford Bow, LMA P88/MRY1/002.	An East Indian.
358.	1638	St. James, Clerkenwell, London	Burial. 19 October: “ffrancis Blackamore, a poor widow.”	*True Register of St James, Clerkenwell*, p. 236.	
359.	1638	St. Olave, Hart Street, London	Baptism of a 16-year-old female [n.d.]: “Indian Chirugeon [surgeon]” who is named “Loreto” in the church of St. Olave, Hart Street in 1638.	Greater London Council Publication, cited by Visram, *Asians in Britain*, p. 5.	Probably dies there in 1681; vide: “14 June 1681, burial of ‘Loreta, an India woaman, buryed in the near [new?] churchyard in Seething Lane, from Mr. Pewseye’s” (GL 28869, and *Registers of St. Olave Hart Street*, p. 222).
360.	1639	St. James, Clerkenwell, London	Burial. 6 August: “Mary d. of Raph Blackamore.”	*True Register of St James, Clerkenwell*, p. 239.	There are many entries for this person, “Raph Blackmore,” over several decades in this parish.
361.	1640	Church of Christ Broadmead, Bristol	Preacher’s memoir: n.d.: “By the goodness of God they had one Memmorable member aded unto them namely a Blackymore maide named Francis (a servant to one that lived upon ye Back of Bristoll) which thing is somewhat rare in our dayes and Nation, to have an Ethyopian or Blackmore to be truly Convinced of Sin; and of their lost State withoUt ye Redeemer and to be truly Converted to ye Lord Jesus Christ, as she was: which by her profession or declaration at ye time of her reception: together with her Sincere Conversation; she	*Records of a Church of Christ in Bristol*, p. 9, 101–2; cited Fryer, *Staying Power*, p. 32; cited Dresser, *Slavery Obscured*, p. 11.	Also see statement at the web page of Port Cities Bristol: “Many of the black people living in Bristol were Christians, and were baptised, married or buried in church. The church records often refer to their nationality or colour. One individual who appears in the church records of a Baptist chapel was called Frances. She was referred to as ‘an Ethiopian or blackamoor’. Ethiopia was often used to refer to the whole of Africa, rather than to the country in the North East. So the term Ethiopian probably meant that she was a black African,

			gave greate ground for Charity to believe she was truly brought over to Christ, for this poor Aethiopian's soule savoured much of God, and she walked very humble and blamelesse in her Conversation, to her end; and when she was upon her death bed: She sent a Remarkable Exhortation, unto ye whole Church with whom she walked, as her last request unto them: which argued her holy, childlike fear of ye Lord; and how precious the Lord was to her Soule; as was observed by the manner of her Expressing it. Which was this: one of the Sisters of ye Congregation coming to visit her, in her Sicknesse, She solemnly took her leave of her, as to this world: and pray'd ye Sister, to remember her to ye whole Congregation, and tell them, that she did Begg every soule, To take heed that they did lett The glory of God to be dear unto them a word meet for ye Church ever to remember; and for every particular member to observe, that they doe not loose ye glory of God in their families, neighbourhoods or places where God casts them: it being ye dyeing words of a Blackmoore, fit for a White heart to store. After which this Aethiopian yielded up ye Spirit to Jesus that redeemed her and was		not that she was from Ethiopia. Frances was a servant to a man who lived 'upon the Back of Bristol' (now known as Welshback). Frances was a valued member of the Baptist congregation in the Broadmead area of Bristol. She died in 1640." <http://www.discoveringbristol.org.uk/showNarrative.php?narId=471&nacId=474>. Seen 7.2.04.

			Honourably Interred being carryed by y^{e} Elders, & y^{e} chiefest of note of y^{e} Brethren in y^{e} Congregation (Devout men bearing her) to y^{e} grave, where she must rest untill our Lord doth come who will bring his Saints with him. By this in our days, we may see, Experimentally, that Scripture made good … that is God is no respecter of faces: But among all nations, &c. Acts 10: 34:35."		
362.	1640	St. Andrew's, Plymouth	Burial. 8 August: "a neager who was employed by Mr Abraham Jennings."	Registers of St. Andrew's, Devon Record Office.	
363.	1641	St. James, Clerkenwell, London	Burial. 3 March: "Eliz. Blackamore."	*True Register of St. James, Clerkenwell*, p. 252.	
364.	1641	St. Margaret's, Westminster (London)	Christening. n.d.: "James Blackman, *s* of Robert and Ann."	*Memorials of St. Margaret's Church, Westminster*, p. 173.	
365.	1642	London	Christening. 31 July: "Jehan Vannaigre."	IGI (Film no. 170591, p. no. 79, ref. no 3525.	
366.	1644-45	St. Margaret's, Westminster (London)	Marriage. 2 March: "Zachary Blackman to Anne Rivett."	*Memorials of St. Margaret's Church, Westminster*, p. 355.	
367.	1645	Newark, Parish, Nottinghamshire	Baptism. 30 March: "'John Americanus' a 'blackamore.'"	Nottinghamshire Archives; Cited in: <http://www.casbah.ac.uk//cats/print/105/NCCARCP01.htmq>. Seen 12.2.06.	Almost certainly an American Indian.
368.	1645	Lincoln's Inn Fields, Westminster (London)	Newspaper article. 10–17 April: *Sunday April 13* Give us leave to insert somewhat this day, and pardon the digression both to the day and also of the matter, it being not upon the subject of *Mars*, which is our business, but of *Venus*	*The Moderate Intelligencer*, VII, 10–17 April 1645, p. 53.	

			and *Bacchus*, It's a strange custome in *Lincolne's Inn-fields*, not far from the *Portugall* Ambasadours house, the practice we conceive every way as bad, as any that were used when the book of Recreations commanded or permitted maygames, and revellings: but not to keep you from the matter any longer: There gathers many hundreds of men, women, maids, and boyes together, then comes Negers, and others of like rankes, these make sport with our English women and maids, offer in the *Venetian* manner, by way of introduction to that used in their *Stewes*: why these black men should use our English maids and women upon the Lords day, or any other, in that manner, we know no reason for: but the truth is, the fault is wholly in those loose people that come there, and in the Officers of those Parishes where it is done.		
369.	1645	St. James, Clerkenwell, London	Burial. 4 September: "Humphrye s. of widow Blackamore."	*True Register of St James, Clerkenwell*, p. 264.	
370.	1645	St. James, Clerkenwell, London	Burial. 7 September: "Jone Blackamore, a poor woman."	*True Register of St James, Clerkenwell*, p. 264.	
371.	1646	London	Philosophical discourse: "On the Blackness of Negroes," "Of the same," "A Digression concerning Blackness."	Thomas Browne, *Pseudodoxia Epidemica*, Book VI, chapters 10, 11, 12, in *Works*, ed. Keynes, 2: 460–81.	
372.	1647	St. Benet, Paul's Wharf, London	Marriage. 6 April: "Phillip Hollybury and Grace Blackmurre."	*Registers of St. Benet and St. Peter, Paul's Wharf*, p. 287.	"blackmurre" is yet another version of "blackamoore."

373.	1647 (to 1667)	London and Bristol	1. Preacher's memoir. 31 May: Henry Jessey's account of the spiritual distress of "Dinah 'the Moor', as confessed to Sarah Wight: "*Mrs. S.* Do you see a want of faith? *Maid.* I am a filthy wretched sinner. *Mrs. S.* Are you tempted against your life? *Maid.* I am often tempted against my life, *Mrs. S. Why, what causeth it?* *Maid.* Sometimes this, because I am not as others are, I do not look so as others do." 2. Miscellaneous notation of a court document of July 1667. "A curious example of the practice of kidnapping human beings for transportation to America is recorded in the minutes of the Court of Aldermen in July. The justices note that one Dinah Black had lived for five years as servant to Dorothy Smith, and had been baptized, and wished to lived under the teaching of the Gospel; yet her mistress had recently caused her to be put aboard a ship, to be conveyed to the plantations. Complaint having been made, Black had been rescued, but her mistress (who had doubtless sold her) refused to take her back; and it was therefore ordered that she	1. *The Exceeding Riches of Grace Advanced*, 1651 and 1658, pp. 122–25. 2. Latimer, *Annals of Bristol*, p. 344; cited Shyllon, *Black People*, pp. 19–20.	

			should be free to earn her living until the case was heard at the next quarter sessions. The Sessions Book has perished. From the peculiar manner in which she is described, it may be assumed that Dinah was a negro woman captured on the African coast, and had lived as a slave in Bristol."		
374.	1647	St. Benet, Paul's Wharf, London	Marriage. 27 December: "Winfeild Blackamore & Elizabeth Benson."	*Registers of St. Benet and St. Peter, Paul's Wharf*, p. 28.	
375.	1647/48	St. Benet, Paul's Wharf, London	Baptism. 11 February: "Elizabeth d. of Winfeild Blackamore."	*Registers of St. Benet and St. Peter, Paul's Wharf*, p. 25.	Editorial note: "This entry is misplaced at the end of this year."
376.	1648/49	Sedgefield, Durham	Christening. 12 February: "Ana Negros."	IGI (Batch no. C000818).	"Negros"—another variant for Negro.
377.	1650	Sedgefield, Durham	Christening. 27 June: "Mariana Negro."	IGI (Batch no. C000818).	
378.	1652/53	St. Stephen, Walbrook, London	Marriage. 9 January: "Henry Studfeuld [Studfeild], of Alluhallowes the lessee, & Eliza. Blackmore, of this parish."	*Registers of St. Stephen Walbrook and St Benet, Sherehog*, p. 63.	
379.	1655	St. Margaret's, Westminster (London)	Burial. 1 November: "Elizabeth Blackman."	*Memorials of St. Margaret's Church: Registers*, p. 642.	
380.	1656	Leyton, Essex	Baptism. 2 October: "Joseph, the sonne of Master George Swanley gentleman and Barbare his wife was born the 28th of September baptized the 2nd of October."	Kennedy, *History of the Parish of Leyton*, p. 116.	
381.	1656-57	St. Margaret's, Westminster (London)	Christening. 22 February: "Elizabeth Blackmoore, *d* of Edward and Elizabeth."	*Memorials of St. Margaret's Church, Westminster*, p. 246.	
382.	1657	St. Margaret's, Westminster (London)	Burial. 2 June: "Elizabeth Blackmoore."	*Memorials of St. Margaret's Church, Westminster*, p. 648.	

383.	1658	Chulmleigh, Devon	Burial. 1 June: "Luce the Blackamoor."	Devon Record Office.	
384.	1658	(Middlesex) London	Court document. 21 October: accusation of Martin Francis against Elizabeth Simpson "That Katherine Hutchins, and Elizabeth Simpson and Mary Biggins pretended to make a marriage between Martin Francis (a blackamoore) and the said Elizabeth, thereby defrauding him of seventeen pounds in money."	Middlesex County Sessions of Peace, LMA Roll 1658: 1189/117, 281; cited by Hendricks, "Feminist Historiography," p. 372.	
385.	1659	St. Dunstan, Stepney, London	Baptism. 31 March: "31/Sara Reide of ye age of 27 years a Blackamore this day baptized."	Registers of St. Dunstan, Stepney, LMA P93/DUN/258.	
386.	1659	London	Newspaper notice. 4–11 August: "Advertisement A Negro boy about nine years of age, in a grey serge suit, his hair cut close to his head, was lost on Tuesday last August 9, at night in S. Nicholas Lane, London. If anyone can give notice of him to Mr. Tho. Barker, at the Sugar Loaf in that lane, they shall be well rewarded for their pains."	*Mercurius Politicus*, August 1659, no. 582, p. 654; cited Fryer, *Staying Power*, p. 22.	
387.	1659	St. Margaret's, Westminster (London)	Burial. 25 October: "Sarah Blackmore."	*Memorials of St. Margaret's Church, Westminster*: *Registers*, p. 658.	
388.	1659/60	St. Katherine by the Tower, London	Marriage. 19 January: "Joseph Lisbone married Martha Cradwell."	*Register of St. Katherine by the Tower*; cited Chater, "Hidden from History," p. 382.	
389.	1659/0	St. Margaret's, Westminster (London)	Burial. 28 February: "Adam Moore."	*Memorials of St. Margaret's Church, Westminster*: *Registers*, p. 655.	

390.	1660	St. Margaret's, Westminster (London)	Christening. 1 August: "Martha Blackmore, *d* of Edward and Elizabeth."	*Memorials of St. Margaret's Church: Registers*, p. 262.	
391.	1661	Leadenhall Street, London	Personal account. 22 May: "Early on the morning of the 22nd of May, the day being Monday, the king left Whitehall, by water, for the Tower, in order that he might, according to ancient custom, proceed through the city to Westminster Abbey… . Arriving at the great arch in Leadenhall Street, his ears were greeted by sounds of trumpets and drums playing marches; when they had finished, a short scene was enacted on a balcony of the arch, by figures representing Monarchy, Rebellion, and Loyalty. Then the great procession wended its way to the East India House, situate in the same street, when the East India Company took occasion to express their dutiful affections, in a manner 'wholly designed by person of quality.' As the king advanced, a youth in an Indian habit, attended by two blackamoors, knelt down before his majesty's horse, and delivered himself of some execrable verse, which he had no sooner ended than another youth in an Indian vest, mounted on a camel, was led forwards and delivered some lines praying his	Molloy, *Royalty Restored*, p. 28.	Also see the book version of this source at <http:// www.worldwideschool.

			majesty's subjects might never see the sun set on his crown or dignity."		
392.	1660	St. Giles in the Fields, (Middlesex) London	Baptism. 17 July: "frauncis Honey a Blackamoor."	Registers of St. Giles in the Fields, Middlesex, LMA 60.531 (St. Gl)/002.	
393.	1660	London	Diary entry. 9 October: "Among all the tales that passed among us to-day, he told us of one Damford, that, being a black man, did scald his beard with mince-pie and it came up again all white in that place and continued to his dying day."	Pepys, *Diary*, 1: 262.	
394.	1661	London	Personal diary. 27 March: "At last we made Mingo, Sir W. Batten's black, and Jack, Sir W. Pen's, dance, and it was strange how the first did dance with a great deal of seeming skill …	Pepys, *Diary*, 2: 61.	
395.	1661	Cardington, Bedfordshire	Baptism. 14 July: "Robart the blake more servant of Sr George Blundell was baptized the 14 day of July by doctor Thorne."	*Bedfordshire Registers*, 8 (1934): 18; cited Fryer, *Staying Power*, p. 32; Bedfordshire and Luton Archives and Records Service.	
396.	1661	St. Dunstan, Stepney, London	Baptism. 24 September: "Daniel Thomas a Negro servant to Mr. Hutchinson of stepnie baptized being 18 years old."	Registers of St. Dunstan, Stepney, LMA P93/DUN/258.	
397.	1662	London	Diary. 30 May: "Here we saw a little Turk and a negro, which are entended for pages to the two young ladies."	Pepys, *Diary*, 3: 95; cited Fryer, *Staying Power*, p. 21.	
398.	1662	St. Benet Fink, London	Burial. 20 November: "Emanuell Feinande, Mr Adams' friend's slave, a blackmore."	Registers of St. Benet Fink, GL 4098.	

399.	1662	St. Martin in the Fields, Westminster	Burial. 25 November: “Georgius Blackmore.”	Registers of St. Martin in the Fields, West.Arch. .	
400.	1662/63	Tyburn Tree, London	Personal journal entry. 7 March: “On the 7th we saw at Tyburn eleven people being hanged, three of the King’s bodyguard, two women, and one negress or coloured woman.”	Schellincks, *Journal*, p. 176.	
401.	1663	St. Martin in the Fields, Westminster (London)	Burial. 23 April: “Samuell Blackmore.”	Registers of St. Martin in the Fields, West.Arch.	
402.	1663 (1663 to 1730)	St. Martin’s (St. Martin in the Fields), Westminster (London) and Castle Cornet, Guernsey, and Gretton, Northamptonshire	1. Baptism. [n.d.]: “James Chapell, a Negro boy of 15, servant to Lord Christopher Hatton.” 2. Citation in Will of Sir Christopher Hatton. (signed) 7 May 1695: “And to my servant James Chapell I give one annuity of £20 a year during the term of his life.” 3. Burial. 17 February 1730: “James Chappell.”	1. Personal Communication from Nikki Taylor, Northamptonshire County Record Office. 2. NatArch Records of the Prerogative Court of Canterbury Prob 11/492, Poley Quire Numbers: 1–44 (document dated 19 February 1707). 3. Gretton Registers, Northamptonshire County Record Office.	
403.	1663	St. Mary, Putney	Baptism. 30 August: “John Brant a Neger Baptized at 22 yeares of age.”	Registers of St. Mary, Putney, LMA P95/MRY1/002.	
404.	1663/64	St. Katherine by the Tower, London	Baptism. 31 January: “son of Joseph Lisbone and Martha Cradwell.”	Chater, “Hidden from History,” p. 382.	Joseph Lisbone’s burial notice describes him as a “blackemore.”
405.	1663/64	St. Katherine by the Tower, London	Burial. 1 February: “Joseph Lisbone, a blackemore.”	*Register of St. Katherine by the Tower*, cited Chater, p. 382.	

406.	1663/64	St. Margaret's, Westminster (London)	Burial. 5 February [day]: "Ed. Blackmore *ch.*"	*Registers of St. Margaret's, Westminster*, i: 76.	
407.	1664	St. Vedast, Foster Lane, London	Baptism. 11 July: "Hannah Foster, and [*sic*] Indian, was baptized July the 11th, 1664. The Witnesses were John Woods, Mary Baily, and Elizabeth Weston; by Dr Shute."	*Registers of St. Vedast, Foster Lane*, p. 76.	
408.	1664	Little Stanmore, London	Baptism. [n.d.] October: "Richard Indem a Blackamoor catechized and baptized October."	Registers of Little Stanmore, LMA DRO/109/001.	"Indem" is most probably a variation/corruption of "Indian."
409.	1664/65	Chepsted, Chevening county, Kent	Baptism. 12 February: "John an Ethiopian a blackamoor Servant to the Lady Katharine Strode of Chepsted being 18 years of age or thereabouts as is supposed."	Chevening County Registers CMB 1564–1812, Centre for Kentish Studies; personal communication, Marika Sherwood.	
410.	1665	St. Olave Hart Street, London.	Burial. 29 July: "A negro man servant of Mr. John Newton's, from Mr. Raworthe; new chu [*sic*], y'd."	*Registers of St. Olave, Hart Street*, p. 200.	
411.	1665	London	Diary. 7 September: "a black boy that he had that died of a consumption; and being dead, he caused him to be dried in a Oven, and lies there entire in a box."	Pepys, *Diary*, 6: 215; cited Fryer, *Staying Power*, p. 25.	
412.	1665	St. Mary, Putney, London	Baptism. 10 September: "Edward Dedford, a black at John Turner's, being [blank] years, bap."	Registers of St. Mary, Putney, LMA P95/MRY1/365; cited Gerhold, "Black People," p. 22.	
413.	1666	St. James, Clerkenwell, London	Marriage. 4 April: "Phillip Waddleworth & Anne Nagar."	*True Register of St James, Clerkenwell*, p. 123.	
414.	1666	Pannier (Panyer) Alley, Farringdon, London	Diary. 13 April: "Called upon an old woman in Pannier Alley to agree for ruling some paper for me and she will	Pepys, *Diary*, 7: 98; cited Drake, *Black Folk*, 2: 287.	

			do it pretty cheap. Here I found her have a very comely black mayde to her servant which I liked very much."		
415.	1667	Arundell House, Strand, London	Diary entry. 30 May: "Anon, comes the Duchesse [of Newcastle], with her waiting woman attending her; amonst others, that Ferrabosco of whom so much talk is that her lady would bid show her face and kill the gallants. She is indeed black, and hath good black little eyes, but otherwise but a very ordinary woman, I do think; but they say sings well."	Pepys, *Diary*, 8: 243.	
416.	1667	Arundell House, Strand, London	Diary entry. 30 May: "a very pretty black boy that ran up and down the room, somebody's child in Arundell-house"	Pepys, *Diary*, 8: 243.	
417.	1667	Leyton, Essex	Baptism. 19 June: "Robert poppogunde blackeomore was baptized the same day *i.e.* as Mickele sonne to Sir William Hicks."	Kennedy, *History of the Paris of Leyton*, p. 116; partially cited by Fryer, *Staying* Power, p. 32 n. 33.	"Robert" is the first black entry in this register, but in the next 70 years the incidence of blacks jumps: they appear once every decade (albeit mostly in the baptism lists), including in 1778 "an East India Black" on 18 March, by the name of "Cœsar Giner."
418.	1667	St. James, Clerkenwell, London	Marriage. 26 September: "John Blackmore & Ane Hartley."	*True Register of St. James, Clerkenwell*, p. 131.	
419.	1667	Harwich, Essex	Will of Sir William Batten, keeper of the lighthouses at Harwich, Essex. 22 November: "Item I give and bequeath to my servante Mingoe a Negroe That now dwelleth with mee the	NatArch PROB 11/325, q 144. Digital copy of the record and a transciption of a partial extract of it available at: <http://www.nationalarchives.gov.uk/pathways/blackhistory/work_	

			somme of Tenne pounds to be paid within Twelve monethes next after my decease And I doe alsoe give unto him the said Mingoe the Custody and keeping of my Light houses Att Harwich, and the somme of Twenty pounds a yeare of lawfull money of England during the Terme of his naturall life for his paines therein."	community/docs/batten_will.htm>. Seen 9.14.04.	
420.	1667/68	St. Giles in the Fields, London	Baptism. 25 February: "John Paul a negro."	Registers of St. Giles in the Fields, LMA 60.531 (St. Gl)/002.	
421.	1667/68	St. Giles in the Fields, London	Baptism. 25 February: "Thomas Paul a negro."	Registers of St. Giles in the Fields, LMA 60.531 (St. Gl)/002.	
422.	1668	St. Saviour's, Southwark, London	Baptism. 11 October: "Ralph Trunckett, a blackamoore aged 20 years willingly bapt at Church p Mr. Webb."	Registers of St. Saviour's, Southwark, LMA P92/SAV/3003.	Is "willingly" a rare admission that some were *not* "willingly" baptized?
423.	1668	Arlingham, Gloucestershire	Baptism. 4 December: "Hannah, daughter of Thomas Liston, a Barbados merchant, was baptized."	Gloucestershire Archives, MS P23 IN 1/3.	According to James Turtle of the Gloucestershire Record office, this is a black person. See <http://www.irespect.net/history/Historic%20Records.htm>. Seen on 7.28.04.
424.	1669	St. Mary, Lambeth, London	Baptism. 4 April: "John the son of Abimelech Potter a blackamoor."	Registers of St. Mary, Lambeth, LMA P85/MRY1/342.	Probably a Muslim.
425.	1669	London	Diary entry. 5 April: "A black-moore of Mr. Belcher's (Doll), who dresses our meat mighty well and we mightily pleased with her."	Pepys, *Diary*, 9: 510; cited Fryer, *Staying Power*, p. 24.	
426.	1669	St. Paul, Covent Garden, Westminster, London	Burial. 22 July: "Clemen, a blackamore."	Registers of St. Paul, Covent Garden, West.Arch.	

427.	1670	Tichborne, Hampshire	"Lady Day," 25 March: Painting of Lord Tichborne handing out the dole in front of his country estate with his full household staff, and villagers, "[b]ut prominently placed in the foreground on the left edge of the painting—foregrounded, though marginalized—is a liveried dark-skinned (perhaps native American or East Indian) male servant who, with two other high ranking white male servants, is holding a basket of bread."	Gillis Van Tillborough, *Lord Tichborne Handing out the Dole*, English Heritage; McBride, *Country House Discourse*, pp. 88 and 90 (reproduction of painting).	Also see the statement on Hampshire County Council web page: "The manor of Tichborne is first identified in a grant of land to Denewulf, Bishop of Winchester, by King Edward the Elder in 909. In 938 Athelston gave certain lands at Tichborne to the monks of St. Peter and St. Paul at Winchester, and in 964 King Edgar granted Tichborne to Winchester Cathedral. There is no entry for Tichborne in the Domesday Book as it was probably included with Twyford. The Tichborne family has held the manor from the twelfth century onwards, and Tichborne House is the present manor house from which the Tichborne Dole is distributed annually on Lady Day (25th March). The ceremony originated in 1150 when Lady Tichborne lay dying and Sir Roger consented to provide a charity from as much land as his wife could walk round holding a lighted torch. Lady Mabel rose from her death-bed and managed to crawl around an area of land (still known as The Crawls) before the torch blew out. Before she died she prophesied that the House of Tichborne would fall if the charity were discontinued." Available at: <http://www.hants.gov.uk/

					localpages/central/alresford/ tichborne/>. Seen 10.17.04.
428.	ca. 1670	London and Paris	Personal citation. “When I was sent Ambassador from the late King to Paris, in the Year 1670. I took over with me a young Black-a-moor Boy, who could just make a Shift to be understood in *English*; and this boy one Holy-day Morning went along with some of my Gentlemen to see the Curiosities of so remarkable a City, and all of them at last went into *Notredame* church, as the Priest was celebrating Mass, at the high Mass. The Lad was perfectly surpriz’d at their rich Habits, and fine Musick; and when the Priest came to the *Elevation,* he ask’d one of my Gentlemen, what that white Thing was, which the Man in the Part-coloured Coat held up in his Fingers? Why, (replies he) these People believe it to be God Almighty. Not long after, at a side Altar he saw a Priest giving the Wafer to a parcel of People upon their Knees, and putting it into their Mouths. What, What, (cries he to the Gentleman) do they eat their God after they have so Solemnly worshipp’d him? Yes, answers he, this is their Belief. The Boy was so strangely confounded at what he had observed, that he spoke not a Syllable when he came home; but was moping	*A Conference on the Doctrine of Transubstantiation*, pp. 11–13; cited Fryer p. 24.	.

			and musing by himself. I could not but take notice of the Alteration in him at Dinner; So *Tom*, (says I to him) what's the matter with thee, if thour't ill go down to the House-keeper: No, cries he, I am not sick, but I have seen a very odd sight this Morning; which I can't help thinking on. I saw a Man in fine Cloaths show the People God, and they fell upon their knees, and beat their Brests; and afterwards I saw this Man put God into their Mouths, and they swallowed him. Well, says I, and where's the Harm in that, *Tom*? I don't know, says the Boy, why they should eat God, since he does us no Harm; but if they have the same power over the Devil, I wish we had a hundred or two of these fine men to eat the *Devil* for us; for we cannot rest for him a Nights, he pinches us in the Arms; sowrs our Palm Wine, spoils our Victuals, and is so Plaguy Mischievous, he and his young Cubs, that we should be glad to get rid of him at any Rate. And this Reflection a poor ignorant Lad, just come from *Guinea*, made of himself. "		
429.	1670	St. Nicholas, Deptford, London	Baptism. 24 July: "Robert a blacke."	Registers of St. Nicholas, Deptford, LMA P78/NIC/003.	
430.	1671	London—Lisbon	Government (consular) certificate. 5 October: "Thomas Maynard Consul Generall of the English Nation in all the Dominions of the Prince of	NatArch SP 89/11.	

			Portugall. We testifie to whom it may concerrn, that about the Middle of the Month of Sept last, the officers of the Inquisicon Seized a Negro boy called John Adue of about the age of Seventeen years, belonging to Richard Borthwick of London; wch Negro Boy was carried prisoner to the Inquisicon, upon the pretence that if he remained with his Master that he would make him a Heretick of which the said Richard Borthwick complaining to me, I drew up a Memoriall wch I delivered to the $Inquisito^{rs}$ of the great Table or Board, complaining of the great injuries, which they had done to his Ma^{ts} Subjects & violated the Treaty of Commerce betwixt the two Crownes: Especiall the afore said John Adue being borne a Subject of his Ma^{ts}. as I have been informed by the said Richard Borthwick; wch took of all Scruples of their pretences that they would noy have none of the Prince of Portugall's Subjects transported into England to be turned from the Roman Catholic Religion: Notwithtanding all and my often presing them to Restore the said Negro or the value of him they still retaine him in their power without giving any satisfactory answer, saying only that all Blacks, are within their Jurisdiction, and they will not		

			suffer them to become Hereticks. In witness … 5/15 of October 1671."		
431.	1672	St. Paul, Covent Garden, Westminster (London)	Burial. 6 April: "Thomas, a blackmore."	Registers of St. Paul, Covent Garden, West.Arch.	
432.	1672	St. Botolph, Aldersgate, London	Baptism. 12 May: "Joseph, a blackamore about 20 years of age."	Registers of St. Botolph, Aldersgate, GL 3854/1.	
433.	1672	St. Giles in the Fields, London	Baptism. 23 June: "James Mooty, Henry Cushdy, John Bonock, David Assica, Moores."	Registers of St. Giles in the Fields, LMA 60.531/002.	
434.	1672	St. Katherine Cree, London	Marriage. 26 September: "Paul Peache, a blackemore and Rosamond Key (by licence)."	Registers of St. Katherine Cree, GL 7890/1.	
435.	1672/73	St. Martin in the Fields (London) and Gretton, Northamptonshire	1. Marriage. 1 January: "Jacobi Chappell married Elizabethae [*sic*] Chappell." 2. Marriage. 7 May 1705: "James Chappel and Mercy Peach both of this parish."	1. Personal Communication, Nikki Taylor, Northamptonshire Record Office. 2. Gretton Registers, Northamptonshire Record Office, Wootton Hall Park, Mereway, Northampton NN4 8BQ.	
436.	1673	Savernake, Wiltshire	Deed. [n.d.] "Copy deed between John, Duke of Somerset and Alice Long (daughter of a blackamore, Britannia, a daughter of the King of Morocco), making provision for her descendants, and concerning a house between Brimslade Park and Burbage. Inclosures, and other property."	Wiltshire and Swindon Record Office, Savernake Estate, File 9/22/212 – date: 1673.	
437.	1674	Kensington, London	Burial. 26 March: "Theophilus Cock, a Blackamore, S[r] john Thorowgoods foot-boy."	*Registers of Kensington*, p. 145.	

438.	1674	St. Mary, Lambeth, London	Baptism. 29 March: "Thomas Springe, a blackemore supposed to bee about Eight uears of age."	Registers of St. Mary, Lambeth, LMA P85/MRY1/342.	
439.	1674	Winiwick, Northampton	Burial. 17 December: "A Guinean boy, Servt. Sr. Wm. Craven, baptized y[e] summer before and named Winiwick, was buried December 17."	WRNCRO.	
440.	1675	Holy Trinity, Knightsbridge, London	Marriage. 25 April: "Daniel Price and Jane Blackamore."	*Registers of Holy Trinity, Knightsbridge*, p. 58.	
441.	1675	St. Olave, Hart Street, London	Public baptism. 29 April: "George, an Indian servant of Mr. Robert Andrews, chirugeon, aged 16 yeares or thereabouts, Christened in ye publique congregation."	Registers of St. Olave, Hart Street, GL 28868; *Registers of St. Olave, Hart Street*, p. 81.	
442.	1675	St. Mary Woolnoth, London	Burial. 26 June: "A blackamore boy of Mr. John Temple, *Goldsmith*."	*Registers of St. Mary Woolnoth and St Mary Woolwich*, p. 241.	
443.	1675	St. Clement Danes, London	Baptism. 21 December: "Charles, a black, his name Hercules."	Registers of St. Clement Danes, West.Arch.	
444.	1675/76	Christchurch Newgate Street, London	Baptism. 22 January: "Thomas Dingley," "Hannah Botun," 'blackamores.'"	Registers of Christchurch Newgate Street, GL 3713/1.	
445.	1676	Leyton, Essex	Burial. 30 July: "Anne daughter of Robert the Black from Mile End."	Kennedy, *History of the Paris of Leyton*, p. 128.	
446.	1676	Gretton, Northamptonshire	Baptism. 9 October: "Elizabeth the daughter of James Chappell baptised 1676."	Gretton Registers, Northamptonshire County Record Office, Wootton Hall Park, Mereway, Northampton NN4 8BQ.	
447.	1676	St. Margaret's, Westminster (London)	Marriage. 12 December: "Jo. Johnson to Eliz. Blackmoore. L."	*Registers of St. Margaret's, Westminster*, 1: 66.	"L" = by license.

448.	1677	London	Court ruling: "Trover for 100 Negroes, and upon *Non Culp* it was found by special Verdict, that the Negroes were Infidels, and the Subjects of an Infidel Prince. and are usually bought and sold in America as Merchandise. by the Custom of Merchants, and that the Plaintiff bought these. and was in possession of them until the Defendant took them. And Thompson argued, there could be no Property in the Person of a Man sufficient to maintain Trover. and cited Co. Lit. 116. That no Property could be in Villains hut by Compact or Conquest. But the Court held, that Negroes being usually bought and sold among Merchants, and so Merchandise, and also being Infidels, there might be a Property in them sufficient to maintain Trover, and gave Judgmem for the Plaintiff, *nisi Causa*, this Term:"	"Butts v. Penny," Catterall, *Judicial Cases*, 1: 9.	

Works Cited

Primary Sources

Libraries and Archives

Bedfordshire and Luton Archives and Records Service, Riverside Building, County Hall, Bedford MK42 9AP. <http://www.casbah.ac.uk/surveys/archivereportBLARS.stm> 7.5.05.

Bodleian Library, Oxford, Broad Street, Oxford OX1 3BG.

Bristol Record Office, 'B' Bond Warehouse, Smeaton Road, Bristol BS1 6XN.

British Library, 96 Euston Road, London, NW1 2DB.

Canterbury Register Office, Wellington House, St Stephen's Road, Canterbury, CT2 7RD.

Centre for Kentish Studies, Sessions House, County Hall, Maidstone ME14 1XQ, . <http://www.kent.gov.uk/leisure-and-culture/archives-and-local-history/archive-centres/centre-for-kentish-studies.htm > 13.5.05.

City of Westminster Archives, 10 St Ann's Street, London SW1P 2DE.

Devon Record Office, Great Moor House, Bittern Road, Sowton, Exeter, EX2 7NL. <devrec@devon.gov.uk>

East Kent Archives Centre, Enterprise Zone, Honeywood Road, Whitfield, Dover CT16 3EH, . <http://www.kent.gov.uk/leisure-and-culture/archives-and-local-history/archive-centres/east-kent-archives-centre.htm> 14.8. 06.

Family Tree Legends Genealogical website at <http://www.familytreelegends.com/trees/patlowe/1/data/613> 12.9.06.

Folger Shakespeare Library, 201 E. Capitol Street, Washington, DC.

Gloucestershire Archives, Clarence Row, Alvin Street, Gloucester, GL1 3DW. <archives@gloucestershire.gov.uk> and <http://www.irespect.net/history/Historic%20Records.htm>

Guildhall Library, Aldermanbury, EC2P 2EJ, London.

Hampshire Record Office, Sussex Street, Winchester, SO23 8TH. <http://www.hants.gov.uk/record-office/> 22.7.06.

International Genealogical Index. Electronic Access at <www.familysearch.org/> 24.11.05

Libraries and Heritage HQ, Wiltshire County Council, Bythesea Road, Trowbridge, BA14 8BS, Wiltshire. <http://www.wiltshire.gov.uk/leisure-and-culture/access-to-records/wiltshire-and-swindon-record-office.htm> 1.7.05.

Local Studies and Archives, Bromley Public Libraries, Bromley, Kent BR1 EX. <www.bromley.gov.uk/libraries/librariesintheborough/bromley_archives.htm>

Local Studies Centre, London Borough of Lewisham, Town Hall, Catford, London SE6 4RU.

London Metropolitan Archives, 40 Northampton Road, Clerkenwell, London, EC1R 0HB.

National Archives, Kew, Richmond, Surrey TW9 4DU. <www.nationalarchives.gov.uk>

National Archives of Scotland, Edinburgh, HM General Register House, 2 Princes Street, Edinburgh Eh13Y. <www.nas.gov.uk>

Northamptonshire County Record Office, Wootton Hall Park, Mereway, Northampton NN4 8BQ. <http://www.northamptonshire.gov.uk/Community/record/about_us.htm> 24.2.06.

North Devon Record Office, Tuly Street, Barnstaple EX31 1EL. <http://www.devon.gov.uk/index/community/the_county/record_office/> 3.3.06.

Nottinghamshire Archives, County House, Castle Meadow Road, Nottingham, NG2 1AG, . <www.nottscc.gov.uk/libraries/archives/index.htm> and <www.nottinghamshire.gov.uk/archives> 10.1.05.

Printed Sources

The Accounts of the Lord High Treasurer of Scotland, ed. Thomas Dickson, Sir James Balfour Paul, C. T. McInnes, and Athol L. Murray. 13 vols. Edinburgh: H. M. General Register House, 1877.

Acts of the Privy Council of England (1542–1604). Ed. John Roche Dasent. 32 vols. 1890; Nendeln, Liechtenstein: Kraus Reprint, 1964.

Adams, Simon, ed. *Household Accounts and Disbursement Books of Robert Dudley, Earl of Leicester, 1558–1561, 1584–1586*. London: Cambridge University Press, 1995.

Africanus, John Leo. *A Geographical Historie of Africa*. London: John Bishop, 1600.

Anglo, Sydney, ed. *The Great Tournament Roll of Westminster: A Collotype Reproduction of the Manuscript*. Oxford: Clarendon Press, 1968.

Arnold, Janet, ed. *Queen Elizabeth's Wardrobe Unlock'd : The Inventories of the Wardrobe of Robes Prepared in July 1600, Edited from Stowe Ms 557 in the British Library, Ms Lr 2/121 in the Public Record Office, London, and Ms V.B.72 in the Folger Shakespeare Library, Washington DC*. Leeds: Maney, 1988.

Aubrey, John. *Aubrey's Brief Lives*. Ed. Oliver Lawson Dick. Ann Arbor: University of Michigan Press, 1957.

——. *Brief Lives*. Ed. Richard Barber. Totowa, N.J.: Barnes and Noble, 1982.

Beaugue, Jean de. *The History of the Campagnes 1548 and 1549: Being an Exact Account of the Martial Expeditions Perform'd in Those Days by the Scots and French on the One Side, and by the English and Their Foreign Auxiliaries on the Other* (1556). N.p., 1707.

Beaven, Alfred B. *The Aldermen of the City of London, Temp. Henry III–1908*. London: Corporation of the City of London, 1913.

Bedfordshire Parish Registers. Ed. F. G. Emmison. 30 vols. Bedford, Bedfordshire: County Record Office, 1931–53.

Best, George. *A True Discourse of the Late Voyages of Discouerie, for the Finding of a Passage to Cathaya, by the Northvveast, under the Conduct of Martin Frobisher Generall, Deuided into Three Bookes*. London: Henry Bynnyman, seruant to the right Honourable Sir Christopher Hatton Vizchamberlaine, 1578.

Birdwood, George, and William Foster, eds. *The Register of Letters &C. Of the Governour and Company of Merchants of London Trading into the East Indies, 1600–1619*. London: B. Quaritch, 1893.

"Black Presence." Web essay. Corporation of London web page. <www.corpoflondon.gov.uk/Corporation/lma_learning/schoolmate/Bal/sm_bal_stories_detail.asp?ID=31> 30.8.04.

Boyd's Marriage Index. Electronic Database. <www.originsnetwork.com/help/popup-helpbo-bmi.htm> 10.8.05.

Browne, Thomas. *The Works of Sir Thomas Browne*. Ed. Geoffrey Keynes. Chicago: University of Chicago Press, 1964.

Burke, Bernard. *A Genealogical History of the Dormant Abeyant, Forfeited, and Extinct Peerages of the British Empire* (1866). Baltimore: Genealogical Publishing Co., 1978.

Calendar of Letters, Despatches, and State Papers Relating to the Negotiations between England and Spain, Preserved in the Archives at Simancas and Elsewhere (CSP Spanish) (1862). Ed. G. A. Bergenroth. 13 vols. Nendeln, Leichtenstein: Kraus Reprint, 1969.

Calendar of State Papers, Domestic: James I, 1603–1610 (1857). 2006. Electronic database. <www.british-history.ac.uk/report.asp?compid=15003&strquery=paul%20bayning> 20.4. 2006.

Calendar of State Papers, Domestic Series, of the Reign of Edward VI 1547–1553. Ed. C. S. Knighton London: H. M. Stationer's Office, 1992.

Calendar of State Papers, Domestic Series, of the Reigns of Edward VI, Mary, Elizabeth, and James I. Preserved in the Public Record Office. Ed. Mary Anne Everett Green. Vol. X: 1619–22. London: Longman, Brown, Green, Longmans and Roberts, 1856–72.

Calendar of State Papers, Domestic Series, of the Reign of Charles I. Preserved in the Public Record Office. Ed. John Bruce. Vol. II: 1627–28. London: Longman, Brown, Green, Longmans, & Roberts 1858–90.

Camden, William. *Britannia or a Chorographical Description of the Most Flourishing Kingdoms, England, Scotland and Ireland, and the Islands Adjoining, out of the Depth of Antiquity: Beautified with Maps of the Several Shires of England . . .* (1586). London: A Churchill, 1722.

Cameron, Annie I., ed. *The Scottish Correspondence of Mary of Lorraine*. Edinburgh: Scottish History Society, 1927.

Carr, Cecil T. *Select Charters of Trading Companies 1530–1707* (1913). New York: Burt Franklin, 1970.

Catterall, H. T., David Maypole Matteson, and James J. Hayden. *Judicial Cases Concerning American Slavery and the Negro*. Washington, D.C.: Carnegie Institution of Washington, 1926–37.

Chambers, E. K. *The Elizabethan Stage*. 4 vols. Oxford: Clarendon Press, repr. 1997.

Chanter, J. R., *Sketches of the Literary History of Barnstaple*. Barnstaple, Devon: E. J. Arnold, 1866.

——, and Thos. Wainwright. *Reprint of the Barnstaple Records*. 3 vols. Barnstaple, Devon: A. E. Barnes, 1900.

Charles I. *Charles I in 1646: Letters of King Charles the First to Queen Henrietta Maria.* Ed. John Bruce. London: Camden Society, 1856.

Chater, Kathy. "Hidden from History: Black People in Parish Records." *Genealogists' Magazine* 26/10 (2000): 381–85.

Chronicles of London. Ed. C. L. Kingsford. Derby: Alan Sutton, 1977.

Cokayne, George E. *Some Account of the Lord Mayors and Sheriffs of the City of London.* London: Phillimore and Co., 1897.

A Collection of State Papers Relating to Affairs of the Reigns of King Henry VIII, King Edward VI, Queen Mary and Queen Elizabeth from the Year 1542 to 1570. Ed. S. Haynes. 2 vols. London: William Bowyer, 1740.

The Commissions for Building Fifty New Churches: The Minute Books, 1711–27, a Calendar. 1986. Electronic database. London Record Society. <www.british-history.ac.uk/report.asp?compid=38869> 2.7.06.

Complete State Papers Domestic. Microform. Brighton: Harvester Press, 1977–81.

The Complete State Papers Domestic 1509–1702. Microform. Woodbridge, CT: Research Publications International, 1993–95.

Copland, Patrick. *Memoir of Reverend Patrick Copland.* Ed. Edward D. Neill. New York: Charles Scribner and Sons, 1871.

——, and Peter Pope. *Virginia's God Be Thanked, or a Sermon of Thanksgiving for the Happie Successe of the Affayres in Virginia This Late Yeare. Preached by Patrick Copland at Bow-Church in Cheapside before The ... Virginia Company ... 18 of April, 1622 ... Hereunto Are Adjoyned Some Epistles Written First in Latine (and Now Englished) in the East Indies by Peter Pope, an Indian Youth ... Who Was ... Baptised ... In London, December 22, 1616*. London: John Dawson, 1622.

Davenant, William. *Sir William Davenant's* Gondibert. Ed. David F. Gladfish. Oxford: Clarendon Press, 1971.

Davenport, Frances Gardiner, ed. *European Treaties Bearing on the History of the United States and Its Dependencies to 1648*. Washington, DC: Carnegie Institution of Washington, 1917.

Debrett, John. *The Peerage of the United Kingdom of Great Britain and Ireland.* 2 vols. London: J. Moyes, 1812.

The Diary of Henry Machyn Citizen and Merchant-Taylor of London from A.D. 1550 to A.D. 1563. Ed. J. B. Nichols. London: Camden Society, 1848.

The Diary of Lady Anne Clifford. Ed. V. Sackville-West. London: Heinemann, 1923.

The Diaries of Lady Anne Clifford. Ed. D. J. H. Clifford. Stroud, Gloucestershire: Alan Sutton, 1990.

A Dictionary of London (1918). 2006. Electronic database. Centre for Metropolitan History. <www.british-history.ac.uk/report.asp?compid=8>. 17.4. 06.

Dictionary of National Biography. Ed. Sidney Lee and Leslie Stephen. London: Elder Smith, 1901.

Dictionary of the Scottish Language. Electronic Database. <www.dsl.ac.uk/dsl/2005> 9.7.05.

Dillingham, John. *The Moderate Intelligencer*. London: R. W., 1645–49.

Documents of the Rose Playhouse. Revised Edition. Ed. Carol Chillington Rutter. New York: Manchester University Press, 1999.

Donnan, Elizabeth, ed. *Documents Illustrative of the History of the Slave Trade to America*. 4 vols. Washington, DC: Carnegie Institute of Washington, 1930.

Dunbar, William. *The Poems of William Dunbar*. Ed. David Laing. 2 vols. Edinburgh: Laing and Forbes, 1834.

——. *The Poems of William Dunbar*. Ed. James Kinsey. London: Oxford University Press, 1970.

Eden, Richard. *The Decades of the New World and West Indies*. London: Guilhelmi Powell, 1555.

——. *The History of Travel*. Ed. Richard Willes. London: R. Iugge, 1577.

Evelyn, John. *The Diary of John Evelyn*, ed. E. S. de Beer. London: Oxford University Press, 1959.

The Exceeding Riches of Grace Advanced. London: Printed by J. C. for Henry Mortlock, 1658. Early English Books Online. <eebo.chadwyck.com>

Fanshawe, Ann, Lady. *The Memoirs of Ann, Lady Fanshawe*. Whitefish, MT: Kessinger, 2005.

ffarington, William. *The Derby Household Books; Comprising an Account of the Household Regulations and Expenses of Edward and Henry, Third and Fourth Earls of Derby; Together with a Diary Containing the Names of the Guests Who Visited the Latter Earl at His Houses in Lancashire*. Stanley Papers, Pt. 2. Ed. Revd. F. R. Raines. Vol. 31. Manchester: Chetham Society, 1853.

Fletcher, Francis. *The World Encompassed by Sir Francis Drake: Being His Next Voyage to That to Nombre De Dios* (1628). Hakluyt Society Publications 16. New York: Burt Franklin, n.d.

Fortescue, John Sir. *De Laudibus Legum Angliae*. Trans. S. B. Chrimes. Cambridge: Cambridge University Press, 1942.

Foster, John. *The Statesmen of the Commonwealth of England: With a Treatise on the Popular Progress in English*. London: Longman, Orme, Brown, Green & Longmans, 1840.

Fuller, Thomas. *The Worthies of England*. Ed. John Freeman. London: George Allen and Unwin Ltd., 1952.

Gardiner, Samuel Rawson. *History of England from the Accession of James I, to the Outbreak of the Civil War 1603–1642*. London: Longman, Green and Co., 1884.

——, ed. *Letters and Papers Relating to the First Dutch War*. London: Navy Records Society, 1930.

Glanville, John. *The Voyage to Cadiz in 1625: Being a Journal Written by John Glanville, Secretary to the Lord Admiral of the Fleet*. Ed. A. B. Grossart. London: Camden Society, 1883.

Hakluyt, Richard. *Diverse Voyages Touching the Discovery of America and the Islands Adjacent*. Ed. John Winter Jones. London: Hakluyt Society, 1850.

——. *The Principal Navigations, Voyages, Traffiques of the English Nation*. Ed. Edmund Goldsmid. 16 vols. Edinburgh: E. & G. Goldsmid, 1889.

——. *Voyages of the Elizabethan Seamen to America: Thirteen Original Narratives from the Collection of Richard Hakluyt*. Ed. E. J. Payne. London: T. De La Rue & Co., 1880.

Harrison, William. *Harrison's Description of England in Shakespere's Youth*. The New Shakspere Society Publications. Ed. Frederick J. Furnivall. Vaduz: Kraus Reprint Ltd., 1965. 2 vols.

——. *The Description of England*. The Folger Shakespeare Library. Ed. Georges Edelen. Ithaca, New York: Cornell University Press, 1968.

Harvey, P. D. *Maps in Tudor England*. London: The Public Record Office and The British Library, 1993.

Hasted, Edward. *The History and Topographical Survey of the County of Kent* (1797). 12 vols. Menaton, Yorkshire: Scolar Press, Ltd, 1972.

Hawkins, John. *The Hawkins' Voyages during the Reigns of Henry VIII, Queen Elizabeth, and James I*. Ed. Clements R. Markham. New York: Burt Franklin.

Henry, L. W. "The Earl of Essex as Strategist and Military Organizer (1596–97)." *English Historical Review* 68/268 (1953): 363–93.

Hentzner, Paul, and Sir Robert Naunton. *Travels in England during the Reign of Queen Elizabeth and Fragmenta Regalia*. London: Cassell, 1892.

Hinson, Colin. "Clerkenwell History." 2006. Electronic Essay. GENUKI: English and Irish Genealogy. <homepages.gold.ac.uk/genuki/MDX/Clerkenwell/ClerkenwellHistory.html> 13.6.06.

——. "Hackney: Description and History from 1868 Gazetteer." 2006. Electronic Essay. GENUKI. <homepages.gold.ac.uk/genuki/MDX/Hackney/HackneyHistory.html> 18.7.2006.

Historical Gazetteer of London before the Great Fire: Cheapside; Parishes of All Hallows Honey Lane, St Martin Pomary, St Mary Le Bow, St Mary Colechurch and St Pancras Soper Lane (1987). Electronic Database. Centre for Metropolitan History. <www.british-history.ac.uk/report.asp?compid=1618&strquery=thomas%20barber. > 4.10.06.

History of Collections: Or an Exact Account of the Proceedings of the Four Last Parliaments of Q. Elizabeth (1680). 2006. Electronic Database. History of Parliament Trust. <www.british-history.ac.uk/report.asp?compid=43562&strquery=stallenge> 15.9.06.

A History of the County of Bedford, Volume 3 (1912). Electronic Database. Victoria County History. <http://www.british-history.ac.uk/report.asp?compid=42422> 28.3.06.

A History of the County of Essex, Volume 6 (1973). Ed. W. R. Powell. Electronic Database. Victoria County History. <http://www.british-history.ac.uk/source.asp?pubid=283> 2.10.06.

A History of the County of Lancashire, Volume 3 (1907). Electronic Database. Victoria County History. <http://www.british-history.ac.uk/report.asp?compid=41314> 17.9.03.

A History of the County of Middlesex, Volume 4: Harmondsworth, Hayes, Norwood with Southall, Hillingdon with Uxbridge, Ickenham, Northolt, Perivale, Ruislip, Edgware, Harrow with Pinner (1971). Electronic Database. Victoria County History. <www.british-history.ac.uk/report.asp?compid=22419&strquery=robert%20vyner> 8.8.06.

A History of the County of Middlesex, Volume 5: Hendon, Kingsbury, Great Stanmore, Little Stanmore, Edmonton Enfield, Monken Hadley, South Mimms, Tottenham (1976). Electronic Database. Victoria County History. <www.british-history.ac.uk/report.asp?compid=26993> 30.6.06.

A History of the County of Middlesex, Volume 10: Hackney. Electronic Database. Victoria County History. <www.british-history.ac.uk/report.asp?compid=22694> 18.7.06.

A History of the County of Middlesex, Volume 11: Stepney, Bethnal Green. Ed. T. F. T. Baker, 1998. Electronic Database. <www.british-history.ac.uk/report.asp?compid=22740> 9.5. 2006.

A History of the County of Northamptonshire, Volume 5: The Hundred of Cleley. 2002. Electronic Database. Victoria County History. http://www.british-history.ac.uk/report.asp?compid=22788. 23.1.2006.

A History of the County of Surrey (1912). Electronic Database. Victoria County History. www.british-history.ac.uk/report.asp?compid=43035&strquery=putney. 20.6.2006.

A History of the County of Wiltshire, Volume 16: Kinwardstone Hundred (1999). Electronic Database. Victoria County History. http://www.british-history.ac.uk/report.asp?compid=23049. 24.9.05.

Hortop, Job. *The Rare Travails of Job Hortop*. Ed. G. R. G. Conway. 1st ed. Marsella, Mexico: no pub., 1928.

Howell, Thomas Bayly, et al. *A Complete Collection of State Trials and Proceedings for High Treason and Other Crimes and Misdemeanors from the Earliest Period to the Year 1783*. 34 vols. London: T. C. Hansard for Longman, Hurst, Rees, Orme, and Brown . . ., 1816.

Hume, M. A. S., ed. *Chronicle of King Henry VIII, Being a Contemporary Record of Some of the Principal Events in the Reigns of King Henry VIII and Edward VI.* London: George Bell, 1889.

The Inhabitants of London in 1638 (1931). 2006. Electronic Database. Centre for Metropolitan History. <www.british-history.ac.uk/report.asp?compid=32035&strquery=st.%20mary%20mounthaw> 14.6.06.

James I. *The Political Works of James I*. Ed. Charles Howard McIlwain. New York: Russell and Russell, 1965.

Journal of the House of Commons, Volume 2: *1640–1643* (1802). 2006. Electronic Database. The History of Parliament Trust. <www.british-history.ac.uk/report.asp?compid=7253&strquery=paul%20banning> 19. 4.06.

Journal of the House of Commons, Volume 3: *1643–1644* (1802). 2006. Electronic Database. The History of Parliament Trust. <www.british-history.ac.uk/report.asp?compid=6715&strquery=portugal%20ambassador> 25.7.06.

Journal of the House of Commons, Volume 5: *1646–1648* (1802). 2006. Electronic Database. The History of Parliament Trust. <www.british-history.ac.uk/report.asp?compid=25308&strquery=thomas%20love> 21.6.06.

Journal of the House of Lords: Volume 5: *1642–1643* (1802). 2006. Electronic Database. History of Parliament Trust. <www.british-history.ac.uk/report.asp?compid=34840&strquery=antonio%20de%20sousa> 24.7.06.

Justinian, *The Digest of Justinian*, ed. A. Watson. 2 vols. Philadelphia: University of Pennsylvania Press, 1998.

Kennedy, John. *A History of the Parish of Leyton, Essex*. Leyton, Essex: Phelps Brothers, 1894.

Knighton, C. S., and David Loades. *Letters from the Mary Rose*. Thrupp Stroud, Gloucestershire: Sutton Publishing Ltd., 2002.

Lancashire, Ian. *Early Modern English Dictionaries Database* (EMEDD), Online Database. <www.chass.utoronto.ca/english/emed/emedd.html>

Letters and Papers, Foreign and Domestic, of the Reign of Henry VIII. Ed. (var.) James Gairdner, J. S. Brewer, R. H. Brodie. 2nd ed. 21 vols. in 32 pts. Vaduz: Kraus Reprint Ltd., 1965.

Letters and Papers Illustrative of the Reigns of Richard III and Henry VII. Rerum Britannicarum Medii Aevi Scriptores. Ed. James Gairdner. 2 vols. London: Longman, Green, Longman, and Roberts, 1861–63.

Letters Received by the East India Company from Its Servants in the East, ed. Frederick Charles Danvers and William Foster. 6 vols. London: S. Low Marston, 1896.

Lindsay, Robert, of Pitscottie. *The History and Cronicles of Scotland*. The Scottish Text Society. Ed. by AE. J. G. Mackay. 3 vols. New York: Johnson Reprint Corp., 1966.

Locke, J. Courteney. *The First Englishmen in India: Letters and Narratives of Sundry Elizabethans Written by Themselves*. New York: AMS Press, 1970.

Locke, John. *The Second Treatise on Civil Government*. Buffalo, NY: Prometheus Books, 1986.

Mandeville, John. *The Travels of John Mandeville* (1324). Ed. by A. W. Pollard. New York: Dover, 1964.

Marlowe, Christopher. *Dr. Faustus*. Ed. by Michael Keefer. New York: Broadview Press, 1991.

Memorials of St. Margaret's Church, Westminster: The Parish Registers 1539–1660. Ed. by Arthur Meredith Burke. London: Eyre and Spottiswoode, Ltd., 1914.

Memorials of Stepney Parish; That Is to Say the Vestry Minutes from 1579 to 1662, Now First Printed, with an Introduction and Notes. Ed. George Hill and Walter Frere. Guildford: Billing and Sons, 1890–91.

Mercurius Politicus Comprising the Sum of Foreign Intelligence with the Affairs Now to Foot in the Three Nations of England, Scotland and Ireland. Weekly Serial, nos. 1 (6–13 June 1650) to 615 (5–12 April 1660) London: R. S. White, 1659.

Moneys Received and Paid for Secret Services of Charles II and James II from 30th March, 1679, to 25th December, 1688. Ed. John Yonge Akerman, William Selby Lowndes, and Henry Guy. Camden Society (Publications of the Royal Historical Society) 52. London: J. B. Nichols and Son, 1851.

More, Thomas. *The Correspondence of Sir Thomas More*. Ed. Elizabeth Francis Rogers. Princeton: Princeton University Press, 1947.

——. *Selected Letters: St. Thomas More*. Ed. Elizabeth Francis Rogers. New Haven: Yale University Press, 1961.

——. *Utopia* (1516), trans. Ralph Robinson, ed. Edward Arber (1866). New York: AMS Press, 1966.

Nabbes, Thomas. *Tottenham Court*. London: Richard Oulton, 1638. Electronic edition in Chadwyck-Healey's English Verse Drama Full Text Database (1994) at the Electronic Text Center, University of Virginia.

A New History of London: Including Westminster and Southwark (1773). 2006. Electronic Database. Centre for Metropolitan History. <www.british-history.ac.uk/report.asp?compid=46777&strquery=britain's%20burse> 25.7.06.

New Light on Drake: A Collection of Documents Relating to His Voyage of Circumnavigation 1577–1580. Works Issued by the Hakluyt Society (Second Series, No. 34). Ed. Zella Nuttall. Nendeln/Leichtenstein: Kraus Reprint, 1987.

Nicholas V, Pope. "Romanus Pontifex." 1455. In Davenport.

Nichols, Philip. *Sir Francis Drake Revived*. Whitefish, MT: Kessinger Publications, 2004.

Old and New London. 2006. Electronic Database. Centre for Metropolitan History. <www.british-history.ac.uk/report.asp?compid=45131&strquery=portugal%20row> 25.5.06.

Paul III, Pope. "Sublimus Dei." 1537. <www.newadvent.org/library/docs-pa03sd.htm>.

Pelling, Margaret. *Physicians and Irregular Medical Practitioners of London*. 2004. Electronic Database. <www.british-history.ac.uk/report.asp?compid=17428&strquery=stone%20house,%20st,%20botolph> 14.5.06.

Pepys, Samuel. *The Diary of Samuel Pepys*. Ed. Robert Latham and William Matthews. 11 vols. Berkeley: University of California Press, 1970.

—— and Mynors Bright, Richard Griffin Braybrooke, Henry Benjamin Wheatley. *The Diary of Samuel Pepys: For the First Time Fully Transcribed from the Shorthand Manuscript in the Pepysian Library, Magdalen College, Cambridge*. 18 vols. New York: Croscup and Sterling, 1900.

Pillsbury, Parker. *Acts of the Anti-Slavery Apostles*. Concord, NH: Clague, Wegman, Schlicht, and Co., 1883.

Pinks, W. J. *The History of Clerkenwell*. Ed. Edward J. Woods. London: Charles Herbert, 1881.

Platter, Thomas. *Travels in England*. Trans. Clare Williams. London: Jonathan Cape, 1937.

Pollard, A. F. *The Reign of Henry VII: From Contemporary Sources*. NY: AMS Press, 1967.

Prokter, Adrian, and Robert Taylor, eds. *The A to Z of Elizabethan London*. London: Guildhall Library, 1979.

Purchas, Samuel. *Hakluytus Posthumus, or Purchas His Pilgrimes: Contayning a History of the World in Sea Voyages and Land Travells by Englishmen and Others*. 20 vols. Glasgow: J. Maclehose and Sons, 1905–7.

——. *Purchas His Pilgrimage, or, Relations of the World and the Religions Obserued in All Ages and Places Discouered . . .* London: Printed by William Stansby for Henrie Fetherstone, 1613.

Raleigh, Sir Walter. *The Discovery of Guiana, and the Journal of the Second Voyage Thereto*. London: Cassell, 1897.

Rauchenberger, Dietrich. *Johannes Leo der Afrikaner: Seine Beschreibung des Raumes zwischen Nil und Niger nach dem Urtext*. Orientalia Biblica et Christiana 13. Wiesbaden: Harrassowitz Verlag, 1999.

The Receyt of the Ladie Kateryne. Ed. Gordon Kipling. Oxford: Early English Text Society, 1990.

The Records of a Church of Christ in Bristol, 1640–1687. Edward Terrill. Ed. Roger Hayden. Vol. 27. Bristol: Bristol Record Society, 1974.

Records of Early English Drama (REED), "Devon." Online Database. <www.archive.org/details-db.php?mediatype=texts&identifier=devonREED00wassuoft > 17.7.05.

The Register Book of St. Dionis Backchurch, London: 1538–1774. Ed. Joseph Lemuel Chester. London: The Harleian Society, 1878.

The Register of All the Christeninges, Burialles & Weddinges within the Parish of Saint Peters Upon Cornhill: Beginning at the Raigne of Our Most Soueraigne Ladie Queen Elizabeth. Ed. Granville W. G. Leveson Gower. London: Mitchell and Hughes, 1877–79.

The Register of Baptisms, Marriages and Burials of the Parish of St. Andrew's, Plymouth, Co. Devon. Ed. Margaret C. S. Cruwys. Exeter: Exeter, Devon and Cornwall Record Society, 1954.

The Register of Baptisms, Marriages, and Burials in the Parish of St. Martin in the Fields, in the County of Middlesex. Ed. John Mason. London: Mitchell & Hughes, 1898–1936.

The Register of St. Dunstan in the East, London. Ed. A. W. Hughes Clarke. London: Harleian Society, 1939–58.

The Register of St. Mary Mounthaw, London, 1568–1849. Ed. A. W. Bruce Bannerman. London: Harleian Society, 1928.

The Register of St. Mary Somerset, London. Ed. A. W. Bruce Bannerman. London: John Whitehead and Son, 1929–30.

The Register of St. Matthew Friday Street, London. Ed. A. W. Bruce Bannerman. London: Harleian Society, 1933.

The Register of the Chapel of the Holy Trinity, Knightsbridge, 1658–1681. Ed. J. Harvey Bloom. London: Mitchell, Hughes and Clarke, 1926.

The Registers of All Hallows, Bread Street, and St. John, the Evangelist, Friday Street. Ed. A. W. Bruce Bannerman. London: Mitchell, Hughes and Clark, 1913.

The Registers of Christchurch, Newgate Street, 1558–1574. Ed. Willoughby A. Littledale. Harleian Soc. Pubs. London: Mitchell and Hughes, 1895.

The Registers of Kensington Co., Middlesex. Ed. Fn. Macnamara and A. Stpry-Maskelyne. London: Mitchell and Hughes, 1890.

The Registers of Marriages of St. Mary Le Bone, Middlesex, 1668–1812: And of Oxford Chapel, Vere Street, St. Mary Le Bone, 1736–1754. Ed. A. W. Bruce Bannerman. London: John Whitehead and Son, 1917–27.

The Registers of St. Benet and St. Peter, Paul's Wharf, London. Ed. Willoughby A. Littledale. London: Mitchell, Hughes and Clark, 1909.

The Registers of St. Botolph, Bishopsgate, London. Ed. A. W. Cornelius Hallen. Edinburgh: T. and A. Constable, 1889–95.

The Registers of St. Helen's Bishopgate, London. Ed. A. W. Bruce Bannerman. London: Mitchell & Hughes, 1904.

The Registers of St. Margaret's, Westminster. Ed. Lawrence Tanner. 3 vols. London: Harleian Society, 1935–77.

The Registers of St. Martin Outwich, London. Ed. A. W. Bruce Bannerman. London: Mitchell, Hughes and Clarke, 1905.

The Registers of St. Mary Magdalene, Bermondsey. Exeter: W. Pollard and Co., 1894.

The Registers of St. Mary the Virgin, Aldermanbury, London. Ed. W. Bruce Bannerman. London: John Whitehead and Sons, 1931.

The Registers of St. Mildred Bread Street and of St. Margaret Moses, Friday Street. Ed. A. W. Bruce Bannerman. London: Mitchell, Hughes and Clarke, 1912.

The Registers of St. Olave, Hart Street, London. Ed. A. W. Bruce Bannerman. *1563–1700*. London: Roworth and Co., 1916.

The Registers of St. Stephen Walbrooke and St Benet Sherehog, London. Ed. A. W. Bruce Bannerman. 2 vols. London: Roworth and Co., 1914.

The Registers of St. Vedast, Foster Lane and St. Michael Le Quern. Ed. Willoughby A. Littledale. London: Mitchell and Hughes, 1902–3.

Report and Transactions of the Devonshire Association for the Advancement of Science, Literature and Art. n.p.: Devonshire Association for the Advancement of Science, Devonshire Press, 1906.

Returns of Aliens Dwelling in the City and Suburbs of London from the Reign of Henry VIII to that of James I (1900–8). Ed. R. E. G. and Ernest F. Kirk. Vol. 10, Parts I, II, III. Nendelin, Leichtenstein: Kraus Reprint, 1969.

Returns of Strangers in the Metropolis, 1593, 1627, 1639: A Study of an Active Minority. Ed. Irene Scouladi. London: Huguenot Society Publications, 1985.

Roe, Sir Thomas. *The Embassy of Sir Thomas Roe to the Court of the Great Mogul, 1615–1619, as Narrated in His Journal and Correspondence. Edited from Contemporary Records*. The Hakluyt Society. Ed. William Foster. 2nd series, Vols. 1–2. Nendeln, Leichtenstein: Kraus Reprints, 1967.

Rushworth, John. *Historical Collections of Private Passages of State, Weighty Matters in Law, Remarkable Proceedings in Five Parliaments Beginning the Sixteenth Year of King James, Anno 1618, and Ending . . . [with the Death of King Charles the First, 1648]*. London: Printed by J. A. for Robert Boulter . . . 1680.

Rye, Willam Brenchley, ed. *England as Seen by Foreigners: In the Reigns of Elizabeth and James 1*. New York: Benjamin Blom, 1967.

Schellinks, William. *The Journal of William Schellinks in England, 1661–1663*. Trans. Maurice Exwood and H. L. Lehmann. University College, London: Offices of the Royal Historical Society, 1993.

Select Pleas in the Court of the Admiralty. Ed. Reginald G. Marsden. 2 vols. London: Bernard Quaritich, 1894.

Shakespeare, William. *The Norton Shakespeare: Based on the Oxford Shakespeare*. Ed. Stephen Greenblatt. New York: W.W. Norton & Company, 1997.

——. *The Riverside Shakespeare*. Ed. G. Blakemore Evans. Boston: Houghton Mifflin, 1997.

Shaw, William. *The Knights of England: A Complete Record from the Earliest Times to the Present Day*. 2 vols. London: Sherrat and Hughes, 1906.

Smith, Sir Thomas. *De Republica Anglorum*. Ed. Mary Dewar. New York: Cambridge University Press, 1982.

Stow, John. *A Survey of London: Reprinted from the Text of 1603*. Ed. Charles Lethbridge Kingsford. 2 vols. Oxford: Oxford University Press, 1971.

Stuart Royal Proclamations. Ed. James F. Larkin. 2 vols. Oxford: Clarendon Press, 1983.

Stubbes, Phillip. *Phillip Stubbes's Anatomy of the Abuses in England in Shakspere's Youth, A. D. 1583*. Ed. Frederick James Furnivall. London: Trubner and Co. for the New Shakespeare Society, 1583.

Supplement to Volume I and II of Letters, Despatches, and State Papers. Ed. G. A. Bergenroth. London: Longmans, Green, Reader, and Dyer, 1968.

Terry, Edward. *A Voyage to East-India*. London: J. Martin and J. Allestrye, 1655.

Towerson, William. "Voyage to Guinea in 1555." In *A General History and Collections of Voyages and Travels*, ed. Robert Kerr. Edinburgh: no pub., 1824.

Townshend, Dorothy Baker. *The Life and Letters of the Great Earl of Cork*. London: Duckworth and Company, 1904.

Transcript of the Registers of the United Parishes of S. Mary Woolnoth and S. Mary Woolchurch Haw, in the City of London, from Their Commencement 1538 to 1760. London: Bowles & Sons, 1886.

True Register of All Christenings, Marriages, and Burials in the Parish of St. James, Clerkenwell. Ed. Robert Hovenden. London: Mitchell and Hughes, 1884–93.

Tudor Royal Proclammations. Ed. P. L. Hughes and J. F. Larkin. 3 vols. New Haven: Yale University Press, 1969.

Tudor Tracts 1532–88. Ed. A. F. Pollard. New York: Cooper Square Publishers, 1964.

Two Tudor Subsidy Rolls for the City of London 1541 and 1582. An edition of the National Archives documents E.179/144/120 and E.179/251/16, plus the 1541 Orphans' Books of London, prepared by the London Record Society, ed. R. G. Lang. 1993. Electronic Database. London Record Society. <www.british-history.ac.uk/report.asp?compid=36139&strquery=blackamore> 02.7.2006.

Villers, George, Duke of Buckingham. *A Conference on the Doctrine of Transubstantiation between His Grace, the Duke of Buckingham, and Father Fitzgerald, an Irish Jesuit*. London: Ferdinand Burlegh & A. Dodd, 1714.

"The Virginia Charters." 2006. Electronic Documents. Department of Alfa-informatica, University of Groningen. <www.let.rug.nl/usa/D/1601-1650/virginia/chartxx.htm> 9.16.2006.

Visitation of London 1568. Ed. Sophia W. Rawlins. London: John Whitehead, 1963.

The Voyage of Nicholas Downton to the East Indies, 1614–15, as Recorded in Contemporary Narratives and Letters. Ed. William Foster. London: Hakluyt Society, 1939.

Walton, Izaak. *The Compleat Angler*, ed. Geoffrey Keynes. New York: Modern Library, 1939.

Wedel, Lupold von. "Journey through England and Scotland . . . In 1584 and 1585." Ed. Victor von Klariwill. In *Queen Elizabeth and Some Foreigners*, trans. T. H. Nash, 301–43. London: John Lane, 1928.

Zurara, Gomes Eanes de. *The Chronicle of the Discovery and Conquest of Guinea*. Trans. C. Raymond Beazley and Edgar Prestage. London: Hakluyt Society, 1896, 1897.

Secondary Sources

Abram, Annie. *English Life and Manners in the Later Middle Ages*. London: E. P. Dutton and Co., 1913.

Ackroyd, Peter. *The Life of Thomas More*. London: Chatto and Windus, 1998.

——. *London: The Biography*. New York: Doubleday, 2000.

Agamben, Giorgio. *Homo Sacer: Sovereign Power and Bare Life*. Stanford: Stanford University Press, 1998.

Alexander, Catherine M. S., and Stanley W. Wells. *Shakespeare and Race*. New York: Cambridge University Press, 2000.

Andrews, K. R. "Christopher Newport of Limehouse, Mariner." *William and Mary Quarterly* 11/1 (1954): 28–41.

——. "English Voyages to the Caribbean, 1596 to 1604: An Annotated List." *William and Mary Quarterly* 31/2 (1974): 243–54.

——. *Ships, Money and Politics: Seafaring and Naval Enterprise in the Reign of Charles I*. New York: Cambridge University Press, 1991.

——. "Sir Robert Cecil and the Mediterranean Plunder." *English Historical Review* 87/344 (1972): 513–32.

——. *Trade, Plunder and Settlement: Maritime Enterprise and the Genesis of the British Empire 1480–1630*. Cambridge: Cambridge University Press, 1984.

Anim-Addo, Joan. *Sugar, Spices, and Human Cargo: An Early Black History of Greenwich*. Greenwich: Greenwich Leisure Services, 1996.

Anozie, Frederick N. *Khoekhoe*. New York: The Rosen Publishing Group, 1997.

Appleby, John C. "Abraham Jennings of Plymouth: The Commercial Career of a 'Western' Trader, c. 1602–1649." *Southern History: A Review of the History of Southern England* 18 (1996): 24–42.

Archer, Ian. "Material Londoners?" In Lena Cowen Orlin, ed., *Material London ca. 1600* (Philadelphia: University of Pennsylvania Press, 2000), pp. 174–92.

——. *The Pursuit of Stability*. Comparative Studies in Early Modern British History. New York: Cambridge University Press, 1991.

Armstrong, Alan, ed. *The Economy of Kent 1640–1914*. New York: Boydell and Brewer, Inc., 1995.

Arthur, William. *An Etymological Dictionary of Family and Christian Names*. New York: Sheldon, Blakeman and Co., 1857.

Ashley, Maurice. *Great Britain to 1688: A Modern History*. Ann Arbor: University of Michigan Press, 1961.

Ashton, Robert. "The Parliamentary Agitation for Free Trade in the Opening Years of the Reign of James I." *Past and Present* 38 (1967): 40–55.

"Attempts towards Colonization: The Council for New England and the Merchant Venturers of Bristol, 1621–23." *American Historical Review* 4/4 (1899): 678–702.

Baker, Bernadette. "What Is Voice? Issues of Identity and Representation in the Framing of Reviews." *Review of Educational Research* 69/4 (1999): 365–83.

Baker, Sir John. "Human Rights and the Rule of Law in Renaissance England." *Journal of International Human Rights* 2 (2004). Electronic Journal <www.law.northwestern.edu/journals/jihr/v2/3> 6.10.04.

Balibar, Etienne, and Immanuel Wallerstein. *Race, Nation, Class*. New York: Verso, 1991.

Bardsley, Charles Wareing. *A Dictionary of English and Welsh Surnames*. New York: H. Frowde, 1901.

——. *English Surnames: Their Sources and Significations*. London: Chatto and Windus, 1895.

Bartels, Emily. "Imperialist Beginnings: Richard Hakluyt and the Construction of Africa." *Criticism* 34 (1992): 517–38.

——. "Making More of the Moor: Aaron, Othello and Renaissance Refashionings of Race." *Shakespeare Quarterly* 41/4 (1990): 433–54.

——. "Othello and Africa: Postcolonialism Reconsidered." *William and Mary Quarterly* 54/1 (1997): 45–64.

——. "Too Many Blackamoors: Deportation, Discrimination and Elizabeth." *Studies in English Literature, 1500–1700* 46/2 (2005): 305–22.

Barthelemy, Anthony Gerard. *Black Face, Maligned Race: The Representation of Blacks in English Drama from Shakespeare to Southerne*. Baton Rouge: Louisiana State University Press, 1987.

——, ed. *Critical Essays on Shakespeare's* Othello. New York: G. K. Hall, 1994.

Bean, Richard. "A Note on the Relative Importance of Slaves and Gold in West African Exports." *Journal of African History* 15 (1974): 351–56.

Becher, A. B. "The Voyages of Martin Frobisher." *Journal of the Royal Geographical Society of London* 12 (1842): 1–20.

Beck, Sanderson. *Ethics of Civilization*. Goleta, CA: World Peace Communications, 2004.

Beier, A. L. "Social Problems in Elizabethan London." *Journal of Interdisciplinary History* 9 (1978): 203–21.

——, and Roger Finlay, eds. *London 1500–1700: The Making of the Metropolis*. London: Longman, 1985.

Berger, Ronald M. "The Development of Retail Trade in Provincial England, ca. 1550–1700." *Journal of Economic History* 40/1 (1980): 123–28.

Bergeron, David M. "The Elizabethan Lord Mayor's Show." *Studies in English Literature, 1500–1700* 10/2 (1970): 269–85.

Billings, William. "The Cases of Fernando and Elizabeth Key: A Note on the Status of Blacks in Seventeenth-Century Virginia." *William and Mary Quarterly*, 3rd series 30/3 (1973): 467–74.

Bisson, Michael S., Terry Childs, Philip De Barros, and Augustin F. C. Holl. *Ancient African Metallurgy: The Sociocultural Context*. Lanham, MD: Rowman and Littlefield Publishers, 2000.

Blackburn, Robin. "The Old World Background to European Colonial Slavery." *William and Mary Quarterly*, 3rd series 54/1 (1997): 65–102.

Boogaart, Ernst Van Den. "The Trade between Western Africa and the Atlantic World 1600–90: Estimates of Trends in Composition and Value." *Journal of African History* 33/3 (1992): 369–85.

Boose, Lynda. "'The Getting of a Lawful Race': Racial Discourse in Early Modern England and the Unrepresentable Black Woman." In *Women, "Race," and Writing in the Early Modern Period*. Ed. by Margo Hendricks and Patricia Parker, 35–54. New York: Routledge, 1994.

Boulton, Jeremy P. *Neighbourhood and Society: A London Suburb in the Seventeenth Century*. Cambridge: Cambridge University Press, 1987.

Bowen, H. V., Margarette Lincoln, and Nigel Rigby. *The Worlds of the East India Company*. Woodbridge: The Boydell Press, 2002.

Braddick, Michael. *State Formation in Early Modern England c. 1550–1700*. Cambridge: Cambridge University Press, 2000.

Braude, Benjamin. "The Sons of Noah and the Early Modern Construction of Ethnic and Geographic Identities in the Medieval and Early Modern Periods." *William and Mary Quarterly*, 3rd series 54/1 (1997): 103–42.

Brenner, Robert. *Merchants and Revolution: Commercial Change, Political Conflict, and London's Overseas Traders, 1550–1653*. Princeton: Princeton University Press, 1991.

Brodsky, Vivian. "Widows in Late Elizabethan London: Remarriage, Economic Opportunity, and Family Orientations." In *The World We Have Gained: Histories of Population and Social Structure*, ed. Lloyd Benfield, Richard Smith, and Keith Wrightson, 122–54. Oxford: Oxford University Press, 1986.

Bryan, Lindsay. "Marriage and Morals in the Fourteenth Century: The Evidence of Bishop Hamo's Register." *English Historical Review* 121 (2006): 467–86.

Butterworth, Andrew. "How Sir Kit Was Rescued from the Rubble." *Taking Stock. The Annual Magazine from Gretton Local History Society* 2 (1993): 10–11.

——. "Sir Kit and the Weird Old Woman." *Taking Stock. The Annual Magazine from Gretton Local History Society* 1 (1992): 4–5.

Caffentzis, George. "On the Notion of a Crisis of Social Reproduction: A Theoretical Review." *The Commoner* (Autumn 2002): 1–14. An ejournal at <www.thecommoner.org>. 10.14.04.

Callo, Joseph F., and Alastair Wilson. *Who's Who in Naval History: From 1550 to the Present*. London: Routledge, 2004.

Capp, Bernard. *When Gossips Meet*. Oxford: Oxford University Press, 2003.

Celebrating Black History in Wandsworth. 2002. Electronic Pamphlet. Wandsworth Council. <www.lmal.org.uk/uploads/documents/wandsworth_resource_pack.pdf> 21.5.06.

Certeau, Michel de. *The Mystic Fable*. Chicago: University of Chicago Press, 1992.

——. *The Writing of History*. New York: Columbia University Press, 1988.

Chalklin, Christopher. "The Towns." In *The Economy of Kent*, ed. Alan Armstrong, 205–34. New York: Boydell & Brewer, Inc., 1995.

Chambers, R. W. *Thomas More*. London: Jonathan Cape, 1938.

Chesnutt, David R., and C. James Taylor, eds. *The Papers of Henry Laurens*. Columbia, SC: University of South Carolina Press, 2000.

Chidester, David. *Savage Systems: Colonialism and Comparative Religion in South Africa*. Charlottesville, VA: University of Virginia Press, 1996.

Chrimes, S. B. *Henry VIII*. London: Methuen, 1972.

Claremont, Francesca. *Catherine of Aragon*. London: Robert Hale, 1939.

Claridge, William Walter. *A History of the Gold Coast and Ashanti: From the Earliest Times to the Commencement of the Twentieth Century*. London: John Murray, 1915.

Clark, Peter. *English Provincial Society from the Reformation to the Revolution: Religion, Politics and Society in Kent 1500–1640*. Madison, NJ: Farleigh Dickinson University Press, 1977.

Clay, C. G. A. *Economic Expansion and Social Change: England 1500–1700*. 2 vols. Cambridge: Cambridge University Press, 1984.

Clegg, Cyndia Susan. "Archival Poetics and the Politics of Literature: Essex and Hayward Revisited." *Studies in the Literary Imagination* 32/1 (1999): 115–32.

Cleveland, Catherine Lucy Wilhelmina Powlett. *The Battle Abbey Roll: With Some Account of the Norman Lineages*. London: J. Murray, 1889.

Cliffe, John Trevor. *The World of the Country House in Seventeenth-Century England*. New Haven: Yale University Press, 1999.

Cogswell, Thomas. "The Politics of Propaganda: Charles I and the People in the 1620s." *Journal of British Studies* 29/3 (1990): 187–215.

Colarucio, Michael J. *The Province of Piety*. Durham, NC: Duke University Press, 1995.

Colvin, Ian Duncan. *South Africa*. Edinburgh: T. C. & E. C. Jack, 1909.

Connell-Smith, G. "The Ledger of Thomas Howell." *Economic History Review* 3/3 (1951): 363–70.

Conrad, Lawrence I., Michael Neve, Vivian Nutton, Roy Porter, and Andrew Wear. *The Western Medical Tradition: 800 BC–1800 AD*. Cambridge: Cambridge University Press, 1995.

Cooke, Alan. "Best (Beste), George." 2002. Dictionary of Canadian Biography Online. Available at: <www.biographi.ca/EN/ShowBioPrintable.asp?BioId=34182> 13.5.06.

Cotton, A. N. B. "John Dillingham, Journalist of the Middle Group." *English Historical Review* 93/369 (1978): 817–34.

Cowhig, Ruth. "Blacks in English Renaissance Drama and the Role of Shakespeare's Othello." In *The Black Presence in English Literature*, ed. David Dabydeen, 1–25. London: Manchester University Press, 1985.

Cox, J. Charles. *The Parish Registers of England*. Totowa, NJ: Rowman and Littlefield, 1974.

Crescinsky, Herbert. "An Oak-Panelled Room in Barnstaple." *The Burlington Magazine for Connnoisseurs* 40/231 (1922): 296–303.

Croft, Pauline. “Trading with the Enemy 1585–1604.” *Historical Journal* 32/2 (1989): 281–302.

Curtin, Philip D. *The Atlantic Slave Trade: A Consensus.* Madison: University of Wisconsin Press, 1969.

Dabydeen, David. *The Black Presence in English Literature*. London: Manchester University Press, 1985.

Dailey, Barbara Ritter. “The Visitation of Sarah Wight: Holy Carnival and the Revolution of the Saints in Civil War London.” *Church History* 55/4 (1986): 418–55.

D’Amico, Jack. *The Moor in English Renaissance Drama.* Tampa: University of South Florida Press, 1991.

Davies, C. S. L. “Slavery and Protector Somerset: The Vagrancy Act of 1547.” *Economic History Review* 19/3 (1966): 533–49.

Davies, K. G. *The Royal African Company*. New York: Octagon Books, 1975.

Dawson, Giles E., and Laetitia Kennedy-Shipton. *Elizabethan Handwriting 1500–1650: A Manual*. New York: W. W. Norton and Company, 1966.

Deleuze, Gilles, and Felix Guattari. *Anti-Oedipus: Capitalism and Schizophrenia*, trans. Robert Hurley, Mark Seem, and Helen R. Lane. New York: Viking Press, 1977.

Denkinger, Emma Marshall. “Actor’s Names in the Registers of St. Botolph Aldgate.” *PMLA* 31/4 (1926): 91–109.

Derrida, Jacques. “Archive Fever.” *Diacritics* 25/2 (1995): 9–63.

deSonghai, Oumani. *The Sultana and Her Sisters: Black Women in the British Isles before 1530*. 2005. Electronic Essay <theafricancommune.com/print.php3?id_article=828> 11.15.05.

Dimock, Arthur. “The Conspiracy of Dr. Lopez.” *English Historical Review* 9/35 (1894): 440–72.

Douglas, Robert Dick. *Three Boy Scouts in Africa*. London: G. P. Putnam’s Sons, 1929.

Drake, St. Clair. *Black Folk Here and There*. 2 vols. Los Angeles: Center for Afro-American Studies, University of California, 1990.

Dresser, Madge. *Slavery Obscured: The Social History of the Slave Trade in an English Provincial Port*. New York: Continuum, 2001.

Duffy, Eamon. *The Voices of Morebath: Reformation and Rebellion in an English Village*. New Haven: Yale University Press, 2001.

Earle, T. F., and K. J. P. Lowe. *Black Africans in Renaissance Europe*. Cambridge: Cambridge University Press, 2005.

“East India Company.” Encyclopedia entry. Online. <http://59.1911encyclopedia.org/E/EA/EAST_INDIA_COMPANY.htm> 16.7.04.

Edwards, Paul. “The Early African Presence in the British Isles.” In *Essays on the History of Blacks in Britain*, ed. Jagdish S. Gundara and Ian Duffield, 9–29. Aldershot and Brookfield, VT: Ashgate Publishing, 1992.

——, and James Walvin. *Black Personalities in the Era of the Slave Trade*. Baton Rouge: Louisiana State University Press, 1983.

Edwards, Tudor. *Bristol*. London: Batsford, 1950.

Elbl, Ivana. "The Volume of the Early Atlantic Slave Trade, 1450–1521." *Journal of African History* 38 (1997): 31–75.

Elton, G. R. *Studies in Tudor and Stuart Politics and Government: Papers and Reviews 1946–72*. Vol. I: *Tudor Politics/Tudor Government*. Cambridge: Cambridge University Press, 1974.

——. *The Tudor Revolution in Government: Administrative Changes in the Reign of Henry VIII*. Cambridge: Cambridge University Press, 1953.

Erickson, Peter. "The Moment of Race in Renaissance Studies." *Shakespeare Studies* 26 (1998): 27–36.

——. "Representation of Blacks and Blackness in the Renaissance." *Criticism* 35/4 (1993): 495–527.

——, and Clark Hulse, eds. *Early Modern Visual Culture: Representation, Race, Empire in Early Modern England*. Philadelphia: University of Pennsylvania Press, 2000.

Fabricius, Johannes. *Syphilis in Shakespeare's England*. Bristol, PA: Jessica Kingsley, 1994.

Farrer, J. A. *Paganism and Christianity*. London: A. and C. Black, 1910.

Finlay, Roger, and Beatrice Shearer. "Population Growth and Suburban Expansion." In Beier and Finlay, eds., *London 1500–1700*, pp. 37–57.

Fleissner, Robert. "Herbert's Aethiopessa and the Dark Lady: A Mannerist Parallel." *College Language Association Journal* 19 (1976): 458–67.

——. "The Moor's Nomenclature." *Notes & Queries* 25 (1978): 143.

——. "William Dunbar's Sultry Pre-Shakespearean Dark Lady." *The Upstart Crow* 3 (1980): 88–96.

Floyd-Wilson, Mary. *English Ethnicity and Race in Early Modern Drama*. Cambridge: Cambridge University Press, 2003.

Forbes, Thomas. *Chronicle from Aldgate: Life and Death in Shakespeare's London*. New Haven: Yale University Press, 1971.

Foucault, Michel. *The Archaeology of Knowledge and the Discourse on Language*, trans. A. M. Sheridan Smith. New York: Pantheon Books, 1972.

Fraser, Antonia. *The Wives of Henry VIII*. New York: Alfred A. Knopf, 1992.

Frier, Bruce W. "Roman Slave Law." *American Historical Review* 95/4 (1988): 1026–27.

Frobenius, Leo. *The Voices of Africa*. London: Hutchinson and Co., 1913.

Fryer, Peter. *Staying Power: The History of Black People in Britain*. London: Pluto Press, 1984.

Fumerton, Patricia. "London's Vagrant Economy: Making Space for 'Low Subjectivity.'" In *Material London: Ca. 1600*, ed. Lena Cowen Orlin, 206–26. Philadelphia: University of Pennsylvania Press, 2000.

Fury, Cheryl A. *Tides in the Affairs of Men: The Social History of Elizabethan Seamen, 1580–1603*. Westport, CT: Greenwood Press, 2002.

Gardiner, Juliet, and Neil Weinborn. *The Columbia Companion to British History*. New York: Columbia University Press, 1996.

Gerhold, Dorian. "Black People in 17th and 18th Century Putney." *Black and Asian Studies Association Newsletter* 37 (2003): 22–24.

——. "Celebrating the Black Presence in Wandsworth." Electronic essay sponsored by Wandsworth Museum, Education and Outreach Service. <http://www.lmal.org.uk/uploads/documents/wandsworth_resource_pack.pdf> 03.12.2005.

Gerzina, Gretchen H. *Black London.* New Brunswick, NJ: Rutgers University Press, 1995.

Gibson, James. *Kent.* Toronto: University of Toronto Press, 2002.

Gnammankou, Dieudonne. *The Past: A Model for the Future*? 2001. Electronic essay <www.gnammankou.com/thepast.pdf> 26.4.05.

Goldstone, Jack A. "State Breakdown in the English Revolution: A New Synthesis." *American Journal of Sociology* 92/2 (1986): 257–322.

Grant, Alison. "Breaking the Mould: North Devon Maritime Enterprise." In *Tudor and Stuart Devon: The Common Estate and Government*, ed. Todd Gray, Margery Rowe, and Audrey Erskine, 119–40. Exeter: University of Exeter Press, 1992.

Griffiths, Paul. "Secrecy and Authority in Sixteenth and Seventeenth Century London." *Historical Journal* 40/4 (1997): 925–51.

——, J. Landers, M. Pelling, and R. Tyson. "Population and Disease, Estrangement and Belonging 1540–1700." In *The Cambridge Urban History of Britain*, ed. Martin Daunton, 195–234. Cambridge: Cambridge University Press, 2001.

Gunn, S. J. *Early Tudor Government 1485–1558.* New York: St. Martin's Press, 1995.

Guy, John. "Henry VII." 2005. Encarta Online Encyclopedia. <http://uk.encarta.msn.com> 31.1.06.

——, ed. *The Reign of Elizabeth I: Court and Culture in the Last Decade.* Cambridge: Cambridge University Press.

Habib, Imtiaz. "East Indians in Early Modern England as 'The First Fruits of India': Colonial Effacement and Postcolonial Re-inscription." *Journal of Narrative Theory* 36/1 (2006): 1–19.

——. "Elizabethan Racial Medical Psychology, Popular Drama, and the Social Programming of the Late-Tudor Black: Sketching an Exploratory Postcolonial Hypothesis." In *Disease, Diagnosis, and Cure on the Early Modern Stage*, ed. Stephanie Moss and Kaara Peterson, 93–112. Aldershot and Burlington, VT: Ashgate Publishing, 2004.

——. "'Hel's Perfect Character' or the Blackamoor Maid in Early Modern English Drama: The Postcolonial Cultural History of a Dramatic Type." *Literature Interpretation Theory* 11 (2000): 277–304.

——. "Othello, Sir Peter Negro, and the Blacks of Early Modern England: Colonial Inscription and Postcolonial Excavation." *Literature Interpretation Theory* 9/1 (1998): 15–30.

——. *Shakespeare and Race: Postcolonial Praxis in the Early Modern Period.* Lanham, MD: University Press of America, 2000.

——. "Shakespeare's Spectral Turks: The Postcolonial Poetics of a Mimetic Narrative." *Shakespeare Yearbook* 14 (2004): 237–70.

Hair, P. E. H. "Attitudes to Africans in English Primary Sources on Guinea up to 1650." *History in Africa* 26 (1999): 43–68.

Hall, Kim. "'I Would Rather Wish to Be a Black-Moor': Beauty, Race and Rank in Lady Mary Wroth's *Urania*." In *Women, 'Race,' and Writing in the Early Modern Period*, ed. Margo Hendricks and Patricia Parker, 178–94. New York: Routledge, 1994.

——. "Object into Object: Some Thoughts on the Presence of Black Women in Early Modern Culture." In *Early Modern Visual Culture: Representation, Race, Empire, in Renaissance England*, ed. Peter Erickson and Clark Hulse, 346–79. Philadelphia: University of Pennsylvania Press, 2000.

——. "Reading what Isn't There: 'Black' Studies in Early Modern England." *Stanford Humanities Review* 3/1 (1993): 23–33.

——. *Things of Darkness: Economies of Race and Gender in Early Modern England*. Ithaca: Cornell University Press, 1995.

Hamlin, William. "Imagined Apotheosis: Drake, Harriot, and Raleigh in the Americas." *Journal of the History of Ideas* 57/3 (1996): 405–28.

Hammock, W. G. *Leytonstone and Its History*. London: Baten and Davies, 1904.

Handover, P. M. *The Second Cecil: The Rise to Power 1563–1604 of Sir Robert Cecil, Later First Earl of Salisbury*. London: Eyre and Spottiswoode, 1959.

Hank, Patricia, and Flavia Hodges. *A Dictionary of Surnames*. New York: Oxford University Press, 1988.

Harding, Vanessa. "City, Capital, Metropolis: The Changing Shape of Seventeenth-Century London." In *Imagining Early Modern London: Perceptions and Portrayals of the City from Stow to Strype 1698–1720*, ed. J. F. Merritt, pp. 117–43. Cambridge: Cambridge University Press, 2000.

——. *The Dead and the Living in Paris and London, 1500–1670*. Cambridge: Cambridge University Press, 2002.

Hardt, Michael, and Antonio Negri. *Empire*. Cambridge, MA: Harvard University Press, 2000.

Harris, Tim. "The Bawdy House Riots of 1668." *Historical Journal* 29/3 (1986): 537–56.

Harrison, Francis Burton. "Footnotes on Some XVII Century Virginians." *Virginia Magazine of History and Biography* 51/1 (1943): 24–35.

Hatfield, April Lee. *Atlantic Virginia: Intercolonial Relations in the Seventeenth Century*. Philadelphia: University of Pennsylvania Press, 2003.

Hauben, Paul J. "A Spanish Calvinist Church in Elizabethan London, 1559–65." *Church History* 34/1 (1965): 50–56.

Hawkins, Mary W. S. *The Hawkins Family* (1888). 2006. Electronic book at <www.welbank.net/hawkins/pah/chap2.html> 16.9.06.

Haynes, Alan. *Robert Cecil: 1st Earl of Salisbury*. London: Peter Owen, 1989.

Hazlewood, Nick. *The Queen's Slave Trader: John Hawkins, Elizabeth I, and the Trafficking in Human Souls*. New York: Harper Collins, 2004.

Hendricks, Margo. "Feminist Historiography." In *A Companion to Early Modern Women's Writing*, ed. Anita Pacheco, 361–76. London: Blackwell Publishing, 2001.

——. "Obscured by Dreams: Race, Empire and Shakespeare's *A Midsummer Night's Dream*." *Shakespeare Quarterly* 47/1 (1996): 35–72.

——. "Surveying Race." In *Shakespeare and Race*, Ed. Catherine M. S. Alexander and Stanley Wells, 1–22. New York: Cambridge University Press, 2000.

——, and Patricia Parker, eds. *Women, Race and Writing in Early Modern England.* New York: Routledge, 1994.

Henry, L. W. "The Earl of Essex as Strategist and Military Organizer (1596–97)." *English Historical Review* 68/268 (1953): 363–93.

Higginbotham, A. Leon. *In the Matter of Colour*. Oxford: Oxford University Press, 1980.

Hill, Christopher. *A Nation of Novelty and Change: Radical Politics, Religion and Literature in Seventeenth-Century England.* New York: Routledge, 1990.

"The History of Kent." 2005. Electronic Essay. Kent County Council. <http://www.kent.gov.uk/Community/kent-and-its-people/history-of-kent/> 11.02.05.

Hoerder, Dirk. *Cultures in Contact*. Durham, NC: Duke University Press, 2002.

Hoskins, W. G. "The Rebuilding of Rural England 1570–1640." *Past and Present* 4 (1953): 44–59.

Hulse, Lynn. "The Musical Patronage of Robert Cecil, First Earl of Salisbury (1563–1612)." *Journal of the Royal Musical Association* 116/1 (1991): 24–40.

Hunter, G. K. *Dramatic Identities and Cultural Traditions: Studies in Shakespeare and His Contemporaries*. Liverpool: Liverpool University Press, 1978.

Hyamson, Albert Montefiore. *A History of the Jews in England.* London: Macmillan, 1907.

Ingram, William. *The Business of Playing: The Beginnings of Adult Professional Theater in Elizabethan London*. Ithaca: Cornell University Press, 1992.

Inikori, Joseph E. *Africans and the Industrial Revolution in England: A Study in International Trade and Economic Development.* Cambridge: Cambridge University Press, 2002.

——. "The Volume of the British Slave Trade 1655–1807." *Cahiers d'Etudes Africaines* 32/4 (1992).

Jacobs, Reginald. *Covent Garden: Its Romance and History*. London: Simpkin, Marshall, Hamilton, Kent & Co., 1913.

JanMohammed, Abdul R. *Manichean Aesthetics: The Politics of Literature in Colonial Africa*. Amherst: University of Massachusetts Press, 1986.

Japtok, Martin, and Winfried Schleiner. "Genetics and 'Race' in *The Merchant of Venice*." *Literature and Medicine* 18/2 (1999): 155–72.

Jones, Eldred. *The Elizabethan Image of Africa*. Charlottesville, VA: University Press of Virginia, 1971.

——. *Othello's Countrymen: The African in English Renaissance Drama*. London: Oxford University Press, 1965.

Jones, Emrys. "London in the Early Seventeenth Century." *London Journal* 6/2 (1980): 123–33.

Jones, Pip, and Rita Youseph. *The Black Population of Bristol in the Eighteenth Century*. Local History Pamphlets, ed. Peter Harris. Bristol: Bristol Branch of the Historical Association, 1994.

Jones, S. J. "The Growth of Bristol: The Regional Aspect of City Development." *Transactions and Papers (Institute of British Geographers)* 11/46 (1946): 57–83.

Jourdain, M. "Lace as Worn in England until the Accession of James I." *Burlington Magazine for Connoisseurs* 10/45 (1906): 162–68.

Kassel, Lauren. "How to Read Simon Forman's Casebooks: Medicine, Astrology, and Gender in Elizabethan London." *Social History of Medicine* 12/1 (1999): 3.

Katz, David. *Jews in the History of England.* Cambridge: Cambridge University Press, 1994.

Kenyon, J. P. *Stuart England.* Harmondsworth: Penguin, 1985.

Kim, Keechang. *Aliens in Medieval Law: The Origins of Modern Citizenship.* New York: Cambridge University Press, 2004.

Kisby, Fiona. "Music and Musicians of Early Tudor Westminster." *Early Music* 23/2 (1995): 223–28 and 31–40.

——. "Royal Minstrels in the City and Suburbs of Early Tudor London: Professional Activities and Private Interests." *Early Music* 25/2 (1997): 199–219.

Knutson, Roslyn L. "A Caliban in St. Mildred Poultry." In *Shakespeare and Cultural Traditions*, ed. Tetsuo Kishi, Roger Pringle, and Stanley Wells, 110–26. Newark: University of Delaware Press, 1991.

Labrum, E. A. *Civil Engineering Heritage: Eastern and Central England.* London: Thomas Telford, 1994.

Lacey, Robert. *Sir Walter Ralegh.* New York: Atheneum, 1974.

Lane, Kris E. *Pillaging the Empire: Piracy in the Americas, 1500–1750.* Armonk, NY: M. E. Sharpe, 1998.

Laslett, Peter. "Demographic and Microstructural History in Relation to Human Adaptation: Reflections on Newly Established Evidence." In *How Humans Adapt: A Biocultural Odyssey*, ed. Donald J. Ortner, 343–70. Washington, DC: Smithsonian Institution Press, 1983.

Latimer, John. *Annals of Bristol.* Bristol: George and Sons, 1900.

Lawson, John. *A New Voyage to Carolina.* Whitefish, MT: Kessinger Publications, 2004.

Lefevre, Peter, and Joseph K. Lange. *Precursors of Nelson: British Admirals of the Eighteenth Century.* London: Stackpole Books, 2001.

Leppert, Richard. *The Sight of Sound: Music, Representation, and the History of the Body.* Berkeley: University of California Press, 1995.

Lester, Anthony, and Geoffrey Bindman. *Race and Law in Great Britain.* Cambridge, MA: Harvard University Press, 1972.

Lind, Vera. *Africans in Early Modern German Society: Identity – Difference – Aesthetics – Anthropology.* Electronic essay. <www.ghi-dc.org/bulletin28S01/b28lind.html> 9.12.05.

Lindegaard, D. P. *Black Bristolians of the Seventeenth, Eighteenth, and Nineteenth Centuries.* Bristol: Privately published, n.d.

Linebaugh, Peter, and Marcus Buford Rediker. *The Many-Headed Hydra: Sailors, Slaves, Commoners, and the Hidden History of the Revolutionary Atlantic.* Boston: Beacon Press, 2000.

Little, Arthur L. "'An Essence That's Not Seen': The Primal Scene of Racism in Othello." *Shakespeare Quarterly* 44/3 (1993): 304–24.

——. *Shakespeare Jungle Fever: National-Imperial Re-Visions of Race, Rape, and Sacrifice.* Stanford, CA: Stanford University Press, 2000.

Little, K. L. *Negroes in Britain: A Study of Racial Relations in English Society*. International Library of Sociology and Social Reconstruction, ed. Karl Mannheim. London: Kegan Paul, Trench, Trubner & Co, Ltd., 1947.

Littleton, Thomas. *Tenures*. London: R. Pynson, 1510.

Loades, David. *The Mid-Tudor Crisis*. New York: St. Martin's Press, 1992.

Lockyear, Roger. *The Early Stuarts: A Political History of England*. New York: Longman, 1999.

Loomba, Ania. "The Color of Patriarchy: Critical Difference, Cultural Difference and Renaissance Studies." In *Women, 'Race', and Writing in the Early Modern Period*, ed. Margo Hendricks and Patricia Parker, 17–34. New York: Routledge, 1994.

——. *Gender, Race, Renaissance Drama*. Manchester: Manchester University Press, 1989.

——. "Shakespeare and Cultural Difference." *Alternative Shakespeares*, Vol. 2, ed. Terence Hawkes, 164–91. London: Routledge, 1996.

——. *Shakespeare, Race, Colonialism*. Oxford and New York: Oxford University Press, 2002.

Lopes, David. "The Destruction of the Kingdom of Kongo." *Civil Rights Journal* 6/1 (2002): 31–39.

Lounsbery, Anne. "Russia's Literary Genius: The Great Grandson of an African Slave." *Journal of Blacks in Higher Education* 27 (2000): 105–8.

Lovejoy, Paul E. *Transformations in Slavery*. Cambridge: Cambridge University Press, 2000.

—— "The Volume of the Atlantic Slave Trade: A Synthesis." *Journal of African History* 23/4 (1982): 473–501.

Macdonald, Joyce Green. "The Force of the Imagination: The Subject of Blackness in Shakespeare, Jonson and Ravenscroft." In *Renaissance Papers*, ed. George Walton Williams and Barbara Bain, 54–69. Raleigh, NC: Southeastern Renaissance Conference, 1991.

——. "Sex, Race, and Empire in Shakespeare's *Antony and Cleopatra*." *Literature and History* 5/1 (1996): 60.

Macdougall, Norman. *James IV*. East Lothian: Tuckwell Press Ltd., 1997.

Maddocks, Sydney. *Ratcliff*. 2006. Electronic version of print essay originally published in *The Copartnership Herald* III.26 (1933). Tower Hamlets History Online. <www.mernick.co.uk/thhol/ratcliff.html> 3.26.06.

——. *Stepney in Other Days*. 2006. Electronic version of print essay originally published in *The Copartnership Herald* 2.19 (1932). Tower Hamlets History Online. <www.mernick.co.uk/thhol/stepney1.html> 26.4.06.

Maesters, Al. *Amazing Treasure Ship of the California Desert*. 2006. Sand Razor. Electronic pamphlet at: <www.google.com/search?q=cache:gwmQfDvgX_IJ:sandrazor.com/linkCounter.php%3FlinkID%3D144+california+expedition+of+captain+cordone&hl=en&gl=us&ct=clnk&cd=3&client=safari> 2.12.06.

Mainwaring, Henry. *The Life and Works of Sir Henry Mainwaring*. London: Navy Records Society, 1922.

Manley, Lawrence. *Literature and Culture in Early Modern London*. Cambridge: Cambridge University Press, 1995.

Marsden, R. G. "The Vice-Admirals of the Coast." *English Historical Review* 23/92 (1908): 736–57.

Martin, Steve. "Revealing London's Black History: A Case Study." Electronic essay <http://64.233.167.104/search?q=cache:EzrEyY22ZPwJ:www.lmal.org.uk/uploads/documents/Paper_5.doc+blackamore+in+hackney&hl=en&ie=UTF-8> 27.9.04.

Marx, Robert, and Jennifer Marx. *Treasure Lost at Sea: Diving to the World's Great Shipwrecks*. New York: Firefly Books, 2003.

Masonen, Pekka. "Leo Africanus: The Man with Many Names." *Al-Andalus-Magreb. Revista de estudios árabes e islámicos* VIII–IX.fasc. 1 (2002): 115–43.

——. *The Negroland Revisited: Discovery and Invention of the Sudanese Middle Ages*. Helsinki: The Finnish Academy of Science and Letters, 2000.

Mattingly, Garrett. *Catherine of Aragon*. Little Brown: Boston, 1941.

Mayhew, A. L., and Walter W. Skeat. *A Concise Dictionary of Middle English A.D. 1150 to 1580*. Oxford: Clarendon Press, 1888.

McBride, Kari Boyd. *Country House Discourse in Early Modern England: A Cultural Study of Landscape and Legitimacy*. Aldershot and Burlington, VT: Ashgate Publishing, 2001.

McCabe, Joseph. *A Rationalist Encyclopaedia: A Book of Reference on Religion, Philosophy, Ethics, and Science*. Ann Arbor: Gryphon Books, 1971.

McFarlane, K. B. *The Nobility of Later Medieval England*. Oxford: Oxford University Press, 1973.

McIntosh, Marjorie Keniston. *Working Women in English Society, 1300–1620*. Cambridge: Cambridge University Press, 2005.

Mellor, Ronald J. "Roman Empire: Life in Imperial Rome." Encarta Online Encyclopedia. <http://encarta.msn.com/> 19.12.05.

Merritt, J. F. *The Social World of Early Modern Westminster*. Manchester: Manchester University Press, 2005.

Meyers, Charles. *Elizabethan Marranos Unmasked*. Electronic essay <www.kulanu.org/unmasked.html> 23.3.05.

——. "Lawsuits in Elizabethan Courts of Law: The Adventures of Dr. Hector Nunez, 1566–591: A Precis." *Journal of European Economic History* 25/1 (1996): 157–58.

Migeod, F. W. H. "Personal Names among Some West African Tribes." *Journal of the Royal African Society* 17/65 (1917), 38–45.

Miles, Theodore. "Place Realism in a Group of Caroline Plays." *Review of English Studies* 18/72 (1942): 428–40.

Millar, Gilbert John. *Tudor Mercenaries and Auxiliaries 1485–1547*. Charlottesville, VA: University of Virginia Press, 1980.

Miller, W. E. "Negroes in Elizabethan London." *Notes and Queries* 206 (1961): 138.

Milton, Giles. *Big Chief Elizabeth: The Adventures and Fate of the First English Colonists in America*. New York: Farrar, Strauss, and Giroux, 2001.

Molloy, John Fitzgerald. *Royalty Restored or London under Charles II*. London: Downey and Co., 1897.

Morrill, John S. *The Oxford Illustrated History of Tudor and Stuart Britain*. Oxford: Oxford University Press, 2000.

Mukerji, Chandra. *From Graven Images: Patterns of Modern Materialism*. New York: Columbia University Press, 1983.

Neill, Michael. "'Mulattos,' 'Blacks,' and 'Indian Moors': *Othello* and Early Modern Constructions of Human Difference." In his *Putting History to the Question: Power, Politics, and Society in English Renaissance Drama*, 269–84. New York: Columbia University Press, 2000.

——. "Unproper Beds: Race, Adultery and the Hideous." *Shakespeare Quarterly* 40/4 (1989): 383–412.

Nethercot, A. H. *William Davenant: Poet Laureate and Playwright Manager*. New York: Russell and Russell, 1967.

Neve, Le, Peter, and George W. Marshall. *Neve's Pedigrees of the Knights Made by King Charles II, King James II, King William III, and Queen Mary, King William Alone, and Queen Anne*. London: Harleian Society Publications, 1873.

Newton, Arthur Percival, ed. *Travel and Travellers of the Middle Ages*. Freeport, New York: Books for Libraries Press, Inc., 1967.

Newman, Karen. "'And Wash the Ethiop White': Femininity and the Monstrous in *Othello*." In *Fashioning Femininity and English Renaissance Drama*, ed. Karen Newman, 71–94. Chicago: University of Chicago Press, 1991.

Nicholson, Bradley. "Legal Borrowing and the Origins of Slave Law in the British Colonies." *American Journal of Legal History* 38/1 (1994): 38–54.

Niebrzydowski, Sue. "The Sultana and Her Sisters: Black Women in the British Isles before 1530." *Women's History Review* 10/2 (2001): 187–210.

Oldham, James. "New Light on Mansfield and Slavery." *Journal of British Society* 27/1 (1988): 45–68.

Orkin, Martin. "*Othello* and the Plain Face of Racism." *Shakespeare Quarterly* 38/2 (1987): 166–88.

——. *Shakespeare against Apartheid*. Craighill (S. Africa): A. D. Donker, 1987.

Orlin, Lena Cowen, ed. *Material London: Ca. 1600*. Philadelphia: University of Pennsylvania Press, 2000.

Orser, Charles E. *Encyclopedia of Historical Archaeology*. London: Routledge, 2002.

Oxford English Dictionary (the Compact Edition of the Oxford English Dictionary: Complete and Reproduced Micrographically) [*OED*]. 3 vols. Oxford: Oxford University Press, 1971.

Pacheco, Anita, ed. *A Companion to Early Modern Women's Writing*. London: Blackwell Publishing, 2001.

Patten, John. "Urban Occupations in Pre-Industrial England." *Transactions of the Institute of British Geographers* 2/3 (1977): 296–313.

Patterson, Catherine. "Conflict Resolution and Patronage in Provincial Towns, 1590–1640." *Journal of British Studies* 37/1 (1998): 1–25.

Paul, John E. *Catherine of Aragon and Her Friends*. London: Burns and Oates, 1966.

Peabody, Sue. "'A Nation Born to Slavery': Missionaries and Racial Discourse in Seventeenth-Century French Antilles." *Journal of Social History* 38/1 (2004): 113–26.

Perkinson, Richard. "Topographical Comedy in the Seventeenth Century." *English Literary History* 3/4 (1936): 270–90.

Perreault, Melanie. "'To Fear and to Love Us': Intercultural Violence in the English Atlantic." *Journal of World History* 17/1 (2006): 71–93.

Perry, Albert. "Abraham Hannibal, the Favorite of Peter the Great." *American Journal of Legal History* 8/4 (1923): 359–66.

Phillips, G. A. "Crown Musical Patronage from Elizabeth to Charles I." *Music & Letters* 58 (1977): 29–42.

Picard, Liza. *Elizabeth's London: Everyday Life in Elizabethan London*. New York: St. Martin's Press, 2004.

Pilkinton, Mark C. *Bristol*. Toronto: University of Toronto Press, 1997.

Pine, L. G. *The Story of Surnames*. Rutland, VT: Charles E. Tuttle Company, 1969.

Pinkerton, W. "Cats, Dogs, and Negroes as Articles of Commerce." *Notes and Queries* 3rd ser. 2 (1862): 345–46.

Plant, David, "British Civil Wars and Commonwealth." Web essay at <http://www.british-civil-wars.co.uk/biog/index_b.htm> 14.7.05

Pollit, Ronald. "John Hawkins's Troublesome Voyages: Merchants, Bureaucrats and the Origins of the Slave Trade." *Journal of British Studies* 12/2 (1973): 26–40.

——. "'Refuge of the Distressed Nations': Perceptions of Aliens in Elizabethan England." *Journal of Modern History* 52.1 (1980): D1001–D19.

Pollock, F., and F. W. Maitland. *The History of English Law before the Time of Edward I*. 2 vols. Cambridge: Cambridge University Press, 1968.

Poos, L. R. "Historical Demography of Renaissance Europe: Recent Research and Current Issues." *Renaissance Quarterly* 49/4 (1989): 794–811.

Pope-Hennessy, James. *Sins of the Fathers: A Study of the Atlantic Slave Traders, 1441–1807*. New York: Alfred A. Knopf, 1968.

Port Cities Bristol web page. Electronic statement. <http://www.discoveringbristol.org.uk/showNarrative.php?narId=471&nacId=474> 24.3.04.

Porter, Carolyn. "Are We Being Historical Yet?" In *The States of 'Theory': History, Art, and Critical Discourse*, ed. David Carroll, 27–62. New York: Columbia University Press, 1990.

Porter, R. "The Crispe Family and the African Trade in the Seventeenth Century." *Journal of African History* 9/1 (1968): 57–77.

Powell, Anthony. *Some Poets, Artists and 'a Reference for Mellors'*. London: Timewell Press, 2005.

Power, M. J. "The East and West in Early-Modern London." In *Wealth and Power in Tudor England*, ed. R. J. Knecht, E. W. Ives, J. J. Scarisbuck, 167–85. London: The Athlone Press, 1978.

Pryor, Alton. *Classic Tales in California History*. Roseville, CA: Stagecoach Publications, 1999.

Questier, Michael C. *Catholicism and Community in Early Modern England*. Cambridge: Cambridge University Press, 2006.

Quigley, William P. "Five Hundred Years of English Poor Laws, 1349–1834: Regulating the Working and Nonworking Poor." *Akron Law Review* 30/1 (1996): 73–128.

Quinn, D. B., and A. N. Ryan. *England's Sea Empire 1550–1642*. London: George Allen and Unwin, 1983.

Rabb, Theodore K. *Enterprise and Empire: Merchant and Gentry Investment in the Expansion of England, 1575–1630*. Cambridge, MA: Harvard University Press, 1967.

Raman, Shankar. *Framing 'India': The Colonial Imaginary in Early Modern Culture*. Stanford, CA: Stanford University Press, 2001.

Ramsay, G. D. "Clothworkers, Merchants Adventurers and Richard Hakluyt." *English Historical Review* 92/364 (1977): 504–21.

Rawley, James A. *The Transatlantic Slave Trade*. New York: W. W. Norton and Co., 1981.

Raymond, Joad, ed. *News Networks in Seventeenth-Century Britain and Europe*. London: Routledge, 2006.

Read, Jason. "A Universal Contingency: Deleuze and Guattari on the History of Capitalism." *Borderlands* An ejournal. <www.borderlandsejournal.adelaide.edu.au/vol2no3_2003/read_contingency.htm> 2.3.03.

Reaney, Percy H., and R. M. Wilson, *A Dictionary of English Surnames*. Oxford Oxford University Press, 1997.

Rice, Douglas Walthew. *The Life and Achievements of Sir John Popham, 1531–1607*. Madison, NJ, 2005.

Richards, Judith. "'His Nowe Majesty' and the English Monarchy: The Kingship of Charles I before 1640." *Past and Present* 113 (1985): 70–96.

Rickard, J. "Admiral Sir William Batten (d. 1667)." Web essay <http://www.historyofwar.org/articles/people_batten.html> 17.10.05.

Robertson, Karen. "Pocahontas at the Masque." *Signs* 21/3 (1996): 551–83.

Robinson, Cedric. "The Inventions of the Negro." *Social Identities* 7/3 (2001): 329–61.

Rogers, J. A. *Nature Knows No Color Line*. St. Petersburg, FL: Helga M. Rogers, 1980.

Rogozinski, Jan. *Pirates!: Brigands, Buccaneers, and Privateers in Fact, Fiction, and Legend*. New York: Da Capo Press, 1996.

Romero, Aldemaro, Suzanna Chilbert, and M. G. Eisenhart. "Cubagua's Pear-Oyster Beds: The First Depletion of a Natural Resource Caused by Europeans in the American Continent." *Journal of Political Ecology* 6 (1999): 57–78.

Rowse, A. L. *Ralegh and the Throckmortons*. London: Macmillan & Co Ltd, 1962.

——. "Tudor Expansion: The Transition from Medieval to Modern History." *William and Mary Quarterly* 14/3 (1957): 309–16.

Ruddock, Alwyn A. "Alien Merchants in Southampton in the Later Middle Ages." *English Historical Review* 61/239 (1946): 1–17.

Sacks, David Harris. "The Corporate Town and the English State: 'Little Businesses' 1625–1641." *Past and Present* 110 (1986): 69–95.

——. "London's Dominion: The Metropolis, the Market Economy, the State." In *Material London ca. 1600*, ed. Lena Cowen Orlin, 20–54. Philadephia: University of Pennsylvania Press, 2000.

——. *The Widening Gate: Bristol and the Atlantic Economy 1450–1700*. Berkeley and Los Angeles: University of California Press, 1991.

Salkeld, Duncan. "Black Lucy and the 'Curtizans' of Shakespeare's London." *Signatures <www.ucc.ac.uk/signatures/* 2 (2000): 1.1–1.10.

——. "Making Sense of Difference: Postmodern History, Philosophy and Shakespeare's Prostitutes." *Chronicon* 3/1 (1999): 1–23. An electronic history journal availabe at <www.ucc.ie/chronicon> 7.13.06.

Saunders, A. C. De C. M. *A Social History of Black Slaves and Freedmen in Portugal 1441–1555*. New York: Cambridge University Press, 1982.

Scammell, G. V. "English Merchant Shipping at the End of the Middle Ages: Some East Coast Evidence." *Economic History Review* 13/3 (1961): 327–41.

——. "Shipowning in the Economy and Politics of Early Modern England." *Historical Journal* 15/3 (1972): 385–407.

Schleiner, Winfried. *Medical Ethics in the Renaissance*. Washington, DC: Georgtown University Press, 1995.

Schoenbaum, Samuel. *William Shakespeare: A Documentary Life*. New York: Oxford University Press, 1975.

Schwarz, Marc L. "James I and the Historians: Towards a Reconsideration." *Journal of British Studies* 13/2 (1974): 114–34.

Scott, Tom. *Dunbar: A Critical Exposition of His Poems*. Edinburgh: Oliver and Boyd, 1966.

Seed, Patricia. "Taking Possession and Reading Texts: The Authority of Overseas Empires." *William and Mary Quarterly* 49/2 (1992): 183–209.

Shapiro, James. *Shakespeare and the Jews*. New York: Columbia University Press, 1996.

Sharpe, Jim. "Social Strain and Social Dislocation, 1585–1603." In John Guy, ed., *The Reign of Elizabeth I*, pp. 193–211.

Sharpe, Kevin. *Criticism and Compliment: The Politics of Literature in the England of Charles I*. Cambridge: Cambridge University Press, 1989.

——. "Private Conscience and Public Duty in the Writings of Charles I." *Historical Journal* 40/3 (1997): 643–65.

Sherwood, Marika. "Black People in Tudor England." *History Today* 53/10 (2003): 40–42.

——. "Black History Month." *Feversham Society Newsletter* No. 450. October 2001. <www.faversham.org/pages/directory_item.aspx?i_PageID=11927>.

Shyllon, Folarin Olawale. *Black People in Britain 1556–1833*. London: Oxford University Press, 1972.

——. *Black Slaves in Britain*. London: Institute of Race Relations, 1974.

Silva, Çhandra de. "Beyond the Cape: The Portuguese Encounter with the Peoples of South Asia." In *Implicit Understandings: Observing, Reporting, and Reflecting on the Encounters between Europeans and Other Peoples in the Early Modern Era*, ed. Stuart B. Schwartz, 295–322. Cambridge: Cambridge University Press, 1994.

Slack, Paul. *The English Poor Law 1531–1782*. New Studies in Economic and Social History. New York: Cambridge University Press, 1995.

——. *Rebellion, Popular Protest, and the Social Order in Early Modern England*. Past and Present. Cambridge: Cambridge University Press, 1984.

——, and Ryk Ward. *The Peopling of Britain: The Shaping of a Human Landscape*. New York: Oxford University Press, 2002.

S., M. G. "Strode of Chepsted." *Notes & Queries*. 6th ser. 10 (1884): 331.

Smallwood, Arwin D. *Bertie County: An Eastern Carolina History*. Charleston, SC: Arcadia Publishing, 2002.

Smith, Alan G. R. *The Emergence of a Nation State: The Commonwealth of England*. Foundations of Modern Britain. Longman: New York, 1997.

Smyth, W. H. *Chapman the Sailor's Lexicon: The Classic Source for More than 15,000 Nautical Terms*. New York: Hearst Books, 2005.

Spivak, Gayatri. "Can the Subaltern Speak?" In *Marxism and the Interpretation of Culture*, ed. Cary Nelson and Lawrence Grossberg, 271–313. London: Macmillan, 1988.

Stallybrass, Peter, and Allon White. *The Politics and Poetics of Transgression*. London: Methuen, 1986.

Starkey, David. *Six Wives: The Queens of Henry VIII*. New York: HarperCollins, 2003.

Statt, Daniel. "The City of London and the Controversy over Immigration 1660–1722." *Historical Journal* 33/1 (1990): 45–61.

Stavert, W. J. "Note on the Cravens of Appletreewick." *Yorkshire Archaeological Journal* 13 (1895): 441–536.

Steele, Jess. *Turning the Tide: The History of Everyday Deptford*. London: Deptford Forum, 1993.

"Stepney Folk Vestrymen." 2006. Electronic essay <website.lineone.net/~fight/Stepney/vestrymn.htm> 7.18.06.

Stevens, David. *Scotland's Last Royal Wedding: The Marriage of James VI and Anne of Denmark*. Edinburgh: John Donald, 1997.

Stewert, Julia. *African Names: Names from the African Continent for Children and Adults*. New York: Citadel Press, 2005.

Stoler, Ann Laura. *Carnal Knowledge and Imperial Power: Race and the Intimate in Colonial Rule*. Berkeley: University of California Press, 2002.

Stone, Lawrence. "The Anatomy of Elizabethan Aristocracy." *Economic History Review* 18/1–2 (1948): 1–53.

——. *The Family, Sex and Marriage in England 1550–1800*. New York: Harper and Row, 1972.

——. "Social Mobility in England 1500–1676." *Past and Present* 33 (1966): 16–55.

Studnicki-Gizbert, Daviken. *Pearls*. Electronic essay <bell.lib.umn.edu /Products/pearls.html> 2.12.06.

Sutton, Jean. *Lords of the East: The East India Company and Its Ships*. London: Conway Maritime Press, 1981.

Sweet, James. "Spanish and Portuguese Influences on Racial Slavery in British North America, 1492–1619." In *Collective Degradation: Slavery and the Construction of Race. Proceedings of the Fifth Annual Gilder Lehrman Center International Conference at Yale University*, 2003, 1–33. Electronic copy available at <www.yale.edu/glc/events/race/Sweet.pdf, 2003> 1.10.05.

Tate, W. E. *The Parish Chest: A Study of the Parochial Administration in England.* Cambridge: Cambridge University Press, 1969.

Thirsk, Joan. *Economic Policy and Projects: The Development of a Consumer Society in Early Modern England.* Oxford: Oxford University Press, 1978.

Thomas, Hugh. *The Slave Trade*. New York: Simon and Schuster, 1997.

Thomson, A. T., and Philip Wharton. *The Wits and Beaux of Society*. London: Harper and Brothers, 1861.

Thornton, John. *Africa and Africans in the Making of the Modern World, 1400–1800.* Cambridge: Cambridge University Press, 1998.

Tokson, Eliott H. *The Popular Image of the Black Man in English Drama*. Boston: G. K. Hall, 1982.

Traister, Barbara. *The Notorious Astrological Physician of London: Works and Days of Simon Forman.* Chicago: University of Chicago Press, 2001.

Travitsky, Betty S. "Reprinting Tudor History: The Case of Catherine of Aragon." *Renaissance Quarterly* 50/1 (1997): 164–74.

Trevillian, Russell. *The Rearview Mirror*. Philadelphia: Xlibris Corporation, 2000.

Trill, Suzanne, Kate Chedzgoy, and Melanie Osborne, eds. *Lay by Your Needles Ladies, Take the Pen: Writing Women in England, 1500–1700*. Oxford: Oxford University Press, 1997.

Trimble, William Raleigh. "The Embassy Chapel Question." *Journal of Modern History* 28/2 (1946): 97–107.

Tuan, Yi-Fu. *Dominance and Affection: The Making of Pets*. New Haven: Yale University Press, 1984.

Tudor Hackney. 2006. Internet essay. <www.learningcurve.gov.uk/tudorhackney/localhistory/lochlp.asp> 18.4.06.

Turner, T. H. *Manners and Household Expenses of England in the Thirteenth and the Fifteenth Centuries*. London: W. Nicol, 1841.

Twombly, Robert C., and Robert H. Moore. "Black Puritan: The Negro in Seventeenth-Century Massachusetts." *William and Mary Quarterly* 24/2 (1967): 224–42.

Tytler, Patrick F. *Lives of Scottish Worthies*. London: John Murray, 1831.

Underdown, David. *A Freeeborn People: Politics and Nation in Seventeenth-Century England.* Oxford: Clarendon Press, 1996.

Ungerer, Gustav. "Prostitution in Elizabethan England: The Case of Mary Newborough." *Medieval and Renaissance Drama in England* 15 (2003): 138–223.

——. "Recovering a Black African's Voice in an English Lawsuit." *Medieval and Renaissance Drama in England* 17 (2005): 255–71.

Unwin, George. "The Merchant Adventurers' Company in the Reign of Elizabeth." *Economic History Review* 1/1 (1927): 35–64.

Unwin, Raynor. *The Defeat of John Hawkins: A Biography of His Third Slaving Voyage*. New York: Macmillan, 1960.

Valdes y Cocom, Mario de. *The Blurred Racial Lines of Famous Families: Pushkin Genealogy*. Frontline WGBH Boston. Web essay, <www.pbs.org/wgbh/pages/frontline/shows/secret/famous/pushkingenealogy.html> 24.12.2005.

Vaughan, Alden T., and Virginia Mason Vaughan. "Before *Othello*: Elizabethan Representations of Sub-Saharan Africans." *William and Mary Quarterly* 54/1 (1997): 19–44.

——. *Roots of American Racism: Essays on the Colonial Experience*. New York: Oxford University Press, 1995.

——. "Sir Walter Ralegh's Indian Interpreters 1585–1618." *William and Mary Quarterly* 59/2 (2002): 341–76.

—— "Tales from the Vault: In Search of Slavery's English Roots." *Common-Place* 1/4 (2001). Electronic journal at *www.common-place.org*.

——. "Trinculo's Indian: American Natives in Shakespeare's England. '*The Tempest and Its Travels*, ed. Peter Hulme and William Sherman, 49–59. Philadelphia: University of Pennsylvania Press, 2000.

Vaughan, Virginia Mason. *Othello: A Contextual History*. Cambridge: Cambridge University Press, 1994.

—— and Alden T. Vaughan. *Shakespeare's Caliban: A Contextual History*. Cambridge: Cambridge University Press, 1991.

Visram, Rozina. *Asians in Britain: 400 Years of History*. London: Pluto Press, 2002.

Voss, Paul J., and Marta L. Werner. "Towards a Poetics of the Archive: Introduction." *Studies in the Literary Imagination* 32/1 (1999): i–viii.

Walvin, James. *Black and White: The Negro and English Society 1553–1945*. London: Allen Lane, 1973.

——. *The Black Presence: A Documentary History of the Negro in England, 1555–1860*. New York: Schocken Books, 1971.

Watson, Alan. "Roman Slave Law and Romanist Ideology." *Phoenix* 37/1 (1983): 53–65.

Webster's New Universal Unabridged Dictionary, ed. Jean L. McKechnie. 2nd edn. New York: Simon and Schuster, 1972.

Weinman, Ken. *Treasure Galleon of the Mohave Desert*. 2006. Electronic pamphlet <www.losttreasure.com/newsletter/6-1-2000/6-1-2000.html> 2.12.06.

White, Micheline. "Women Writers and Literary-Religious Circles in the Elizabethan West Country: Anne Dowriche, Anne Lock Prowse, Anne Lock Moyle, Ursula Pulford, and Elizabeth Rous." *Modern Philology* 103 (2005): 187–214.

Wiecek, William M. "Somerset: Lord Mansfield and the Legitimacy of Slavery in the Anglo-American World." *University of Chicago Law Review* 42/1 (1974): 86–146.

Wild, Anthony, *The East India Company, Trade and Conquest from 1600*. New York: The Lyons Press, 1999.

Willan, T. S. "Some Aspects of the English Trade with the Levant in the Sixteenth Century." *English Historical Review* 70/276 (1955): 399–410.

Willen, Diane. "Women in the Public Sphere in Early Modern England: The Case of the Urban Working Poor." *Sixteenth Century Journal* 18/4 (1988): 559–75.

Williams, Ethel Carleton. *Anne of Denmark: Wife of James VI of Scotland, James I of England*. London: Harlow Longmans, 1970.

Williams, Penry. *The Later Tudors: England 1547–1603*. Oxford: Clarendon Press, 1995.

Williams, William Retlaw. *Kidderminster, Bromsgrove and Pershore, from the Earliest Times to the Present Day, 1213–1897. With Biographical and Genealogical Notices of the Members*. London: Jakeman and Carver, 1897.

Williamson, George C. *Lady Anne Clifford, Countess of Dorset, Pembroke and Montgomery, Her Life, Letters, and Work*. Kendal: Titus Wilson, 1922.

Williamson, James A. *Hawkins of Plymouth*. New York: Barnes and Noble, 1969.

——. *Sir John Hawkins: The Man and the Times*. Westport, CT: Greenwood Press, 1970.

Wilson, Kristen. "Deptford, England, the East India Company and the Global Economy in Geography." Electronic essay <http://www.personal.psu.edu/users/k/d/kdw1003/paper> 18.2.03.

Withycombe, E. G., ed. *The Oxford Dictionary of English Christian Names*. Oxford: Clarendon Press, 1950.

Worth, Richard Nicholls. *History of Plymouth: From the Earliest Period to the Present Time*. Plymouth: W. Brenden, 1890.

Wright, George. "Statistics of the Parish of St. George the Martyr, Southwark." *Journal of the Statistical Society of London* 3/1 (1840): 50–71.

Wrightson, Keith. *Earthly Necessities: Economic Lives in Early Modern Britain*. New Haven: Yale University Press, 2000.

Wrigley, E. A. "How Reliable Is Our Knowledge of Demographic Characteristics of the English Population in the Early Modern Period?" *Historical Journal* 40/3 (1997): 571–95.

——. "A Simple Model of the Importance of London in the Changing English Society and Economy 1650–1750." *Past and Present* 37 (1967), 44–70.

Yungblut, Laura Hunt. *Strangers Settled Here among Us: Policies, Perceptions, and the Presence of Aliens in Elizabethan England*. New York: Routledge, 1996.

Žižek, Slavoj. *The Plague of Fantasies*. London: Verso, 1997.

Zook, George Fredrick. "The Royal Adventurers in England." *Journal of Negro History* 4/2 (1919): 143–62.

Index

Milton Keynes UK
Ingram Content Group UK Ltd.
UKHW020523260924
448819UK00016B/157